Handbooks of Sociology and Social Research

Series Editor
John DeLamater
University of Wisconsin-Madison
Madison, Wisconsin
USA

Each of these Handbooks survey the field in a critical manner, evaluating theoretical models in light of the best available empirical evidence. Distinctively sociological approaches are highlighted by means of explicit comparison to perspectives characterizing related disciplines such as psychology, psychiatry, and anthropology. These seminal works seek to record where the field has been, to identify its current location and to plot its course for the future.

If you are interested in submitting a proposal for this series, please first contact the publishing editor, Esther Otten: esther.otten@springer.com.

More information about this series at http://www.springer.com/series/6055

John DeLamater • Rebecca F. Plante
Editors

Handbook of the Sociology of Sexualities

Springer

Editors

John DeLamater
Department of Sociology
University of Wisconsin-Madison
Madison
Wisconsin
USA

Rebecca F. Plante
Department of Sociology
Ithaca College
Ithaca
New York
USA

ISSN 1389-6903
Handbooks of Sociology and Social Research
ISBN 978-3-319-17340-5 (hardcover)   ISBN 978-3-319-17341-2 (eBook)
ISBN 978-3-319-44743-8 (softcover)
DOI 10.1007/978-3-319-17341-2

Library of Congress Control Number: 2015940322

Springer Cham Heidelberg New York Dordrecht London

Printed on acid-free paper

Springer International Publishing AG Switzerland is part of Springer Science+Business Media (www.springer.com)

We dedicate this Handbook to the scholars and researchers who worked hard, and in some cases, fought, to legitimize the study of sexuality as a topic of sociological inquiry. They created a scientific discourse to supplant the religious and biomedical perspectives that dominated discussion of sexuality until recently. We acknowledge the social, political and economic hardship that some of them endured to lay the essential groundwork for the broad array of scholarship reflected in this volume. We recognize that some contemporary researchers continue to endure social, educational and political harassment for persisting in the study of topics in this field. It is our hope that this collection of superb reviews of scholarship on sexuality will give pause to the critics and facilitate the motivation and work of the next generation of scholars.

John DeLamater
Rebecca F. Plante

Contents

Contributors

Susannah Bartlow Gender and Sexuality Resource Center, Marquette University Milwaukee, Milwaukee, WI, USA

Alexis A. Bender Behavioral and Social Health Outcomes Program (BSHOP), Army Institute of Public Health, US Army Public Health Command (USAPHC), Aberdeen, MD, USA

Amy M. Burdette Department of Sociology, Florida State University, Tallahassee, FL, USA

Thea Cacchioni Department of Women's Studies, University of Victoria, Victoria, BC, Canada

Laura M. Carpenter Department of Sociology, Vanderbilt University, Nashville, TN, USA

John DeLamater Department of Sociology, University of Wisconsin-Madison, Madison, WI, USA

Aaron H. Devor Sociology Department, University of Victoria, Victoria, BC, Canada

Susan Dewey Department of Gender and Women's Studies, University of Wyoming, Laramie, WY, USA

Kimi Dominic Sociology Department, University of Victoria, Victoria, BC, Canada

Breanne Fahs Women and Gender Studies Program, Arizona State University, Glendale, AZ, USA

Jessica Fields Sociology, San Francisco State University, San Francisco, CA, USA

Katherine Frank Department of Sociology, American University, Washington, DC, USA

Justin R. Garcia The Kinsey Institute & Department of Gender Studies, Indiana University, Bloomington, IN, USA

Amin Ghaziani Department of Sociology, University of British Columbia, Vancouver, Canada

Jen Gilbert York University, Toronto, ON, Canada

Andrew Gorman-Murray School of Social Sciences and Psychology, University of Western Sydney, Penrith, NSW, Australia

Adam Isaiah Green Department of Sociology, University of Toronto, Toronto, Ontario, Canada

Carol Haefner Psychology Department, Sofia University, Palo Alto, CA, USA

Angelique Harris Social and Cultural Sciences, Marquette University, Milwaukee, Milwaukee, WI, USA

Terrence D. Hill School of Sociology, University of Arizona, Tucson, AZ, USA

Phil Hubbard School of Social Policy, Sociology and Social Research, University of Kent, Canterbury, UK

Amanda M. Jungels Behavioral and Social Health Outcomes Program (BSHOP), Army Institute of Public Health, US Army Public Health Command (USAPHC), Aberdeen, MD, USA

Amy C. Lodge Center for Social Work Research, University of Texas, Austin, TX, USA

Lauren Jade Martin Sociology Department, Pennsylvania State University, Berks, Reading, PA, USA

Sean G. Massey Women, Gender, & Sexuality Studies Program, Binghamton University, Binghamton, NY, USA

Ann M. Merriwether Departments of Psychology and Human Development, Binghamton University, Binghamton, NY, USA

Michelle Miller York University, Toronto, ON, Canada

Kyl Myers Department of Sociology, University of Utah, Salt Lake City, UT, USA

Catherine J. Nash Department of Geography, Brock University, St. Catharines, ON, Canada

Anthony Paik Department of Sociology, University of Massachusetts-Amherst, Amherst, MA, USA

María Pérez-y-Pérez School of Social and Political Science, University of Canterbury, Christchurch, New Zealand

Rebecca F. Plante Department of Sociology, Ithaca College, Ithaca, NY, USA

Ira L. Reiss University of Minnesota, Minneapolis, Minnesota, USA

Susan M. Seibold-Simpson Decker School of Nursing, Binghamton University, Binghamton, NY, USA

Elisabeth Sheff Sociology, Oglethorpe University, Atlanta, GA, USA

Amy L. Stone Sociology and Anthropology, One Trinity Place, Trinity University, San Antonio, TX, USA

Eric Swank Arizona State University, Glendale, AZ, USA

Megan M. Tesene Sociology Department, Georgia State University, Atlanta, GA, USA

Jill D. Weinberg Sociology, DePaul University, American Bar Foundation, Chicago, IL, USA

Michael W. Wiederman University of South Carolina School of Medicine-Greenville, Greenville, SC, USA

Kassia R. Wosick Department of Sociology, New Mexico State University, Las Cruces, NM, USA

The Sociological Study of Sexuality: An Introduction

John DeLamater and Rebecca F. Plante

Sexuality is a major influence on individual health and well being, an important component of many types of social relationships, and an increasingly visible feature of social life. Not surprisingly, it has been the focus of a great deal of scholarly inquiry and research. In the early decades of the twentieth century, much of the "scientific" writing about sexuality focused on what were considered problematic forms of sexual cognitions and behaviors. These works reflected an essentialist view (DeLamater and Hyde 2004) of sex, sexual orientation, and sexual behavior. The empirical base of this work was largely case studies of people seen in therapeutic settings. As a result, the literature had an individualistic, psychological focus.

The first large-scale surveys of "typical" sexual behavior were conducted by Alfred Kinsey and colleagues (1948, 1953). They conducted individual interviews with thousands of men and women, questioning them in detail about sexual behavior and the types of partners with whom they engaged in intimacy. Kinsey was an entomologist and brought a biological perspective to the study of sexual behavior. He focused on the six "outlets" a man or woman could use to ex-perience sexual pleasure, recognizing that only two of the six were heterosexual. However, in analyzing and reporting his results, he systematically considered variation by gender, race and social class, taking into account variation by social structure.

In the 1950s, Winston Ehrmann and Ira Reiss applied survey methods to the study of premarital sexuality. Ehrmann collected surveys from undergraduate students for several years, focused on a model of "stages" of premarital behavior, ranging from kissing to heterosexual intercourse. His major publication was *Premarital Dating Behavior* (1959), which documented the connection between the nature of the relationship and its sexual intimacy. Reiss focused on the role of attitudes ("standards") in premarital sexuality, arguing that attitudes reflected the influence of social institutions, including religion and the family. His book was published one year later (1960), and was subtitled "a sociological investigation." Reiss describes the development of his research and theory in Chap. 4.

In 1974, *Sexual Conduct* by John Gagnon and William Simon was published. Their social constructionist view of sexual behavior represented a sharp break from the then dominant essentialist, biological perspective. They argued that sexual interactions are not "hard-wired." Sexual behavior is influenced by cultural norms, the ongoing interaction of the participants, and each participant's past experiences and current desires. This view laid the groundwork for a truly social psychological analysis of sexuality. This perspective

J. DeLamater (✉)
Department of Sociology, University of Wisconsin-Madison, 53706 Madison, WI, USA
e-mail: delamate@ssc.wisc.edu

R. F. Plante
Department of Sociology, Ithaca College, 14850 Ithaca, NY, USA
e-mail: rplante@ithaca.edu

J. DeLamater, R.F. Plante (eds.), *Handbook of the Sociology of Sexualities,* Handbooks of Sociology and Social Research, DOI 10.1007/978-3-319-17341-2_1, © Springer International Publishing Switzerland 2015

and the research and writing it inspired is summarized by Michael Wiederman in Chap. 2.

From these pioneering efforts, a large body of theory, research and commentary has developed over the past 45 years that treats sexual cognitions, behaviors, and relationships as social phenomena that can be analyzed using the theories and methods of contemporary sociology. In this *Handbook* we aim to bring together work reflecting the contributions of sociological analysis to understandings of human sexuality in the contemporary world, with a particular emphasis on North America.

Of course, the organization and content of this *Handbook* reflects the perspective of its editors. We believe that all scientific work is based on theory. As implied above, sociology provides a distinctive set of theories that identify particular issues/questions regarding sexuality and ways of thinking about them. Thus, the first part presents these theories. In addition to script theory (Chap. 2) and macro perspectives (Chap. 4), we present two recent perspectives that are having a major impact. Field theory is developing a meso- or mid-level analysis of the influence of context on social behavior. Adam Isaiah Green (Chap. 3) applies it insightfully to sexuality. The life-course perspective considers the role of earlier experiences on later outcomes, and how lives are structured by the larger society, and Laura Carpenter (Chap. 5) applies it systematically to the study of sexual lives.

Several research methods widely used in social psychology and sociology have been fruitfully applied to the study of a variety of personal and social aspects of sexuality. Part 2 provides thoughtful analyses of three of these. Following the pioneering research by Kinsey and his collaborators, surveys of groups and populations to measure attitudes and behavior have been a staple of the subfield. Anthony Paik provides a very balanced analysis of the strengths and weaknesses of this use of the survey method, and discusses the rapid growth in online surveys to reach certain populations (Chap. 6). A variety of techniques have been used to illuminate the quotidian and often hidden features of sexual interactions in various settings, or 'sex worlds.'

Maria Pérez-y-Pérez provides a very insightful analysis of the social and personal dimensions of the researcher's active involvement in a "sexy setting" (Chap. 7). Kate Frank, drawing on her extensive experience, describes the strengths and weaknesses of a variety of observational methods (Chap. 8).

A common criticism of sociological research and writing about sexuality in the late twentieth century was the lack of attention to the biology of sexuality, except in discussions of reproduction and sexually transmitted infections (STIs). Particularly missing was thoughtful, critical discussion of the sexual body and how it is implicated in diverse forms of sexual relationships and sexual activities. Fortunately, scholars have turned their attention to the topic in the past 15 years. Part 3 presents three chapters dealing with bodies and sexuality. Breanne Fahs and Eric Swank address two main aspects in Chap. 9, the role of the body in sexuality, and the uses of the body to resist social control efforts. Bodies take center stage when we consider the sexual lives of persons with differently abled bodies ('disabilities'). Amanda Jungels and Alexis Bender carefully review the small amount of research in this area and point to important directions for future work (Chap. 10). Bodies and embodiment also play a major role in the lives of trans* people and their experiences of sexual intimacy and relationships. Skilled contributors to the growing literature in this area, Aaron Devor and Kimi Dominic provide a detailed, nuanced look at the body and sexuality for trans* people (Chap. 11).

The editors share Laura Carpenter's belief that a biopsychosocial model of sexuality is necessary if we are to understand the various influences on sexual expression across the life-course. While Part 3 introduces the *bio-* dimension, Part 4 considers sexuality in the micro-social context, along with the accompanying cognitions, motivations, and emotions (the *psycho* dimension). A major contextual influence on partnered sexual expression is the *nature of the relationship* between participants. The first several chapters in Part 4 consider diverse relational contexts. Justin Garcia, Susan M. Seibold-Simpson, Sean G. Massey, and Ann M. Merriwether discuss sexual activity in casual or uncommitted contexts (Chap. 12) from three perspectives: casual sex, public health/sexual risk-taking, and sexual pleasure. Elizabeth Sheff and Megan Tesene shed light on several types of consensual non-monogamous relationships, covering both sexual and non-sexual aspects (Chap. 13). Amy Lodge analyzes a range of sexual expressions in long-term relationships (Chap. 14). Scholars studying race were the first to focus attention on *intersectionality*, the fact that each of us has multiple demographic/social characteristics (e.g., race, class, gender) that interact to influence our identities and behavior. Angelique Harris and Susannah Bartlow reflect on how intersectionalities can be better applied in sexualities research (Chap. 15). Carol Haefner and Rebecca F. Plante review the literature on asexuality, a sexual identity that challenges several taken-for-granted assumptions about relationships and sexualities (Chap. 16).

A relatively new topic in sociological analyses is consideration of spatial factors or the built environment. As we think about sexual expression, it is obvious that cities (or suburbs), and distinctive spaces within them, provide important contexts for sexual relationships and lifestyle. In Chap. 17, Phil Hubbard, Andrew Gorman Murray, and Catherine J. Nash summarize the ways in which cities operate to frame or constrain sexualities. Of course, the role of urban environments in providing a base for gay lives and sexualities has been studied for several decades. Those literatures, and recent changes in the "queer metropolis," are comprehensively reviewed by Amin Ghaziani (Chap. 18).

Part 5 deconstructs the *social* dimension. As sociologists, we are particularly interested in how social institutions shape, facilitate, and restrict various forms of sexual expression. We organized this section using a mental image of concentric circles. Closest to the individual in space and time is 'the family'; Lauren Jade Martin reviews the family's role in sexuality and reproduction (Chap. 19). Religion, as Reiss recognized 55 years ago, is a major institutional influence on individuals and families. Amy Burdette, Terrence Hill, and Kyl Myers consider the wide influence of religion on sexuality and sexual health

(Chap. 20). Formal sexuality education has been part of social context for about 40 years, and is sensitively analyzed here by Jessica Field, Jen Gilbert, and Michelle Miller (Chap. 21). Perhaps the most prominent feature of sexuality in the contemporary United States is its commodification; sex and exploitation sell. The role of sex work, or "commercial sexual activity," is carefully analyzed by Susan Dewey (Chap. 22). And in Chap. 23, Kassia Wosick addresses the vast scope and impacts of pornography.

A major recent contribution of sociological analysis to the study of human sexuality has been attention to the increasing hegemony of medicine over sexual and reproductive life. More and more aspects of everyday sexual life have been defined as illnesses, in need of medical treatment, including drugs, surgical procedures and various "therapies." Thus, no coverage of institutional influences on sexuality would be complete without a thorough analysis of this phenomenon of the medicalization of sexuality, provided by Thea Cacchioni (Chap. 24).

Last, but by no means least, social movements have played an important role in bringing about change in attitudes, norms and laws governing sexual relationships and sexual expression. Amy Stone and Jill Weinberg explore this ever-shifting topic (Chap. 25).

Our goal was to provide a comprehensive overview of the contributions of social psychological and sociological analyses to the understanding of human sexual expression in much of its diversity. As usual in such an undertaking, the chapters included here reflect the availability of knowledgeable scholars to write them. We were unable to include a chapter on online research methods, though these are covered by Paik, and by several other authors in part. We also were unable to include a chapter on mass media and sexuality. And certainly this handbook reflects the editors' perspectives, blind spots, and omissions.

The alert reader will notice that there are no chapter(s) specifically devoted to sexual orientation. We decided at the outset that we would ask each author to include coverage of literature on sexual orientation as it related to their substantive topic. We believe that there is now enough literature on diverse aspects of LGB sexuality and relationships to allow integrated coverage, and we think it makes sense to model inclusive ways to address a range of sexual orientations. And although we do have a chapter about intersectionalities, we also asked authors to be attentive to research addressing race, class, and gender. In the cases where these literatures are missing, authors are clear about what future researchers will need to do to rectify the gaps in our collective studies of sexualities.

We are very grateful to Esther Otten, Senior Publishing Editor at Springer, for her enthusiastic support for adding this *Handbook of Sexualities* to the prestigious Springer Handbook Series of Sociology and Social Research. We were thrilled when the American Sociological Association announced that the theme of the 2015 Annual Meeting will be "Sexualities in Society." Our authors, and Springer's production staff, especially Hendrikje Tuerlings, deserve our gratitude for making it possible to have this Handbook published in August 2015, in conjunction with the Annual Meeting.

References

DeLamater, J., & Hyde, J. (2004). Conceptual and theoretical issues in studying sexuality in close relationships. In J. H. Harvey, A. Wenzel & S. Sprecher (Eds.), *The handbook of sexuality in close relationships* (pp. 7–30). Mahwah: Lawrence Erlbaum.

Ehrmann, W. (1959). *Premarital dating behavior*. New York: Holt.

Gagnon, J., & Simon, W. (1974). *Sexual conduct: The social sources of human sexuality*. Chicago: Aldine.

Kinsey, A., Pomeroy, W., & Martin, C. (1948). *Sexual behavior in the human male*. Philadelphia: W.B. Saunders.

Kinsey, A., Pomeroy, W., Martin, C., & Gebhard, P. (1953). *Sexual behavior in the human female*. Philadelphia: W.B. Saunders.

Reiss, I. L. (1960). *Premarital sexual standards in America: A sociological investigation of the relative social and cultural integration of American sexual standards*. Glencoe: Free Press.

Part I
Theories

Sexual Script Theory: Past, Present, and Future

2

Michael W. Wiederman

All the World's a stage,
And all the men and women merely players.
(Shakespeare, As You Like It)

In their book *Sexual Conduct*, John Gagnon and William Simon (1973) described their *sexual script theory* perspective on human sexual behavior. Its basic premise was that all social behavior, including sexual behavior, is socially scripted. Of course, as the quote from Shakespeare attests, Simon and Gagnon were hardly the first to liken human behavior to scripted performance. Still, their book represented a watershed moment in sex research, and has been deemed one of the top 25 classic works of sexual theory (Weis 1998b). Bancroft (2009) referred to sexual scripting theory as "one of the, if not *the* most frequently cited theoretical models in post-psychoanalytic sexual science" (p. 10), McCormick (2010) declared that "No single theoretical perspective better accounts for the complexity of human sexual motivation and behaviors" (p. 91), and Kimmel (2007) concluded that Gagnon and Simon's book "heralded the new paradigm from which all subsequent readings of sexuality in the social sciences and humanities have sprung" (p. ix).

If the basic tenet of sexual script theory was not novel, why has it proven itself such a pivotal and long-lasting theoretical perspective? An attempt to answer that question requires both an explanation of sexual script theory and consideration of its place in history.

2.1 Sexual Script Theory

Central to sexual script theory is the notion of social constructionism—the interpretation of reality, including human behavior, is derived from shared beliefs within a particular social group (DeLamater and Hyde 1998). In this case, the human behaviors in question are sexual, and the meanings attached to those behaviors, including what makes them "sexual" behaviors, derives from metaphorical scripts individuals have learned and incorporated as a function of their involvement in the social group (Simon 1996; Simon and Gagnon 1986, 1987, 2003). "Scripts are involved in learning the meaning of internal states, organizing the sequencing of specifically sexual acts, decoding novel situations, setting the limits on sexual responses and linking meanings from nonsexual aspects of life to specifically sexual experience" (Gagnon and Simon 1973, p. 17).

Social scripts are conceptualized as the mental representations individuals construct and then use to make sense of their experience, including their own and others' behavior.

> Scripts are a metaphor for conceptualizing behavior within social life. Most of social life most of the time must operate under the guidance of an operating syntax, much as language is a precondition for speech. For behavior to occur, something resembling scripting must occur on three distinct levels: cultural scenarios, interpersonal scripts, and intrapsychic scripts. (Simon and Gagnon 1984, p. 53)

Although cultural scenarios are at the most abstract level of scripting, they are necessary for

M. W. Wiederman (✉)
University of South Carolina School of Medicine-Greenville, Greenville, SC 29605, USA

J. DeLamater, R.F. Plante (eds.), *Handbook of the Sociology of Sexualities,* Handbooks of Sociology and Social Research, DOI 10.1007/978-3-319-17341-2_2, © Springer International Publishing Switzerland 2015

providing the context for roles, and contain institutional arrangements and symbols that comprise collective life (Simon and Gagnon 1986, 1987, 2003). Mass media certainly play an important role in conveying cultural scenarios, but sexual norms are conveyed even through the ways in which cultural institutions such as government, law, education, and religion are experienced on a daily basis (Gagnon 1990; Simon 1996). Because particular sexual behaviors are illegal, stigmatized, and warned against, whereas others are instructed, encouraged, and envied, individuals learn the general contexts for sexual activity. In a sense, cultural scenarios lay out the playing field of sexuality; what is deemed desirable and undesirable, and where the broad boundaries lie between appropriate and inappropriate sexual conduct.

As important as *sexual cultural scripts* are, they are not synonymous with sexual behavior. "The enactment of virtually all roles must either directly or indirectly reflect the contents of appropriate cultural scenarios. These cultural scenarios are rarely entirely predictive of actual behavior, and they are generally too abstract to be applied in all circumstances" (Simon and Gagnon 1984, p. 53). So cultural scenarios lay out the general cast of characters (roles) and the relationships among them, yet usually do not provide enough concrete direction to guide actual interpersonal behavior in specific situations. This is where the interpersonal level of sexual scripts enters.

Interpersonal scripts rest on the roles and general circumstances provided by cultural scenarios, yet they entail adaptation to the particulars of each situation. Accordingly, each social actor helps create interpersonal scripts by adapting the general guidelines he or she learned from his or her experiences in the culture to the specifics presented in each social encounter (Simon and Gagnon 1986, 1987, 2003). At the interpersonal level, the script was said to provide "the organization of mutually shared conventions that allows two or more actors to participate in a complex act involving mutual dependence" (Gagnon and Simon 1973, p. 18). When the two or more actors involved share similar scripts, the social interaction may play out with relative harmony.

However, there is always room for differences in the interpersonal scripts followed by each actor, with potentially troublesome results (Wiederman 2005). Also, the specifics of each circumstance differ, requiring modification and improvisation of previously adopted scripts. Especially when alternative outcomes are available in a particular scenario, the ability to engage in mental rehearsal is important for choosing among potential behaviors. This internal, individual experience of scripts is the intrapsychic level within script theory.

Intrapsychic scripts may entail specific plans or strategies for carrying out interpersonal scripts, but they are so much more (Simon and Gagnon 1986, 1987, 2003).

> This intrapsychic scripting creates fantasy in the rich sense of that word: the symbolic reorganization of reality in ways to more fully realize the actor's many-layered and sometimes multivoiced wishes. Intrapsychic scripting becomes a historical necessity, as a private world of wishes and desires that are experienced as originating in the deepest recesses of the self must be bound to social life: individual desires are linked to social meanings (Simon and Gagnon 1984, p. 54).

Intrapsychic scripts include fantasies, memories, and mental rehearsals, and it is within the intrapsychic scripts that individuals work out the difficulties involved in enacting interpersonal scripts within the general context of cultural scenarios (Gagnon 1990; Simon and Gagnon 1986, 1987, 2003).

Whereas cultural scenarios and interpersonal scripts may be thought of as more narrative in structure, intrapsychic scripts need not be.

> When dealing with erotic elements in the intrapsychic we are dealing with a more complex set of layered meanings which has much more to do with non-narrative tradition in literary representation and imagery. What is arousing may not be the plan to have sex, but fragmentary symbolic materials taken from mass media or from local experience. (Gagnon 1990, p. 7)

In this way, intrapsychic scripts represent the particulars of each individual's unique sexuality, including those aspects that cannot be formed into words.

As described here, each of the three levels of sexual scripts may seem rather static. For descriptive purposes, it may be necessary to characterize cultural scenarios, interpersonal scripts, and intrapersonal scripts as "things" in the sense that each exists on its own. However, Gagnon and Simon viewed all three levels of scripts as dynamically related, and frequently in flux as a result. As actually played out in behavior in the context of peoples' lives, there is potentially perpetual interplay among the three levels of sexual scripts. Unfortunately, this potential complexity is difficult to describe, capture, or examine in all its richness.

Gagnon and Simon also noted that the relevance of each of the three levels of scripting varies across settings. For example, in what they termed "paradigmatic societies," cultural scenarios and a specified set of ritualized variations may be all that is required to provide instructions such that social participants understand their respective roles and the meanings ascribed to their behaviors. In these societies, cultural scenarios and prescribed variations are sufficient to provide direction for successful enactment of scripts. In "postparadigmatic societies," in contrast, there are substantially fewer shared meanings and more disjunctures of meaning across different spheres of life. "As a result, the enactment of the same role within different spheres of life or different roles within the same sphere routinely requires different appearances, if not different organizations, of the self" (Simon and Gagnon 1984, p. 54). Postparadigmatic societies entail so much variability in meanings of sexual behavior that each social situation may require a unique adaptation of the individual to that situation.

Although Gagnon and Simon focused on sexual behavior in application of scripting theory, within their view there is nothing inherently special about sexual behavior or its motivation.

> From a scripting perspective, the sexual is not viewed as an intrinsically significant aspect of human behavior; rather, the sexual is viewed as becoming significant either when it is defined as such by collective life—sociogenic significance; or when individual experiences or development assign it a special significance—ontogenic significance. (Simon and Gagnon 1984, p. 54)

Sexual activities gain their special status simply because the society ascribes such status or because of the individual's own unique experiences.

Sexual scripting theory also entails a developmental or life-cycle aspect. Gagnon and Simon noted that particular scripts, or aspects of scripts, have age requirements, such as "You cannot engage in X until you are Y years of age," or "By age Y you must have done X." Common scripts themselves may have variants based on the relative ages of the actors, or at least the actors within a particular script are evaluated differently based on their respective ages. Adolescence and early adulthood are the most troubling stages for individuals and for the culture to which such individuals belong; it is during these stages that individuals are developing and refining their interpersonal and intrapsychic sexual scripts. "The major cultural scenarios that shape the most common interpersonal scripts tend to be almost exclusively drawn from the requirements of adolescence and early adulthood. There are virtually none tied to the issues of subsequent segments of life" (Simon and Gagnon 1984, p. 58). Accordingly, Simon and Gagnon (1984) noted that the extreme ends of the lifecycle might be thought of as the presexual (childhood) and the postsexual (old age), at least in terms of predominant, shared scripts. "Not that sexually significant events do not occur during these periods, but they are not or only rarely anticipated in prevailing cultural scenarios dealing with the very young and the very old" (Simon and Gagnon 1984, p. 58).

Interpersonal and intrapsychic scripts fashioned in adolescence and early adulthood frequently take on a conservative nature in that, once successful, individuals are motivated to retain them and not stray too far from what has worked in the past.

> Once they have found a formula that works—in other words, the realization of sexual pleasure, as well as the realization of sociosexual competence—there is an obvious tendency on some level to para-ritualize that formula. Variations can occur, but variations generally occur within the limits of a larger, stabilizing body of scripts both interper-

sonal and intrapsychic. The stabilizing of sexual scripts, often confused with the crystallization of a sexual identity, occurs partly because it works by insuring adequate sexual performance and providing adequate sexual pleasure. It also represents an effective accommodation with the larger self-process, in which sexual practice and sexual identity do not disturb the many components of one's nonsexual identities. (Simon and Gagnon 1984, p. 57)

To contemporary readers, sexual script theory is likely to be non-controversial. If so, this level of comfort attests to how constructionist perspectives have become inherent in Western thought about human experience. Why Gagnon and Simon's ideas took hold when they did remains an open question. They certainly were not the first to describe and discuss the importance of membership in society for providing individual members with explanations for human behavior, or the process of meaning making. Indeed, sexual script theory is a logical extension of symbolic interactionism, a term coined by sociologist Herbert Blumer in the 1930s based on the work of his mentor, sociologist George Herbert Mead. "Symbolic interactionism focuses on how meaning is created, modified, and put into action by individuals in the process of social interaction" (Brickell 2006, p. 94), and has its own history in the study of sexuality (Gecas and Libby 1977; Longmore 1998; Waskul and Plante 2010).

Similarly, Gagnon and Simon were not the first to employ the script metaphor to social interactions. For example, the sociologist Erving Goffman (1959) famously presented dramaturgy as a sociological perspective, likening human social interaction to performance of assumed roles in a theatrical production (see Henslin and Biggs 1971, for an early example of applying dramaturgy to sexuality). If the ideas underlying sexual script theory were not unique, but instead applications and extensions of symbolic interactionism, dramaturgy, and other social constructionist theories, why did the elaboration of sexual script theory come to represent such an important point in the history of sex research?

2.2 Sexual Script Theory in Historical Context

Sexual script theory emphasizes that social context is extremely important for understanding human behavior, including the behavior of widespread adoption of the theory itself. There are several social factors that may have facilitated the proliferation of sexual script theory. First, Gagnon and Simon explicitly applied the sociological principles described earlier specifically to sexual behavior. Although such application seems commonplace decades after the fact, at the time such a perspective was novel. Second, the cultural milieu may have been ripe for such a social constructionist perspective on sexuality. As Simon and Gagnon (1984) noted, their perspective was a reaction to the dominant theoretical views of human sexuality at the time: psychoanalytic and biological (see Plummer 1982, for comparison of social scripting to these then-dominant, perspectives in sex research). Within these dominant perspectives, sexual behavior was seen as essentially determined, either by instincts or drives, inherently tied to human biology. For example, Freud based his psychoanalytic theory on an assumed instinct toward life and procreation—Libido—that may find natural and healthy expression or may be distorted into psychopathology.

Freudian psychoanalytic perspectives on sexuality continued to hold sway even as biological perspectives rose to attention. Perhaps the most famous of the "new" biological perspective on sexuality was Alfred Kinsey and his colleagues (1948, 1953) who catalogued sexual behaviors of respondents and plotted them against such variables as age, sex, and social class. Whereas some variables Kinsey and his colleagues considered relevant were societal in nature (e.g., social class, education), the underlying assumption seemed to be that these social variables distorted otherwise natural expressions of sexuality. Similarly, William Masters and Virginia Johnson (1966, 1970) focused their research and therapy on bodily response to sexual stimuli; work based on the assumption that there is universal, and therefore

natural, sexual functioning. Even casual examination of the titles of the books by Kinsey and his colleagues (1948, 1953), and Masters and Johnson (1966, 1970), reveals the assumption they were working under; that there were inherent sexual universals for humans that could be analyzed and described by researchers such as themselves.

Unlike the psychoanalytic and biological perspectives, Gagnon and Simon believed that nothing could be assumed about sexuality, apart from the notion that anything considered "sexual" arose because those meanings were attached to the stimuli, or situation, or behavior by the individuals so involved. This social constructionist approach may have been especially appealing to a growing number of researchers in the late 1960s and 1970s as cultural events called into question essentialist perspectives that had been taken for granted previously. Similarly, Gagnon and Simon (1973) considered sexual scripts as explicitly interwoven with gender scripts, and feminist movements at the time were calling into question assumptions about male and female, and the extent to which these assumptions were inevitable versus products of culture and socialization (see Simon and Gagnon 2003 for discussion of cultural changes that shaped sexual script theory). So, sexual script theory may have benefitted from coming along at the right time in history as it presented a framework very much in tune with changing cultural values in the United States.

2.3   Similar Theoretical Perspectives in Social Science

The previous section included a brief discussion of the intellectual history from which sexual script theory emerged, including social constructionism generally, and symbolic interactionism and dramaturgy more specifically. Given that sexual script theory took shape through the late 1960s and into the 1970s, there were other theoretical perspectives present at the time (and some developed shortly thereafter) that shared some important features with sexual script theory. The most prominent ones are described briefly here, in hopes of more clearly illuminating both similarities and differences with social scientific perspectives that may be related, at some level, to sexual script theory.

In examining script theories, and those that share similarities with script theories, an important and early distinction becomes apparent based on academic discipline. That is, some script theories, including sexual script theory, emerged out of sociology, thereby resting on the foundations of social constructionism, symbolic interactionism, and dramaturgy. Other script theories, however, emerged out of psychology and psychiatry, thereby resting more on psychoanalytic assumptions or mentalistic models in which the emphasis is on the individual and his or her cognitive experience, created by past experience.

In 1964, psychiatrist Eric Berne published his most famous book, *Games People Play*, popularizing Transactional Analysis (TA). Generally, TA appropriated particular psychoanalytic concepts, renamed them, and embedded them in interpersonal interactions between individuals. Berne's TA provided a framework for analyzing and describing the "moves" within social transactions between two or more people, including the parts of the personality from which particular aspects of interpersonal interactions derive, as well as the psychological "pay offs" for engaging in particular ritualized sets of transactions. It was these ritualized, or scripted, interpersonal interactions that Berne termed "games." One could say that the fact that some games were common enough to be documented implied that such interpersonal interactions are at least loosely scripted, and a specific set of games Berne (1964) described had to do with sexual encounters. Interestingly, Berne (1973) also used the term "life scripts" to refer to overarching patterns of behavior that seemed to characterize some individuals' lives, resulting in repetitive types of interpersonal relationships and ultimate psychological pay offs (also see Steiner 1974). One important difference between TA and sexual script theory, however, is that Berne, perhaps by nature of being a psychiatrist, seemed most interested in games and scripts that were pathological and caused problems in some way.

Similar to Berne, Aaron Beck (1967) focused on pathological experience, primarily with individuals suffering from clinical depression. Beck's model focused on rigid, maladaptive ways of perceiving the world, which subsequently resulted in depressive emotion. Beck (1967) termed the mental mechanism through which people perceive the world as "cognitive schemas," which he defined as: "A (mental) structure for screening, coding, and evaluating the stimuli that impinges on the organism. On the basis of the matrix of schemas, the individual is able to orient himself in relation to time and space, and to categorize and interpret experiences in a meaningful way" (p. 283). In a general sense, cognitive schemas are mental representations individuals construct regarding their knowledge pertaining to a particular concept. Such concepts could be things (e.g., schools, apples), events (e.g., one's 16th birthday, religious services generally), roles (e.g., parents, police officers), and particular people (e.g. one's sibling, a coworker), including oneself (so called "self-schemas"). The importance of cognitive schemas is that they allow us to organize mental material according to the concepts to which that material relates.

The cognitive schemas that seem most closely related to script theory are those pertaining to events, and more specifically, to events as general concepts (e.g., "having sex") rather than specific events that have already occurred. Indeed, some theorists elaborated such cognitive conceptualizations of scripts (e.g., Abelson 1976, 1981). In that way, sociological script theory and cognitive script theory both entail mental material about how to act, what to expect from others involved in the particular scenario, and how to interpret stimuli and happenings within the delineated episode. The primary difference, however, seems to arise out of the emphasis placed on the dynamic and social nature of scripts (sociological perspective) versus the internal and enduring nature of scripts as held by individuals (psychological perspective). Also, sociological scripting perspectives have been applied to human sexuality much more frequently and extensively than have psychological scripting perspectives.

The cognitive schema perspective on scripts has been incorporated into a well-established line of theory and research: attachment theory. Based on the notion that our earliest experiences with caregivers create mental representations of what can be expected in close relationships with others (Bowlby 1969), attachment theory has been a rich source of theoretical and empirical work on a variety of types of emotionally close relationships (Howe 2011). More recently, theorists and researchers in that area have extended the mental representations inherent in attachment theory into the realm of "generalized event representations," or "scripts," that entail what the individual has come to expect in particular kinds of emotional interpersonal relationships (Fivush 2006; Waters and Waters 2006). In particular, attention has been paid to the "maternal secure base script" as the ideal that results from interactions between an infant and a mother who consistently meets the infant's needs (Vaughn et al. 2006). This notion of attachment scripts has apparent relevance for sexual scripts (Dewitte 2012) to the extent that sexual activity occurs within ongoing, emotionally close relationships that provoke caregiving schemas (Peloquin et al. 2014).

A more direct application of mentalistic scripts to romantic relationships was elaborated by Sternberg (1996, 1998), who hypothesized that people each build "stories" about romantic love relationships, based both on personal experience as well as exposure to such stories in one's culture. Based on analyses of both mass media portrayals of romantic love as well as responses from interviews of American adults, Sternberg identified 25 primary love stories, or scripts, that his respondents seemed to follow in their enactments of romantic love relationships. Couples who followed the same or complementary love stories (scripts) were most satisfied with their respective romantic relationships. Although Sternberg did not employ the term "script," or include sexual aspects of romantic relationships, there are apparent conceptual similarities to sexual script theory.

In addition to using script theory to conceptualize mental representation of relationship behavior and meaning, some theorists have extended the script metaphor into the individualistic realm of personality (most notably, Tomkins 1979, 1987). Within these perspectives, the assumption is that personality is organized around emotionally significant experiences, or "scenes."

> To understand and deal with such emotionally significant experiences [scenes], people cognitively but nonconsciously link scenes based on their similarities. This co-assembling of scenes results in 'scripts,' which are implicit assumptions for anticipating and dealing with life experiences so as to maximize positive emotions and minimize negative emotions. (Demorest 2013, p. 583)

An individual's personality is the collection scenes experienced as well as the set of expectations that result from these past experiences. Of course this is a perspective very much rooted in the cognitive schema tradition in psychology, and although not explicitly tied to sexuality, it presumably encompasses stable aspects of sexuality presumed to be part of the individual's personality.

From this brief review of behavioral science theories seemingly tied by the use of the term "script," we see that most have occurred in the psychological tradition of cognitive schema theory. Sexual script theory, in contrast, emerged and developed from a sociological perspective. That is not to say that the two lines of theory and research are entirely unrelated, but they do appear to maintain important differences, and the identification of one set of theories with psychology and psychiatry and the other with sociology likely discourages integration. Returning to Gagnon and Simon's sexual script theory, the section below is dedicated to consideration of how scripts are typically measured in research that employs their theory.

2.4 Methods and Application in Research on Sexual Scripts

What types of scripts, respondents, and topics have been addressed in research employing sexual scripts theory? How have researchers evaluated or measured scripts? Comprehensive answers to these questions are beyond the scope of this chapter, but general answers, and some exemplars, are offered. Still, any attempt to answer these questions entails particular difficulties. As Gagnon (1990) noted, researchers may explicitly or implicitly employ sexual script theory in their work. In other words, some research and the rationale and explanations offered by the researchers may fit sexual script theory particularly well, even when those researchers never mention or reference such theory. At the same time, researchers may make reference to script theory explicitly, yet interpret or apply the theory in ways that are inaccurate or unjustified. An additional complication is that frequently researchers appear to use the term "script" synonymously with terms such as "socialization," "mass media," "cultural messages," and "social roles." With these problematic issues in mind, the published work reviewed here entails explicit reference to sexual script theory consistent with Gagnon and Simon's work.

2.4.1 Critical Review Approaches

In evaluating sexual scripts, researchers have used two broad approaches. One entails deciphering cultural scripts ("cultural scenarios" to Gagnon and Simon) by critically reviewing either cultural artifacts such as mass media, or the collective research published previously. As an example of the cultural analysis approach, Mosher and Tomkins (1988) drew on numerous cultural sources in making the case that particular sexual and gender scripts defined a subpopulation of hypermasculine ("macho") males. In particular, they examined the socialization of boys to acknowledge particular emotions but not others, male adolescent rites of passage, and mass media as evidence that males are commonly provided hypermasculine scripts that result in machismo.

Other researchers have relied on examination of previously published research for examining sexual scripts. For example, Hill (2006) elucidated a common sexual script for feminine heterosexual males based on what previous research revealed about male-female relationships among men considered feminine. Although femininity may impair a man's sexual attractiveness to women, Hill concluded that "feminine heterosexual subvert overly restrictive heteropatriarchal sexual scripts, freeing both traditional and nontraditional men to explore ways of being sexual with women outside a dominant-submissive dialect" (p. 145).

Monto and Carey (2014) examined shifts in national data on sexual behavior collected over 25 years to determine whether sexual scripts for young adults in the U.S. appeared to have shifted toward a more casual, "hook-up" orientation. They found that, although the number of sex partners had not changed over time, contemporary young adults were more likely to report having had sex with a friend or acquaintance, thereby demonstrating some changes in normative sexual scripts. Other writers have reviewed published research to make the case that traditional sexual scripts facilitate sexual aggression from men toward women (Beyers 1996), as well as the case that sexual scripts in the US have become more egalitarian over previous decades (McCormick 2010) Also relying on published research, Eaton and Rose (2011) examined the research published in the journal *Sex Roles* over a span of 35 years to determine the ways in which traditional dating scripts and premarital sexual scripts for males and females in the US may have changed. They concluded, however, that dating relationships in early adulthood remained firmly tied to traditional gender roles and traditional cultural scripts.

Other researchers have analyzed mass media in attempts to uncover what may be prevalent sexual scripts. For example, Kim et al. (2007) analyzed episodes from the top 25 primetime television programs broadcast in the US to elaborate what they termed "the heterosexual script." In contrast, Markle (2008) examined episodes from a popular cable television program in the US that featured sexually assertive female characters, and in so doing determined that the primary female characters enacted a traditionally masculine sexual script. Kelly (2010) analyzed dramatic television series aimed at teen girls in the US to describe scripts related to loss of virginity. Kelly identified three primary virginity loss scripts, and elaborated the positive and negative components

and implications of each script, as well as the meanings ascribed to virginity and its loss within each script.

2.4.2 Self-Report Approaches

In addition to analyzing published research or cultural artifacts such as mass media, the other broad approach to the evaluation of sexual scripts entails researchers gathering self-report data directly from research participants. In essence, respondents are asked to generate or describe particular sexual scripts, or are asked to validate the existence of particular sexual scripts. This latter approach may involve presenting various possible elements of a sexual script and asking respondents to rate how likely it is that each element would be included in the scenario the respondents are provided (e.g., first date). To the extent that the research participants exhibit consensus, the researchers conclude that the respondents shared a cultural script for the given scenario.

As an example of this approach, Krahe et al. (2007) asked teen respondents to rate the likelihood of several script elements for having sex with a new partner for the first time. Ratings of the individual script elements were compared under instructions to consider adolescents in general versus the respondent him- or herself. Interestingly, respondents' personal scripts contained less risk elements and more positive outcomes compared to their general cultural scripts. Similarly, Littleton and Axsom (2003) asked college student respondents to rate how typical several script elements were for "seduction" and "rape." The researchers found that, although there were clear differences between to two scripts, there were several elements that overlapped, which may explain why some instances of sexual assault are viewed ambiguously, even by the victims.

The second general self-report method entails asking research participants to generate a verbal (written or spoken) description of either what did occur in a defined sexual event, or might occur in a hypothetical scenario presented by the researchers (e.g., Clark and Carroll 2008; Eaton and Rose 2012; Krahe et al. 2007). The assumption is that themes that emerge from respondents' descriptions of their sexual experiences represent common cultural scripts. With responses to a hypothetical scenario, the assumption is that respondents rely on their cultural scripts to generate the anticipated events and elements comprising the scenario.

There are numerous examples illustrating the primary self-report approaches that have been employed to collect data from respondents concerning sexual scripts. Consider Masters et al. (2013) who conducted individual, face-to-face interviews with heterosexual young adults. The researchers were interested in potential differences between respondents' cultural sexual scripts and personal sexual scripts, and how they negotiated any such discrepancies. They found that respondents seemed to fall into three broad categories: those whose cultural and personal scripts coincided, those who accepted gender-based cultural scripts as reality yet created exceptions for their own such behavior, and those who attempted to either transform cultural scripts or view their own variation on those scripts as equally valid. Whittier and Melendez (2004) conducted multiple interviews with a small sample of gay men, examining how the respondents viewed their own sexuality. "Analysis revealed that intersubjectivity, or what individuals thought others thought of them, is a common process in participants' intrapsychic sexual scripting" (p. 131).

Interviews have been a common method of data collection in sexual script theory research. For example, Karlsen and Traeen (2013) interviewed young adult women regarding their experiences in "friends with benefits" relationships, Mutchler (2000) interviewed gay men about their sexual lives, and Hussen et al. (2012) interviewed African American men regarding their early sexual socialization and subsequent sexual experiences. In each of these studies, respondent narratives were analyzed for themes indicative of what the researchers considered predominant sexual scripts. The interview or focus group approaches to gathering data, with subsequent analysis of themes emerging in responses, has been employed to examine sexual scripts among African American teen girls (French 2013) and women (McLellan-Lemal 2013), Nigerian adolescents (Barnett et al. 2011), women living in urban cities in the US (McLellan-Lemal 2013; Ortiz-Torres et al. 2003), deaf adults (Gilbert et al. 2012), adults with cerebral palsy (Dune 2013), adults with physical impairments affecting sexual functioning (Dune and Shuttleworth 2009; Mitchell et al. 2011), female family clinic clients (Dworkin et al. 2007), HIV-positive men who have sex with other men while under the influence of alcohol (Parsons et al. 2004), and those seeking casual sex partners through web sites designed for that purpose (Sevcikova and Daneback 2011).

2.4.2.1 Innovative Approaches

In addition to the typical means of gathering data on sexual scripts, there have been some particularly novel approaches to measurement. For example, Stulhofer et al. (2010) were interested in the extent to which young adult men had incorporated scripts displayed in mainstream pornography into their scripts for sexual activity with actual partners. Initially, a sample of young men and women were asked to list separately the things, activities, and sensations that are important for (1) pornographic depictions of sexual activity, and (2) personal experience of great sex. A set of 42 elements that emerged from analyses of the free responses was then presented to a large sample of young adult men who were asked to rate the items as to importance, first when the set was presented in the context of "great sex" followed by the context of depictions of sex in pornography. The researchers compared each respondent's rating of each pair of matched items in the two contexts to create a difference score. The lower the overall score, the more similarly the respondent rated the importance of elements required for good sex and for pornographic depictions of sex. The researchers interpreted relatively low scores (high similarity between sets of ratings) as indicative of greater overlap between the sexual scripts respondents maintained for personal sexual activity and for sexual activity in pornography.

Lenton and Bryan (2005) also started by asking college students to generate scripts; however the context was initiation of sexual activity within two types of dating relationships—casual vs. committed. Based on the themes that emerged, these researchers constructed scenarios representing each of the two types of sexual scripts and presented them to a second sample of college students. Lenton and Bryan intentionally left out particular script elements in their constructed scenarios, and respondents were each tested as to whether they remembered particular elements as having been present in the scenarios they read. The researchers assumed that elements that were falsely remembered as having been present must be part of the respondent's script for sexual activity with that particular type of dating relationship. That is, if a respondent incorrectly recalled a particular element as having been included in the scenario he or she read, Lenton and Bryan concluded that the respondent misremembered the element because it is part of the respondent's sexual script pertaining to the given scenario. In this way, the researchers approached assessment of individuals' sexual scripts in an innovative way.

Alvarez and Garcia-Marques (2008), who were interested in the extent to which college students' scripts for casual versus stable sexual relationships included use of condoms, also took a multi-stage approach to examining sexual scripts. These researchers began by asking a sample of college students to each create lists of about 20 typical actions or situations, in sequential order, involved during an episode of sexual intimacy within either a casual or stable relationship. In addition to examining the incidence of condom use in these reported scenarios, Alvarez and Garcia-Marques constructed prototypical scripts from the responses, and presented those to a second sample of college students. The second set of respondents were asked to construct the endings to the presented scenarios, each of which stopped short of sexual intercourse, and the authors examined the incidence of mentioning condoms. Last, Alvarez and Garcia-Marques (2008) presented a series of written scenarios, only some of which were sexual, to a third sample of col-

lege students. The sexual scenarios included script-typical and script-atypical elements, and respondents were tested on their memory of the presence of each element subsequent to a cognitive distraction task. The respondents' abilities to correctly remember condom-related elements of particular scenarios were compared to their abilities to remember script-typical or script-atypical elements. From such comparisons, the authors examined whether condom use appeared to be a typical element of college students' sexual scripts in casual versus stable sexual relationships.

The review thus far has featured published research in which sexual script theory was used explicitly to frame the research methodology chosen. However, there are numerous instances in which researchers employed sexual script theory in their interpretation of results that were based on data gathered from respondents with traditional, non-script methods. For example, such research has entailed examining the influence of gender in judgments about casual sex (Reid et al. 2011), the initiation of sexual activity within dating relationships (La France 2010; Vannier and O'Sullivan 2011), reactions to first sexual intercourse (Pinquart 2010), young women's negotiation of cunnilingus in dating relationships (Backstrom et al. 2012), whether oral sex is considered "sex" (Dotson-Blake et al. 2012), and how heterosexual men are able to perform in gay pornography (Escoffier 2003). In each of these examples, the researchers gathered data in conventional ways, yet used a sexual scripts framework for interpreting their data.

2.5 Sexual Script Theory: Critique and Future Directions

Despite its popularity, some important concerns have been raised regarding sexual script theory. A primary criticism involves its status as a formal theory. Ideally, theories facilitate prediction in the form of testable hypotheses. With accumulating knowledge based on those tests, the theories offer the ability to explain causal connections among variables. It is with regard to explaining causal relationships among the variables of interest where sexual script theory is lacking (Bancroft 2009; Weis 1998a). Instead, sexual script theory appears to offer a metaphor; its greatest strength lies in providing a language and way of conceptualizing the cognitive schemas individuals hold, and the exemplary scenarios provided by one's culture, pertaining to sexuality.

Due to its lack of explanatory power, many fundamental questions regarding sexual scripts remain unanswered. In particular, why are particular cultural scripts institutionalized, becoming prevalent or common, whereas other are not? How do we explain cultural shifts over time? What are the mechanisms through which individuals acquire and maintain their respective sets of sexual scripts? How do individuals' sexual scripts exert influence over behavior, and when and why are sexual scripts more or less influential in this regard? And perhaps the most complex question is how do sexual scripts at all three conceptual levels interact dynamically with one another at the level of the individual? These particular concerns about sexual script theory as a full-fledged scientific theory were raised by Weis (1998a), and he provided some provisional answers, or least possibilities. Weis called for research on these and other questions, yet little if any progress has been made along those lines.

With these deficits in conceptual foundation and elaboration through empirical data, sexual script theory's status as a scientific theory is debatable. Indeed, Bancroft (2009) summarized his perspective this way: "What are my conclusions about Gagnon and Simon's sexual script approach? I consider their dramaturgical metaphor to be useful as a way to grasp what are otherwise highly complex psychological processes; in other words, a good example of a simplified model of reality" (p. 12). However, he goes on, "(Gagnon and Simon's) sole use of a dramaturgical model, which has the advantage of being comprehensible in a vernacular sense, effectively puts their work into the folk-theory category" (p. 12).

To be fair, however, Gagnon and Simon were consistent across their writings in stating that they never intended their sexual scripting perspective to be a scientific theory, and perhaps over time became even less concerned about the issues raised here. That is, in their earlier work they relied on principles of social learning to at least partially explain the processes through which individuals acquired scripts (Gagnon and Simon, 1973). However, by 30 years later they noted that their thinking had gradually shifted from social learning to a more social constructionist perspective (Simon and Gagnon 2003). Indeed, when Gagnon (1990) was asked to review the connections between sexual script theory and published research on sexuality, he did so, but questioned the validity of the exercise given that scientific research itself is socially constructed and any results thereby subjectively interpreted. Ironically, as Bancroft (2009, see p. 12) noted, the lack of empirical evidence behind sexual script theory did not prevent Gagnon and Simon from making strong, sweeping statements regarding the existence and power of sexual scripts.

Despite a professed lack of faith in results of supposedly empirical research, Simon and Gagnon occasionally relied on such data for drawing conclusions regarding sexual scripts. For example, Gagnon and Simon (1987) concluded that there had been cultural shifts in the scripts pertaining to oral-genital contact in the United States. What was the basis for their conclusion? Gagnon and Simon reviewed published research results, including the results of surveys on the incidence and contexts of oral sex experience. Similarly, Laumann et al. (1994) conducted the National Health and Social Life Survey (NHSLS), an impressive nationally representative survey of sexuality in the US, and sexual script theory was one of only three theoretical models the authors stated as being the basis for their empirical work.

With such an extensive data set as the NHSLS, Laumann et al. (1994) seemed poised to resolve some lingering questions regarding sexual script theory. However, as those authors noted, analyzing scripts directly is difficult in a cross-sectional survey, because doing so entails examining the sequencing of behavior, the interactions between sexual partners, and so forth (see Laumann et al. 1994, p. 7). Instead, the NHSLS contained questions regarding respondents' respective sexual histories, their most recent sexual activity, preferences, attitudes, and so forth, and inferences were drawn about sexual scripts from those data. Even so, Bancroft (2009, p. 11) noted that sexual script theory played an extremely minor role in the interpretation and presentation of results by Laumann et al. (1994).

Mahay et al. (2001) examined NHSLS data to explicate the intersection of sexual scripts with race, gender, and social class in the U.S. On its face, the endeavor seemed promising for answering some basic theoretical questions regarding the functioning of sexual scripts. However, because of the nature of the NHSLS data, the three levels of sexual scripts were operationally defined in ways fundamentally different from Gagnon and Simon's concepts: cultural scripts/scenarios were represented by respondents' attitudes, interpersonal scripts by actual practices with sex partners, and intrapsychic scripts by respondents' sexual preferences. Depending on each respondent's pattern of responses across these domains, he or she was designated as following one of three scripts determined by the researchers: Traditional, Relational, or Recreational. Bancroft (2009) raised these concerns about the approach Mahay et al. (2001) took:

> No consideration is given to the extent to which such aspects of human sexuality are meaningful illustrations of sexual scripts, and one is left with the distinct impression that this was a post-hoc attempt to use the NHSLS data to support a scripting approach rather than evidence that scripting theory had influenced the design of the survey in the first place. (p. 11)

The difficulties with measurement of sexual script variables is a lingering issue in need of clarification if sexual script theory is to advance. In this chapter I summarized the primary ways researchers have attempted to gather data pertaining to scripts, but there have been other, less frequent approaches that appear more problematic. For example, Sakaluk et al. (2014) set out to construct a self-report scale to quantify sexual scripts in emerging adulthood. These researchers started with small focus groups of college students, asking a wide-ranging set of questions pertaining to sexual beliefs, especially pertaining to men's and women's roles in sexual activity. From the responses, Sakaluk et al. compiled a set of verbatim statements, and administered these to a large sample of college students for their rating of agreement or disagreement with each. Factor analysis revealed six factors, yet it was the individual items that seem problematic from a sexual script perspective. Each item referred to males or females in general and spanned a wide range of beliefs about men compared to women. It's unclear how these disparate attitudinal items relate to the three levels of sexual scripts as defined by Gagnon and Simon.

The critical commentary on the results from Sakaluk et al. (2014) are meant simply as an illustration of a larger problem: researchers appear to have taken great liberty in their conceptualization and measurement of what they consider sexual scripts. Frequently "sexual scripts" seem to be used synonymously for what other researchers might simply call sexual attitudes, beliefs, and norms. One might argue that attitudes and beliefs are aspects of intrapsychic scripts; however, even intrapsychic scripts were conceptualized as more complex, and equating sexual attitudes and beliefs with sexual scripts generally, or even cultural scenarios specifically, does not seem warranted.

Frith and Kitzinger (2001) raised another potentially serious concern regarding how sexual scripts have been studied. Recall that typically sexual scripts are elicited in the context of focus group discussions, or asking respondents to write out scenarios provided a specific context or prompt. Frith and Kitzinger proposed that the narratives that result from such methodology may not reflect pre-existing scripts but may be formulated as the result of the process of asking respondents to generate such narratives. In other words, respondents may produce a narrative script based on assumed cultural norms, yet not carry such scripts with them outside of the research context. Indeed, other researchers have noted an apparent need for people to construct narratives to explain their sexual experiences and identities (Plante 2007; Plummer 1995). To illustrate their point, Frith and Kitzinger (2001) conducted focus groups with female college students, asking them about handling unwanted sexual activity. The researchers analyzed responses with an eye toward how focus group participants responded to each other in the creation of shared scripts. Frith and Kitzinger concluded that the scripts respondents produced seemed to emerge from a social process, and served the function of alleviating respondents from personal responsibility for unwanted sexual experiences.

The implications of Frith and Kitzinger's proposal are important, as sexual script theory rests on the assumption that sexual scripts, at all three levels, exist as cognitive entities that individuals maintain over time. If instead people produce sexual scripts when asked to do so for research purposes, the importance of such scripts for influencing behavior is called into question. For example, consider Dworking et al. (2007) who examined women's sexual scripts both before and after an intervention designed to promote condom use. At follow-up they found that in both the intervention group and the control group, women introduced condoms earlier in the sequence when asked to generate a sexual script for having sexual intercourse with a new male partner than they had done at initial assessment. The researchers attributed the effect to the fact that both groups had undergone extensive evaluation, regardless of whether they received the intervention, thereby leading the women to become more comfortable with introduction of condoms with new partners. To extend Frith and Kitzinger's (2001) concern, however, it seems possible that the women discerned what was expected of them by the researchers (given their emphasis on safe sex) and thereby constructed a set of sexual scripts to match those expectations. If so, that's an important distinction from having made changes to their enduring personal sexual scripts that, theoretically, influence their behavior.

The issue of differences between cultural scripts/scenarios and interpersonal/intrapersonal scripts is an important distinction in need of further study. Researchers employing sexual script theory tend to focus on cultural scripts, perhaps because a focus on themes and commonalities is more manageable than the potential diversity across individuals and their intrapersonal scripts. However, if those intrapersonal and interpersonal scripts are more relevant for peoples' behavior, beliefs, and so forth, research pertaining to those scripts is all the more valuable. It seems clear that researchers cannot assume correspondence between cultural and interpersonal and intrapersonal scripts, as past research focused on such comparisons has shown important differences (e.g., Allison and Risman 2014; Masters et al. 2013; McCabe et al. 2010).

In addition to examining all three levels of sexual scripts, as well as their relationships to each other and to behavior, further research is needed simply on investigation of sexual scripts across a variety of types of people. Although the published research reviewed in this chapter illustrates a fair degree of variability in the types of people whose scripts have been studied, typically only one study has been published on any one given group. Especially with studies employing focus groups, samples are typically small (e.g., 20–50), making it even less likely that one study on the sexual scripts of a particular demographic group adequately captures the diversity present in the population from which the sample was drawn. Also, although there have been some studies on sexual scripts with samples outside of the US, they are relatively few in nature and typically from Western cultures. In other words, there is tremendous need for research on possible similarities and differences in cultural sexual scripts across ethnic and subcultural groups.

Last, most research on sexual scripts has been focused on heterosexual, cisgender respondents, especially college students. In other words, non-heterosexual and transgender samples have been conspicuously rare or absent in published research on sexual scripts. In searching the published research literature, the rare examples with regard to non-heterosexual respondents involved gay men, with an emphasis on problematic aspects of sexuality such as engaging in risky sex. I was unable to find a single example of published research on sexual script theory with transgender individuals. Gender and sexuality are inherently intertwined in sexual script theory, and notions of a traditional sexual script revolve around male-female sexual interactions (Wiederman 2005). So, investigation of the interactions among gender identity, gender roles, gender pairings of sexual partners, and sexual scripts seems especially important (Iantaffi and Bockting 2011).

In closing, Gagnon and Simon's sexual script theory has been a mainstay in social scientific research on human sexuality for more than four decades. Still, its future as a formal theory rests on much needed additional work at both the conceptual and empirical levels. For all of its intuitive and descriptive appeal, sexual script theory lacks explanatory and predictive power. Also, as popular as sexual script theory has been, there remain numerous topics and demographic groups to which the script perspective has not been applied. Sexual script theory is likely to remain a popular conceptual framework in researchers' repertoire, but the development of the approach beyond its current status requires attention paid to that developmental process, rather than simply the continued application of the theory when convenient.

References

Abelson, R. P. (1976). Script processing in attitude formation and decision making. In J. S. Carroll & J. W. Payne (Eds.), *Cognition and social behavior* (pp. 33–46). Hillsdale: Erlbaum.

Abelson, R. P. (1981). Psychological status of the script concept. *American Psychologist, 36,* 715–729.

Allison, R., & Risman, B. J. (2014). "It goes hand in hand with the parties:" Race, class, and residence in college student negotiations of hooking up. *Sociological Perspectives, 57,* 102–123.

Alvarez, M. J., & Garcia-Marques, L. (2008). Condom inclusion in cognitive representations of sexual encounters. *Journal of Sex Research, 45,* 358–370.

Backstrom L., Armstrong, E. A., & Puentes, J. (2012). Women's negotiation of cunnilingus in college hookups and relationships. *Journal of Sex Research, 49,* 1–12.

Bancroft, J. (2009). *Sexuality and its problems* (3rd ed.). London: Churchill Livingstone.

Barnett, J. P., Maticka-Tyndale, E., & The HP4RY Group. (2011). The gift of agency: Sexual exchange scripts among Nigerian youth. *Journal of Sex Research, 48,* 349–359.

Beck, A. T. (1967). *Depression: Causes and treatments.* Philadelphia: University of Pennsylvania Press.

Berne, E. (1964). *Games people play: The basic handbook of transactional analysis.* New York: Grove Press.

Berne, E. (1973). *What do you say after you say hello?* New York: Bantam.

Bowlby, J. (1969). *Attachment and loss, Vol. 1: Attachment.* New York: Basic Books.

Brickell, C. (2006). The sociological construction of gender and sexuality. *The Sociological Review, 54,* 87–113.

Byers, E. S. (1996). How well does the traditional sexual script explain sexual coercion? Review of a program of research. *Journal of Psychology & Human Sexuality, 8,* 7–25.

Clark, M. D., & Carroll, M. H. (2008). Acquaintance rape scripts of women and men: Similarities and differences. *Sex Roles, 58,* 616–625.

DeLamater, J. D., & Hyde, J. S. (1998). Essentialism versus social constructionism in the study of human sexuality. *Journal of Sex Research, 35,* 10–18.

Demorest, A. P. (2013). The role of scripts in psychological maladjustment and psychotherapy. *Journal of Personality, 81,* 583–594.

Dewitte, M. (2012). Different perspectives on the sex-attachment link: Towards an emotion-motivational account. *Journal of Sex Research, 49,* 105–124.

Dotson-Blake, K. P., Knox, D., & Zusman, M. E. (2012). Exploring social sexual scripts related to oral sex: A profile of college student perceptions. *The Professional Counselor, 2*(1), 1–11.

Dune, T. M. (2013). Understanding experiences of sexuality with cerebral palsy through sexual script theory. *International Journal of Social Science Studies, 1*(1), 1–12.

Dune, T. M., & Shuttleworth, R. P. (2009). "It's just supposed to happen:" The myth of sexual spontaneity and the sexually marginalized. *Sexuality and Disability, 27,* 97–108.

Dworkin, S. L., Beckford, S. T., Ehrhardt, A. A. (2007). Sexual scripts of women: A longitudinal analysis of participants in a gender-specific HIV/STD prevention intervention. *Archives of Sexual Behavior, 36,* 269–279.

Eaton, A. A., & Rose, S. (2011). Has dating become more egalitarian? A 35 year review using *sex roles. Sex Roles, 64,* 843–862.

Eaton, A. A., & Rose, S. (2012). Scripts for actual first date and hanging-out encounters among young heterosexual Hispanic adults. *Sex Roles, 67,* 285–299.

Escoffier, J. (2003). Gay-for-pay: Straight men and the making of gay pornography. *Qualitative Sociology, 26,* 531–555.

Fivush, R. (2006). Scripting attachment: Generalized event representations and internal working models. *Attachment & Human Development, 8,* 283–289.

French, B. (2013). More than Jezebels and freaks: Exploring how black girls navigate sexual coercion and sexual scripts. *Journal of African American Studies, 17,* 35–50.

Frith, H., & Kitzinger, C. (2001). Reformulating sexual script theory: Developing a discursive psychology of sexual negotiation. *Theory & Psychology, 11,* 209–232.

Gagnon, J. H. (1990). The explicit and implicit use of script theory in sex research. *Annual Review of Sex Research, 1,* 1–43.

Gagnon, J. H., & Simon, W. (1973). *Sexual conduct: The social sources of human sexuality*. Chicago: Aldine.

Gagnon, J. H., & Simon, W. (1987). The sexual scripting of oral genital contacts. *Archives of Sexual Behavior, 16*, 1–25.

Gecas, V., & Libby, R. (1976). Sexual behavior as symbolic interaction. *The Journal of Sex Research, 12*, 33–49.

Gilbert, G. L., Clark, M. D., & Anderson, M. L. (2012). Do deaf individuals' dating scripts follow the traditional sexual script? *Sexuality & Culture, 16*, 90–99.

Goffman, E. (1959). *The presentation of self in everyday life*. New York: Anchor.

Henslin, J. M., & Biggs, M. A. (1971). Dramaturgical desexualization: The sociology of the vaginal examination. In J. M. Henslin (Ed.), *Studies in the sociology of sex* (pp. 243–272). New York: Appleton-Century-Crofts.

Hill, D. B. (2006). "Feminine" heterosexual men: Subverting heteropatriarchal sexual scripts? *The Journal of Men's Studies, 14*, 145–159.

Howe, D. (2011). *Attachment across the life course*. London: Palgrave.

Hussen, S. A., Bowleg, L., Sangaramoorthy, T., & Malebranche, D. J. (2012). Parents, peers and pornography: The influence of formative sexual scripts on adult HIV sexual risk behavior among Black men in the U.S. *Culture, Health & Sexuality, 14*, 863–877.

Iantaffi, A., & Bockting, W. O. (2011). Views from both sides of the bridge? Gender, sexual legitimacy, and transgender people's experiences of relationships. *Culture, Health & Sexuality, 13*, 355–370.

Karlsen, M., & Traeen, B (2013). Identifying "friends with benefits" scripts among young adults in the Norwegian cultural context. *Sexuality & Culture, 17*, 83–99.

Kelly, M. (2010). Virginity loss narrative in "teen drama" television programs. *The Journal of Sex Research, 47*, 479–489.

Kim, J. L., Sorsoli, C. L., Collins, K., Zylbergold, B. A., Schooler, D., & Tolman, D. L. (2007). From sex to sexuality: Exposing the heterosexual script on primetime network television. *Journal of Sex Research, 44*, 145–157.

Kimmel, M. (2007). John Gagnon and the sexual self. In M. Kimmel (Ed.), *The sexual self: Construction of sexual scripts* (pp. vii–vxi). Nashville, TN: Vanderbilt University Press.

Kinsey, A., Pomeroy, W., & Martin, C. (1948). *Sexual behavior in the human male*. Philadelphia: W. B. Saunders.

Kinsey, A., Pomeroy, W., Martin, C., & Gebhard, P. (1953). *Sexual behavior in the human female*. Philadelphia: W. B. Saunders.

Krahe, B., Bieneck, S., & Scheinberger-Olwwig, R. (2007). Adolescents' sexual scripts: Schematic representations of consensual and nonconsensual sexual interactions. *The Journal of Sex Research, 44*, 316–327.

La France, B. H. (2010). What verbal and nonverbal communication cues lead to sex?: Analysis of the traditional sexual script. *Communication Quarterly, 58*, 297–318.

Laumann, E. O., Gagnon, J. H., Michael, R. R., & Michaels, S. (1994). *The social organization of sexuality: Sexual practices in the United States*. Chicago: University of Chicago Press.

Lenton, A. P., & Bryan, A. (2005). An affair to remember: The role of sexual scripts in the perception of sexual intent. *Personal Relationships, 12*, 483–498.

Littleton, H. L., & Axsom, D. (2003). Rape and seduction scripts of university students: Implications for rape attributions and unacknowledged rape. *Sex Roles, 49*, 465–475.

Longmore, M. (1998). Symbolic interactionism and the study of sexuality. *The Journal of Sex Research, 35*, 44–57.

Mahay, J., Laumann, E. O., & Michaels, S. (2001). Race, gender, and class in sexual scripts. In E. O. Laumann & R. T. Michael (Eds.), *Sex, love, and health in America: Private choices and public policies* (pp. 197–238). Chicago: University of Chicago Press.

Markle, G. (2008). "Can women have sex like a man?" Sexual scripts in *Sex in the City*. *Sexuality & Culture, 12*, 45–57.

Masters, W. H., & Johnson, V. E. (1966). *Human sexual response*. Boston: Little, Brown.

Masters, W. H., & Johnson, V. E. (1970). *Human sexual inadequacy*. Boston: Little, Brown.

Masters, N. T., Casey, E., Wells, E. A., & Morrison, D. M. (2013). Sexual scripts among young heterosexually active men and women: Continuity and change. *Journal of Sex Research, 50*, 409–420.

McCabe, J. M., Tanner, A. E., & Heiman, J. (2010). The impact of gender expectations on meanings of sex and sexuality: Results from a cognitive interview study. *Sex Roles, 63*, 252–263.

McCormick, N. B. (2010). Preface to sexual scripts: Social and therapeutic implications. *Sexual and Relationship Therapy, 25*, 91–95.

McLellan-Lemal, E., Toledo, L., O'Daniels, C., Villar-Loubet, O., Simpson, C., Adimora, A. A., & Marks, G. (2013). "A man's gonna do what a man wants to do:" African American and Hispanic women's perceptions about heterosexual relationships: A qualitative study. *BMC Women's Health, 13*, 27–41.

Ménard, A.D., & Cabrera, C. (2011). Whatever the approach, Tab B still fits into Slot A: Twenty years of sex scripts in romance novels. *Sexuality & Culture, 15(3)*, 240–255.

Mitchell, K. R., Wellings, K., Nazareth, I., King, M., Mercer, C. H., & Johnson, A. M. (2011). Scripting sexual function: A qualitative investigation. *Sociology of Health & Illness, 33*, 540–553.

Monto, M. A., & Carey, A. G. (2014). A new standard of sexual behavior? Are claims associated with the "hook-up culture" supported by General Social Survey data? *Journal of Sex Research, 51*, 605–615.

Mosher, D. L., & Tomkins, S. S. (1988). Scripting the macho man: Hypermasculine socialization and enculturation. *Journal of Sex Research, 25,* 60–84.

Mutchler, M. G. (2000). Young gay men's stories in the States: Scripts, sex, and safety in the time of *AIDS. Sexualities, 3,* 31–55.

Ortiz-Torres, B., Williams, S. P., & Ehrhardt, A. A. (2003). Urban women's gender scripts: Implications for HIV prevention. *Culture, Health & Sexuality, 5,* 1–17.

Parsons, J. T., Vicioso, K. J., Punzalan, J. C., Halkitis, P. N., Kutnick, K., Velasquez, M. M., (2004). The impact of alcohol use on the sexual scripts of HIV-positive men who have sex with men. *Journal of Sex Research, 41,* 160–172.

Peloquin, K., Brassard, A., Lafontaine, M., & Shaver, P. R. (2014). Sexuality explained through the lens of attachment theory: Attachment, caregiving, and sexual satisfaction. *Journal of Sex Research, 51,* 561–576.

Pinquart, M. (2010). Ambivalence in adolescents' decisions about having their first sexual intercourse. *Journal of Sex Research, 47,* 440–450.

Plante, R. F. (2007). In search of sexual subjectivities: Exploring the sociological construction of sexual selves. In M. Kimmel (Ed.), *The sexual self: Construction of sexual scripts* (pp. 31–48). Nashville: Vanderbilt University Press.

Plummer, K. (1982). Symbolic interactionism and sexual conduct: An emergent perspective. In M. Brake (Ed.), *Human sexual relations: Towards a redefinition of sexual politics* (pp. 223–241). New York: Pantheon Books.

Plummer, K. (1995*). Telling sexual stories: Power, change and social worlds*. New York: Routledge.

Reid, J. A., Elliott, S., & Webber, G. R. (2011). Casual hookups to formal dates: Refining the boundaries of the sexual double standard. *Gender & Society, 25,* 545–568.

Sakaluk, J. K., Todd, L. M., Milhausen, R., Lachowsky, N. J., & Undergraduate Research Group in Psychology (2014). Dominant heterosexual sexual scripts in emerging adulthood: Conceptualization and measurement. *Journal of Sex Research, 51,* 516–531.

Sevcikova, A., & Daneback, K. (2011). Anyone who wants sex? Seeking sex partners on sex-oriented contact websites. *Sexual and Relationship Therapy, 26,* 170–181.

Simon, W. (1996). *Postmodern sexualities*. London: Routledge.

Simon, W., & Gagnon, J. H. (1984). Sexual scripts. *Society, 22*(01), 53–60.

Simon, W., & Gagnon, J. H. (1986). Sexual scripts: Permanence and change. *Archives of Sexual Behavior, 15,* 97–120.

Simon, W., & Gagnon, J. H. (1987). A sexual scripts approach. In J. H. Geer & W. T. O'Donohue (Eds.), *Theories of human sexuality* (pp. 363–383). New York: Plenum.

Simon, W., & Gagnon, J. H. (2003). Sexual scripts: Origins, influences and changes. *Qualitative Sociology, 26,* 491–497.

Stein, A. (1989). Three models of sexuality: Drives, identities, and practices. *Sociological Theory, 7,* 1–13.

Steiner, C. (1974). *Scripts people live: Transactional analysis of life scripts*. New York: Grover Press.

Sternberg R. J. (1996). Love stories. *Personal Relationships, 3,* 59–79.

Sternberg, R. J. (1998). *Love is a story: A new theory of relationships*. New York: Oxford University Press.

Stulhofer, A., Busko, V., & Landripet, I. (2010). Pornography, sexual socialization, and satisfaction among young men. *Archives of Sexual Behavior, 39,* 168–178.

Tomkins, S. (1979). Script theory: Differential magnification of affects. In C. Keasey (Ed.), *Nebraska Symposium on Motivation* (Vol. 26, pp. 201–236). Lincoln: University of Nebraska Press.

Tomkins, S. (1987). Script theory. In J. Aronoff, A. Rabin & R. Zucker (Eds.), *The emergence of personality* (pp. 147–216). New York: Springer.

Vannier, S. A., & O'Sullivan, L. F. (2011). Communicating interest in sex: Verbal and nonverbal initiation of sexual activity in young adults' romantic dating relationships. *Archives of Sexual Behavior, 40,* 961–969.

Vaughn, B. E., Waters, H. S., Coppola, G., Cassidy, J., Bost, K. K., & Verissimo, M. (2006). Script-like attachment representations and behavior in families and across cultures: Studies of parental secure base narratives. *Attachment & Human Development, 8,* 179–184.

Waskul, D. D., & Plante, R. F. (2010). Sex(ualities) and symbolic interaction. *Symbolic Interaction, 33,* 148–162.

Waters, H. S., & Waters, E. (2006). The attachment working models concept: Among other things, we build script-like representations of secure base experiences. *Attachment & Human Development, 8,* 185–197.

Weis, D. L. (1998a). Conclusion: The state of sexual theory. *Journal of Sex Research, 35,* 100–114.

Weis, D. L. (1998b). The use of theory in sexuality research. *Journal of Sex Research, 35,* 1–9.

Whittier, D. K., & Melendez, R. M. (2004). Intersubjectivity in the intrapsychic sexual scripting of gay men. *Culture, Health, & Sexuality, 6,* 131–143.

Wiederman, M. W. (2005). The gendered nature of sexual scripts. *The Family Journal:Counseling and Therapy for Couples and Families, 13,* 496–502.

Sexual Fields

3

Adam Isaiah Green

3.1 Introduction

The sociological study of modern sexual life now enjoys a rich, 40 year history, one inaugurated roughly in the early 1970s when Laud Humphreys (1975), Gagnon and Simon (1974), and other scholars brought the investigation of sexuality out from under the thumb of deviance and into the framework of social constructionism. Thereafter, the sociology of sexuality branched outward, from historical examinations of sexual communities (Kennedy and Davis 1993; Levine 1998; Rupp 2009) and sexual identities (Greenberg 1988; Hennen 2008; Stein 1997), to the study of sex work and sexual regulation (Bernstein 2007; Brock 1998); courtship (Adams 1999; Bailey 1998), transgendered practices and subjectivities (Newton 1972; Rupp and Taylor 2008; Schilt and Windsor 2014), and epistemological investigations of sexual classifications (Stein and Plummer 1996), among still others. To the extent that one may identify theoretical currents within this broad literature, it is clear that social constructionism developed alongside of and gave way to a critical poststructural impulse which, in the wake of Foucault (1980), crystallized in "queer theory" (Epstein 1996; Seidman 1996). Though the queer theoretical enterprise of the 1990s and early 2000s did not

replace social constructionism, it nevertheless captured the subfields' theoretical energies and took them in new directions, deepening the constructionist emphasis on anti-essentialism (Rupp and Taylor 2008; Valocchi 2005), and coupling it with an antihumanist epistemology that conceives of sexuality as an effect of power and political economy (Fox and Alldred 2013; Weiss 2012).

The incisive epistemological insights of queer theory aside, sexuality scholars with interests in sexual identities, communities and practices have needed to look elsewhere for analytic guidance (Edwards 1998; Gamson 2000; Green 2007). This need has grown ever more apparent given advances in communication technologies since the early 1970s when Gagnon and Simon (1974) were postulating the first systematic theoretical rendering of sexuality in the sociology of sexuality—scripting theory. Over this stretch of time, the evolution of sexual life via the digital revolution, from dating sites to erotic chat rooms to mobile apps designed for hookups, has brought a palpable sense of the centrality of collective sexual life and its complexity for even the most mainstream of sexual actors.

But how to make sense of the impact of these developments for intimate partnership? And how to think about contemporary sexual life in a way that retains the pragmatist and symbolic interactionist insights regarding micro-level interaction—a fundamental element of constructionist scholarship—while at the same time accounting for broader, macro-level structures, discourses

A. I. Green (✉)
Department of Sociology, University of Toronto, Toronto, Ontario, Canada
e-mail: AdamIsaiah.Green@Utoronto.ca

and processes, like the state, medicine, psychiatry and media, illuminated by queer theory?

To be sure, earlier scholarship in the sociology of sexuality had detailed the power of sexual subcultures and sexual institutions in shaping sexual life (Fitzgerald 1986; Tewksbury 2002; Weinberg and Williams 1975). Here, attention was ceded neither to individuals nor to the institutional and discursive domains in which they were embedded. Levine (1998), for example, showed how post-World War II gendered scripts were institutionalized in the fabric of the New York City clone subculture, the latter which mirrored and amplified each individual clone's internalized masculine script into new sexual norms and lifestyles. And Kennedy and Davis (1993) showed how the discourse of "butch and fem" had come to constitute identities, subjectivities and social organization in one 1950s lesbian community of Buffalo, New York. Nevertheless, overall, this body of work tended to be anthropological in focus and did not gesture in the direction of a comprehensive framework for thinking about collective sexual life more generally (Green 2014). That is, analysis stopped at the borders of the sexual communities under investigation, and broader lines of inquiry around the structural similarities between erotic worlds and their modes of organization, remained undeveloped (Green 2014).

More recently, scholars of the sociology of sexuality have pushed forward constructionist research through the *sexual fields approach*, conceiving of collective sexual life as a particular kind of social life in its own right (Green 2008b, 2014). A *sexual field* "emerges when a subset of actors with potential romantic or sexual interest in one another congregate in physical or virtual space and orient themselves toward one another according to a logic of desirability imminent to their collective relations …" (Green 2014, p. 27). Hailing from other areas of sociological work—mainly, the sociology of culture and inequality—the theoretical impetus for the sexual fields approach originates in Bourdieusian field theory (1977, 1990) and the analysis of routine practice (Martin and George 2006; Green 2008a). Regarding collective sexual life as comprised of multiple erotic worlds, each with their own particular sociodemographic composition and internally constituted status order, scholars of the sexual field aim to demonstrate how fields shape desire and desirability in a manner irreducible to individual desires alone. Thus, as I draw out in greater detail below, the sexual fields approach entails an analysis of the ways in which partnership preferences, including preferences for partner characteristics around sexual, economic and social attributes, are forged in the context of sexual fields whereby the field organizes both what we desire in another and how we understand ourselves within the sexual status order.

Below, I trace some of the broader social and historical factors that bear on and make possible the sexual field and then turn more directly to an overview of the sexual fields framework.

3.2 Historical Factors Shaping Sexual Life in the West

The post-World War II era has been characterized both by the increasing autonomy of the sexual sphere and the increasing specialization of sexual subcultures. This is not to suggest that people today are more sexually active or more sexually desirous than in generations past but, rather, that the pathways to partnership and the rules of engagement between them have grown increasingly varied, disembedded from traditional institutions of social control (Bailey 1998; D'Emilio 1983) such as the family and the church. Hence actors have both more autonomy in directing their intimate lives and more specialized options to consider in the pursuit of intimate relations (Giddens 1992; Weiss 2012).

The increasing autonomization and specialization of sexual life is attributable to a confluence of historical and social factors. Modern capitalism may be one of the most important of these. To the extent that capitalism creates a wage labor system that disembeds individual workers from birth families, permitting if not necessitating geographic mobility, so the family has diminishing social control over sexual practices (Almagueur 1993; D'Emilio 1983).

Furthermore, the creation of wage labor and the diminution of agricultural economies has meant that the economic advantages of large families have eroded, thus freeing up the time and energies of contemporary married women in their childbearing years. In place of a reproductive imperative (Herdt 1996), and in conjunction with therapeutic and cultural discourses that emphasize the importance of sexual pleasure, heterosexual coupling no longer implies chastity in courtship nor sustained reproduction over the course of the marital relationship. And in a related vein, women (and men) have gained increasing control over reproduction, with radical consequences for sexual norms and practices (Giddens 1992). For example, birth control, abortion, and fertility treatments permit a degree of control over reproduction such that sexual life need not be tied so tightly to it, either because sexually active women can simply remain sexually active without the fear of pregnancy, or because pregnancy can be cultivated at ever-older ages among formerly post-reproductive women. In short, in the late nineteenth, twentieth and now twenty-first centuries, we enjoy a semblance of sexual life for which pleasure is the central aim, thus bringing a degree of sexual freedom perhaps unrivalled in historical terms.

But if sexual life has grown increasingly autonomous from traditional sources of social control, it is at the same time ever more specialized, catering to highly specific preference structures and sexual subcultures. Websites oriented around partnership—from a fling to a marital relationship—make this point especially clear. Today online, one may select from racial, ethnic and religious preferences (e.g., Jdate.com, AsiaFriend-Finder.com), class preferences (e.g., Sugardaddie.com, Millionaire Matchmaker.com), age preferences (e.g., SeniorMatch.com, Cougarlife.com), body type preferences (BigMuscleBear.com, Chubbychasersdating.com) and relationship type preferences (AshelyMadison.com, Fling.com), among still others. And the increasing acceptance of alternative, non-heteronormative lifestyles has fostered equivalent queer possibilities online, in social apps designed for quick hook ups, and in real-time sites such as bars, bathhouses, gay-designated neighborhoods, nightclubs, circuit parties and bookstores. Here, queer and trans individuals congregate in collective sexual life, in part, to facilitate sexual sociality and cultivate a variety of intimate partnerships.

In total, when one considers the sociosexual landscape outside the bedroom of the monogamous dyad, one finds a staggering array of permutations of collective sexual life that illustrate the growing autonomy of sexual fields along with their manifold specificities. Advances in the development of capitalism, the erosion of traditional institutions of social control, the increasing sophistication and availability of abortion, birth control and fertility, the changing status of women, and the increasing acceptance of a sexual pleasure norm, constitute some of the major historical factors that underpin transformations in the sexual field over the last 120 years, or so. And more recently, the digital revolution has ushered in an era of sexual sociality unencumbered by time and space, intensifying changes in real-time sexual life that were already underway.

Having provided some introductory context for the emergence of modern sexual fields and the sexual fields approach, I turn now to a more detailed account of the sexual fields framework, including its key concepts and theoretical emphases.

3.3   The Sexual Fields Approach

3.3.1   Field theory

Over the past three decades, sociologists have moved toward what some have called the "practice turn" (Schatzki et al. 2001). The practice turn signals a concerted movement away from prior rationalist, functionalist and poststructural accounts of action that reduced practice to the consequence of self-calculation, objective forces or subjective interpretations. In its place, a more integrated conception of action that synthesizes these domains within a single framework (Schatzki et al. 2001) has emerged, including structuration (Giddens 1984), critical realism (Archer 1995) and field theory (Bourdieu 1977,

1990; Bourdieu and Wacquant 1992), among others.

Bourdieu's analysis of routine practice, which brings together the core concepts of field, capital and habitus under the umbrella of field theory, has been an especially productive analytic within the practice turn. The chief theoretical insight of field theory is the notion that actors exist relationally in social space, their distinct positions arising as the consequence of differential resources (i.e., the distribution of capital) coupled with field-specific logics of practice. Such logics invest field objects (e.g., "fine art") and positions (e.g., "artists") with meaning and status, and thereby establish the terms of struggle. Actors are motivated to maintain or improve their field positions and, in this sense, they reconstitute the very boundaries of the field in their routine practices. Fields then are constructed configurations of social space that bring together actors within an objective domain of "organized striving" (Martin 2003), establishing the stakes of "the game" and the patterning of lines of action within its boundaries. Fields also confer value through capital—e.g., social, economic and cultural—which, in turn, provide both the means for achieving the rewards of the field and a stake in the struggle for dominance itself. In this sense, capital is a property of individuals but, at the same time, a property of the field (Green 2014), for capitals have no essential value (Bourdieu 1990); rather, they represent arbitrary designations, the value of which is field dependent, if interconvertible across fields (Bourdieu 1990; Bourdieu and Wacquant 1992).

Bourdieu's field theory is a paradigmatic instance of the practice turn because it works to transcend the classical (and poststructural) bifurcation of objectivity and subjectivity in accounts of action. To accomplish this task, Bourdieu develops the concept of habitus, a subconscious, psychic structure acquired early in life on the basis of prolonged exposure to systems of stratification—primarily, the conditions of possibility and constraint made possible by class. Habitus represents the objectification of the external, "objective" social structure at the level of psychic organization, whereby the social conditions of ones' childhood and adolescence are "inculcated" and "somatised" within the mind/body (Bourdieu 1990; Bourdieu and Wacquant 1992; Bourdieu 2001). Thus, concretely, a working-class and a middle-class young adult approaching a college application will have distinct habitus—distinct dispositions, habits of action, perceptual schema—that will bear on where (or if) they apply, what they write in the application, and how they perceive the value and purpose of their education, should they be admitted. Practice (e.g., in this case, applying to college) thus follows *not* from deliberate, purposeful lines of action but, instead, from non-deliberate and automatic cognitions that are shaped by and reflective of the larger social order (social structure) within which one spent her formative years. Though practices are not entirely subconscious, they are largely under the control of the habitus which, via analogic processes (Lizardo 2004), can be applied to a nearly infinite range of experiences without rule-following or conscious forethought. Hence the durability of the habitus and the tendency for actors to reproduce their practices, for once the habitus has taken form it operates subconsciously to shape lines of action, even when such actions have the consequence of reproducing one's marginal position within the field.

The recent extension of field theory to the domain of sexual life does not represent an entirely uniform movement but a range of paths forward that recognize the power of field theory for explaining desire, desirability and sexual practice (Green 2014). Chief differences among sexual field theorists include differential emphases on the degree to which fields are domains of struggle (Hennen 2014), and the degree to which fields are autonomous from the broader field of power (George 2014)—both topics I return to below.

3.3.2 The Sexual Fields Framework

While a growing body of work now draws from field theory in one way or another in the analysis of sexual life (Prieur 1998; Schilt and Windsor 2014; Weinberg and Williams 2010), the approach has received systematic development in my work and the sexual fields framework (Green 2008a, b, 2011, 2014). The sexual fields framework uses the concepts of Bourdieu's approach to routine practice and develops a theoretical approach to explain sexual desires, desirability and practice within contemporary sexual life, including the array of local, internally stratified, erotic worlds that characterize collective sexual life today. Concepts of the sexual fields framework include the conceptual corpus of field theory—i.e., field, capital and habitus—and adds to these the key concepts: sexual sites, structures of desire, and sexual circuits. Here the chief theoretical insight regards the patterning of desire and desirability—that is, the things sexual actors want in an intimate partner, and the things that sexual actors need in order to attract such an intimate partner. In the sexual fields framework, desire and desirability are understood to emerge, in part, as *field effects*, a product of ecological, social learning, and social psychological processes associated with the field. But before the core theoretical insight of the sexual fields framework can be rendered effectively, I first review its component parts, below.

A *sexual field* materializes as actors orient themselves toward one another with the effect of producing a system of stratification around the process of intimate partnership. Sexual fields, then, represent a configuration of social spaces, anchored to physical and virtual *sites*, that are inhabited by actors who strive to obtain the rewards of the field (Bourdieu 1977; Martin and George 2006). Their strivings are organized insofar as they follow the institutionalized logic of practice which is largely internally constituted and wherein status emerges on account of the differential distribution of field-specific capitals.

In Bourdieu's (1977, 1990) work, two guiding metaphors capture the effects of a field with relevance for collective sexual life (Martin 2011). First, Bourdieu suggests that fields operate as "fields of force" (1977), like a field of gravity, for instance, that bring into alignment the otherwise diverse elements that enter its orbit. In terms of a sexual field, the metaphor directs the analyst to consider how collective sexual life is shaped by the logics of any given field, be it the

logic of an online dating website, a debutante ball, a gay leather bar, a college keg party, or a big-city speed-dating event. That is, upon entering and becoming an actor in any one of these sexual fields, one finds that certain lines of action are required to be a relevant participant, to occupy social space and command the rewards of the field. These lines of action may include self-presentation, such as style, comportment, and the cultivation of a particular body type, along with social practices related to how to approach another, deference, demeanor, the enactment of courting practices, sexual repertoires, nightlife and lifestyle preferences. And sexual fields may require an even broader array of individual characteristics and group associations for participation, including one's occupation, income, race and ethnic background, with whom one socializes, where, religious affiliations, and the like. As a simple and stark contrast, compare the sexual actor with interest in meeting a Christian partner via a church group or ChristianMingle.com, versus the sexual actor with interest in meeting a "muscle bear" partner (i.e., a hirsute, husky gay man) at a gay bear bar or BigMuscleBear.com. To be sure, these distinct sexual fields will attract different kinds of actors with pre-existing dispositions and practical repertoires related to presentation, value commitments, and the like, but they will also have an impact above and beyond these starting points, bringing into further alignment distinct ways of being a viable "player" in "the game" and distinct ways of experiencing and understanding sexual value—one's own and that of others. Put differently, the sexual field acts as a field of force, like a field of gravity, increasing homogeneity around partner preferences via processes of socialization and somatic incorporation whereby partnership preferences are refined and transformed at the level of the erotic habitus (Green 2008a).

Second, Bourdieu (1977) suggests that fields are like a sporting field or a battlefield (Martin 2011)—i.e., a field of struggle. To the extent that fields are domains of organized striving, field actors occupy social space on account of their distinct, relative positions to one another, as these positions confer a sense of appropriate lines of action. In a sexual field—say the co-ed keg party of big campus Greek life—not all fraternity men will have access to the most popular, desired sorority women, and *vice versa*. To the extent that men and women may vie for the same subset of potential intimate partners, or even simply for significance in this social space, so Greek social life can be regarded as the site of a kind of battlefield whereby one's status is determined relative to other players in the field. Put in the terms of the sexual fields framework, we might say that co-eds within Greek social life operate with differential degrees of sexual capital that stratify sexual actors in their pursuit of field esteem and its rewards—i.e., intimate partnership with a partner of one's choosing. One's relative status within this field will, in turn, shape who will approach whom and how, and subsequent practices related to self-presentation and the management of self.

This brings us to a second key concept in the sexual fields framework—*sexual capital.*

Sexual capital is that species of capital (among other species, including economic, cultural and social capitals) associated with attractiveness that confers advantage upon those who possess it within a sexual field, including field significance and the ability to obtain an intimate partner of one's choosing. As developed in the sexual fields literature (Farrer and Dale 2014; Green 2014; Martin and George 2006), the concept has at least three elements that render it analytically richer than a simple notion of sexual attractiveness.

First, sexual capital is not simply a characteristic of individuals—e.g., having a fit body or pleasing facial features[1]—but rather, is at once a property of individuals *and* a property of the sexual field. This is so because the individualistic elements that confer value in a sexual field—including physical, affective, and presentational characteristics—are not strictly personal features but, rather, acquire their value in the context of the specific collective attributions of sexual attractiveness that hold in a given sexual field.

Thus, sexual capital is not an essential "thing" that an individual owns, like a personal portfolio that one can take from one field to another (Farrer and Dale 2014), but is field dependent, varying between fields and, sometimes, even within a field.[2] In analytic terms, this insight means that the analyst of the sexual field must be especially attentive to context and the ways in which desirability may hold different forms across fields.

Second, in a related vein, to the extent that desired attributes in a partner include characteristics beyond sexual appeal, such as cultural and economic capital, so sexual capital is but one part of a larger portfolio of capitals that is attributed with differential value between communities, social strata, and sexual fields. Indeed, while in some instances economic, cultural or social capital may simply be "sexy" (Martin 2005), in which case one has the conversion of non-sexual capitals to sexual capital, in other instances these capitals are desirable in a partner but not themselves sexy, in which case one has a *capital portfolio* (Green 2014), comprised of a range of capitals that differentially determines status in a sexual field. As an example, if common wisdom holds true, we can say that men, on the whole, value sexual capital more than other capitals in their prospective female partners, while women, on the whole, value economic and cultural capital more than sexual capital in their prospective male partners (Buss et al. 1991). Of course, the extent to which this holds true will vary systematically between sexual fields that are populated by distinct social strata across time and space, and which place differential value on partner characteristics. Thus among contemporary college-aged university students, sexual capital may strongly trump other capitals with respect to an actor's desirability, whereas this may have been less true among sorority sisters in the 1950s, or among those middle-aged and divorced today. This example underscores the essential point that partner desirability is socially constructed, historically specific and field-dependent.

---

[1] For a contrasting formulation, see Hakim's notion of "erotic capital" (2011). For a refutation of Hakim's formulation, see Green (2013).

[2] For more on this point, see Green's (2014) discussion of sexual fields with multiple structures of desire.

And third, finally, the determinants and effects of sexual capital are not delimited to the sexual fields in which they most immediately matter. In the first instance, the determinants of value in a sexual field are historically dependent and may be traceable to the broader field of power, including the state and elite "metasexual authority" (George 2014). Thus, building on a critical sexualities literature that couples sexology, colonialism, state-building and sexual identity, George (2014) argues that sexological and psychiatric writing in the nineteenth and twentieth centuries were consecrated by the state to ensure that particular kinds of sexual value were inculcated in populations, including characteristics associated with race and class hierarchies (see more below). In this sense, sexual fields, like fields more generally, operate with a degree of heteronomy, reproducing (and contesting) the very terms of sexual identity and sexual desirability within their bounded interactional domains.

But if the determinants of sexual value are not captured fully in the immediate, visible relations of position with a sexual field, neither are the effects of the sexual field. This is to say that not all sexual fields are created "equal" in terms of their salience for and impact on local and national cultures. In fact, some sexual fields—including, as an example, the NYC, largely white, upper-middle class sexual field dramatized by the hit television series, *Sex and the City*—have greater power to capture the cultural imaginary and in turn, reshape the various and sundry alternative sexual fields in which cultural consumers socialize. Thus the elite sexual fields occupied by top female models and their rich and powerful male suitors (Mears 2011) may have much greater power to establish the terms of sexual attractiveness than those of their working class and poor counterparts employed at the bottom of the service sector. The increased salience of one sexual field over another for the culture as a whole may itself be explained via the field of power, whereby cultural elites consecrated by the state are endowed with greater capacity to set the terms of a sexual capital in macrohistorical terms, in ways that ramify throughout the landscape of sexual fields more generally.

Because the sexual fields framework shifts the focal unit of analysis from individual sexuality to group life, it requires the analyst to conceptualize desire in collective terms. A third core concept, *structure of desire*, conceives of desire as the aggregation of individual wants and attitudes in the form of "hegemonic systems of judgement" (Martin and George 2006). These systems of judgment materialize as institutionalized matter at the site of the sexual field and are observable in the representations and patterned interactions of the field. On the side of representation, sexual fields communicate a sexual status order through a variety of sign vehicles. For example, a sexual field that emerges around a site of consumption, as in a bar, a lounge, or a dating website, will usually broadcast idealized representations of what is and what should be important to the clientele, including representations of the perfect "couple" on the front page of a dating website (e.g., including characteristics related to race, age, class, affect, body type, presentational style, etc.), the appearance of the bartenders (e.g., including characteristics related to race, age, class, affect, body type, etc.), the décor (e.g., compare the gay leather bar with the upscale martini bar), the name of the site (e.g., the Ramrod), patterns in the fronts of patrons (e.g., dress, adornment, affect), and the patterned written content of website profiles, including descriptions of the likes and dislikes of website members (e.g., "no Asians;" "no old daddies;" "under 30 only;" "no fats or fems").

Interactionally, structures of desire are enacted via patterns in sociality, including the talk about who is desirable and who is not, observable patterns in who is favored and who is ignored (i.e., who is popular), who is bought drinks and who is left paying for one's self, who gets let in first by the bouncer and who is stalled or denied entrance altogether, and who earns the most hits, hearts, flowers or kisses on a dating website.

Taken together, these elements of a structure of desire both reflect and put into alignment how individuals understand desirability, including the attractiveness of others but also themselves. That is, to the extent that actors in a sexual field have an intuitive awareness of the relational nature of "the game," they are bound to engage in comparison processes whereby they assess the degree to which a given person of interest possesses sexual capital within the field, along with the degree to which they possess the requisite capitals to hold a significant field position and command its rewards, including the attention of such a desired person. Put differently, rather than understand desirability in purely idiosyncratic or essentialist terms, players in the sexual field act as lay social scientists who construct theories around others' desirability and their own. Hence, structures of desire become crucial to the extent that actors apprehend them as a kind of probability matrix determining their opportunities for partnership, including hegemonic standards of desirability against which they themselves are judged. Moreover, as I explore further below, structures of desire can have the effect of socializing first-order desires, such that the things we originally thought we desired change over time following repeated exposure to the field.

Though structures of desire are best conceived to operate at the level of the field, the comparison processes by which actors determine the sexual status of others and themselves are usually anchored to aggregations of recurring networks of actors who occupy a given set of field sites and, in turn, provide the most salient "data" from which one constructs a theory of sexual value. These networks—*sexual circuits*—are made up of those with whom we regularly "rub elbows" in the field but which lack stronger ties of dependence (Adam and Green 2014) and with whom we may have no personal relationship. Sexual circuits have "circuit" like structures insofar as they represent patterned flows of sets of individuals and groups that populate particular sexual sites and sexual fields. For example, in Toronto, Adam and Green (2014) distilled ten distinct circuits using factor analysis of surveys from a sample of Pride attendees. These circuits represent imperfect but patterned assemblages of individuals who report attending particular sets of sites in the prior year. The first major circuit was comprised of individuals who had frequented a core set of nine bars, four dance clubs, four recurring special events and one bathhouse. By contrast, a second major circuit consisted of a unique set of quick sex sites, including four bathrooms, a park and a phone line. A third circuit included four bars typically identified with the leather and denim scene (Adam and Green 2014). And so on. Thus, circuits gain their composition based on common characteristics that include shared interests in particular sexual fields over others, shared lifestyle practices, and once can assume a similar range of sociodemographic characteristics. More than any particular representational character of a given site of a sexual field, it is the sexual circuits that we regularly encounter in collective sexual life that establish the most important source upon which we apprehend a field's structure of desire, distribution of capital and corresponding status order.

Having reviewed some of the major sensitizing concepts of the sexual fields framework, I turn below to a brief discussion of the framework's central theoretical insight concerning the transformation of desire and desirability in collective sexual life.

3.3.3　Desire and Desirability in Collective Sexual Life

If a sexual field's analysis has one central theoretical argument, it is that desire and desirability are transformed over time as individuals enter collective sexual life and become exposed to field forces. To date, I (Green 2014) have identified three central, interrelated ways in which fields transform desire and desirability such that we may speak of both, in part, as *field effects*. These include: (1) the popularity tournament; (2) socialization; and (3) aggregation and intensification processes. I explore each one individually below.

To the extent that sexual fields are comprised of actors who are positioned in relation to one another on the basis of differential capital portfolios, one has the basis of a stratified social order. However, as I argue above, sexual capital is not a fixed, essential property of individuals, but a field-dependent resource amenable to change over time and context. One of the most simple examples of this is found in the popularity tournament (Green 2014; Martin and George 2006; Waller 1937). Here, one's relative standing in the sexual field has the tendency to reinforce and even intensify that standing subsequently at the individual level and then, recursively, at the collective level. Thus, Waller (1937) finds that at college co-ed parties, "nothing succeeds like success"—i.e., the popular become even more popular. Conversely, one may infer that the unpopular become even less popular over time. Put differently, individual partner preferences in a sexual field are not reducible to pre-existing, individual dispositions but, rather, are to varying degrees transformed as they enter the gravitational pull of the sexual field (Green 2014). Thus one's initial field reception is consequential for future assessments of sexual capital.

A second central way in which sexual fields act on sexual desires and desirability relates to general processes of socialization. Here, exposure to a given sexual subculture within a sexual field can resocialize desire (and desirability) such that we acquire a deeper taste for that which we were previously only mildly interested, or an aversion to things we previously desired. Thus, the twenty-something Hamptons vacationer may have previously preferred the company of well-off men, but when she witnesses her friends pursuing men who own multiple pieces of real estate, including a condo in Manhattan and two summer homes, she finds soon enough that her standards for attractive partners have changed as economic capital becomes an even more important element within the capital portfolios of desired partners. In a slightly different vein, in Shanghai, Western Caucasian men are favored by a certain contingent of local Chinese women who occupy key "ethnosexual contact zones" (Farrer and Dale 2014). Chinese women who seek out this ethnosexual contact zone are typically younger, on average, then their Western expat-sisters, and highly deferential to expat men. In this context, Western men find that they have decreasing desire for Western women over time (Farrer and Dale 2014). Put in different terms, the desires of Western expat men are resocialized at the level of the habitus to favor local Chinese women and

to disfavor their Western female counterparts. Here, we have an instance of the transformation of racialized desires—toward local Chinese women and away from Western expat women—within a sexual field that encourages expat men to cultivate a taste for ethnicity. And at a female transgender bar, otherwise "heterosexual men" encounter highly feminized and flirtatious transgender women and, over time, develop an erotic taste for them that overcomes the disjuncture between anatomy and gender such that the trans women's hyper-sexualized feminine affect becomes a source of sexual desire (for more, see below) (Weinberg and Williams 2013).

Finally, a third critical way in which desire and desirability arise, in part, as field effects, draws from Fischer's (1975) ecological theory of urbanism and subcultures. Here, when individual desires are aggregated at the sites of a sexual field such that they obtain a critical mass, they become amplified, exceeding the desires of any given individual to constitute a new, intensified structure of desire. Put in different terms, the hegemonic systems of judgment (Martin and George 2006) of the sexual field are not calculable as a kind of plural, "multicultural" desire that reflects the addition of each new player's particular desires but, rather, follow a multiplicative construction that extracts and magnifies the overlapping facets of desire to produce a "hyper" realized structure of desire. In gay male culture, a clear example of this is found in circuit parties (Westhaver 2005) that are often populated by unusually muscular men, some of whom train in preparation for the parties themselves. But what may have been a desirable, fit body back home at the local bar no longer acts as sexual capital at the circuit party, where the sheer number of muscular bodies has the effect of producing an intensified structure of desire that represents the amplification of any given party participant's desire. Sexual capital is now reserved for men with bulging ripped bodies and hard, prominent abdominal muscles. Hence both the desires and desirability of party participants have been transformed as actors enter the gravitational field of the circuit-party sexual field.

Having considered some of the most important ways a sexual field can act back on sexual desire and desirability, I turn now to a discussion of the ways in which a sexual field analysis may incorporate a range of considerations that are exogenous, micro and macro to the field itself.

3.3.4 Sexual Fields and Levels of Analysis

A sexual field is a meso-level configuration that transcends the idiosyncrasies of micro-level interactions to shape and structure desire and desirability over time. But precisely because of the complexity of intimate partnership and sexual desire, the field itself is not a fully autonomous configuration, but is shaped by elements that are both micro and macro to its social spaces. In this sense, the analyst of a sexual field is confronted with multiple points of entry for understanding its structure and processes, from the intrapsychic life of desiring individual players who may already hold a pre-existing set of sexual scripts, to the most macrohistorical factors related to the state and globalization that may bear on the character of the field.

Individuals who come to the sexual field typically do so with pre-existing ideas about intimate life and preconstituted schema around desire and desirability, though these may change over time in the context of field sociality. Hence, scholars of the sexual field may consider the ways in which exposure to a given sexual field bears on individual desires. Here, the analyst might ask: how does sociality in a given sexual field shape or transform the sexual desires of study participants?; how does sociality in a given sexual field shape or transform sexual repertoires of study participants?; what is the impact of sexual sociality in a sexual field upon study participants' sense of self-esteem, locus of control, and the ability to procure the rewards of the field, including social significance and choice of desired partner?

At the level of interaction, a sexual field may be analyzed via ethnographic observation to account for patterns in sociality as these take form around sexual circuits, structures of desire, and the dispersion of sexual capital. Here, the analyst might ask: how do individuals and groups negoti-

ate structures of desire, how do they apprehend and make sense of them and how do they respond (e.g., do they change fields?; do they hold themselves up as objects of scrutiny and work to transform their own capital portfolios in an effort to exercise greater command of the field?)?; what are the predominant sexual circuits that characterize the primary reference group of actors in the field, how do actors fit into these sexual circuits and under what conditions do they depart from the prevailing norms around intimate partnership?; how does the distribution of sexual capital in a field shape interactional patterns, the physical location of actors in social space, and patterns of deference, affect and deportment attendant to sociosexual interaction?

At the level of the field, the analyst may ask: what is the sociodemographic composition of the circuits of a given sexual field and a given domain of collective sexual life?; how do sexual circuits articulate with epidemiological trends in sexually transmitted infections?; what structures of desire characterize the sexual field—i.e., what are the preferred capital portfolios and how are these distributed between field actors?; how is a field's structure of desire communicated representationally and interactionally?; what kinds of sexual fields are available to a given population or within a given bounded locale, and how does one sexual field relate to another?

Finally, at the macrolevel, the analyst of the sexual field may consider a wide range of factors that may bear on the sexual field, including the relationship of the state to the sexual field, HIV/ AIDS, racial histories, and sexological "meta-authority", including sexologists, psychiatrists, and feminists.

3.3.5 Sexual Fields Scholarship

Given the recent development of the sexual fields approach (Martin and George 2006; Green 2008a, 2011), published scholarship in the area is as yet limited. Indeed, while published work uses terms from the framework, either in direct reference to it (Farrer 2011; Weinberg and Williams 2010, 2013) or in a semblance of parallel analyses (Hennen 2008; Paul and Choi 2009; Prieur 1998), systematic application of the approach is in its infancy.

One of the first articulations of a sexual fields approach develops a critique of the reigning market approaches to sexuality in favor of a field theoretical framework (Martin and George 2006). Market approaches to partnership choices typically come in one of two varieties: (1) analyses that observe "market-like" properties in sexual exchange processes such that one may employ the market model metaphorically and incorporate some of its concepts (e.g., choices, costs, utilities, and so on); and (2) analyses that use a strong market model that produce predictions about partnership choices based on exchange theories (Martin and George 2006). According to Martin and George (2006), neither approach is sufficient. In the first instance, "market-like" approaches appear to propose a strong market model but, in fact, have no predictive power, only retrospective interpretive capacity (Martin and George 2006). In the second instance, strong market models falter because they are predicated on the notion of an exchange of equal utilities, and are therefore unable to account for instances when a *dis*utility is a utility—such as, for example, when a sexual capital deficit may be an advantage insofar as it may minimize the tendency to roam. Moreover, market models make sexual desire superstructural to the analysis—i.e., they cannot explain why we desire what we desire, or what makes something desirable in the first place, beyond a simple supply and demand dynamic (Martin and George 2006). Thus, in the place of a market model, Martin and George (2006) argue for the application of Bourdieusian field theory to the problem of intimate pairing or, more precisely "the social organization of sexual *desiring* [*sic*]" (Martin and George 2006, p. 108). In their focus, the central aim for sexual field analysis is to explain how and why sexual valuations obtain "supra-individual consistencies" (Martin and George 2006) that mark certain individuals/groups more and less attractive than others—i.e., that endow certain individuals/groups with differential degrees of sexual capital.

From a macrohistorical perspective, George (2014) notes the rise of "meta-sexual field" in the nineteenth and twentieth centuries and the effects of "meta-sexual authority" on shaping some of the fundamental organizing principles of the late modern sexual field. By meta-sexual authority, George refers to those social and biological sciences and their practitioners who generated theories about human sexuality, from Freud to Kinsey and Masters and Johnson. These sexual "experts" were consecrated by the state because they served state interests around asserting national identity and the social control of ethnic minorities. In fact, the initial conditions for the development of a coherent meta-sexual field arose from state and public concerns to regulate and control immigrant and deviant populations. By "discovering" and isolating sexual motivations, meta-sexual authority and the "sexual sciences"—mainly, sexology—allowed for implicit social regulation of WASP norms, including through the vehicles of vigorous sex education, screening and surveillance of immigrants, migrants, vagrants, criminals and military personnel.

One of the signal accomplishments of the nineteenth century sexology was the creation of sexual orientation categories. George (2014) argues that this classificatory system gained traction not because of the power of sexology to disseminate its particular vision of the sexual, but because the state built sexological categories into policy directives as a means to execute its political will, including control over the definition of citizenship and the ownership of public space. Today, the landscape of sexual fields is broadly constituted through the separation of fields by sexual orientation—a historical vestige of nineteenth and twentieth century sexology and state building.

Race, class and nationality are also key issues for Farrer (2011) in his study of "ethnosexual contact zones" in Shanghai. Here, Farrer discovers a sexual field characterized by stratified sexual capital that maps onto postcolonial national and racial categories. In this context, white European and North American men are labelled "loawai," or "foreigners" by local Chinese women who hold them in high regard, attributing to them "glamour and sex appeal" (Farrer 2011, p. 756). This attribution itself is a vestige of the prior colonial world order which provided the economic and symbolic structures that secured the superior status of Western men in China. Some local Chinese women prefer foreign men because they are primarily attracted to their exotic appearance and its association with beauty and sex appeal (Farrer 2011). Others prefer foreign men because they desire the economic and cultural capital that these men often hold. Interestingly, the precise mix of preferred capitals within foreign men's capital portfolios is shaped, in part, by sexual subfields within the ethnosexual contact zone. That is, local Chinese women are well aware that some sites cater to a particularly well-off expatriate crowd, while other sites much less so. Hence, these women tailor their field participation to match the particular capital portfolio that is of greatest interest to them. Subsequently, tensions exist between foreign men and ethnically Chinese men who may compete for status via women's favor. These tensions are played out in racialized contact zones within bars and night clubs wherein Chinese men typically reserve a table and purchase bottles of liquor, while foreign men typically drink at the bar. This distinct spatial placement in the site is significant because it demonstrates the degree to which racialized men are reflexive about their particular sexual capital and the ways in which they must deploy this to meet women. That is, expat men use their sexual capital to attract women, while Chinese men, who cannot rely on their sexual capital, must use their economic capital to be competitive players.

Race and racialization are also the foci of my (Green 2008b, 2011) analysis of sexual stratification in the gay sexual fields of Chelsea, New York, and Toronto, Ontario. In the former, I find a largely middle-class, white dominated gay sexual field wherein white men's collectivized desires stratified men of color along lines of the hypermasculine "thug," on the one hand, or undesirable "others," on the other. In response to this structure of desire, men of color who had attraction to white men developed reflexive strategies to either "play up" race through a rough affect and aggressive style of speech (i.e., linguistic code switching), or "play down" race through adopting urban white sign vehicles, including

style of dress but, also, physical signifiers such as light colored contact lenses and straightened hair. Moreover, some men of color who felt a particularly significant deficit in sexual capital translated their perceived disadvantaged status into sexual practice, including reduced sexual agency when negotiating desirable sex and safe sex with white partners.

In Toronto, I (Green 2011) studied a similar middle-class, white dominated sexual field rife with racialized sexual circuits that, generally, disadvantage men of color. Here, I focused on the processes by which actors become aware of, cognize, and negotiate sexual status orders, including six key moments likely to hold across sexual fields: (1) a recognition of the stratified social spaces of the field; (2) a recognition of a structure of desire that confers differential valuations of attractiveness upon individuals and groups; (3) a formulation of one's own position within the sexual status order; (4) an assessment of the dispersion of sexual capital, including the status of desired others; (5) knowledge concerning how to conduct a successful performance, including field-specific demeanor; and (6) the ability to save face.

One especially important finding in this research concerns the subjective, perceptual basis upon which each individual formulates a sense of the status order within the sexual field. This perceptual moment is, in fact, imperfect insofar as it entails not just the assessment of whether a given actor finds another person to be attractive but, more, whether the field's collectivity finds a given actor or group attractive—i.e., whether or not another actor or set of actors are endowed with sexual capital in the field. In this sense, the fallibility of such an assessment aside, desirability is not the simple attribution of attractiveness of one person to another, but rather enters the orbit of the field as actors formulate a sense of the structure of desire and collective, "hegemonic systems of judgment" (Martin and George 2006). This means that even if person "Y" initially finds person "X" unremarkable, when person "X" is perceived to hold significant sexual capital, person "Y" will adjust his or her demeanor toward person "X" and, potentially, develop a "taste" for them over time (via the popularity tournament). It also means that structures of desire are not simply about desire, but also about attitudes toward others, as when the otherwise sexy "slut" of the sorority is stigmatized by sorority sisters and, as a consequence, loses desirability among fraternity men (Armstrong 2010).

But if competition—or the "field of struggle"—appear to mark the center of a sexual fields analysis, this is not always the case. Hennen (2014) takes up the question of the formation of a sexual field and the ways in which fields may produce new desires. In this work, Hennen is critical of the Bourdeusian formulation that marries structured hierarchy to field organization, preferring instead a more flexible account of the sexual field that can, in certain instances, understand the field as a field of force alone, rather than as both a field of force and a field of struggle. Hennen bases his argument, in part, on the historical formation of the gay leather sexual subculture. Leathermen are men who typically find leather clothing and accessories erotic, have a hypermasculine affect, and engage in some variety of BDSM practice (bondage, discipline, sadomasochism). Examining the origin of the gay leather sexual subculture, Hennen is especially sensitive to place its development in the historical context of World War II. In the late 1940s and 1950s, the leather sexual field congealed around the wounded masculinities of World War II veterans who sought the company of other such men on account of their traumatic experiences on the battlefield. At this time, not all male participants were expressly gay but, rather, were drawn to the homosociality of the leather subculture and its BDSM practices. For them, the leather subculture had a kind of therapeutic value commensurate with their outsiders' status more generally. In Hennen's (2014) words: "I suggest that the horrors of war so traumatized these men that they found it necessary to seek out the company of men with similar experiences, to organize a furtive alternative culture rather than return to the mainstream" (p. 74).

Once the gay leather subculture materialized among veterans, it attracted non-veterans who developed a sexual affinity for BDSM and leather, most of whom were more explicitly gay-identified. Such men underwent a process of deliberate inculcation as they trained in BDSM play and, in the process, acquired a new sexual disposition that favored leathermen and sexual subculture. In this sense, the field did less to liberate existing desires than provide a social space for the constitution of new desires—i.e., the specificity of desire in the leatherman sexual subculture emerged as a field effect. Nevertheless, from this vantage point, Hennen (2014) finds less the presence of a field of struggle—i.e., a field of stratified players vying for sexual capital—than a field of force in the sense of a magnetic field that pulls into alignment the elements within its scope. Here, the gay leather sexual field began as a historical homosocial formation related to the collective psychological trauma of war, and grew into a full fledged sexual subculture that transformed desires and practices in the process of field cooperation, rather than field competition. Distinguishing the first forerunners of the leather sexual subculture from its later, non-veteran participants, Hennen (2014) notes: "Without extending the analogy too far, one might say that this corresponds roughly to the difference between the original conditions constituting the field of force around a magnet and the mental shards that are subsequently attracted to it" (p. 76).

Weinberg and Williams' (2013) analysis of Mabel's in San Francisco puts a similar emphasis on the ways in which a sexual field may work as a field of force, but in this case, to bring into alignment the sexual desires of otherwise heterosexual men in response to the advances of transgender women. At Mabel's, transgender women socialize and solicit sexual relations with men who generally identify as "heterosexual." Some of this interaction takes the form of paid sex work. Typically, men come to drink and be entertained by the trans women, the latter whom comport themselves in a highly sexually suggestive, feminine manner, including in their dress, affect, posture, speech, and the like (Weinberg and Williams 2013). The trans women are flirtatious with the male patrons, and eager to engage them verbally and through provocative touching. The sexual capital of the transwomen is largely based on their ability to pass as a biological female; the more female they appear, the higher their erotic value—of which the transwomen are well aware.

Weinberg and Williams found that most (though not all) male patrons of Mabel's eroticized women who were assigned 'female' at birth (*not* transwomen or men); thus the transwomen faced a significant obstacle in order to procure a sexual relationship with those men. That is, transwomen had to increase the distance between their assigned-at-birth sex and their trans status in order to arouse and sustain the interests of the male patrons. This was accomplished, in part, via processes specific to the sexual field, through what Weinberg and Williams (2013) refer to as "sensory embodiment" (p. 63). Within Mabel's, the transwomen were highly practiced in the art of seduction, and the dance between them and the collectively titillated men served to "structure and intensify desire" such that the environment itself induced desire on the part of the men (Weinberg and Williams 2013). Here, the interpretive work required to find another's embodiment erotic—i.e., sensory embodiment—was accomplished in the patterned interactions between transwomen and men, producing a structure of desire that overrode the fact of the transwomen's assigned-at-birth sex and allowed for the illusion to feel real (enough). In short, via the structure of desire of the sexual field, "transwomen fit into the eroticized schema the straight men had of an attractive woman" (Weinberg and Williams 2013, p. 65).

Having considered a range of published sexual fields scholarship, I now reflect upon future directions in sexual fields analysis.

3.4   Future Directions in Sexual Fields Research

The application of field theory to collective sexual life is a recent venture in the sociology of sexuality. Nevertheless, the approach offers a new generation of sexuality scholars a rich framework of sensitizing concepts for making sense of and exploring modern collective sexual life. As I (Green 2014) have previously written, some of

the most pressing questions for any sexual fields analysis include:

> a) What is the relationship of sexual desires to the sexual field?; b) What kinds of capital confer value in a sexual field, why and how are these distributed across actors, and with what effects?; c) What is the structure of a sexual field with respect to its circuits and horizontal and vertical stratification?; d) How do sexual fields relate to one another, to other kinds of fields, and to larger structures and processes, such as immigration, gentrification, urban renewal, and the rise and fall of sexually transmitted infections? (pp. 51–52)

These general questions aside, there are substantive lines of inquiry that demand attention from the sexual fields approach. From the broadest macrohistorical vantage point, one may wonder how the current distribution of sexual capital in any given field is shaped by histories around colonialism, segregation, state-building, globalization, and those structures and processes that confer unequal value upon groups based on their national, racial, ethnic and religious identities. As well, to the extent that the last few decades have ushered in a "new" phase of the life course—"emerging adulthood" (Arnett 2000)—it becomes imperative for analysts of collective sexual life to consider how the delay of full adult independence will bear on sexual practice, desire and desirability, and the capital portfolios that determine the value of an intimate partner. If Kimmel (2008) is correct, changes in the economy of the developed Western world from the 1980s forward render both young women but especially young men ever more dependent upon parents later into the life course, with fewer opportunities for earning a living wage, higher demands for post-graduate credentials and training, and prolonged internal struggles around identity and self-mastery. Under these conditions, heterosexual (and perhaps same-sex) marriage and child rearing are substantially delayed as young women and men struggle to establish careers and independent adult lifestyles. Hence it stands to reason that such tectonic shifts in the life course are likely to have powerful effects on intimate partnerships, including patterns of participation in collective sexual life and the kinds of expectations and desires actors will bring with them to the sexual field. Of course, these expectations and desires will be heavily mediated by race, class and sex, and should be part and parcel of any future sexual fields analysis of emerging adulthood and collective sexual life. This general observation underscores the point that while much of the extant sexual fields research has been conducted by scholars doing LGBTQ studies, the sexual fields approach is by no means limited to queer sociology but has general applicability across social contexts, including those characterized as heteronormative.

Alongside the rise of emerging adulthood, the digital revolution and social media have transformed the social organization of collective sexual life to such a profound degree that entire neighborhoods—including "gayborhoods"— may be vanishing (Ghaziani 2014) as actors prefer virtual to real-time channels in the search for partnership. But the private nature of online life means that its effects on individuals and groups, including who and how they choose desirable partners, and how desirability is constituted in the first place, are largely obscured. To be sure, the Internet collapses time and space in a process Giddens (1981) has referred to as "time-space distanciation." This transformation has surely facilitated intimate connections, extending possibilities for partnering well beyond the traditional boundaries of time and space. Yet virtual sites, be they dating websites or social applications with GPS technologies (e.g., "Tinder;" "Grindr") are also social in the sense that they are comprised of actors who become visible to one another and who must navigate status expectations in ways not altogether different from real-time sites of sociality. Moreover, because many websites and social apps allow users to search on particular criteria, they facilitate the development of ever-narrower preference structures around age, race, class, ethnicity, religion, body type, relationship type, and so on. This fact is likely to transform how actors, *en masse*, think about and construct desirability in ways that will surely bear on future iterations of the sexual field and the ways in which its participants produce and negotiate sexual stratification.

As well, the relationship of the sexual field to sexually transmitted infections is a substantive line of inquiry that demands immediate attention.

Among men who have sex with men (MSM), for example, the introduction of promising HIV pre-exposure prophylactic medications (PrEP) and emerging data on the success of anti-retroviral treatment (ARV) in preventing HIV transmission are likely to transform the social organization of collective sexual life as new sexual identities, such as the HIV "positive but undetectable" and "PrEP user" change the assessment of sexual risk and the subsequent patterning of intimate partnership. But precisely if and how the successful treatment of HIV will bear on collective sexual life, on attributions of desirability, and on the norms of acceptable and "underground" sexual practices, remain as yet unknown and call out for sexual field analysis.

To conclude, the study of sexual fields is in its infancy and much work remains to be done. As a framework trained on the phenomenon of sexual stratification, the sexual fields approach offers sexuality scholars a range of sensitizing conceptual tools to make sense of desire and desirability as these take form in collective sexual life. By problematizing our sexual desires and practices in the context of the sexual field, sexual fields' scholars unearth the social organization of sexuality, bringing a robust sociological analysis to what too often has been ceded to psychology, psychoanalysis, and the intrapsychic processes of the individual.

References

Adams, M. L. (1999). *The trouble with normal. Postwar youth and the making of heterosexuality*. Toronto: University of Toronto Press.

Adam, B. D., & Green, A. I. (2014). Circuits and the social organization of sexual fields. In A. I. Green (Ed.), *Sexual fields: Toward a sociology of collective sexual life* (pp. 123–142). Chicago: University of Chicago Press.

Almagueur, T. (1993). Chicano men: A cartography of homosexual men and behavior. In H. Abelove, M. Aina Barale, & D. Halperin (Eds.), *The lesbian and gay studies reader* (pp. 255–273). New York: Routledge.

Archer, M. (1995). *Realist social theory: The morphogenetic approach*. Cambridge: Cambridge University Press.

Armstrong, E. (2010). *Sluts. Paper presented at "bringing Bourdieu to sexual life."* Toronto: University of Toronto.

Arnett, J. J. (2000). Emerging adulthood: A theory of development from the late teens through the twenties. *American Psychologist, 55,* 469–480.

Bailey, B. (1998). *From front porch to back seat.* Baltimore: Johns Hopkins University Press.

Bernstein, E. (2007). *Temporarily yours.* Chicago: University of Chicago Press.

Bourdieu, P. (1977). *Outline of a theory of practice.* Cambridge: Cambridge University Press.

Bourdieu, P. (1990). *The logic of practice.* Stanford: Stanford University Press.

Bourdieu, P. (2001). *Masculine domination (trans: Nice, R.).* Stanford: Stanford University Press.

Bourdieu, P., & Wacquant, L. (1992). *Invitation to a reflexive sociology.* Chicago: University of Chicago Press.

Brock, D. (1998). *Making work, making trouble: Prostitution as a social problem.* Toronto: University of Toronto Press.

Buss, D. M., Shackelford, T. K., Kirkpatrick, L. A., & Larsen, R. J. (1991). A half century of mate preferences: The cultural evolution of values. *Journal of Marriage and Family, 63,* 491–503.

D'Emilio, J. (1983). *Sexual politics, sexual communities: The making of a homosexual minority in the United States, 1940–1970.* Chicago: University of Chicago Press.

Edwards, T. (1998). Against the queer turn. *Sexualities, 1,* 471–484.

Epstein, S. (1996). A queer encounter: Sociology and the study of sexuality. In S. Seirdman (Ed.), *Queer theory, sociology* (pp. 145–167). Cambridge: Blackwell.

Farrer, J. (2011). Global nightscapes in Shanghai as ethnosexual contact zones. *The Journal of Ethnic and Migration Studies, 37,* 747–764.

Farrer, J., & Dale, S. (2014). Sexless in Shanghai: Gendered mobility strategies in a transnational sexual field. In A. I. Green (Ed.), *Sexual fields: Toward a sociology of collective sexual life* (pp. 143–170). Chicago: University of Chicago Press.

Fischer, C. (1975). Toward a subcultural theory of urbanism. *American Journal of Sociology, 80,* 1319–41.

Fitzgerald, F. (1986). *Cities on a hill.* New York: Simon and Schuster.

Foucault, M. (1980). *The history of sexuality* (Vol. I). New York: Vintage.

Fox, N. J., & Alldred, P. (2013). The sexuality-assemblage: Desire, affect, anti-humanism. *The Sociological Review, 61,* 769–789.

Gagnon, J., & Simon, W. (1974). *Sexual conduct. The social sources of human sexuality.* New York: Aldine.

Gamson, J. (2000). Sexualities, queer theory, and qualitative research. In N. Denzin & Y. Lincoln (Eds.), *Handbook of qualitative research* (2nd ed., pp. 347–365). Thousand Oaks: Sage.

Ghaziani, A. (2014). *There goes the gayborhood?* Princeton: Princeton University Press.

George, M. (2014). The state, society and meta-sexual field. Paper in progress.

Giddens, A. (1981). *A contemporary critique of historical materialism: Power, property and the state.* London: Macmillan.

Giddens, A. (1984). *The constitution of society: Outline of the theory of structuration.* Cambridge: Polity Press.

Giddens, A. (1992). The *transformation of intimacy: sexuality, love and eroticism in modern societies.* Stanford: Stanford University Press.

Green, A. I. (2007). Queer theory & sociology: Locating the subject and the self in sexuality studies. *Sociological Theory, 25,* 26–45.

Green, A. I. (2008a). Erotic habitus: Toward a sociology of desire. *Theory and Society, 37,* 597–626.

Green, A. I. (2008b). The social organization of desire: The sexual fields approach. *Sociological Theory, 26,* 25–50.

Green, A. I. (2011). Playing the (sexual) field: The interactional basis of sexual stratification. *Social Psychology Quarterly, 74,* 244–266.

Green, A. I. (2013). Erotic capital and the power of desirability: Why "Honey Money" is a bad collective strategy for remedying gender inequality. *Sexualities, 16,* 137–158.

Green, A. I. (2014). *Sexual fields: Toward a sociology of collective sexual life.* Chicago: University of Chicago Press.

Greenberg, D. (1988). *The construction of homosexuality.* Chicago: University of Chicago Press.

Hakim, C. (2011). *Honey money: The power of erotic capital.* London: Allen Lane.

Hennen, P. (2008). *Faeries, bears, and leathermen: Gay men in community queering the masculine.* Chicago: University of Chicago Press.

Hennen, P. (2014). Sexual field theory: Some theoretical questions and empirical considerations. In A. I. Green (Ed.), *Sexual fields: Toward a sociology of collective sexual life* (pp. 71–100). Chicago: University of Chicago Press.

Herdt, G. (1996). *Third sex: Third gender.* New York: Zone Books.

Humphreys, L. (1975). *Tearoom trade: Impersonal sex in public places.* Chicago: Aldine.

Kennedy, E. L., & Davis, M. D. (1993). *Boots of leather, slippers of gold: The history of a lesbian community.* New York: Routledge.

Kimmel, M. (2008). *Guyland: The perilous world where boys become men.* New York: Harper Collins.

Levine, M. (1998). *Gay macho.* New York: New York University Press.

Lizardo, O. (2004). The cognitive origins of Bourdieu's habitus. *Journal for the Theory Of Social Behavior, 34,* 2–32.

Martin, J. L. (2003). What is field theory? *American Journal of Sociology, 109,* 1–49.

Martin, J. L. (2005). Is power sexy? *American Journal of Sociology, 111,* 408–446.

Martin, J. L. (2011). *The explanation of social action.* New York: Oxford University Press.

Martin, J. L., & George, M. (2006). Theories of sexual stratification: Toward an analytics of the sexual field and a theory of sexual capital. *Sociological Theory, 24,* 107–132.

Mears, A. (2011). *Pricing beauty: The making of a fashion model.* Los Angeles: University of California Press.

Newton, E. (1972). *Mother camp: A history of female impersonation in America.* Chicago: University of Chicago Press.

Paul, J. P., Ayala, G., & Choi, K. (2009). Internet sex ads for partner selection criteria: the potency of race/ethnicity online. *Journal of Sex Research, 46,* 1–11.

Prieur, A. (1998). *Mema's house, mexico city: On transvestites, queens and machos.* Chicago: University of Chicago Press.

Rupp, L. (2009). *Sapphistries: A global history of love between women.* New York: New York University Press.

Rupp, L., & Taylor, V. (2008). *Drag queens at the 801 cabaret.* Chicago: University of Chicago Press.

Schatzki, T. R., Knorr Cetina, K., & Von Savigny, E. (2001). *The practice turn in contemporary theory.* London: Routledge.

Schilt, K., & Windsor, E. (2014). Negotiating sexuality through gender: The sexual habitus of transgender men. *The Journal of Homosexualities, 61*(5), 732–748

Seidman, S. (1996). *Queer theory/sociology.* London: Blackwell.

Stein, A. (1997). *Sex and sensibility: Stories of a lesbian generation.* Berkeley: University of California Press.

Stein, A., & Plummer, K. (1996). I can't even think straight. In S. Seidman (Ed.), *Queer theory/sociology* (pp. 129–144). London: Blackwell.

Tewksbury, R. (2002). Bathhouse intercourse: Structural and behavioral aspects of an erotic oasis. *Deviant Behavior, 23,* 75–112.

Valocchi, S. (2005). Not yet queer enough: The lessons of queer theory for the sociology of gender and sexuality. *Gender and Society, 19,* 750–770.

Waller, W. (1937). The rating and dating complex. *American Sociological Review, 2,* 727–734.

Weinberg, M. S., & Williams, C. J. (1975). Gay baths and the social organization of impersonal sex. *Social Problem, 23,* 124–136.

Weinberg, M. S., & Williams, C. J. (2010). Men sexually interested in transwomen (MSTW): Gendered embodiment and the construction of sexual desire. *Journal of Sex Research, 47,* 374–383.

Weinberg, M. S., & Williams, C. J. (2013). Sexual field, erotic habitus, and embodiment at a transgender bar. In A. I. Green (Ed.), *Sexual fields: Toward a sociology of collective sexual life* (pp. 57–71). Chicago: University of Chicago Press.

Weiss, M. (2012). *Techniques of pleasure: BDSM and the circuits of sexuality.* Durham: Duke University Press

Westhaver, R. (2005). "Coming Out of Your Skin:" Circuit parties, pleasure and the subject. *Sexualities, 8,* 347–374.

Macro Theory in Sexual Science

4

Ira L. Reiss

4.1 Part One: Macro Theory and the Birth of Two Disciplines

In the late nineteenth and early twentieth century two new disciplines came to the attention of the Western world—sociology and sexual science. The problems of the industrializing and urbanizing world led people to search for a new way of gaining knowledge about their changing social and sexual lives. There were people who helped these newborn disciplines grow by honing new lenses with which to see more clearly the new world in which they lived. Part of this dramatic process was the building of explanatory macro theories that could theoretically draw a portrait of the intertwining segments of the rapidly changing Western societies.

Theory, whether macro or micro, refers to explanations that help us understand how certain changes occur, how social problems can be contained, and hopefully how our overall society works. *Theory,* more formally put, is composed of logically interrelated concepts, that put forth propositions about what is being studied, in a way that can be empirically researched. Macro theory focuses on comparing societies or studying major segments of a human society such as our social classes, our sexual customs, or our basic institutions. These macro units are the structural

parts of a society and they were of great interest in the very beginning years of sociological theory and still require our attention today (Comte 1835/1896; Spencer 1901; Stark 2009).

The difference between macro and micro theory is rooted in the size of the unit studied. Micro theory would explain how people in a marital dyad or a friendship triad communicate with each other or how small groups of people work to create changes they desire in the broader society. Bear in mind that these two levels of analysis logically have to relate to each other because micro and macro units impact each other (Collins 1988; Hechter 1983; Stark 2009).

To illustrate the interaction of macro and micro theory one need only examine the classic macro study of suicide by Emile Durkheim wherein he stated that the degree of integration or cohesion in a large group would determine the suicide rate in that group (Durkheim 1951). Durkheim was dealing with individual acts of suicide in different groups and thus there is a micro aspect (individual) and a macro aspect (group) to this theory and one can choose to focus upon either one or both of them. Group integration is built from the acts and feelings of individuals and so the two basic variables in Durkheim's theory—integration and suicide-- both have a macro and micro theoretical level that can be explored. Durkheim chose to focus on the macro level of relationships in different groups and so he stressed "social facts" above individual facts. To him this macro level was the key sociological level of analysis that had been overlooked by other disciplines.

I. L. Reiss (✉)
University of Minnesota, Minneapolis,
Minnesota 55455, USA
e-mail: irareiss@comcast.net

J. DeLamater, R.F. Plante (eds.), *Handbook of the Sociology of Sexualities,* Handbooks of Sociology and Social Research, DOI 10.1007/978-3-319-17341-2_4, © Springer International Publishing Switzerland 2015

In sum then, there is no impassable separation or invidious distinction between micro and macro theory. The choice is a matter of what excites a scholar's interest rather than being a better or worse choice. Both structure (social forces) and agency (individual power) go together in the real world just like micro and macro do in the theoretical world. The researcher and theoretician can separate these levels but in reality they flow into each other (Collins 1988; Mead 1934; Skinner 1985).

I have used sociologists like Durkheim to illustrate macro theoretical levels because they are very well known in the social science community and their work clearly illustrates macro theory (Marx 1859/1904; Weber 1930). There also were macro theories in the early years of sexual science put forth by people like Sigmund Freud, Havelock Ellis, and Magnus Hirschfeld (Ellis 1936; Freud 1957, 1962; Hirschfeld 1932, 1936). But Durkheim's work more formally presents tested macro theoretical ideas.

The beginning of sexual science in the U.S. was focused on social problems like prostitution, venereal disease and "purity" issues while in Europe the focus was more on homosexuality and transvestites. There were major debates over whether research or societal reform should be the focus of sexual science. This new field was also seen as a therapeutic discipline dealing with sexual "pathologies." The focus here was on sexual "illnesses" of people, and the analysis was done by medical doctors (Krafft-Ebing 1886). Both Ellis and Hirschfeld believed that homosexuality was determined by heredity but there was much debate on this issue with the politicians of that day. In 1907, Dr. Iwan Bloch, a dermatologist, moved to broaden the field by including social scientists in the study of sexuality. It was he who proposed an all inclusive name for the study of sexuality—*sexualwissenschaft*—sexual science (Bloch 1908/1928).

The very promising development of sexual science in Europe came to a sudden halt in the early 1930s when Hitler took power in Germany. One of his earliest actions was to burn the books and papers at the Institute for Sexual Science that had been founded by Magnus Hirschfeld (Hirschfeld

1932). Of course, the work of Sigmund Freud was also important in the development of sexual science. But it was controversial and the English sexual scientist, Havelock Ellis, took issue with a number of Freud's psychoanalytic concepts such as the Oedipus Complex (Ellis 1936; Freud 1962; Grosskurth 1980). There were many important ideas in the work of men like Hirschfeld, Freud and Ellis, but there was also a good deal of competitiveness and at that time there was not an abundance of research and theory work that could enter into such disputes.

Sociology became a department in the 1890s in both Europe and America, but sexual science did not gain acceptance as an academic department in those early years. In my mind, Ellis's work was the most central to those with a social science interest. Ellis stressed comparing our ideas about sexuality by seeing whether they held up when analyzing sexuality in other societies. He used studies in anthropology by Malinowski to test out and critique some of Freud's ideas (Malinowski 1929; Ellis 1936).

After Hitler attacked sexual science, the curtain fell on sexual science work in Europe for the next two or three decades. The leadership baton was passed to America in the work of Alfred Kinsey starting in the late 1930s (Kinsey et al. 1948, 1953). Kinsey's work was very important and influential but it was basically descriptive and not theoretically presented. We can't go into more historical detail here but for a most interesting account of the development of the field of sexual science in both Europe and America there are good sources to consult (Bullough 1994; Haeberle 1978; Money and Musaph 1977). For our purposes here we will now turn to some of the macro theoretical work in America starting in the 1960s and going up to the present day.

4.2   Part Two: Macro Studies on Sexuality in the United States

In Parts 2 and 3 of this chapter, I present two of my macro theories on sexuality and compare each of them with macro theory work done by other social scientists. I aim to illustrate some of the diversity of macro theory projects and increase awareness of the processes by which macro theory is created in America. In Part 4 I will present more recent macro work and also review work by Harvard biologist Edward Wilson, in order to show how biological macro theoretical work on sexuality fits with social science macro theoretical work on sexuality today.

4.2.1 The Autonomy Theory of Premarital Sexuality

The family textbooks in the 1950s stressed abstinence and portrayed premarital sexuality as involving predominantly lust and selfishness and having no redeeming characteristics. In these textbooks the double standard in premarital sexuality was only lightly touched upon. Also, the work of Kinsey and his colleagues on sexual behavior was often ignored or cherry picked to fit with the text author's preconceptions. In addition, I strongly felt that we were neglecting the scientific study of sexual attitudes toward premarital sexuality. At that time I believed that we were about to witness a major increase in premarital sexuality and so we needed a more thorough and unbiased perspective on premarital sexuality (Reiss 1960).

In 1958 I began work on a scale measuring premarital sexual permissiveness. With the help of four hard working senior sociology majors I built two 12-item scales measuring premarital sexual attitudes towards males and towards females. I tested my scales in 1959 at two high schools and two colleges in Virginia. Comparing answers in the male and female scales afforded a measurement of a double standard attitude. Each scale had questions on premarital kissing, petting and coital behavior. For each of those three sexual behaviors there were four questions asking about acceptance of the behavior under different levels of affection. In 1989 I revised the scale into a short four item scale that focused on premarital coitus using four questions that varied the degree of affection. This new form was tested successfully in both the U.S. and Sweden (Schwartz and Reiss 1995). Both the original and

the short form of the scales are still in use by researchers (Reiss 1967, 2011a).

Using research funds that I received from the National Institute of Mental Health, I was able to add my premarital scale questions to a questionnaire for a national sample of 1500 respondents fielded in 1963 by the National Opinion Research Center (NORC) at the University of Chicago. I also administered the scales at two more colleges, one in New York and one in Iowa. The scales met all the Guttman Scale requirements in the national sample and in all the school samples. Guttman scales rank answers to the questions in a ladder formation, with specific steps from low to high (Stouffer et al. 1950). The successful laddering of the questions on premarital sexual permissiveness in the national and all six student samples implied that there was an American cultural ranking of the acceptability of these different sexual behaviors that my scales were measuring.

The NORC national sample also enabled me to test a number of demographic variables that could be used to build and test ideas concerning factors that promote or inhibit changes in premarital sexual permissiveness. There were questions on education, income, occupation, marital status, number of children, region of the country, religion, age, race, gender, happiness, school segregation, racial integration, and political preference (Nixon vs. Kennedy). This national sample was the first representative national probability sample validating scales measuring premarital sexual permissiveness (Reiss 1964a, b, 1965). The 1963 attitude responses have been used as a baseline from which to measure attitude changes toward premarital sexuality over the past half century (Hopkins 2000; Reiss and Miller 1979; Reiss 2001, 2006).

The premarital sexual revolution in America is best dated as being clearly underway by 1965 and proceeding in an upward arc until about 1975 when it leveled off. The percent accepting premarital coitus in my 1963 national sample was 20%; in 1965 another NORC national sample found 28% accepting premarital coitus; in 1970 another NORC national sample showed 52% acceptance; and in 1975 the General Social Survey (GSS) fielded by NORC showed 69% acceptance

(GSS 2013; Klassen et al. 1989; Reiss 1967; Scott 1998). A move from 20 to 69 % in 12 years can be called a sexual revolution. The acceptance rate in the 2012 GSS was 73 %, not much of a change in this measure since 1975 (GSS 2013). My major goal in my study, besides testing the reliability and validity of my scale, was to understand the social factors that could change people's premarital sexual permissiveness.

The student data covered a number of similar variables but it added additional variables such as dating experiences, love conceptions, sexual behaviors, guilt reactions, and perceived sexual permissiveness of parents, peers and close friends (Reiss 1967, Appendices). Note that these questions involve individual factors concerning dyadic reactions, experiences and perceptions—these were micro variables being used in a macro study of our shared national premarital sexual attitudes. In addition, the demographic factors that I mentioned above were macro variables related to social class, race, age, gender and such.

Since there was little existing social science knowledge of what would influence a person's views of premarital sexual permissiveness, I had to use an inductive approach in which I carefully examined the relationships of the different variables in my data and then induced my theoretical explanation. I will spell out, below, the seven propositions and the overarching theory that I developed.

4.2.2   Proposition One

First, I searched for a variable in the national sample that I felt could impact premarital sexual permissiveness (PSP). Religiosity as measured by church attendance seemed to fit that bill. Organized religion generally promotes a conservative, restrictive view of what is premaritally sexually acceptable. Religiosity did show a strong negative relationship to my PSP scales in both the student samples and the national sample. I found that the relationship of church attendance to PSP was much stronger among females compared to males and much stronger among whites compared to blacks. These race and gender ta-

bles specified the relation of church attendance to PSP (Reiss 1967, Chap. 3). Now the question was, could I derive one proposition, one theoretical explanation, that would explain the race and gender differences in the relationship?

I sought to find what common factor blacks and males have that distinguishes them from whites and females. I concluded that in American society blacks and males are both more accepting of PSP than are whites and females, and so perhaps the theoretical explanation is that the lower a group is on acceptance of PSP the more likely they are to be impacted by factors such as church attendance. Whites and females are traditionally lower on PSP than blacks and males and their attitudes did seem to be more alterable by social factors such as the rate of church attendance. So the data fit with my explanation.

I checked this relationship and found it held in each of my student samples. Of these four race/ sex groups, the one with the lowest PSP and thus most likely to move up in PSP if their church attendance or other conservative influences decreased would be white females. That prediction has been checked over the decades since my study. White females have made the most dramatic changes in PSP (Hofferth et al. 1987; Laumann et al. 1994; Singh and Darroch 1999). These findings build confidence in the explanation I devised.

Proposition One States The lower the traditional level of sexual permissiveness in a group, the greater the likelihood that social pressures will alter individual levels of sexual permissiveness.

4.2.3   Proposition Two

The second proposition grew out of my check on the relation between one's social class and PSP. The student samples and the national sample surprised me by not showing any relationship between social class and PSP—I had expected a negative relationship, which was what Kinsey had found (Kinsey et al. 1948, 1953). I searched for a socio/cultural factor that might alter this lack of a relationship between social class and

PSP. I found to my surprise that when I controlled on the dimension of liberal/conservative (in non-sexual areas) the social class relationship changed dramatically. In a liberal group the relation between social class and PSP was positive but in a conservative group it was negative! Put these liberal and conservative groups together and they cancel each other out. However, examine them separately and the relationship is no longer masked and it appears in two different forms.

Liberal groups are the most likely to maintain high levels of PSP despite factors like church attendance that can reduce PSP. The upper classes showed the greatest differences between liberal and conservative groups—the lower classes showed the least difference between liberal and conservative groups (Reiss 1967). So these first two propositions would logically imply that the most likely group to maintain high PSP would be an upper class liberal group of males. I should add here that this proposition on class and liberalism in my data works better with whites than with blacks. The small size of the black upper class sample may be a factor here. Blacks overall showed a general negative relation of social class and PSP.

Proposition Two States The higher the amount of general liberality in a group, the greater the likelihood that social forces will maintain high levels of sexual permissiveness.

4.2.4 Proposition Three

Proposition three addresses family influences on PSP. There are more ties to the marital and family institutions for females than for males and the third proposition states that these family ties restrict the ease with which female sexual permissiveness will change. For example, in my student samples romantic love and exclusiveness of dating showed a positive relationship to PSP but mostly for females. Males had high PSP regardless of love and exclusiveness. The accepted PSP level in the family institution was much lower than the accepted level in the youth groups. So the more closely bound you are to your parents

the less likely you were to increase your PSP. We have seen in propositions 1 and 2 that these family ties can be altered for various sub groups. Nevertheless, the family ties still are a factor that has influence.

Proposition Three States Male and female differences in ties to the family institution will create differences in the factors (such as affection) that influence their premarital sexual permissiveness.

4.2.5 Proposition Four

Proposition four deals with issues of gender equality. In my results there is gender inequality in abstinence; males were allowed more petting than are females, and also in the double standard where males were allowed more coital rights than women have. Believers in abstinence and the double standard are of course lower in PSP than those who accept coitus equally for men and women. There is thus support for increased permissiveness leading to increased gender equality. Inequality is surely still with us since even today only 20 % of congress is female, there are no female Catholic priests, more University professors are male, and men still earn more than women. Such structural inequality in basic institutions means that we'll find gender inequality in sexuality as well but less of it in high PSP groups.

Proposition Four States Within the abstinence and double standard codes, the higher the overall level of permissiveness in a group the greater the extent of equalitarianism.

4.2.6 Proposition Five

The fifth proposition examines the influence of parental values. I found that parental values influence a person's starting level of PSP, but how long did the influence last? Behavior seemed to generally come first, and acceptance (not rejection) of that behavior, most often followed. This process of change once one starts dating is explained in part by the first four propositions concerning the impact of sexual acceptance, liberality, family ties, and gender equality but parental values also play a part in determining the speed at which PSP will increase.

Proposition Five States The level of permissiveness in the values one derives from parents will be a key determinant of the number, rate and direction of changes in one's premarital sexual standards.

4.2.7 Proposition Six

Here in proposition six we have another determinant of PSP—peer influence. The finding that older and more permissive young people see themselves as more distant from their parents supports the view of an increasing tendency to free oneself from parental controls.

Proposition Six States There is a general tendency for the individual to perceive his/her parents' permissiveness as a low point on a permissive continuum and his/her peers' permissiveness as a high point, and over time to increasingly place his/her self closer to peers, and close friends.

4.2.8 Proposition Seven

Proposition seven, the last proposition, deals with another way that the family impacts a young person's PSP. Older siblings were found to be lower on PSP than their younger sibs, and divorced parents were higher on PSP than married parents. Finally we found that children who had no siblings were the highest on premarital sexual permissiveness. The battle lines between courtship and family pushes and pulls are writ large in this proposition.

Proposition Seven States Responsibility for other family members (as a sibling or as a parent) diminishes one's premarital permissiveness and the more courtship involvement one has (as a

young person or as a divorced parent) the higher the level of permissiveness.

4.2.9 Summary Statement of the Autonomy Theory

The final and most important step in my research was to see if I could formulate a single theoretical statement from which all seven propositions could be derived. The crucial question was: Is there some common element that can be found in all seven of these propositions?

After careful analysis I concluded that the element that was present in all seven propositions was autonomy. Whether you're speaking of a courtship group or a single person, the greater the level of autonomy, the greater the level of permissiveness will be and so my overall theoretical statement was:

Within a modern society the higher the degree of autonomy of an individual or a courtship group, the higher the level of premarital sexual permissiveness.

I call this summary statement the Autonomy Theory. The assumption underlying the power of autonomy is that there is individual and group pressure pushing towards high levels of premarital sexuality and so if given autonomy the move will be toward more PSP. All seven propositions show this power of autonomy regarding PSP and they also display the underlying assumption of this theory that there is pressure (societal and biological) to increase PSP. The very fact that we found social and cultural aspects aimed at inhibiting autonomy implies that many people believe there is a tendency to increase PSP. The sexual revolution of the 1960s and 1970s changed the social world towards higher youth autonomy (Reiss 1960, 2006). I believe that one major reason for the change was the higher proportion of women employed who had preschool children. The percent was 12 % in 1950 and in 2011 it had grown to about 70 % (Kreider and Elliott 2010). This gave more autonomy to children and also to women. Of course, there were many other factors as well. This autonomy theory is derived from American data but I believe my theory is also relevant for societies in Western Europe from which our culture derives. See my account of sexuality and gender in Sweden for data on differences and many similarities (Reiss 1980c).

How closely are attitudes linked or tied to behaviors? The NORC has studied this and they report quite significant correlations between attitudes and behaviors (Reiss 2001). Was I able to predict attitudes and behaviors using the autonomy theory? One test was to examine the results found by other professionals who tested my theory and its propositions. Together with a graduate student of mine, Brent Miller, we examined the outcomes of such research (Reiss and Miller 1979). The retests generally supported my propositions. I mentioned earlier that my prediction that white females would change the most in the sexual revolution also was supported. I believe my 1963 national sample can be used as a measure of the public views at the beginning of the sexual revolution that occurred 1965–1975.[1]

Finally, let me note some limitations of my study. The national sample was of people 21 and above and is representative of the country but the student sample came from just three states. So to more accurately test social factors impacting both adults and younger people we must utilize more representative youth samples. Also, my measure of liberality and conservatism was a proxy measure and it would be much better if I could have had an established scale to do this measurement. There also is the question of whether my Autonomy Theory can be applied to all segments of our society, or to other Western societies or to non-industrial societies. Finally, my study was limited to heterosexuality and so the question is open regarding whether it applies to GLBT attitudes and behaviors.

4.2.10 The National Health and Social Life Survey

To expand the reader's view of Macro theory I turn to a 1992 comprehensive study of human sexuality from a sociological point of view, undertaken by Edward Laumann, John Gagnon,

Robert Michael and Stuart Michaels. The advent of HIV/AIDS in the early 1980s led to increased interest in learning more about sexuality in order to contain the spread of this new deadly disease. Laumann et al.'s research was aimed at doing just that and at first it was supported by federal government grants. However, after political attacks by right wing politicians the government support was retracted and Laumann and his colleagues had to find private foundation funding. This clash with political reality when one is doing sex research is not an uncommon event (Reiss 2014).

The theoretical basis of the study chosen by the authors focuses on scripting theory, choice theory and social network theory. These "theories" are orientations and are different from the "substantive theory" that I developed in my own work. A substantive theory refers to specific hypotheses relating variables. To illustrate, proposition two affirms the difference between liberal and conservative groups in maintaining high levels of permissiveness. An orientation may tell you to pay attention to specific liberal and conservative variables but it will not state how those variables relate to changes in sexuality. As Robert Merton stated, orientations are a "point of departure" toward theorizing (Merton 1967, p. 142). The three orientations that Laumann mentioned do not spell out propositions regarding how a specific "script, choice or network" relates to a specific type of sexual attitude or behavior. To develop specific, substantive propositions you need to examine the variables used in a study and see how they relate to each other. I don't reject orientations. I take an eclectic view of them and use them mainly when they fit into the problem area I am examining.

Laumann et al. states that the design of their study, the National Health and Social Life Survey (NHSLS), limited the measurements of factors in the script, choice or network orientations and so they instead focused on six "master statuses" that they use throughout the book to break down the results. These six statuses are gender, race/ethnicity, age, education, marital status, and religious affiliation. These are six of the statuses used by Alfred Kinsey and his colleagues in their work (Kinsey et al. 1948, 1953). The NHSLS sample represents the 18-to-59-year-old American population and the 90 min interview they used cov-

---

[1] My 1963 national sample can be obtained from the Kinsey Institute.

ered in depth a great many areas related to sexual behavior and attitudes. They had a good response rate of 79% and a sample of 3432 people interviewed by the NORC.

Here are some significant findings from their survey. Masturbation is not a frequently studied area of sexuality and that adds value to their findings. They found that among married couples 57% of the husbands and 37% of the wives had masturbated in the past year (Laumann et al. 1994). They report also that blacks masturbated less than whites and that for both racial groups, about half of those who did masturbate felt guilty about it. Laumann and his colleagues did not attempt to build explanations of the racial or marital difference in masturbation. They examined the differences in masturbation behavior by educational background—a measure of social class. One interesting finding was that for those whose education was less than high school the male/female difference in achieving orgasm during masturbation was 60 vs 46%. But for those in the highest educational group (masters degree or more) the difference was 95% males vs. 87% females (Laumann et al. 1994). The male/female differences in orgasmic masturbation are somewhat less in highly educated people but more importantly they support the idea that the higher educational groups have much more success in reaching orgasm in masturbation. In addition they reported that higher educated people masturbated more frequently than lower educated people and that the masturbation rates were not associated with frequencies of other sexual behaviors. So masturbation was not predominantly due to a lack of other sexual outlets. These findings would be worth exploring further.

Laumann's study defined homosexual behavior by asking about desire and self-definition. By self-definition they report 2.8% of the men and 1.4% of the women responded that they were homosexual or bisexual (Laumann et al. 1994, Chap. 8). Using behavior as the definition of homosexuality, they report 4.9% of the men and 4.1% of the women had a same gender sexual experience after turning 18. Measuring homo-

sexuality since puberty they found 9.1% of the men and 4.3% of the women had some same gender sexual behavior. The authors report that in the 12 largest cities in the U.S., where one third of the U.S. population lives, they found 16% of the men and 5% of the women had same gender sexual relationships since puberty. Further some 17% of the men and 10% of the women in these cities said they felt sexual attraction for the same gender (Drescher 1998).

Sexual frequency reported by men and women was quite similar. Ten percent had no sex in the past year and going up to about a third who had sex two or more times a week (Laumann et al. 1994). The definition of having sex used in this survey was very broad: It included any sexual activity with a person that involved "genital contact and sexual excitement" (Laumann et al. 1994, p. 67). So this could be oral sex or anal sex or penile/vaginal sex or mutual masturbation, etc. Laumann and his colleagues did break down the frequency of sex by marital status and reported just under seven times a month for marital couples and just under nine times a month for cohabiting partners.

The lack of multivariate analysis in all the data analysis was a limitation in this study. For example, they report similar rates of sexual relations for fundamental Protestants and for moderate Protestants. However, other studies reported lower rates for fundamental Protestants (Billy et al. 1993) and so there is reason to check further as to why this was not found by Laumann et al. To be sure that this finding is not a spurious relationship one would want to be sure that fundamentalist Protestants were not younger or more likely to be married than were moderate Protestants. If age and marital status are related to type of Protestant, then controlling on them could change the relation of rates of sexual relations and type of Protestant. Laumann et al. did analyze some of the bivariate tabular results using sophisticated logistic regression techniques but other tables were left in bivariate format.

When looking at men and women ages 18–29 and checking sex during the last 5 years we find that more than 60 % of this group had two or more partners—in fact about 25 % of this group has five or more partners in the last 5 years (Laumann et al. 1994). Their data does show that over half the cohabiting relationships end within 1 year and extra dyadic sexuality occurs often before the final break. In marriage 25 % of married men and 15 % of married women report having extramarital sex.

Laumann and his colleagues used a threefold classification of sexual norms or attitudes: Reproductive, Relational or Recreational. Not having direct measures they took questions from earlier NORC studies that they thought would be useful in measuring the three types of sexual norms. They did a cluster analysis of the responses to these nine questions and found correlational patterns that they then tried to relate to the three types of sexual norms. Perhaps others will work further on scales measuring these concepts. We also need to examine whether these three types of sexual norms fully cover the field of sexual norms and to what degree these three types overlap with each other.

Their data could be used to develop theoretical explanations, or assess theory proposed by others. For example, there are findings that can be used to assess some of my propositions. They report that from the 1970s to the 1990s females and whites increased their sexual behavior more than did males and blacks (Laumann et al. 1994). That fits very well with my proposition one.

This study was one of the most important additions to our knowledge of sexuality since the work of Kinsey. Bear in mind that Kinsey's studies were also basically descriptive but they were quite influential. Descriptive studies can have considerable value if other people will analyze the data in terms of a theory. It was from just such a study, as the 1963 NORC research, that I developed my autonomy theory. Laumann has published other work in which his theoretical stance is much more visible (Laumann and Michael 2000; Laumann et al. 2004, 2006). There are also more recent studies that can bring up to date some of the Laumann et al. findings and afford additional sources for formulating theoretical explanations (Bruckner and Bearman 2005;

Chandra et al. 2011; Collins 2004; Herbeneck et al. 2010; Reece et al. 2010).

4.3   Part Three: Cross Cultural Macro Theories

4.3.1   The Cross Cultural PIK Linkage Theory

We turn now to two macro research studies, both seeking to develop a sociological theory that can explain human sexuality in a way that would cover virtually all types of societies in our world today. I will first present my macro theory and the research testing it and then compare it to another major theory and research project.

In 1980 I was looking for a new challenge. The most exciting project that I could think of was to analyze sexuality customs in cultures around the world to identify what parts of human society are universally related to the sexual behavior and attitudes in a society. Assuming those universal linkages are found, the theoretical task would then be to explain how each of these universal linkage areas operate to structure sexual customs in our societies. I also wanted to examine the differences in the way these universal linkages are operationalized in various societies.

I spent 4 years reading everything I could find on sexuality customs in a great many societies (Reiss 2004). I also spoke to anthropologists, psychologists, sociologists, therapists, and philosophers to obtain their guidance and suggestions on my project. I used the Standard Cross Cultural Sample (SCCS) of the best-studied 186 non-industrial societies to empirically check my theoretical propositions (Murdock and White 1969). In addition I used what good quality research there was of sexual customs in the U.S. and other industrialized societies.

Much of our confusion in comparing societies stems from lack of clarity and precision in our definitions. One key term is gender. I use the term gender role to refer to the set of scripts that societies apply to males and females' sexual customs.

There are societies with more than two genders— the traditional Navajo American Indian group is one of them—but the Western world has just two (Reiss 1980a, p. 57, 1986, p. 85). Gender is a socially defined category but gender roles are not 100% socially produced (Fausto-Sterling 2000). There may well also be biological reasons for the particular scripts that are assigned to males and females and I will discuss that later. However, in this project my focus was predominantly on finding and explaining the universal *sociological* linkages that organize our sexual lives.

I define human sexuality in a particular culture as consisting of those scripts shared by a group that are supposed to lead to erotic arousal and in turn to genital response. Of course, I recognize that there are attitudes and behaviors that lead to genital arousal and response that are not in the shared cultural scripts of a particular group in a society. When such unscripted acts become common, they often are then added to the shared script. To illustrate: The increased popularity of oral sex once the sexual revolution began in 1965 was one such sexual innovation that led to oral sex taking a larger role in today's sexual repertoire (Laumann et al. 1994). So macro theorists need to pay attention to how individual micro scripts influence our broad macro cultural scripts (Chafetz 1984; Collins 2004). No matter what kind of theory we are portraying and what discipline we call home, it takes more than one brush to paint the complexity of our social system

I started with the assumption that the two most common outcomes of sexual relationships are physical pleasure and self-disclosure. Physical pleasure is rather obvious although by no means is it always guaranteed. Self-disclosure requires a bit more of an explanation. First, note that the very act of being seen enjoying the pleasure of sexual intercourse is itself a self disclosure—you don't usually do that in front of just anyone. Further, a person's character is revealed by the degree to which they pay attention to self pleasure versus partner pleasure. In this and other ways we self disclose to our sexual partners many things about ourselves—some verbally, many unintentionally.

In all cultures the meaning of sexuality will be connected in some fashion with pleasure and disclosure. This is so whether sexuality is encouraged or discouraged, approved or disapproved. Also, cultures seem aware at some level that pleasure and disclosure in any relationship can lead to bonding between people. Some cultures, in order to avoid bonding, may encourage rapid change of partners or sex with prostitutes. Other pleasure-oriented cultures will encourage sexuality but see it in a playful fashion as when Professor Elwin describes how the Muria in central India view sexuality: "…the penis and the vagina are in a 'joking relationship' to each other… sex is great fun…it is the dance of the genitals." (Elwin 1947, p. 419). Other societies pressure people to save sexuality for love or other serious affectionate relationships. The double standard is always underlying all these sexual standards, even though Western cultures today are less restrictive of female sexuality—sexuality is still not an even playing field.

After all my explorations, I identified three areas of social life that strongly influence the way sexuality is integrated in all societies. The first universal societal linkage is to *Power Differences by Gender*. I define power, as Max Weber did, as the ability to influence others despite their resistance. The second linkage was to *Ideological Beliefs of Normality*. Ideologies are the emotionally powerful beliefs in a society that are the sources of judging many behaviors as good or bad and as "normal or abnormal." The third universal societal linkage of sexuality was to *Kinship as in Extramarital Jealousy Norms*. These norms define how each gender should express or inhibit marital sexual jealousy. These three universal societal linkages compromise the heart of my theory of the universal determinates of the basic structure of sexual customs in any human society. My acronym for this theory comes from the key concept in each linkage area (Power, Ideology, Kinship) and so I refer to this theory as the PIK Linkage Theory.

The SCCS is a secondary data source; it does not have the full set of questions I would have liked but it was the best data source we have on non-industrial societies. This sample was a good testing ground for my ideas. Any universal linkage of sexuality to other social structures would have to be present in these 186 societies.

Power and Gender Differences The first thing to examine in gender power differences is the tie to the raising of children in different types of societies. The mother is almost always tied closer than the father to children. In a hunting and gathering society of perhaps 50–100 people, the childrearing role is ranked close to equal with the hunting role that males predominantly perform. Accordingly, these small hunting and gathering societies are higher in gender equality than are most other types of societies.

With the development of agriculture about 10,000 years ago the male/female power difference increased radically. This change is particularly seen in the intensive agricultural societies where male strength becomes a factor. Agricultural societies lead to cities and to thousands of people living near each other. Class systems are formed and institutions become more specialized. Women are respected but they are not given equal power. Women's tie to the childrearing role limits what she can do in the economic and political institutions and that lowers the power she has in that society. The male advantage in power outside the home then structures the sexuality scripts for men and women. Here are the building blocks of the double standard edifice in sexuality and most other areas of life. As expected, the SCCS data showed that intensive Agricultural societies were likely to define women as inferior to men.

When we get to modern industrial societies, the power of women does increase especially as they enter the marketplace but clearly males still dominate the power roles in the economic and political institutions in Western industrial societies. If you wish to afford women greater equality with men, then you will need to accommodate changes in women's ties to child rearing. You find movements in this direction in Western European countries that provide leaves with pay when a child is born and more flexible hours of work. In addition you need to pursue more equality in the economic and political institutions for women. The 20% female share in the U.S. Congress is one of the lowest in the Western world and our less than 80% pay for women in the same line of work clearly hinders equality (Stark 2009). Men and women are still far from equal. In the SCCS we see evidence of greater equality when we look at horticultural societies wherein women's work is highly valued for it involves a great deal of the planting and gathering of essential foods (Chafetz 1984; Roos 1985; Whyte 1978). In fact the Hopi Indians in our southwest have been defined by anthropologist Alice Schlegel as very close to gender equal (Schlegel 1977). But even there you find that males will often develop methods for increasing their power (Reiss 1986).

I used the SCCS to evaluate my position concerning gender equality being different in hunting and gathering and agricultural groups. My first check using the SCCS was to search for the determinants of the belief that "females are inferior to males." The code a society received for that belief was surely a measure of male power. I used path analysis in my data checks in order to try to understand how different factors impacted the belief in female inferiority (Reiss 1986). I found that the extent of agriculture did significantly correlate with a belief in female inferiority. In addition I saw that agriculture also increased class stratification, and tightened the tie of the mother to the care of her infant and increased the acceptance of a machismo ethic that stressed male strength and aggressiveness. All these changes in agricultural societies tied the mother to domestic tasks and isolated her from the public sphere where societal power is exercised.

My interest in gender power differences was aimed at showing how this can affect sexual relationships in human societies. My theoretical assumption asserts that powerful people seek to maximize their control over the valuable elements in their societies. Sexuality is one of the valuable elements in a society–power can be used to either maximize or minimize sexual interactions. Evidence of this in the SCCS data showed that as gender inequality decreases, the frequency of women's premarital and extramarital sexual behavior approaches that of men. More on this when we get to the third linkage.

Ideological Beliefs of Normality Any part of culture that is highly valued will be regulated in the moral codes of that society and those codes will be buttressed by strong emotions or ideologies. Moral systems are based upon the assumptions that a society makes concerning the nature of human beings and how they should and can behave. These fundamental assumptions about human nature form the core of what we call our ideologies. The sexual norms that are accepted or rejected vary considerably in different cultures but I found that the linkage of sexuality to the docking area of ideology is always present.

The General Social Survey (GSS) is a widely used source of data on American society. That national sample is now carried out every 2 years by the National Opinion Research Center (NORC) at the University of Chicago. These biannual surveys can be used to examine trends in the acceptance of different sexual behaviors and attitudes. The most striking trend in the U.S. in recent years comes from the sharp rise in the acceptance of homosexuality since the early 1990s. Homosexuality is a behavior that arouses strong emotional responses and so it fits into the ideological category we are discussing here (Drescher 1998). In 1973 the GSS showed that 19 % of the respondents accepted homosexual behavior as "wrong only sometimes" or "not wrong at all." In 1993 that percent rather suddenly increased to 29 %. The rate then rose consistently and by 2012 it was 51 % (GSS 2013). Given the supportive 2013 U.S. Supreme Court ruling on homosexual marriage I assume that this percent will continue to rise.

Ronald Inglehart reported similar increases in the acceptance of homosexuality in many countries in his 1990 world survey (Inglehart 1997). Homosexuality is an important area to study because for many generations feelings about homosexuality had been strongly negative. Both the changes in attitudes toward homosexuals and the changes in premarital sexual attitudes in 1965–1975 exemplify that rapid changes in traditional sexual attitudes can occur (Reiss 2001, 2006, 2014).

The sexual ideology of normality derives its meaning from the values of the power structures in the broader society. We can see this in the concept of premature ejaculation. If we go back 100 years we would find a society in which the male's concern for the female's orgasm would be of far lesser importance than it is today. As our gender roles became more equal in the post WW2 world we became more concerned about female orgasm and the notion of premature ejaculation came into vogue. Males who reached orgasm in 15 s after entering the vagina were viewed as having a psychological problem—a "disorder." However, if a female reached orgasm in 15 s would she be thought of as having a sexual disorder? So clearly the basic moral culture is the basis for defining some sexual acts as "abnormal" and that holds in all the societies I examined. In East Bay in Melanesia most males reach orgasm in 15–30 s and the male who doesn't is considered to have a "delayed ejaculation" (Davenport 1965, p. 185). The sexual ideology may change but everywhere I looked I saw societies morally evaluating sexuality—nowhere was it just a private act.

In Western culture, especially in the past, religion had a key role in defining sexual normality. Religion is more powerful in the U.S. than in most Western European societies but even here we see contraception and abortion behaviors increasingly influenced by other parts of our society (Reiss 2014). Societies can change the evaluation of some forms of sexuality, but they can't remove it from ideological beliefs about how our sexual life should be choreographed.

Kinship and Extramarital Sexual Jealousy This is the third and last universal linkage area for sexual customs. Marriage is a key institution in our kinship system. As a sociologist I would define jealousy as a boundary protecting mechanism for what a society feels are important relationships. In this sense jealousy is an alarm system, a protective emotion aimed at maintaining an important relationship when it is threatened by an intruder. When this happens the primary emotional feelings one has are anger, hurt, and depression, which we label as jealousy. Societies spell out when, if ever, an extramarital sexual relationship is allowed and if that blueprint is violated, jealousy and other emotional reactions may occur.

When we look cross culturally we find that women often react to extramarital sexual jealousy with depression and men often respond more with anger. Buunk and Hupka's (1987) research on seven nations–U.S., Mexico, Netherlands, Ireland, Soviet Union, Hungary and Yugoslavia– shows this to be the case. They report that in extramarital sexuality the more affluent the society, the more the rights of people to be autonomous will be stressed. But in all seven societies, men were clearly given more autonomy. This lesser power of women in a society makes the depression response to jealous situations understandable. But we can see from these seven countries, as well as from the SCCS societies, that all societies are aware of sexual jealousy in marriage and in other important relationships. And most importantly, the ways of dealing with extramarital sex reflects the overall level of gender equality in that society (Banfield and McCabe 2001; Glass and Wright 1992; Reiss 1980c; Reiss et al. 1980b).

The awareness by people of the pleasure and the bonding properties of sexuality alerts all societies that if they want a relationship like marriage to last, they best develop norms that give marriage priority over other sexual relationships even in situations where extradyadic relationships are, under some conditions, accepted (Blumstein and Schwartz 1983). On a more psychological level, jealousy is seen as produced by the threat that a person feels when their partner violates the priority of their relationship. This is the psychological core of the jealous reaction in non-industrial societies as well as in our Western societies. Attitudes toward extramarital sexual behavior have not become more accepting in the last 50 years. The GSS in 2012 found that, in America, only 11 % thought it was acceptable.

Despite the power differential of men and women around the world, extramarital sexual relationships are not only for husbands. In the Turu culture of Tanzania a wife may find a man she wants as a lover. She will become friendly with that man's wife and help arrange for her husband to work together with that man in cultivation and cooperative labor projects (Schneider 1971,

p. 66). At times the husband may object to her choice but the wife then may throw his double standard in his face by showing how he has a mistress but is trying to forbid her a lover.

Philip Blumstein and Pepper Schwartz (1983) studied extramarital relationships in a large sample of heterosexual married couples, cohabiting couples and homosexual couples and found that all three of these types of relationships there were norms regulating extra-dyadic sexual relationships. There always are some boundaries that should not be crossed. These boundaries support the priority of the stable relationship over the affair. The lesbian couples were the least likely to accept extradyadic relationships. Married couples had stronger restrictions than did cohabiting or gay male couples. The overall aim of these restrictive norms appears to be to segregate the extramarital relationship and keep it from weakening the existing dyadic relationship. Sexual jealousy and other emotions will result if these limits are violated.

To further test some of my ideas about sexual jealousy and gender power I analyzed the 80 non industrial cultures from the SCCS that Ralph Hupka studied in his analysis of jealousy (Hupka 1981). In these 80 cultures I found three direct determinants of the severity of husband's sexual jealousy—the importance of property, the importance of marriage, and the presence of a male kin group (Reiss 1986). I see all three of these variables as proxy measures of male power. For example, in virtually all cultures property is owned by men and so the more property is emphasized, the more support there will be for male power. Marriage importance also is a proxy for male power in that its importance goes with the passing of power to descendants. Male kin groups are also an indirect measure of power because in a patrilineal society power and other resources are passed down through the male line.

The three male power variables have positive relationships with each other, which further supports their integration as male power measures. When these indices of male power are present, men feel justified in displaying sexual jealousy if their wives stray from their restraints. I should add here that female premarital sexuality was more restricted in societies with high scores on the three male power variables. No such control was placed on male premarital sexuality. As female power increases there is more open display of female jealousy and female feelings of depression decrease (Hupka 1981).

Basically of the three universal linkages I see the gender power linkage as the most important variable in my explanation of human sexuality (Crawford and Popp 2003). As I have shown, power comes into play in the other two linkages of ideologies and extramarital jealousy. Nevertheless, both ideology and extramarital linkages have their own influences as I've tried to indicate. And it is difficult to disaggregate the feedback loops that exist between these three linkages of human sexuality. It would be of great theoretical value to have someone study the interaction of these three universal linkages. Also, I believe that using the PIK Linkage Theory as a guide to study sexuality in any society will move our field to a higher level of understanding of the sociological basis of human sexuality. I should also note that autonomy is a measure of power and so there are ties between my autonomy theory and my PIK theory that can be explored.

For those with more applied interest, I mention that the PIK Linkage Theory has been analyzed in Europe as an aid to managing the risks of HIV infections (Devin and Meredith 1997). Also, Edward Laumann's 2006 work on subjective sexual well being in 29 cultures is a study that can be helpful to those working in applied areas such as therapy or those interested in theoretizing regarding causes of feelings of sexual well being (Laumann et al. 2006).

4.3.2   A Post-Industrialization Theory

Now let's turn to a macro cross cultural theory concerning the important changes that are occurring as Western societies move from industrial to post-industrial societies. Ronald Inglehart used the World Values Survey (WVS) of 43 societies in 1980 and 1990 and later studies, covering over 70% of the world's population. He used these data to build a theoretical explanation of societal

change. Almost all of the 43 societies were studied with a nationally representative sample (Inglehart 1971, 1997; Inglehart et al. 1998; Inglehart and Norris 2003; Inglehart and Welzel 2009).

His theoretical approach starts with the assertion that major changes happened after WW2 in Western European countries. He sees a new generation being raised with high degrees of economic security. Starting around 1970 that generation led the world into a late stage of industrialization. The industrial revolution promoted an emphasis on material things, and gave some societies a chance at creating economic security for their peoples. The post-World War II generation in Europe maximized that sense of security by developing welfare states. In the U.S. we had the development of Social Security, Medicare and Medicaid, all of which promoted our sense of economic security. Inglehart's theory then asserts that good economic security leads to a growth of non-materialist values. Instead of just seeking financial success people start to emphasize well-being and quality of life. Autonomy and self-participation in government processes accompany these changes. Here is a possible theoretical tieup to my autonomy theory and the power dimension in my PIK theory.

Important for our interests in sexuality and gender are Inglehart's findings that between 1980 and 1990 major changes toward more equal gender roles and more acceptant attitudes towards gays and lesbians were occurring. I have earlier in this chapter discussed some of these changes in sexuality and gender. One area of disagreement between Inglehart's findings and the GSS survey findings I presented was in the increased acceptance of extramarital sexuality in Inglehart's World Value Samples. To compare, the GSS showed a rise of acceptance of extramarital sexuality in the U.S. during the 1970s to 16% and then a drop in the 1980s to 8%, and in 2012 it was 11% (GSS 2013; Reiss 2006). One question Inglehart used to measure extramarital sexual attitudes was: "Married men/women having an affair is never justified" (Inglehart 1997, p. 367). The GSS also used one question: "What is your opinion of a married person having sexual relations with someone other than the marriage partner?" So the different wording could make for different answers. What is needed are well tested scales to measure these attitudes (Fisher et al. 2011; Reiss 1980b, 2011b). This is not easy to always do but using good methodology is an essential part of creating good theory.

Inglehart sees the increased economic security and the changes in cultural beliefs and values in the area of sexuality and elsewhere as interrelated processes. His view places the interactive process between security and cultural beliefs as taking place in a political context. He paints a macro view of these interactions. In addition, Inglehart more directly brings in agency, or individual impact, on these macro structures of society as an additional factor involved in these changes. He sees this new type of society as a post-industrial society. I believe he dropped the term "postmodern" that he originally used to describe this new society because to many people, that term focuses on a relativistic and subjective view of individual and social life.

Some understanding of postmodernism can be very helpful to anyone working in sexual science. Michel Foucault, a French philosopher, was one of the founders of the postmodern approach that viewed power, rather than knowledge, as the key element in the human sciences (Foucault 1980; Skinner 1985). The human sciences would include such fields as sociology, psychology, anthropology and Medicine. This move away from knowledge to power thereby removed human science as a path to understanding. Postmodernism then is a relativist position questioning any "outsider" view of the world such as all science proposes. Pierre Bourdieu a noted French sociologist calls this postmodern perspective a form of "epistemological agnosticism"—a denial of knowing any way to obtain a scientific view of the world (Bourdieu and Wacquant 1992, p. 48). I agree and I too see postmodernism as a form or relativism and irrationality. Without human science as a source of knowledge, what basis do we have for understanding our social world (Reiss 1999, 2006; Skinner 1985)?

Inglehart's data shows how the richer societies are the first ones that have solved the economic security problems enough for new values to de-velop and the poorer societies are more likely to seek security in religion and traditional gender roles than are people in the rich societies. His data did generally show that there was a trend over the decades towards self-expressive values in most countries studied. The Nordic countries are the leaders in this move towards post-industrialism values and they display the economic and political changes that go with that trend (Kontula 2009; Reiss 1980c).

There are two key hypotheses in his Post Industrial theory upon which his full explanation is based. First is the Search Hypothesis that states that the greatest value goes to things in short supply. So in wealthier nations economic security loses value and new values develop. Secondly, the Socialization Hypothesis that posits that the values influencing you during your first 25 years of life will continue to be important to you. This hypothesis supports the future growth in wealthy nations of Post Industrial values that influenced the post WWII generation. Inglehart examined the data on births out of wedlock and divorce rates. He notes that both of these are much more common and more accepted normatively today. These value changes go with a reduction in the felt value of religion. He asserts that in this change agency and structure show reciprocal relations with each other and this exemplifies how individual actions can impact macro social structures.

He points out the greater pluralism in views on homosexuality and abortion and in the lives of those who are living in more post-industrial societies rather than industrial societies. He notes that general sexual permissiveness is higher in post-industrial societies. As I've noted, his views here fit with my autonomy theory by showing that greater sexual permissiveness goes with greater autonomy in post-industrial societies. Another value change he reports among post-industrialists is the rise in the percent who say that a child needs a two parent home but at the same time there is increased acceptance of extramarital sexual permissiveness. Perhaps this seeming conflict disappears if the post-industrialists are in more "open" marriage arrangements so that extramarital sex may be less likely to lead to divorce. The broader acceptance of extramarital sexuality may well go with the generally more pluralistic set of post industrial values. In line with pluralism, post-industrial societies seem to have a minimalist philosophy regarding constraints on choices, i.e., use them only when absolutely necessary.

One basic caveat I have is that the trend toward post-industrial values is very attractive to most people who consider themselves liberals. I am a liberal and as I went over his research and theory I kept asking myself, can today's world with all its problems really be moving towards such an attractive liberal society? When your results fit so well with your basic values, it is time to re-check them very carefully. I want to be sure we can be confident of the validity of the measures used for the key value changes. I fully endorse Bourdieu's concept of *reflexivity* where he asks all of us to subject ourselves to the same careful analysis as we use on our data (Bourdieu and Wacquant 1992, p. 41). Perhaps in the next WVS Inglehart could utilize alternate measures of some of the key concepts to see if they agree with the older findings. Another way to build confidence in the results would be to examine more findings of other surveys and see if they support his findings and his predictions. Inglehart's work and his ideas are exciting and well worth exploring further.

4.4 Part Four: Recent Macro Theoretical Studies

We have covered four major macro theory studies in Parts Two and Three. I will here very briefly point to three recent macro theory award winning journal articles. These have all been published between 2008 and 2011, so macro theory is still very much in style today.

Richard Lippa, a psychologist, compared biological evolutionary models and social structural models concerning gender differences in 53 countries with 200,000 participants in a BBC Internet Survey (Lippa 2009). He explored sex drive, sociosexuality (restricted vs. unrestricted sexual attitudes & behaviors), height, gender equality, and economic development. He found both models could predict some of the variables and concludes that we need a hybrid model of biological and social structural influences. For example, he found women more variable than men and found that gender equality and economic development predated sex differences in sociosexuality. But he found sex drive and height fit more with a biological model. He also asked for more precise and nuanced predictions about sex differences across nations in order to better design an integrated socio-biological theory that would be a valid Hybrid Model.

A study by Deanna Carpenter, a psychologist, and her colleagues tested new scales to measure sexual inhibition and sexual excitation (Carpenter et al. 2008). This study tested the scales on over 2000 undergraduates to examine women and men's similarities and differences. The researchers reported that women, compared with men, scored higher on sexual inhibition and lower on sexual excitation. They present a factor analysis of men's and women's scores to find shared and unshared themes. The women reported less attraction to casual sex, and more attraction to their own gender. Despite these and other differences the gender factor structures were quite similar. The authors discuss the relative role of biological and socio/cultural factors in the similarities and differences noted.

A third and final recent award winning journal article used macro theoretical ideas from the work of Sari van Anders and her colleagues (Van Anders et al. 2011). They start with a theory that the responses of hormones to social contexts are the proximate mechanism of evolutionary pathways to pair bonds and other social bonds. Van Anders et al., cite the importance of testosterone and oxytocin in pair bonding in other species. Their theory is that testosterone and peptides provide a set of predictors and a classification system for social behavioral contexts related to social bonds. Testosterone is found in the outcomes of both antagonistic and protective aggression. The authors further examine evidence in this study for developing further their macro theory.

These three recent articles indicate the increasing attempts to deal with biological and sociological factors in a unified fashion. None of them are by sociologists but it is surely time for more sociologists to venture forth and see what macro theoretical formulations can be developed out of a union of sociological and biological macro theory.

I would also suggest that we start to develop more sociological research and theory on the area of sexual ethics. To that end I suggest that the reader examine the 1997 book where my wife and I found strong evidence for the proposition that asserted if the U.S. were to change its sexual ethic from its current restrictive traditional ethic to the ethic of sexual pluralism we would significantly lower our rates of rape, AIDS, teen pregnancy and child sexual abuse (Jones et al. 2012; Reiss and Leik 1989; Reiss and Reiss 1997).

4.4.1 Sociology and Biology: A Scientific Match?

The plea for sociologists becoming more conversant with evolutionary theory and other aspects of biology has been raised by at least two past presidents of the American Sociological Association (Lieberson and Lynn 2002; Massey 2002). Biology is a far better fit with sociological research and theory than is physics or chemistry. A major division of biology is concerned with humans and thus it, like sociology, is in part a human science. Developing macro theory concerning human sexuality by sexual scientists who are knowledgeable in both biology and sociology would be of extraordinary importance for the future of sexual science.

To illustrate the kind of macro theoretical work that sociobiologists today are doing, I will review an exciting 2012 book by the founder of sociobiology, Edward O. Wilson of Harvard University. It will display some of the theory and methods used by biology today and some of the controversies that exist. No single book can represent a discipline but Wilson is an important person in Biology. His new perspective brings society into a clearer focus for biologists. So controversial or not, his work is worth discussing here. My review should afford the reader some insights regarding whether sociological approaches to the study of sexuality can fruitfully combine with biological science (Salk and Hyde 2012).

The book's title: *The Social Conquest of Earth* shows the macro scope of Wilson's theoretical treatise. He begins with three very broad philosophical questions: "Where do we come from? What are we? and Where are we going?" He sees today's civilization as composed of people with stone-age emotions, medieval institutions, and Godlike technology. He feels we are in trouble and his book is intended to help find a way out. Wilson proposes a controversial new perspective on evolutionary theory and compares it to the reigning perspective in evolutionary theory. This new perspective is his answer to the three questions about human beings that he raises. He seeks to add to the evolutionary approach a focus on the importance of group life. So this should surely interest us as social scientists.

He starts by explaining how humans developed a "eusocial" type of society. A eusocial society contains people who are concerned about the welfare of each other—a society with cooperation and altruistic acts being performed. He sees this type of society beginning about 1 million years ago with the control of fire and the development of campsites and the growth of our ability to handle tools. Eusocial development in humans is portrayed by Wilson as the key to the survival of human groups. It led to a division of labor and more bonding between men and women who were sexually involved with each other (Mead 1934).

The prevailing evolutionary theory concerning humans that he critiques is called the "kin selection theory", aka "inclusive fitness theory." Basically this accepted theory states that altruism developed from behavior towards very close genetic kin with whom one was "nested" at these early campsites. The closer the genetic kinship tie, the more likely altruistic behavior would develop. He argues that this theory is not supported by the evidence and he offers his eusocial evolutionary theory as a needed restatement (Wilson 2012). His evolutionary theory proposes a dual-level selection instead of just an individual selection assumption. He accepts selection as targeting individual traits of members of the group (the old view) *but* he adds to that the importance of forces of selection that target traits of one's group compared to other groups (the new view). Wilson sees altruistic acts by some individuals as necessary for the survival of the group. He believes his dual selection theory should now replace the old kin selection theory.

The old evolutionary theory stated that the individual level of genetic fitness depended on acts that were helpful to the survival of that individual whereas the group level of fitness that Wilson stresses depended on acts that supported the group in competition with other groups. The group level promotes altruistic actions and pressures individuals to think of survival as not just of themselves but of others in that group. The tribal group afforded security to all those in the group. As noted, there is a sexual bonding element in his view that is strengthened by the event of camp-sites using fire and people staying together.

He does give a significant role to cultural changes and talks of the interaction of culture and genetics and how this can lead to genetic changes where it advantages survival due to culturally healthier diets, or disease preventing cultural beliefs that advantage certain people or groups. He sees this as creating genetic changes for future generations. Wilson's disagreements with kin selection theory are illustrated in studies of eusocial societies in ants and bees where their development fits best with his multilevel individual/group selection and its reproductive advantages. He feels there is little support for the older kin selection theory except as a secondary force in selectivity (Wilson 2012).

The integration of cultural and genetic changes is more accepted today in biology than it was a few decades ago, before the genome research was undertaken and completed (Salk and Hyde 2012). Wilson states that the true core of human nature today are the epigenetic rules between genetic and cultural forces. He discusses the gene/culture evolution and sees some of these rules going back a few million years. Epigenetics refers to heritable changes in gene expression that are not caused by changes in DNA but related to environmental effects (Salk and Hyde 2012; Rutter 2002). Those gene/culture interconnections

are not hardwired and are changeable over time. He notes that cultural evolution can smother genetic evolution by lifestyle changes that limit the expression of some genes but major genetic changes also occur as when 60,000 years ago people broke out from Africa and there was an explosion of new mutations.

Wilson illustrates his epigenetic gene/culture evolutionary perspective by examining incest taboos. He sees the cultural incest taboo as based in part on the lack of sexual interest that occurs when people during the first 30 months of their life are raised together. The cultural incest norm here fits with the genetic finding that incest can lead to serious biological handicaps for offspring. Incest taboo is an example of gene/cultural co-evolution. Wilson notes that in general the bias or strong impact on behavior of some genes is high as in incest taboos but it can be very low as in things like clothing customs. Low genetic bias means that cultural input can impact a gene or set of genes and keep them from having a powerful impact on behavior. Genes vary in the bias or power of their input and culture enters in easily in low genetic bias areas but has some input even in high bias areas.

The ending of the book surprised me. It is there that Wilson puts forth his belief that God doesn't exist and organized religion is a form of tribalism. The existence of God is not an issue debated much in sociology. Perhaps the God issue comes in as a result of the clashes biologists have had with right wing conservatives about evolutionary theory in the schools. However, this is hardly something that can be settled by scientific research. Science deals with the natural world, not the supernatural world. At the start of the book Wilson took a swipe at philosophy and states that philosophers can't answer his three questions (Where do we come from? What are we? and Where are we going?) because philosophy is a maker of "failed models of the human mind" (Wilson 2012, p. 9). When Wilson states that neither religion nor philosophy can answer his three questions, he seems to be eliminating other sources of knowledge and thereby expanding what biology is capable of dealing with. I see science as one source of knowledge, one epistemological source, but not the only such source (Kagan 2009; Longino 1990, 2002; Proctor 1991). Science is the preferred source for the natural world but as I've indicated, there are questions that cannot be answered by any science and the existence of God is one such question (Reiss 1993).

Obviously, the study of human sexuality is a major concern of both social science and biology. However, bear in mind that to work together we will have to learn new concepts such as Wilson's dual level selection evolution theory. Also, we need to learn more about the kin selection theory and certainly epigenetics, and see the contrast in the "proximate" causation interests of social science (how a structure or process works today) vs. the "ultimate" causation interests of much of biology (why the structure or process exists in the first place). The same type of exposure to social science concepts must be faced by any biologist who wants to utilize sociological concepts and theories such as those I have covered in this chapter. That person would have to become familiar with concepts of agency, structure, post-industrialization, covert culture, latent and manifest functions, role taking, etc. We need some "bridge" people to help smooth out the complex theoretical and research passage way between our disciplines before we can more easily produce interdisciplinary works of theory and research. We have to more fully understand each other before we can work together. A union of disciplines will also require efforts to arrive at some common definitions of shared concepts as basic as gender, sexuality, and culture.

In addition, despite the seemingly important role of the social group in his proposed evolutionary concept, in the last chapter of the book he sums things up by saying: "Humanity is a biological species in a biological world….Our lives are restrained by the two laws of biology: all of life's entities and processes are obedient to the laws of physics and chemistry; and all of life's entities and processes have arisen through evolution by natural selection" (Wilson 2012, p. 287). It's difficult to find in this statement any explicit recognition of the role of culture and society in evolution or elsewhere. I do not see a clear place

for macro theory in sociology in this summation. It seems to imply that culture and society are subsidiaries of biological forces, rather than independent influences. His words elsewhere in the book contradict this conclusion but this statement in the last chapter did make me wonder about the *independent role* that culture plays in his thinking. Perhaps Wilson was just reflecting his devotion to biology but his words did cause me concern.

I see all humans as being born into the pushes and pulls of both culture and genetics. There is not just a genetic low and high "bias" but there is also a low and high "bias" socio/cultural force that must be dealt with. These two culture/gene influences interact and impact each other in ways that we are just now discovering. I see no way to fully separate these two major influences on our lives. The power of *both genes and culture* must vary by what type of situation we are investigating and in what type of socio/cultural system and what set of genes are involved. Studying the variation in that complex interaction should be our focus (Reiss 2006; Rutter 2002).

Nevertheless, now is the time for the more adventurous individuals in sexual science to join with those exploring the interactions of biology and sociology in research, theory, concepts and assumptions regarding sexuality (Salk and Hyde 2012). These efforts can greatly expand our knowledge of who we are and what we can scientifically explain about our lives. I feel confident that some of you reading this will take up this challenge and build a unifying bridge between our two disciplines.

4.4.2 The Future of Sexual Science

I cannot close this chapter without saying a few words about the crucial importance of PhD programs in sexual science for theoretical development. As of 2015 we have two PhD programs in Human Sexuality in fully accredited universities. In 2013 Widener University in Chester, Pennsylvania activated the first fully accredited American PhD program awarding a degree in human sexuality. In 2014 the California Institute of Integral Studies in San Francisco opened a new PhD program in human sexuality. PhD programs with a multidisciplinary and scientific approach will afford us the background in sociology and biology that will enable us to integrate our work in these two disciplines. My wish is that the Kinsey Institute at Indiana University will institute a PhD program in sexual science, with emphasis on a scientific approach within a multidisciplinary framework. That bold move by the university that supported the birth of the Kinsey institute would greatly advance the legitimacy of our field of study and contribute significantly to its future growth.

I would conclude with the plea for more emphasis in our published research efforts on theoretical development and more encouragement for those who do this sort of work (Bancroft 2000; Finkelhor 2013; Reiss 2006). My analysis and suggestions regarding theory development are aimed at advancing our field of sexual science, particularly in the area of the social science study of human sexuality. We need to move toward an answer to the question raised by Robert Lynd in 1939 in the title of his book *Knowledge for What?* Explaining human sexuality in our theoretical work will more clearly show the world that scientific knowledge can enhance our lives and help us build a better society (Deven and Meredith 1997; Reiss and Reiss 1997; Reiss 2014).

The field of sociology has been split since its beginning among those who emphasize descriptive data, those who stress theory and philosophical approaches, and those who are reformers and want to focus on our social problem areas (Turner and Turner 1990). I would support integrating all three approaches in our work. Each of us can favor one approach, but let's be pluralistic rather than combative or evangelical about our different choices (Reiss 2014). At this point I give priority to the development and testing of theoretical explanations that can be helpful in the containment of our many sexual problem areas (Reiss and Reiss 1997; Reiss 2006). I believe we should always keep in mind that our work in sexual science is not just about theory and research—our efforts should also be designed to help people make their sexual lives less troubling and more rewarding.

References

Bancroft, J. (Ed.). (2000). *The role of theory in sex research.* Bloomington: Indiana University Press.

Banfield, S., & McCabe, M. P. (2001). Extra relationship involvement among women: Are they different from men? *Archives of Sexual Behavior, 30,* 119–142.

Billy, J., Tanfer, K., Grady, W. R., & Klepinger, D. H. (1993). The sexual behavior of men in the United States. *Family Planning Perspectives, 25,* 52–60.

Bloch, I. (1908/1928). *The sexual life of our time* (6th ed.). New York: Allied Book Company.

Blumstein, P., & Schwartz, P. (1983). *American couples.* New York: Morrow.

Bourdieu, P., & Wacquant, L. J. D. (1992). *An invitation to reflective sociology.* Chicago: University of Chicago Press.

Bruckner, H., & Bearman, P. (2005). After the promise: The STD consequences of adolescent virginity pledges. *Journal of Adolescent Health, 36,* 271–278.

Bullough, V. L. (1994). *Science in the bedroom: A history of sex research*; New York: Wiley.

Buunk, B., & Hupka, R. B. (1987). Cross-cultural differences in the elicitation of sexual jealousy. *Journal of Sex Research, 23,* 12–22.

Carpenter, D., Janssen, E., & Graham, C., Vorst, H., & Wicherts, J. (2008). Women's scores on the sexual inhibition/sexual excitation scales (SIS/SES): Gender similarities and differences. *Journal of Sex Research, 45,* 36–48.

Chafetz, J. (1984). *Sex and advantage: A comparative macrostructural theory of sex stratification.* Totowa: Rowman and Allenheld.

Chandra, A., Mosher, W. D., Copen, C., & Sionean, C. (2011). Sexual behavior, sexual attraction, and sexual identity in the U.S.: Data from the 2006–2008 National Survey of Family Growth. National Health Statistics Report No. 36. Hyattsville, MD, National Center for Health Statistics.

Collins, R. (1988). The micro contribution to macro sociology. *Sociological Theory, 6,* 242–253.

Collins, R. (2004). *Interaction ritual chains.* Princeton: Princeton University Press.

Comte, A. (1835/1896). *The positive philosophy* (trans: H. Martineau). London: George Bell and Sons. (Original work published 1835).

Crawford, M., & Popp, D. (2003). Sexual double standards: A review and methodological critique of two decades of research. *Journal of Sex Research, 40,* 13–26.

Davenport, W. (1965). Sexual patterns and their regulation in a society of the Southwest Pacific. In F. A. Beach (Ed.), *Sex and behavior* (pp. 164–207). New York: Wiley.

Deven, F., & Meredith, P. (1997). The relevance of a macrosociological perspective on sexuality for an understanding of the risks of HIV infection. In L. V. Campenhoudt, M. Cohen, G. Guizzardi, & D. Hausser (Eds.), *Sexual interactions and HIV risk: New conceptual perspectives in European research*. London: Taylor & Francis.

Drescher, J. (1998). *Psychoanalytic therapy and the gay man*. New York: Routledge.

Durkheim, E. (1897/1951). *Suicide* (trans: J. A. Spaulding & G. Simpson). Glencoe: The Free Press.

Ellis, H. (1936) *Studies in the psychology of sex* (Vols. 1–2). New York: Random House.

Elwin, V. (1947). *The Muria and their Ghotul*. London: Oxford University Press.

Fausto-Sterling, A. (2000). *Sexing the body: Gender politics and the construction of sexuality*. New York: Basic Books.

Finkelhor, D. (November 2013). The decline of sexual abuse and sexual assault. Paper presented at the meeting of the Society for the Scientific Study of Sexuality.

Fisher, T., Davis, C. M., Yarber, W. L., & Davis, S. L. (Eds.). (2011). *Handbook of sexuality-related measures* (3rd ed.). New York: Routledge.

Foucault, M. (1980). *The history of sexuality: An introduction* (Vol. 1). New York: Vintage Paperback.

Freud, S. (1905/1962). *Three contributions to the theory of sex*. New York: E.P. Dutton & Co.

Freud, S. (1920/1957). *The future of an illusion*. New York: Doubleday Anchor Books.

General Social Survey (GSS). (2013). *Cumulative codebook*. Storrs: Roper Center for Public Opinion Research.

Glass, S. P., & Wright, P. I. (1992). Justifications for extramarital relationships: The associations between attitudes, behaviors and gender. *Journal of Sex Research, 29*, 361–387.

Grosskurth, P. (1980). *Havelock Ellis: A biography*. New York: Alfred A. Knopf.

Haeberle, E. J. (1978). *The sex atlas: A new illustrated guide*. New York: The Seabury Press.

Hechter, M. (Ed.). (1983). *The microfoundations of macrosociology*. Philadelphia: Temple University Press.

Herbeneck, D., Reece, M., Schick, V., Sanders, S. A., Dodge, B., & Fortenberry, D. (2010). Sexual behavior in the U.S.: Results from a national probability sample of men and women ages 14–94. *Journal of Sexual Medicine, 7*(Supp. 5), 255–265.

Hirschfeld, M. (1932). *Sexual pathology: Being a study of the abnormalities of the sexual functions* (trans: J. Gibbs). Newark: Julian Press.

Hirschfeld, M. (1936). *Sex in human relationships* (trans: J. Rodker). London: John Lane The Bodley Head.

Hofferth, S. L., Kahn, J. R., & Baldwin, W. (1987). Premarital sexual activity among U.S. teenage women over the past three decades. *Family Planning Perspectives, 19*, 46–53.

Hopkins, K. W. (2000). Testing Reiss's autonomy theory on changes in non-marital coital attitudes and behaviors of U.S. teenagers: 1960–1990. *Scandinavian Journal of Sexology 3*, 113–125.

Hupka, R. (1981). Cultural determinants of jealousy. *Alternative Lifestyles, 4*, 310–356.

Inglehart, R. (1971). The silent revolution in Europe: Intergenerational change in post-industrial societies. *American Political Science Review, 65*, 991–1017.

Inglehart, R. (1997). *Modernization and post modernization: Cultural, economic, and political change in 43 societies*. Princeton: Princeton University Press.

Inglehart, R., & Norris, P. (2003). *Rising tide: Gender equality and cultural change around the world*. New York: Cambridge University Press.

Inglehart, R., & Welzel, C. (2009). Development and democracy: What we know about modernization today. *Foreign Affairs*, July/August, 1–15.

Inglehart, R., Basanez, M., & Moreno, A. (1998). *Human values and beliefs: A cross-cultural sourcebook*. Ann Arbor: University of Michigan Press.

Jones, J., Mosher, W., & Daniels, K. (2012). Current contraceptive use in the U.S., 2006–2010, and changes in patterns of use since 1995. *National Health Statistics Reports, 60*, 1–27.

Kagan, J. (2009). *The three cultures: Natural science, social science, and the humanities in the 21st century*. New York: Cambridge University Press.

Kinsey, A., Pomeroy, W., & Martin, C. (1948). *Sexual behavior in the human male*. Philadelphia: W. B. Saunders.

Kinsey, A., Pomeroy, W., Martin, C., & Gebhard, P. (1953). *Sexual behavior in the human female*. Philadelphia: W. B. Saunders.

Klassen, A. D., Williams, C. J., & Levitt, E. E. (1989). *Sex and morality in the U.S.* Middletown: Wesleyan University Press.

Kontula, O. (2009). *Between sexual desire and reality: The evolution of sex in Finland*. Helsinki: Population Research Institute.

Krafft-Ebing, R. von. (1886). *Psychopathia sexualis: A medico-forensic study*. New York: G.P. Putnam's Sons.

Kreider, R. M., & Elliott, D. B. (August 2010). Historical changes in stay-at-home mothers: 1969–2009. Paper presented at the meeting of the American Sociological Association.

Laumann, E. O., & Michael, R. T. (Eds.). (2000). *Sex, love, and health in America: Private choices and public policies*. Chicago: University of Chicago Press.

Laumann, E. O., Gagnon, J., Michael, R. T., & Michaels, S. (1994). *The social organization of sexuality: Sexual practices in the United States*. Chicago: University of Chicago Press.

Laumann, E. O., Ellingson, S., Mahay, J., Paik, A., & Youm, Y. (Eds.). (2004). *The sexual organization of the city*. Chicago: University of Chicago Press.

Laumann, E. O., Paik, A., Glasser, D. B., Kang, J., Wang, T., Levinson, B., Moreira, E. D., Nicolosi, A., & Gingell, C. (2006). A cross national study of subjective sexual well being among older women and men: Findings from the global study of sexual attitudes and behaviors. *Archives of Sexual Behavior, 35*, 145–161.

Lieberson, S., & Lynn, F. B. (2002). Barking up the wrong branch: Scientific alternatives to the current model of sociological science. *Annual Review of Sociology, 28,* 1–19.

Lippa, R. A. (2009). Sex differences in sex drive, sociosexuality, and height across 53 nations: Testing evolutionary and social structural theories. *Archives of Sexual Behavior, 38,* 631–651.

Longino, H. (1990). *Science as social knowledge: Values and objectivity in scientific inquiry.* Princeton: Princeton University Press.

Longino, H. (2002). *The fate of knowledge.* Princeton: Princeton University Press.

Lynd, R. S. (1939). *Knowledge for what? The place of social science in American culture.* New York: Grove Press, Inc.

Malinowski, B. (1929). *The sexual life of savages.* New York: Reader's League of N.Y.

Marx, K. (1859/1904). *A contribution to the critique of political economy* (trans: N. I. Stone). New York: International Publishing Company.

Massey, D. S. (2002). A brief history of human society: The origin and role of emotion in social life. *American Sociological Review, 67,* 1–29.

Mead, G. H. (1934). *Mind, self and society.* Chicago: University of Chicago Press.

Merton, R. K. (1967). *On theoretical sociology: Five essays, old and new.* New York: The Free Press of Macmillan.

Money, J., & Musaph, H. (1977). *Handbook of sexology.* Amsterdam: Excerpta Medica.

Murdock, G. P., & White, D. R. (1969). Standard cross cultural sample. *Ethnology, 8,* 329–369.

Proctor, R. N. (1991). *Value-free science? Purity and power in modern knowledge*; Cambridge: Harvard University Press.

Reece, M., Herbenick, D., Schick, V., Sanders, S. A., Dodge, B., & Fortenberry, J. D. (2010). Condom use rates in a national probability sample of males and females ages 14–94 in the U.S. *Journal of Sexual Medicine, 7*(Supp. 5), 266–276.

Reiss, I. L. (1960). *Premarital sexual standards in America.* Glencoe: The Free Press.

Reiss, I. L. (1964a). Premarital sexual permissiveness among negroes and whites. *American Sociological Review, 29,* 688–698.

Reiss, I. L. (1964b). The scaling of premarital sexual permissiveness. *Journal of Marriage and the Family, 26,* 188–198.

Reiss, I. L. (1965). Social class and premarital sexual permissiveness: A re-examination. *American Sociological Review, 30,* 747–756.

Reiss, I. L. (1967). *The social context of premarital sexual permissiveness.* New York: Holt, Rinehart and Winston.

Reiss, I. L. (1980a). *Family systems in America* (3rd ed.). New York: Holt, Rinehart & Winston.

Reiss, I. L. (1980c). Sexual customs and gender roles in Sweden and America: An analysis and interpretation. In H. Lopata (Ed.), *Research on the interweave of social roles: Women and men* (pp. 191–220). Greenwich: JAI Press.

Reiss, I. L. (1986). *Journey into sexuality: An exploratory voyage*; Englewood Cliffs: Prentice Hall Inc.

Reiss, I. L. (1993). The future of sex research and the meaning of science. *Journal of Sex Research, 30,* 3–11.

Reiss, I. L. (1999). Evaluating sexual science: Problems and prospects. *Annual Review of Sex Research, 10,* 236–271.

Reiss, I. L. (2001). Sexual attitudes and behavior. In N. J. Smelser & P. B. Baltes (Eds.), *International encyclopedia of the social and behavioral sciences* (Vol. 21, pp. 13969–13973). Oxford: Elsevier Science Limited.

Reiss, I. L. (2004). An introduction to the many meanings of sexological knowledge. In R. T. Francoeur & R. Noonan (Eds.), *International encyclopedia of Sexuality* (pp. 1–9). New York: Continuum Publishing Group.

Reiss, I. L. (2006). *An insider's view of sexual science since Kinsey.* Lanham: Roman & Littlefield.

Reiss, I. L. (2011a). Reiss premarital sexual permissiveness scale. In T. Fisher, C. Davis, W. Yarber, & S. Davis (Eds.), *Handbook of sexuality related measures* (3rd ed., pp. 509–510). New York: Routledge.

Reiss, I. L. (2011b). Reiss extramarital sexual permissiveness scale. In T. Fisher, C. Davis, W. Yarber, & S. Davis (Eds.), *Handbook of sexuality related measures* (3rd ed., pp. 253–255). New York: Routledge.

Reiss, I. L. (2014). Exploring the relation of values, power and advocacy in American sexual science. *International Journal of Sexual Health, 26,* 1–12.

Reiss, I. L., & Leik, R. K. (1989). Evaluating strategies to avoid AIDS: Number of partners vs. use of condoms. *Journal of Sex Research, 26,* 411–433.

Reiss, I. L., & Miller, B. (1979). Heterosexual permissiveness: A theoretical analysis. In W. Burr, R. Hill, I. Nye, & I. L. Reiss (Eds.), *Contemporary theories about the family: Research based theories* (Vol. 1, pp. 57–100). New York: The Free Press of the Macmillan Co.

Reiss, I. L., & Reiss, H. M. (1997). *Solving America's sexual crises.* Amherst: Prometheus Books.

Reiss, I. L., Anderson, R., & Sponaugle, G. C. (1980b). A multivariate model of the determinants of extramarital sexual permissiveness. *Journal of Marriage and the Family, 42,* 395–411.

Roos, P. A. (1985). *Gender and work: A comparative analysis of individual societies.* Albany: SUNY Press.

Rutter, M. (2002). Nature, nurture, and development: From evangelism through science toward policy and practice. *Child Development, 73,* 1–21.

Salk, R., & Hyde, J. (2012). Contemporary genetics for gender researchers: Not your grandma's genetics anymore. *Psychology of Women Quarterly, 36,* 395–410.

Schlegel, A. (1977). *Sexual stratification: A cross cultural view.* New York: Columbia University Press.

Schneider, H. K. (1971). Romantic love among the Turu. In D. S. Marschall & R. C. Suggs (Eds.), *Human sexual behavior: Variation in the ethnographic spectrum* (pp. 59–70). New York: Basic Books.

Schwartz, I. M., & Reiss, I. L. (1995). The scaling of premarital sexual permissiveness revisited: Test results of Reiss's new short form version. *Journal of Sex and Marital Therapy, 21,* 78–86.

Scott, J. (1998). Changing attitudes to sexual morality: A cross-national comparison. *Sociology, 32,* 815–845.

Singh, S., & Darroch, J. E. (1999). Trends in sexual activity among adolescent American women: 1982–1995. *Family Planning Perspectives, 31,* 212–219.

Skinner, Q. (Ed.). (1985). *The return of grand theory in the human sciences.* Cambridge: University of Cambridge Press.

Spencer, H. (1876/1901). *The principles of sociology* (3rd ed.). New York: D. Appleton and Company.

Stark, R. (2009). *Sociology* (10th ed.). Belmont: Wadsworth Publishing.

Stouffer, S. A., Guttman, L., Suchman, E. A., Lazarsfeld, P. F., Star, S. A., & Clausen, J. (1950). *Measurement and prediction* (Vol. 4). Princeton: Princeton University Press.

Turner, S. P., & Turner, J. H. (1990). *The impossible science: An institutional analysis of American sociology.* Newbury Park: Sage Publications.

Van Anders, S. M., Goldey, K. L., & Kuo, P. X. (2011). The steroid/peptide theory of social bonds: Integrating testosterone and peptide responses for classifying social behavior contexts. *Psychoneuroendocrinology, 36,* 1265–1275.

Weber, M. (1905/1930). *The Protestant ethic and the spirit of capitalism* (trans: T. Parsons). New York: Charles Scribner & Sons.

Whyte, M. K. (1978). *The status of women in preindustrial societies.* Princeton: Princeton University Press.

Wilson, E. O. (2012). *The social conquest of earth.* New York: Liveright Publishing Corporation.

Studying Sexualities from a Life Course Perspective

5

Laura M. Carpenter

5.1 Introduction

In June 2014, the *New York Times* published an article about sexuality in assisted living facilities. It told the story of Trulah and Lewis Mills, a couple married in 1941 and sexually active until their deaths in 2013, despite their advanced age, less-than-private accommodations, and Trulah's increasing dementia. According to Glenna Mills, the couple's daughter, Trulah had always been "a sexual kitten," sitting on her husband's lap and holding hands "all the time." Sexual desire and activity may commonly be viewed as the province of the young, but research consistently finds that people who exhibit high levels of interest in sex, relative to their peers, when they are young continue to do so as they age, even as they experience some decline in sexual thoughts and frequency.

The Millses were fortunate to reside in a facility where the staff viewed emotional and physical intimacy between older adults as normal and acceptable—if a bit "cute" or "disgusting," depending on the staff member and the nature of the activity. They were also legally married to one another. Many facilities discourage sexual behavior between consenting but unmarried older adults, separate them, or report them to family members,

who may disapprove (especially if cognitive decline is a factor). In fact, as author Paula Span (2014) pointed out, many heterosexual women Trulah Mills's age—in their 80s—are widows, owing to the tendencies of heterosexual men to partner with women younger than themselves and of women to live longer on average than men. That gender difference in mortality also means a shrinking pool of potential partners for older gay men and a relatively expansive pool for older lesbians. Yet, sexual minority elders remain "an invisible population," in the words of Ann Christine Frankowski of the Center for Aging Studies at the University of Maryland, Baltimore County, one of Span's sources for the article.

Lesbian, gay, bisexual, and queer (LGBQ) elders are bound to become more visible, however, with the aging of Baby Boomers and Generation Xers, who are far more likely than their older peers to have been "out" for most or all of their adult lives. Also due to change are the sexual values of the people residing in assisted living facilities. Couples like the Millses developed their attitudes about sexuality during the relatively restrictive 1940s and 1950s, whereas women and men who came of age during or after the sexual "revolution" of the 1960s and 1970s tend to hold more permissive views. For example, most Baby Boomers do not believe that sexual conduct should be limited to marital relationships and many favor more sexual and social equality between men and women than do folks just a decade or two older (DeLamater 2012). Those attitudes are not likely to change as Boomers

L. M. Carpenter (✉)
Department of Sociology, Vanderbilt University,
Nashville, TN 37235, USA
e-mail: laura.carpenter@vanderbilt.edu

J. DeLamater, R.F. Plante (eds.), *Handbook of the Sociology of Sexualities,* Handbooks of Sociology and
Social Research, DOI 10.1007/978-3-319-17341-2_5, © Springer International Publishing Switzerland 2015

enter old age. Quipped Span (2014), "You hope the [assisted living] industry recognizes that the people who will move in 20 years from now may have different ideas."

The Millses' story highlights a number of important issues in sexualities research today. Why do some women and men enjoy rollicking sex lives from youth through old age while others never obtain such pleasures, or find them diminishing over time? Can people whose early sex lives are frustrating or even unpleasant have more positive sexual encounters later on? Why are some individuals more profoundly affected by negative sexual experiences, like rape, than others? How do physical and mental health shape sexual feelings and conduct over time, and how do biological factors interact with psychological, social, and structural forces? In what ways does the broader social and historical context influence sexual life? What happens when a person changes sexual orientation or gender? How do gender, race, ethnicity, social class, religion, and other aspects of social identity intersect to affect sexual beliefs and behavior from birth until death?

Taking a life course perspective on sexuality can help address all of these issues. This chapter outlines the history of, and rationale for, such a perspective and considers methodological issues that arise when using it. The chapter also presents a comprehensive, transferrable conceptual framework for studying gendered sexualities over the life course. This framework posits that sexual beliefs and conduct result from individuals' lifelong accrual of advantageous and disadvantageous experiences, and adoption or rejection of sexual scripts, within specific social and historical contexts. Men and women follow distinctive sexual trajectories insofar as they accumulate gender-specific scripts and experiences and as their gender and sexuality trajectories intertwine. The chapter concludes with a review of exemplary recent studies of sexualities across the life course and promising directions for future research.

5.2 Studying Sexualities Over the Life Course

5.2.1 Background

The first major wave of scholarship on sexualities over the life course began in the early 1990s when a group of researchers funded by the MacArthur Foundation decided to collect their sexuality-related studies in a single location. The result was the path-breaking *Sexuality Across the Life Course* (1994), edited by sociologist Alice Rossi. In 14 chapters by 18 authors, the book addressed different stages of the life course, such as adolescence and old age; different demographic groups, such as African American men and homosexual youth; and specific issues, such as sexual victimization and sexual dysfunction. Contributors employed a variety of quantitative and qualitative methods. In her introduction, Rossi stressed that scholars studying sexuality should use an interdisciplinary model encompassing biological, social, and psychological dimensions, because those dimensions are present in actual lives. That insight remains influential today. Rossi's volume helped to make sexuality a legitimate area of study for life course scholars, although in retrospect it is striking how seldom the contributors explicitly employed concepts from the life course literature.

Subsequent research drew on Rossi et al.'s theorizing and empirical research and incorporated new developments in both life course and sexuality scholarship. Whereas *Sexuality Across the Life Course* presented life course stages as relatively isolated "snapshots," later studies increasingly sought to explain how events at one stage of life did, or did not, affect events at another stage. For example, Browning and Laumann (1997) used the concepts of pathways and turning points to explore how sexual abuse in childhood leads to adverse outcomes in later life for some, but not all, abused women. They found that women who were abused as children were more likely to engage in consensual sex before age 16, which in turn made them more likely to have had 11 or more partners by the time of the survey, which in turn increased the chances of contracting one or more sexually transmitted infections (STIs). Women who had been abused but delayed first sex tended to follow different, less troubled trajectories. Donnelly et al. (2001) brought life course concepts to bear on involuntary celibacy, focusing on the timing and sequencing of sexual and social experiences. Those men and women who initiated sexual activity "late" found it increasingly difficult to find romantic and sexual partners as they aged; conversely, people who became sexually inactive "too young" (e.g., through a partner's illness) expressed more intense frustration and sadness than those who experienced such transitions "on time."

Other scholars in this first wave deployed life course ideas to challenge then-prevailing linear models of sexual identity development. Savin-Williams and Diamond (2000) demonstrated that gay or lesbian identity emerges as individuals achieve four distinct "milestones": same-sex attraction, self-labeling, same-sex sexual contact, and disclosure ("coming out"). Gender influences at what ages, how rapidly, and in what order individuals reach these milestones; sexual minority girls and boys typically follow different pathways. Historical context further shapes these processes. The increasing presence of openly gay adults in public life following the HIV/AIDS epidemic of the 1980s has made it easier for queer youth to recognize and act on their desires.

Other scholars showed how transitions between life stages represent points at which individuals may adopt new sexual scripts. For example, in their research on the dissolution of marital and cohabiting relationships, Wade and DeLamater (2002) found that heterosexual men and women often adopted new, more permissive sexual scripts shortly after transitioning from partnered to single, but returned within about a year to scripts more "typical" of people with similar social backgrounds and initial beliefs about sex.

These innovative forays notwithstanding, by the mid 2000s, researchers had yet to articulate a comprehensive, transferrable conceptual framework for studying sexualities over the life course

that could be applied to diverse phenomena. Moreover, although scholars of sexuality and gender had increasingly begun to theorize gender and sexual identity as inextricably intertwined with race, ethnicity, and social class (not to mention religion, disability, and other aspects of identity), as opposed to seeing them as separable or statistically "controllable" (Collins 1990; McCall 2005), much of the published research had yet to employ such an intersectionality framework. For example, *Sexuality Across the Life Course* relegated sexual minorities and specific racial/ethnic groups to separate chapters rather than integrating analyses by race, class, and gender in every chapter. Most researchers' reliance on predominantly White, middle-class, heterosexual samples exacerbated this deficiency.

Recognizing these concerns as well as the promise of a comprehensive conceptual model, I joined forces with fellow sociologist John DeLamater to organize a special panel on "Sexuality over the Life Course" for the 2007 Annual Meeting of the American Sociological Association (ASA). I had begun to think about sexuality from a life course perspective pursuant to my research showing how virginity loss encounters are shaped by, and give shape to, the sexual and social experiences that precede and follow them (Carpenter 2005). Following his work with Wade, DeLamater had been routinely employing life course concepts in his analyses of sexuality in later life (DeLamater and Moorman 2007; DeLamater and Sill 2005). The ASA panel inspired not only the development of a model for studying gendered sexualities over the life course (Carpenter 2010), but also the first edited volume on sexualities over the life course (Carpenter and DeLamater 2012) since Rossi's 1994 book.

Published in 2012, *Sex for Life: From Virginity to Viagra, How Sexuality Changes Throughout our Lives* marked the emergence of a second major wave of research and theorizing on sexualities over the life course. It articulated a more sophisticated conceptual framework than previous efforts and broke new ground by including an extremely wide range of life stages, from childhood to very old age; by showcasing studies that explicitly linked two or more stages of life (e.g., childhood, adolescence, and young adulthood; midlife and old age); and by featuring life transitions typically not viewed in terms of sexuality, such as immigration and physical disability onset. The volume emphasized an intersectional approach, with virtually every chapter demonstrating how sexual identity or conduct was influenced by gender and its intersections with race, ethnicity, social class, or other aspects of social location. The book also pointed to notable gaps remaining in the literature—more on those gaps follows.

5.2.2 The Gendered Sexuality Over the Life Course (GSLC) Framework

A comprehensive framework for studying gendered sexualities over the life course must attend to trajectories, transitions, and turning points in the life course and the cumulative advantages and disadvantages they produce; health and physiological factors; human agency; social-historical context and birth cohorts; the accomplishment of gender and sexual identity and their intersections with race, ethnicity, social class, and other aspects of social identity; and sexual scripting processes (Carpenter 2010; Carpenter and DeLamater 2012). It must also take account of social structures and institutions and the linking of lives within and across generations (DeLamater and Carpenter 2012). Table 5.1 depicts these elements, along with key questions to ask when applying the framework to specific cases. Let us consider each of these elements in turn.

5.2.2.1 Life Course Basics
Every life course can be conceptualized as composed of multiple simultaneous *trajectories* through different dimensions of life, such as education, family, and sexuality. Each trajectory spans from birth until death and is punctuated by various *transitions*, or movements from one social role to another (Elder 1985; O'Rand 2003). For example, a person's education trajectory might include the transitions from pre-school to elementary student, from college student to graduate, and in and out of vocational

or other adult education programs. Similarly, an individual's sexuality trajectory might include transitions in and out of sexual subcultures like BDSM (bondage and discipline/sadism and masochism) and the adoption and discontinuation of specific sexual practices like fellatio or rimming (oral-anal contact). Social norms generally dictate the order and pace at which transitions are "supposed" to occur; deviating from the typical or prescribed order—for example, engaging in genital sex before ever kissing another person—can leave people feeling distressed or dissatisfied and may increase instability in their personal relationships. Some transitions represent *turning points*, changes that dramatically alter the course of a person's life (Clausen 1995), such as being expelled from school or coming out as gay or lesbian. Though analytically distinct, in practice, trajectories are intertwined, such that events in one trajectory may affect events in another. For example, matriculating at a college where all students live on campus facilitates casual sexual interactions, including "hooking up" (Allison and Risman 2014).

Many transitions have more than one potential outcome and not everyone undergoes every possible transition in every trajectory. For instance, some people never engage in genital sex with a partner; among those who do, a first experience may lead immediately to more sexual encounters with the same partner or may be followed by no further sexual activity with any partner for months or years (Carpenter 2005). Moreover, transitions and turning points may occur in different sequences and at different times of life, and they may vary in duration. For example, one woman might work from age 25 to 35 as an exotic dancer before agreeing to have sex for money; another might start dancing at 18 and quickly transition to massage parlor work. Consequently, different individuals may experience distinctive forms of the same trajectory. Trulah Mills was likely a virgin when she married, at a young age; had children only after she married; and stayed married, and sexually active, with her husband until her death. Other heterosexual women marry later in life, or not at all; have sex and sometimes children before they marry; or experience long

Table 5.1 Elements to consider when examining gendered sexualities over the life course

Element	Questions to ask
Transitions	Between what social roles are people moving? How are those transitions timed (on-time, early, late) and ordered?
Turning points	Do some transitions represent major changes in life course? With what consequences?
Cumulative (dis)advantages processes	How do experiences at one life stage impact later experiences? Are these chains of experience positive, negative, mixed?
Intersections among trajectories	How does the sexuality trajectory affect other life trajectories (e.g., family, work, education), and vice versa?
Physiological processes	How might physiological changes and illness/treatment, including those related to aging, affect this aspect of sexual life?
Agency	In what ways are people exercising agency (short- and long- term)? What constraints do biology and social structures impose?
Social-historical context and birth cohort	How might major historical changes affect this aspect of sexuality? In what social structures and institutions are individuals embedded? Do they promote specific norms, or constrain and enable certain practices, pertaining to sexuality? To what extent do members of different birth cohorts have distinctive experiences?
"Doing" gender and sexual identity	What gender and sexual identities are being accomplished via sexual conduct? How are gender and sexuality co-constructed?
Other aspects of social identity	How do race, ethnicity, social class, religion, and other aspects of social identity—intersecting with gender and sexual identity—affect GSLC dynamics?
Sexual scripts	What sexual scripts are available? Which do people choose? Which do they reject?
Linked lives	To whom is this individual linked—in their own generation and in the generations born before and after their own? What sexual values do those intimate others hold? In what ways do they constrain or enable the sexual lives of people to whom they are linked?

periods of sexual inactivity due to a partner's illness, or to divorce or widowhood.

Each life transition creates opportunities and constraints that condition future transitions, leading in turn to additional opportunities and constraints—a dynamic life course scholars refer to as *cumulative advantages and disadvantages* (O'Rand 1996). Frequently, positive or advantageous transitions pave the way for additional positive transitions, as when (so one imagines) Trulah and Lewis's enjoyable first kiss led to pleasurable petting, which laid the groundwork for orgasms during more intimate subsequent encounters. Conversely, negative or disadvanta-geous transitions often lead to further negative transitions, as when pain during one sexual interaction causes a person to be so tense during a second interaction that more intense pain is almost inevitable (Labuski 2011). How any given transition or turning point should be assessed depends on individual preferences, social norms, and social-historical context. For example, although most people in the contemporary USA view divorce as an undesirable transition, it is now viewed far less negatively than it was in the 1950s and 1960s. A person who chooses to divorce an unfaithful or abusive spouse may experience that transition as highly positive, whereas an individual who is divorced by a spouse who represents her or his sole source of income may find that transition extremely distressing and deleterious, and become quickly sexually active in an attempt to find a new provider (Lichtenstein 2012; Wade and DeLamater 2002).

People grow older in sociological terms as they accumulate positive, negative, or neutral life transitions—that is, as they acquire new social roles or exit old ones. At the same time, they are also aging in physiological terms (Riley 1987). Puberty, menopause, and andropause entail hormonal changes which alter bodily appearance in ways that may signal sexual readiness (e.g., appearance of secondary sexual characteristics at puberty) or suggest its diminishment (e.g., changes in skin and hair texture with declining estrogen or testosterone) and which may affect sexual desire and sexual functioning (e.g., increased vaginal dryness after menopause; decreased strength of erection after andropause). Physical and mental health also vary over the life course, in ways that may influence sexual life. Some illnesses and some treatments for illnesses inhibit sexual desire or function. For example, high blood pressure and certain medications intended to ameliorate it may dampen libido and interfere with ejaculation; clinical depression and prescription anti-depressants alike may reduce sexual desire. Individuals who are themselves healthy may find their sexual lives profoundly affected by a partner's poor health or physical changes, as when Lewis Mills had to adapt to Trulah's greater physical frailty and cognitive decline. Scholars taking a life course perspective on sexualities must attend carefully to physical aging, health, and illness.

5.2.2.2 Human Agency, Social-Historical Context, and Linked Lives

Although people make the choices that shape their life trajectories, they do not choose the circumstances in which they do so (Elder 1985; Mills 1959). Consequently, it behooves sexuality researchers to take account of human agency and social-historical context. Individuals endeavor to direct the course of their lives, in both the short and long term, and they typically do so in ways

that are consistent with their sense of self (Hitlin and Elder 2007). Such choices often feel so routine that people do not experience them as choices. For example, Trulah and Lewis Mills, who clearly saw physical intimacy as crucial to their identity as individuals and as a couple, might not have given much thought to engaging in whatever activity resulted in "a thunk" issuing "from their studio apartment" and "Mrs. Mills, then 89, on the floor" (Span 2014). Significant changes or disruptions in the life course typically prompt more conscious decision making, however, and those decisions are generally guided by people's preexisting understandings of who they are, where they have been, and what they value (Hitlin and Elder 2007).

Whether conscious or "automatic," the choices people make inevitably occur within the constraints of biology and of social structures and institutions. For example, heterosexual couples who prefer the "missionary" position for vaginal sex may find it physically impossible to assume during the third trimester of a pregnancy. Institutions like assisted living facilities provide single old people with opportunities for sexual companionship by bringing them together with other old singles, but they also limit romantic and sexual activity by permitting only certain kinds of sexual conduct (if any)—such as "conventional" sex, in private, between married, heterosexual couples like the Millses.[1]

Social structures and institutions change over time, however, as do population dynamics, scientific technologies, and social norms. Hence, it is critical to locate individual, agentic lives in the broader social-historical context. For example, although an increasing proportion of US school districts have provided formal sex education from the 1970s onward—initially in response to climbing rates of teen pregnancy brought about by increasingly permissive attitudes toward sexual activity and childbearing outside marriage, and later to the HIV/AIDS epidemic—the content and comprehensiveness of curricula vary considerably across districts and regions, in turn conditioning

---

[1] Scare quotes are mine, not Span's.

young people's sense of sexual options, including what they know about contraception and safer sex (Fields 2008). Importantly, even as social structures and institutions influence individual lives, changes in life course patterns shape institutions (Riley 1987). For instance, as standards for sexual behavior have become less restrictive, assisted living facilities have been pressured to rescind rules forbidding consensual sexual activity among unmarried residents (Span 2014).

Life course scholars often link broad historical processes to birth cohorts—groups of people born around the same time—taking care to distinguish dynamics related to aging from those related to cohorts. Lewis and Trulah Mills were part of the cohort that grew up during the Great Depression, their lives shaped by conservative sexual mores, unsettled times, and the desire for family stability; their daughter, Glenna, is part of the Baby Boom cohort, the millions of children born between 1946 and 1964, whose experiences of economic plenty, highly effective contraceptives, and sheer demographic abundance led to the loosening of sexual attitudes; and their grandchildren are part of the Generation-X cohort, born between 1964 and 1979, their beliefs about sex shaped by the permissive attitudes that preceded them as well as by the HIV/AIDS epidemic, resurgence of moral conservatism in the 1980s and 1990s, and ever-increasing popular and legal tolerance for homosexual identity and activity.

It is also critical to recognize that people are linked to one another both within and across generations, through romantic partnerships, family relationships, and intimate friendships (Giele and Elder 1998). These connections, which scholars call *linked lives*, can have a profound impact on sexuality trajectories. For example, Trulah Mills's ability to be a "sexual kitten" depended in part on the presence and cooperation of husband Lewis, as well as on daughter Glenna's comfort with seeing her aging parents as sexual beings. Similarly, Elliott (2012) documented how US adolescents' sexual behavior is influenced not only by interactions with peers, especially close friends and romantic partners, but also by interactions (or lack of interactions) with parents, especially mothers.

5.2.2.3 Gender and Sexuality as They Intersect with Other Social Statuses

Gender shapes the life course in complex ways. In virtually every known society, men and women follow at least somewhat distinctive work, education, family, and health trajectories, both because of gendered social norms and expectations and because of gender differences in access to material resources and power (Moen 1996). Sexual trajectories are no exception to this gendering (Carpenter 2010). Increasingly, scholars acknowledge that gender is not simply a set of cultural predispositions that people learn early in life and replicate ever after; gender is rather an aspect of identity that individuals actively reproduce—and potentially change—through social interaction throughout their lifetimes (West and Zimmerman 1987).[2] In contexts like the contemporary United States, where only two genders are legally and socially recognized, people are held accountable for doing gender "well enough" to be recognized as men or women. Yet, individuals "do" gender in diverse ways—think Oprah Winfrey and Beyoncé Knowles, both recognizably, but differently, feminine (and African American). People also modify their gendered behavior in response to others, and they may resist doing gender in conventional ways (Lucal 1999). Often, doing femininity "properly" entails enacting subservience or submissiveness, whereas doing masculinity "properly" entails enacting dominance and assertiveness, although these aspects of gender are becoming less pronounced and rigid than in the past.

Scholars generally agree that gender, sexuality, and sexual identity are interrelated, although the precise nature of that relationship is much debated (Rubin 1984; Ingraham 1996). According to Valentine (2004), whether gender determines sexuality dynamics or vice versa should be ap-

---

[2] Sociologists generally recognize a distinction between sex—the chromosomes, hormones, and genital configurations used to distinguish female and male bodies—and gender, the social and cultural meanings and practices associated with femininity and masculinity (Lorber 1993). Both sex and gender are increasingly recognized as socially constructed.

proached as an empirical question, with different possible answers in different locations and eras. Developing a thorough understanding of any aspect of sexuality from a life course perspective requires thinking about how gender and sexual identity are *mutually constructed* in the context in question. For example, when Lewis and Trulah Mills were teenagers, in the 1930s, beliefs about appropriate goals and behaviors for women and men were more sharply differentiated than they are today (albeit less differentiated than in, for instance, South Korea). One might surmise that their views about gender influenced their sexualities more than the other way around.

Gender and sexual identity influence and are influenced by race, ethnicity, and social class, as well as by religion, disability, and other aspects of social identity. These effects are not additive—one cannot simply tally and compare the dimensions of oppression or privileges any two people experience—but rather intersecting, deeply intertwined and mutually constitutive. Scholars refer to this phenomenon as *intersectionality* (Collins 1990; McCall 2005). For example, staff members might have interpreted Lewis Mills's sexual behavior as more predatory, or Trulah's as more out-of-control, if they had been African American rather than White. Moreover, middle-class White couples like the Millses may be better able to afford assisted living facilities with progressive policies about resident sexuality than many middle-class African American couples who, despite high levels of education and white-collar occupations, tend to lack the wealth (savings and assets) that facilitates such choices (Jackson and Williams 2006). A full understanding of sexualities over the life course requires analyses that go beyond "controlling" for social location to engage explicitly with the complex intersections of sexuality, gender, race, ethnicity, and social class.

5.2.2.4 Sexual Scripting

Transitions and turning points represent junctures at which people can reaffirm old ways of negotiating sexual life—or adopt new ones (Wade and DeLamater 2002). Many scholars conceptualize such ways of negotiating as sexual scripts, the socially created and socially learned patterns of desire and conduct that govern people's sexual lives, in addition to (or instead of) biological or psychological imperatives (Gagnon and Simon 1973). At the broadest level, *cultural scenarios* for sexuality, such as movie plots and religious texts, provide "roadmaps" indicating when, where, why, with whom, and in what ways one should be sexual (Simon and Gagnon 1986). *Interpersonal scripts* are constructed when two or more individuals interact in sexual ways. Parties who bring different cultural scenarios to their "drama" may need to improvise and reconcile those divergent scenarios, possibly creating new scripts in the process. People's desires, fantasies, and intentions—their *intrapsychic scripts*—are shaped by cultural scenarios and interpersonal scripts, and also influence people's sexual lives in their own right.

In most societies, women and men are encouraged to follow different sexual scripts (Laws and Schwartz 1977). Insofar as the scripts individuals enact at one stage of life partly govern what scripts are accessible and appealing to them at later stages, sexual scripting is a gendered process that tends to produce distinctive cumulative dynamics for men and women. For example, men who embrace scripts that equate masculinity with sexual uncontrollability may be more likely to have extramarital affairs, which may lead to an increased likelihood of divorce and of contracting STIs. Sexual identity, race, ethnicity, social class, religion, and other aspects of social identity also shape life trajectories by creating opportunities and introducing constraints and shaping preferences for sexual scripts (or sanctions for using the "wrong" script). For example, "hooking up" may have replaced dating as the expected route to relationship formation among college students, but in practice, hooking up is relatively uncommon among racial/ethnic minority, working class, and sexual minority students, especially those who live with family members instead of on campus or independently (Allison and Risman 2014).

Looking for and engaging with these elements can help scholars to create a rich, detailed, and informative picture of any aspect of sexuality from a life course perspective—and to predict how certain sets of circumstances might play out in real human lives.

5.2.3 A Related Conceptual Framework

In their contribution to *Sex for Life*, Das et al. (2012) developed a conceptual framework that shares several elements with Carpenter and DeLamater's gendered sexuality over the life course (GSLC) model. Das et al. propose that scholars should be cognizant of three broad domains that influence sexuality over the life course. First, instead of viewing people as "entrained," sexually or otherwise, in adolescence and young adulthood (as scholars have tended to do), researchers should conceptualize individuals' sexual careers as entailing periods of stability and change, prompted by constraints and opportunities in local contexts. Change may occur at any point in the life course, as individuals confront "branching points" with more than one possible outcome. This "'punctuated equilibrium' model of the sexual career" (p. 239) corresponds to the "life course basics," social-historical context, and agency components of the GSLC framework.

Second, insofar as the bulk of human sexual activity takes place between two people (rather than alone or in groups of three or more), scholars should investigate dyads along with individuals. Partnerships structure sexual patterns, as when a man adapts his sexual tastes to mesh with those of his new boyfriend. According to Das and colleagues, sex should be understood as a kind of extended "transaction" or negotiation in which members of the dyad deploy "local" and "cultural" resources, like gender, relative income, physical capacity, and social ties, to get what they want (Das et al. 2012, p. 239). This focus on dyads and transactions has its counterpart, respectively, in the linked lives and sexual scripts elements of the GSLC model.

Also mapping to the linked lives component of the GSLC model is the third element in Das, Waite, and Laumann's framework: attention to the ways social networks shape sexual practices. All individuals and dyads are embedded in "stakeholder networks" which include close friends and family members. Think, for example, of Glenna Mills and her potential influence on workers in her parents' care facility. Such relationships can facilitate or limit people's behavior, not least by creating contexts in which some kinds of behavior are permissible and normative and other kinds are beyond the pale. Different groups maintain different norms, depending on their race, ethnicity, religious beliefs, geographical location, and so forth.

5.3 Methods for Studying Sexualities Over the Life Course

A wide range of research methods are suitable for studying sexualities over the life course (Carpenter and DeLamater 2012; Giele and Elder 1998), whichever conceptual framework one might opt to employ. Qualitative methods such as in-depth interviews, focus groups, and participant observation are invaluable for gaining insight into people's subjective beliefs and experiences, the meanings they attach to those experiences, and the complex processes, sexual and otherwise, that constitute human life. Quantitative methods, such as surveys and vignette-based experiments, which employ standardized questionnaires and protocols, yield data that are more consistent across study participants. When data are gathered using probability sampling techniques, as in many national surveys, research findings are representative of, and can be generalized to, the populations from which the samples are taken. Meta analyses, in which findings from multiple quantitative studies on a single topic are combined to create summary statistics, can help integrate findings from smaller studies and make sense of conflicting findings.

In general, qualitative methods emphasize depth—fewer cases explored in greater detail and nuance—whereas quantitative methods boast breadth, examining substantially more cases at a less microscopic level. Studies that draw on both kinds of data can provide tremendous insight into the complexities of gendered sexual lives by capturing subjective, nuanced, hard-to-quantify aspects of sexuality without losing generalizability and representativeness. For example, Lyons et al. (2014) used quantitative survey and qualitative interview data from the Toledo Adolescent Relationship Study (TARS) to explore young women's and men's experiences with casual sex. Specifically, they used the third wave of the TARS survey to identify broad patterns of beliefs and behaviors among the 239 young adults who reported casual sexual encounters and employed 44 in-depth relationship narratives completed by a subsample to glean how participants understood and experienced "transitional" relationships—those occurring between, or in lieu of, longer, more intimate relationships. Combining these types of data helped Lyons and colleagues to conclude that young adults' motives for engaging in casual sex were often, though not always, associated with their stage in the life course. Many spoke of being too busy, geographically mobile, or young for committed intimate relationships, although "some of the older respondents claimed that they believed that they were getting too old for casual sex" (Lyons et al. 2014, p. 96).

Studies of sexualities over the life course typically focus on individuals, but other units of analysis may prove equally fruitful. Research on dyads may be especially illuminating, as an increasing number of scholars are discovering. Heiman et al. (2011) charted the links between relationship satisfaction and sexual satisfaction by surveying heterosexual men, aged 39–70, and their female partners, aged 25–76, in Brazil, Germany, Japan, Spain, and the United States. Researchers asked the couples, who had been in committed relationships lasting from 1 to 51 years, not to compare their questionnaire responses so that their answers would be independent; discrepancies between partners' answers can be instructive. Other studies have examined intergenerational family units, such as parents and their adolescent children (e.g., Elliott 2012; Garcia 2012). Also valuable are studies designed to permit analyses across and within important institutional contexts. For example, the National Longitudinal Study of Adolescent Health drew its sample of adolescents from a sample of middle and high schools, enabling researchers to explore how peer group dynamics in specific schools influenced such phenomena as sexual abstinence (Brückner and Bearman 2005).

In many ways, longitudinal data represent the gold standard of life course research (Giele and Elder 1998). Tracking the same individuals (or couples or "swingers" clubs) over time helps scholars apprehend how beliefs and experiences at earlier life stages are connected to those at later stages. Longitudinal data also enable researchers to disentangle age from cohort dynamics. For instance, following two groups of individuals born 20 years apart can help one determine the extent to which differences in the sexual attitudes of 30- and 50-year-olds are due to changes in those individuals' beliefs and behaviors as they matured or to the different time periods in which they came of age. Recent advances in statistical analysis, such as fixed effects analysis, propensity score matching, and growth curve models, have greatly enhanced the ability of scholars using longitudinal data to account for change within individuals, to delineate different life pathways, and to compensate for the differential selection of study participants into (or out of) specific behaviors and statuses (Sassler 2010).

However, longitudinal studies are expensive, complicated, and time-consuming to conduct. Accordingly, DeLamater (2012, p. 139) recommends conducting multiple "small-scale longitudinal studies of clearly defined populations," such as specific ethnic groups or social class strata. Some researchers use synthetic cohort or quasi-panel research designs, which pool cross-sectional data collected from different groups at multiple points in time, but which do not track specific individuals, to assess changes within and across birth cohorts. For example, Das et al. (2012) created synthetic cohorts by linking the National Health and Social Life Survey (NHSLS), which included US adults aged 18–59 in 1992; the Global Study of Sexual Attitudes and Behaviors (GSSAB), which interviewed English-speaking non-European Westerners aged 40–80 in 2001–2002; and the National Social Health and Aging Project (NSHAP), which targeted US adults aged 57–85 in 2005–2006.

Although a number of major longitudinal surveys have included basic questions related to sexuality (e.g., whether respondents engaged in vaginal intercourse in the preceding year), vanishingly few have asked a sufficient number of detailed questions about diverse aspects of sexuality as to permit answering complex research questions about sexualities over the life course. One invaluable exception is the National Longitudinal Study of Adolescent Health (generally referred to as Add Health), which gathered its first wave of data, including a great many questions about a wide range of sexual beliefs and behaviors, from US boys and girls in grades 7–12 (and some of their parents and school administrators) in 1995–1996. Three subsequent waves of data have been collected, in 1996, 2001–2002, and 2007–2008, at which point respondents were aged 24–32. Life course sexuality scholars would benefit tremendously if Add Health participants were to be followed even further in time. Another notable longitudinal survey, focusing on the opposite end of the life course, is NSHAP. Like Add Health, NSHAP includes numerous, detailed questions about sexual attitudes and experiences, past and present. The first wave of NSHAP was collected in 2005–2006 from household-dwelling US women and men aged 57–85; the second wave was collected in 2010–2011.

Both Add Health and NSHAP used probability-based methods to ensure that their samples are representative of, and can be generalized, to the US population overall. Both studies oversampled for Blacks and Hispanics, who represent too small a proportion of the national population for ordinary probability techniques to yield a large enough sample to permit detailed statistical analyses by race and ethnicity. Add Health additionally oversampled for certain Asian groups; NSHAP oversampled for people 75–85. The same sampling principle applies to sexual minorities, who represent somewhere between 3 and 13 % of the US population, depending on the cohort in question and the definition used (Savin-Williams and Ream 2007; Laumann et al. 1994); however, neither Add Health nor NSHAP has oversampled for sexual minority respondents (indeed, doing so would likely prove difficult in practice).

Other longitudinal surveys that include some (but not necessarily very detailed) questions pertinent to sexuality include the aforementioned TARS, which collected five waves of data, in 2001, 2002, 2004, 2006, and 2011, from students registered in 2000 for the 7th, 9th, and 11th grades in Lucas County, Ohio, which is racially and socioeconomically diverse; the National Longitudinal Survey of Youth 1997 (NLSY97), which has interviewed a nationally representative sample of individuals born between 1980 and 1984 annually since 1997; and the National Survey of Family Growth (NSFG), especially Cycle 6 (2002), which asked detailed questions about the sexual partnering and fertility experiences of women and men age 15–45 (see Sassler 2010). Considerable progress could be made by encouraging more major surveys, longitudinal and retrospective alike, to include more nuanced questions about sexuality and gender identity and behaviors.

Fortunately, a great deal can be learned about sexualities over the life course even when longitudinal data collection is neither possible nor practical. Retrospective interviews and questionnaires have enabled many researchers to reconstruct key life course sexualities dynamics (e.g., Albanesi 2010; Carpenter 2005; Montemurro 2014a). Although retrospective accounts are subject to recall bias—that is, people may forget details of what happened to them—research suggests that individuals generally have good recall of events that they experience as highly salient, like first sex with a partner or sexual assault, even at considerable distance in time (Berk et al. 1995). Scholars relying on retrospective accounts must bear in mind that people may interpret past events in light of new beliefs or understandings—although such reinterpretations can themselves represent interesting findings. Sexualities researchers collecting retrospective accounts may find the life history calendar method, in which participants enter key time markers (e.g., high school graduation, birth of first child) on a calendar in order to facilitate recall of other, less salient events, particularly helpful (Nelson 2010).

Collecting data on theoretically relevant cases, as recommended by grounded theory experts (Charmaz 2006), may also help to build a fuller picture of sexualities over the life course. Scholars might focus on particular sexual or social subcultures, like polyamorists or self-identified asexuals; on understudied stages of the life course, including childhood and old age; on sexual turning points, such as the beginning of new relationships or changes in religious affiliation; or on specific social locations, given that social class, race, and ethnicity pattern work, family, and health trajectories. Many fresh insights into gendered sexualities over the life course could come from studying people whose lived experiences of gender and/or sexuality defy convention, such as individuals who have transitioned from one gender to another (trans men and women), whose biological sex does not neatly fit traditional male nor female designations (intersex), or who identify as both masculine and feminine or as neither (gender fluidity and androgyny). More research on links between life stages is also highly desirable; we still know too little about the "black boxes" of social and sexual transitions, even though times of transformation are likely to be particularly edifying.

5.4   Recent Sexualities Research Drawing on, or Consistent with, the Life Course Perspective

A strong second wave of scholarship on sexualities over the life course is now under way. Although space constraints prevent acknowledging of all this research here, it is worth highlighting some standout examples. Readers interested in a broad overview of research may be interested in the 13 original empirical studies, by 19 contributors, collected in *Sex for Life* (Carpenter and DeLamater 2012). These studies run the gamut of qualitative and quantitative methods, from surveys and meta-analysis to in-depth interviews and ethnography, and have roots in diverse disciplines, including criminology, education, ethnic studies, disability studies, political science, psychology, social work, sociology, and women's

and gender studies. They explore a wide range of sexuality-related topics, including interest in sex and sexual behavior among Black and White 7- to 12-year-olds; the impact of childhood sexual abuse on intimate relationships in adulthood; resiliency among sexual minority youth; effects of parental divorce on adolescent sexual behavior; gender differences in "hooking up" as young people transition from high school to college; how exclusion from legal marriage has shaped local gay sexual cultures and gay men's sexual relationships in North America; White and Black men's sexual trajectories after spinal cord injury; how migration between the Philippines and United States shaped sexual mores across two generations; Black and White women's experiences with dating and STIs after relationship dissolution in midlife; broad patterns of sexual expression in midlife and old age; White and Black women's experiences of menopause as influenced by their childbearing histories; body image and sexuality among old gay men and lesbians; and intimacy among very old (aged 90 and up) women and men.

5.4.1   Adolescence and Young Adulthood

One rich vein of life course-influenced research focuses on adolescence and young adulthood. Many studies have employed multiple waves of Add Health data to examine change and stability over time. For example, Haydon et al. (2012) used Add Health Waves 1 and 4 to group respondents into five categories based on the "variety, timing, spacing, and sequencing of oral-genital, anal, and vaginal sex." About half of the youth began their trajectories with vaginal sex, around age 16, and waited at least a year before engaging in oral or anal sex. Another third became sexually active at slightly older ages and engaged in oral and vaginal sex within the same year. Black respondents were more likely than White respondents to follow pathways beginning with vaginal sex; youth from economically less-advantaged backgrounds were disproportionately likely to follow trajectories characterized by early initiation.

Other intriguing studies draw on data from TARS. Halpern-Meekin et al. (2013) used TARS Wave 4 to examine "relationship churning"—on and off sexual relationships with former romantic partners. They posit that relationship churning, which was common across the sample but especially among Black participants and among those who grew up in families with atypical structures (i.e., structures other than two parents, a parent and stepparent, or a single parent), is a feature of emerging adulthood, "a life stage associated with exploring relationship possibilities … and learning about various ways of viewing and negotiating relationships" (Halpern-Meeking et al. 2013, p. 167). Insofar as "during emerging adulthood people learn the roles and skills they will employ in their lives going forward" (p. 181), the authors anticipate that women and men who enact these patterns in youth may continue them in later life stages.

Another series of illuminating analyses come from Sprecher et al., who administered the same survey to undergraduate students at a single US university for 23 years. In one "cohort-longitudinal" analysis, Sprecher et al. (2013) found that respondents from the 1995–1999 cohort reported somewhat less permissive sexual attitudes than the 1990–1994 and 2005–2012 cohorts, a pattern they attributed to cultural factors like increasing awareness of HIV and STIs. In contrast to findings from other studies, gender differences in sexual permissiveness changed little over time; women in every cohort were less permissive than men. In another "panel-longitudinal" analysis, focused on emotional reactions to first sex, Sprecher (2014) found that each successive cohort of men reported lower levels of anxiety while each successive cohort of women reported higher levels of pleasure and lower levels of guilt. Higgins et al. (2010, 2011) made creative use of a cross-sectional survey of students at four US universities to examine gender differences in first vaginal intercourse—which more women than men described as unsatisfying or worse—and satisfaction with one's current sex life, which differed little by gender. The authors concluded that a "marked catch-up effect" occurred among the women in the time between first sex and the sur-

vey (3.5 years on average), underlining "the need for a life-course perspective on sexual health that recognizes the different needs and profiles particular to various stages in the life cycle" (2011, p. 1652).

Other exemplary studies employ qualitative methods to delve into the complexities of adolescents' and young adults' sexuality trajectories. Albanesi (2010) investigated how 18- to 23-year-olds' deep sense of themselves as gendered affects their sexual agency. Her analysis, which focused on the junctures at which 83 women and men acted agentically, eschewed agency, or transitioned from agentic to non-agentic, demonstrated how gender identity—which is relatively stable and develops before sexual identity—exerts a "steady influence" on "the enactment of sexual agency [as] an interactive process that can be renegotiated throughout life" (p. 135). Most participants, whatever their racial/ethnic and social class backgrounds, modified their sexual behavior to better fit their personal sense of gender.

5.4.2 Sexual Identity and Orientation

An especially important strand of life course-inflected research examines the development and effects of sexual identity and sexual orientation, especially among adolescents and young adults. Add Health has greatly facilitated these efforts. In a compelling analysis of the survey's first three waves, Savin-Williams and Ream (2007) assessed the fluidity of same-sex romantic attraction, sexual behavior, and sexual identity. Participants, especially girls, who reported any same-sex attractions in earlier waves were more likely to report subsequent shifts in their attractions than were participants who reported no same-sex attractions. Savin-Williams and Ream caution other researchers not to presume the stability of sexual orientation among individuals in a stage of life marked by sexual experimentation, lack of experience, and a tendency toward deception (of self and others).

Jager and Davis-Kean (2011) used Add Health Waves 1, 2, and 3 to examine how sexual identity trajectories affect mental health. Youth, especially boys, who reported same-sex attractions consistently from early adolescence onward exhibited lower levels of psychological well-being than their heterosexual counterparts, but often experienced later adolescence as a "recovery period when disparities narrowed over time" (Jager and Davis-Kean 2011, p. 1). This rapid narrowing may be linked to broad social changes, specifically growing tolerance for homosexuality in the USA. Ueno et al. (2013) brought a cumulative (dis)advantages perspective to bear on Add Health Waves 1 through 4 to evaluate how different trajectories of same-sex contact in adolescence and young adulthood influence educational attainment. Women who reported same-sex contact in both life stages completed less education than other young women, a pattern the authors attribute in part to "increased levels of interpersonal problems and depressive symptoms in adolescence, which in turn limit academic performance and expectations in secondary schools" (Ueno et al. 2013, p. 136). In contrast, men who delayed same-sex contact until young adulthood—possibly because of the greater stigma of such contact for males—obtained higher degrees than other men, an advantageous trajectory resulting from a greater ability, lacking social and sexual distractions, to concentrate on school.

Qualitative interviews and participant observation also have shed light on the dynamics and meanings of sexual identity over the life course. For over a decade, Diamond (2009) followed nearly 100 young US women, initially aged 16–23, who had experienced same-sex attractions (though not necessarily same-sex activity or self-identification as lesbian or bisexual); most were White and middle class. Through biannual interviews, Diamond documented the considerable fluidity and context-dependency of love and sexual desire throughout women's (early) life course. Better (2014) analyzed retrospective accounts from 39 women, aged 20–62, most of whom were White, to trace changes in sexualities over time. Some women revised their sexual identity to accommodate new understandings of the self; others wondered if their desire for other women was authentic if they also dated or had

sex with men. Trying to fit established categories of sexual identity and seeking approval from queer adults or peers loomed large for many women during adolescence; Better (2014) posited this as "a step in this developmental process" (p. 30). Moore (2011) drew on participant observation, 58 in-depth interviews, a small survey, and focus groups to explore how working- and middle-class Black women living with other women in New York City understood their sexual orientation, experienced desire, expressed gender, found partners, and formed families over time. Like Better, she found that gender, race, and class identities, formed early in life, influenced women's perceptions and enactment of sexual identity later on.

Far less research has focused on men's sexual identity trajectories. Green (2006) drew on interviews with 60 gay and 50 heterosexual men, aged 21–52 and currently residing in New York City, to demonstrate how the possibility or impossibility of marriage influenced men's sexual and relationship histories. All of the men learned the same sexual script involving heterosexual desire and activity and, ultimately, marriage and children. But where the heterosexual men were able to live out that script, the gay men had to reconcile it with their own desires and the unavailability of legal same-sex marriage. Race and social class additionally inflected the men's trajectories. For example, the (mostly) middle-class Black men who frequented predominantly White gay venues in Manhattan—which Green (2008) conceptualizes as a "sexual field"—enjoyed different degrees of "erotic capital," and therefore opportunities for sex and romance, depending on their age, appearance, personal histories and predilections, and other factors, including the mix of patrons at a particular bar at a particular time.

More research focusing on the intersections of race, gender, class, and sexual identity among specific groups (as Moore did with Black lesbians and Green did with Black gay men) would represent a tremendous contribution to the literature (see McCall 2005 on this strategy), as would studies conducted outside major metropolitan centers such as New York and San Francisco.

5.4.3 Sexualities from Young Adulthood Onward

In a field where examinations of the entire life course remain rare, Beth Montemurro's research stands out. In her book, *Deserving Desire*, Montemurro (2014a) used in-depth, retrospective interviews with 95 (mostly) heterosexual, racially, ethnically, and socioeconomically diverse women, aged 20–68, to explore when and how "women experience changes in their sexuality" (p. 2). Drawing on Carpenter and DeLamater's (2012) conceptual framework, Montemurro charted a complex, six-step process through which women develop sexual agency and subjectivity from youth into old age. Women moved through the six stages—developing a stance on sexuality; learning through doing; validation, affirmation, and encouragement (often linked to a first committed sexual partner); self-discovery through role and relationship changes; self-discovery through embodied changes; and self-acceptance—at different paces, and their personal experiences influenced when, how, and whether they moved from stage to stage. The sexual trajectories of women born before 1960 typically took a different shape from the trajectories of women born after 1960.

Elsewhere, Montemurro (2014b) drew on the same data and conceptual framework to explore how changes in relationship status constrain or foster women's sexual self-confidence. Theorizing marriage, separation, and divorce in terms of turning points and cumulative (dis)advantages, Montemurro found that women born before 1960 experienced marriage as more of a sexual turning point than women born after 1960, not least because it gave them "permission" to be sexual. Women who divorced at relatively young ages often described that transition as enhancing their sexual subjectivity; although some women who divorced at older ages reported similar experiences, many indicated that divorce had severely limited opportunities for future (heterosexual) partnering. Developing similar themes for a popular audience, journalist Iris Krasnow (2014) interviewed dozens of women, aged 20 to over 90, from diverse racial/ethnic backgrounds and

sexual identities, about "sex after..." such life course events as childbirth, divorce, coming out, and a (male) partner's illness.

Most research, especially qualitative research, that takes such a broad view of sexualities over the life course, has focused on women. This may be because women's sexuality is more often seen as problematic (e.g., because of the possibility of pregnancy) or in need of "saving" (e.g., because women are sexually "repressed" in Western culture), or because men's sexuality is assumed to be largely non-problematic (with the exception of issues like erectile dysfunction). Researchers also may assume that men will be more reluctant than women to talk about intimate life—even though many scholars (including several cited here) have collected extremely nuanced data about sexuality from men. Kimmel's (2008) interviews with racially diverse, mostly college-educated men between the ages of 16–26—that is, the life stage of "emerging adulthood"—revealed how gender norms and social structures encourage many young men to consume (heterosexual) pornography, to favor "hooking up" over dating and committed relationships, and, in some cases, to become sexual predators. Studies that trace diverse men's sexualities across multiple stages of the life course would be very welcome additions to the literature.

5.4.4 Sexualities and Parenthood

Surprisingly few scholars have brought a life course perspective to bear on the relationship of sexuality to pregnancy or parenthood. Hipp et al. (2012) analyzed 304 retrospective accounts from heterosexual women who had recently given birth, finding that women's desire for partnered sex during the postpartum period was influenced far more by how male partners behaved around the birth than by individual factors like vaginal injury, breastfeeding, and subjective evaluations of the birth experience. Conceptualizing the transition to motherhood as a life course event that affects sexuality, Montemurro and Siefkin (2012) reported that two thirds of the 50 women they interviewed felt that women's sexual expression ought to change when they become mothers. Of the 27 mothers in the study, 26 reported that their level of sexual desire, the way they felt about sex, or their sexual appeal changed during pregnancy or after childbirth. Fatigue and the responsibilities of parenthood left many women feeling disconnected from their sexuality, at least temporarily.

Cancel Tirado (2011) turned the life course spotlight on fatherhood to show how some young Mexican immigrant men adopted lower-risk sexual behavior, such as monogamy or more consistent use of birth control, after they became fathers. New ideas about gender and sexuality, to which men were exposed via the immigration process, also contributed to changing behavior (see also Gonzáles-López 2005). Overall, however, fatherhood altered the young men's ideas and perceptions about family planning and sexual behavior more than it affected their actual conduct. Much more remains to be learned about fatherhood and sexuality at various stages of the life course. How parenthood affects the sexual beliefs, behaviors, and identities of lesbians and gay men also deserves more attention, especially in light of the "gayby boom" that began in the 1990s and intensified in the 2000s.

5.4.5 Sexualities in Midlife

An increasing number of scholars are addressing sexualities in midlife. Lindau and Gavrilova (2010) combined data from the 1995–1996 National Survey of Midlife Development in the United States (MIDUS) and wave 1 (2005–2006) of NSHAP to develop the concept of sexually active life expectancy: the average number of years of remaining life a person spends as sexually active. At age 30, sexually active life expectancy was about 20 years lower than demographic life expectancy for women (30.7 versus 50.6 years) and 10 years lower for men (34.7 versus 44.8 years), including people without current partners.[3] Sexually active life expectancy was closely related

to men's health, affecting men directly (poor health impeded men's sexual activity) and their heterosexual women partners indirectly (an effect exacerbated by women's tendency to partner with men older than themselves). Older women's sexual interest was more resistant to illness and sexual problems than men's, even though sexually active older women reported sexual problems such as low desire, vaginal dryness, and orgasm difficulties, which were associated in turn with lower levels of sexual satisfaction.

Many researchers have wondered how the duration of relationships affects sexual satisfaction. Analyzing data from the International Survey of Relationships (ISR), which targeted men aged 40–70 and their female partners in Brazil, Germany, Japan, Spain, and the United States, Heiman et al. (2011) found that men reported higher levels of sexual satisfaction and relationship happiness with each increasing category of relationship length. In contrast, women expressed less sexual satisfaction than men in relationships shorter than 10 years, more sexual satisfaction in relationships of 25–50 years' duration, and less happiness in relationships lasting from 20 to 40 years.

5.4.6 Sexualities in Later Life

The study of sexualities in later life has benefited considerably from the rich data collected by NSHAP (Suzman 2009). Several research teams linked the first wave of NSHAP data to other major data sets to create synthetic cohort and quasi-panel studies, which make it easier to disentangle the effects of aging, cohort dynamics, and shifting social contexts (e.g., Das et al. 2012; Lindau and Gavrilova 2010). London and Wilmoth (2014) supplemented NSHAP data with comments posted by readers of two online news stories to explore attitudes about extramarital sex on the part of spouses of people with Alzheimer's disease. Non-spouse family members caring for Alzheimer's patients were far less likely to approve of such extramarital relations than were spouses taking care of husbands or wives with the disease. This stands to reason, given that "the

---

[3] Most, but not all, respondents in this analysis self-identified as heterosexual.

person living with cognitive impairment may no longer recognize their spouse, which undermines feelings of connectedness and desire," although it also "raises questions about consent in sexual relations" (p. 105). As London and Wilmoth note, this dilemma will become increasingly common as members of the Baby Boom cohort reach old age.

The second wave of NSHAP, collected in 2010–2011, included new interviews with partners of wave 1 respondents. A special issue of *Journal of Gerontology: Social Sciences*, drawing on research from NSHAP waves 1 and 2, was published in November 2014. Now that data from the second wave of NSHAP have become publicly available, life course sexualities scholars at many institutions will be poised to investigate a wide range of sexual phenomena among US men and women in midlife and old age. These data will not, however, be particularly useful for scholars who wish to focus on older lesbian, gay, bisexual, queer, transgender, and intersex individuals, about whom we still know far too little (though see Witten and Eyler 2012).

Other scholars are employing qualitative methods to address meanings and processes of sexualities in later life. Sandburg (2013) gathered narratives about sexuality from 22 Swedish heterosexual men aged 67–87. The men spoke of intimacy, by which they meant the decentering of erection and penetration, both as an adaptation to aging-related bodily and social changes (e.g., erection difficulties, retirement from paid employment) and as an opportunity to develop pleasurable new sexual subjectivities. Sandburg (2013) concluded that "intimacy may be a way for older heterosexual men to navigate between current binary discourses of asexual old age and 'sexy seniors'" or, worse, "dirty old men" (p. 261). Drawing on life history interviews with 40 Japanese women and men aged 60 and older, Moore (2010) demonstrated that men were less likely to engage in extramarital sex as they aged, sometimes because of flagging sexual potency, but more often because of declining opportunities to meet potential partners and changes in the balance of power within marriage, often precipitated by the death of the husband's parents.

Although many couples developed "sibling-like" relationships as they grew older, many respondents, especially men, stressed the continuing importance of sexual desire to their sense of self. Nyanzi's (2011) ethnographic study of widows and widowers in urban Uganda revealed striking interactions between gender and age, such that widowers and younger widows were more likely to remarry than older widows. The cultural institution of widow inheritance worked further to control widowed women's sexual lives and often prompted sexual cleansing rituals.

5.4.7 Other Life Transitions and Experiences

Surprisingly little research has explored how military service shapes sexualities over the life course, especially considering how many people have served in their nations' armed services. Using data from the 1992 NHSLS, London et al. (2012) found that US veterans (especially men) are significantly more likely than non-veterans to have engaged in extramarital sex and to have ever divorced, even after controlling for early-life factors. In another study, which pooled data from three surveys, London and Wilmoth (in review) found that, among US men who turned 18 between 1922 and 2010, military veterans were more likely than other men to have ever paid for sex. Indeed, the odds of having paid for sex increased the longer the men had served. The patterns revealed in both analyses arguably result from differences between the military and civilian life course, including factors predisposing some individuals to enter the military (e.g., orientation to risk); constraints and opportunities during deployment (e.g., bases' proximity to commercial sex industries); norms for masculinity in the military; and post-military factors, such as employment in travel-intensive occupations. Examining the same phenomena among women veterans—which London and Wilmoth were unable to do, given scant data on women service members—would be especially edifying, as would examining the life course effects of sexual assault within the armed forces, which affects women disproportionately (For a journalistic ac-count of service women's experiences, sexual and otherwise, over time, see Benedict 2010.)

Another transition on which scholars are beginning to train a life course perspective is movement into, and out of, sex work. McCarthy et al. (2014) collected data from a racially- and sexually-diverse sample of 212 US and Canadian sex workers, most of them women, using both a life-history calendar approach and a life-event checklist. Although early-life trauma and other misfortunes propelled a majority of their respon-dents into sex work, economic emergencies and other contingencies in adulthood also precipitated pathways into sex work. Similarly, using a "life story" method rooted in narrative theory, Cox et al. (2013) discovered that all but one of the Ni-caraguan women sex workers in their study "nar-rated the entry into sex work as the culmination of a downward spiral of life events" (p. 1466), typi-cally beginning with family conflict and leaving home, alleviated briefly via a period of indepen-dence and self-support, and followed by losing access to regular child care, losing a job, or both.

Along the same lines, Cobbina and Oselin (2011) found that US women who became street prostitutes in adolescence typically did so to re-claim control of their sexuality or because they saw such work as normal, whereas women who became street prostitutes during adulthood spoke of doing so to sustain a drug addiction or in order to survive. Those who began sex work as teen-agers remained in the trade longer than those who began such work as adults. Women who exited street prostitution emphasized the impetus provided by certain life transitions and turning points, including pregnancy and childbirth, being arrested, getting sober, being hospitalized, and aging (Oselin 2010). Barton (2006) found that women's feelings about working as exotic danc-ers typically evolved from positive and empow-ering to negative and oppressive the longer they stayed in the occupation.

5.5 Future Directions for the Field

As far as the field has come, much remains to be learned about sexualities over the life course.

5.5.1 Transgender and Intersex

As noted, the experiences of people who are transitioning or have transitioned from one gen-der to another can offer a great deal of insight into the interrelationship and co-construction of gender and sexualities, including sexual identity. Although some scholars have begun to train a life course perspective on transgender women's and men's lives (e.g., a "transgender and the life course" panel at the 2014 annual meeting of the Eastern Sociological Society), they have focused so far chiefly on physical and mental health, gen-der, and family relations. For example, in a study of transgender men using testosterone replace-ment therapy, DuBois (in progress) found that men whose physical characteristics "fit" their gender ideals experience a greater overnight dip in blood pressure (indicating lower stress levels) than men whose physical characteristics diverge from their gender ideals.

Issues around sexual identity have received far more attention than sexual behavior thus far.[4] In a review of the literature on transgender and aging, Witten and Eyler (2012) briefly discuss sexuality and intimacy, focusing more on identity than sex-ual practice, as well as how transitioning affects established relationships (some couples adapt, some do not); these discussions reference very few sources (because few exist). Several popular biographies of trans men and women (e.g., Green 2004; Boylan 2003) have discussed how sexual identity does or does not change—for the trans* person and for her or his partner—during gender transition, but more systematic research would be very welcome.

One promising ongoing study is the Transgen-der Social Life, Family, and Health Project, by Carrie Elliott, Andrew London, Natalee Simpson, Rebecca Wang, and Tre Wentling at Syracuse University. These scholars interviewed 39 US adults who express a gender different from what would be expected based on their assigned sex at birth. The semi-structured interviews inquired

---

[4] This is true of research about sexual minorities and aging more generally. (Thanks to Moira Carmody for this insight.)

about gender identity and expression, health and health care, family relationships within and across generations, parenting and the desire for children, military service, and the intersections of race and ethnicity with gender transition. Participants also spoke about how gender transition affected their sexual desire, behavior, and identity. The extent to which published analyses will address sexualities is not yet clear, however (London, personal communication).

Another area ripe for a life course approach concerns individuals with intersex conditions, often referred to as Disorders of Sex Development (DSD) in the medical literature. How people who do not fit the traditional gender binary negotiate sexual relationships and develop sexual identity deserves more attention, especially in a cultural context where sexual identity is typically seen as contingent on the existence of two, and only two, genders. Relatively little is known about how diagnosis and treatment of intersex conditions, which may include surgical intervention and hormone therapies, affect sexual feelings, behavior, and identity. Gender "assignment" surgeries typically damage nerves and remove or reconfigure erogenous tissue; outcomes may include reduced sexual sensation and pain (Karkazis 2008). Treatments for some intersex conditions begin in infancy and continue for decades; a life course perspective would help to chart their effects, sexual and otherwise, on individuals over time (Talley and Casper 2012). A life course perspective would also help us understand how changing approaches to diagnosis and treatment, and the evolution of popular knowledge and attitudes about intersex, affect the sexual lives of people with intersex conditions. (For a list of 15 pressing research questions about intersex and sexuality over the life course, see Talley and Casper 2012.)

5.5.2 Seldom-Studied Life Stages and Links Among Them

Several periods of life have been especially neglected by sexualities scholars. This is partly an artifact of researchers' and funders' tendency to focus on social groups and life phases that are perceived as somehow problematic or dangerous. As noted, scant research has examined sexualities in childhood prior to adolescence; most of the few studies that exist focus on children whose sexuality is deemed problematic in some way (Thigpen 2012). This lack can be traced to the widespread cultural assumption, especially pronounced in the United States, that "normal" children lack sexual feelings and behaviors; institutional and ethical constraints on studying sexualities among a population who are too young to consent to be studied (and who many lay people believe will be contaminated by such study); and the limitations of what even young adults can retrospectively recall from their childhood, especially the earliest years. The ultimate effect, as Thigpen (2012) notes, is that little is known about sexual feelings and behaviors among "ordinary" children, including how they may vary by gender, race, ethnicity, and social class.

Another life stage on which sexualities research is lacking is midlife, although this gap is gradually being filled. Although demographers have long studied fertility in young adulthood and midlife, few researchers have attended to sexual beliefs, behavior, and identities of adults (heterosexual or LGBTQ) who are married or in long-term committed relationships. Sex and parenthood, including sex during pregnancy, is surprisingly understudied (with a few exceptions; see above). Nor have many scholars carefully considered how having children from previous relationships affect the sexual lives of single or divorced women and men (see Lichtenstein 2012 for an exception). Sassler (2010) recommends asking

> how children affect the earlier stages of relationships—such as decisions to enter into a dating relationship, the tempo of relationship progression to sexual involvement and coresidence, the form such unions take (marriage, cohabitation, or cohabitation that transitions to marriage). (p. 14)

Finally, sexualities in very old age have been badly neglected. One important exception is Loe's (2012) nuanced analysis of intimacy and sexuality among women and men in their 90s and 100s. This study is especially notable for including people of color and people with limited socioeconomic resources—a challenge given disproportionately high mortality rates among African Americans, Native Americans, and Latinos and among the economically disadvantaged. (Indeed, as noted above, there is a paucity of life course research on people of color at any age.) Research on the sexual feelings and behavior of older sexual minorities is particularly sparse; as with transgender and intersex individuals, the focus thus far has been primarily on sexuality identity rather than behavior (Witten and Eyler 2012). More interrogations of these topics are likely forthcoming as larger numbers of people who openly self-identify as gay, lesbian, or bisexual reach old age.

In addition to studying seldom-examined stages of the life course, we desperately need more research that spans larger segments of life and draws links between those segments. Several aforementioned studies, especially those using longitudinal data from Add Health, TARS, or NSHAP, connect sexual ideas and experiences across adolescence and young adulthood or midlife and (young or old) old age, respectively, as do multiple contributions to the edited volume *Sex for Life* (Carpenter and DeLamater 2012). Montemurro's (2014a) analysis of US women's retrospective sexual life histories represents an important corrective, spanning childhood (in some women's narratives) to the early 60s (for the oldest respondents). The time is ripe for similar investigations of sexuality as it changes and stabilizes over the life course for heterosexual men and for gay, lesbian, and bisexual women and men. Moreover, as Sassler (2010) notes,

> Greater attention to not just the number of prior sexual partners and coresidential unions but also the quality of those relationships could shed much light on the relationship patterns of today's Americans and enable researchers to explore what individuals learn from prior (terminated) partnering experiences. (p. 14)

5.5.3 Other Understudied Phenomena

It is worth highlighting a few additional sexual phenomena that deserve more attention from a life course perspective. Strikingly, pleasure and desire remain two of the least-examined aspects of sexuality, from any perspective. In general, positive aspects of sexuality, such as pleasure and desire, have received far less scholarly attention than those aspects considered troubled or troubling, such as STIs and sexual violence; this is especially true for groups whose sexuality is widely stereotyped as somehow suspect (e.g., teenagers, people of color). Overall, women's sexual pleasure and desire are largely ignored or surmised to be absent or unimportant (or pathological, in the case of African American and Latina women), whereas sexual pleasure and desire are assumed to come easily and naturally to men, especially White men; low desire or pleasure in men is typically medicalized, particularly at older ages (Loe 2004). Most research that examines sexual desire and pleasure tends to do so in a "snapshot" manner rather than from a life course perspective, with the exception of several studies noted above. Hopefully more scholars will follow these researchers' lead.

How sexualities are affected by, and affect, physical and intellectual disabilities and acute and chronic illnesses also merits more scrutiny from a life course perspective. Two groups of scholars have paid increasing attention to the relationships among disability, chronic illness, and sexuality. Biomedical researchers and clinicians have focused chiefly on the effects of bodily impairment, looking at what can be "fixed" or accommodated. Scholars drawing on an alternative, social model have framed disabilities as issuing from the social world (e.g., discriminatory attitudes) and built environment (e.g., inhospitable dwellings). The latter perspective is quite consistent with a sociological approach, especially when combined with an understanding of impairments as having specific physiological consequences; for example, vision impairments affect sexual life differently than do mobility impairments.

To date, the bulk of non-clinical research on sexualities and disabilities has emanated from scholars in the humanities, especially English literature (e.g., McRuer and Mollow 2012). The field is ripe for sociological insights, including—and perhaps especially—a life course perspective. One excellent example of this approach can be found in Bender's (2012) study of working- and middle-class Black and White men with spinal cord injury. Another key study, bridging disability and chronic illness, is Schlesinger's (1996) analysis of the sexual lives of women who experience chronic pain. To date, most life course-inflected analyses of chronic illness and sexuality have addressed conditions with "obvious" implications for sexual conduct, such as STIs (e.g., Nack 2008; Lichtenstein 2012), breast cancer (Martinez 2009), and prostate cancer (Asencio et al. 2009). More research assessing the sexual impact of physical and mental illnesses not typically viewed in sexual terms (e.g., diabetes, high blood pressure, depression, schizophrenia) would be very welcome. For example, McClelland et al. (in press) are studying how women with terminal cancer view and experience sexuality and intimacy.

Movement in and out of sexual subcultures, such as swinging, BDSM, and zoophilia (sex between humans and animals), also deserves more attention. Sexual subcultures are rarely investigated, much less from a life course perspective. However, several empirical studies demonstrate how beneficial such an approach could be. Sheff (2013, 2015) provides an excellent model in her remarkably rich ethnographic study of polyamorous relationships—committed sexual partnerships involving three (or occasionally more) adults—showing how, over the course of 16 years, emotional and sexual aspects of poly relationships commenced, evolved, and sometimes ended due to partners' shifting interests, needs, and health status. Williams and Weinberg (2003) demonstrate how early-life sexualized experiences with animals prompted certain men to pursue sexualized interaction with animals in adulthood. Their thoughtful analysis of zoophilic desire and conduct could be enhanced with a conscious application of concepts like trajectories and turning points.

5.5.4 Attending to Intersectionality and International Diversity

As noted throughout this chapter, it is crucial to consider how not only gender and sexual iden-

tity, but also race, ethnicity, social class, and other aspects of social location intersect to influence sexual life (and are influenced by sexual life in turn). Sexualities researchers have made great strides in this regard. Surveys are increasingly over sampling for racial/ethnic minorities and other groups of theoretical interest (e.g., religious communities, identical twins); more and more qualitative studies draw on socially-diverse samples; more scholars are choosing to focus on specific intersections of identities (e.g., Moore on Black lesbians, Espiritu on heterosexual Filipinas); and edited volumes are threading race, gender, and class analyses throughout every chapter rather than segregating social groups by chapter.

Yet, much remains to be done. Many scholars continue to rely on samples that are largely White and/or largely middle class, often for reasons of convenience or accessibility. Poor and working-class respondents and people of color more often appear in research on aspects of sexuality that are considered problematic (e.g., unintended pregnancy), whereas positive aspects of sexuality (e.g., pleasure) are typically investigated among predominantly White middle-class populations (especially college students). Scholarship on a specific sexuality-related topic often begins with White middle-class samples and then gradually extends to encompass more diverse populations. For example, the contributors to Witten and Eyler's (2012) edited book, *Gay, Lesbian, Bisexual, and Transgender Aging: Challenges in Research, Practice, and Policy*, one of the first of its kind, uniformly lament the lack of research on—and call for more attention to—racial/ethnic minorities and poor and working-class people in studies of sexual minorities.

Sociologists who study sexualities could also benefit from attending more closely to contexts outside highly economically-developed nations, especially the United States. Life courses and sexual mores differ across societies, such that comparing multiple sites on the globe, within or across studies, may illuminate important processes. For example, Green (2012) offers new insight into the ways gay men think about marriage and partnering by comparing the USA, where same-sex marriage was illegal in most states (at the time he collected his data), and Canada, where same-sex marriage had recently been legalized. Similarly, Witten and Eyler (2012) encourage us to think in new ways about the life course of transgender women and men by noting that, in contemporary Iran, some people who transition from one gender to another are gay men or lesbians who do so to avoid (illegal and highly stigmatized) homosexuality rather than because they feel a disjuncture between their biological sex and personal sense of gender identity.

5.6 Conclusion

The study of sexualities from a life course perspective has come a long way in just a few decades. Each successive wave of scholars has expanded what we know about the links between sexual and social experiences at one point in time to experiences later on—which are often complex and non-deterministic—and revealed the complicated processes through which individual beliefs and behavior are shaped by, and shape, social and historical context. The growing body of knowledge these researchers are producing will help shed light on the sexual lives of people like Trulah and Lewis Mills, and of the women and men in the cohorts that will grow up and grow old in their wake.

Challenges remain, of course. In particular, sexualities researchers need to move beyond taking "snapshots" of single life stages to exploring processes as they unfold across multiple periods of life, and to pay more thoroughgoing attention to the intersections of gender and sexual identity/orientation with race, ethnicity, and social class (for a start). Every aspect of sexuality can benefit from having a life course perspective trained on it. This is an exciting juncture, with many new insights looming on the horizon.

References

Albanesi, H. (2010). *Gender and sexual agency: How young people make choices about sex*. Lanham: Lexington Books.

Allison, R., & Risman, B. J. (2014). "It goes hand in hand with the parties": Race, class, and residence in college student negotiations of hooking up. *Sociological Perspectives, 57,* 102–123.

Asencio, M., Blank, T., Descartes, L., & Crawford, A. (2009). The prospect of prostate cancer: A challenge for gay men's sexualities as they age. *Sexuality Research & Social Policy, 6*(4), 38–51.

Barton, B. (2006). *Stripped: Inside the lives of exotic dancers*. New York: New York University Press.

Bender, A. (2012). Secrets and magic pills: Constructing masculinity and sexual "normalcy" following spinal cord injury. In L. M. Carpenter & J. DeLamater (Eds.), *Sex for life* (pp. 198–214). New York: New York University Press.

Benedict, H. (2010). *The lonely solider: The private war of women serving in Iraq*. Boston: Beacon Press.

Berk, R., Abramson, P. R., & Okami, P. (1995). Sexual activities as told in surveys. In P. R. Abramson & S. D. Pinkerton (Eds.), *Sexual nature/sexual culture* (pp. 371–386). Chicago: University of Chicago.

Better, A. (2014). Redefining queer: Women's relationships and identity in an age of sexual fluidity. *Sexuality & Culture, 18,* 16–38.

Boylan, J. F. (2003). *She's not there: A life in two genders*. New York: Broadway Books.

Browning, C. R., & Laumann, E. O. (1997). Sexual contact between children and adults: A life course perspective. *American Sociological Review, 62*(4), 540–560.

Brückner, H., & Bearman, P. (2005). After the promise: The STD consequences of adolescent virginity pledges. *Journal of Adolescent Health, 36*(4), 271–278.

Cancel Tirado, D. I. (2011). *Family planning and sexual risk-taking among Mexican immigrant men: How does fatherhood matter?* Dissertation in Human Development and Family Studies. Oregon State University.

Carpenter, L. M. (2005). *Virginity lost: An intimate portrait of first sexual experiences*. New York: New York University Press.

Carpenter, L. M. (2010). Gendered sexuality over the life course: A conceptual framework. *Sociological Perspectives, 53*(2), 155–178.

Carpenter, L. M., & DeLamater, J. (Eds.). (2012). *Sex for life: From virginity to Viagra, how sexuality changes throughout our lives*. New York: New York University Press.

Charmaz, K. (2006). *Constructing grounded theory*. Thousand Oaks: Sage.

Clausen, J. A. (1995). Gender, contexts, and turning points in adult lives. In P. Moen, G. H. Elder, & K. Lüscher (Eds.), *Examining lives in context* (pp. 365–389). Washington, D.C.: American Psychological Association.

Cobbina, J. E., & Oselin, S. S. (2011). It's not only for the money: An analysis of adolescent versus adult entry into street prostitution. *Sociological Inquiry, 81*(3), 310–332.

Collins, P. H. (1990). *Black feminist thought*. New York: Routledge.

Cox, K. S., Casablanca, A. M., & McAdams, D. P. (2013). "There is nothing good about this work": Identity and unhappiness among Nicaraguan female sex workers. *Journal of Happiness Studies, 14*, 1459–1478.

Das, A., Waite, L., & Laumann, E. O. (2012). Sexual expression over the life course. In L. M. Carpenter & J. DeLamater (Eds.), *Sex for life* (pp. 236–259). New York: New York University Press.

DeLamater, J. (2012). Sexual expression in later life: A review and synthesis. *The Journal of Sex Research, 49*, 125–141.

DeLamater, J., & Sill, M. (2005). Sexual desire in later life. *The Journal of Sex Research, 42*, 138–149.

DeLamater, J., & Moorman, S. (2007). Sexual behavior in later life. *Journal of Aging and Health, 19*, 921–945.

DeLamater, J., & Carpenter, L. M. (2012). Toward an interdisciplinary science of lifelong sexualities for the twenty-first century. In L. M. Carpenter & J. DeLamater (Eds.), *Sex for life* (pp. 299–316). New York: New York University Press.

Diamond, L. (2009). *Sexual fluidity: Understanding women's love and desire*. Cambridge: Harvard University Press.

Donnelly, D., Burgess, E., Anderson, S., Davis, R., & Dillard, J. (2001). Involuntary celibacy: A life course analysis. *Journal of Sex Research, 38*(2), 159–169.

DuBois, L. Z. (In progress). *Stress response and experience during major life transitions: A study of transgendered men using hormonal replacement therapy*. Doctoral dissertation in Anthropology. University of Massachusetts, Amherst.

Elder, G. H., Jr. (1985). Perspectives on the life course. In G. H. Elder, Jr. (Ed.), *Life course dynamics: Trajectories and transitions* (pp. 23–49). Ithaca: Cornell University Press.

Elliott, S. (2012). *Not my kid: What parents believe about the sex lives of their teenagers*. New York: New York University Press.

Fields, J. (2008). Risky lessons: *Sex education and social inequality*. New Brunswick: Rutgers University Press.

Gagnon, J. H., & Simon, W. (1973). *Sexual conduct*. Chicago: Aldine.

Garcia, L. (2012). *Respect yourself, protect yourself: Latina girls and sexual identity*. New York: New York University Press.

Giele, J. Z., & Elder, G. H., Jr. (Eds.). (1998). *Methods of life course research: Qualitative and quantitative approaches*. Thousand Oaks: Sage.

González-López, G. (2005). *Erotic journeys: Mexican immigrants and their sex lives*. Berkeley: University of California Press.

Green, J. (2004). *Becoming a visible man*. Nashville: Vanderbilt University Press.

Green, A. I. (2006). "Until death do us part?": The impact of differential access to marriage on a sample of urban men. *Sociological Perspectives, 49*(2), 163–189.

Green, A. I. (2008). The social organization of desire: The sexual fields approach. *Sociological Theory, 26*, 25–50.

Green, A. I. (2012). The symbolic power of civil marriage on the sexual life histories of gay men. In L. M. Car-

penter & J. DeLamater (Eds.), *Sex for life* (pp. 146–160). New York: New York University Press.

Halpern-Meekin, S., Manning, W. D., Giordano, P. C., & Longmore, M. A. (2012). Relationship churning in emerging adulthood: On/off relationships and sex with an ex. *Journal of Adolescent Research, 28*(2), 166–188.

Haydon, A. A., Herring, A. H., Prinstein, M. J., & Halpern, C. T. (2012). Beyond age at first sex: Patterns of emerging sexual behavior in adolescence and young adulthood. *Journal of Adolescent Health, 50*(5), 456–463.

Heiman, J. R., Long, J. S., Smith, S. N., Fisher, W. A., Sand, M. S., & Rosen, R. C. (2011). Sexual satisfaction and relationship happiness in midlife and older couples in five countries. *Archives of Sexual Behavior, 40*, 741–753.

Higgins, J. A., Trussell, J., Moore, N. B., & Davidson, J. K. (2010). Virginity lost, satisfaction gained? Physiological and psychological sexual satisfaction at heterosexual debut. *The Journal of Sex Research, 47*(4), 384–394.

Higgins, J. A., Mullinax, M., Trussell, J., Davidson, J. K., & Moore, N. B. (2011). Sexual satisfaction and sexual health among university students in the United States. *American Journal of Public Health, 101*(9), 1643–1654.

Hipp, L. E., Low, L. K., & Van Anders, S. M. (2012). Exploring women's postpartum sexuality: Social, psychological, relational, and birth-related contextual factors. *Journal of Sexual Medicine, 9*, 2330–2341.

Hitlin, S., & Elder, G. H., Jr. (2007). Time, self, and the curiously absent concept of agency. *Sociological Theory, 25*, 170–191.

Ingraham, C. (1996). The heterosexual imaginary: Feminist sociology and theories of gender. In S. Seidman (Ed.), *Queer theory/sociology* (pp. 168–193). Oxford: Blackwell.

Jackson, P. B., & Williams, D. (2006). The intersection of race, gender, and SES: Health paradoxes. In A. J. Schulz & L. Mullings (Eds.), *Gender, race, class, and health: Intersectional approaches* (pp. 131–162). San Francisco: Jossey-Bass.

Jager, J., & Davis-Kean, P. E. (2011). Same-sex sexuality and adolescent psychological well-being: The influence of sexual orientation, early reports of same-sex attraction, and gender. *Self Identity, 10*(4), 417–444.

Karkazis, K. (2008). *Fixing sex: Intersex, medical authority, and lived experience*. Durham: Duke University Press.

Kimmel, M. (2008). *Guyland: The perilous world where boys become men*. New York: Harper Collins.

Krasnow, I. (2014). *Sex after… Women share how intimacy changes as life changes*. New York: Gotham Books.

Labuski, C. (2011). "It's hard to say": Moving beyond the mystery of female genital pain. In C. Bobel & S. Kwan (Eds.), *Embodied resistance: Challenging the norms, breaking the rules* (pp. 143–155). Nashville: Vanderbilt University Press.

Laumann, E. O., Gagnon, J., Michael, R., & Michael, S. (1994). *The social organization of sexuality: Sexual practices in the United States*. Chicago: University of Chicago Press.

Laws, J. L., & Schwartz, P. (1977). *Sexual scripts: The social construction of female sexuality*. Hinsdale: Dryden Press.

Lichtenstein, B. (2012). Starting over: Dating risks and sexual health among midlife women after relationship dissolution. In L. M. Carpenter & J. DeLamater (Eds.), *Sex for life* (pp. 180–197). New York: New York University Press.

Lindau, S. T., & Gavrilova, N. (2010). Sex, health, and years of sexually active life gained due to good health: Evidence from two US population based cross sectional surveys of ageing. *BMJ, 340,* c810. doi:10.1136/bmj.c810.

Loe, M. (2004). *The rise of Viagra: How the little blue pill changed sex in America*. New York: New York University Press.

Loe, M. (2012). Pleasure in old age. In L. M. Carpenter & J. DeLamater (Eds.), *Sex for life* (pp. 278–295). New York: New York University Press.

London, A. S., & Wilmoth, J. M. (2014). Extramarital relationships in the context of spousal Alzheimer's disease: A mixed-methods exploration of public attitudes. In J. H. McCormick & S. L. Blair (Eds.), *Family relationships and familial responses to health issues (Contemporary Perspectives in Family Research, Volume 8A)* (pp. 103–134). Bingley: Emerald Group.

London, A. S., & Wilmoth, J. M. (Under review). *Veteran status and paid sex among American men: Results from three national surveys*.

London, A. S., Allen, E., & Wilmoth, J. M. (2013). Veteran status, extramarital sex, and divorce: Findings from the 1992 National Health and Social Life Survey. *Journal of Family Issues, 34*(11), 1452–1473.

Lorber, J. (1993). Believing is seeing: Biology as ideology. *Gender & Society, 7,* 568–582.

Lucal, B. (1999). What it means to be gendered me: Life on the boundaries of a dichotomous gender system. *Gender & Society, 13,* 781–797.

Lyons, H. A., Manning, W. D., Longmore, M. A., & Giordano, P. C. (2014). Young adult casual sexual behavior: Life-course-specific motivations and consequences. *Sociological Perspectives, 57*(1), 79–101.

Martinez, G. (2009). "My body is not the same": Body and sexuality for White and Latina long-term breast cancer "survivors." In R. F. Plante & L. M. Maurer (Eds.), *Doing gender diversity: Readings in theory and real-world experience* (pp. 232–244). Boulder: Westview Press.

McCall, L. (2005). The complexity of intersectionality. *Signs, 30,* 1771–1800.

McCarthy, B., Benoit, C., & Jansson, M. (2014). Sex work: A comparative study. *Archives of Sexual Behavior* Permalink. https://escholarship.org/uc/item/0gd9h8f0. Accessed 21 June 2014.

McClelland, S. I., Holland, K. J., & Griggs, J. J. (In press). Vaginal dryness and beyond: The sexual health needs of women diagnosed with metastatic breast cancer. *The Journal of Sex Research*.

McRuer, R., & Mollow, A. (Eds.). (2012). *Sex and disability*. Durham: Duke University Press.

Mills, C. W. (1959). *The sociological imagination*. New York: Oxford University Press.

Moen, P. (1996). Gender, age, and the life course. In R. H. Binstock & L. K. George (Eds.), *Handbook of aging and the social sciences* (pp. 171–187). San Diego: Academic Press.

Montemurro, B. (2014a). *Deserving desire: Women's stories of sexual evolution*. New Brunswick: Rutgers University Press.

Montemurro, B. (2014b). Getting married, breaking up, and making up for lost time: Relationship transitions as turning points in women's sexuality. *Journal of Contemporary Ethnography, 43*(1), 64–93.

Montemurro, B., & Siefken, J. M. (2012). MILFS and matrons: Images and realities of mothers' sexuality. *Sexuality & Culture, 16,* 366–388.

Moore, K. L. (2010). Sexuality and sense of self in later life: Japanese men's and women's reflections on sex and aging. *Journal of Cross Cultural Gerontology, 25,* 149–163.

Moore, M. (2011). *Invisible families: Gay identities, relationships, and motherhood among black women*. Berkeley: University of California Press.

Nack, A. (2008). *Damaged goods: Women living with incurable sexually transmitted diseases*. Philadelphia: Temple University Press.

Nelson, I. (2010). From quantitative to qualitative: Adapting the life history calendar method. *Field Methods, 22*(4), 413–428.

Nyanzi, S. (2011). Ambivalence surrounding elderly widows' sexuality in urban Uganda. *Ageing International, 36,* 378–400.

O'Rand, A. M. (1996). The cumulative stratification of the life course. In R. H. Binstock & L. K. George (Eds.), *Handbook of aging and the social sciences* (pp. 188–207). San Diego: Academic Press.

O'Rand, A. (2003). The future of the life course: Late modernity and life course risks. In J. T. Mortimer & M. J. Shanahan (Eds.), *Handbook of the life course* (pp. 693–701). New York: Kluwer Academic/Plenum.

Oselin, S. S. (2010). Weighing the consequences of a deviant career: Factors leading to an exit from prostitution. *Sociological Perspectives, 53*(4), 527–550.

Riley, M. W. (1987). On the significance of age in sociology. *American Sociological Review, 52,* 1–14.

Rossi, A. S. (1994). *Sexuality across the life course*. Chicago: University of Chicago Press.

Rubin, G. (1984). Thinking sex: Notes for a radical theory of the politics of sexuality. In C. S. Vance (Ed.), *Pleasure and danger* (pp. 267–319). Boston: Routledge.

Sandberg, L. (2013). Just feeling a naked body close to you: Men, sexuality and intimacy in later life. *Sexualities, 16,* 261–282.

Sassler, S. (2010). Partnering across the life course: Sex, relationships, and mate selection. *Journal of Marriage and the Family, 72*(3), 557–575.

Savin-Williams, R. C., & Diamond, L. (2000). Sexual identity trajectories among sexual-minority youths: Gender comparisons. *Archives of Sexual Behavior, 29*(6), 607–627.

Savin-Williams, R. C., & Ream, G. L. (2007). Prevalence and stability of sexual orientation components during adolescence and young adulthood. *Archives of Sexual Behavior, 36,* 385–394.

Schlesinger, L. (1996). Chronic pain, intimacy, and sexuality: A qualitative study of women who live with pain. *The Journal of Sex Research, 33*(3), 249–256.

Sheff, E. (2013). *The polyamorists next door: Inside multiple-partner relationships and families.* Lanham: Rowman & Littlefield.

Sheff, E. (2015). Failure or transition? Redefining the "end" of polyamorous relationships. In T. S. Weinberg & S. Newmahr (Eds.), *Selves, symbols, and sexualities: An interactionist anthology* (pp. 201–214). Los Angeles: Sage.

Simon, W., & Gagnon, J. H. (1986). Sexual scripts: Permanence and change. *Archives of Sexual Behavior, 15*(2), 97–120.

Span, P. (10 June 2014). Sex in assisted living: Intimacy without privacy. *New York Times.*

Sprecher, S. (2014). Evidence of change in men's versus women's emotional reactions to first sexual intercourse. *The Journal of Sex Research, 51*(4), 466–472.

Sprecher, S., Treger, S., & Sakaluk, J. K. (2013). Premarital sexual standards and sociosexuality: Gender, ethnicity, and cohort differences. *Archives of Sexual Behavior.* doi:10.1007/s10508-013-0145-6. (Published online 11 July 2013).

Suzman, R. (Ed.). (2009). The national social life, health, and aging project: An introduction. *Journal of Gerontology B: Psychological Science, Social Science, 64B*(Suppl 1), i5–i11. doi:10.1093/geronb/gbp078.

Talley, H. L., & Casper, M. J. (2012). Intersex and aging: A (cautionary) research agenda. In T. M. Witten & A. E. Eyler (Eds.), *Gay, lesbian, bisexual, and transgender aging* (pp. 270–289). Baltimore: Johns Hopkins University Press.

Thigpen, J. (2012). Childhood sexuality: Exploring culture as context. In L. M. Carpenter & J. DeLamater (Eds.), *Sex for life* (pp. 45–69). New York: New York University Press.

Ueno, K., Roach, T. A., & Peña-Talamantes, A. E. (2013). The dynamic association between same-sex contact and educational attainment. *Advances in Life Course Research, 18,* 127–140.

Valentine, D. (2004). The categories themselves. *GLQ, 10*(2), 215–220.

Wade, L. D., & DeLamater, J. D. (2002). Relationship dissolution as a life stage transition: Effects on sexual attitudes and behaviors. *Journal of Marriage and the Family, 64*(4), 898–914.

West, C., & Zimmerman, D. H. (1987). Doing gender. *Gender & Society, 1*(2), 125–151.

Williams, C. J., & Weinberg, M. S. (2003). Zoophilia in men: A study of sexual interest in animals. *Archives of Sexual Behavior, 32*(6), 523–535.

Witten, T. M., & Eyler, A. E. (Eds.). (2012). *Gay, lesbian, bisexual, and transgender aging: Challenges in research, practice, and policy.* Baltimore: Johns Hopkins University Press.

Part II
Methods

Surveying Sexualities: Minimizing Survey Error in Study of Sexuality

6

Anthony Paik

6.1 Introduction

Sex surveys have been around for more than 100 years. The first survey asking questions about sex was conducted by Clelia Mosher, a graduate student at the University of Wisconsin, in 1892 (Ericksen and Steffen 2009). However, it was *Sexual Behavior in the Human Male* (1948) and *Sexual Behavior in the Human Female* (1953) by Alfred Kinsey et al. that highlighted the notion that people's private sexuality could be revealed through surveys, setting the stage for the later introduction of probabilistic sampling and modern survey techniques in sex research. Today, the use of surveys to study sexualities is widespread, but their deployment has been the target of intense criticism. While reviewing the landmark National Health and Social Life Survey (NHSLS), Richard Lewontin (1995) wrote sarcastically, "Anyway, why should anyone lie on a questionnaire that was answered in a face-to-face interview with a total stranger?" Lewontin's position was polemical: he was skeptical of the entire enterprise of self-reports. Ironically, he targeted a sex survey that in many ways was a significant improvement, compared to prior studies, in terms of minimizing survey error. Nevertheless, issues of minimizing lies about sexuality and maximizing the representativeness of these answers—

Lewontin's primary criticisms—are critical in the study of sexualities.

This chapter provides an overview of potentials and pitfalls of survey research on sexualities. Below, I review the use of survey methods in the study of sexualities, including design, populations studied, and methodological issues across several key sex surveys. While all sex surveys suffer from some degree of bias or error; the use of survey research methods in the study of sexualities are focused on minimizing the amount of *total survey error*, comprised by (1) coverage error between sampling frames and populations, (2) sampling error, (3) nonresponse error, (4) measurement error, and (5) processing or coding errors (Groves et al. 2004). In this chapter, I draw heavily on Groves et al. (2004) and focus on the importance of four types for error in sex surveys: coverage, nonresponse, measurement, and coding issues. I also examine the use of several nonprobability sampling designs: respondent-driven sampling (RDS), time-location sampling (TLS), and internet surveys. Finally, I discuss error in the context of three probability surveys: the Chicago Health and Social Life Survey (CHSLS), the National Longitudinal Study of Adolescent to Adult Health (Add Health), and the New Family Structures Study (NFSS). The CHSLS highlights a probability-based sampling strategy for studying sexual minorities as well as sexualities at the intersection of race and class; the Add Health shows the importance of measurement error by looking at repeated measures over time for the same respondents; and the NFSS underscores

A. Paik (✉)
Department of Sociology, University of Massachusetts-Amherst, Amherst, MA 01003, USA
e-mail: apaik@soc.umass.edu

J. DeLamater, R.F. Plante (eds.), *Handbook of the Sociology of Sexualities,* Handbooks of Sociology and Social Research, DOI 10.1007/978-3-319-17341-2_6, © Springer International Publishing Switzerland 2015

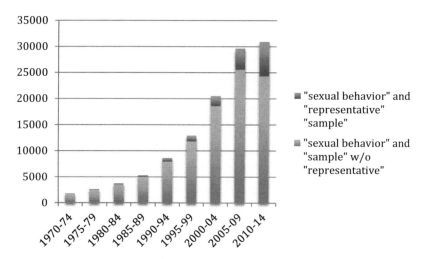

Fig. 6.1 The number of Google Scholar hits using "sexual behavior" and "sample"

the pitfalls of a probability-based internet survey as well as measurement issues. By highlighting the presence of survey error across several probability samples, this chapter seeks to provide a roadmap for minimizing these issues in future surveys of sexualities.

6.2 Background

Surveys are a key methodology for studying sexualities. The social scientists behind the NHSLS argued that sexuality is just another set of social facts amenable to standard data collection techniques (Laumann et al. 1994). Indeed, compared to other social-science methods, surveys are particularly useful for illuminating sexuality. Whereas qualitative interviewing, ethnography, and "big data" analyses rely on, respectively, nonrepresentative interviews with small groups, observations in specific contexts, and digital traces, sex surveys are suited for measuring what occurs behind closed doors for entire populations. Sex surveys, it is worth noting, may have another effect, a hegemonic one. In this account, the measurement of sexualities may contribute to the social construction of sexualities by defining quantitatively what is "normal" and "abnormal" and by reifying sexual categories (Ericksen and Steffen 2009). Regardless, the goal of survey research on sexualities is to assess aspects of sexu-

ality among a sample of respondents and to draw inferences based on their responses.

Figure 6.1, which shows results of two searches in Google Scholar from 1970 to 2014, illustrates the growth of research on sexuality, generally, and survey research, specifically. The number of articles using the terms "sexual behavior" and "sample" has grown rapidly over the last 40 years.[1] Not surprisingly, this pattern shows burgeoning interest in the study of sexual behavior over time. At the same time, the proportion of these articles using the terms "representative sample" has grown from 6 % from 1970 to 1974 to more than 20 % during the last 5 years. This pattern aligns well with a review of the public health literature, which found that from 1990 to 1992 only 3 of 152 articles employed probability sampling to study sexual minorities (Sell and Petrulio 1996). Thus, despite Lewontin's criticism of the NHSLS in 1995, interest in representative studies of sexual behavior is apparently at an all-time high. This figure is by no means an accurate measure of the number of articles, books, and reports that focus on representative sex surveys. Rather, the goal here is to simply illustrate that surveying sexualities, or at least discussion

---

[1] Unlike "sexualities," the search term "sexual behavior" has been used continuously from 1970 to 2014. I also employed this term because it is likely to have fewer false positives in comparison to "sexuality."

of them, has become more common and that, although the modal approach is likely to be sex surveys of convenience samples, reliance on representative surveys is rapidly increasing.

6.3 Survey Error in the Study of Sexualities

Both convenience and representative samples have advantages and disadvantages when surveying sexualities. Nonrepresentative convenience samples are a primary means to study small or hard-to-find populations or to gather data with limited resources, such as when researchers survey college students in their courses or patients at a treatment facility. Although the study results may generate theoretical expectations or hypotheses, making inferences, such as prevalence estimates or conclusions about relations among measures, about larger populations is unsound. For example, a sex survey given to college students taking an introductory psychology or sociology course will allow researchers to make inferences to this population of students and to develop expectations about college students more generally. These data, however, have unknown selection biases that limit researchers' abilities to make inferences, based on their results, to college students taking introductory courses in psychology or sociology more generally, let alone all college students. It is worth noting that some nonprobabilistic sampling approaches—RDS, TLS, and internet surveys seek to approximate probability sampling, thereby allowing for inferences to populations. I discuss these below.

Studies using representative samples generated through survey research methods have greater ability to make inferences to populations, but can be quite expensive and may not be well suited for hard-to-find populations, which is often the case in the study of sexualities. Survey research is built on a number of interrelated stages, including the target population, the sampling frame, the sample, responses to survey items, and analysis; consequently, the study of sexualities, at least from a survey perspective, must deal with multiple types of error (Groves et al. 2004). The first

is *coverage error* between the target population (e.g., adolescents in the United States) and the sampling frame (e.g., adolescents who were attending school at the time of the survey). The second is *sampling error*, which specifies the extent to which units did or did not have a chance for inclusion into the sample. The third is *nonresponse error*; high levels of nonresponse may cause the obtained sample to be biased in comparison to the sampling frame. The fourth deals with *measurement error* related to data collection. Finally, there are *processing errors* related to analysis, such as coding problems that lead to errors in inference. Convenience samples, by definition, suffer from substantial coverage and sampling error, but researchers could seek to minimize nonresponse, measurement, and processing errors. The objective of survey research is to minimize error across these various stages. Below, I focus primarily on coverage, nonresponse, measurement, and coding errors in survey research on sexualities.[2]

6.3.1 Populations, Sampling Frames, and Coverage Error

The principal strength of survey research is the ability, in theory, to make inferences about a target population based on an analysis of survey responses from a sample of individuals drawn from the former. A key issue is whether a probability sample remains representative when coverage error or nonresponse is high (Baker et al. 2013). In this context, having access to a sampling frame, a listing of most-to-all units or clusters of units in a population, from which a representative sample can be drawn, is critical. The problem of coverage error refers to the degree to which a sampling frame omits elements of a population or includes incorrectly those not part of the population, such that obtained samples are biased and nonrepresentative (Groves et al. 2004).

---

[2] Sampling error is another type of survey error that I do not focus in this chapter. It is worth noting, however, that convenience samples suffer from substantial sampling error.

Sex surveys typically utilize known sampling frames, such as lists of households, schools, or phone numbers, which are not exclusively focused on sexualities, and then seek to identify subpopulations within the obtained sample. For example, the NHSLS (Laumann et al. 1994), the General Social Survey (GSS), and Census have been mentioned as high-quality surveys utilizing household sampling frames that produced demographic estimates of gay and lesbian populations (Black et al. 2000). The National AIDS Behavioral Study (NABS) utilized random digit dialing to generate representative samples of men who have sex with men, both nationally and in high-risk urban centers (Catania et al. 1990). An issue here is that without oversampling, sample sizes need to be quite large to produce analyzable numbers of respondents reporting gay and lesbian identities as well as same-sex attraction and behavior. Hence, although this approach is extremely useful for generating population estimates as well as allowing for examining correlations among variables, it is a costly strategy for studying "hard-to-find" populations. Indeed, if the primary objective is to study small populations, such as sexual minorities, this strategy of surveying a general population is often cost prohibitive.

Importantly, several studies have employed sampling frames in ways that generated higher proportions of respondents who were gay men and men who have sex with men (MSM). The Urban Men's Health Study (UMHS) focused on zip codes in four major cities where the density of households with MSMs was high and then employed screeners to identify MSM respondents (Catania et al. 2001). Catania and his collaborators completed 2881 interviews, or 78 % of the identified MSM households. The CHSLS included a household community sample targeting a neighborhood in Chicago known to have a concentration of gay men. Out of 175 male respondents in the Shoreland community sample of the CHSLS, 36 % reported some level of being sexually attracted to other men; 30 % of the women in this sample reported some same-sex sexual attraction as well (Van Haitsma et al. 2004).

Two major issues related to sampling frames are coverage error and their nonexistence for important populations. First, representative samples of adults in households and students in school, for example, may miss subpopulations that are particularly important for sexuality. For example, although the Add Health is frequently employed to make inferences about adolescent sexuality, the school sampling frame omits individuals who dropped out of school. Similarly, household surveys like the NHSLS and GSS omit the homeless and institutionalized populations, whereas telephone surveys, such as NABS, miss individuals without phones.

Second, a frequent problem is the absence of sampling frames exclusively focused on sexualities populations. Populations such as men who have sex with men (MSMs), lesbians, bisexuals, and gay men are hard to find, denoting the nonexistence of sampling frames containing complete listings of individuals in these populations, or a comprehensive listing of clusters of these individuals. For many, the strategies employed by the UMHS and the CHSLS described above are cost prohibitive. Consequently, researchers typically draw on alternative, nonrepresentative sampling approaches, such as snowball, facility-based, respondent-driven, and time-location sampling (Magnani et al. 2005; Stueve et al. 2001). None of these approaches can yield representative estimates, but under certain conditions and assumptions some may approximate populations. I discuss some of these in greater detail below.

6.3.2 Nonprobability Sampling

Researchers have adopted a number of nonprobability sampling approaches to survey difficult-to-find sexualities populations. Here, I focus on three recent developments: time-location sampling (TLS), respondent-driven sampling (RDS), and internet surveys. These approaches build on earlier nonprobability designs, such as snowball, facility, and targeted sampling, which are reviewed elsewhere (Magnani et al. 2005). TLS seeks to generate a sampling frame of places and spaces where hard-to-find populations congregate (Stueve et al. 2001; Magnani et al. 2005). A key issue is that of developing a comprehensive list of spaces or locations where the population of interest congregates. The problem is that this approach likely suffers from unknown amounts of coverage error. Appropriate sites may be omitted, but inappropriate sites may also be included. In addition, population members who are infrequent users of these places will likely be missed.

Another approach is RDS. Similar to snowball sampling, RDS relies on a chain-referral process where initial respondents recruit a limited number of network partners into the study; researchers then elicit a limited number of new contacts from the new respondents, and so on. The objective of RDS is to produce long referral chains (Magnani et al. 2005), which make it more likely that hard-to-reach portions of a population are included; limits on the number of referrals allow for calculating selection probabilities. RDS uses estimation procedures to generate sample estimates that may approximate population parameters if assumptions are met (Gile and Handcock 2010). A recent comparison of RDS, snowball sampling, and TLS among MSM in Brazil found that the latter two produced samples of men with more than 50 % hailing from the highest social classes; the comparable figure in the RDS sample was just 3 % (Kendall et al. 2008). The RDS approach was inexpensive as well. These differences highlight the potentially large impacts of sampling bias in nonprobability designs.

Nonprobability internet surveys are perhaps the newest entrant into the world of sex research. Internet surveys provide the opportunity to collect many cases at low cost and to approximate the diversity of respondents typically captured in national probability surveys. Here, I exclude the Knowledge Networks panel, since it is a probability-based internet survey. I focus on internet surveys that use "opt-in methods"—that is, recruitment occurs primarily through displaying banner ads. In general, internet surveys using opt-in methods are convenience samples.

For example, Durex's Sexual Wellbeing Survey utilizes an internet panel from Harris Interactive (Durex 2006). Harris Interactive's approach is to widely distribute invitations to take surveys via banner ads. In this case, the sampling frame is unknown, but the attained panel can be matched on demographics. A national field ex-periment comparing RDD probability sampling, Knowledge Networks' probability-based internet sample, and Harris Interactive's nonprobability sample found that the latter had substantial sampling bias based on the content of the survey (i.e., interest in politics), but these respondents tended to perform better, thereby reducing measurement error in survey responses (Chang and Krosnick 2009). Similarly, a recent study compared a Swedish national probability sample with a sexual health internet survey advertised through banner ads. The website had 1.7 million visitors, but less than 1 % accessed the study through banner ads, and only a third actually took the survey (Ross et al. 2005). The results showed that the two had comparable statistics for relationship characteristics, but the internet sample was demographically different (e.g., better educated, younger, more students) and drew larger proportions of individuals who were attracted to the same sex and more sexual experienced. Finally, a comparison between the National Survey of Lifestyles and Attitudes and an opt-in internet sample of MSM in Great Britain also found differences across demographic characteristics and sexual behaviors (Evans et al. 2007). Taken together, internet surveys are likely to be a poor match for assessing population characteristics, which is where probability samples are likely to excel (Yeager et al. 2011; Baker et al. 2013).

The strength of internet surveys, in contrast, is the ability to gather data on hard-to-find populations, such as transgender individuals (Miner et al. 2011), quickly and at the low cost. Moreover, the use of sample matching and estimation and propensity weighting adjustments can make nonprobability samples similar to probability samples (Schonlau et al. 2004), but obtained estimates are often highly dependent on the assumptions of these techniques being met (Baker et al. 2013). While nonprobability samples are a poor match for describing population characteristics, some suggest that nonprobability samples can be used at least in an exploratory way, assuming model-based assumptions are met, to examine relationships among variables (Baker et al. 2013). Thus, the rewards of internet surveys—access, cost, efficiency—come with risks. As indicated in the summary report of the AAPOR task force on nonprobability sampling (Baker et al. 2013), the amount of risk is salient for probability and nonprobability approaches:

> Probability sampling approaches, while using models to adjust for undercoverage and nonresponse, provide some protection against the risk of substantial biases. Non-probability approaches rely more heavily on the appropriateness of the models, and, in most cases, on the selection, availability, and quality of the variables used for respondent selection and post hoc adjustment. (p. 93)

6.3.3 Nonresponse in Surveys

Samples are drawn from sampling frames. Groves et al. (2004) discuss several types of error associated with sampling, including when samples are biased due to zero probabilities of inclusion for some units, sampling variance, and nonresponse. Here, I focus primarily on nonresponse bias in the context of sexualities research. Nonresponse is generated in multiple ways, including refusals as well as when surveys are not delivered or respondents cannot participate (Groves et al. 2004).

In general, sex researchers have been quite successful in generating probability samples with high response rates. The NHSLS, a face-to-face, household survey, attained a response rate of 79%, whereas the Add Health's response rates across multiple waves were well over 70%. It is worth noting that, at the time, there was substantial skepticism that individuals would be willing to participate in sex surveys. Household surveys, however, are often time and cost prohibitive for many researchers. Despite claims of being probability samples, a number of sex surveys, often collected by market research firms, attained low response rates, raising the likelihood of sampling bias. The Global Study of Sexual Attitudes and Behaviors, for example, used random digit dialing in a number of countries and had an average response rate of just 15.3%. With decreasing landline connection rates and declining response rates, researchers have turned to probability-based internet surveys.

Knowledge Networks, for example, recruited panel members via random digit dialing and mail contacts; individuals who are successfully recruited into the panel then complete web sur-

veys using laptops, with incentives coming in the form of free internet access (Chang and Krosnick 2009). The devil is in the details, however. Panel members appear to be surveyed quite frequently, an average of one survey per week, and could be removed if they refused after eight consecutive surveys. More importantly, this particular incentive might attract individuals who do not have internet access.

Chang and Krosnick (2009) estimated a response rate of just 25% for Knowledge Networks, but this number may frequently be quite a bit lower since they assume that 56% of households contacted via random digit dialing agreed to participate in the panel. Other Knowledge Networks panels, for example, had overall response rates of 20 (Smith 2003) and 7% (Brashears 2011). Regnerus (2012a) did not report a response rate for the NFSS, which was based on Knowledge Networks's panel, but indicated that the panel response rate to surveys generally, but not specifically for his study, was 65%. This number, however, does not account for the much larger percentage of unit nonresponse associated with the random digit dialing and panel recruitment procedures. In a comparison with the GSS, Smith concluded that differences in results from probability-based internet surveys and household probability samples "are likely to be common and notable" (2003, p. 176).

6.3.4 Measurement and Coding Errors in Survey Responses

Surveys ask questions, and the hope is that respondents provide accurate answers. Much can go awry, particularly when asking sensitive questions related to sexuality. Measurement error refers to the gap between "the true value of a measurement" and the response obtained (Groves et al. 2004, pp. 51–52). Indeed, there is a substantial literature focused on measurement error related to gathering data on sexuality (for reviews, see Catania et al. 1990; Weinhardt et al. 1998; Fenton et al. 2001).

Here, I focus on respondent-level error related to the mode of administration, questionnaire structure, and survey items as well as interviewer-related error. Questions about sexuality are often thought to fall into the class of survey items termed "sensitive questions," which includes topics such as criminal behavior, substance use, and income. Sensitive questions may be particularly likely to elicit nonresponses, including refusals and "don't knows," responses biased by social desirability, and misreporting, which might be motivated by embarrassment, the presence of third parties, and other factors. As suggested by Michaels (2013) and Groves et al. (2004), there are a number of survey techniques—decisions about the mode of administration, the use of self-administered items, audio computer-assisted self interviewing (ACASI), and the design of questionnaires—that may reduce nonresponse, social desirability biases, and question order effects.

6.3.4.1 Item-specific Error

Survey questions can elicit error in the form of nonresponses or inaccurate answers. Nonresponse occurs when respondents skip questions or provide answers in the form of refusals or "don't knows." In sex research, nonresponse has been linked to the use of self-administered questionnaires (Catania et al. 1990) and questions that might be particularly embarrassing. Social desirability biases typically come in two forms: overreporting and underreporting (Catania et al. 1990). Overreporting may be induced by motives to brag about sex, underreporting by the desire to avoid embarrassment. A well-known finding in sex research is tendency for male respondents to report on average more partners than female respondents. From an accounting perspective, this might be possible if same-sex partnerships among men are sufficiently high and prevalent among men, but the more likely scenario is that male respondents are overreporting, female respondents are underreporting, or both. Indeed, experimental evidence does appear to suggest that gender differences in reported sexual behaviors are related to social desirability biases (Alexander and Fisher 2003). Additionally, survey items may also prime respondents into giving answers that are perceived to be consistent with their identities (Brenner and DeLamater 2014).

6.3.4.2 Mode of Administration

Although the mode of administration is key for response rates, they also have implications for measurement error linked to survey items. A key issue for face-to-face interviews is social desirability bias, where respondents may overreport or underreport (Catania et al. 1990). On the flip side, face-to-face interviews may elicit more accurate, complete responses when interviewers successfully establish trust and rapport, probe, and provide answers to respondent's questions. They also allow for more complicated skip patterns in surveys. In general, several high quality samples have utilized computer-assisted technologies, such as audio computer-assisted self-interviewing (ACASI) to maximize privacy during face-to-face interviews; research supports this strategy (Weinhardt et al. 1998).

Self-administered questionnaires (SAQs) may reduce biases related to privacy, embarrassment and social desirability, but these surveys or sections of surveys also tend to have higher levels of nonresponse (Catania et al. 1990; Turner et al. 1997). To the best of my knowledge, researchers have not identified the mechanism generating higher nonresponse, but I would speculate that it may be induced by the tendency for more sensitive questions to be administered in this mode, respondent fatigue, and, as my research shows, interviewer fatigue or misreporting when SAQs are embedded in face-to-face interviews (Paik and Sanchagrin 2013). Finally, telephone interviews may also be less susceptible to social desirability biases, but comparisons with SAQs suggest that the latter are superior (Turner et al. 1997). The relative anonymity of these interviews may decrease embarrassment and privacy concerns related to reporting unconventional sexual behavior (Catania et al. 1990).

6.3.4.3 Questionnaire Design and Interviewer Effects

Question Order Relatively little attention has been devoted to the issue of order effects in the context of sex research. Some researchers have examined order effects in SAQs administered to college students and found none (DeLamater and MacCorquodale 1975; Catania et al. 1990). This is, however, counterintuitive, as one would expect order effects depending on the sequencing of more or less sensitive questions and the length of surveys. There is a need for more research on this topic.

Question Wording In sex research, the wording of questions is likely to have tremendous implications for the answers a researcher gets. Catania et al. (1990) discuss two strategies for asking questions about sexuality: "standard" or "poetic." Questions relying on standard terms will tend to utilize language one might find in a sex education class; in contrast, poetic terms are more closely related to slang or colloquial phrases. Surprisingly, there have been relatively few recent studies examining wording effects.

Interviewer Effects Although the demographic characteristics and training of interviewers may affect the answers provided, older research suggests that the findings are mixed (Catania et al. 1990). That said, more recent research focusing on the listing of network partners have found substantial interviewer effects, which resulted in a downward bias in network size (Paik and Sanchagrin 2013). To the extent that similar types of questions are used to gather sex-partner specific information, it might be that similar interviewer effects will be found in the context of sex research.

6.3.4.4 Coding Error

A final class of measurement errors in sex research is coding error. Respondents may sometimes answer questions using an incorrect answer from what they intended. This may seem trivial, but when one is dealing with small populations, such as those less than 2 or 3% of the overall population, a small percentage of mistaken entries can drastically change statistical estimates. Alternatively, sexuality variables can be fairly complex; thus, decisions by researchers can have major implications for coding error.

An important example of coding problems is the measurement of gay and lesbian respondents in the Census. Using the 1 and 5% public use microdata of the 1990 Census, Black et al. (2000) estimated the size of the gay and lesbian partnerships in the United States based on an analysis of 5.3 million households. They used a sophisticated but complex coding scheme and highlighted the possibility of error related to miscoding of the gender of either partners or respondents among unmarried partners. For example, to identify cohabiting gay and lesbian couples, they excluded households comprised by two unrelated adults who did not report marriage-like relationships. Only a small percentage of miscodings among heterosexual cohabiters, for example, can have sizable effects on estimates of the number of gay and lesbian partnerships. With the 2000 Census allowing for reporting of same-sex marriages, this coding problem is even more severe. With the ratio of heterosexual marriages to same-sex marriages at 100 to 1, DiBennardo and Gates (2014) estimated that 40 and 28% of same-sex couples in the 2000 and 2010 Census, respectively, were miscoded heterosexual couples (DiBennardo and Gates 2014).

6.4 Applications

I now focus on survey errors in three different surveys: two household probability samples and a probability-based internet sample. Specifically, I focus on the CHSLS, Add Health, and NFSS. Following the landmark NHSLS, which drew a cross section of the U.S. adult population in 1992, the CHSLS is an urban community sample focused on how social contexts are linked to sexualities. Similarly, the Add Health can be seen as a complementary study focused on adolescents; it also added longitudinal information to examine changes over the life course. The NFSS represents an important attempt to use probability-based internet survey to examine the highly politicized issue of same-sex parenting.

6.4.1 Chicago Health and Social Life Survey (CHSLS)

The CHSLS, collected primarily in 1995 as a community-level follow-up to the NHSLS, is a representative cross-sectional, household sample of adults, ages 18–60, residing in Cook

County, which is a county in the state of Illinois that contains the city of Chicago and much of its inner suburbs. The probability sample of Cook County ($n=890$), which had a response rate of 71%, was representative of a population of more than 5 million Cook County residents in 1995. In addition, the CHSLS included neighborhood samples of four specific geographic areas in the city of Chicago. The neighborhood samples were designed to target specific populations, including neighborhoods with concentrations of gay men and MSMs ($n=358$), working-class Mexican Americans ($n=349$), Puerto Rican Americans ($n=210$), and working-class African Americans ($n=307$). Thus, this study allowed for examining sexuality at the intersection of gender, race, and class with particular attention to the social contexts of these areas. The neighborhood samples also included key informant interviews. The response rates for the neighborhood samples were, respectively, 66, 70, 78, and 60%. Van Haitsma et al. (2004) provide a detailed description of the study design.

A notable feature of the CHSLS is that it utilized many of the same practices that made the NHSLS successful. Unlike most sex surveys, interviewers were provided "Q-by-Q's"—questions-by-question explanations, definitions, and probes for each item in the survey (Van Haitsma et al. 2004). Interviewers received extensive training and mock interviewing beforehand to practice asking questions about sexuality. They used procedures to maximize the chances that interviews were conducted without the presence of third parties. Surveys were conducted in person, utilizing computer assisted program interviewing and self-answered questionnaires (SAQ), and hand cards were employed to maximize privacy for sensitive questions.

The CHSLS is one of the few surveys to focus on geographic areas with high concentrations of gay men. It includes a social network section that collects up to six social network partners for each respondent. Importantly, it is, I believe, the first social network name generator that asked whether each network partner considered themselves lesbian, gay or bisexual. It also includes a SAQ on sexual orientation, which included questions on sexual attraction, sexual identity, the sexual identity of friends, "coming out," and going to gay bars and clubs.

Coverage Error The CHSLS is a household probability sample of adults, ages 18 and 60, residing in Cook County. Like other household probability samples, the CHSLS is likely to miss institutionalized populations. Analyses of the CHSLS, however, are not generalizable to the larger U.S. adult population.

Nonresponse Error Overall, unit nonresponse was a bit higher compared to the NHSLS, Add Health, and the General Social Survey, all of which utilized the CHSLS's contractor, the National Opinion Research Center at the University of Chicago, to conduct their household surveys. Van Haitsma et al. (2004) explain that the fielding of the survey was temporarily suspended, which led to the loss of many "in-process" interviewee contacts. When the survey resumed in 1997, response rates were pushed up quite a bit, except in the 60% response rate neighborhood, which was not included in the second field effort. As such, the lower response rate does not appear to reflect difficulties in getting eligible individuals to take the survey.

Measurement and Coding Error There have been relatively few assessments of measurement error in the CHSLS. However, one notable issue that has been detected is the presence of interviewer-level error (Paik and Sanchagrin 2013). In my research, I found an intraclass correlation (ICC) of almost 0.3 for the CHSLS's network name generator—this is the question asking respondents to list the names of network partners. An ICC of 0.3 suggests that 30% of the variance in network size can be explained at the interviewer level, and one can hypothesize from the results of my analysis of the GSS that this interviewer-level variance reflects the tendency of interviewers to skip this section by coding respondents' answers as having no network partners. There are a number of sections on sexuality in the CHSLS survey with similar skip patterns, and it is quite possible that interviewers may have been motivated to skip these sections as well.

6.4.2 National Longitudinal Study of Adolescent to Adult Health (Add Health)

The Add Health was initially a representative sample of students in grades 7 through 12 in 1994 and 1995. It utilized a school-based, cluster sampling design consisting of four waves collected from 1994 to 2008. The fielding of Wave V will begin in 2015. Using a stratified approach, Add Health selected 80 high schools, designed to be representative of all U.S. high schools, and obtained a response rate of 70%; schools that refused to participate were replaced with another from the same stratum (Add Health 2014). In addition, one feeder school (i.e., a school with a seventh grade) for each high school was selected based on the probability proportional to its size. Based of this sample design, a number of samples were drawn, including a school administrators sample, a parents sample, and an adolescent sample.

The first survey in Wave I was a cluster sample of all students attending school on the day that the survey was administered. Over 90,000 respondents took the survey. Wave I also consisted of a probability-based, in-home survey that was drawn from school rosters ($n=20,745$). Approximately 8000 of these respondents were included in oversamples, such as 16 schools, pairs of siblings (i.e., genetic samples of twins and nontwins), individuals with reported disabilities, and specific racial and ethnic categories. Wave II ($n=14,738$) was administered in-home in 1996 to students, so it excluded 12th graders in Wave I, whereas Waves III ($n=15,197$) and IV ($n=15,701$) consisted of all Wave I respondents who could be reinterviewed in-home in 2001–2002 and 2008–2009, respectively. All in-home interviews utilized computer-assisted personal interview (CAPI) for less sensitive questions, audio computer-assisted self interview (ACASI) for more sensitive ones, and some SAQs.

Coverage Error As a school-based cluster sample, Add Health is representative of the student population in 1994 and 1995. It is also designed to be representative of this cohort of individuals as they age. This is a remarkable feature of this study, and researchers of sexuality are fortunate to have access to this important data. It is important to remember that the sampling frame did not include adolescents who were not in school in 1994 and 1995. This means that the Add Health was not representative of adolescents in the United States. Those who left school ("drop outs") may be of particular interest to sex researchers, since one of most important push factors, adolescent fertility, is linked to sexuality, and their sexual behavior may be less conventional. Given compulsory schooling laws, it is worth noting that some of the younger cohorts in the Add Health data, such as grades 7–9 at Wave I, are likely to be representative of adolescents in the United States, whereas the higher grades are impacted by increasing drop-out rates.

Nonresponse The response rates in the Add Health data are very good. For the in-home survey of Wave I, it was 79%. Attrition related to the inability to locate respondents and unit nonresponse across Waves II-IV was fairly low. These waves had response rates of 89, 77, 80%, respectively. Overall, this suggests that unit nonresponse initially and in subsequent waves is unlikely to bias the Add data substantially.

Measurement and Coding Error Although it is fairly standard to warn readers of research articles about the possibility of measurement error, there are relatively few assessments of measurement error in the Add Health data. In a comparison with three other national probability surveys, Santelli et al. (2000) compared prevalence estimates of the Add Health with the National Survey of Family Growth, the National Survey of Adolescent Males and the Youth Risk Behavior Survey and found significant differences for experience with sexual intercourse, condom use, and contraceptive use. They highlight the possibility of measurement error as a factor leading to discrepant prevalence estimates.

A number of unusual response patterns have highlighted the possibility of measurement error in the Add Health. In an analysis of virginity pledging, Rosenbaum (2006) found that more than half of Wave I pledgers recanted at Wave II, particularly among those who became sexually active. Conversely, 28% of sexually active adolescents at Wave I who took pledges at Wave II recanted their sexual behavior. Regnerus and Uecker (2007) found that respondents who interviewers assessed as embarrassed were less likely to report having had sex, but social desirability, candidness, and embarrassment were not associated with giving logically inconsistent answers about sexual experience across Waves I and II. Fan et al. (2006) examined the paper-and-pencil survey administered at schools (an SAQ) and found significant numbers of respondents who they described as being "jokesters." Specifically, they operationalized jokesters as respondents who gave two or more answers about being adopted, being born in the U.S., and having an artificial limb in the school SAQ and then later recanted in the in-home interviews.

More recently, a controversy erupted over prevalence estimates of lesbian, gay, and bisexual youth based on Wave I of the Add Health. At stake, according to the researchers involved, are findings suggesting linkages between sexual orientation and health disparities. With respect to sexual orientation, researchers can utilize behavioral measures as well as an attraction question. The latter, however, focused on *romantic* attraction—an unusual phrase that may have significant measurement bias. Specifically, the Add Health questionnaire includes the following items: "Have you ever had a romantic attraction to a female?" and "Have you ever had a romantic attraction to a male?" Savin-Williams and Joyner (2014) summarized the research as having unexpectedly high percentages of boys and girls reporting same-sex attraction (7 and 5%, respectively), but in subsequent waves, this percentage dropped precipitously. For example, among men, 80% of those reporting same-sex romantic attraction at Wave I reported being exclusively heterosexual at Wave IV; the corresponding percentage for women was 60% (Savin-Williams and Joyner 2014, p. 415). They suggest two possible mechanisms—confusion due to the question wording and mischievous respondents—as the likely suspects and rule out the notion that gay,

lesbian, and bisexual youth have become more "closeted." A fourth possibility, not mentioned, is the possibility that the fluidity of sexual attraction varies over the life course (Diamond 2009).

Critics of Savin-Williams and Joyner (2014) have acknowledged that measurement error is possible in the form of intentional misreporting by respondents, but have argued that such biases are likely to be insubstantial (Li et al. 2014; Katz-Wise et al. 2015). In my view, measurement error in the form of misreporting is a serious concern; researchers should proceed cautiously. Much of the controversy has centered on comparisons between Wave I and adult responses in Waves III and IV. However, Waves I and II provide a more direct comparison. Respondents were still adolescents and were asked the same question at two time points. Based on Udry and Chantala's (2005) discussion, there was substantial instability observed between the two waves. This may reflect fluidity in sexual attraction, measurement error, or both. Finally, it is worth noting that falsified data are a major concern when a variable being studied is fairly rare (e.g., same-sex attraction), on the one hand, and is attractive to respondents to joke about, on the other. The conditions are ripe for misreporting. Even if jokesters represent 1 or 2% of the overall population, their answers can significantly alter population-based estimates of lesbian, gay, and bisexual youth.

6.4.3 New Family Structures Study (NFSS)

The NFSS, fielded from July 2011 to February 2012, is a national probability sample of almost 3000 adults between the ages of 18 and 39. According to Regnerus (2012a), the data are based on Knowledge Network's internet panel, which was also employed in the 2009 National Survey of Sexual Health and Behavior. Recruitment into the panel employed dual sampling: original participants were recruited primarily by random digit dialing of household phones, but the firm transitioned to address-based sampling in 2009 and mail recruitment procedures as landline connection rates have declined in U.S. households. Incentives for participation in the panel are fairly extensive. In return for answering weekly surveys, individuals without internet access were offered monthly free internet service and use of a laptop; those with internet service were awarded cash based on the rate of participating in surveys. Recruitment into surveys typically utilizes simple random samples, but stratified random sampling is also an option. Incentives for survey response were $ 5 for regular panelists and $ 20 for former members of the internet panel.

The NFSS incorporated a number of unique fielding procedures compared to the typical Knowledge Network survey. First, the NFSS was fielded for a substantially longer period in order to increase participation among existing panelists. Knowledge Networks contacted former internet panel members for recruitment beginning in November 2011. According to study documentation, the survey participation rate was 62 % (12,756 survey responses out of 20,711) for current panel members and 22 % among former panelists (2302 responses out of 10,657 sampled); thus, the overall survey participation rate in the screener was 48 %.

Second, the NFSS used a screener that asked respondents whether either of their parents had ever had a "romantic relationship with someone of the same sex" while they were being raised at home. If respondents indicated that this had happened, they were asked a follow-up question about whether respondents had lived with parents while they were having a same-sex relationship. Of the 15,058 who completed the screener, a subset was selected to complete the full survey. The procedures here are not specific, but it would appear that the NFSS oversampled "unconventional" families and randomly sampled among those reporting two biological parents (i.e., labeled the "control" in study documentation). Presumably, NFSS included all respondents answering "yes" to the first question and randomly selected respondents answering "no" to the first question; this is not clear from the documentation. In total, 2988 respondents took the main survey; 236 of these respondents appear to have answered yes to the first question. By my calculation, 109 of these respondents reported living in a same-sex household for 4 months or more. It is not clear

what the attrition rate was between the screener and the main survey. Regnerus does not report an overall response rate.

Coverage The RDD was based on the universe of residential telephone numbers; the address-based sampling (ABS) utilized the U.S. Postal Service's Delivery Sequence File. The NFSS utilizes a fairly complete sampling frame.

Nonresponse The complex sampling approach of the NFSS raises a number of issues. First, the NFSS relies on fairly strong incentives to recruit panel members, particularly for those without internet service. A possibility here is that individuals without internet service may be highly motivated to participate, whereas individuals with internet service will not be. Consequently, there may be some sampling bias here. To the extent that this sampling bias is correlated with NFSS variables, then there may be bias. It is worth noting that this bias is likely to be somewhat controlled, since weighting procedures are likely to focus on demographic features as well as internet access.

Unit nonresponse is another issue in these data. With a survey completion rate to the screener at 48 %, I calculated the number of eligible, according to the survey documentation, as 3277; thus 91 % of those eligible, based on the screener, completed the main survey. Based on 2010 data and ABS recruitment, Brashears (2011) reported recruitment rates at initial contact and profile completion rates of 18.8 and 57.4 %, respectively. Thus, excluding panel attrition and assuming these 2010 figures are similar to Regnerus's rates in late 2011 and early 2012, then I estimate an overall response rate to be 4.7 % ($0.188 \times 0.574 \times 0.480 \times 0.91$). This is clearly a high level of unit nonresponse. Taken together, the possibility of biased sampling is clearly an issue.

Measurement and Coding Error A major criticism directed at Regnerus's (2012a) use of the NFSS data was his coding for family structure. Specifically, he constructed codes for respondents who had "lesbian mothers" (LM) and "gay fathers" (GF) based on any reported same-sex romantic relationship from birth until age 18, or until the respondent left their home. There are several things to note. This categorization utilizes a behavioral measure and reports it as an identity measure; it does not assess whether respondents lived with lesbian mothers or gay fathers; it ignores available information about respondents who lived in a same-sex household; and it includes other family statuses, such as single parents and divorced parents. He also constructed an "intact biological family" (IBF) category for those who lived with their parents from ages 0 to 18 *and* the latter were still married at the time of the interview. This excludes, intentionally, respondents who were raised by biological parents who divorced after the age of 18. He also constructed categories for heterosexual respondents raised in stepfamilies or by single parents, among others.

Regnerus focused his attention on comparing LMs and GFs against his IBF category, and not surprisingly, found significant differences on a host of outcomes. The problem, as noted by others (e.g., Sherkat 2012), is that not only do the LM and GF categories conflate same-sex relationships and family transitions, but the IBF category has been selected to reflect the most stable families. In his response to these criticisms, Regnerus (2012b) published more fine-grained analyses of the LMs, GFs, and nonIBFs, but maintained the IBF category. With the exception of comparing the problematic IBF category to LMs and GFs, Regnerus (2012a, b) only reports mean differences with no controls in either paper.

Based on this information, LMs who lived with their mothers' partners are quite similar to heterosexual respondents raised by single mothers. Table 1 reports 1 statistically significant difference out of 45 comparisons when comparing LMs to heterosexual respondents raised by single mothers, 6 out of 41 in Table 2, and 3 out of 33 in Table 3. Out of these 10 significant differences, 5 are in favor of LMs. Finally, it is worth noting that, similar to single mothers, more than 70% of mothers of LMs received welfare growing up.

A final issue, not raised previously, to the best of my knowledge, is the possibility of miscod-

ings by respondents, which has plagued Census estimates of same-sex households. Only 236 out of 15,038 respondents indicated that their parents had same-sex romantic relationships. If one were to assume that 0.5% of respondents miscoded their answers as "yes," then it could be possible that nearly 30% (75/248) of those coded as LMs or GFs are miscodes.

6.5 Conclusion

Research reports based on results of sex surveys rely on the assumption that survey error has been minimized. This review suggests that researchers have been quite successful in fielding sex surveys, but the careful attention to survey methods, which were a hallmark of the sex surveys of the 1990s, may have waned over the years. Indeed, the research trend may be heading towards increased use of nonprobability methods, especially given considerable interest in RDS and internet surveys. Certainly, the ability to match samples and use propensity weighting to make nonprobability samples more representative is quite seductive. Yet, these approaches have considerable risks, especially when post-hoc adjustments cannot fully account for the variables that researchers will eventually use. Thus the likelihood of biased samples is considerable.

In the context of probability samples, the total survey error approach of Groves et al. (2004) highlights the importance of vigilance throughout the data collection process. The probability-based internet survey did not fare well in this review. When very low response rates are obtained, questions about the representativeness of these data are legitimate. In contrast, the CHSLS and Add Health appear to be of high quality in terms of coverage and nonresponse, but all three appear to have measurement or coding error. This suggests the need for renewed attention to measurement issues when asking questions about sex.

Much of the research on survey methods in sex surveys is now more than a decade old. It may be time for assessing methodological issues of emerging techniques and revisiting the topic of measurement error. On the one hand, there is a need for evaluating strengths and limitations of sample matching and propensity weighting techniques in the context of internet surveys. Internet surveys will become more common, and I fully expect researchers to claim that their data are representative after employing weighting techniques and other *post hoc* adjustments. What is not clear is whether these techniques can adequately correct biases in the data for the many variables of interest. On the other, my review identified that measurement error is a persistent problem in sex surveys. A renewed effort to assess measurement error when asking questions about sex would be an important contribution going forward. Sex surveys are of considerable interest not only to researchers and policymakers, but also to the public. There is considerable demand for "sex factoids," including percentages of "this" and "that" and "risk factors." Because sex surveys play a key role in supplying these numbers, researchers may need to be more circumspect as long as the specter of survey error looms.

References

Add Health. (2014). The National Longitudinal Study of Adolescent to Adult Health. http://www.cpc.unc.edu/projects/addhealth/design/designfacts/index.html#samples. Accessed 31 Dec 2014.

Alexander, M. G., & Fisher, T. D. (2003). Truth and consequences: Using the bogus pipeline to examine sex differences in self reported sexuality. *Journal of Sex Research, 40*(1), 27–35.

Baker, R., Brick, J. M., Bates, N. A., Battaglia, M., Couper, M. P., Dever, J. A., et al. (2013). Summary report of the AAPOR task force on non-probability sampling. *Journal of Survey Statistics and Methodology, 1*, 90–143.

Black, D., Gates, G., Sanders, S., & Taylor, L. (2000). Demographics of the gay and lesbian population in the United States: Evidence from available systematic data sources. *Demography, 37*(2), 139–154.

Brashears, M. E. (2011). Small networks and high isolation? A reexamination of American discussion networks. *Social Networks, 33*(4), 331–341.

Brenner, P. S., & DeLamater, J. (2014). Measurement directiveness as a cause of response bias: Evidence from two survey experiments. *Sociological Methods & Research*. doi:10.1177/0049124114558630.

Catania, J. A., Gibson, D. R., Chitwood, D. D., & Coates, T. J. (1990). Methodological problems in AIDS behavioral research: Influences on measurement error and

participation bias in studies of sexual behavior. *Psychological Bulletin, 108*(3), 339–362.

Catania, J. A., Osmond, D., Stall, R. D., Pollack, L., Paul, J. P., Blower, S., et al. (2001). The continuing HIV epidemic among men who have sex with men. *American Journal of Public Health, 91*(6), 907–914.

Chang, L., & Krosnick, J. A. (2009). National surveys via RDD telephone interviewing versus the internet: Comparing sample representativeness and response quality. *Public Opinion Quarterly, 73*(4), 641–678.

DeLamater, J., & MacCorquodale, P. (1975). The effects of interview schedule variations on reported sexual behavior. *Sociological Methods & Research, 4*(2), 215–236.

Diamond, L. M. (2009). *Sexual fluidity: Understanding women's love and desire*. Cambridge: Harvard University Press.

DiBennardo, R., & Gates, G. J. (2014). Research note: US census same-sex couple data: Adjustments to reduce measurement error and empirical implications. *Population Research and Policy Review, 33*, 1–12.

Durex Sexual Wellbeing Survey. (2006). https://www.durex.com/en-lat/sexualwellbeingsurvey/methodology/pages/participantsselected.aspx. Accessed 31 Dec. 2014.

Ericksen, J. A., & Steffen, S. A. (2009). *Kiss and tell: Surveying sex in the twentieth century*. Harvard University Press: Cambridge.

Evans, A. R., Wiggins, R. D., Mercer, C. H., Bolding, G. J., & Elford, J. (2007). Men who have sex with men in Great Britain: Comparison of a self-selected internet sample with a national probability sample. *Sexually Transmitted Infections, 83*(3), 200–205.

Fan, X., Miller, B. C., Park, K. E., Winward, B. W., Christensen, M., Grotevant, H. D., & Tai, R. H. (2006). An exploratory study about inaccuracy and invalidity in adolescent self-report surveys. *Field Methods, 18*(3), 223–244.

Fenton, K. A., Johnson, A. M., McManus, S., & Erens, B. (2001). Measuring sexual behavior: Methodological challenges in survey research. *Sexually Transmitted Infections, 77*(2), 84–92.

Gile, K. J., & Handcock, M. S. (2010). Respondent-driven sampling: An assessment of current methodology. *Sociological Methodology, 40*(1), 285–327.

Groves, R. M., Fowler, F. J., Jr., Couper, M. P., Lepkowski, J. M., Singer, E., & Tourangeau, R. (2004). *Survey methodology*. Hoboken: Wiley.

Katz-Wise, S. L., Calzo, J. P., Li, G., & Pollitt, A. (2015). Same data, different perspectives: What is at stake? Response to Savin-Williams and Joyner (2014a). *Archives of Sexual Behavior, 44*(1), 15–19.

Kendall, C., Kerr, L. R., Gondim, R. C., Werneck, G. L., Macena, R. H. M., Pontes, M. K., et al. (2008). An empirical comparison of respondent-driven sampling, time location sampling, and snowball sampling for behavioral surveillance in men who have sex with men, Fortaleza, Brazil. *AIDS and Behavior, 12*(1), 97–104.

Kinsey, A. C., Pomeroy, W. B., & Martin, C. E. (1948). *Sexual behavior in the human male*. Philadelphia: WB Saunders.

Kinsey, A. C., Pomeroy, W. B., Martin, C. E., & Gebhard, P. H. (1953). *Sexual behavior in the human female*. Philadelphia: WB Saunders.

Laumann, E., Gagnon, J., Michael, R., & Michaels, S. (1994). *The social organization of sexuality: Sexual practices in the US*. Chicago: University of Chicago Press.

Lewontin, R. (1995, April). Sex, lies, and social science. *New York Review of Books, 42*(7), 24–29.

Li, G., Katz-Wise, S. L., & Calzo, J. P. (2014). The unjustified doubt of add health studies on the health disparities of non-heterosexual adolescents: Comment on Savin-Williams and Joyner (2014). *Archives of Sexual Behavior, 43*(6), 1023–1026.

Magnani, R., Sabin, K., Saidel, T., & Heckathorn, D. (2005). Review of sampling hard-to-reach and hidden populations for HIV surveillance. *AIDS, 19*, S67–S72.

Michaels, S. (2013). Sexual behavior and practices: Data and measurement. In A. K. Baumle (Ed.), *International handbook on the demography of sexuality* (pp. 11–20). New York: Springer.

Miner, M. H., Bockting, W. O., Romine, R. S., & Raman, S. (2011). Conducting Internet research with the transgender population: Reaching broad samples and collecting valid data. *Social Science Computer Review, 30*(2), 202–211.

Paik, A., & Sanchagrin, K. (2013). Social isolation in America: An artifact. *American Sociological Review, 78*(3), 339–360.

Regnerus, M. (2012a). How different are the adult children of parents who have same-sex relationships? Findings from the New Family Structures Study. *Social Science Research, 41*(4), 752–770.

Regnerus, M. (2012b). Parental same-sex relationships, family instability, and subsequent life outcomes for adult children: Answering critics of the new family structures study with additional analyses. *Social Science Research, 41*(6), 1367–1377.

Regnerus, M. D., & Uecker, J. E. (2007). Religious influences on sensitive self-reported behaviors: The product of social desirability, deceit, or embarrassment? *Sociology of Religion, 68*(2), 145–163.

Rosenbaum, J. E. (2006). Reborn a virgin: Adolescents' retracting of virginity pledges and sexual histories. *American Journal of Public Health, 96*(6), 1098.

Ross, M. W., Månsson, S. A., Daneback, K., Cooper, A., & Tikkanen, R. (2005). Biases in internet sexual health samples: Comparison of an internet sexuality survey and a national sexual health survey in Sweden. *Social Science & Medicine, 61*(1), 245–252.

Santelli, J. S., Lindberg, L. D., Abma, J., McNeely, C. S., & Resnick, M. (2000). Adolescent sexual behavior: Estimates and trends from four nationally representative surveys. *Family Planning Perspectives, 32*(4), 156–194.

Savin-Williams, R. C., & Joyner, K. (2014). The dubious assessment of gay, lesbian, and bisexual adolescents of add health. *Archives of Sexual Behavior, 43*(3), 413–422.

Schonlau, M., Zapert, K., Simon, L. P., Sanstad, K. H., Marcus, S. M., Adams, J., et al. (2004). A comparison between responses from a propensity-weighted web survey and an identical RDD survey. *Social Science Computer Review, 22*(1), 128–138.

Sell, R. L., & Petrulio, C. (1996). Sampling homosexuals, bisexuals, gays, and lesbians for public health research: A review of the literature from 1990 to 1992. *Journal of Homosexuality, 30*(4), 31–47.

Sherkat, D. E. (2012). The editorial process and politicized scholarship: Monday morning editorial quarterbacking and a call for scientific vigilance. *Social Science Research, 41*(6), 1346–1349.

Smith, T. W. (2003). An experimental comparison of knowledge networks and the GSS. *International Journal of Public Opinion Research, 15*(2), 167–179.

Stueve, A., O'Donnell, L. N., Duran, R., San Doval, A., & Blome, J. (2001). Time-space sampling in minority communities: Results with young Latino men who have sex with men. *American Journal of Public Health, 91*(6), 922.

Turner, C. F., Miller, H. G., & Rogers, S. M. (1997). Survey measurement of sexual behavior. In J. Bancroft (ed.), *Researching sexual behavior: Methodological issues* (pp. 37–60). Bloomington: Indiana University Press.

Udry, R. J., & Chantala, K. (2005). Risk factors differ according to same-sex and opposite-sex interest. *Journal of Biosocial Science, 37*(04), 481–497.

Van Haitsma, M., Paik, A., & Laumann, E. O. (2004). The Chicago health and social life survey design. In E. O. Laumann, S. Ellingson, J. Mahay, A. Paik, & Y. Youm (Eds.), *The sexual organization of the city* (pp. 39–65). Chicago: University of Chicago Press.

Weinhardt, L. S., Forsyth, A. D., Carey, M. P., Jaworski, B. C., & Durant, L. E. (1998). Reliability and validity of self-report measures of HIV-related sexual behavior: Progress since 1990 and recommendations for research and practice. *Archives of Sexual Behavior, 27*(2), 155–180.

Yeager, D. S., Krosnick, J. A., Chang, L., Javitz, H. S., Levendusky, M. S., Simpser, A., & Wang, R. (2011). Comparing the accuracy of RDD telephone surveys and internet surveys conducted with probability and non-probability samples. *Public Opinion Quarterly, 75*(4), 709–747.

Ethnography in a "Sexy Setting:" Doing Research in a New Zealand Massage Parlour

7

María Pérez-y-Pérez

7.1 Introduction

Over the last decades, social scientists have made significant contributions to the interdisciplinary study of sexuality. Some examples include: research on sexual consent (Burkett and Hamilton 2012; Powell 2010); teenage sexuality (Tolman 2002; Vares et al. 2011); the sociology of sexual stories (Plummer 1995); postmodern sexualities (Plummer 2003; Simon 1996); sexual politics and ethics (Besnier and Alexeyeff 2014; Carmody and Ovendon 2013); sexual practices and nonconformity (Broom and Tovey 2009; Gamson 1998; Newmahr 2008); heterosexism and heteronormativity (Frei 2012; Ingraham 2004); and prostitution (Brewis and Linstead 2000a; Ditmore et al. 2010; Weitzer 2009). Sexuality researchers have succeeded in producing knowledge in areas of public health and social policy, sexual behaviour, sexual functioning, and historical and ethnographic studies of sexual communities and cultures. Sexuality research has succeeded in challenging biomedical and essentialist discourses of early sexology, effectively asserting that sexuality is profoundly historical and social. However, this has not been without struggle to attain academic and professional legitimacy for this body of work, with researchers often encountering challenges in disseminating their research—experiencing censorship, limited funding sources, public controversy, and significantly, criticisms levied at methodological approaches and value of their work (Irvine 2014).

The often-overlooked work of early scholars in the Chicago School of Sociology proved to be the foundation of a radical approach to sexuality (Heap 2003). The studies undertaken provided the foundation for a radical new understanding of sexuality that emphasized the social context and meaning of sexual practices, rather than biological or essentialist discourses. They focused primarily on investigations of a wide range of "nonnormative sexualities," including prostitution, cross-racial sexuality and homosexuality. Most importantly, researchers at the Chicago School spoke out against the expectations of positivism that demanded a "scientific" and objective approach to inquiry. Instead they championed ethnographic methods to enable them to capture snapshots of the lives of men and women in the inner city. The School promoted active "field research" to study urban sexual practices and cultural constructions of sexuality, with the city as a social laboratory (Heap 2003, p. 465). This tradition of immersive research has since influenced the research methods of those who have studied marginalised sexualities, particularly through the use of small scale, intimate methodologies.

Empirical studies following the tradition of the Chicago School have managed to challenge the tired stereotypes associated with marginalized or controversial sexualities. Indeed, as a

M. Pérez-y-Pérez (✉)
School of Social and Political Science, University of Canterbury, Christchurch, New Zealand
e-mail: maria-victoria.perez-y-perez@canterbury.ac.nz

J. DeLamater, R.F. Plante (eds.), *Handbook of the Sociology of Sexualities,* Handbooks of Sociology and Social Research, DOI 10.1007/978-3-319-17341-2_7, © Springer International Publishing Switzerland 2015

subject of research, sexuality has been described as a broad social domain involving diverse fields of power, systems of knowledge, and sets of institutional and political discourses (Irvine 2003). Thus, new approaches/forms of empirical research have evolved to respond to changes in political/policy agendas, legislative reforms, and pedagogical shifts. For example, in sex work studies, research frameworks have included evaluation strategies of welfare and support services/activities (Wahab 2006) and of course, "what works" reports to assist in gaining knowledge for public health and safety (Ward and Day 1997) and "exiting" information (transition out of prostitution) (Oselin 2014). Further, qualitative studies drawing on ethnographic methods have provided in-depth explorations of sex workers' experiences and motivations (see McKeganey and Barnard 1996; Sanders 2005), and the extent of and response to violence against sex workers, particularly women (O'Connell Davidson 1998; Sanders 2001). Moreover, ethnographic studies in particular, have succeeded in providing the space for the voices of sex workers and their clients. Following this tradition of sex work research—I undertook two ethnographic studies to map the complexities and differences of sex work markets in a New Zealand city. Like researchers before me (Nencel 2001; Agustín 2005; Sanders 2006), I argue that ethnographic methods are the most fruitful means to enter, observe and participate in sex worlds so that we may trace and map accounts of sex work and sex work assemblages.

This chapter begins by reflecting on ethnography as a research approach/methodology in the social sciences and in particular, the evolving ethnographic strategies for researching sex worlds. I then proceed to discuss how ethnography has been undertaken within these settings, with a specific focus on sex work. The frameworks commonly used to study sex work have been fixed almost exclusively on the women who sell sex and increasingly the men who purchase services. In order to unpack and follow the complexities of sex work worlds, Agustín (2005) suggests that we approach commercial sex as culture rooted in everyday practices and systems, and thereby try to examine its intersec-

tions with everyday activities, institutions and social practices. With this in mind I present an example of assembling identity in a massage parlour. This "snapshot" of sex work presents my own approach to ethnography that draws together Agustín's (2005) proposal and the ethnographic strategies of Law (2004) and Actor Network Theory (ANT). This ethnographic approach can be applied to sex research in general to trace local sex worlds/cultures, networks, or subcultures. Moreover, a thorough acquaintance with the objects or artefacts that also inhabit sex worlds can help us to better understand and describe both the material and physical circumstances of sex worlds.

7.2 Ethnography and "Climbing into the Worlds of Participants"

Ethnography typically involves researchers spending extended periods of time in one or more settings recording what Murphy and Dingwall (2007) refer to as the "situated rationality of action" (p. 2224). Key to such recording has been to explore the ways in which, in a context, people's actions make sense, even when they seem to others outside the situation to be inappropriate or counter-productive, or simply mundane and irrelevant. Indeed, ethnographic studies of this sort have a long and distinguished history in sociological research. Classic examples of ethnographic studies include Goffman (1961) on mental institutions, Whyte's (1955) study of street corner life in a Boston "slum" area, Becker (1951) on professional dance musicians, Van Maanen's (1983) study of a London Metropolitan Police Department, and Gubrium's (1975), study of a residential care facility for the elderly. In this way, as Agar (2006) notes, the basic premise of using an ethnographic approach to research is that if you are interested in some corner of the world, "you climb inside it and spend time with its inhabitants" (p. 18). The researcher then, looks for connections or links among the diverse pieces of that world and between that world and other social worlds (see Agar 1996; Mattingly 2005; Kondo 1990, Strathern 1999).

At its best then, ethnography, has the power to richly communicate the complexity of human experience. Indeed, a mark of the skillful ethnographic researcher is the ability to observe/participate and record the lived complexities of the social worlds. We can argue then that the best ethnographies write about this in a way that offers up in-depth and detailed accounts of lived experience, the discourses that surround us, and the webs of meaning and relations that we weave ourselves. In studies of work for example, no other methodological approach has been more effective in uncovering the tacit skills, decision-making practices, the controversies and complexities, in other words, the activities that have been labeled routine, mundane, and trivial (see Glucksman 2000; Seymour and Sandiford 2005; Van Maanen 1992).

Recently, studies have increasingly explored and extended the scope or *gaze* of the ethnographic approach. Such studies emphasise the following and describing of actions, activities and relationships of the worlds we wish to understand or *peer into* (Latour 2005; Law 2004; Mol 2002). In this way, extending conventions of anthropological study, the researcher learns to trace, follow or map assemblages of human actors and non-human objects or *things,* and their centrality in the bringing together or the assembling of a phenomenon or action (see Law and Singleton 2013; Gherardi 2000; Star 1999). Thus, researchers have become increasingly interested in the roles performed by objects or non-human actors in everyday life worlds.

7.3 Ethnography and Sex Worlds

As ethnographers, what we learn from our observations and "hanging out" (see Murphy and Dingwell 2003) is different from the kind of information provided in response to interview questions. This is particularly pertinent for researchers of sex worlds in which participation has often meant immersion or "going native." Laud Humphreys' *Tearoom Trade* (1975) is an early example. Humphreys posed as a "watchqueen," or "lookout" in order to observe/document public sex among men. Though Humphreys' methodological challenges were straightforward, his strategies for solving them could be considered creative, and were highly criticized for their privacy violations and deceit (see Goodwin et al. 1991). Nevertheless, *Tearoom Trade* can be seen as a valuable contribution to interpretive social research into diverse sexual worlds. Like Humphreys (1975), Bolton's (1995, 1996) approach to ethnographic fieldwork (sexual participant-observation) further underlines the advantages of the researcher becoming a participant in a study rather than a passive observer. Bolton immersed himself in a particular gay community to experience and address the processes of adaptation and change towards issues such as AIDS. Like Humphreys' approach, Bolton's ethnographic research has also been considered unorthodox (see Wengle 1988). However, what is significant here, is that Bolton (1995) in his work, clearly highlights the inadequacy of "rapid assessment procedures" or more structured techniques of data collection, (focus group interviews, surveys and structured interviews) to provide insights and understanding into the behaviours and sexual practices of individual gay men with regards to HIV and AIDS.

Other less controversial studies in sex settings following the tradition of Humphreys (1975) and Bolton's (1995, 1996) active participation, are Frank (2002), Rambo Ronai (1998) and Wahab (2003), who not only conducted observations in strip clubs but also participated in these sex work venues as exotic dancers. They argue that to really understand the job and culture, it had to be lived. Similarly, Flowers (1998a) worked as a phone sex operator, positioning herself both as a worker and researcher in the phone sex market. In this way, she was able to gain access to informal networks and understandings of the phone sex market not normally accessible through interviews alone.

There are practical, ethical and personal aspects to fieldwork in sex settings. There are some sites of fieldwork where sexuality and sexual status are part of the everyday talk and activity. Further, the sexual dimension of the social setting can have implications for the conduct of fieldwork and the sexual engagement of the researcher, where sex and sexual activity are explicitly present (see Frank, Chap. 8, this volume). Examples include strip clubs (Frank 2002; Rambo Ronai 1998), brothels and massage parlours (Albert 2001; Pérez-y-Pérez 2003), streets designated as "redlight" areas (McKeganey and Barnard 1996), and sexual health clinics (Day and Ward 1990). As sex settings they structure the context of fieldwork. Everyday activities and conversations will include sex. Sex will be part of the vocabularies and routines of the setting and the fieldwork. As Coffey (1999) suggests, in such settings the sexual dimension informs and contextualizes the data and the personal fieldwork experience. Similarly, Agustín (2007) contends that, ethnographers "engage in situations that they don't define, delimit or control" (p. 140). As ethnographers, we occupy a precarious position in this kind of prolonged fieldwork.

Participant observation is key in the building of intimate knowledge as the researcher weaves herself/himself into the diverse worlds that constitute the research field (Perez-y-Perez and Stanley 2005). As researchers, we enter the homes, bedrooms, work spaces and private lives of the people we spend time with. It is this "entering" and "following" (Latour 1999), the discovery of connections (Agar 2006), and the stories and experiences research participants share with us that is crucial to the meanings and the findings we are able to describe (see Pérez-y-Pérez 2003; Stanley 1999; O Connell Davidson 1994). Thus, particularly in sexual settings, *participation* can raise a number of questions for researchers in terms of what exactly participation entails and means, and the consequences for those inhabiting these worlds (see O'Connell Davidson 2008; Perez-y-Perez and Stanley 2011; Frank, Chap. 8, this volume). As Hodgson (1999) contends, "what makes ethnographically based cultural critique so much richer—that is, our engagement with peoples as well as 'texts'—is what from another perspective makes it so problematic, in terms of the potential repercussions of our work for those we study" (p. 202). How the research is conducted and how data are collected are questions that are particularly relevant. Both personal and disciplinary ethics make us accountable in unique ways to the

people we study for the possible consequences of our work and writing—however intended or unintended.[1]

7.3.1 Getting into Sex Worlds

For sex work researchers, entry into sex settings has often entailed strategies to negotiate closed sex work environments through the collaboration with various gatekeepers, thereby overcoming initial hostilities, ambivalence or inaccessibility (see Sanders 2005; O'Connell Davidson 1998). Specific outreach projects have been the most prolific gatekeepers with their established and trusted ties with sex work industry markets and personnel (see Cooper et al. 2001; Day and Ward 2004; Matthews 1990). For example, McKeganey and Barnard (1996) used outreach/volunteer work as their points of entry as a means to observe and interact with street sex workers. Researchers have also aligned themselves with regulators in sex work markets (brothel owners, police, key informants, prostitute collectives/groups) in order to learn the local sex work context (see Eden 1997; Sterk 1996; O'Neill and Barberet 2000), sexual health clinics (Day and Ward 1990; Harcourt and Philpot 1990; Pyett 1996), attending court or probation centres, or accompanying police on their rounds (Benson and Matthews 2000; Sharpe 1998).

In order to pursue my study of sex work without the obligations attached to sponsored research, I chose to work in a massage parlour. Indeed, as a woman researching sex work, I had the potential for greater mobility within the sex work markets without the need for on-going sponsorship from a particular group or organisation (see Pérez-y-Pérez 2003). Like Becker's art worlds (Becker 1963), the sex industry, as I found out, primarily utilised informal networks and referrals or recommendations as a means for personnel

---

[1] For a detailed discussion of the implications of intimate ethnographies please refer to Pérez-y-Pérez and Stanley 2011.

recruitment.[2] Thus, it was from a chance conversation over drinks at the New Zealand Prostitutes' Collective (NZPC) Friday night gathering,[3] that I learned about the urgent need for a massage parlour receptionist/shift manager. Though I did not provide sexual services, I was nonetheless part of the massage parlour assemblage. As a shift manager/receptionist: I got to hold the condoms, oils, and lubricants; pass the towels and sheets; follow, listen and reflect with the people with whom I became inextricably linked. My embedding within my research worlds meant that I was able to follow and map the social organisation of sex work in all its complexities (O'Neill 1997). In particular, I could uncover/unpack and follow the configuration of networked actors that produced sex markets (Pérez-y-Pérez and Stanley 2005).

7.3.2 The Right "Currency:" Staying in Sex Worlds

As Barnard (1992) suggests, it is one thing to locate a study population but it is quite another to initiate the type of contact that enables the development of a good enough relationship that will enable the researcher to hang out and be part of the field. The development of "deep familiarity" (Goffman 1989), or "currency" (Pérez-y-Pérez and Stanley 2005) provides the researcher with a certain amount of "legitimacy" to move around the field and proceed to network. This is crucial in circumstances where the research subjects operate within illegal or legally ambiguous contexts and are stigmatised. My currency was based on multiple factors: being a woman, my age, being

what could be considered an "outsider" not simply in terms of sex work, but also in terms of the New Zealand context. Thus my Spanish/English background (accent, lack of local knowledge etc.), Latina/Spanish "looks"—provided a point of difference and a talking point. In addition, I entered the field as a novice in terms of practical sex work experience. Nevertheless, I shared with them the stigma associated with participation in sex work markets (see Perez-y-Pérez 2003).[4]

I needed actors to collaborate with me and allow my entry into their sex work worlds. Who was spoken to, the sites I was able to access, and the degree of candidness and issues spoken to were dependent upon the relationships I was able to build, and the nature of these relationships. Thus, like many researchers before me, I too established rapport and forged personal relationships—thus weaving myself into the diverse worlds that constitute the research field (see Bolton 1995; Perez-y-Perez and Stanley 2011; Rambo Ronai 1998). Trust is key for this currency to be viable, not only for the purpose of access into, but also mobility within and across markets particularly when studying legally compromised worlds (see: Nencel 2001; Sanders 2006; Barnard 1992). My willingness to assume and learn the role of massage parlour manager in order to understand the organisation of sex work allowed the women to position themselves as experts in relation to me, rather than as the passive observed. As Agar (1996) argues, when entering the field, the researcher essentially becomes the student in order to begin to understand, observe, and participate. Thus, the role of "apprentice" provides the researcher the opportunity to experience group interpretations of their daily realities. In addition, the willingness of the researcher to participate in the democratising process of "ap-

---

[2] I received three referrals from women—who then proceeded to recommend me. For further details see:Pérez-y-Pérez (2003). Discipline, autonomy and ambiguity: Organisations, markets and work in the sex industry, Christchurch, New Zealand. Unpublished doctoral thesis, University of Canterbury, Christchurch, New Zealand.

[3] I regularly attended the Friday night social drinks at the NZPC drop-in centre. This social gathering provided me with an opportunity to network with people involved with and active in the sex work markets.Attendees included: sex workers and clients, fellow researchers, NZPC volunteers, local and national government representatives, community and local NGO members, etc.

[4] I frequently encountered a level of suspicion and, occasionally, a certain amount of animosity when my "other" job was disclosed during conversations. My (then) partner, confessed that he had wondered if I would, or had been tempted to "give it a go," and that he had received constant harassment from his friends about my "role" at the massage parlour.It was common practice for sex workers to claim to be a *receptionist* to explain their presence in a massage parlour.

prenticeship" to the group can be critical in terms of group acceptance and the establishment of trust (Agar 1996; Punch 1993). The peculiarity of my apprenticeship was that I entered the industry as a manager.

My hybrid status as a worker/researcher provided me with experiences that had not been detailed by other researchers in the sex industry. As the manager of a massage parlour, I was positioned to understand the parlour as a business. This was my job, to coordinate the work of a parlour and present it to clients and the Police in such a way that it ran as a *normal* business. I had to operate competently in my job. My positioning as manager provided me with a new perspective on the world of sex work that also differed from the sex workers but at the same time placed me in constant proximity to them. I was fixed in place in my work but the others revolved around me. I mediated between the actors that made up the field (see Green, Chap. 3, this volume).

7.4   On Following Sex Work

I discovered, like Maher (2000) that "ethnography is a messy business" (p. 232). My fieldwork took place in the workplace, this meant that I carried out my daily tasks as a participant within the field—in my case a shift manager of a busy inner city massage parlour—alongside the activities of a researcher, following/observing/hanging out with diverse actors and keeping a research journal. Indeed, being part of the field meant that what, why and how I did what I did was just as important in the scheme of "massage parlour things."

Furthermore, my research and work took place within an uncertain context. Massage parlours operated as "quasi-legal" businesses,[5] though

many activities associated with sex work were criminalised (see Pérez-y-Pérez 2009).[6] Subsequently, fieldwork consisted of many activities that were both unstructured and uncertain as mobile/transient actors entered and left sex work networks and assemblages.

In spite of the potential "mess" of this methodological approach, I chose ethnography because I questioned the validity of research frameworks that begin with specific views at the outset, labeling the buying and selling of sexual services as deviance, victimization or violence. I wanted a theoretical space that would allow me to resist moralizing—moreover an approach that is considerate of Agustin's (2005) call to take a "cultural-studies approach" for researching sex work (p. 619). Thus, extending his suggestion to look at commercial sex as a culture, with a focus on the social actors and everyday practices involved in the sex industry, I include the non-human or material actors equally involved in the assembling of sex markets and practices. Though these actors often appear in accounts of sex in terms of "settings" (see Atkins and Laing 2012; Hammers 2009; Kaufman 2009), sex work practice (see Brewis and Linstead 2000a; Colosi 2010; O'Connell Davidson 1998) or the identity work of sex workers and researchers (see Coffey 1999; O'Connell Davidson 1994; Rambo Ronai 1998), such studies hint at the work that these non-human actors do and privilege human agency. Thus, ethnographic work that draws on an Actor Network Theory (ANT) toolkit recognizes and gives credit to "things" such as condoms, sex toys, towels, sheets, alcohol in the assembling of

---

[5] Following Brants' "regulated tolerance" (1998), "quasi-legal" in the New Zealand context combines elements of criminalisation (legislation regulating prostitution related activities), and informal regulatory arrangements of containment/surveillance. The Massage Parlours Act (1978) was an attempted organisational solution to facilitate increased surveillance of massage parlours, rather than to eradicate prostitution. Key to this approach was licensing

and registration practices (for a more detailed discussion see: Pérez-y-Pérez, 2003, 2009).

[6] Summary Offences Act 1981, 8.26, in which it is an offence to offer sex for money in a public place, but it is not an offence to offer to pay for sex. Crimes Act 1961: s.147, it is an offence to keep or manage a brothel; this involves the managing of rooms or any kind of place for the purpose of prostitution for one woman or more. s.148(a) it is an offence to live on the earnings of the prostitution of another person, this means that partners of sex workers could be committing an offence by being supported by their spouses. s.149, it is an offence for any person for gain or reward, to procure any woman or girl to have sexual intercourse with any male who is not her husband.

sex work. ANT encouraged me to embrace the "mess" of this social reality and resist editing and privileging social actors (see Law 2004).

7.4.1   Applying ANT Sensibility

The attraction of an *Actor Network Theory* (ANT) approach is that it attunes the researcher to new ways of asking questions, new ways of approaching research, analysis and writing (see Law and Singleton 2013; Mol 2002). For Law (2009), ANT provides,

> a disparate family of material-semiotic tools, sensibilities and methods of analysis that treat everything in the social and natural worlds as a continuously generated effect of the webs of relations within which they are located. It assumes that nothing has reality or form outside the enactments of those relations. Its studies explore and characterize the webs and the practices that carry them. (p. 141)

In this way, ANT can be viewed in terms of "tools," "sensibilities" and "methods of analysis" (Law and Singleton 2013). An ANT sensibility draws our attention to the numerous "everyday" ways that non-humans guide, enable and constrain social life (Latour 1993). We are encouraged to see the ways in which non-humans mediate everyday life, how they "transform, translate, distort, and modify the meaning or the elements they are supposed to carry" (Latour 2005, p. 39). As researchers, our task is to describe how human and non-human "assemblages" act together (Law 1992). We don't treat social and material actors as discrete and separate from one another; moreover, our attention is drawn to the work that they do together (Law 1994). Thus, it is not surprising that ANT has now been drawn upon by researchers in a variety of social science disciplines, mapping in their studies how humans and non-humans are actively involved in the making of social worlds (see Bruni 2005; Law and Mol 2002).

One of ANT's primary points of focus is on the world-building capacities of the actors themselves (see Latour 1999a; Latour 2005). ANT tells us that we are what we are by virtue of our associations (see Law 1994) in the ways that "our" identities, thoughts, and actions are produced and spread through people, things, situations, and structures (see also Jerolmack and Tavory 2014; Lave 1988). Here, "the idea is not that there are no differences between people and things, but that they are not and cannot be separated" (Nespor 2011, p. 2). Thus, we are able to move through different settings, use different objects and tools, and interact with other people in diverse ways, but we simply can't get outside such relations. However, this does not mean that non-humans are privileged over that of human actors.

A central term used in versions of ANT is that of the "assemblage." Law (1994) discusses how utilising the notion of the assemblage essentially reverses our conventional conceptions of agency. A person can be viewed as "an assemblage of different components, and therefore an effect of this particular arrangement" (Kerr 2010, p. 19). In this way, like Kerr's (2010) "gymnast assemblage," the sex worker can be referred to as the "sex worker assemblage" in recognition that the sex worker is an assemblage of a body + skills + condoms + sex toys + clothing etc. Through viewing sex work as a network of continuously shifting assemblages, the unstable nature of sex work can be revealed.

ANT researchers avoid imposing theoretical frameworks onto the data they collect. They argue against the traditional sociological method of beginning with a framework or theory before commencing fieldwork (see Latour 2005; Callon 1986; Law and Singleton 2005). For Latour (2005), this is considered to be taking an analytical short cut, and thereby failing to adequately trace the associations made between actors. Moreover, ANT avoids reductionist accounts of power and social structures such as ethnicity, class and gender, and looks for the unexpected forms of power and how these work (see Law and Singleton 2013, p. 496). Thus, by not relying on these structures to guide analysis, other lines of inquiry may be opened up. As Law and Singleton (2013) explain, ANT sensibility can still reveal these conventional types of power relationships, but it is also interested in "ethnographic surprises" (p. 500), and thus tries to illuminate other forms of power that may be at play. An ANT sensibility enables the tracing of unexpected forms of power and how these work to determine the shape of an activity.

Using ANT, I was able to trace the work that I did both *in* and *on* the social worlds that I inhabited—becoming part of a world of practices: the temporalities, the massage parlour setting, the friendships with co-workers, the techniques of sex work, the technologies of safe sex, the alcohol, the authority of the owner and police, the actions of clients, and so forth. Importantly, using an ANT sensibility focusing on working *in* the world and being sensitive *to* the world (see Ingold 2011), I was able to put aside notions about the character of actors and proceed to learn how actors become assembled in practices and their relations within these assemblages. The following sections provide small snapshots of *ethnographic surprises,* alluding to how *power* works/ is done in the assembling of the professional hooker and massage parlour manager.

7.4.2   Following Identity Work: Assembling the Manager

Identities are not simply given; fieldwork inevitably requires the researcher to undertake "identity work" (Coffey 1999). For ANT researchers, identities can be conceived of as multiple and shifting, and emerging through an assemblage of actors. To achieve a certain level of "fit" or acceptability was key to my ability to competently operate as a manager and circulate within the massage parlour network. In this way, identity work was both for my own sense of comfort, wishing to blend in, as well as to avoid enacting identities of difference that could impede building trust and rapport. Like many fieldworkers, my choice of clothing, demeanour, and speech constituted an important part of my impression management (see Coffey 1999; Hammersly and Atkinson 1995). As researchers, we locate our bodies alongside those of others as we negotiate the spatial context of the field (Coffey 1999). We concern ourselves with the positioning, visibility and performance of our own embodied self. This

is most easily illustrated in the context of a massage parlour where bodies are displayed, sexualised, disciplined, desired, shaped, touched and talked about.

Latour (1995) argues that we should learn from our participants, and in my case I am surprised at how much I was a *naïve inquirer.* I needed to consider the work undertaken by sex workers in assembling their identities, when bringing together actors to co-produce my fieldwork body. I thus paid attention to the actors I associated myself with when in the field. Despite elements of my identity aligning with many of those within the massage parlour (we were all women), much effort and learning was invested into presenting myself in terms appropriate to the setting. Often this was a matter of "hit and miss" as I experimented with the inclusion/exclusion of actors in my manager assemblage, such as shoes, makeup, clothes, perfume. Like Jerolmack and Tavory (2014), I observed and noted how clothing could shape social interactions and social identities. Further, they suggest that an individual's anticipations of other people's reactions shapes their choice in clothing, and as such can provide the materials to mold the social self in ways that set up desired social interactions. Through learning the norms and how to *be* in this setting, as well as the knowledge and skills to "carry this off," my personal style of manager evolved over time. The (re)actions, comments, complements of those within the field helped me in my choice of actor to invite into the assemblage of manager. In turn, actors within the assemblage were key in the enrolment of other actors. For example a "Wonderbra" required a low-cut top (or the other way around).

I was attentive to the "realities" of needing to able to present and perform in a certain style, in order to achieve routine acceptance of the actors within the field. I would certainly have seemed out of place amidst the sumptuous décor, furnishings, and lighting of the massage parlour in my *usual* choice of clothing.[7] Further, the cloth-

---

[7] I had a section in my wardrobe containing what I referred to as my *parlour clothes.* I invested in and applied dramatic make-up (rich red lipstick), a different perfume,

ing and arrangement of actors within the setting affected change in aspects of my posture, how my body moved and interacted. For example, I wore heels not solely for the purpose of aesthetics (make my legs look longer in an outfit) but importantly to perform authority.[8] Heels encouraged me to take stronger slower (purposeful) strides, increased my 5'2" height by 6", and enabled me to comfortably appear at the reception window at the front desk. Authority was also enacted through the presence of a large set of (master) keys and phones that I carried with me at all times. Similar to Allison's (1994) experience as a hostess in a Tokyo hostess club, I needed to establish the inaccessibility of my body to clients. Thus these *authority* objects worked to differentiate me from others within the setting. However, ANT reminds us too that non-human actors are not docile and can misbehave "acting back upon us in unexpected ways" (Jerolmack and Tavory 2014, p. 67). My heels, make-up, clothing, keys and phones did not always make me "bulletproof," as I learned on a couple of occasions.

I also learned to enact particular physical emotions and articulations, not only for the role of manager, but to *fit* into the setting. I learned to greet and engage clients, facial expressions of interest and engagement, and convey disapproval. I was able to piece together a repertoire for a manager learning the norms of different massage parlour settings, the knowledge and skills to "carry them off," and draw on my own workplace and life experiences. I learned through watching the women I worked with, and their relations to the actors within the setting, and from them I pieced together my own identity, just as any other worker introduced to this work context has to do.

7.4.3   Following Identity Work: Assembling the "Professional Hooker"

Through my own experience of assembling identity, I noted that like service work, a characteristic of sex work is the hybridity of the work and hybrid identities conceptualised in the workplace (Crang 1994; Sanders 2005). For Crang's (1994) service workers, hybridity is the bringing together of the ways in which service workers buy into the culture of their workplace,[9] as well as the cultural capital they bring. Similarly in a massage parlour such activities could be described as "personalised services." The key aim is the generation and retention of regular clients and the reputation of the massage parlour. Service work literature stresses the increasing importance of image, and the construction of a specific work identity; in turn this sets the service workers above or beyond other service workers (see Crang 1994). Massage parlour workers also sought to assemble identities that differentiated them from other sex work assemblages (street work, private escorts etc.). Such identities were aligned to notions of what was often referred to as being *professional*.

The general criteria for a "professional" or a "good sex worker" set out by massage parlour management do not differ greatly from that set out by employers in any other service work context: punctuality, reliability, efficiency, loyalty, and the ability to do the job proficiently (see Pérez-y-Pérez 2003). In addition, there are the expectations of healthy and safe work practices, and the formation of a regular client base. To unpack the *professional* massage parlour worker, saw me mapping the individual and collective work that went into producing this identity, and tracing the actors within this assemblage. One aspect of this work that I followed was boundary defining/setting.

The *professional* worker in the settings I inhabited required the enrolment of specific non-human actors. For example, Claudia talks about the importance she placed upon what she de-

---

and found myself browsing in stores I would not normally enter for my *parlour clothes.*

[8] There was no "bouncer" on the door to screen clients—this was up to me as manager/receptionist. I was required to "eject" unruly or difficult clients from the premises, to settle any disputes between workers and clients and between workers.I monitored behaviour of workers and clients within the massage parlour using a *bricolage* of methods.For further details see: Pérez-y-Pérez (2003).

---

[9] In Crang's (1994) study, this was a restaurant.

scribes as her *work kit*, that she aligned with a professional sex worker:

> [i]t is definitely important to have a good work kit. How could you not? Not having your own condoms and lube is just stupid, no, no. I used to see girls turn up to work without any condoms. It's not exactly hard to get yourself sorted out with what you need for work, you can buy condoms at any garage or dairy. I mean would a plumber turn up to work without his tools? (Claudia, parlour worker)

The condom, personal lubricant and tissues were central actors in a *work kit*. Further, health professionals and sex worker groups such as the New Zealand Prostitutes' Collective (NZPC) promoted the endorsement of these actors within the professional assemblage. However, Latour (1991) points out that identities can be reliant upon the associations an actor has built with other actors, and argues that identities are not fixed, as an actor can become involved in new networks, whereby an actor takes on new characteristics. Thus the *professional* identity can be disrupted when a sex worker moved onto another massage parlour with a less *professional* reputation—associated with sex work "bads" (disreputable actors and practices). For example, Claudia's *professional* reputation was questioned or compromised when she moved on, and became associated with the identity/reputation of another massage parlour.

In sex work literature, the management of a sex worker identity is often talked about in terms of sex workers maintaining boundaries between commercial and non-commercial lives (Phoenix 2000; Sanders 2005). Further, sex workers have been documented achieving some form of boundary definition through the use of discursive strategies/techniques, and importantly through the inclusion (or "use" in such accounts) of non-human actors to achieve a "distance" from the work, such as, nicotine, alcohol, marijuana, caffeine, amphetamines, and valium (see McKeganey and Barnard 1996; Phoenix 1999). Within the massage parlour setting, attempts were made to exclude, edit or "tinker with" (see Mol 2010) a number of these actors from the sex worker assemblage in order to enact *professional sexwork*. The result of this editing or tinkering is that certain realities are strengthened while others are weakened: some massage parlour practices are enabled, while others are constrained from being enacted. For example, marijuana and "hard drugs" were excluded from the massage parlour, and the purchase and consumption of alcohol on the premises was permitted, [10]albeit monitored.

ANT offers a different way to think about the compromises and dilemmas that take place between actors (Mol 2008; Mol et al. 2010). Compromise is not about one actor's wishes winning out over others—here the massage parlour management wishing to make a profit by selling alcohol and restricting the consumption by sex workers. Instead, as Mol (2008) found, compromise is about the tinkering that occurs so that actors may come together to produce a new assemblage that suits their diverse aims and needs. The presence of the bar and alcohol created a "gentlemen's club setting," along with the leather sofas, billiard table, music, lighting and soft furnishings. Having a drink helped to "break the ice," and maintain the *professional* or "upmarket" façade of the setting, adding to the reputations of both workers and massage parlour.

7.5 Conclusion

Sexuality researchers have the responsibility to avoid producing more of the same accounts, but rather to question or choose to research areas or topics that are often pushed to one side or ignored completely. A methodological approach that enables the detailed description of context and of the actors within sex settings will facilitate the challenge of stereotypes. Like many researchers before me, I had this in mind when I planned and undertook my research. I entered the field of research to better understand the organisation of sex work in a massage parlour. I sought to provide an insight into the complexity of relationships and arrangements within sex work networks.

My version of ANT offers a different form of ethnography of sex work, one that is interested

---

[10] The massage parlour had a licensed bar and I was a licensed bar manager.

in studying the assemblages of massage parlour work—how actors framed and configured their worlds. The following of the actors and avoiding the editing/tidying of their activities and narratives allowed me to capture the ways in which sex work was practiced and assembled. I was positioned in such a way that it made it possible to discover the field by connecting with its key actors or, rather, actors coming to me and then following actors (Latour 1987). By considering that both human and non-human actors mutually define each other I avoided reducing my account of sex work to that of the dyadic sex worker/client encounters. I was able to explore and participate, in the work undertaken to assemble particular identities. Moreover, by accepting that the researcher does not hold expert knowledge unobtainable to the participants themselves, I avoided the imposition of conventional social frames or structures. Instead, by taking an ANT approach, the focus was on how both human and non-human actors contribute to the development of social practice, meaning making and experience within the massage parlour.

ANT requires the researcher to trace webs of relations by following the actors and following actors' associations with other actors (Latour 1987). In this way, the researcher's own terms of reference may be redefined, and room is made for multiplicity, contradiction and ambivalence; that is, the mess of social realities. By opening what Latour (1987) refers to as "black boxes", and attending to how realities are enacted in practices, I was able to develop a different focus to massage parlour research to highlight the work of heterogeneous actors involved in producing sex work realities that are often sidelined/ignored in other accounts.

For sexuality researchers, an ANT approach can offer the researcher new ways of asking questions, and new ways to approach research, analysis and writing. ANT offers an alternative to current ethnographic strategies, making it possible to investigate the relationship between material and social actors (bodies) in order to understand how subjectivities are formed. An ANT sensibility enables the tracing of unexpected forms of power or "ethnographic surprises" and how these

work to determine or configure sexual activities, practices and identities. Moreover, following the interactions between actors enables the researcher to document complexities in the assemblages that would otherwise remain hidden.

References

Agustín, L.M. (2005). New directions: The cultural study of commercial sex. *Sexualities, 8*(5), 618–631.

Agustín, L.M. (2007). *Sex at the margins: Migration, labour markets and the rescue industry*. London: Zed Books.

Agar, M. (1996) *The professional stranger: An informal introduction to ethnography*. San Diego: Academic Press.

Agar, M. (2006). *Dope double agent: The naked emperor on drugs*. Lulubooks.

Albert, A. (2001). *Brothel: Mustang ranch and its women*. New York: Random House.

Atkins, M. & Laing, M. (2012). Walking the beat and doing business: Exploring spaces of male sex work and public sex. *Sexualities, 15*(5/6), 622–643.

Barnard, M. (1992). Working in the dark: Researching female prostitution. In H. Roberts (Ed.), *Women's Health Matters* (pp. 141–156). London: Routledge.

Becker, H. S. (1951). The professional dance musician and his audience. *American Journal of Sociology*, 136–144.

Becker, H. (1963). *Outsiders: Studies in the sociology of deviance*. New York: Free Press.

Benson, C., & Matthews, R. (2000). Police and Prostitution: Vice squads in britain. In R. Weitzer (Ed.), *Sex for Sale: Prostitution, pronography and the sex industry*. New York: Routledge.

Besnier, N., & Alexeyeff, K. (2014). *Gender on the edge: Transgender, gay, and other Pacific Islanders*. Honolulu: University of Hawaii Press.

Bolton, R. (1995). Tricks, friends, and lovers: Erotic encounters in the field. In D. Kulick & M. Wilson (Eds.), *Taboo: Sex, identity, and erotic subjectivity in anthropological fieldwork* (pp. 140–167). London: Routledge.

Bolton, R. (1996). Coming home: The journey of a gay ethnographer in the years of the plague. In E. Lewin and W.C. Leap (Eds.), *Out in the field: Reflections of lesbian and gay anthropologists* (pp. 147–168). Chicago: University of Illinois Press.

Brewis, J., & Linstead, S. (2000a). *Sex, work and sex work: Eroticizing organisation*. London: Routledge.

Brewis, J., & Linstead, S. (2000b). "The worst thing is the screwing:" Consumption and the management of identity in sex work. *Gender, Work and Organization, 7*(2), 84–97.

Broom, A, & Tovey, P. (2009). *Men's health: Body, identity and social context*. Chichester: Wiley-Blackwell.

Burkett, M., & Hamilton, K. (2012). Postfeminist sexual agency: Young women's negotiations of sexual consent. *Sexualities, 15*(7), 815–833.

Callon, M. (1986). Some elements of a sociology of translation: Domestication of the scallops and the fishermen of St. Brieuc Bay. In J. Law (Ed.), *Power, action and belief: A new sociology of knowledge?* (pp. 196–223). London: Routledge & Kegan.

Carmody, M., & Ovendon, G. (2013). Putting ethical sex into practice: Sexual negotiation, gender and citizenship in the lives of young women and men, *Journal of Youth Studies, 16*(6), 792–807.

Coffey, A. (1999). *The ethnographic self: Fieldwork and the representation of identity*. London: Sage.

Colosi, R. (2010). *Dirty dancing?: An ethnography of lapdancing*. New York: Willan Publishing.

Cooper, K., Kilvington, J., Day, S., Ziersch, A., & Ward, H. (2001). HIV prevention and sexualhealth services for sex workers in the UK. *Health Education Journal, 60*(1), 26–34.

Crang P. (1994). It's showtime: On the workplace geographies of display in a restaurant in southeast England. *Environment and Planning D: Society and Space, 12*(6), 675—704.

Day, S., & Ward, H. (1990). The praed street project: a cohort of prostitute women in London. In M. Plant (Ed.) *AIDS, Drugs and Prostitution*. London: Routledge.

Day, S., & Ward, H. (2004). *Sex work, mobility and health in Europe*. London: Kegan Paul.

Ditmore, M.H., Levy, A., & Willman, A. (Eds.) (2010). *Sex work matters: Exploring money, power, and intimacy in the sex industry*. London: Zed Books.

Eden, P. (1997). Sex industry worlds: Massage parlours, escort agencies, and the social organisation of sex work in Christchurch. Unpublished Master of the Arts, University of Canterbury, Christchurch.

Flowers, A. (1998a) *The fantasy factory: An insider's view of the phone sex industry*. Philadelphia: Pennsylvania University Press.

Flowers, A. (1998b). Research from within: Participant observation in the phone-sex work place. In J.E. Elias, V.L. Bullough, V. Elias, & G. Brewer (Eds.) *Prostitution: On whores, hustlers, and Johns* (pp. 390–395). New York: Prometheus Books.

Frank, K. (2002). *G-Strings and sympathy: Strip club regulars and male desire*. Durham: Duke University Press.

Frei, D. (2012). *Challenging heterosexism from the other point of view: Representations of homosexuality in queer as folk and the L word*. New York: Peter Lang.

Gamson, J. (1998). *Freaks talk back: Tabloid talk shows and sexual nonconformity*. Chicago: University of Chicago Press

Gherardi, S. (2000). Practice-based theorizing on learning and knowing in organizations. *Organization, 7*(2), 211–224.

Glucksmann, M. (2000). *Cottons and casuals: The gendered organisation of labour in time and space*. Durham: Sociology Press.

Goodwin, G. A., Horowitz, I. L., & Nardi, P. (1991). Laud Humphreys: A pioneer in the practice of social science. *Sociological Inquiry, 61,* 139–147.

Goffman, E. (1961). *Asylums: Essays on the social situation of mental patients and other inmates*. Garden City: Doubleday.

Goffman, E. (1989). On field work. *Journal of Contemporary Ethnography, 18*(2), 123–132.

Gubrium, J. F. (1975). *Living and dying at Murray Manor*. New York: St.Martin's Press.

Hammers, C. (2009). An examination of lesbian/queer bathhouse culture and the social organization of (im) personal sex, *Journal of Contemporary Ethnography, 38*(3), 308–335.

Harcourt, C., & Philpot, R. (1990). Female Prostitutes, AIDS, drugs, and alcohol in New South Wales. In M.A. Plant (Ed.), AIDS, *Drugs and Prostitution*. London: Routledge.

Heap, C. (2003). The city as a sexual laboratory: The queer heritage of the Chicago school, *Qualitative Sociology, 26*(4), 457–87.

Hobbs, D. (1993). Peers, careers, and academic fears: Writing as field-work. In D. Hobbs, & T. May (Eds.), *Interpreting the field: Accounts of ethnography* (pp. 45–66). Oxford: Clarendon Press.

Hodgson, D.L. (1999). Critical interventions: Dilemmas of accountability in contemporary ethnographic research. *Identities, 6*(2–3), 201–224.

Humphreys, L. (1975). *Tearoom trade, enlarged edition: Impersonal sex in public places*. New Jersey: Transaction Publishers.

Ingold, T. (2011). *Being alive: Essays on movement, knowledge and description*. New York: Routledge.

Ingraham, C. (2004). *Thinking straight: The power, the promise, and the paradox of heterosexuality*. New York: Routledge.

Irvine, J. M. (2003). The sociologist as voyeur: Social theory and sexuality research, 1910–1978. *Qualitative Sociology, 26*(4), 429–456.

Irvine, J.M. (2014). Is sexuality research "dirty work?" Institutionalized stigma in the production of sexual knowledge. *Sexualities, 17*(5/6), 632–656.

Jerolmack, C., & Tavory, I. (2014). Molds and totems: Nonhumans and the constitution of the social self. *Sociological Theory, 32*(1), 64–77.

Kaufman, M.R. (2009). "It's just a fantasy for a couple of hours:" Ethnography of a nude male show bar. *Deviant Behavior, 30,* 407–433.

Kerr, R. F. (2010). *Assembling high performance: An actor network theory account of gymnastics in New Zealand* (Doctoral thesis, University of Canterbury, Christchurch, New Zealand).

Kondo, D. K. (1990). *Crafting selves: Power, gender, and discourses of identity in a Japanese workplace*. Chicago: University of Chicago Press.

Latour, B. (1987). *Science in action: How to follow scientists and engineers through society*. Harvard University Press.

Latour, B. (1993). *We have never been modern*. Cambridge: Harvard University Press

Latour, B. (1999). *Pandora's hope: Essays on the reality of science studies*. Cambridge: Harvard University Press.

Latour, B. (2005). *Reassembling the social*. Oxford: Oxford University Press

Lave, J. (2011). *Apprenticeship in critical ethnographic practice*. Chicago: Chicago University Press.

Law, J. (1994). *Organizing modernity*. Oxford: Blackwell.

Law, J. (2004). After method: Mess in social sciences research. London: Routledge.

Law, J. (2009). Actor network theory and material semiotics. In B. Turner (Ed.), *The new Blackwell companion to social theory* (pp. 141–158). Malden: Blackwell.

Law, J., & Singleton, V. (2005). Object lessons. *Organization, 12*(3), 331–355.

Law, J., & Singleton, V. (2013). ANT and politics: Working in and on the world. *Qualitative Sociology, 36*, 485–502. doi:10.1007/s11133-013-9263-7

Law, J., & Mol, A. (Eds.) (2002). *Complexities. Social studies of knowledge practices*. Durham: Duke University Press.

Matthews, L. (1990). Outreach work with female prostitutes in Liverpool. In M. Plant (Ed.), *AIDS, drugs and prostitution* (pp. 76–87). London: Routledge.

Mattingly, C. (2005). Toward a vulnerable ethics of research practice. *Health: An Interdisciplinary Journal for the Social Study of Health, Illness and Medicine, 9*(4), 453–471.

Mol, A. (2002). *The body multiple: Ontology in medical practice*. London: Duke University Press.

Mol, A. (2008). The logic of care: Health and the problem of patient choice. London: Routledge.

Mol, A. (2010). Actor-network theory: Sensitive terms and enduring tensions. *Kölner Zeitschrift für Soziologie und Sozialpsychologie. Sonderheft, 50*, 253–269.

Mol, A., Moser, I., & Pols, J. (Eds.). (2010). *Care in practice: On tinkering in clinics, homes and farms*. Bielefeld: Transcript Publishers.

Murphy, E. A., & Dingwall, R. (2003). *Qualitative methods and health policy research*. New York: Aldine de Gruyter.

Murphy, E., & Dingwall, R. (2007). Informed consent, anticipatory regulation and ethnographic practice. *Social Science & Medicine, 65*, 2223–2234.

McKeganey, N., & Barnard, M. (1996). *Sex work on the streets: Prostitutes and their clients*. Buckingham: Open University Press.

Nencel, L. (2001). *Ethnography and prostitution in Peru*. London: Pluto Press

Nespor, J. (2011). Devices and educational change. *Educational Philosophy and Theory, 43*(s1), 15–37.

Newmahr, S. (2008). Becoming a sadomasochist integrating self and other in ethnographic analysis. *Journal of Contemporary Ethnography, 37*(5), 619–643.

Oselin, S. (2014). *Leaving prostitution: Getting out and staying out of sex work*. New York: New York University Press.

O'Connell Davidson, J. (1994). On power. Prostitution and pilchards: The self-employed prostitute and her clients. Paper presented at the 12th Annual Labour Process Conference 23–25 March, Aston, University of Birmingham.

O'Connell Davidson, J. (1998). *Prostitution, power and freedom*. London: Polity.

O'Connell Davidson, J. (2008). If no means no, does yes mean yes? Consenting to research intimacies. *History of the Human Sciences, 21*(4), 49–67

O'Neill, M. (1997). Prostitute women Now. In G. S. A. Scambler (Ed.), *Rethinking prostitution: Purchasing sex in the 1990s*. London: Routledge.

O'Neill, M., & Barberet, R. (2000). Victimization and the social organization of prostitution in England and Spain. In R. Weitzer (Ed.), *Sex For Sale: Prostitution, pornography, and the sex industry*. New York: Routledge.

Pérez-y-Pérez, M. (2003). *Discipline, autonomy and ambiguity: Organisations, markets and work in the sex industry*, Christchurch, New Zealand (Doctoral thesis, University of Canterbury, Christchurch, New Zealand).

Pérez-y-Pérez, M. (2009). "Doing it with the lights on:" The decriminalisation of New Zealand sex work. *The International Journal of Interdisciplinary Social Sciences, 4*(8): 139–152.

Pérez-y-Pérez, M., & Stanley, T. (2005). Researching sex: "Getting our hands dirty." *Social Work Review, 17*(4), 30–38.

Pérez-y-Pérez, M., & Stanley, T. (2011). Ethnographic intimacy: Thinking through the ethics of social research in sex worlds. *Sociological Research Online, 16*(2), 13.

Phoenix, J. (1999). *Making sense of prostitution*. Basingstoke: Palgrave.

Phoenix, J. (2000). Positive identities: Men money and violence. *British Journal of Criminology, 40*, 37–55.

Plummer, K. (1995). *Telling sexual stories: Power, change and social worlds*. New York: Routledge.

Plummer, K. (2003). Queers, bodies and postmodern sexualities: A note on revisiting the "sexual" in symbolic interactionism, *Qualitative Sociology, 26*(4), 515–530

Powell, A. (2010). *Sex, power and consent: Youth culture and the unwritten rules*. Melbourne: Cambridge University Press.

Punch, M. (1993). Observation and the police: The research experience. In M. Hammersley (Ed.), *Social research: Philosophy, politics and practice*. London: Sage Publications in association with The Open University Press.

Pyett, P. M. (1996). Who Works in the Sex Industry? A Profile of female prostitutes in Victoria. *Australian journal of public health, 20*(3), 431–433.

Rambo Ronai, C., & Cross, R. (1998). Dancing with Identity: Narrative resistance strategies of male and female stripteasers. *Deviant Behaviour: An Interdisciplinary Journal, 19*, 99–119.

Sanders, T. (2001). Female street sex workers, sexual violence, and protection strategies. *Journal of Sexual Aggression, 7*(1), 5–18.

Sanders, T. (2005). *Sex work. A Risky business*. Cullompton: Willan.

Sanders, T. (2006). Sexing up the subject: Methodological nuances in researching the female sex industry. *Sexualities, 9*, 449–468.

Seymour, D., & Sandiford, P. (2005). Learning emotion rules in service organisations: socialisation and training in the UK public-house sector. *Work, Employment and Society, 19*(3), 547–564.

Sharpe, K. (1998). *Red light, blue light: Prostitutes, punters and the police.* Aldershot: Ashgate Publishing Ltd.

Simon, W. (1996). *Postmodern sexualities.* New York: Routledge.

Sterk, C. (1996). Prostitution, drug use, and AIDS. In C. D. Smith, & W. Kornblum (Eds.), *In the field: Readings on the field research experience.* Westport: Praeger.

Stanley, T.W. (1999). *Positive sex and risk: social and sexual negotiation with HIV* (MA thesis, University of Canterbury, Christchurch, NZ).

Star, S.L. (1999). The ethnography of the infrastructure. *American Behavioral Scientist, 43*(3), 377–91.

Strathern, M. (1999). *Property, substance and effects: Essays on persons and things.* New Brunswick: Athlone Press.

Tolman, D. (2002). *Dilemmas of desire: Teenage girls talk about sexuality.* Cambridge: Harvard University Press.

Van Maanen, J. (1983). The fact of fiction in organizational ethnography. In J. Van Maanen (Ed.), *Qualitative methodology* (pp. 37–55). Beverly Hills: Sage.

Van Maanen, J. (1992). Drinking our troubles away: Managing conflict in a British policy agency. In D. M. Kolb, & J. M. Bartunek (Eds.), *Hidden conflict in organisations: Uncovering the behind-the-scenes disputes* (pp. 32–62). London: Sage

Vares, T., Jackon, S., & Gill, R. (2011). Preteen girls read "tween" popular culture: Diversity, complexity and contradiction, *International Journal of Media & Cultural Politics, 7*(2), 139–154.

Wahab, S. (2003). Creating knowledge collaboratively with female sex workers: Insights from a qualitative, feminist, and participatory study. *Qualitative Inquiry, 9,* 625–642.

Wahab, S. (2006). Evaluating the usefulness of a prostitution diversion project. *Qualitative Social Work, 5*(1), 67–92.

Ward, H., & Day, S. (1997). Health care and regulation: New perspectives. In G. Scambler, & A. Scambler (Eds.), *Rethinking prostitution* (pp London: Routledge.

Weitzer, Ronald (2009). Sociology of sex work. *Annual Review of Sociology,* 35 (1): 213–234.

Wengle, J.L. (1988). *Ethnographers in the field: The psychology of research.* Tuscaloosa: University of Alabama.

Whyte, W. F. (1955). *Street comer society.* Chicago: The University of Chicago Press.

Observational Methods in Sexuality Research

8

Katherine Frank

Research methods are ideally value-neutral—that is, each method is a potential means of gathering information about the world—but researchers develop "favorites" and academic disciplines value certain methods over others. The study of human sexuality often requires a researcher to work across disciplinary boundaries, however, and to deploy multiple methods. In my own research, I have used observation, participant observation, multiple in-depth interviews with each participant, one-time interviews, surveys, case studies, archival research, and so on. Each method, I have come to believe, has strengths and weaknesses. We should choose our methods not on tradition ("everyone in anthropology does ethnography" or "if you don't collect quantitative data, no one will take you seriously in sociology") but for their appropriateness for the questions being asked, the research setting, and each researcher's traits, skills, and personality.

Many researchers have noted the difficulty in obtaining data on human sexual behavior (Berk 1995; Orbuch 1991; di Mauro 1995). Social stigmas and taboos influence how willing individuals are to talk about their practices, and sexual behaviors have a significant fantasy component as well as being shaped by personal histories, remembered or not. Specific challenges further arise when using observation in the study of sexuality.

Much actual sexual behavior occurs in private; an observer would change the nature of the encounter. Thus, while social scientists can observe people's self-presentation (*How do people signal erotic interest?*), mate choices (*Do women tend to marry men who are taller than themselves?*), or negotiations before sex (*How do potential customers approach sex workers on the street?*), many aspects of sexual behavior cannot easily be observed. Sex can potentially be witnessed in sex clubs or bathhouses, although these venues present their own challenges and limitations.

Still, when carried out skillfully and under the right conditions, observation can generate extensive insight into human sexual behavior. Observational methods in sexuality research are discussed here from this perspective—as one tool in a toolkit for understanding sexual behavior. First, I differentiate between ethnography, participant observation, and observation, because these terms are sometimes conflated. Next, the core components of observation—perception and interpretation—are discussed in terms of research undertaken by human observers. Consideration of the researcher as part of the process of knowledge construction thus emerges as central to debates about the use of observational methods. The historical roots of the tension between insider and outsider perspectives are explored next, and I argue that *all* researchers should practice *reflexivity*, or a self-conscious awareness of how who we are affects what we see and believe about the world. The later sections of the chapter are concerned with the practical decisions facing researchers using observational

K. Frank (✉)
Department of Sociology, American University,
Washington, DC 20016, USA
e-mail: katherinefrank@mac.com

J. DeLamater, R.F. Plante (eds.), *Handbook of the Sociology of Sexualities,* Handbooks of Sociology and
Social Research, DOI 10.1007/978-3-319-17341-2_8, © Springer International Publishing Switzerland 2015

methods, as well as a few of the ethical issues associated with research on human subjects: overt versus covert research and a researcher's sexual participation in the field.[1]

To discuss the interactive and participatory elements of interviewing would require another chapter; however, some of the same concerns about insider/outsider statuses, identity, objectivity, reflexivity, and so on remain salient in those discussions.

8.1 Ethnography, Observation, and Participant Observation— Clarifying the Terms

Unfortunately, the terms "ethnography," "observation," and "participant observation" are often used as if they are interchangeable with each other, or without enough specificity.

Ethnography is systematic and holistic research on a given society or in a specific locale, conducted by an individual or a team. Although ethnographic research is premised on the idea of "fieldwork"—the researcher gains first-hand knowledge by living, working, or studying in a particular place for a period of time, often more than a year—data are usually collected through multiple methods in such projects. (Some researchers use the term "fieldwork" to denote any research that takes place in a "field," or somewhere other than a laboratory, although such studies are not always ethnographies). Observation and participant observation are methods that can be used in ethnographic research—and probably cannot be avoided, to some extent in field research—although they can be deployed in other types of studies as well. Ethnographers observe behavior as they interact with people at their field sites, but they may also collect data by drawing charts and maps, photographing or videotaping events, examining historical documents, recording physiological measurements, or conducting focus groups, surveys, or interviews. The term ethnography may sometimes also refer to the end product of such multi-method investigation—the analysis and representation of the data with the aim of offering holistic understanding of a setting. To simply claim that one is "doing an ethnography" is thus imprecise and vague.

Observation, in the broadest sense, concerns the collection of visual data, although the other senses also contribute information. Visual data becomes meaningful through processes involving both perception and interpretation—what a researcher *sees*, or thinks she sees, and the meanings and explanations used to make sense of it.

Observation is used in many types of studies, and can generate quantitative or qualitative data, descriptive narratives, and further research questions. Some information is difficult to attain *except* through observation. Researchers may want to understand how encounters or negotiations between individuals unfold; observation can provide greater perspective and context than asking questions of individuals. Observations of people's nonverbal behavior in specific situations can also provide information that may be difficult or impossible for them to vocalize. People do not always know *why* they do the things they do; sometimes, they do not even know *what* they are doing. Further, as there is often a discrepancy between what people say they do and what they actually do, observation can shed light on these inconsistencies.

Experimental observation allows researchers to manipulate an environment and to record and analyze participant responses, as in a laboratory. Experimental observations can be conducted on animals or humans. In the 1800s, a researcher used a glass tube shaped like a penis to observe women masturbating to orgasm in a laboratory; his observations supported the belief that women's orgasms resulted in physiological changes (Bullough 1995). *Naturalistic observation* refers to observing animals or people in everyday environments or without using experimental interventions. Naturalistic observation opens up many social situations to possible study, especially those occurring in public or semi-public places.

Observations can be *structured*, where the focus is on counting behaviors or assessing a

---

[1] Some of the material in these sections is adapted from an appendix in Frank, K. (2013) Plays Well in Groups: A Journey Through the World of Group Sex. Rowman & Littlefield Publishers, Inc.

particular variable, or *unstructured*, where as much as possible about the scene is recorded. Researchers have conducted structured observations when observing women's "flirting behaviors" (Moore 1985), customer tipping behavior in strip club patrons (Brewster 2003), or negotiations between potential clients and street prostitutes, for example. Depending on the field site and the questions being asked, researchers may use sampling strategies or alternate the hours of the day or night at which they observe. Unstructured observations do not necessarily have such parameters, but can lead to important and even unanticipated insights. Teela Sanders (2004) conducted 10 months of research with female sex workers in the UK during 2000 and 2001 to study their perception and management of occupational hazards. In addition to interviews, she socialized with sex workers informally and kept field notes. Sanders (2004) recorded instances where she became the "butt of the joke" in a room full of workers; as time went on, she was included in the women's humor. When she reflected on the pervasiveness of joking, sarcasm, and practical gags in this environment, she came to understand humor as a social and psychological distancing technique: a way for sex workers to manage emotions about clients, create supportive networks, and communicate important information to each other, such as how to defend themselves in an attack (Sanders 2004). Humor was not something she had set out to study, but her observations revealed its importance in this social setting.

Sometimes observation is preferable over other methods for ethical reasons. It would be extremely difficult, even unethical, to study some risky, dangerous, or aggressive behaviors in a laboratory or to provoke individuals in a naturalistic setting. Graham et al. (2014), for example, were interested in aggression during male-female interactions, especially during sexual advances, so they conducted observational research in nightclubs. They watched from different locations in the clubs, and recorded participants' gender, intoxication level, the intent of interactions that occurred, and the responses of third parties. They observed 258 aggressive instances, 90 % of which involved male initiators and female targets.

The term *participant observation* is used in a variety of ways, from indicating that a researcher lived among the people being studied to suggesting that the researcher was an on-going participant in that group's activities or way of life to varying extents. Unfortunately, despite this variation in choices that researchers make about how they conduct observations and interact with others at their field sites, "participant observation" is sometimes used loosely to describe any field study. Philosophically, of course, any observer of human behavior is also at some level a participant simply by being present, regardless of how unobtrusive he attempts to be. Even a sociologist sitting in a Starbucks and logging whether men or women are most likely to order fancy coffees, for example, is still a social actor. Other people may ignore him, engage him, wonder what he is writing, or frown at him for taking up space, but his presence could theoretically alter people's behavior. He is also a participant in that his observations are filtered through who he is as a person—his research will reflect his perspective rather than an unadulterated "reality." Methodologically, however, researchers must decide exactly how to engage with individuals at their field sites, and how to handle the specific practical and ethical issues arising out of that decision. Researcher intention does matter, and how much one is willing or able to participate in a social setting can potentially impact one's data collection and analysis—*or not*. How much one is willing or able to participate may also have ethical implications. Rather than using "participant observation" as a vague catchall phrase, researchers would be better served by revealing the specifics of the extent and purpose of their participation *and* their observation.

8.2 Seeing Is Believing—Or Is It?

Have you noticed how nobody ever looks up? Nobody looks at chimneys, or trees against the sky, or the tops of buildings. Everybody just looks down at the pavement or their shoes. The whole world could pass them by and most people wouldn't notice.—Julie Andrews Edwards, The Last of the Really Great Whangdoodles

As with all research methods, observational methods have limitations. Human observers are prone to numerous biases, some of which are particularly relevant to observation. Some biases are the result of human cognitive limitations, while others arise from "deep-seated personal, social, economic, or political interests and values" (Poland and Caplan 2004, p. 9). Some researchers are more skilled than others at observation; techniques for improving one's observational skills exist but are rarely taught in graduate schools. Some critics argue that observational research is ultimately flawed because of the potential multiple sources of error. Other scientists believe that there is never an unbiased or truly objective position from which to conduct research, and instead emphasize that the researcher should be seen as a *tool*: When we understand how these limitations—cognitive and otherwise—affect our research, we can mitigate their effects and use them to further develop our understanding.

Human observers are necessarily imperfect. We are visually gifted compared to some animals—we laugh when our dog can't find a treat on the floor in front of his nose—but the range of our vision and our attention to detail is relatively pathetic in comparison to other species. We cannot properly "see" certain things without technological interventions, whether a microscope, MRI machine, or computer simulations. Ducks initially appeared to be sexually monogamous to biologists, who observed the same male/female adult pairs each mating season, later followed by broods of wobbly ducklings. But when researchers began using DNA testing to determine the paternity of the chicks, they realized it was necessary to distinguish between social and sexual monogamy (Birkhead 2002). Because perception is necessarily coupled with the process of interpretation, observations can be tinged with ethnocentrism, racism, sexism, heterosexism, classism, cultural ideologies, and power relations. In the 1600s, early sex researchers reported seeing distinctly male or female sperm with a microscope, or that the sperm of a donkey looked like a miniature donkey (Bullough 1995). Early sex research on masturbation and homosexuality in humans was marked by a tendency to view these practices as unhealthy or even pathological; when the cultural climate changed, the science changed as well—one study at a time.

Selective perception, or the tendency to pay more attention to the things that one expects or wants to see, is an example of a cognitive limitation that can impact social science research. Starting in infancy, humans unconsciously filter out some stimuli while attending to other patterns and details. By allowing us to tune out seemingly extraneous sensory information, this tendency frees us up to perform complex mental tasks—but at the same time, it can make us "blind" to other aspects of our environments. According to experimental psychologist Daniel Simons (Simons and Chabris 1999), what we see when we look around us appears to be a stable and continuous world, but is actually an illusion, dependent on perspective and on interpretation. Sometimes, we see *only* what we expect to see in a given setting or interaction—and anyone who doubts this should try their hand at his famous "selective attention test:" https://www.youtube.com/watch?v=vJG698U2Mvo). In this experiment, subjects were asked to count how many times a basketball was passed between players. Subjects focused so intently on the task that most failed to notice an adult in a gorilla suit who ambles through the middle of the basketball court, beats his chest, and then leaves. For researchers, selective perception might result in focusing more attention on certain types of individuals than others when recruiting subjects or recording data—basketball players rather than gorillas, for example—or only "seeing" the behaviors that they are interested in.

Numerous techniques exist for mitigating the impact of selective perception on research. Perspective matters, and observers may focus on different things in the same setting. Multiple observers can thus be used, who then compare data. Dates and times of observations can be randomized, or at least spread across the known spectrum of possibilities, to obtain a fuller picture of an environment. A researcher would gain a better understanding of campus dormitory life, for example, if he observed in the hallways as well as the cafeteria, and at 3 a.m. in addition to the daylight hours. As information supporting our own theories, beliefs, or expectations is also more readily *remembered*, sometimes resulting in confirmation bias (an issue that is not unique to observation), researchers often document their observations and then develop coding systems to analyze their data.[2] Fieldnotes or observation logs can help with both the recording of detail and recall; audio and video recording can further preserve events and encounters for repeated viewing.

Sometimes, biases arise in observational research because behavior is defined or produced in such a way as to make it more likely to observe. When scientists believed that male rats controlled the mating process, for example, they defined sexual receptivity in female rats as adoption of the lordosis position—arched back, tilted hips—or allowing a male rat to mount. They also designed studies likely to produce this behavior by using small experimental cages where, as one researcher suggested, "a temporarily resistant female" was "deprived of corners in which she can crouch and prevent the male's mounting response" (Beach 1938, p. 358). When rats were observed in these small, barren cages, researchers confirmed that female rats passively assumed the lordosis position when a male rat was introduced, doing little else to either thwart or court him. But when a pair of researchers observed rats in a more "spacious, semi natural setting," they found female rats engaged in multiple solicitation behaviors— making the initial approach, then "grooming, crawling over the male's head, or presenting her hindquarters (in the case of an unresponsive male)" or running away with a "dart-hop gait" or a "stiff-legged run" (Strum and Fedigan 2002, p. 282). The small cages used previously were not conducive to seduction, playing "hard to get," or even to female avoidance.

When studying humans, researchers are often limited to convenience samples, for both practical and ethical reasons, and have fewer opportunities to manipulate the environment to produce

certain behaviors, especially when it comes to sex. We cannot always see what we want to see in naturalistic environments either. People may change their behavior when they think they are being watched, especially if they are engaging in stigmatized practices. Much relevant behavior occurs relatively out-of-sight of researchers. Some enclaves where sexual activity takes place have few barriers to entry, while others erect multiple road-blocks—cover charges, membership requirements, participation rules, and so on. More research has been done on bathhouses and sex clubs than on sex parties in private homes, for example. Sociologist Charles Moser (1998) wrote retrospectively about his visits to BDSM parties, some of which were held in private homes and others in commercial spaces, to describe the rules and expectations of participants. His access to the private parties was premised on the fact that he had been interacting with the community for 25 years. Researchers must be cautious not to generalize if their access to "backstage" or diverse environments was limited.

Some populations are more visible than others, something that must be taken into account in study designs and in analyses of the data that is collected. Anti-prostitution activist and researcher Melissa Farley (Farley et al. 2004) conducted research on sex workers and found that 68 % suffered from Post Traumatic Stress Disorder. Farley's work has been criticized, however, because her sample was composed of the most visible and accessible sex workers—street or brothel workers rather than those seeking customers online— or the most marginalized populations, such as those seeking community services. Her finding of high rates of PTSD, then, may have been due to poverty, stigmatization due to their visibility, vulnerability to client violence, and police harassment rather than to the act of exchanging sex for money. Farley et al. (2004) administered psychological instruments to participants and did not rely on observation alone to collect data, but her sample suffered from sampling bias, where subjects recruited for a study are not representative of the entire population in question.

Each of us is a particular race, class, gender, and sexuality; these social positions impact our

---

[2] Confirmation bias can also occur in other ways, as when behavior is defined, or studies are designed, in such a way that the behavior of interest is more likely to be observed.

perceptions and interpretations. Gender identification bias, which has been revealed in both
animal and human studies, can lead to male and
female researchers observing different behaviors
or interpreting those behaviors differently. Biologist Sarah Hardy's (2000) work on primates challenged prevailing beliefs that only male mammals were non-monogamous by arguing that
promiscuity might have an adaptive advantage
for females. Perhaps because male scientists focused more intently on male primate behaviors,
and perhaps also because beliefs in female monogamy and male promiscuity were so culturally
salient, male scientists had missed significant female primate mating behaviors *and* failed to interpret the behaviors they did observe as part of a
unique evolutionary strategy.

Community members draw on a system of
shared meanings that is not immediately apparent to researchers and can further affect observational data. While researching swinging in the
United States, I noted that some academics and
journalists reported witnessing "barebacking," or
penetration without a condom, when visiting sex
clubs, something usually interpreted as "unsafe
sex" and disturbing from a public health perspective. This observation did not fit with my experiences as a participant and observer in the lifestyle
community, what I had learned conducting interviews with swingers, or what I had witnessed
in sex clubs. Lifestylers, I had come to believe,
were very cautious about avoiding STDs and
barebackers were forcefully stigmatized. So what
could account for the discrepancy? Upon reflection, I realized I was using the more nuanced definitions of sex that I had come to take for granted. Lifestylers referred to unprotected sex with
outside partners as barebacking. But, similar to
married or committed couples more generally in
the US, they did not refer to condomless sex with
a spouse (or primary partner) as barebacking,
"unsafe," or even "unprotected." Further, even
though lifestylers allow recreational sex with outside partners, emotional monogamy tends to be
highly valued and presenting as a strong couple
is important. Condomless sex between primary
partners at clubs, events, and parties was often
expected as one way to demonstrate commitment

and the specialness of that relationship. Swingers' clubs often post rules requiring condom use
during intercourse, but condoms are not expected
between committed partners who do not use them
at home. Here, then, the same act—penetration
without a condom—means completely different
things depending on the relationships of the individuals involved. In fact, this distinction affected
my interpretations of the behavior *as I perceived
it*. I hadn't witnessed barebacking, but I *had* witnessed penetration without a condom between
committed partners. Does it matter?

It depends, of course, on the question.

8.3 Insiders and Outsiders: A Brief History

We don't know who discovered water, but it wasn't
a fish.
—Anonymous

Don't judge a man until you have walked a mile in
his shoes
—Native American proverb

The idea that fish would never discover water exemplifies the value of an outsider's perspective—
a detached, or distanced, observer can notice
things that are so customary or essential to a practice or way of life that they are taken for granted
by participants. On the other hand, an insider's
perspective is also valuable—by "walking a mile
in his shoes," we believe we can at least begin
to grasp another's subjective reality. Some social
scientists refer to these perspectives as "emic" and
"etic," contrasting them in a variety of ways: en-
gaged/detached; local/global; particular/univer-
sal; insider/outsider, "ground up"/"top down" or
"subjective"/"objective."[3] Sometimes, emic and
etic perspectives become associated with particular research methods, theories, or academic disciplines, with one view privileged as more accurate
or essential than the other; other times, researchers attempt to strike a balance between them.

---

[3] The terms emic and etic may be used slightly differently
across fields, and are deployed across fields from marketing to counseling to social science research.

A brief discussion of the history of the tension between insider and outsider perspectives is necessary, as this history influences methodological decisions made today and the philosophical debates surrounding them.

Anthropology developed during an historical period marked by widespread colonialism, when distinctions between "civilized" and "primitive" became loaded with meaning. Supposedly "primitive" cultures were often idealized—as more natural or peaceful, for example (Shangri-La)—or denigrated—as childlike or inferior. Understanding native cultural groups was important to Western European colonizers for multiple reasons, including being able to better control the populations and support theories of racial hierarchy. Participant observation developed hand-in-hand with ethnography in this early anthropology. In the nineteenth and early twentieth centuries, anthropologists wanting to study native cultures would often live in those communities at length. In addition to conducting their "official" academic inquiries—which could include taking physical measurements, charting kin relations, or performing psychological experiments—early fieldworkers thus also necessarily became social actors, though to different extents. They learned native languages, developed relationships with key "informants," ate the local food, and encountered what anthropologist Bronislaw Malinowski (1922) called "the imponderabilia of everyday life" (pp. 24–25). The *process* (ideally) of actually participating in daily life was believed to cultivate a richer understanding of people's worlds than mere observation. "Do as the natives do," he suggested, in order to understand their point of view. Insights into deep cultural meaning were expected through the process by which "the strange becomes familiar and the familiar becomes strange"; recreating this experience for readers was a goal of writing ethnography. Immersion became imbued with an aura of authenticity, although written reports required a delicate balance between subjective insight and scientific distance. Intellectually, such a move challenged "armchair anthropologists," who studied other cultures from afar,

as well as those who made their observations from "the colonial veranda," or a safe position of privilege.

Actual levels of participation varied, of course. As Ralph Bolton (2002) asks, "How many anthropologists studying peasant working conditions have actually spent time plowing, sowing, or reaping? More than likely, they sat at the edge of the field and observed" (p. 148). Despite this variation, and despite the fact that turn-of-the-century fieldworkers did not blend seamlessly into their new social environments, their experiences of near-total immersion in unfamiliar settings did indeed lead to valuable insights. In *Coming of Age in Samoa* (1928), for example, Margaret Mead shocked many of her contemporaries not just by suggesting that young Samoan women engaged in casual sex before marriage, but that such behavior could be considered "natural" in another cultural context. Her comparison of Arapesh, Mundugumor, and Tchambuli societies in *Sex and Temperament in Three Primitive Societies* (1935) again caused a stir by proposing that gender norms and dispositions were culturally constructed rather than inherent to biological sex. Mead's research has been criticized over the years, but her influence on American society and social movements was immense.

For a researcher in the field, the flip side to obtaining a coveted insider's perspective was the risk of "going native"—identifying so strongly as a member of the group that one lost objectivity, became unable to relay findings back to the home culture, and possibly even lost interest in returning. Proving that one had maintained proper boundaries took numerous forms in early ethnographies, from the language used in the texts to the patterned ways that research tales were told: first, the researcher appears on the scene as an isolated outsider, then passes a test or challenge to gain the trust and acceptance of the group; in the end, however, the researcher passes another test by abstaining from local practices that would be interpreted as indicative of losing perspective, such as sex, marriage, or religious conversion. In Malinowski's *The Sexual Life of Savages* (1929), for example, he argued that sexuality permeated everyday life for the natives; the implication, of course, was that this was not the case for people in more civilized societies. His claims of both accessing a native's point of view and remaining distanced enough to be objective, however, were later questioned when it was discovered that his personal desires had been relegated to his diary.

From the turn of the century until after World War II, sociologists and criminologists in the US were also becoming more interested in "fieldwork" and in enhancing cross-cultural—or "subcultural"—understanding through observation and participant observation. Sociologists at the University of Chicago began using anthropological methods to study urban environments and "closed" communities with barriers to entry, such as ethnic neighborhoods, gangs, or social clubs. The Chicago School especially privileged the idea of "naturalistic observation," and viewed the city as a living laboratory in which to study social problems. Robert Park, a Chicago School sociologist, argued that,

> the same patient methods which anthropologists… have expended… might be even more fruitfully employed in the investigation of the customs, beliefs, social practices, and general conceptions of life prevalent in Little Italy or on the lower North Side of Chicago, or in recording the more sophisticated folkways of the inhabitants of Greenwich Village.
> (Bulmer 1986, p. 92)

Park told his students that although they had been taught that real research required "getting your hands dirty" by "grubbing in the library… accumulating a mass of notes and liberal coating of grime," "first hand observation" was also needed:

> Go and sit in the lounges of the luxury hotels and on the doorsteps of the flophouses; sit on the Gold Coast settees and on the slum shakedowns; sit in the Orchestra Hall and in the Star and Garter Burlesk. In short, gentlemen [sic], go get the seat of your pants dirty in *real* research. (McKinney 1966, p. 71)

Although Park instructed researchers to study across social classes, the fact is that some people are more visible than others, and some trigger more voyeuristic fantasies. Getting the seat of one's *pants* dirty, it seems, was supposedly

more likely in a back alley than at the Orchestra Hall. Similar to anthropologists who set off for remote jungle outposts, many sociologists turned their eyes toward the "exotic others" of their city milieus—hobos, criminals, juvenile delinquents, and the disenfranchised.

Although some researchers believed in becoming a "fly on the wall" in their chosen field sites—that is, to refrain from disrupting or intervening in social interactions in ways that might bias their analysis—others sought access to the inner lives of their informants and to understand the subjective meanings of their actions through varying degrees of participation. Symbolic interaction theory, which had been gaining favor in those years, proposes that human reality is constructed through our interactions with others. Researchers, then, could use their own experiences as data, as they learned to "think and feel" like the people they were studying—sometimes referred to as "sympathetic introspection" (Cooley 1909, p. 7). Once again, immersion experiences generated important insights. By respecting the meanings generated in various communities, researchers tried (and sometimes succeeded) at humanizing individuals who were often seen only as social problems. The focus on deviance as a social process involving labeling, stigma, and power relations unsettled the view that "deviants" were born psychologically damaged or inferior. On the topic of sexuality, sociologists produced work on "gay ghettos" and street prostitution, for example, exploring the ways that individuals acquired and managed stigmatized identities.

Today, researchers no longer usually face the possibility of complete isolation at a field site as early anthropologists did. Few tribal groups, if any, lack contact with outsiders. Even places that are geographically remote are economically, politically, and technologically linked to a global network. Many researchers now study close to "home" for practical, ethical, or other reasons. In such a world, it is more difficult to know what "total immersion" would look like and field sites are not necessarily distinguishable from one's everyday social world. And although social scientists continue to study in social enclaves with barriers to entry, they can no longer claim to access a single privileged or authentic "insider perspective." Community members may critique research findings or become researchers themselves. Still, questions that arose decades ago about the potential for, and usefulness of, developing insider versus outsider perspectives, and about whether researchers should engage with the individuals and social settings they are studying or remain distanced observers, continue to animate discussions of observational methods and to influence the decisions with which contemporary researchers are faced.

8.4 Reflexivity as Practice

The idea of the researcher as a tool has occupied a great deal of intellectual thought and debate. Humans are visual mammals, yet we are also prone to numerous biases, misperceptions, and misinterpretations. Do we trust our own eyes? Do we trust a particular researcher's observations or interpretations? Why or why not? How do we know if one is gaining objective knowledge about the world or merely offering a subjective description? Although these questions are clearly relevant to all types of research, they are particularly salient when it comes to studying the world of human meaning.

8.4.1 Degrees of Engagement

Because the tension between insider and outsider perspectives is so fundamental to observational and participatory methods, much intellectual effort has gone into trying to characterize researchers' engagement with the communities they study. Gold's (1958) typology of researcher roles included 4 modes of data gathering: complete participant, participant as observer, observer as participant, and complete observer. Sociologist James Spradley (1980) also developed a continuum based on researcher involvement, ranging from non-participatory (no contact), passive (bystander role), moderate (a balance between insider and outsider roles), active ("going native"), and complete (the researcher is already a member

of the group). Adler and Adler (1987) focused on a researcher's belongingness—not just participation—in groups being studied. They thus distinguished between researchers with peripheral membership (just observing), active membership (participation in at least some activities) and full membership (full participation). Sociologist Loic Wacquant (2011) used the term "observant participation" to suggest that a researcher can prepare to "go native" by equipping himself both with the tools and training of a social scientist and also by learning the bodily dispositions and practices of the community being studied. Wacquant trained as a boxer for his ethnography, *Body and Soul: Notebooks of an Apprentice Boxer* (2000).

None of these characterizations are appropriate for describing every type of group or fieldwork situation, however. Further, we are still left with the question of how precisely one is to distinguish between statuses when the distinction between insider and outsider is not straightforward. My own research on the male customers of strip clubs might be considered "active" or "full participation"—I was, after all, working as a stripper. I learned the bodily dispositions of a stripper (see Frank 2002b, 2005) and was often primarily viewed by others as a stripper, not a researcher (Frank 2002a). But as I was studying the *customers* instead of the dancers, wasn't I in some respects also observing as a participant? What are the criteria that should be used in determining whether a researcher should be called a participant observer, an observant participant, a non-participatory observer, or something else? Is it how much time is spent in a particular field site? Whether there were return visits? Is it whether the researcher engaged in *all* of the activities as the other people present? And how does identity come into play? That is, if a researcher identifies as a BDSM practitioner, can she be termed a "complete" participant observer if she refrains from playing at her field sites for ethical reasons? What if she only takes part in a BDSM scene because she is conducting research and is curious about how it feels? How would we categorize a gay man who studies heterosexually identified men-who-have-sex-with-men at sex clubs?

Research is also a dynamic process—our methods, questions, and theories may change based on our experiences in the field. Joseph Styles (1979) set out to study men's sexual encounters in bathhouses as "a nonparticipating insider"; however, after being groped in the crowded corridors to the point of losing his towel and realizing that his attempts at conversation were being interpreted as sexual interest, he thought, "to hell with it" and became a participant (as cited in Goode 1999, p. 305). In doing so, he gained a deeper understanding of the subtle sexual negotiations taking place inside the venues. Researchers need to negotiate complicated relationships with individuals at their field sites; participation in everyday activities may increase or decrease as friendships develop and deepen. As a researcher gains knowledge about a field site and comfort with previously foreign practices, his observations and interpretations may change. A researcher unfamiliar with group sex, for example, might at first be overwhelmed by the nudity in a sex club and focus his initial observations on the tangle of bodies on a mattress; later, though, his attention may turn to how space is demarcated for socializing or on the types of conversations unfolding along the sidelines.

8.4.2 Practicing Reflexivity

The focus on whether or how much a researcher participates, I believe, has overwhelmed consideration of other aspects of observational methods. More important than trying to characterize the researcher's role through static terminology, I believe, is the practice of *reflexivity*.

Reflexivity "involves an awareness that the researcher and the object of study affect each other mutually and continually in the research process" (Alvesson and Skoldberg 2000 as cited in Haynes 2012, p. 73). More than "a simple reflection on the research process and its outcomes," reflexivity is multi-layered contemplation that includes "considering the complex relationships between the production of knowledge (epistemology), the processes of knowledge production (methodology), and the involvement and impact of the

knowledge producer or researcher (ontology)" (Haynes 2012, p. 73). Actual reflexive practices thus vary depending on a researcher's assumptions about the nature of reality, or what there is to know about the world, and how we best learn about it. Some researchers, for example, place critical emphasis on reflection about the data gathering process, while others focus more on the acts of recording observations or writing up results. Ideally, however, reflexivity can be practiced at each stage of the research process and for every type of observational method. What C. Wright Mills (1959) called the "sociological imagination" is an ability to grasp the interplay between individual experience and social structures in one's analysis. Reflexivity, then, requires social scientists to analyze *themselves* as well as others—asking, how are my questions, methods, values, and goals in this research influenced by the social structures around me? The answers to these questions are not always crystal clear, especially at the beginning of a project, which makes the development of reflexivity—or "reflexivities"—more like practicing piano than climbing a mountain.

Researchers need to develop an awareness of how broader power relations impact the very definition of "research," as well as interactions with research subjects and their interpretations of those interactions. Social, economic, political, cultural and historical contexts influence research questions and processes. Consider what some researchers have called the "politics of visibility." Much as colonial history and persistent global inequities situated some people and places as the likely objects of anthropological study, social marginalization makes some groups and individuals more visible and accessible to social scientists in the US. We have far more studies of sex workers who work the streets or in brothels than of those who use the Internet to find clients. More research is conducted on poor drug users in crack dens than on Fortune 500 CEOs who use cocaine.

Just as privilege allows certain groups to escape the prying eyes of social scientists, who we are influences what we choose to study, the questions we ask, and how we try to answer them. Our individual characteristics—race, class, sexuality, gender, and so on—affect how we perceive and interact with others in the field—and they with us. These characteristics can limit our access to certain spaces, which roles we can adopt, and how we interpret our experiences. Understanding our positionality, then, is an essential part of reflexivity.

Male researchers studying in strip clubs with female dancers, for example, have tended to adopt distanced roles such as "non-tipping customer" with little attention paid to positionality (Brewster 2003; Erickson and Tewksbury 2000). Female researchers, on the other hand, have often taken a more reflexive stance, perhaps because of their conspicuous presence or because of an assumed or actual involvement as dancers. Female researchers have also focused more on the complexity of gendered power relations in stripping (Barton 2001; Egan and Frank 2005; Frank 2007). But what does it mean when a male researcher positions himself in the audience to view stage performances but refrains from tipping or purchasing dances, as several have done? Is this approach more ethical, respectful, or likely to elicit a deeper understanding of the transactions occurring than interacting like a typical customer would be? Is either approach more *risky*, personally or professionally? Male researchers may be stigmatized even more than female researchers when they choose to study the sex industry, seen as lecherous by their peers (Barton 2001). Such fears of stigma influence methodological and analytical decisions, such as a desire to limit certain kinds of involvement or to focus one's analysis on the "safer" aspects of the encounters. The experience of doing research can be fraught with a sense of danger, vulnerability, risk, and transgression; sometimes, explicitly acknowledging this complexity can lead to a more nuanced analysis.

As broader social contexts shape each of us and influence our interactions with others, researchers should thus be reflexive about how their own characteristics and privileges impact the research process, affecting everything from gaining access to a community to how much we participate to how we interpret our results. Some

characteristics, such as our gender, race, ethnicity, age, height, and so on, directly affect how others respond to us and how we see the world. Other characteristics, such as social class or sexuality, may have a more indirect influence on our interactions through how we look or speak. Examining our own beliefs, upbringing, relationships, and personal histories in these shifting contextual fields presents additional opportunities for understanding the meanings we make in the field.

On-going reflexivity with regard to our emotional responses during our research can also guide theoretical, methodological and analytical decisions. When I began studying the male customers of strip clubs, for example, I focused strictly on the men's relationships with the dancers. In writing about those interactions, I tried to maintain an awareness of how my observations and experiences were shaped by my positionality as a white American woman from a working class background, a graduate student well versed in feminist theory and an "out" exotic dancer. Consciously traversing a complex web of privileges and stigmas was part of my study design. I wanted to move beyond the deviance framework for understanding stripping and reverse the usual mode of inquiry—from "*Why do some women do this?*" to "*Why do some men want to pay for this?*" Yet my roles as "researcher" and "stripper" were not the only ones that shaped my experiences. As I continued both working in the clubs and conducting interviews off-site, I found that customers repeatedly inquired about my wedding ring, asking, "How does your husband feel about your dancing?" The question was uncomfortable for me because I had worried about his feelings prior to beginning the project. The query also made me wonder how my interactions with customers in the clubs affected the other women in their lives. How would these women feel about *me*? How would *I* feel about my marriage if I found out that *my* husband visited strip clubs? As George Devereux (1967) points out, anthropological data can arouse anxiety in researchers and this anxiety can influence our observations and analysis. Eventually, I reversed the question, asking, "How does your wife or partner feel about your visits to strip clubs?" I focused more on how these men's outside relationships influenced the meanings of their visits to the clubs as my own problematic status and experience as a married person in this environment became evident to me. Reflecting on my emotional responses influenced my decision to explore customer beliefs about monogamy, and affected my interpretations of our exchanges in the clubs and during the interviews.

How much of this process of critical reflection is shared with readers varies. Social scientists traditionally included discussions of how they gained acceptance to a community, disclosing mistakes and breakthroughs as a way to authenticate their observations and assure readers that objectivity was maintained—the researcher got close enough to understand people's behavior, but not so close that perspective was lost. After these initial discussions, however, a researcher tended to maintain an authoritative presence, regardless of how much he had privately thought about his role in the production of knowledge. More recent reflexive writers tend to be forthcoming about their positionalities and their political and personal investments in their field sites, situate their research "story" within a wider social context, and consider the ethics of the research at each stage of the process, sometimes to a distracting extent. The detached observer is thus one extreme; Van Maanen's (1988) "confessional ethnography," where the researcher takes center stage in the narrative, is another. Critics view reflexive ethnography as "a largely egocentric, asocial activity" (Webster 2008, p. 67)—philosophical naval-gazing or confessional writing that tells us more about the author than the world. Many of us do not want ethnography to turn into autobiography, though precisely how much one should disclose about one's identity, engagement in a field site, political ties, and so on, is still debated.

A key to resolving the debate lies in revisiting the reasons that we turned to reflexivity in the first place. The underlying issue is a philosophical dilemma about what it means to study others, especially when using observational methods. What is revealed to readers, then, should be information that helps them evaluate the researcher's conclusions. We can thus consider the researcher's positionality as a source of information rather than bias, and the *process* of reflexivity—regardless of how much is directly shared with readers—as a technique for mitigating some of the limitations inherent to observation.

In her research on women's bathhouse events, sociologist Corie Hammers (2009) suggests that her identity as a lesbian/queer woman allowed for easier access and made her seem trustworthy to the organizers. Hammers decided against participating at the events, however, and thus thought carefully about how to remain unobtrusive. She carried a tape recorder and tablet, but kept them concealed except during interviews. She chose to wear a long sleeve shirt and jeans to indicate "unavailability" and "seriousness," but also recognized that her attire set her apart from the crowd (Hammers 2009, p. 317). During the events, Hammers disclosed her research role to individuals who inquired or seemed interested in her erotically. Because several hundred women were in attendance, though, most participants were unaware of her objectives. Overall, she did not believe that her presence interfered with patron's sexual activities, and her observations suggest interesting differences between men's and women's bathhouse cultures: men's sex was often with strangers, while women's bathhouse sex was more personalized; in contrast to men's silence, women were often loud and celebratory; and women's events had a strong emphasis on sociality. She raises questions, however, about whether her physical disengagement affected respondents' honesty in reporting their motivations. Few women admitted visiting the bathhouse purely for sex in her interviews, for example. But were these lesbians/queer women potentially less willing to admit an interest in casual sex due to anxiety or vulnerability in the presence of a non-participant (Hammers 2009)? By analyzing how her personal characteristics and methodological decisions may have affected her interactions, Hammers (2009)? helps readers contextualize and evaluate her observations and interpretations.

8.5   Covert Versus Overt Research

Observation may be covert, where the researcher does not divulge her purpose and may even mask it, or overt, where people are aware that they are being studied and may or may not know why.

8.5.1   Covert Observation

Covert research is sometimes considered necessary in settings where people's behavior would change significantly in the presence of a researcher. One of the most famous sociological studies of sexual behavior using covert observational methods is *Tearoom Trade: Impersonal Sex in Public Places* by Laud Humphreys (1975). When Humphreys wanted to study men who utilized "tearooms," or public restrooms known for same-sex activity, he found that the layout of each facility and the reactions of participants to his presence affected his ability to *only* observe. He initially pretended to be a straight man entering the restroom, but because the men worried about being arrested or observed accidentally, a lookout, or "watchqueen," would alert the others to cease their activity when someone was approaching. Eventually, Humphreys (1975) adopted this role of lookout, as it allowed him to observe without being expected to join in. Alternately keeping watch and retreating to his car to write notes, Humphreys recorded the types of sexual acts engaged in, and examined the strategies used and roles adopted by participants in sexual negotiations. Because tearoom participants were so concerned about not being observed, there was little chance of an outsider accidentally witnessing any sexual activity. Police stings, Humphreys argued, were thus not really combatting a significant public problem, but being used as a form of harassment and stigmatization.

In a more contentious part of the study, Humphreys (1975) added an element of deception. Because he believed that the men would decline an interview if he approached them in the restroom, he recorded the license plate numbers of some tearoom participants. He then tracked them down at their homes and interviewed them about their attitudes towards homosexuality under the pretenses of conducting a public health survey. He found that 54% of the men were actually married and living relatively conventional lives; he also argued that many put on a "breastplate of righteousness" (p. 135), publicly condemning the same behavior they privately engaged in. Humphrey's research was fascinating as it was uniquely able to address the disjunction between what people say and what they do. Still, his decision to conduct the interviews under false pretenses and to collect personal information that might have put his research subjects at risk sparked controversy (Humphreys 1975).

An account of how men negotiate anonymous sex in bathhouses or restrooms is concerned with patterns of behavior, does not require the identification of any particular individual, and should ideally pose no risk to the men who were observed. Places and people can be given pseudonyms and identifying details can be changed in researcher notes and publications. Richard Tewksbury (2002), also a sociologist, presented himself as a "potential participant" in covert research on two gay male bathhouses. Spending several hours at each location, he "circulated with and among patrons," carefully observing "their activities, movements, interactions and the use of the physical features of the environment" (Tewksbury 2002, p. 85). Periodically, he retreated to private areas to write notes. But when Humphreys (1975) decided to examine the links between the men's sexual practices, their social identities, and their political beliefs, however, he needed to collect more detailed information on each participant. Had the men's activities somehow been inadvertently revealed to their families, neighbors, or employers, the results could have been devastating.

Some critics dislike all covert research because the individuals being observed have not had the opportunity to give informed consent. On the other hand, we are observed and "studied" in many everyday situations without having been asked for our consent. Even online, information is collected about us incessantly, whether we are posting on Facebook or shopping on Amazon.com. If the observations are conducted in a public place, individuals have no risk of being identified, and the possibility of causing harm is negligible, requiring researchers to obtain informed consent may be counterproductive and unnecessary.

The potential risk involved, rather than the simple fact of covert observation—or even deception—is what should weigh most heavily in ethical assessments. Potential harms vary, of course. Subjects are occasionally exposed to potential physical harm, as in some medical or pharmaceutical research, or psychological harm, as in Stanley Milgram's (1963) famous experiments in obedience to authority, which caused distress in participants. Institutional Review Boards (IRBs) were created to mitigate these harms by carefully reviewing research involving human subjects. In IRB proposals, researchers detail the aims of their study, the methods used to recruit subjects, how data is collected and stored, potential risks to participants, and how findings will be used and disseminated.

Academic researchers are also bound by disciplinary ethical codes that apply even in covert situations. Social scientists undertaking covert research generally take care to maintain the anonymity of those involved—unlike when journalists undertake an exposé or spectators post videos of public behavior on YouTube. Sociologist Eric Anderson conducted covert research on the website AshleyMadison.com, a "married dating service for discreet encounters," by monitoring conversations between potential partners (Luscombe 2014). Individuals were often unaware that their online conversations were being viewed and analyzed. Anderson was later accused in the press of spying on members, but the terms and conditions provided at sign up had indicated that user communications might be monitored—a good reason to read the fine print! Further, anonymity of members was maintained (Luscombe 2014).

Social scientists are further expected to take care not to cause physical or emotional harm and to adhere to scientific standards in study design, data collection, and publication. This is not the case, however, for all writers. In a problematic endeavor, for example, Charles Orlando (2014), a "relationship expert" and popular author, went "undercover" and dated women from Ashley Madison to "find out why women cheat." With seemingly no ethical qualms except a worry about actually cheating on his wife, he set up three fake profiles "to see which would resonate fastest" with women on the site, then started chatting with and dating women who responded. He admits lying to the women about his intentions and personal circumstances; his published descriptions of his encounters include evidence of the women's psychological distress at his eventual rejections (Orlando 2014). Orlando's deceptive "experiment" would not have passed institutional review.

Unfortunately, more and more researchers are finding their studies unduly scrutinized when the research topic is sex. Many types of naturalistic observation are exempt from formal institutional review; studies involving sexual behavior, however, may be deemed "sensitive" and subjected to additional protocols. Some institutional review boards assume that asking *any* questions about a person's sexuality can potentially cause psychological distress, although this concern may reflect the individuals reviewing the research more than the actual risks. I have interviewed people about their sex lives for years, providing consent forms warning of possible discomfort with my questions and offering therapists' contact information. Overwhelmingly, though, interviewees describe the experience in positive terms, as more "like therapy" than interrogation.

Regardless of whether one's institution requires official review for a particular study, researchers should think carefully about the impact of the research on participants. When people engage in stigmatized or illegal behaviors, there is a risk of exposure to peers or authorities. Exposure could result in legal or social penalties, depending on the context, or cause personal distress. Even when anonymity is maintained for individuals, researchers may worry about disseminating findings that reinforce stereotypes or are damaging to a group as a whole. Researchers working on highly politicized issues such as teen sexuality or "gay parenting," for example, may find that their work attracts more negative publicity to already stigmatized groups or that their findings are coopted by the media or special interest groups.

8.5.2 Overt Observation

In overt studies, researchers are generally forthcoming about their purposes and participants may be asked to give informed consent, although how this is done may vary. Self-identified lesbian researchers Catherine Nash and Allison Bain (2006) observed women's behavior at bathhouse events. On the evenings of the events, the researchers presented themselves as both voyeurs and potential participants to the other patrons, although they avoided sexual activity. Patrons were not asked to sign consent forms; some knew the women were researchers and others did not. The organizers of the events, however, were aware of the women's ongoing research, and Bain and Nash (2006) had also been conducting interviews with patrons and gathering survey data, practices for which they sought informed consent.

Sometimes, the nature of one's research or the particulars of a field site require mixed strategies. In my research on strip club customers, my initial interactions with potential interviewees necessarily took place in my role as a stripper. I was an employee of the clubs, and thus club managers were invested in my performances as a dancer, not as an anthropologist. There were far too many men in the clubs each night for me to approach every one, much less describe my study to him. Further, my focus was on the regular customers, the men who used the clubs relatively frequently and considered it an important part of their erotic repertoire. Working as a dancer enabled me to identify the regulars. If conversation allowed, I discussed my project with them and asked for an interview off-site at another time. The constraints of the environment, then, meant that I observed hundreds of men each week, some who knew I was an anthropologist and some who did not even care to know my stage name, much less my real name. This design made sense to me practically and ethically. Informed consent was relatively meaningless in the public workplace setting of the strip club because I was not collecting data that could identify customers and was using pseudonyms for the clubs. Informed consent became very important during in the in-depth interviews, however. The interviewees provided substantial amounts of personal information, unlike other customers of the clubs, and participated in an additional transaction—the interview. Thus, interviewees were provided with consent forms stating the purpose of the research, and knew that they could refuse to answer questions or stop the interview at any time.

Technological innovations pose new questions about the meaning of observation and participation, and raise new ethical concerns (Binik et al. 1999). What exactly does informed consent mean, or require, in a virtual world? Are online forums "public" or "private"? How can researchers respect and protect those whom they virtually "observe" in online interactions? Researchers may participate to varying extents in online worlds. Researchers working in virtual communities should learn enough about computer security to be able to protect the identities of individuals they interact with online; care should be taken using screen names and direct quotes that can be found easily through search engines, as personal information could be revealed inadvertently.

Each discipline in the social sciences has a code of ethics that should be respected whether research is covert, overt, or a mix of the two.

8.6 Researcher Sexuality and Sexual Interactions

Some researchers believe that sexual involvement with research subjects—and sometimes even eroticized interactions—should always be avoided for both practical and ethical reasons. Still, it happens. Anthropologists return from the field with a spouse or children. Researchers have flings and affairs. Researchers who *admit* crossing sexual boundaries, though, can face censure or stigmatization, and transgressions are often relegated to informal conversation or gossip. Malinowski (1967) wrote about his sexual desires in his diary, never expecting it to be published posthumously. Some ethnographers allude to sexual experiences in their writing, although fewer are completely open about them. Erich Goode (2002) argues that gay men and women have been more likely to write about sexual encounters in the field than heterosexuals, and that anthropologists have been more likely to disclose than sociologists.[4] Women risk sexual harassment and violence during fieldwork, which might be one reason why female researchers have addressed sex more frequently and directly in their academic work. Further, involvements between female researchers and male informants or between gay men may be "less likely to conjure up an image of traditional exploitation," which may make it easier for those individuals to write about their experiences without professional repercussions (Goode 2002, p. 502). That does not mean that male researchers have not had sexual experiences with female informants, of course—just that such interactions are potentially judged more harshly and thus do not become a part of the published record. Maintaining an artificially distanced academic persona, however, does not rectify existing power differentials; in fact, it may reproduce them.

One justification for abstinence has been to prevent exploitation and ensure that subjects are not coerced into either sexual activity or participation in a project. But while the potential for an abuse of power should always be considered, research carried out in naturalistic settings involves complex social relations. As researchers can be exploitative or dishonest in any relationship with informants, and vice versa, why should sexual relationships be singled out as somehow more problematic? Researchers may also be more or less privileged than their informants, or members of the communities they are studying. Unlike in the early days of field research, people who are written about can now often comment on or publicly reject a scholar's results. In 1969, Humphreys could claim that an observer in a tearoom is not yet "suspected as being a social scientist," but this is not necessarily the case nowadays. BDSM communities, for example, have been extensively studied in the past few decades and members now often engage proactively with researchers or even conduct research themselves.

Organizations like the Community-Academic Consortium for Research on Alternative Sexualities (CARAS) promote communication between activists, participants, and researchers in alternative sexual communities, recognizing that these roles are not mutually exclusive. Whether or not researchers identify as members of the communities that they study, they must always think critically about how they will balance their various roles and interests, handle issues of consent and disclosure, and manage close relationships at their field sites.

As with other forms of researcher participation, concerns have also been raised that sexual involvement will distort a researcher's judgment and ability to present her findings objectively. Goode (1999) suggests that researchers who are intimately involved during fieldwork are not inclined to romanticize the people they are studying, as being acquainted with the mundane details of their lives actually prevents unabashed advocacy. Still, he argues, sex with informants *does* affect what a researcher can write about—to disclose some details would be inappropriate, harmful, or even just embarrassing to the individuals involved (Goode 1999). Whether or not—and which—details *need* to be shared with readers in the first place, of course, is a question that should be carefully considered. Anthropologist Kate Altork (1995), who writes eloquently about her erotic experiences while researching firefighters, warns that the point of reflecting on such experiences is not "to encourage sensationalistic, National Enquirer-type confessionals" about one's sex life. Instead, researchers should simply remain open to discussing the possible ways that sex "changed, enhanced, or detracted from what we felt, witnessed, and interpreted in the field" (Altork 1995, p. 121).

For researchers studying in explicitly sexualized environments, and especially those using observational methods with any element of participation, the ethical issues at stake can be intensified and potential stigmas multiply. Sexual interaction can occasionally enhance rapport or speed acceptance into a community. Some critics view this claim as a self-serving attempt at justification after the fact (Bryant 1999), but a more

---

[4] *Out in the Field* and *Taboo* are edited volumes where anthropologists have written about their decisions with regard to sexual engagements during research.

tempered view would be that it depends on local social norms, what and where one is studying, and how one's sexual relationships are handled. In his research on gay leathermen in the Netherlands during the 1990s, Maurice van Lieshout (1997) used an "opportunistic research strategy," suggesting that sociologists might take advantage of familiar social situations. As he had already participated in the Dutch gay leather scene, he gained rapid entry into the setting he wished to study and easily developed rapport with participants (van Lieshout 1997). In a study of sex and romance among members of the National Association to Aid Fat Americans (NAAFA), Goode (2002) recalls his legitimacy being called into question by a male NAAFA member. "I really don't think you belong here if you are not attracted to fat women" (p. 508). Answering the man's questions about his erotics became a test of his loyalty and good will towards the community; his affirmations that he *really* had desire for fat women were a prerequisite for gaining access. But sexual relationships can also negatively impact access if researchers make mistakes. Goode also admits, for example, that he dated too many of the women in NAAFA too quickly, causing irreparable damage to his reputation in the community. Still, he points out that such issues are not unique to sexual relationships, but to any relationships generating strong emotion.

Anthropologist Ralph Bolton (2002) suggests that *participant* observation—in the fullest sense of the term—has a place in sex research because it allows access to private space and encourages the development of intuitive understanding. "Unless the observer has had wide-ranging sexual experience," he writes, "it is unlikely that he or she can even know what questions to ask or imagine all of the permutations and complexities of sexual events" (Bolton 2002, p. 148). Anthropologists Charles and Rebecca Palson (1972), a married couple, were involved in swinging before they decided to formally study it. The Palsons (1972) claimed that, "most of our important insights into the nature of swinging could only have been found by actually experiencing some of the same things that our informants did" (p. 29). English professor Tim Dean (2009) admits to participat-

ing in unprotected sex in his book on barebacking. Dean does not consider his work to be ethnographic; he is not a social scientist and didn't conduct formal interviews. He did, however, listen and observe. He also had sex. Barebacking, he claims, is an "underground sexual subculture" that "tends to resist conventional research methods." After "uninhibited, multipartner sex," he writes, "men tend to speak more freely." Being in an "overtly sexual space" such as the back room of a gay bar helped "dissolve some of the barriers and pretensions that constrain verbal exchanges elsewhere" (Dean 2009, pp. 29–34). Sociologist Russell Westhaver (2003), who writes on gay male circuit parties, was a participant at events and worked for a company involved in their production. He situates himself as an insider who engaged in "sensuous scholarship," which he explains as ethnography "grounded in a commitment to seeing, hearing, feeling, smelling, and tasting the body through poetic processes of transcribing, revisiting, and elaborating bodily experiences and memories as fieldnotes" (Westhaver 2003, p. 21). Participation was a crucial element in his understanding of the emotional power of the events.

Erotic entanglements may lead to a deeper understanding of social networks in some communities. Bolton found that the line between his personal and professional lives blurred while he was studying gay bathhouses in Brussels. "In gay culture," he writes, "sex is where the action is" (Bolton 1995, p. 142). His relationships with friends and lovers provided him with access to social events and experiences that would have been unlikely had he remained distant:

> I became a player in the scene, reciprocating by introducing my tricks, friends, and lovers to others in my network.... By experiencing them, I came to learn of blow jobs from bartenders when the door was locked at closing time, of jacking off in cruising spots in a park near the Grand Place in partially public view, of sexual encounters in alleyways between someone headed home from the bars and someone on his way to work at dawn, of sexual action in the dunes along the coasts and on the piers in Ostende and in the backrooms of discos and in the bathrooms of ordinary bars. (Bolton 1995, p. 148)

Participation also informed his research in bath-houses and saunas. Although some sites where sex took place were relatively public, such as the steam room and the orgy room, he found that nonparticipants altered the flow of interaction and that the dim lighting presented difficulties with observation. And while interviewing could have been done in nonsexual areas of the sauna such as the bar area or television lounge, most conversation took the form of "post-coital shar-ing" (Bolton 1995, p. 150). These conversations provided valuable information. He did not ask sexual partners to sign consent forms; some did not know he was conducting research on sex and AIDS. Still, Bolton "*never* engaged in sex for the purpose of collecting data," never coerced anyone into having sex with him, and protected people's confidentiality. He also stresses that his partners did not suffer physical or psychological harm from the encounters (beyond the emotional pain of relationships ending on their own). His research objectives were "subordinate" to his participation as a member: "I never engaged in any behavior that I would not have engaged in had my research objectives been different" (Bolton 1995, p. 151). His identity as a gay man did not stop him from reporting negative findings about men's risky sexual encounters.

Sometimes, abstaining from participation can disrupt one's investigation and relationships. During fieldwork in Mozambique among margin-alized young men known as *moluwenes*, anthro-pologist Christian Groes-Green (2010) found that because of differences in gender, race, and status, his informants perceived him as "morally righ-teous" and were wary of discussing their sexual practices with him. Groes-Green (2010) slowly earned their trust by drinking with them, party-ing, "being wild," and "celebrating spontaneity, naughtiness, and excess." But when he turned down a local woman's offer to participate in an orgy one evening, he suddenly reverted back to being an outsider, even a "traitor," and realized his access to the community was at stake in such decisions. His awareness of his privileged posi-tion in relation to the community he was studying often led him to withdraw from lust-provoking situations and "create social boundaries and

physical distance." Yet, the social milieu also re-quired managing his ambivalence. He continued to experience anxiety and guilt when confronted with scenes of unsafe sex, feeling "complicit" in their risky activity because he was unable to in-tervene without losing his ability to observe. Yet, Groes-Green (2012) grasped that "delimited in-volvement"—by which he meant being in close proximity without including "direct sexual or carnal merging"—was critical both to his access to the community and to his aim of understanding why *moluwenes* made the choices they did with regard to sexual behavior.

Researchers Bain and Nash (2006) defended their decision not to participate at the women's bathhouse events they studied on the grounds that one researcher was monogamous and that their "feminist ethics" prohibited them from doing so. Not surprisingly though, their decision to wear street clothes and position themselves on the out-skirts of the activity meant they felt "awkward" when play began. They worried about being per-ceived as inappropriately voyeuristic, inhibited, or judgmental by other attendees. Observers, after all, can themselves be observed. The orga-nizers of the events, whom Bain and Nash (2006) interviewed prior to attending the bathhouse events, made the researchers feel they were not being "honest" in their research if they did not participate. This was not just because their deci-sion was made ahead of time, but because they also were not "using the space in the ways [the organizers] had envisioned" (Bain and Nash 2006, pp. 99–106). When Nash and Bain broke etiquette in such a relatively small and tight-knit community, their fantasy of maintaining a "fly on the wall" researcher position was smashed by the "elephant in the room."

If anthropological and feminist ethics sug-gest attention to power differentials, what are the ethics of academic voyeurism, especially if it causes discomfort or confusion for others? When researchers decide ahead of time what they are willing to experience, might they become like tourists, disrespectful of local customs and obliv-ious to their own social impact? Do prior inten-tions *not* to engage sexually in particular settings protect researchers against the vulnerability that participants expect and experience, and thus inhibit a researcher's ability to understand a field site? Bolton (1995) suggests that the social and emotional risks to the researcher, at times, can be equivalent to or greater than the risks to any of the participants—the researcher, after all, may be far from her comfort zone. The researcher role, Bain and Nash (2006) admit, served as a "cover," providing psychological safety by offering little opportunity to "dwell on, or even discuss" insecurities about their attractiveness to other women (p. 103). Hammers (2009) wonders:

> Had I participated more directly, would I have had a deeper understanding when it comes to sexual negotiations and the exposure, vulnerability, and empowering appeal that spaces such as these induce? Having set myself apart from the scene, did I, like Styles, miss out on the subtleties, cues, and complexities when it came to body language and negotiations of sex? (p. 317)

Likewise, Groes-Green (2012) acknowledges that despite his ambivalences about risky sex, his understanding of his informants grew when he personally experienced the "bodily momentary intensities that drive youngsters to play with death and danger, ecstasy and annihilation, orgies and frenzy" (p. 56).

To their credit, these researchers raise these questions themselves in their published work. Researchers should never be required to participate in activities that violate their personal, ethical, or emotional commitments in the name of science. The point, however, is that neither participation nor abstention from sexual activity is *inherently* unethical or problematic. Rather, decisions about sexual participation are made by particular individuals in specific contexts and should be evaluated as such. Every research method has strengths and limitations. Survey research may suffer from low response rates or from a community's dislike of being studied by outsiders. When limiting themselves to observation, researchers may not have access to back rooms, semiprivate exchanges, or less visible individuals. Participant-observers enjoy greater access but may feel conflicted over disseminating findings that portray a community negatively or find themselves stigmatized in the academic community. All researchers should reflect on the appropriateness of their methods to their questions and on power dynamics in the field, not just when contemplating sexual involvement with a particular informant but at each stage of the process, from the choice of where to study to deciding what questions should be asked and of whom. Researchers should also follow the code of ethics for their discipline. Some researchers suggest that anthropologists have somewhat more flexibility with regard to sexual encounters in the field than psychologists (Montes Penha et al. 2010), although anthropologists would also be expected to respect local norms and practice a high degree of reflexivity.

Goode (2002) asks several provocative questions that can guide ethical reflection about sexual involvement:

> One: Can sex with informants harm them—that is, over and above what ordinary, nonsexual interaction does? Two: Does sex with informants alter what the researcher writes about? Three: Is sex with informants *categorically* unethical? Four: Does sex with informants gain access to information and insight that is otherwise inaccessible? (p. 527)

And to these questions I would add a fifth: What are my personal erotic investments in my interactions with informants, and how do they affect my research? As in all research, the process of reflexivity is key to developing a deep understanding of what we see and how we interpret it; the answers to why we found ourselves there in the first place may not be immediately clear. Outsiders sometimes want to study strange or "deviant" sexual practices with little reflection on their own sexuality; researchers may be seeking many things in addition to knowledge that affect their choice of questions and field sites—healing, affirmation, excitement, adventure, and so on.

Some insights generated by emotional or physical intimacy can help a researcher better understand his or her questions or the population being studied. Sharing some of those insights may help readers understand how questions developed or research progressed. Other times, however, details about a researcher's intimate encounters are irrelevant.

Well-trained researchers can conduct careful, thorough studies regardless of the methods they choose, how much they participate, and their personal identities. In 2010, anthropologist Margot Weiss and sociologist Stacey Newmahr each published books on BDSM in the United States, based on research conducted during roughly the same time period. Weiss (2010) observed in a BDSM community without participating, while Newmahr (2010) became a BDSM player during her fieldwork. Their resulting ethnographies take different theoretical approaches: Weiss focuses intently on BDSM as part of capitalist consumer culture while Newmahr spends more time exploring the creation of authentic "scenes." What each researcher observed, experienced, and concluded about BDSM was related to who she was and how she interacted with others at her field sites. Still, their descriptions of BDSM are factually similar, and both discerned the importance of authenticity for many contemporary BDSM practitioners. Weiss doesn't seem to have "missed" significant aspects of BDSM because of her nonparticipant status, although she contextualizes the scene more broadly in US culture than Newmahr does. Newmahr doesn't appear to have become too "close" to the community to analyze it effectively, although she homes in on the nuances of interaction and the phenomenology of BDSM play more than Weiss.

8.7   Some Practical Suggestions

> The world is still a weird place, despite my efforts to make clear and perfect sense of it.
> —Hunter S. Thompson

Observation is a skill that requires practice and ongoing reflection, but there are some practical ways to make the most of one's abilities.

Reflect on the politics of visibility and mobility as you are designing your study and during fieldwork Unfortunately, some students are sent out to practice conducting observations without any discussion of power dynamics or having done even a cursory literature review. Street sex workers, homeless people, strippers, and other

visible, but marginalized, groups are frequently chosen as research subjects because they seem intriguing and edgy—the exotic others. When I was working in strip clubs, I sometimes found myself more offended by the intrusive questions and disrespectful behavior of unprepared researchers than by any of the regular customers. Reflecting on your motivations for selecting a field site and your assumptions about the individuals you interact with can make the difference between voyeurism and observation.

Some researchers interested in alternative sexual practices tend to study only within identity communities, recruiting from BDSM groups, polyamorous groups, and so on. Although identity-based communities are easier to observe—they may hold meetings, host events, and congregate in known places—such a strategy can miss individuals who do not embrace existing labels. The organized polyamory "community," for example, tends to be privileged in terms of race, class, and education; individuals in other social strata, however, still purposefully engage in multiple sexual/emotional relationships.

Determine which environments are conducive to answering your research questions and then strategically gain access Too often, researchers use the most accessible potential field site or do not adequately match their questions to their sites—many questions, for example, cannot be answered by observing in a *single* sex club or through observation alone. While it is obviously important to select a site where you will eventually gain entry, encountering barriers may be a sign that more preparation is necessary.

If one wishes to study a group that has been historically targeted by social scientists, sensitivity to community concerns about previous research will pay off. Groups like CARAS (https://carasresearch.org) can help with linking researchers to potential participants and designing studies that have the potential to "give back" to the community (or are at least respectful). Some groups may prefer that researchers follow established pathways when announcing studies or attending events.

Design your study to allow for maximum coverage Observing a given environment at different times of the day, on different days of the week, and in different seasons of the year can generate essential information.

Reflect on the specifics of your participation Participation may not be possible or desirable for illegal behaviors, such as drug use or prostitution. In other cases, deciding how you will interact ahead of time is beneficial even if you change your mind later. Will the boundaries you set for yourself be perceived as respectful or offensive by the other people around you?

Reflect critically on your positioning, appearance, and behavior How you literally position yourself during your observations will impact how insiders interact with you. Understanding as much as possible about the norms of the environment can aid immensely. If you are attending an erotic event, for example, try to ascertain how you will indicate your intentions nonverbally. What are participants expected to wear? Are you comfortable in such attire? If so, would wearing it mislead other participants about your intentions? And if not, how might you present yourself so as not to offend participants or cross your own boundaries? Showing up in black leather might work well, but donning a hood so that no one recognizes you could be misunderstood.

Relax If you do not intend to participate, do not also assume that every individual who approaches you is interested in sex or attempt to prevent advances by adopting an avoidant body posture.

Be realistic about your attention span. Shift perspectives, and look away when necessary Merriam (1998) suggests alternating between narrow and wide perspectives when observing a scene. One can also focus for a few minutes, look away, and then focus again. This advice can be taken literally, as when one is watching a performance or ritual unfold, or figuratively, as when one takes a short break from fieldwork.

Document in a way that makes sense for YOU Sure, traditional fieldnotes are the gold standard of fieldwork. But depending on your research site, it may not make sense to record as events unfold. When working in strip clubs, I kept a notebook in my locker so that I could write some things down immediately. But I was far too tired after an 8-h shift to type fieldnotes at my computer after work, so I found it useful to audio record during the drive home. Later, I could either transcribe the recording or listen to it as many times as necessary.

Although some researchers traditionally suggested avoiding computers in the field, today's technology is more omnipresent. Typing notes on a smart phone may work in some field sites, although care must be taken to maintain confidentiality in case the phone is lost, or stolen. Photographs and video-recordings can be legally and ethically problematic in some environments, but acceptable in others. Even if photographs or video-recordings are not prohibited, ask participants before using this technology—individuals engaging in stigmatized activity may have concerns about privacy and anonymity that outweigh the usefulness of preserving the scene and that should be respected. Written permission may be necessary to publish photographs or to use visual materials that are collected for non-research purposes.

Follow the confidentiality guidelines Follow the confidentiality guidelines provided by your Human Subjects Institutional Review Board, or if more stringent, those of your discipline or that you have set for yourself. Some observational projects will be exempt from review, but if multiple methods of data collection are involved, informed consent will eventually become necessary. Confidentiality—or preferably anonymity—is important to maintain during covert and overt research, except under special circumstances. Some types of participant observation can jeopardize the confidentiality of others indirectly. Be careful when writing, storing, and publishing descriptions that could inadvertently be used to identify a place or person. Many researchers are critical of human subjects review boards for making decisions about research based on social acceptability rather than actual risk to participants, and the process of seeking human subjects approval can seem like a bureaucratic nightmare. You may be required to store consent forms separately from interview materials, delete identifying information from field notes, or keep your materials in locked cabinets. Although it is easy to let those steps slide, doing so is a mistake. If you are going to be collecting sensitive data, following the guidelines precisely can also protect YOU from lawsuits, being forced to identify your informants, or causing unintentional harm. One project that I designed, for example, called for multiple, in-depth interviews about cheating and monogamy with spouses, interviewed separately. The human subjects review board strongly suggested one-time interviews rather than repeated interviews, based on the potential for the interview process itself to cause issues in a marriage and to avoid any chance that I might accidentally divulge confidential information from one spouse to another. I accepted the suggestion, which did not substantively change the study. When I learned how little some spouses share with each other, I was glad to have done so.

If you do need IRB approval, start the process early to avoid costly delays if revisions are necessary.

Reflect on the dynamics of your relationships Some theorists term those with whom researchers develop the most important relationships "key informants." Others dislike the term. Either way, a particularly opinionated individual can shape a research project, especially if the researcher is inexperienced or extremely unfamiliar with the setting. On the other hand, gaining the trust and interest of an influential person is often crucial to interacting with a community. Individuals who embrace your research may be

different in some fundamental way than those who avoid you—or not.

Consider ways to substantiate or invalidate your observations Creating a system of checks and balances on your observations is specific to each field site. One possible strategy would be to ask for participant comments on your observations; another strategy would be to use multiple methods of inquiry, balancing observations with interviews, for example.

Don't shy away from documenting the mundane Knowing what is "regular" can help illuminate extraordinary occurrences. Seemingly unimportant events or details may take on new meaning as a project develops.

Don't rely only on your eyes Observation ideally engages all of the senses, not just sight. In your field notes or diaries, try to cover each of the senses when describing a scene or interaction.

Don't interrupt Although interviewing skills deserve a chapter of their own, one of the most useful field techniques is learning how to be quiet. Observational methods often involve informally conversing with people at a field site, and if so, try to allow for digressions and long silences. People often use talk to develop rapport, which means that they quickly fill in silences and sometimes do not even respond directly to what was said, as when stories are shared rapidly among a group. As a researcher, you will want to alternate strategies. Sometimes, we also unconsciously shift conversations in directions that we want or expect them to go. Using talk to develop rapport is fine, but practice shifting your focus to asking questions that you need answered—and giving people the time to answer them.

Pay attention to your mistakes, misunderstandings, and discomfort in the field Part of the reflexive process is to challenge some of your most basic or cherished beliefs—something that is likely to cause discomfort. Certainly, foibles can be a source of embarrassment for researchers, sometimes not even recorded in field notes. But anthropology is rife with examples of misunderstandings that eventually led to a deeper appreciation of the culture being studied (Lee 1969; Bohannan 1966). Irritation with one's informants or the others one encounters in the field may later prove to be illustrative of one's own anxieties; overcoming emotional discomfort might later guide your analysis in new directions.

References

Adler, P. A., & Adler, P. (1987). *Membership roles in field research*. Newbury Park: Sage Publications.

Altork, K. (1995). Walking the fire line: The erotic dimension of fieldwork experience. In D. Kulick & M. Wilson (Eds.), *Taboo: Sex, identity, and erotic subjectivity in anthropological fieldwork* (pp. 107–139). London: Routledge.

Bain, A. L., & Nash, C. J. (2006). Undressing the researcher: Feminism, embodiment and sexuality at a queer bathhouse event. *Area, 38*(1), 99–106.

Barton, B. (2001). Queer desire in the sex industry. *Sexuality and Culture, 5*(4), 3–27.

Beach, F. A., Jr. (1938). Techniques useful in studying the sex behavior of the rat. *Journal of Comparative Psychology, 26*(2), 355.

Berk, R., Paul, R. A., & Paul, O. (1995). Sexual activities as told in surveys. In R. A. Paul & D. P. Steven (Eds.), *Sexual nature, sexual culture* (pp. 371–386). Chicago: The University of Chicago Press.

Binik, Y. M., Mah, K., & Kiesler, S. (1999). Ethical issues in conducting sex research on the Internet. *Journal of Sex Research, 36*(1), 82–90.

Birkhead, T. (2002). *Promiscuity: An evolutionary history of sperm competition*. Boston: Harvard University Press.

Bohannan, L. (1966). Shakespeare in the Bush. *Natural History, 75*(7), 28–33.

Bolton, R. (1995). Tricks, friends, and lovers: Erotic encounters in the field. In D. Kulick & M. Wilson (Eds.), *Taboo: Sex, identity, and erotic subjectivity in anthropological fieldwork* (pp. 140–167). London: Routledge.

Bolton, R. (2002). Mapping terra incognita: Sex research for AIDS prevention—an urgent agenda for the 1990s. In K. Plummer (Ed.), *Sexualities: Critical concepts in sociology* (pp. 142–173). London: Routledge.

Brewster, Z. W. (2003). Behavioral and interactional patterns of strip club patrons: Tipping techniques and club attendance. *Deviant Behavior, 24*(3), 221–243.

Bryant, C. D. (1999). Gratuitous sex in field research: "Carnal lagniappe," or "inappropriate behavior." *Deviant Behavior, 20*, 325–329.

Bullough, V. (1995). *Science in the bedroom: A history of sex research*. New York: Basic Books.

Bulmer, M. (1986). *The Chicago school of sociology*. Chicago: University of Chicago Press.

Cooley, C. (1909). *Social organization: A study of the larger mind*. New York: Charles Scribner's Sons.

Dean, T. (2009). *Unlimited intimacy: Reflections on the subculture of barebacking*. Chicago: University of Chicago Press.

Devereux, G. (1967). *From anxiety to method in the behavioral sciences*. Paris: Mouton & Co.

di Mauro, D. (1995). *Sexuality research in the United States*. New York: The Social Science Research Council.

Egan, R. D., & Frank, K. (2005). Attempts at a feminist and interdisciplinary conversation about strip clubs. *Deviant Behavior, 26*, 297–320.

Erickson, D. J., & Tewksbury, R. (2000). The "Gentlemen" in the club: A typology of strip club patrons. *Deviant Behavior, 21*, 271–293.

Farley, M., Cotton, A., Lynne, J., Zumbeck, S., Spiwak, F., Reyes, M. E., Alvarez, D., & Sezgin, U. (2004). Prostitution and trafficking in nine countries: An update on violence and posttraumatic stress disorder. *Journal of Trauma Practice, 2*(3–4), 33–74.

Frank, K. (2002a). *G-Strings and sympathy: Strip club regulars and male desire*. Durham: Duke University Press.

Frank, K. (2002b). Stripping, starving, and other ambiguous pleasures. In M. L. Johnson (Ed.), *Jane sexes it up: True confessions of feminist desire* (pp. 171–206). New York: Four Walls, Eight Windows.

Frank, K. (2005). Body talk: Revelations of self and body in contemporary strip clubs. In A. Masquelier (Ed.), *Dirt, undress, and difference: Critical perspectives on the body's surface* (pp. 96–121). Bloomington: Indiana University Press.

Frank, K. (2007). Thinking critically about strip club research. *Sexualities, 10*(4), 501–517.

Frank, K. (2013). *Plays well in groups: A journey through the world of group sex*. Rowman & Littlefield Publishers, Inc.

Goode, E. (1999). Sex with informants as deviant behavior: An account and commentary. *Deviant Behavior, 20*(4), 301–324.

Goode, E. (2002). Sexual involvement and social research in a Fat Civil Rights Organization. *Qualitative Sociology, 25*(4), 501–534.

Graham, K., Bernards, S., Wayne Osgood, D., Abbey, A., Parks, M., Flynn, A., Dumas, T., & Wells, S. (2014). "Blurred Lines?" sexual aggression and barroom culture. *Alcoholism: Clinical and Experimental Research, 38*(5), 1416–1424.

Groes-Green, C. (2010). Orgies of the moment: Bataille's anthropology of transgression and the defiance of danger in post-socialist Mozambique. *Anthropological Theory, 10*(4), 385–407.

Groes-Green, C. (2012). Ambivalent participation: Sex, power, and the anthropologist in Mozambique. *Medical Anthropology: Cross-Cultural Studies in Health and Illness, 31*(1), 44–60.

Hammers, C. (2009). An examination of lesbian/queer bathhouse culture and the social organization of (Im) Personal sex. *Journal of Contemporary Ethnography, 38*(3), 308–355.

Hardy, S. B. (2000). *The woman that never evolved.* Boston: Harvard University Press.

Haynes, K. (2012). Reflexivity in qualitative research. In G. Symon & C. Cassell (Eds.), *Qualitative organizational research: Core methods and current challenges* (pp. 72–89). Thousand Oaks: Sage Publications.

Humphreys, L. (1975). *Tearoom trade: Impersonal sex in public places.* Chicago: Aldine.

Lee, R. B. (1969). Eating Christmas in the Kalahari. *Natural History December,* 60–64.

Luscombe, B. (16 August 2014). Cheaters' dating site Ashley Madison Spied on its users. *Time Magazine.* http://time.com/3120241/ashley-madison-cheaters-site-spies-on-its-users/. Accessed 22 Jan 2015.

Malinowski, B. (1922). *Argonauts of the Western Pacific.* New York: Dutton.

Malinowski, B. (1929). *The sexual life of savages in north-western Melanesia: An ethnographic account of courtship, marriage, and family life amoung the natives of the Trobriand Islands, British New Guinea.* New York: Routledge.

Malinowski, B. (1967). *A diary in the strict sense of the term.* Stanford: Stanford University Press.

McKinney, J. C. (1966). *Constructive typology and social theory.* Appleton-Century-Crofts.

Mead, M. (1928). *Coming of age in Samoa: A psychological study of primitive youth for western civiliztion.* New York: Blue Ribbon Books.

Mead, M. (1935). *Sex and temperament in three primitive societies.* New York: Morrow.

Merriam, S. B. (1998). *Qualitative research and case study applications in education.* San Francisco: Jossey-Bass Publishers.

Milgram, S. (1963). Behavioral study of obedience. *The Journal of Abnormal and Social Psychology, 67*(4), 371.

Mills, C. W. (1959). *The sociological imagination.* Oxford: Oxford University Press.

Montes Penha, M., Shedlin, M. G., Reisen, C. A., Poppen, P. J., Bianchi, F. T., Decena, C. U., & Zea, M. C. (2010). Ethnographic fieldwork on sexual behavior: Developing ethical guidelines for native researchers. In D. A. Feldman (Ed.), *AIDS, culture, and gay men* (pp. 155–166). Gainesville: Florida University Press.

Moore, M. (1985). Nonverbal courtship patterns in women: Context and consequences. *Ethology and Sociobiology, 6*(4), 237–247.

Moser, C. (1998). S/M (Sadomasochistic) interactions in semi-public settings. *Journal of Homosexuality, 36*(2), 19–29.

Newmahr, S. (2010). *Playing on the edge: Sadomasochism, risk, and intimacy.* Bloomington: Indiana University Press.

Orbuch, T. L., & Harvey J. H. (1991). Methodological and conceptual issues in the study of sexuality in close relationships. In K. McKinney & S. Sprecher (Eds.), *Sexuality in close relationships* (pp. 9–24). Hillsdale: Lawrence Erlbaum Associates, Publishers.

Orlando, C. (15 May 2014). I went undercover on Ashley Madison to find out why women cheat. *The Daily Dot.* http://www.dailydot.com/opinion/ashley-madison-why-women-cheat/. Accessed 22 Jan 2015.

Palson, C., & Palson, R. (1972). Swinging in Wedlock. *Society, 9*(4), 28–37.

Poland, J., & Caplan, P. (2004). The deep structure of bias in psychiatric diagnosis. *Bias in Psychiatric Diagnosis,* 9–23.

Sanders, T. (2004). Controllable laughter: Managing sex work through humor. *Sociology, 38*(2), 273–291.

Simons, D. J., & Chabris, C. F. (1999). Gorillas in our midst: Sustained inattentional blindness for dynamic events. *Perception-London, 28*(9), 1059–1074.

Spradley, J. (1980). *Participant observation.* New York: Holt, Rinehart and Winston.

Strum, S. C., & Fedigan, L. M. (2002). *Primate encounters: Models of science, gender, and society.* Chicago: University of Chicago Press.

Tewksbury, R. (2002). Bathhouse intercourse: Structural and behavioral aspects of an erotic oasis. *Deviant Behavior, 23,* 75–112.

van Lieshout, M. (1997). Leather nights in the woods: Locating male homosexuality and sadomasochism in a Dutch highway rest area. In G. B. Ingram, A.-M. Bouthillette, & Y. Retter (Eds.), *Queers in space: Communities/public places/sites of resistance* (pp. 339–356). Seattle: Bay Press.

Van Maanen, J. (1988). *"Confessional Tales" in tales of the field: On writing ethnography.* Chicago: Chicago University Press.

Wacquant, L. (2000). *Body and soul: Notebooks of an apprentice boxer.* New York: Oxford University Press.

Wacquant, L (2011). Habitus as topic and tool: Reflections on becoming a prize fighter. *Qualitative Research in Psychology, 8,* 81–92.

Webster, J. (2008). Establishing the "Truth" of the matter: Confessional reflexivity as introspection and avowal. *Psychology & Society, 1*(1), 65–76.

Weiss, M. D. (2010). *Techniques of pleasure: BDSM and the circuits of sexuality.* Durham: Duke University Press.

Westhaver, R. (2003). Party boys: Identity, community, and the circuit (Doctoral Dissertation). Simon Fraser University, Burnaby, British Columbia, Canada.

Part III
Bodies and Sexuality

Unpacking Sexual Embodiment and Embodied Resistance

9

Breanne Fahs and Eric Swank

9.1 Introduction

Understanding the body and its relationship to the social world has long fascinated and perplexed social scientists, natural scientists, feminist theorists, and historians alike. At a basic level, there is no society without bodies. The body serves as a fluid and permeable boundary between our individual selves and the outside world, and has great significance to how we see our identities, our sexualities, and our relationships with others. Grounded in a history of dichotomizing the mind and body and largely ignoring the body outside of its pesky role in inspiring madness and mental illness (Thompson 1999), the body has been historically overlooked by Western scholars; in fact, the notion of embodiment has entered sociological and psychological conversations only quite recently.

Shockingly little social science work has interrogated, until the last 20 years, the role of the body, its impact on gendered relations, and its paramount importance to the study of social inequalities. We know far more about the body as a medical enterprise, a collection of parts and processes, than we do about its social and sexual

functioning. The study of the social concept of embodiment showcases the tense relationship that the body has to its biological and social contexts, particularly as the body connects to sexual feelings, thoughts, and actions (Attwood 2007; Coy and Garner 2012). Further, because embodiment theories and research are grounded in such social contexts, much of the work around embodiment has (both overtly and subtly) a political emphasis. Bodies not only exist, but interact, and as such, social processes, biases, and emotions are written onto the stories of embodiment.

This chapter traces the key conflicts and debates around defining and measuring embodiment, followed by a multifaceted discussion of how different disciplines and scholarly traditions have theorized and studied embodiment. We subsequently review how embodiment has been conceptualized over the lifespan (e.g., childhood, adolescence, adulthood, and old age), followed by a review of the scholarly work on sexual performance and embodiment (e.g., body parts, enhancing the body, exercise, and orgasm). The chapter concludes with a discussion of embodiment as it relates to social identities like LGBT identity, race, gender, and class, followed by a discussion of embodied resistance, or how people with stigmatized bodies fight back, imagine bodies outside of the norm, transform the idea of a "freak," or map on political philosophies like anarchism to the study of embodiment.

B. Fahs (✉)
Women and Gender Studies Program, Arizona State University, Glendale, AZ, 85306 USA
e-mail: Breanne.Fahs@asu.edu

E. Swank
Arizona State University, 85306 Glendale, AZ, USA
e-mail: eric.swank@asu.edu

J. DeLamater, R.F. Plante (eds.), *Handbook of the Sociology of Sexualities,* Handbooks of Sociology and Social Research, DOI 10.1007/978-3-319-17341-2_9, © Springer International Publishing Switzerland 2015

9.2 Part 1: What is Embodiment?

Embodiment refers to the experience of living in, perceiving, and experiencing the world from the physical and material place of our bodies. More precisely, embodiment researchers have studied embodiment as the process of "being embodied" and as the process of "embodying the social," with both conceptualizations overlapping and at times occurring simultaneously (Crossley 1996; Rubin 1984). "Being embodied" refers to the lived embodiment experiences of being in our bodies, having corporeality, and existing in actual skin (Grosz 1994; Young 1990).

Some theorists have theorized the body not as a passive entity in need of cognitions to make sense of the world, but as something capable of genuine experience, that is, having "latent knowledge" (Merleau-Ponty 1945, p. 238). Subjective experiences of the body may occur outside of the cognitions we impose onto our bodies (Young 1990), as we simultaneously embody both an objectified and material self and an experiencing and subjective self (Fahs 2011a). Other embodiment theorists have also suggested that the body can exist through "intersubjectivity" (or shared understandings of reality) or relationships to other people. Within a sexual exchange, for example, people can experience their own bodies and the bodies of another simultaneously as objects and subjects, desiring and being desired (Cahill 2011). This immense theoretical complexity leaves wide open terrain for critical scholars and social scientists to study, measure, and define embodiment.

9.2.1 Key Conflicts and Issues

Theorists and researchers often start with different premises of what constitutes a body and how to understand and theorize the body as it exists in social space. As a key conflict in the theorizing about embodiment, essentialist theorists (that is, those who argue that the body has a biological and scientific reality that is not shaped and contested by social forces) and the social constructionists (those who argue that social and historical contexts influence and impact our bodies) have disagreed about how to understand the body and embodiment (DeLamater and Hyde 1998). Studying sexuality was, for Masters and Johnson (1966), a biological project that looked at the sexual functioning of biological parts outside of a social context. While some recent work in the natural sciences has looked critically at biological understandings of sexuality (Lloyd 2009), most biological research on sexuality ignores both subjectivity and people's own understandings of their embodied sexual experiences (Fahs 2011a).

Social constructionists, on the other hand, understood sexual desire, identities, experiences, and relationships as fundamentally social and dependent on interpretive processes (Plante 2006; Tiefer 2006). Bodies do not have any inherent meanings, but social context and social messages around bodies are created by social interactions of people in specific social situations (e.g., bodies have different meanings and expectations in synagogues, police stations, barber shops, and grocery stores). By saying that people's understandings of bodies are fluid, this does not mean that people simply choose their definitions of the social forces that dictate, discipline, and control bodies (Bartky 1990; Foucault 1978) and how bodily experiences and feelings relate to the (gendered, racialized) social world (Bordo 1993; Young 1990). Rather, people must make sense of the social world as they either internalize or resist the bodily expectations directed at them. Other cultural studies theorists have focused more on how bodies are produced or performed, both consciously and unconsciously, and how embodiment can be "inscribed" for specific people or specific social contexts (Butler 1990). As spinoffs of this, theories of embodiment as related to visible identities (Alcoff 2005), imagined spaces (Gatens 1996), and cyborg or technologically-inscribed bodies (Haraway 1991) have also emerged in recent years.

9.2.2 The Trouble with Defining Embodiment

Building on the conflicts between essentialists and social constructionists, embodiment also has permeable boundaries in terms of what, exactly, it encompasses. Embodiment includes a wide range of topics, identities, and approaches, including areas as vast as medicalization of bodies (Braun 2005), the racialization of bodies (Hill Collins 1990), the aging body (Hillyer 1998), the fat body (Rothblum and Solovay 2009), the disabled body (Inckle 2014), bodily privilege (Bobel and Kwan 2011), the sexual body (Hannabach 2007), the intersexed or trans body (Williams et al. 2013), and the gendering of bodies (Braun 2005; Tiefer 2008), among others. The definitions of embodiment, then, shift in relation to the sorts of approaches employed to "know" or "understand" embodiment.

9.2.3 Methodological Conflicts to Studying and Measuring Embodiment

Struggles about conflicts over embodiment appear most vividly in the methodologies employed to study and understand embodiment. A range of disciplines have worked to unpack and understand embodiment, including critical psychology, sociology, gender studies, queer theory, sexuality studies, rhetoric and literary studies, geography, social theory, and cultural/media studies. One recent methodological review of embodiment research identified some emergent traditions in embodiment work: social theories of the body; histories of the body; analyses of bodily techniques; and studies of embodied experience (Brown et al. 2011).

Primarily understood as an abstract construct, embodiment has appeared most often within the theoretical literatures rather than empirical ones. For example, Michel Foucault's (1977) highly influential work on bodies and embodiment posited that institutional and state power is exercised onto bodies both by force and, more insidiously, through compliance and internalized oppression.

The actual need for discipline and control waned in the face of people's sense that they should keep their bodies and sexualities in control (i.e., "self-surveillance"), thus revealing the chaotic and complicated workings of power as more of a "web" than an act of simple dominance over the powerless. Pierre Bourdieu's (1977) work also similarly fused sociological and anthropological theories of embodiment by emphasizing how taste and disposition are written onto the body. Many theorists have worked to "bring the body back in" via social theorizing around the body (Shilling 2004).

Historical accounts of the body have also worked to incorporate new narratives about how the body has previously existed, and how that relates to the current status of bodies and embodiment. Whether analyzing the histories of sexuality and masturbation (Laqueur 2003), the relationship between language and sexuality (Foucault 1984), or the missing histories of bodily desire and subjectivity (Smith-Rosenberg 1986), historians have unpacked embodiment retrospectively. The histories of embodiment and the uses of the body as a weapon of oppression or empowerment have long haunted historical narratives of embodied lives (Foucault 1977; Thompson 1999).

Methodologies of embodiment have also explored specific bodily practices and performances, looking at subjects as wide reaching as tattoos (Pitts 2003), crying and tearfulness (Hepburn 2006), dizziness (Brown et al. 2011), anorexia and eating disorders (Bordo 1993), cosmetic surgery (Heyes 2007), breast feeding (Schmied and Lupton 2001) and walking (Young 2005b). Studies using video diaries and surveillance of the body (that is, recording its sounds, movements, shapes) have documented the body audibly and viscerally (Bates 2013).

When conceptualized within the framework of sociological and psychological work, embodiment has emphasized the importance of studying subjectivities. How to methodologically engage with embodied feelings, sensations, and engagements with the world from this perspective has produced multiple methodologies for embodiment within the social sciences (Brown et al.

2011). Some empirical research on embodiment, for example, has focused on sweating, pain, and aging (Gillies et al. 2004), while others have focused on discursive accounts of subjectivity (Morgan 2005). In these accounts, the body's "fleshy," desirous, difficult characteristics are emphasized in relation to cognitive processes (Rohrer 2007), though this work also emphasizes emotional experiences and "embodied subjectivity" (Probyn 1993).

Psychology, in particular has had a disjointed relationship with embodiment, seeing it initially as an abstract entity conceptualized only through notions of stimulus-response, reflexes, habits, drives, and behavior; this reading largely neglected social interaction, complex social reasoning, bodily subjectivities, and desires (Glenberg 2010). Methodological disagreements have ensued about the optimal ways to study and measure embodiment. Some social scientists use positivistic approaches to explain people's relationship to body image (Jones 2001), body objectification (Noll and Fredrickson 1998), racial biases (Hunter 2002), and hair removal practices (Martins et al. 2008). Others argue that grounded theory and interpretive phenomenological analysis, which analyzes participants' accounts of their bodies by allowing categories to emerge from the data, constitutes the best way to engage with embodiment (Braun and Clarke 2006; Tolman 2002). However, to date, psychologists have drifted to deductive and quantitative approaches while most of the other social sciences have mostly foregone quantitative studies as they argue for the advantages of using grounded theory. These inductive methods subvert mechanical understandings of causation and correlation, and they challenge the overly reductive tendencies of psychology to characterize participants within pre-generated frames (Tolman 1994).

As another approach to studying embodiment, some researchers posit that people cannot derive knowledge from the body without actually involving their body in the psychological research. These techniques emphasize the moving, living, breathing body as it relates to understanding and self-awareness. For example, memory work—where researchers focus on the body as "being in" rather than "thinking about" experiences, often by using trigger words—constitutes another approach to studying embodied subjectivity (Gillies et al. 2004). Embodiment researchers have also empirically examined holding objects (Niedenthal et al. 2001), head movements (Foster and Stack 1996), and "implicit attitude experiments" (Foroni and Semin 2012) to measure different kinds of embodied experiences.

9.3 Part 2: Theorizing Embodiment

9.3.1 Who Gets to Decide What is "Embodied" or Not?

Embedded within discussion about embodiment are several key tensions about the notion of assessing embodied experience. For example, some theorists have discussed embodiment as an awareness of embodied experiences (Millsted and Frith 2003). Others have described embodiment in more complicated terms, constructing embodiment as an ongoing negotiation of agency, empowerment, and bodily autonomy (Earle 2003). Much like discussions of "agency" within the feminist literatures (Albanesi 2009), conflicts about how to measure, define, and assess participants' embodied experiences persist throughout the literature.

9.3.2 Feminist Contributions to Embodiment

Given that women's worth and meaning have often revolved around appraisals of their attractive or "ugly" bodies, while men's value has been linked more to their minds or functional bodies, feminist theorists have had to grapple with this painful history without neglecting the importance of the body (Grosz 1994). They have argued that the body must be considered in its material, corporeal form while also examining the body as a product of social forces (Irigaray 1985). Rather than separating the body and mind, many argued that the mind and body are inextricably linked together (Grosz 2008).

Feminist theorists have been particularly skilled at describing the impositions of patriarchal culture onto bodies, especially women's bodies. Several feminist theorists have used gender and sexuality as markers of institutionalized heterosexuality, theorizing how bodies perform (or are expected, by male audiences and authority figures, to perform) in particular ways (Bartky 1990; Bordo 1993; Butler 1990). French feminist theorists like Luce Irigaray (1985) and Monique Wittig (1992) theorized the body and embodiment as a product of systems that promote capitalism, value masculinity and patriarchy, and subject women to multiple intrusions and oppressions.

As one of the key contributions of feminist theory to the study of embodiment, feminists argued for intersectional approaches to studying embodiment. Specifically, feminists urged a consideration how social identities like race, class, sexuality, ability, size, and age all intersected with gender and were projected onto the body (Collins 1999). For example, the experience of poverty presents not only economic challenges, but writes itself into how people eat, dress, bathe, work, and live. Corporeality, then, was situated within and constructed around interlocking and multiple forms of oppression, and embodiment provided a way to understand social differences as experienced through (and on) the body (Grosz 1994).

Postcolonial feminist scholars have also taken up notions of embodiment in order to map the experiences of the colonial subject (Minh-Ha 1989; Spivak 1999). With accusations that people of color were "closer to nature," postcolonial feminist theorists have deconstructed and undone some of the damage done by such claims through their embodiment research (Minh-Ha 1989; Spivak 1999). Postcolonial scholars have also challenged hierarchies of power embedded within racialized, sexualized, classed, and gendered dynamics, both within the United States and globally (Morris 2010).

Feminist theorists have also taken up the ways that cultural scripts and norms get imposed onto bodies, forcing them into binaries of female/male and feminine/masculine (Bordo 1993). By examining topics like exercise, dieting, makeup, cosmetic surgery, vaginal "rejuvenation," body hair, and other sites of bodily discipline, feminists have marked the production of femininity and masculinity through the body (Bordo 1993; Chrisler 2012; Fahs 2011b; Weitz 2001). Feminists have also theorized about the shaming of women's bodies; emphases on changing physical appearance via hair straightening for women of color (Hill Collins 1990), surgical reconstruction of noses (Eriksen and Goering 2011), or the compulsive elimination of body hair for women (Fahs 2014) present one mode of doing so. Similarly, shame directed toward women's natural bodily processes also occurs as in discourses of menstrual shame (Bobel 2006). Clearly, women grapple with numerous disciplinary practices that control the presentation of gender, race, class, and sexuality.

9.3.3 Queer Contributions to Embodiment

Queer theorists have also contributed to the study of embodiment, primarily by critically examining the ways that heterosexuality has been produced, institutionalized, and valued above all other forms of sexual identity and expression (Butler 1990; Sedgwick 1990). Queer theory focuses not only on eliminating the binary between heterosexual and homosexual, but also challenging all dominant narratives that produce "normative" bodies and "normative" bodily expression (Warner and Berlant 2000; Butler 1990). By critiquing the construction of "normal" behaviors, practices, and bodies, queer theorists have interrogated the meanings of the more literal aspects of queer life (e.g., butch and drag performances, gay pride parades) but also the more metaphorical and abstract ways of seeing and doing sexuality (e.g., "queering" literature).

Most queer and feminist theorists have been criticized for not addressing corporeal embodiment more closely (that is, the lived experiences of being in a body) (Braidotti 1994; Grosz 2008). By theorizing the discursive production of embodiment, however, queer theorists have worked to upend categories, binaries, and dichotomies that constrain sexuality and gender (Halberstam 1998), emphasizing instead the marginalized or demonized embodied practices and the systems that regulate and control bodies and sexualities (Butler 1990). Particular attention has been paid to those who violate social norms, including feminine men (Connell 2005), masculine women (Halberstam 1998), transgendered people (Feinberg 1996; Stryker 1994), fat bodies (Rothblum and Solovay 2009), and those occupying multiple social locations at once (Grollman 2012; Meyer et al. 2008; Slevin and Linneman 2010).

9.4 Part 3: The Body Becoming Sexual Throughout the Lifespan

9.4.1 Childhood

Studies of childhood and sexuality generally come from a "social problems" perspective; as such, embodiment and sexuality research on childhood generally has focused less on sexuality as a developmentally normal occurrence and more often on sexual abuse (Bancroft 2003; Ryan 2000), the production of heteronormativity (Renold 2005), sexual behaviors that children engage in (Friedrich 2003), and retrospective accounts of people's childhoods (Graham 2003). Not fully constructed as "embodied citizens," most research has focused on how children's bodies and sexualities are understood within a discourse about "innocence," virginity, and the danger of adult appropriation of childhood sexuality, (which can lead to a moral panic) (Fahs et al. 2013; Robinson 2012). Language about sexuality, in particular, plays a key role in shaping children's understandings of their sexuality and their bodies as foreign, scary, and dangerous (Lamb and Coakley 1993).

Most often, children's sexualities and bodies are constructed as immature entities that "evolve" into adult sexuality later on (e.g., "emerging sexualities"), as childhood expressions of sexuality are often seen as playful or as a marker of abuse rather than desirous and "sexual" per se (Hyde 2003; Renold 2005; Robinson 2012). Girls' play

in their cross-gender friendships sometimes signals a shift between "innocence" and sexuality (Hauge 2009), though debates still ensue about how to draw the line between the sexual and the nonsexual for children. Children of both genders clearly identified genitals as exciting, private, and pleasant (Rademakers et al. 2003), and clearly masturbated during childhood (Strachan and Staples 2012). One well-known study by Herdt and McClintock (2000) identified the "magical age of ten," where distinctly sexual feelings emerge and a shift occurs from prepubescence to adolescence. Still, little research has explored what sexual meanings children derive from their bodies, as children's embodiment is almost completely ignored.

9.4.2 Adolescence

Compared to research on childhood embodiment, far more work has examined adolescent embodiment and sexuality, particularly around subjective perspectives of "losing" virginity and first sexual experiences (Loewenson et al. 2004). Studies on adolescent boys often deal with processes that mark a transition into manhood, particularly talking about the sexual appeal of girls and women (Thorne 1993), unsolicited touching of girls and women (Renold 2007), seeking muscularity (McCreary and Sasse 2000), and fighting with other boys (Messerchmidt 2000). Notably, the commonplace focus on girls' sexual experiences assumes that girls either do not act or do not have sexual desires while adolescent boys' sexual desire is assumed to be always already present (Fine 1988; Tolman 2002). Further, assumptions of heterosexuality and the impositions of heterosexism appear in full force during adolescence, inscribing only heterosexual embodiment as valuable and desirable for much of adolescence (Hauge 2009; Renold and Ringrose 2011; Tolman 2002).

Some research on adolescent embodiment has asked girls and boys to contextualize and give meaning to their sexual experiences and to their bodies, particularly within heterosexual relationships (Impett et al. 2011). Many adolescents reported feeling disembodied during their sexual experiences, looking instead to fashion, diet, and denial of the senses to construct the adolescent body (Tolman 2002; Holland et al. 1994). Further, many adolescent girls also struggled with the fear of sexual violence (or actual experiences of sexual coercion) alongside negative reputational risks of expressing sexual desire (Tolman 2002). Along these lines, adolescent girls often felt pressured to meet boys' expectations for sexuality; consequently, many adolescent girls reported faking orgasm or submitting themselves to patriarchal surveillance (Tolman 1994, 2002). Still, other adolescents were able to fight back against both heterosexism and patriarchy by feeling that they had sexual agency or acknowledging the ambivalent meanings of sexuality at their age (Gleeson and Frith 2004; Hauge 2009).

Adolescent sexuality also differed across identity categories, as urban Black and Latina girls' had to negotiate assumptions about hypersexuality and fatness while suburban white girls dealt with the assumption that they lacked sexual desire and were anorexic (Boyd et al. 2011; Le Espiritu 2001; Tolman 2002). The tension between pleasure and coercion informed adolescent girls' sexuality in many ways, particularly in the U.S., as girls' sexual desire remained largely missing within sex education (Fine and McClelland 2006; see also Fields, Gilbert and Miller, this volume). For example, U.S. teen pregnancy rates remain much higher than rates in other Western countries because of the combination of wider economic inequalities, greater gender traditionalism, and social policies that fail to see contraception as a right for young women (Lottes 2002; Singh et al. 2001). Further, international studies about girls' sexuality have shown complicated dynamics for girls as they negotiate "innocence" and sexuality (Curtis 2009; Schalet 2010).

Cultural and social scripts of sexuality have also influenced adolescent embodiment and sexuality, particularly around the performances of heterosexuality and bisexuality (Pascoe 2005) and the search for the "perfect body" and perfect masculinity/femininity via cosmetic surgery. In the past, compulsory heterosexuality manifested as the constant push toward all young people

declaring themselves as solely heterosexual, but sexual scripts have been becoming more liberal in the last several decades. Specifically, sexual fluidity (Diamond 2008) and "performative bisexuality" (Fahs 2009) have encouraged young women to explore experiences outside of heterosexuality, though many of these are still couched as ways to please boys and men (Fahs 2011a). For adolescent boys, studies suggest more fixed and stable identities around sexual desire and greater pressures to perform heterosexuality at all times (Kimmel 2004). Ironically, despite having more access to sexual diversity, cultural and social scripts about sexuality, condoms and contraception, and pornography, adolescents still reported much uncertainty and pain about negotiating their sexuality and embodiment (Fine and McClelland 2006; Holland and Thomson 2010).

9.4.3   Adulthood

Research on adult embodiment and sexuality has focused far more on notions of satisfaction, pleasure, entitlement, wantingness, and relationships compared to studies of adolescents (Fahs 2011a; McClelland 2010, 2014). For women, satisfaction with body image and increased sexual desire occur in mid-life as women age (Woertman and Brink 2012), though experiences with body shame and sexual trauma (by adulthood, a more common occurrence) can also lead to feelings of disembodiment and sexual dissatisfaction for women (Sanchez and Kiefer 2007; Young 1990). Research emphases on sexual satisfaction has also led to controversies about how to measure and assess people's sexual satisfaction, especially for oppressed people (McClelland 2014).

"Controlling images" promoted through the media, schools, families, and in the broader culture also influence not only how women experience their bodies and sexualities but also how they experience sexual desire and pleasure. For women of color, "controlling images" can infuse their embodiment with stereotypes about promiscuity and sexual "deviance" (Hill Collins 1990; Zavella 2008). For fat women, stereotypes about laziness, moral inferiority, and "gross" bodies can also lead to feelings of inadequacy and distress (Bessenoff and Snow 2006). Similarly, for disabled women, stereotypes of frailty and limited bodily control can impact how disabled people feel about their bodies and sexualities (Hassouneh-Phillips and McNeff 2005; Shildrick 2005).

Women in general also face pressures to contain and manage their unruly bodies throughout adulthood. Containment of menstruation, hiding menstrual products, and managing menstrual "odors" are all imposed upon women (Johnston-Robledo et al. 2003; Roberts et al. 2002; Roberts and Waters 2004). Women also experience pressures to remove their body hair and pubic hair as indicators of femininity, heterosexuality, and respectability (Basow and Braman 1998; Fahs 2011b; Fahs and Delgado 2011). Embodiment during pregnancy, childbirth, and breastfeeding has also appeared in the literature in recent years, as women face enormous contradictions and conflicts about their pregnant bodies (Gatrell 2007; Nash 2012; Oliver 2010).

Further, pressures for women to remain thin and men to be muscular and fit are common and both work to discipline and control their bodies (Lanzieri and Hildebrandt 2011; Morrison et al. 2003). Women often use exercise as a means to regulate their bodies, trim down and feel socially acceptable while men often exercise to bulk up and show their physical prowess (Craig and Liberti 2007; Furnham et al. 2002; Strelan et al. 2003). Moreover women are much more likely to turn to invasive surgeries to look young and thin, as one study noted that 48% of women and 23% of men were interested in having cosmetic surgery (Frederick et al. 2007). Notably, far more research has interrogated gay male embodiment (Grogan et al. 2006; Monaghan 2005; Morrison et al. 2004) in comparison to heterosexual men's embodiment (Frith and Gleeson 2004; Marshall and Katz 2002). A few studies have examined men's relationship with their sperm (Moore 2011), but most studies of men's sexual embodiment have focused on "top" and "bottom" identities, experiences of anal penetration, and how those identities and experiences relate to sexual desire, satisfaction, and power (Hoppe 2011; Kippax and Smith 2001; Middelthon 2002).

9.4.4　Old Age

Studies of older adults and their experiences with embodiment are also quite limited. There are few studies on body image among the elderly (Feingold and Mazzella 1998) though one study found that men's self-rated attractiveness actually increased as they aged throughout adulthood (Slevin and Mowery 2012). Other studies have found that aging was not beneficial to women's impressions of their bodies, as women's body image remained the same throughout their senior years (Lewis and Cachelin 2001). Habitual body monitoring and appearance anxiety decreased as women passed middle-age (Tiggemann 2004), but many female senior citizens are still concerned about looking younger, having firmer breasts, and staying thin (Slevin 2010). Some research has examined women's experiences with menopause as a transitional phase of life, finding that women felt most distressed about the loss of bodily control, the possibility of having their motherly roles diminish in importance, and the violation of "normative" femininity that came with menopause (Dillaway 2011). Social identities also connected to women's experiences of menopause, as working class women experienced more intense menopausal symptoms than middle and upper class women (Martin 2001). Further, middle class white women reported more positive feelings about their bodies during menopause compared to women of color and working class women, citing that they no longer needed to worry about contraception and could enjoy sex more as a result (Dillaway 2005; Loe 2004).

Concerns about sexuality also shift and change during old age, as people face personal transitions. For men, pressures to take Viagra and maintain erectile functioning exist as ways to prove their masculinity (Lodge and Umberson 2012) (with new markets supporting these efforts, see Katz and Marshall 2003), while women faced frustration about the lack of male partners and men's loss of sexual functioning (Loe 2004).

Conflicts about feeling disgust toward sexualizing older bodies also appeared (Vares 2009), with clear ideas about who gets to have a "sexual body" clearly internalized in old age. Along these lines, Black women's sexuality remained almost completely invisible in the literature on aging and sexuality (Dickerson and Rousseau 2009), suggesting notable gaps in the existing research on aging and sexuality.

9.5 Part 4: Sexual Performance and Embodiment

9.5.1 Producing Body Parts

Sexual performances also relate deeply to people's ideas about embodiment, particularly as related to worries and concerns about specific parts and regions of their own bodies. Women's breasts are often targeted as sites of anxious embodiment, with women worrying about their breast sizes and shapes in relation to their body images (Millsted and Frith 2003). Cultural prescriptions of attractive breasts relate deeply to patriarchal constructions of "good bodies," leading some women to pursue cosmetic surgery to enlarge their breasts (Young 2005a).

For men, the penis has represented a source of anxious embodiment, as men worried about whether their penises were too small and would disappoint their partners (Del Rosso 2011; Nugteren et al. 2010; Tiggemann et al. 2008). Moreover, racist stereotypes are connected to white men's fears of smaller penises (Wong et al. 2013). Viagra and the push toward the "always hard" penis has also influenced standards for masculinity as perpetually phallic, even into old age (Loe 2004; Maddison 2009). Men who had a tendency to think that their penises were smaller than other men also reported higher levels of self-doubt and shame (Tiggemann et al. 2008).

Further, anxieties around hair—hair on the head, underarm hair, leg hair, and pubic hair— have also appeared in the decades following the sexual revolution, as women feel compelled to remain completely hairless in their pubic, leg, and underarm regions (Fahs 2011b, 2012, 2014). Approximately 99 % of women have reported that they had removed body hair at some point in their lives (Toerien et al. 2005). Women who refused to remove their body hair faced external appraisals of themselves as disgusting, manly, unattractive, and gross (Fahs 2011b). While some men "manscape" or trim their pubic hair (Boroughs et al. 2005), most men feel entitled to choose the degree to which they will remain hairy, while women do not feel entitled to similar levels of choice around their body hair (Braun et al. in press). Conversely, men of all ages reported worries that their masculinity would be ridiculed by other men if their hair styles were too feminine or if they started balding on their heads (Ricciardelli 2011). Women of color in particular faced more severe penalties than white women for choosing to have body hair, particularly when family members expressed concerns with "respectability" (Fahs and Delgado 2011). With regard to pubic hair, younger and partnered women reported that they were more likely to remove pubic hair than older and non-partnered women (Herbenick et al. 2010b), suggesting social and contextual factors in which women remove pubic hair.

Social scientists have also identified women's genital self-image, or how women feel about their vulvas and pubic hair, as relevant to their body images more broadly (Roberts and Waters 2004; Schick et al. 2010). Because women receive messages that their bodies are always failing and inadequate, and that they are not desirable in their natural states, women have internalized the need for cleaning, sanitizing, deodorizing, exfoliating, and even surgically altering their bodies and their genitals (Bartky 1990). Many women, for example, expressed frank disgust at the idea of having menstrual sex (Fahs 2011c) or allowing a partner to perform oral sex on them (Bay-Cheng and Fava 2011). Conversely, more positive genital self-image correlated with greater likelihood of health-seeking behaviors like gynecological exams (DeMaria et al. 2011; Herbenick and Reece 2010). Women with positive genital self-image also reported more frequent vibrator use, masturbation, genital self-examinations, and gynecological appointments (Herbenick et al. 2010a).

In response to pressures to have conforming vulvas and vaginas, women have also faced new pressures to alter their genitals in order to obtain a more standardized (and perhaps "pornified") look. This "disease mongering" has led to pressures for women to engage in labiaplasties, vaginal "rejuvenation," the injection of Botox into women's G-spots, and the tightening of the vagina (Braun 2005; Braun and Tiefer 2010). Women who underwent labiaplasties did not report improvements in their sex lives (Bramwell et al. 2007).

9.5.2 Orgasm

Sexual satisfaction and orgasm also constitute a sizeable portion of the literature on sexual embodiment. Deciding how to measure satisfaction, and how much orgasm factors into such measurements, has preoccupied sex researchers for some time (McClelland 2010). Though sexual frequency and sexual satisfaction were sometimes synonymous (Waite and Joyner 2001), the research on sexual compliance suggests that a large number of women have boring or unpleasurable sex to please their male partners (Katz and Tirone 2009; Vannier and O'Sullivan 2010). One study found that sexual satisfaction and sexual activity were often misaligned, as younger women, women of color, less educated women, and lower socioeconomic status women reported having lower sexual satisfaction and higher sexual activity (Fahs and Swank 2011).

Research on orgasm has revealed much about the relationship between gender, power, and embodiment (Braun et al. 2003). Heterosexual women fake orgasm three times more often than heterosexual men (Muehlenhard and Shippee 2010). Women also often fake orgasms in an other-directed fashion, they want to please their male partners, end the encounter, feel sexually normal, avoid negative reactions, and reinforce a (male) partner's sexual skills (Fahs 2011a; Frith 2013). Conversely, men are more likely to fake orgasm for their own benefit and motivations such as wanting to sleep or feeling too intoxicated to gain an erection (Muehlenhard and Shippee

2010). Orgasm also represents the material, and perhaps capitalistic, impulses toward production of outcomes during sex, and toward embodiment as a concrete entity (Jackson and Scott 2007). Some humanists have also taken up orgasm as a subject of interest, as performance artist Frueh (2003) explored orgasm in relation to artistic expression, while Jagose (2010) characterized the fake orgasm as indicative of the failures of heterosexual sex.

9.5.3 Trans Embodiment

In recent years, more attention has been paid to trans embodiment and the ways that trans bodies can disrupt previously held notions of clear gendered dichotomies (Feinberg 1996; see also Devor and Dominic, this volume). Trans bodies, particularly those in the process of transitioning, are often seen as liminal, "on the edge," in the middle, or completely out of sight, both on television and in material, lived realities (Booth 2011), raising new possibilities for an examination of queer identities and their important, disruptive impact on assumptions about heterosexuality (Nash 2010). Trans people have also fought to have their (often forgotten or obscured) histories recognized and to fight against dichotomies of gender that often ignore the experiences of "third gender" and "middle gender" bodies (Halberstam 2005).

Trans bodies have been terrorized, pathologized, and confined in many different institutional spaces, including the mental health system, which often fails to provide adequate care for trans individuals (Israel et al. 2008; Mohr et al. 2001), and pathologizes transgender identity as "Gender Identity Disorder" (Lombardi et al. 2002; Winter et al. 2009). Prisons are also often places where trans people are discarded, neglected, and much misunderstood (Smith and Stanley 2011). Conflicts between the trans community and the gay, lesbian, and bisexual community have also appeared prominently in recent years (Feinberg 1996; Stone 2009), as whether drag are either celebrities or people to be mocked (Taylor and Rupp 2004) or whether transwomen can enter "women-only" feminist spaces (Goldberg 2014). Ultimately, the emerging debates and theories around trans identities and trans embodiment have provided fruitful new directions for the field of embodiment studies more broadly (Stryker and Whittle 2006).

9.6   Part 5: Embodied Resistance

9.6.1   Who Fights Back and How?

While much of the literature on embodiment has discussed people's compliance with social norms and their desire to conform to socially-acceptable modes of embodiment, there is also a growing, sizeable literature on embodied resistance (Bobel and Kwan 2011; Gagné and Tewksbury 1998). Resistance of this sort uses the body to convey a message that "inverts, contradicts, abrogates" (Pitts 1999, p. 71) culturally prescribed codes. Whether through reframing deviant bodies as healthy, normal, or "cool," or through fighting back against certain social regulations, the body as a site of resistance is ever evolving and changing. For example, fighting back through embracing tattoo art (Atkinson 2002), embracing fatness (Johnston and Taylor 2008; Meleo-Erwin 2012), or engaging in gender-bending modes of physical activity like women's roller derby (Peluso 2011), belly dancing (Moe 2011), or performing as a drag queen (Taylor and Rupp 2004), the body as a site of political, social, and cultural resistance has become an increasingly relevant facet of modern life.

The body has also figured centrally in political activism, as less powerful people use their bodies to engage in hidden or covert resistance. For example, working slowly, feigning sickness, monkey wrenching, or stealing from workplaces all constitute modes of hidden resistance (Scott 1990). During social movements and collective political campaigns, social movements routinely get people to use their bodies to protest at low-risk marches and picket lines (Roscigno and Hodson 2004; Schussman and Soule 2005) or during high-risk periods where public displays of civil resistance are needed (Nepstead 2005;

Swank and Fahs 2013). Religious activists have burned themselves to stop wars (Ben Park 2004), while antiracists have used their bodies to protest Klan marches (Jipson and Becker 2001), and environmentalists have stopped traffic on freeways (St. John 2008). Abortion clinic escorts and pro-choice advocates have also used their bodies to fight back against the forces that seek to strip women's right to abortion away from them (DilOrio and Nusbaumer 1993). While some people consider these potentially dangerous uses of the body as counterproductive, several studies have found that disruptive tactics of this sort can produce positive social change under the right conditions (Cress and Snow 2000; Haines 1984; King 2011).

New social movements like feminism and environmentalism are especially interested in changing social norms and using the body as a key site of resistance. For example, menstrual activists have fought back against the commercial menstrual product industry by citing the dangers of tampons and dioxins (Bobel 2006), arguing against the inclusion of "Premenstrual Dysphoric Disorder" in the DSM (Offrnan and Kleinplatz 2004), and have worked to lessen the shaming and secrecy of menstruation in the culture at large (Bobel 2006). Both within and outside of universities, feminists have fought back against constructions of their bodies as "disgusting" and "failing" (Fahs 2013).

People have also sought to publicly resist "slut shaming" and the treatment of women's sexual selves as inherently shameful and "sinful." The notion that women deserve to be raped, or should be punished for having active sexualities, has been strongly refuted by feminists and sex-positive advocates (Martin 2005; White 1999). Slutwalks (seeking to end the "blame the victim" mentality around rape and to end rape culture) have emerged as one way people have resisted the shaming of women's sexualities (Carr 2013), while plays like The Vagina Monologues have also allowed for more public discourse about women's vaginas and vulvas (particularly on college campuses where the play is performed nearly every Valentine's Day) (Ensler 2007). Work to reclaim women's bodies and sexualities as political entities, often within a feminist lens, have constituted much of the recent work on embodied resistance and liberation.

9.6.2 Bodies Outside of the Norm

Embodied resistance work has also focused on valuing bodies often deemed as "Other" or different from the mainstream. Some of this work includes advocacy for the sexuality of disabled people (Shildrick 2007), fighting for more visibility for women of color (Lee 2000), reclaiming fatness as a space of social resistance (Joanisse and Synnott 1999), and advocacy for "pro-ana" websites that promote solidarity among anorexic people (Dias 2013). Other examples of such work include alternative pornography films (Attwood 2007), more radical conceptualizations of mental health and how to promote bodily wellness (Hendricks and Plummer 2013), and body modification practices (Pitts 2003). Collectively, this work often openly fights not only for the right for Othered bodies to exist, but instead frames these Othered bodies as important tools of resistance.

9.6.3 "Freak" Studies

As an outgrowth of disability studies, postcolonial/subaltern studies, and fat studies, "freak studies" (Chemers 2005) is now an emerging field that encompasses a radical reinvisioning of Othered bodies as themselves worthy of both study and critical interrogation. For example, freak studies takes up not only the literal treatment of the freak in popular culture (Adams 2001), but also the larger issues around bodies that refuse to conform (Stryker 1994). Courses in freak studies and the examination of "freak" bodies have started to appear across the country, often fusing together work that is clearly anti-assimilationist (that is, against the idea that bodies should conform to the mainstream) and radically diverse (Sherry 2004). The field also works to closely interrogate the intersections between trans bodies, disabled bodies, fat bodies, bodies

of color, queer bodies, and other bodies out of bounds (Chemers 2005).

9.6.4 Anarchism and the Sexual Body

Embodiment has also been conceptualized recently within the anarchist literatures, particularly as scholars have started to interrogate the radical potential in envisioning sexuality and love relationships as distinctly political (Heckert and Cleminson 2011). Typically, anarchists have conceptualized sexuality as a mode of resistance against traditional or mainstream scripts of heterosexuality, marriage, coupling, and monogamy (Alexander 2011). More recently, incorporating ideas of asexuality and celibacy as acts of resistance (Fahs 2010) or seeing sexuality and love as fundamentally important to the project of political upheavals and revolution (Heckert and Cleminson 2011) have constituted new lines of thinking about how anarchy, sexuality, and embodiment can fuse together. Using the body as a tool of political protest can unite with the project of seeing the body as sexual (or not) and as deeply connected to other humans (Heckert and Cleminson 2011).

9.7 Conclusion

Ultimately, the study of embodiment presents a complicated array of ideas, practices, realities, and resistances, all of which reveal not only the central importance of the body to individual well-being, but to the very fabric of modern social life. Because institutional and cultural biases praise and condemn specific bodies in specific contexts, embodiment as individual awareness of one's body can be empowering or disempowering, contradictory or straight forward, and it can elicit deep connections to social identities like race, class, sexuality, gender, size, disability, and nationality. Most importantly, the body is a fluid text upon which many contemporary issues are written and rewritten. It can be a regressive, conservative force, framing people within insidious stereotypes and embodied practices, or it can serve as a site of resistance and upheaval, making new ideas and new worlds within which people's bodies can move and exist. As such, embodiment has paramount importance in the study not only of the sexual self, but of the human experience more broadly.

References

Adams, R. (2001). *Sideshow U.S.A.: Freaks and the American cultural imagination*. Chicago: University of Chicago Press.

Albanesi, H. P. (2009). *Gender and sexual agency: How young people make choices about sex*. Lanham: Lexington Books.

Alcoff, L. M. (2005). *Visible identities: Race, gender, and the self*. New York: Oxford University Press.

Alexander, J. (2011). Alexander Berkman: Sexual dissidence in the first wave anarchist movement and its subsequent narratives. In J. Heckert & R. Cleminson (Eds.), *Anarchism & sexuality: Ethics, relationships, and power* (pp. 25–44). London: Palgrave.

Atkinson, M. (2002). Pretty in ink: Conformity, resistance, and negotiation in women's tattooing. *Sex Roles, 47*(5–6), 219–235.

Attwood, F. (2007). No money shot? Commerce, pornography, and new sex taste cultures. *Sexualities, 10*(4), 441–456.

Bancroft, J. (2003). *Sexual development in childhood*. Bloomington: Indiana University Press.

Bartky, S. L. (1990). *Femininity and domination: Studies in the phenomenology of oppression*. Florence: Psychology Press.

Basow, S. A., & Braman, A. C. (1998). Women and body hair: Social perceptions and attitudes. *Psychology of Women Quarterly, 22*(4), 637–645.

Bates, C. (2013). Video diaries: Audio-visual research methods and the elusive body. *Visual Studies, 28*(1), 29–37.

Bay-Cheng, L. Y., & Fava, N. M. (2011). Young women's experiences and perceptions of cunnilingus during adolescence. *Journal of Sex Research, 48*(6), 531–542.

Ben Park, B. C. (2004). Sociopolitical contexts of self-immolations in Vietnam and South Korea. *Archives of Suicide Research, 8*(1), 81–97.

Bessenoff, G. R., & Snow, D. (2006). Absorbing society's influence: Body image self-discrepancy and internalized shame. *Sex Roles, 54*(9–10), 727–731.

Bobel, C. (2006). "Our revolution has style:" Contemporary menstrual product activists "doing feminism" in the third wave. *Sex Roles, 54*(5–6), 331–345.

Bobel, C., & Kwan, S. (2011). *Embodied resistance: Challenging the norms, breaking the rules*. Nashville: Vanderbilt University Press.

Booth, E. T. (2011). Queering queer eye: The stability of gay identity confronts the liminality of trans embodiment. *Western Journal of Communication, 75*(2), 185–204.

Bordo, S. (1993). Feminism, Foucault, and the politics of the body. In C. Ramazanoglu (Ed.), *Up against Foucault: Explorations of some tensions between Foucault and feminism* (pp. 179–202). Florence: Psychology Press.

Boroughs, M., Cafri, G., & Thompson, J. K. (2005). Male body depilation: Prevalence and associated features of body hair removal. *Sex Roles, 52*(9–10), 637–644.

Bourdieu, P. (1977). *Outline of a theory of practice*. Cambridge: Cambridge University Press.

Boyd, E. M., Reynolds, J. R., Tillman, K. H., & Martin, P. Y. (2011). Adolescent girls' race/ethnic status, identities, and drive for thinness. *Social Science Research, 40*(2), 667–684.

Braidotti, R. (1994). *Nomadic subjects: Embodiment and sexual difference in contemporary feminist theory*. New York: Columbia University Press.

Bramwell, R., Morland, C., & Garden, A. S. (2007). Expectations and experience of labial reduction: A qualitative study. BJOG: An International. *Journal of Obstetrics and Gynecology, 114*(2), 1493–1499.

Braun, V. (2005). In search of (better) sexual pleasure: Female genital "cosmetic" surgery. *Sexualities, 8*(4), 407–424.

Braun, V., & Clarke, V. (2006). Using thematic analysis in psychology. *Qualitative Research in Psychology, 3*(2), 77–101.

Braun, V., & Tiefer, L. (2010). The "designer vagina" and the pathologisation of female genital diversity: Interventions for change. *Radical Psychology, 8*(1).

Braun, V., Gavey, N., & McPhillips, K. (2003). The fair deal? Unpacking accounts of reciprocity in heterosex. *Sexualities, 6*(2), 237–261.

Braun, V., Tricklebank, G., & Clarke, V. (in press). "It shouldn't stick out from your bikini at the beach:" Meaning, gender, and the hairy/hairless body. *Psychology of Women Quarterly*.

Brown, S. D., Cromby, J., Harper, D. J., Johnson, K., & Reavey, P. (2011). Researching "experience:" Embodiment, methodology, process. *Theory & Psychology, 21*(4), 493–515.

Butler, J. (1990). *Gender trouble*. New York: Routledge.

Cahill, A. J. (2011). *Overcoming objectification: A carnal ethics*. New York: Routledge.

Carr, J. L. (2013). The SlutWalk movement: A study in transnational feminist activism. *Journal of Feminist Scholarship, 4*, 24–38.

Chemers, M. M. (2005). Introduction: Staging stigma: A freak studies manifesto. *Disability Studies Quarterly, 25*(3).

Chrisler, J. C. (2012). "Why can't you control yourself?" Fat should be a feminist issue. *Sex Roles, 66*(9–10), 608–616.

Collins, P. H. (1999). *Black feminist thought: Knowledge, consciousness, and the politics of empowerment*. New York: Routledge.

Connell, R. W. (2005). *Masculinities*. Berkeley: University of California Press.

Coy, M., & Garner, M. (2012). Definitions, discourses, and dilemmas: Policy and academic engagement with the sexualisation of popular culture. *Gender and Education, 24*(3), 285–301.

Craig, M. L., & Liberti, R. (2007). "Cause that's what girls do:" The making of a feminized gym. *Gender & Society, 21*(5), 676–699.

Cress, D. M., & Snow, D. A. (2000). The outcomes of homeless mobilization: The influence of organization, disruption, political mediation, and framing. *The American Journal of Sociology, 105*(4), 1063–1104.

Crossley, N. (1996). Body-subject/body-power: Agency, inscription and control in Foucault and Merleau-Ponty. *Body and Society, 2*(2), 99–116.

Curtis, D. (2009). *Pleasure and perils: Girls' sexuality in a Caribbean consumer culture*. New Jersey: Rutgers University Press.

Del Rosso, J. (2011). The penis as public art: Embodiment and the performance of masculinity in public settings. *Sexualities, 14*(6), 704–724.

DeLamater, J. D., & Hyde, J. S. (1998). Essentialism vs. social constructionism in the study of human sexuality. *Journal of Sex Research, 35*(1), 10–18.

DeMaria, A. L., Hollub, A. V., & Herbenick, D. (2011). Using genital self-image, body image, and sexual behaviors to predict gynecological exam behaviors of college women. *Journal of Sexual Medicine, 8*(9), 2484–2492.

Diamond, L. (2008). *Sexual fluidity: Understanding women's love and desire*. Cambridge: Harvard University Press.

Dias, K. (2013). The ana sanctuary: Women's pro-anorexia narratives in cyberspace. *Journal of International Women's Studies, 4*(2), 31–45.

Dickerson, B. J., & Rousseau, N. (2009). Ageism through omission: The obsolescence of black women's sexuality. *Journal of African American Studies, 13*(3), 307–324.

Dillaway, H. E. (2005). Menopause is the "good old:" Women's thoughts about reproductive aging. *Gender and Society, 19*(3), 398–417.

Dillaway, H. E. (2011). Menopausal and misbehaving: When women "flash" in front of others. In C. Bobel & S. Kwan (Eds.), *Embodied resistance: Challenging the norms, breaking the rules* (pp. 197–208). Nashville: Vanderbilt University Press.

DilOrio, J. A., & Nusbaumer, M. R. (1993). Securing our sanity: Anger management among abortion escorts. *Journal of Contemporary Ethnography, 21*(4), 411–438.

Earle, S. (2003). "Bumps and boobs:" Fatness and women's experiences of pregnancy. *Women's Studies International Forum, 26*(3), 245–252.

Ensler, E. (2007). *The vagina monologues*. New York: Villard Books.

Eriksen, S., & Goering, S. (2011). A test of the agency hypothesis in women's cosmetic surgery usage. *Sex Roles, 64*(11–12), 888–901.

Fahs, B. (2009). Compulsory bisexuality? The challenges of modern sexual fluidity. *Journal of Bisexuality, 9*(3), 431–449.

Fahs, B. (2010). Radical refusals: On the anarchist politics of women choosing asexuality. *Sexualities, 13*(4), 445–461.

Fahs, B. (2011a). *Performing sex: The making and unmaking of women's erotic lives*. Albany: SUNY Press.

Fahs, B. (2011b). Dreaded "Otherness:" Heteronormative patrolling in women's body hair rebellions. *Gender & Society, 24*(4), 451–472.

Fahs, B. (2011c). Sex during menstruation: Race, sexual identity, and women's qualitative accounts of pleasure and disgust. *Feminism & Psychology, 21*(2), 155–178.

Fahs, B. (2012). Breaking body hair boundaries: Classroom exercises for challenging social constructions of the body and sexuality. *Feminism & Psychology, 22*(4), 482–506.

Fahs, B. (2013). Raising bloody hell: Inciting menstrual panics through campus and community activism. In B. Fahs, M. L. Dudy, & S. Stage (Eds.), *The moral panics of sexuality* (pp. 77–91). London: Palgrave.

Fahs, B. (2014). Perilous patches and pitstaches: Imagined versus lived experiences of women's body hair growth. *Psychology of Women Quarterly, 38*(2), 167–180.

Fahs, B., & Delgado, D. (2011). The specter of excess: Race, class, and gender in women's body hair narratives. In C. Bobel & S. Kwan (Eds.), *Embodied resistance: Challenging the norms, breaking the rules* (pp. 13–25). Nashville: Vanderbilt University Press.

Fahs, B., & Swank, E. (2011). Social identities as predictors of women's sexual satisfaction and sexual activity. *Archives of Sexual Behavior, 40*(5), 903–914.

Fahs, B., Dudy, M. L., & Stage, S. (2013). *The moral panics of sexuality*. London: Palgrave.

Feinberg, L. (1996). *Transgender warriors: Making history from Joan of Arc to Dennis Rodman*. Boston: Beacon Press.

Feingold, A., & Mazzella, R. (1998). Gender differences in body image are increasing. *Psychological Science, 9*, 190–195.

Fine, M. (1988). Sexuality, schooling, and adolescent females: The missing discourse of desire. *Harvard Educational Review, 58*(1), 29–54.

Fine, M., & McClelland, S. I. (2006). Sexuality education and desire: Still missing after all these years. *Harvard Educational Review, 76*(3), 297–338.

Foroni, F., & Semin, G. R. (2012). Not all implicit measures of attitudes are created equal: Evidence from an embodied perspective. *Journal of Experimental Social Psychology, 48*(1), 424–427.

Foster, J., & Strack, F. (1996). Influence of overt head movements on memory for valenced words: A case of conceptual motor compatibility. *Journal of Personality and Social Psychology, 71*, 421–430.

Foucault, M. (1977). *Discipline and punish: The birth of the prison*. New York: Vintage.

Foucault, M. (1978). *The history of sexuality* (Vol. 1). New York: Random House.

Foucault, M. (1984). *The Foucault reader*. New York: Random House.

Frederick, D. A., Lever, J., & Peplau, L. A. (2007). Interest in cosmetic surgery and body image: Views of men and women across the lifespan. *Plastic and Reconstructive Surgery, 120*(5), 1407–1415.

Friedrich, W. (2003). Studies of sexuality of nonabused children. In J. Bancroft (Ed.), *Sexual development in childhood* (pp. 107–120). Bloomington: Indiana University Press.

Frith, H. (2013). Labouring on orgasms: Embodiment, efficiency, entitlement, and obligations in heterosex. *Culture, Health & Sexuality, 15*(4), 494–510.

Frith, H., & Gleeson, K. (2004). Clothing and embodiment: Men managing body image and appearance. *Psychology of Men & Masculinity, 5*(1), 40–48.

Frueh, J. (2003). The aesthetics of orgasm. *Sexualities, 6*(3–4), 459–478.

Furnham, A., Badmin, N., & Sneade, I. (2002). Body image dissatisfaction: Gender differences in eating attitudes, self-esteem, and reasons for exercise. *Journal of Psychology, 136*(6), 581–596.

Gagné, P., & Tewksbury, R. (1998). Conformity pressures and gender resistance among transgendered individuals. *Social Problems, 45*, 81–101.

Gatens, M. (1996). *Imaginary bodies: Ethics, power, and corporeality*. New York: Routledge.

Gatrell, C. J. (2007). Secrets and lies: Breastfeeding and professional paid work. *Social Science & Medicine, 65*(2), 393–404.

Gillies, V., Harden, A., Johnson, K., Reavey, P., Strange, V., & Willig, C. (2004). Women's collective constructions of embodied practices through memory work: Cartesian dualism in memories of sweating and pain. *British Journal of Social Psychology, 43*(1), 99–112.

Gleeson, K., & Frith, H. (2004). Pretty in pink: Young women presenting mature sexual identities. In A. Harris (Ed.), *All about the Girl: Culture, power and identity* (pp. 103–114). New York: Routledge.

Glenberg, A. M. (2010). Embodiment as a unifying perspective for psychology. *Cognitive Science, 1*(4), 586–596.

Goldberg, M. (2014). What is a woman? The dispute between radical feminism and transgenderism. New Yorker. http://www.newyorker.com/magazine/2014/08/04/woman-2. Accessed 9 Aug 2014.

Graham, C. (2003). Methodological issues involved in adult recall of childhood sexual experiences. In J. Bancroft (Ed.), *Sexual development in childhood* (pp. 67–76). Bloomington: Indiana University Press.

Grogan, S., Conner, M., & Smithson, H. (2006). Sexuality and exercise motivations: Are gay men and heterosexual women most likely to be motivated by concern about weight and appearance? *Sex Roles, 55*(7), 567–572.

Grollman, E. A. (2012). Multiple forms of perceived discrimination and health among adolescents and young adults. *Journal of Health and Social Behavior, 53*(2), 199–214.

Grosz, E. (1994). *Volatile bodies: Toward a corporeal feminism*. Bloomington: Indiana University Press.

Grosz, E. (2008). *Chaos, territory, art: Deleuze and the framing of the earth*. New York: Columbia University Press.

Haines, H. H. (1984). Black radicalization and the funding of civil rights, 1957–1970. *Social Problems, 32*(1), 31–43.

Halberstam, J. (1998). *Female masculinity*. Durham: Duke University Press.

Halberstam, J. (2005). *In a queer time and place: Transgender bodies, subcultural lives*. New York: New York University Press.

Hannabach, C. (2007). Anxious embodiment, disability, and sexuality: A response to Margrid Shildrick. *Studies in Gender and Sexuality, 8*(3), 253–261.

Haraway, D. (1991). *Simians, cyborgs, and women*. New York: Routledge.

Hassouneh-Phillips, D., & McNeff, E. (2005). "I thought I was less worthy": Low sexual and body esteem and increased vulnerability to intimate partner abuse in women with physical disabilities. *Sexuality and Disability, 23*(4), 227–240.

Hauge, M. (2009). Bodily practices and discourses of hetero-femininity: Girls' constitution of subjectivities in their social transition between childhood and adolescence. *Gender and Education, 21*(3), 293–307.

Heckert, J., & Cleminson, R. (2011). *Anarchism & sexuality: Ethics, relationships, and power*. London: Routledge.

Hendricks, K., & Plummer, S. (2013). Re-thinking wellness: A feminist approach to health and fitness. *Gender Forum, 45*.

Hepburn, A. (2006). Getting closer at a distance: Theory and the contingencies of practice. *Theory & Psychology, 16*(3), 327–342.

Herbenick, D., & Reese, M. (2010). Development and validation of the female genital self-image scale. *Journal of Sexual Medicine, 7*(5), 1822–1830.

Herbenick, D., Schick, V., Reece, M., Sanders, S., Dodge, B., & Fortenberry, D. (2010a). The female genital self-image scale (FGSIS): Results from a nationally representative probability sample of women in the United States. *Journal of Sexual Medicine, 8*(1), 158–166.

Herbenick, D., Schick, V., Reece, M., Sanders, S., & Fortenberry, D. (2010b). Pubic hair removal among women in the United States: Prevalence, methods, and characteristics. *Journal of Sexual Medicine, 7*(10), 3322–3330.

Herdt, G., & McClintock, M. (2000). The magical age of 10. *Archives of Sexual Behavior, 29*(6), 587–606.

Heyes, C. J. (2007). Cosmetic surgery and the televisual makeover: A Foucauldian feminist reading. *Feminist Media Studies, 7*(1), 17–32.

Hillyer, B. (1998). The embodiment of old women: Silences. *Frontiers, 19*(1), 48–60.

Hill Collins, P. (1990). *Black feminist thought: Knowledge, consciousness, and the politics of empowerment*. New York: Routledge.

Holland, J., & Thomson, R. (2010). Revisiting youthful sexuality: Continuities and changes over two decades. *Sexual and Relationship Therapy, 25*(3), 342–350.

Holland, J., Ramazanoglu, C., & Sharpe, S. (1994). Power and desire: The embodiment of female sexuality. *Feminist Review, 46*, 21–38.

Hoppe, T. (2011). Circuits of power, circuits of pleasure: Sexual scripting in gay men's bottom narratives. *Sexualities, 14*(2), 193–217.

Hunter, M. L. (2002). "If you're light you're alright:" Light skin as social capital for women of color. *Gender & Society, 16*(2), 175–193.

Hyde, J. (2003). The use of meta-analysis in understanding the effects of child sexual abuse. In J. Bancroft (Ed.), *Sexual development in childhood* (pp. 82–91). Bloomington: Indiana University Press.

Impett, E. A., Henson, J. M., Breines, J. G., Schooler, D., & Tolman, D. L. (2011). Embodiment feels better: Girls body objectification and well being across adolescence. *Psychology of Women Quarterly, 35*(1), 46–58.

Inckle, K. (2014). A lame argument: Profoundly disabled embodiment as critical gender politics. *Disability & Society, 29*(3), 388–401.

Irigaray, L. (1985). *This sex which is not one*. Ithaca: Cornell University Press.

Israel, T., Gorcheva, R., Burnes, T. R., & Walther, W. A. (2008). Helpful and unhelpful therapy experiences of LGBT clients. *Psychotherapy Research, 18*(3), 294–305.

Jackson, S., & Scott, S. (2007). Faking it like a woman? Towards an interpretive theorization of sexual pleasure. *Body and Society, 13*(2), 95–116.

Jagose, A. (2010). Counterfeit pleasures: Fake orgasm and queer agency. *Textual Practice, 24*(3), 517–539.

Jipson, A., & Becker, P. (2001). Protesting Klan rallies: What can we learn from community organizations vs. non-local countermovements? *Research in Political Sociology, 9*, 233–268.

Joanisse, L., & Synnott, A. (1999). Fighting back: Reactions and resistance to the stigma of obesity. In J. Sobal & D. Maurer (Eds.), *Interpreting weight: The social management of fatness and thinness* (pp. 49–60). Piscataway: Transaction Publishers.

Johnson-Robledo, I., Ball, M., Lauta, K., & Zekoll, A. (2003). To bleed or not to bleed: Young women's attitudes toward menstrual suppression. *Women & Health, 38*(3), 59–75.

Johnston, J., & Taylor, J. (2008). Feminist consumerism and fat activists: A comparative study of grassroots activism and the Dove real beauty campaign. *Signs, 33*(4), 941–966.

Jones, D. C. (2001). Social comparison and body image: Attractiveness comparisons to models and peers among adolescent girls and boys. *Sex Roles, 45*(9–10), 645–664.

Katz, S., & Marshall, B. (2003). New sex for old: Lifestyle, consumerism, and the ethics of aging well. *Journal of Aging Studies, 17*(1), 3–16.

Katz, J., & Tirone, V. (2009). Women's sexual compliance with male dating partners: Associations with investment in ideal womanhood and romantic well-being. *Sex Roles, 60*(5–6), 347–356.

Kimmel, M. S. (2004). Masculinity as homophobia: Fear, shame, and silence in the construction of gender identity. In P. D. Rothenberg (Ed.), *Race, class, and gender in the United States: An integrated study* (pp. 81–93). New York: Worth.

King, B. G. (2011). The tactical disruptiveness of social movements: Sources of market and mediated disruption in corporate boycotts. *Social Problems, 58*(4), 491–517.

Kippax, S., & Smith, G. (2001). Anal intercourse and power in sex between men. *Sexualities, 4*(4), 413–434.

Lamb, S., & Coakley, M. (1993). 'Normal' childhood sexual play and games: Differentiating play from abuse. *Child Abuse and Neglect, 17*(4), 515–526.

Lanzieri, N., & Hildebrandt, T. (2011). Using hegemonic masculinity to explain gay male attraction to muscular and athletic men. *Journal of Homosexuality, 58*(2), 275–293.

Laqueur, T. (2003). *Solitary sex: A cultural history of masturbation*. Cambridge: Zone Books.

Le Espiritu, Y. (2001). "We don't sleep around like white girls do:" Family, culture, and gender in Filipina American lives. *Signs, 26*(2), 415–440.

Lee, R. (2000). Notes from the (non) field: Teaching and theorizing women of color. *Meridians, 1*(1), 85–109.

Lewis, D. M., & Cachelin, F. M. (2001). Body image, body dissatisfaction, and eating attitudes in midlife and elderly women. *Eating Disorders, 9*(1), 29–39.

Lloyd, E. (2009). *The case of the female orgasm: Bias in the science of evolution*. Cambridge: Harvard University Press.

Lodge, A. C., & Umberson, D. (2012). All shook up: Sexuality of mid to later life married couples. *Journal of Marriage and Family, 74*(3), 428–443.

Loe, M. (2004). Sex and the senior woman: Pleasure and danger in the Viagra era. *Sexualities, 7*, 303–326.

Loewenson, P. R., Ireland, M., & Resnick, M. D. (2004). Primary and secondary sexual abstinence in high school students. *Journal of Adolescent Health, 34*(3), 209–215.

Lombardi, E. L., Wilchins, R. A., Priesing, D., & Malouf, D. (2002). Gender violence: Transgender experiences with violence and discrimination. *Journal of Homosexuality, 42*(1), 89–101.

Lottes, I. L. (2002). Sexual health policies in other industrialized countries: Are there lessons for the United States? *Journal of Sex Research, 39*(1), 79–83.

Maddison, S. (2009). "The second sexual revolution:" Big pharma, porn, and the biopolitical penis. *Topia, 22*, 35–53.

Marshall, B. L., & Katz, S. (2002). Forever functional: Sexual fitness and the ageing male body. *Body and Society, 8*(4), 43–70.

Martin, E. (2001). *The woman in the body: A cultural analysis of reproduction*. Boston: Beacon Press.

Martin, P. Y. (2005). *Rape work: Victims, gender, and emotions in organization and community context*. Florence: Psychology Press.

Martins, Y., Tiggemann, M., & Churchett, L. (2008). Hair today, gone tomorrow: A comparison of body hair removal practices in gay and heterosexual men. *Body Image, 5*(3), 312–316.

Masters, W. H., & Johnson, V. E. (1966). *Human sexual response*. Boston: Little, Brown, & Co.

McClelland, S. I. (2010). Intimate justice: A critical analysis of sexual satisfaction. *Social and Personality Psychology Compass, 4*(9), 663–680.

McClelland, S. I. (2014). "What do you mean when you say that you're sexually satisfied?": A mixed methods study. *Feminism & Psychology, 24*(1), 74–96.

McCreary, D. R., & Sasse, D. K. (2000). An exploration of the drive for muscularity in adolescent boys and girls. *Journal of American College Health, 48*(6), 297–304.

Meleo-Erwin, Z. (2012). Disrupting normal: Toward the "ordinary and familiar" in fat politics. *Feminism & Psychology, 22*(3), 388–402.

Merleau-Ponty, M. (1945). *Phenomenology of perception*. Paris: Gallimard.

Messerschmidt, J. W. (2000). *Nine lives: Adolescent masculinities, the body, and violence*. Boulder: Westview Press.

Meyer, I. H., Schwartz, S., & Frost, D. M. (2008). Social patterning of stress and coping: Does disadvantaged social statuses confer more stress and fewer coping resources? *Social Science & Medicine, 67*(3), 368–379.

Middlethon, A. (2002). Being anally penetrated: Erotic inhibitions, improvisations and transformations. *Sexualities, 5*(2), 181–200.

Millsted, R., & Frith, H. (2003). Being large-breasted: Women negotiating embodiment. *Women's Studies International Forum, 26*(5), 455–465.

Minh-Ha, T. (1989). *Woman, native, other*. Bloomington: Indiana University Press.

Moe, A. M. (2011). Belly dancing mommas: Challenging cultural discourses of maternity. In C. Bobel & S. Kwan (Eds.), *Embodied resistance: Challenging the norms, breaking the rules* (pp. 88–98). Nashville: Vanderbilt University Press.

Mohr, J., Israel, T., & Sedlacek, W. (2001). Counselors' attitudes regarding bisexuality as predictors of counselors' clinical responses. *Journal of Counseling Psychology, 48*, 212–222.

Monaghan, L. F. (2005). Big handsome men, bears and others: Virtual constructions of "fat male embodiment." *Body & Society, 11*(2), 81–111.

Moore, L. J. (2011). *Sperm counts: Overcome by man's most precious fluid*. New York: New York University Press.

Morgan, M. (2005). Hip-hop women shredding the veil: Race and class in popular feminist identity. *South Atlantic Quarterly, 104*(3), 425–444.

Morris, R. (2010). *Can the subaltern speak? Reflections on the history of an idea*. New York: Columbia University Press.

Morrison, T. G., Morrison, M. A., & Hopkins, C. (2003). Striving for bodily perfection? An exploration of the drive for muscularity in Canadian men. *Psychology of Men and Masculinity, 4,* 111–120.

Morrison, M. A., Morrison, T. G., & Sager, C. L. (2004). Does body satisfaction differ between gay men and lesbian women and heterosexual men and women? A meta-analytic review. *Body Image, 1*(2), 127–138.

Muehlenhard, C. L., & Shippee, S. K. (2010). Men's and women's reports of pretending orgasm. *Journal of Sex Research, 47*(6), 552–567.

Nash, C. J. (2010). Trans geographies, embodiment, and experience. *Gender, Place & Culture, 17*(5), 579–595.

Nash, M. (2012). *Making "postmodern" mothers: Pregnant embodiment, baby bumps, and body image*. London: Palgrave.

Nepstad, S. E. (2005). Disciplines and dissenters: Tactical choice and the consequences in the plowshares movement. *Research in Social Movements, Conflicts, and Change, 25,* 139–159.

Niedenthal, P. M., Brauer, M., Halberstadt, J. B., & Innes-Ker, A. H. (2001). When did her smile drop? Facial mimicry and the influences of emotional state on the detection of change in emotional expression. *Cognition and Emotion, 15,* 853–864.

Noll, S. M., & Frederickson, B. L. (1998). A mediational model linking self-objectification, body shame, and disordered eating. *Psychology of Women Quarterly, 22*(4), 623–636.

Nugteren, H. M., Balkema, G. T., Pascal, A. L., Schultz, W. C. M., Nijman, J. M., & Van Driel, M. F. (2010). 18-year experience in the management of men with a complaint of a small penis. *Journal of Sex and Marital Therapy, 36*(2), 109–117.

Offman, A., & Kleinplatz, P. J. (2004). Does PMDD belong in the DSM? Challenging the medicalization of women's bodies. *Canadian Journal of Human Sexuality, 13*(1), 17–27.

Oliver, K. (2010). Motherhood, sexuality, and pregnant embodiment: Twenty-five years of gestation. *Hypatia, 25*(4), 760–777.

Pascoe, C. J. (2005). "Dude, you're a fag:" Adolescent masculinity and the fag discourse. *Sexualities, 8*(3), 329–346.

Peluso, N. M. (2011). "Cruisin' for the brusin:'" Women's flat track roller derby. In C. Bobel & S. Kwan (Eds.), *Embodied resistance: Challenging the norms, breaking the rules* (pp. 37–47). Nashville: Vanderbilt University Press.

Pitts, V. (1999). Body modification, self-mutilation, and agency in media accounts of a subculture. *Body & Society, 5*(2–3), 291–303.

Pitts, V. (2003). *In the flesh: The cultural politics of body modification*. London: Palgrave.

Plante, R. (2006). *Sexualities in context: A social perspective*. Boulder: Westview Press.

Probyn, E. (1993). *Sexing the self: Gendered positions in cultural studies*. Florence: Psychology Press.

Rademakers, J., Laan, M. J. C., & Straver, C. J. (2003). Body awareness and physical intimacy: An exploratory study. In J. Bancroft (Ed.), *Sexual development in childhood* (pp. 121–125). Bloomington: Indiana University Press.

Renold, E. (2005). *Girls, boys and junior sexualities*. New York: Routledge.

Renold, E. (2007). Primary school "studs:" (De)constructing young boys' heterosexual masculinities. *Men & Masculinities, 9,* 275–297.

Renold, E., & Ringrose, J. (2011). Schizoid subjectivities? Re-theorizing teen girls' sexual cultures in an era of "sexualization.". *Journal of Sociology, 47*(4), 389–409.

Ricciardelli, R. (2011). Masculinity, consumerism, and appearance: A look at men's hair. *Canadian Review of Sociology, 48*(2), 181–201.

Roberts, T., & Waters, P. L. (2004). Self-objectification and that "not so fresh feeling:" Feminist therapeutic interventions for healthy female embodiment. *Women and Therapy, 27*(3–4), 5–21.

Roberts, T. A., Goldenberg, J. L., Power, C., & Pyszczynski, T. (2002). "Feminine protection:" The effects of menstruation on attitudes toward women. *Psychology of Women Quarterly, 26*(2), 131–139.

Robinson, K. H. (2012). "Difficult citizenship:" The precarious relationships between childhood, sexuality, and access to knowledge. *Sexualities, 15*(3–4), 257–276.

Rohrer, T. (2007). The body in space: Dimensions of embodiment. In T. Ziemke, J. Zlatev, R. M. Frank, & W. de Gruyter (Eds.), *Embodiment* (pp. 339–377). Berlin: Mouton de Gruyter.

Roscigno, V. J., & Hodson, R. (2004). The organization and social foundations of worker resistance. *American Sociological Review, 69*(1), 14–39.

Rothblum, E., & Solovay, S. (2009). *The fat studies reader*. New York: New York University Press.

Rubin, G. S. (1984). Thinking sex: Notes for a radical theory of the politics of sexuality. In H. Abelove, M. A. Barale, & D. M. Halperin (Eds.), *The lesbian and gay studies reader* (pp. 3–44). New York: Routledge.

Ryan, G. (2000). Childhood sexuality: A decade of study. Part 1—Research and curriculum development. *Child Abuse and Neglect, 24*(1), 33–48.

Sanchez, D. T., & Kiefer, A. K. (2007). Body concerns in and out of the bedroom: Implications for sexual pleasure and problems. *Archives of Sexual Behavior, 36*(6), 808.

Schalet, A. (2010). Sexual subjectivity revisited: The significance of relationships in Dutch and American girls' experiences of sexuality. *Gender & Society, 24*(3), 304–329.

Schick, V. R., Calabrese, S. K., Rima, B. N., & Zucker, A. N. (2010). Genital appearance dissatisfaction: Implications for women's genital image self-consciousness, sexual esteem, sexual satisfaction, and sexual risk. *Psychology of Women Quarterly, 34*(3), 394–404.

Schmied, V., & Lupton, D. (2001). Blurring the boundaries: Breastfeeding and maternal subjectivity. *Sociology of Health & Illness, 23*(2), 234–250.

Schussman, A., & Soule, S. A. (2005). Process and protest: Accounting for individual protest participation. *Social Forces, 84*(2), 1083–1108.

Scott, J. C. (1990). *Domination and the arts of resistance: Hidden transcripts*. New Haven: Yale University Press.

Sedgwick, E. K. (1990). *Epistemology of the closet*. Berkeley: University of California Press.

Sherry, M. (2004). Overlaps and contradictions between queer theory and disability studies. *Disability & Society, 19*(7), 769–783.

Shildrick, M. (2005). Unreformed bodies: Normative anxiety and the denial of pleasure. *Women's Studies, 34*(3–4), 327–344.

Shildrick, M. (2007). Contested pleasures: The sociopolitical economy of disability and sexuality. *Sexuality Research & Social Policy, 4*(1), 53–66.

Shilling, C. (2004). *The body in culture, technology, and society*. New York: Sage.

Singh, S., Darroch, J. E., & Frost, J. J. (2001). Socioeconomic disadvantage and adolescent women's sexual and reproductive behavior: The case of five developed countries. *Family Planning Perspectives, 33*(6), 251–289.

Slevin, K. F. (2010). "If I had lots of money…I'd have a body makeover:" Managing the aging body. *Social Forces, 88*(3), 1003–1020.

Slevin, K. F., & Linneman, T. J. (2010). Old gay men's bodies and masculinities. *Men and Masculinities, 12*(4), 483–507.

Slevin, K. F., & Mowery, C. (2012). Exploring embodied aging and ageism among old lesbians and gay men. In L. Carpenter & J. DeLamater (Eds.), *Sex for life, from virginity to Viagra: How sexuality changes throughout our lives* (pp. 260–277). New York: New York University Press.

Smith, N., & Stanley, E. A. (2011). *Captive genders: Trans embodiment and the prison industrial complex*. Oakland: AK Press.

Smith-Rosenberg, C. (1986). *Disorderly conduct: Visions of gender in Victorian America*. New York: Oxford University Press.

Spivak. G. (1999). *A critique of postcolonial reason: Toward a history of the vanishing present*. Cambridge: Harvard University Press.

St. John, G. (2008). Protestival: Global days of action and carnivalized politics in the present. *Social Movement Studies, 7*(2), 167–190.

Stone, A. L. (2009). More than adding a T: American lesbian and gay activists' attitudes towards transgender inclusion. *Sexualities, 12*(3), 334–354.

Strachan, E., & Staples, B. (2012). Masturbation. *Pediatrics in Review, 33*(4), 190–191.

Strelan, P., Mehaffey, S. J., & Tiggemann, M. (2003). Self-objectification and esteem in young women: The mediating role of reasons for exercise. *Sex Roles, 48*(1–2), 89–95.

Stryker, S. (1994). My words to Victor Frankenstein above the village of Chamounix: Performing transgender rage. *GLQ, 1*(3), 227–254.

Stryker, S., & Whittle, S. (2006). *The transgender studies reader*. New York: Taylor & Francis.

Swank, E., & Fahs, B. (2013). An intersectional analysis of gender and race for sexual minorities who engage in gay and lesbian rights activism. *Sex Roles, 68*(11–12), 660–674.

Taylor, V., & Rupp, L. J. (2004). Chicks with dicks, men in dresses: What it means to be a drag queen. *Journal of Homosexuality, 46*(3–4), 113–133.

Thompson, L. (1999). *The wandering womb: A cultural history of outrageous beliefs about women*. Amherst: Prometheus Books.

Thorne, B. (1993). *Gender play: Girls and boys in school*. New Brunswick: Rutgers University Press.

Tiefer, L. (2006). Female sexual dysfunction: A case study of disease mongering and activist resistance. *PLoS Medicine, 3*(4), e178.

Tiefer, L. (2008). Female genital cosmetic surgery: Freakish or inevitable? Analysis from medical marketing, bioethics, and feminist theory. *Feminism & Psychology, 18*(4), 466–479.

Tiggemann, M. (2004). Body image across the adult lifespan: Stability and change. *Body Image, 1*(1), 29–41.

Tiggemann, M., Martins, Y., & Churchett, L. (2008). Beyond muscles: Unexplored parts of men's body image. *Journal of Health Psychology, 13*(8), 1163–1172.

Toerien, M., Wilkinson, S., & Choi, P. Y. L. (2005). Body hair removal: The "mundane" production of normative femininity. *Sex Roles, 52*(5–6), 399–406.

Tolman, D. L. (1994). Doing desire: Adolescent girls' struggle for/with sexuality. *Gender & Society, 8*(3), 324–342.

Tolman, D. L. (2002). *Dilemmas of desire: Teenage girls talk about sexuality*. Cambridge: Harvard University Press.

Vannier, S. A., & O'Sullivan, L. F. (2010). Sex without desire: Characteristics of occasions of sexual compliance in young adults' committed relationships. *Journal of Sex Research, 47*(5), 429–439.

Vares, T. (2009). Reading the 'sexy oldie': Gender, age(ing) and embodiment. *Sexualities, 12*(4), 503–524.

Waite, L. J., & Joyner, K. (2001). Emotional satisfaction and physical pleasure in sexual unions. *Journal of Marriage and the Family, 63*, 247–264.

Warner, M., & Berland, L. (2000). *Intimacy*. Chicago: University of Chicago Press.

Weitz, R. (2001). Women and their hair: Seeking power through resistance and accommodation. *Gender & Society, 15*(5), 667–686.

White, A. M. (1999). Talking feminist, talking Black: Micromobilization processes in a collective protest against rape. *Gender & Society, 13*(1), 77–100.

Williams, C. J., Weinberg, M. S., & Rosenberger, J. G. (2013). Trans men: Embodiments, identities, and sexualities. *Sociological Forum, 28*(4), 719–741.

Winter, S., Chalungsooth, P., Teh, Y. K., Rojanalert, N., Maneerat, K., Wong, Y. W., Macapagal, R. A., et al. (2009). Transpeople, transprejudice, and pathologization: A seven-country factor analytic study. *International Journal of Sexual Health, 21*(2), 96–118.

Wittig, M. (1992). *The straight mind: And other essays*. Boston: Beacon Press.

Woertman, L., & Brink, F. (2012). Body image and female sexual functioning and behavior: A review. *Journal of Sex Research, 49*(2–3), 184–211.

Wong, Y. J., Horn, A. J., & Chen, S. (2013). Perceived masculinity: The potential influence of race, racial essentialist beliefs, and stereotypes. *Psychology of Men & Masculinity, 14*(4), 452–464.

Young, I. M. (1990). Pregnant embodiment: Subjectivity and alienation. In I. M. Young (Ed.), *Throwing like a girl and other essays in feminist philosophy and social theory* (pp. 160–176). Bloomington: Indiana University Press.

Young, I. (2005a). Breasted experience: The look and the feeling. In I. Young (Ed.), *On female body experience: "Throwing like a girl" and other essays* (pp. 75–96). New York: Oxford University Press.

Young, I. M. (2005b). *On female body experience: Throwing like a girl and other essays*. New York: Oxford University Press.

Zavella, P. (2008). Playing with fire? The gendered construction of Chicana/Mexican sexuality. In M. C. Gutmann, F. V. Matos Rodriguez, L. Stephen, & P. Zavella (Eds.), *Perspectives on Las Americas: A reader in culture, history, and representations* (pp. 229–244). Malden: Blackwell Publishers.

Missing Intersections: Contemporary Examinations of Sexuality and Disability

10

Amanda M. Jungels and Alexis A. Bender

10.1 Introduction

When we were asked to write this chapter we were excited to explore the intersection of sexuality and disability in greater depth than either of us had previously. What we discovered is that while the fields of sexuality and disability studies have existed independently for some time, they have only recently begun to merge together. Moreover, the existing literature represents an unbelievably broad range of definitions, methods, and perspectives, making a synthesized overview of the literature very difficult to accomplish. Other researchers have noted this lack of consistency (see Connell et al. 2014), but the breadth and depth of the diversity in regards to definitions, populations, methods, and findings surprised us.

One of the biggest issues we faced in compiling our review was the broad range of definitions that researchers relied upon. As we discuss in more detail in the following section, disability is a complicated and multidimensional concept that is difficult to define (Altman 2001). First, definitions of disability span the social, medical, political, and legal fields, all of which might be at odds with one another depending on the subject of inquiry and the perspectives of the researchers. Moreover, many researchers were not clear about how they operationalized disability (or sexuality, for that matter), leaving the reader unable to compare one study to another. Second, how these definitions are applied—and who is included in a given definition—can vary greatly. We found ourselves faced with the same challenge that many scholars of sexuality and disability have dealt with, and an issue that is the subject of long-standing debate within disability studies: inclusion.

Finally, our review was complicated by the fact that the methods employed in many studies were underdeveloped or lacked rigor. A great number of articles explored the concepts of disability and sexuality in an enlightening way, but the parameters used to define the population—when it was clearly explained at all—would often reduce the sample to a very niche group, excluding a broad range of people and types of disability. In addition, minority groups, and sexual minorities in particular, were often neglected in the existing literature (Caldwell 2010; Noonan and Taylor Gomez 2011), leaving those populations—and the issue of intersectionality—woefully understudied. Furthermore—perhaps because of the reliance on convenience samples drawn from medical and clinical populations—core definitions and basic elements of the studies' methods were often not clearly explained;

The views expressed here are solely those of the authors and do not represent those of the U.S. Army Public Health Command, the U.S. Army, or the U.S. Government.

A. M. Jungels (✉) · A. A. Bender
Behavioral and Social Health Outcomes Program (BSHOP), Army Institute of Public Health, US Army Public Health Command (USAPHC), Aberdeen Proving Ground–Edgewood Area, Aberdeen, MD 21010, USA
e-mail: amanda.jungels@gmail.com

J. DeLamater, R.F. Plante (eds.), *Handbook of the Sociology of Sexualities,* Handbooks of Sociology and Social Research, DOI 10.1007/978-3-319-17341-2_10, © Springer International Publishing Switzerland 2015

we were often left wondering how the population was selected, how disability was defined, where and how participants were recruited, or whether the instruments used had a history of validity and reliability. The reliance on extremely small sample sizes as well as on autoethnographic research is another major issue we discovered while reviewing the existing literature. These studies, while invaluable in the depth and nuance they add to discussions of sexuality and disability, are by their very nature related to the most micro-level observations about sexuality and disability. The dearth of macro-level, large-scale, and representative sample research leaves a significant gap in our understanding about the relationship between disability and sexuality. While we realize that the field of sexuality and disability studies is in its infancy compared to other fields within the social sciences, these weaknesses only served to underscore our belief that more rigorous, well-developed research is needed at the intersection of disability and sexuality if the field is to continue to grow.

Given these challenges, and our desire to present a cohesive overview of the existing literature, what follows is a broad review of the available literature about sexuality and disability, organized primarily by subject area. First, we review commonly used definitions of disability and sexuality, as well as the controversies about the use of various terms. Next, we discuss popular theoretical perspectives used by contemporary researchers. Then, we present a broad literature review of existing research, including topics related to sexual rights of people with disabilities, attitudes toward and perceptions of the sexuality of adults and adolescents with disabilities, sex education, and finally sexual facilitation and satisfaction.

10.2 Key Terms

Gordon and Rosenblum (2001) argue that unlike other parts of the Western world, American researchers have, historically, taken a "peculiarly un-sociological" approach to studying disability, where most of the research "continues to frame disability along 'traditional' or 'individual' lines, that is by focusing on limitations, medicalization, diagnoses, individual adjustment, etc." (p. 16). In response to this perceived oversight, Gordon and Rosenblum (2001) applied a social constructionist approach to understanding disability, and argued that just as the categories of race, sex, sexual orientation, and gender are socially constructed, so too are our conceptualizations of disability. Social processes that create minority groups—whether that distinction is on the basis of gender, sex, race, sexual orientation, or disability—involve naming and aggregating into two or more groups, as well as segregating, stigmatizing, and devaluing those in the "non-normative" group and excluding them from full and total access to the larger society. Gordon and Rosenblum (2001) argue that the application of this theory, which has been applied to other social groups, should and can be applied to disability studies as well.

One of the challenges of researching sexuality and disability is reconciling the wide variety of definitions and terms that are used in the literature. Grönvik (2007) categorized five different definitions of disability, all of which were generated for different purposes. First, "functional definitions" focus on the individual's functional limitations (e.g., their use of a wheelchair). Second, a "relative" or "environmental definition" of disability focuses not on the individual, but on inaccessible or limited environments that they encounter; similarly, the "social model" of disability constructs disability as occurring entirely in the environment, which prevents individuals from participating in society. The fourth category, "administrative definitions," result from interactions with the government where one is defined as disabled, perhaps because of the use of some sort of mobility device. Finally, "subjective definitions" result from how the individual with the impairment would define themselves. Given the diverse origins and uses of these definitions, it should not be a surprise that they sometimes conflict with one another, creating multiple layers of definitions that may or may not be accepted by the disabled individual, the larger community, or the government/legal system. In our review of the literature, we found that when offering explicit definitions or operationalization of disability, researchers relied upon some or all of these categories.

It is also important to keep in mind that the population under study is very diverse. Disability studies encompass people with acquired and congenital disabilities; intellectual, cognitive, and physical disabilities; disabilities that are the result of trauma or illness; individuals with mild disabilities as well as those with very serious disabilities; those who need very little medical intervention or caretaking, and those who need significant medical management; those who maintain their own residences and those who reside in long-term care facilities. This diversity also includes individuals from a variety of racial/ethnic backgrounds, genders, sexual orientations, socioeconomic statuses, political perspectives, and national origins. Moreover, these differences are also reflected in (and combined with) the diversity of non-disabled individuals often included in disabled sexuality research, such as spouses, family members, caregivers, medical professionals, and members of the general public.

The variety of definitions, Grönvik (2007) argues, can lead to widely disparate (and sometimes contradictory) outcomes for researchers, as well as making it difficult for the reader to assess, evaluate, and apply findings. Researchers often do not discuss specifics of the population under study (instead referring to a sample of "people with cognitive disabilities" or "individuals with acquired physical disabilities"), perhaps because of the broad range of diversity that may be included in the sample. This diversity, though, is one of the factors that necessitates the use of carefully drawn definitions; it becomes almost impossible to compare, recreate, or build upon existing literature in a systematic way if one cannot assess these factors. And, as Gordon and Rosenblum (2001) point out, the language one chooses to use (e.g., "disabled person" versus "person with a disability") reflects different ideological positions held by activists, researchers, and community members alike. Grönvik (2007) encourages researchers to think about the definitions they employ, as well as the consequences

of their choices. Similarly, it is important for researchers and activists to understand the varied theoretical perspectives that can be employed, as one's theoretical perspective often guides key methodological choices, including how disability is operationalized.

10.3   Theoretical Perspectives

Historically, most sexuality and disability research has been grounded in the medical model of disability. This research, which was conducted primarily by clinicians, doctors, and other medical professionals, often regarded an individual's impairment as the cause of any and all disadvantages that were experienced; the solution, then, was treatment and cure of the underlying condition or impairment (Crow 1996). The result of this model, according to its critics, is that it tended to view and treat disabled individuals as

> not only broken or damaged, but also incompetent, impotent, undesirable, or asexual. Their inability to perform gender and sexuality in a way that meets dominant societal expectations is seen as an intrinsic limitation, an 'unfortunate' but unavoidable consequence of inhabiting a disabled body. (Rembis 2010, p. 51)

The social model of disability, which grew out of opposition to the medical model, shifts the focus away from the impairment and toward the disadvantages experienced by individuals. Under this model, the disability is not in the body, but instead is located in the reduced opportunities and discrimination that individuals with impairments face. As Shakespeare (2006) notes, as early as 1975 the Union of the Physically Impaired Against Segregation (UPIAS), a British activist organization, stated "it is society which disables physically impaired people. Disability is something imposed on top of our impairments, by the way we are unnecessarily isolated and excluded from full participation in society" (p. 198).

Shakespeare (2006) argued that the shift away from the medical model and to the social model has been effective in three broad areas. First, it has been effective politically, in large part because it is easily understood and offers terminology and language that can be used to easily separate allies from those who are not supportive of disability rights and/or activism (e.g., use of the term "disabled people," which indicates acceptance of the social model versus "people with disabilities," which does not) (Shakespeare 2006). Second, the social model has been effectively used to identify and critique discriminatory practices, encouraging legislative social change. Finally, the social model has played an important role in the improved psychological well-being of disabled individuals:

> In traditional accounts of disability, people with impairments feel that they are at fault. Language such as "invalid" reinforce a sense of personal deficit and failure. The focus is on the individual, and on her limitations of body and brain… The social model has the power to change the perception of disabled people. The problem of disability is relocated from the individual, to the barriers and attitudes which disable her. It is not the disabled person who is to blame, but society. She does not have to change, society does. Rather than feeling self-pity, she can feel anger and pride. (Shakespeare 2006, pp. 199–200)

Despite the usefulness and successes of the social model, it is not without its detractors. First, some critics have pointed out that the core group of activists responsible for the creation of the social model was primarily comprised of White, heterosexual men with physical impairments, which may have produced a limited view of disability (and possibly, in a limited range of interventions and mechanisms for social change). Second, some activists have argued that the social model minimizes the real, and often negative, impact that impairment has on individuals' lives (Shakespeare 2006; Crow 1996). In addition, the social model's definition of disability creates a tautological argument; under this model, disability and oppression are one and the same, so it is technically impossible to conduct research on individuals who are disabled but not oppressed (Shakespeare 2006). Furthermore, the social model has been critiqued for creating and reifying distinctions between impairment and disability that may not be so clear-cut in the lived experiences of disabled individuals. Finally, the social model hypothesizes the possibility of "bar-

rier-free utopia," which is laudable in its intent but would be impossible to actualize, especially given the wide variety of accommodations that would be required (Shakespeare 2006).

Even under the social model, which was regarded a vast improvement over the medical model of disability, there are major issues regarding the incorporation of sexuality and gender issues in disability research. As Shakespeare (2000) points out, until recently, the public lives of disabled people were analyzed and discussed, while the private lives—including issues of sexuality, identity, and sexual relationships—were hidden. As such, issues related to sexuality went largely unexamined. Additionally, some have argued there is bias present in the existing research. Much of the research, they state, focuses on male-centric, heteronormative perceptions of gender and sexuality, with the result that "straight women and lesbians, especially those with congenital—as opposed to acquired—disabilities, gay men, bisexuals, and racial/ethnic minorities continue to experience the most hostility and/or neglect" (Rembis 2010, p. 54).

Some scholars (see Rembis 2010; O'Toole 2000) have argued that researchers need to take a more intersectional perspective, examining the multiple communities of which one is a member. In their interdisciplinary review of five years of articles published in peer-reviewed journals in sexuality, disability, and rehabilitation, Greenwell and Hough (2008) found that a variety of cultural factors were regularly addressed by researchers (e.g., gender, race), but that only about one-quarter of the studies included information about respondents' sexual orientation. In addition, they point out that although researchers often report demographic information about their sample, those variables are rarely used in analyses, "[raising] the question of whether potential investigative opportunities are being missed" (Greenwell and Hough 2008, p. 194). There has been increased attention regarding the intersection of sexual identities among people with disabilities. As discussions of sexual rights, sexual education and sexual satisfaction have increased, some scholars have noted the absence of voices from lesbian, gay, bisexual, and transgender people with disabilities (Caldwell 2010; Noonan and Taylor Gomez 2011; Tremain 2000). Additionally, as Tilley (1996) and O'Toole and Doe (2002) highlight, for individuals with multiple identities, it can be difficult to find support across groups, resulting in "forced and disempowering compromises and consequences" (Tilley 1996, p. 139).

10.4   Literature Review

In the following sections, we discuss topics that are commonly examined in sexuality/disability social research. We first address the topic of the sexual rights of individuals with disabilities, as it lays the foundation for understanding common barriers and legal issues that hinder the free expression of sexuality for people with disabilities. Attitudes toward, and perceptions of, the sexuality of adults and adolescents with disabilities are frequently addressed in the existing literature. This research focuses in large part on the opinions of those who might have social control over the sexuality of people with disabilities (e.g., parents, caregivers, or medical professionals). Sex education is similarly common as a research topic; researchers often focus on the lack of education available, as well as the types of information that individuals with disabilities themselves believe is still needed. Finally, we address issues of sexual facilitation (and conversely, the social control) of the sexuality of people with disabilities, as well as reviewing studies that explicitly address the topic of sexual satisfaction.

10.4.1   Sexual Rights

As proponents of the social model have pointed out, the private lives of disabled individuals have only recently become a subject of political and social action (Shakespeare 2000). One major development occurred in 2002, when the World Health Organization (WHO) convened a meeting of international experts on sexuality and sexual health to establish the importance of sexual health and sexual rights as part of the WHO agenda (WHO 2006). Part of the culmination of this con-

ference was a working definition of sexual health and sexual rights, which has been frequently applied to discussions concerning the sexual rights and sexual health of individuals with disabilities. The adopted definition, which has been used by researchers and scholars alike, stated:

> …the application of existing human rights to sexuality and sexual health constitute sexual rights. Sexual rights protect all people's rights to fulfill and express their sexuality and enjoy sexual health, with due regard for the rights of others and within a framework of protection against discrimination. The fulfillment of sexual health is tied to the extent to which human rights are respected, protected, and fulfilled…. (WHO 2006)

In addition, the definition outlines how human rights are tied to sexual rights:

> Rights critical to the realization of sexual health include: the rights to equality and non-discrimination; the right to be free from torture or to cruel, inhumane, or degrading treatment or punishment; the right to privacy; the rights to the highest attainable standard of health (including sexual health) and social security; the right to marry and to found a family and enter into marriage with the free and full consent of the intending spouses, and to equality in and at the dissolution of marriage; the right to decide the number and spacing of one's children; the rights to information, as well as education; the rights to freedom of opinion and expression; and the right to an effective remedy for violations of fundamental rights. The responsible exercise of human rights requires that all persons respect the rights of others. (WHO 2006)

Despite the establishment of these criteria, there are many barriers still in existence regarding fully-realized sexual health for individuals with a disability (Shakespeare 2000). Sex education is still lacking for many disabled people, and social, civic, and public places are often inaccessible for people with disabilities, reducing the number of venues through which people meet sexual and intimate partners (Shakespeare 2000). Inaccessible spaces can also make it difficult for individuals and couples to engage in common dating and relationship activities (Bender 2012); public accommodations for individuals with disabilities, while a positive step, often do not allow for individuals to fully express themselves as sexual beings. For example, a respondent in Bahner's

(2012) study of Swedish people with disabilities stated that she and her boyfriend (who was also disabled) were often not able to use public transportation to go out, because only one wheelchair was allowed at a time on the bus. The special disability transportation system—which was unreliable and was more expensive—prohibited passengers who were not disabled from riding unless they were personal assistants or caregivers, which meant the system was "definitely not an option if you wanted to go home with somebody you had picked up from, for example, a bar" (Bahner 2012, p. 344). Barriers such as these are often invisible to the larger, ableist culture, and repeated experiences of exclusion, discrimination, and ableism can impact one's self-esteem and belief in one's self as a sexual being (Bender 2012). As Shakespeare (2000) points out, "being sexual demands self-esteem…yet disabled people, systematically devalued and excluded by modern Western societies, are often not in the right place to begin that task of self-love and self-worth" (p. 161).

Some research has been conducted in Western European countries that offer an interesting international perspective into sexual rights of disabled individuals. Western European nations often acknowledge a broader range of rights for disabled individuals, as well as offering more social supports and accommodations for individuals with disabilities (Bahner 2012). Broader recognition of sexual rights does not eliminate controversy, though. For example, Bahner (2012) discusses conflict around Swedish legislation regarding a disabled individual's right to live autonomously (often with the support of a personal assistant), and that assistant's right to refuse to engage in activities that may violate their personal values and beliefs (e.g., by assisting a disabled individual to prepare for or engage in solo or partnered sexual activities). Denmark, conversely has stated that it is the "personnel's duty to facilitate service users' sexuality, whether it concerns assistance in order to have sex with a partner, to masturbate, or to contact a prostitute" (Bahner 2012, p. 339). These macro-level social and legal supports of the sexual rights of individuals with disabilities share a reciprocal and mutually influential re-

lationship with the more micro-level individual opinions and attitudes regarding the sexuality of disabled individuals.

10.4.2 Attitudes and Perceptions About Disabled Sexuality

A considerable amount of research discusses perceptions of sexuality and disability, assessing the attitudes and opinions of medical professionals and the general public, as well as of disabled individuals themselves. This research is quite diverse, and the studies often cannot be directly compared because they address different populations (nurses, doctors, or parents, for example), focus on different types of disabilities (e.g., intellectual versus physical), or use different scales, forms of measurement, or methods. And as previously mentioned, opinions and attitudes about disabled sexuality often differ based on the type and severity of the disability, as well as the personal characteristics of the disabled person (e.g., age, gender, etc.) This section will provide a brief and general overview of this literature, though it is important to keep the aforementioned limitations in mind.

Some of the existing attitudinal research examines the myths about disabled sexuality that are still commonly endorsed, including the myth that individuals with a disability are asexual. The existence of this myth stems, at least in part, from the belief that "with any level of sexual dysfunction, there would be a resultant decrease in sexual fulfillment and therefore a decrease in sexual needs" (Esmail et al. 2010, p. 1151). Heteronormative attitudes about sex prevail in the general public, among caregivers and medical personnel, as well as in resources for individuals with disabilities. These attitudes are often phallocentric, focusing on genital contact and performance, and assume that individuals with disabilities are heterosexual (Tilley 1996).These assumptions tend to make it difficult for individuals (i.e., non-disabled individuals, individuals with a disability, their partners, or caregivers) to modify their definitions of sex to include the sexual practices of disabled individuals, rendering those practices—and people—invisible (Esmail et al. 2010; Tilley 1996). For example, rehabilitation resources for individuals with physical disabilities may discuss sexuality, but they may focus on heterosexual intercourse as "the only means of sexual expression, and, of course, the woman was in the passive missionary position" (Tilley 1996, p. 141). As previously mentioned, sexual minorities are underrepresented in disability research, perhaps in part because of the assumption of heterosexuality. This lack of recognition of sexual minorities in disability research reinforces the larger issue of heteronormativity and isolation, as well as making complex intersectional research very uncommon (O'Toole 2000; Tilley 1996). In addition, these heteronormative beliefs can combine with cultural norms about attractiveness and beauty to negatively impact disabled individuals' (and their potential partners') views of themselves as sexual beings, as well as color the attitudes of members of the general public toward the acceptability (or existence) of disabled sexuality (Esmail et al. 2010; Tilley 1996).

In addition to the myth of asexuality, common gendered misperceptions exist about individuals with intellectual or cognitive disabilities. Cuskelly and Gilmore (2007) assessed attitudes of the general public about the sexuality of men and women with intellectual disabilities, hypothesizing that men with intellectual disabilities would be seen as sexually deviant (perhaps even dangerous) while women with similar disabilities would be viewed as "sexual innocents" or as vulnerable. Noonan and Taylor Gomez (2011) discussed similar attitudes, and concluded that individuals with intellectual disabilities often have their sexual rights curtailed because of the common perception that they are "potential victims of sexual abuse or [are expressing] ... unacceptable sexual behavior. Either way, they become the focus of protection" (p. 177).

Attitudes of the general public regarding sexuality and disability have also been assessed. As with general attitudes about sexuality, older individuals tended to have more conservative attitudes and opinions about disabled sexuality than younger people, and people with higher levels of education tended to be more liberal than those with lower levels of education, at least with regards to the sexuality of individuals with intellectual disabilities (Gilmore and Chambers 2010; Cuskelly and Bryde 2004). Men and women had very similar attitudes toward disabled sexuality, though there were often different levels of acceptance of sexual expression based on the gender of the disabled individual, the type of disability they had, and the degree of impairment (Gilmore and Chambers 2010).

Attitudes and perceptions of parents and other caregivers (typically, medical professionals/support staff) are also commonly addressed in the literature. In general, parents of individuals with intellectual disabilities tend to be more conservative with regards to disabled sexuality than support staff, though this may be due to age or generational differences between the two groups rather than their relationship to the disabled individual (Gilmore and Chambers 2010; Cuskelly and Bryde 2004). In addition, the type of sexual expression being discussed often garnered different levels of acceptance from different populations; for example, Cuskelly and Bryde (2004) found that parents and medical staff members were less supportive of individuals with intellectual disabilities having children compared to other forms of sexual expression (e.g., masturbation, sexual intercourse, and marriage) than were members of the general public. As Cuskelly and Bryde (2004) point out, the attitudes and beliefs of caregivers can have significant impact on the lives of individuals with intellectual disabilities, and conflicting opinions and attitudes from caregivers could cause confusion for the individual with the disability about appropriate sexual behavior. As sexuality and aging scholars have noted elsewhere (Taylor and Gosney 2011), though attitudes of staff are important to assess, it is equally important to assess the policies and regulation of care facilities and group homes, as those policies inform the daily lives of the residents. As Siebers (2014) notes, structural factors in group homes and long-term care facilities may contribute significant barriers to the sexual expression of individuals with disabilities:

Group homes and long-term care facilities purposefully destroy opportunities for disabled people to find sexual partners or to express their sexuality. Even though inhabitants in group homes pay rent for their rooms, the money buys no functional privacy or right to use personal space. The staff usually does not allow renters to be alone in the room with anyone of sexual interest… in many care facilities, staff will not allow two people to sit together alone in the same room. Some facilities segregate men and women. Add to these restrictions the fact that many people with disabilities are involuntarily confined in institutions, with no hope of escape, and the enormity of their oppression becomes palatable. (p. 379)

Existing institutional and structural barriers are often not discussed in attitude and opinion research, perhaps because the barriers themselves vary from institution to institution. Further research is warranted on the interaction on how micro-level perspectives on disabled sexuality can inform macro-level policies (and vice versa). One area of interaction between these two perspectives that has been studied frequently pertains to the sex education that is available for individuals with disabilities.

10.4.3 Sex Education

While sex education is neglected in general in most American schools, it is especially absent for individuals with disabilities (Tepper 2000). As McCabe (1999) and Gomez (2012) point out, sexuality education is not only key to fulfilling sexual experiences, but is also an essential part of preventing and reporting instances of sexual abuse; this is especially true for individuals with disabilities, who might be at increased risk for physical and sexual abuse victimization and perpetration (Lindsay et al. 2012; Plummer and Findley 2012). In fact, access to education and information about sex is an integral part of the WHO's (2006) definition of sexual rights, and increasing attention has been paid to issues of sexual education for individuals with disability.

Existing research on sex education for disabled individuals tends to focus on the sexual experiences, attitudes, or sexual knowledge of individuals with both physical and cognitive disabilities (both congenital and acquired, and at various types and levels of impairment), though few studies have attempted to compare individuals with physical and cognitive disabilities to members of the general public in terms of the quality and type of sex education received (McCabe 1999). In one exception, McCabe (1999) assessed individuals with physical or cognitive disabilities on measures of sexual knowledge and their frequency of a variety of sexual experiences, and found that individuals in the general public reported the highest rates of sexuality education, followed by individuals with physical disability, then followed by those with a cognitive or intellectual disability. In addition, disabled individuals were less likely than members of the general public to receive their sex education from parents or friends but more likely to receive information from the media, which may signal that disabled individuals may be receiving less accurate or relevant information, and may have fewer outlets to discuss their thoughts, feelings, and experiences (McCabe 1999). Similar research comparing individuals with intellectual disabilities to those without intellectual disabilities found that those with disabilities were significantly less knowledgeable about pregnancy, STIs, contraceptives, and masturbation (Murphy and O'Callaghan 2004). Whether this gap in knowledge was due to low retention of knowledge is unclear, but some literature (Lawrence and Swain 1993; McCabe 1999) has indicated that it may be due to limited exposure to sexuality curriculum and age-inappropriate communication style, rather than retention issues due to the disability. Indeed, less than 50 % of McCabe's (1999) respondents with disabilities had received any sex education at all, compared to over 90 % of the non-disabled participants, reinforcing the notion that lack of access to education may be the underlying issue. In another study among 74 young adults with cerebral palsy (aged 20–24), very few (10 %) had discussions about sexuality during rehabilitation and many reported wanting more information about reproduction, interventions, and problems with partners (Wiegerink et al. 2011). Furthermore, as Tepper (2000) points out, sexual education may be particularly important for individuals with acquired disabilities:

After injury things were "not the same." There were concerns about being sexual in the "normal" way. Feelings of "not the same" were rooted in who, what, where, and how participants learned about sexuality in the larger sexual culture. These changes experienced in comparisons to memories of what was normal for them before injury resulted in intrusive and uncontrollable thoughts during sexual activity. The absence of quality sexuality education combined with learning about sex primarily from having genital intercourse led to sexuality embodied in the genitals and cognitively focused on perfect performance with the goal of orgasm … resulted in consequences like low sexual self-esteem and lost hope. (p. 288)

The kinds of sexual education and counseling available following an acquired disability can also have varying impacts based on race, class, gender, and age at the time of injury (Bender 2012). The emphasis on heteronormative performance during rehabilitation for men following spinal cord injury can negatively impact some men's sense of a sexual self if, for example, they are unable to use medications to achieve an erection because of contraindications with other medications or the cost associated with purchasing such medications or devices.

10.4.4   Sexual Facilitation

One of the unique areas where sexuality and disability research intersects is in the area of sexual facilitation. Like many issues surrounding the study of disability and sexuality, the definitions of sexual facilitation used by researchers (if it is defined at all), can be quite varied, ranging from a caregiver having a sex positive attitude, assisting an individual so they can attend social events like parties or go to a bar, facilitating sexual activities with a partner (or partners), or to arranging for or assisting an individual in hiring a sex worker (Bahner 2013; Earle 2001). Given these broad and wide-ranging definitions, disabled individuals and caregivers alike have different perspectives on the appropriateness and usefulness of sexual facilitation. Many studies have demonstrated that a key to establishing comfort with sexual issues with caregivers and personal attendants was good communication with the care-

giver, establishing boundaries, and the caregiver having received at least some education about the sexual lives of disabled individuals (Bahner 2012; Browne and Russell 2005; Earle 2001).

Caregivers and disabled individuals often had different perspectives and expectations about disabled sexuality in general, as Earle's (2001) findings demonstrate. Earle (2001) interviewed disabled individuals as well as caregivers, and found that caregivers often position sexuality as a "want" or a "desire," rather than a "need," which shaped the way they responded to their clients' requests (real or hypothetical) for sexual facilitation. In addition, Earle's (2001) caregiver respondents often endorsed (or had endorsed in the past) the belief that their disabled clients were asexual, because they believed their clients' physical impairments prevented them from pursuing sexual satisfaction; as one caregiver put it, "if you've never been able to do it for yourself, you won't know what you're missing" (p. 317). In addition to establishing comfort with caregivers, determining boundaries, and overcoming ableist attitudes; social norms and sexual scripts could often act as barriers to sexual expression for some individuals. Bahner's (2012) Swedish participants discussed that there are norms surrounding sex—cultural scripts that most of us abide by; for example, not having sex loudly when other people are within earshot—and non-disabled individuals are often able to disregard these norms when in the privacy of their own home. Disabled individuals with attendants, though, often felt as though they had to abide by these norms even when in their own homes, hampering their rights to sexual expression.

10.4.5   Sexual Satisfaction

Sexual satisfaction is regarded as an integral part of a healthy and fulfilling sexual life, yet historically little attention has been paid to the levels of sexual satisfaction among individuals with disabilities (Tepper 2000). According to Tepper (2000) lack of sexual pleasure and low levels of sexual satisfaction among individuals with disabilities has "not been seen as problematic:"

Neglect of the pleasurable aspect in the discourse of sexuality and disability is perpetuated by the assumptions that people with disabilities are child-like and asexual, a focus on procreative sex to the detriment of pleasure, and the assumption that people with disabilities are not physiologically capable of pleasure or orgasm. (p. 287)

Indeed, much of the existing research indicates that individuals who have an acquired disability reported receiving very little information about how their injury would impact their sexuality (Connell et al. 2014). A number of studies have been conducted to better understand the sexual satisfaction of disabled individuals, though these studies are difficult to compare due to differences in methods, populations, and study tools. Two studies examine the social-psychological impacts of injury/trauma, rather than purely physiological consequences on which much of the existing literature focuses. Tepper et al.'s (2001) phenomenological study of women with spinal cord injuries, proposed a system of understanding post-injury responses, including "cognitive-genital dissociation," "sexual disenfranchisement," and "sexual rediscovery." In their review of existing literature on the "lived experiences of sexuality changes in adult trauma survivors," Connell et al. (2014) expanded this system to include physiological effects on sexuality after injury, including issues related to pain, sexual function, medication side effects, and decreased libido.

Cognitive-genital dissociation refers to "shutting down" sexuality after injury, based on the false assumption that sexual pleasure or sexual functioning is no long possible (Tepper et al. 2001). As Connell et al. (2014) point out in their review of sexual satisfaction and disability literature, this process is linked with the lack of accurate information received in the rehabilitation setting, and this process contributed to sexual difficulties, as well as poor self-esteem and body image. This dissociation and lowered self-esteem and body image could result in sexual disenfranchisement, or avoidance of sex based on the belief that sex would be less satisfying after injury. Interestingly, Connell et al.'s (2014) review of the literature indicates that there were no correlations between the type or severity of injury and decreases in self-esteem, sexual satisfaction, or

frequency of sex, indicating that any injury can significantly impact an individual's sexual life, regardless of the type or severity. Finally, sexual rediscovery, or increased confidence and sexual self-esteem, was correlated with both partners' willingness to expand and explore their sexual repertoire (Connell et al. 2014), demonstrating the importance of education not only for the disabled individual, but for their partner(s). Given the interconnectedness between sexual education, sexual satisfaction, and quality of life, it is critical to understand how increased education or rehabilitation with regards to sex and sexuality could increase the quality of life of individuals with disabilities.

10.5   Conclusion

The spheres of sexuality and disability research are both full of rich and well-developed descriptions of the sexual lives of people and of individuals with disabilities; however the overlap of these two fields is sparse. In this review, we have highlighted the areas with the greatest overlap including sexual rights, education, satisfaction, and sexual facilitation. Within each of these main areas we were cognizant of the variation in definitions and theoretical conceptualizations of disability in the literature, and we acknowledge that in our attempt to be broad and inclusive, we excluded some topics and populations from this review; like researchers, we were faced with the challenge of how to be inclusive when faced with such a diverse, yet understudied, topic.

For us, this review drew attention to a large gap in the recognition of people with disabilities as sexual beings with multiple identities. Few studies examined intersecting identities and hardly any examined sexuality across different types of disabilities (e.g., physical and intellectual). More research, especially representative research, is needed in a great number of areas, as well as more transparency in terms of researchers' definitions and methods. Additional financial support for sexuality and disability research would help to accomplish this goal, as well as more training for sexuality and/or disability researchers who wish to venture into the intersections of their fields, especially in relation to definitional and methodological issues. There is a great potential and urgent need for disability and sexuality scholars to bring their fields together to more fully understand the sexual lives and needs of people with disabilities, especially given the ability to create positive changes in the lived experiences of disabled individuals.

References

Altman, B. M. (2001). Disability definitions, models, classification schemes, and applications. In G. L. Albrecht, K. D. Seelman, & M. Bury (Eds.), *Handbook of disability studies* (pp. 97–122). Thousand Oaks: Sage.

Bahner, J. (2012). Legal rights or simply wishes? The struggle for sexual recognition of people with physical disabilities using personal assistance in Sweden. *Sexuality and Disability, 30*(3), 337–356. doi:10.1007/s11195-012-9268-2.

Bahner, J. (2013). *Whose sexuality is this anyway? The exclusion of sexuality in personal assistance services for disabled people.* In DPR Conference. Greenwich, England. 9–11 April 2013.

Bender, A. A. (2012). Secrets and magic pills. In L. M. Carpenter & J. D. DeLamater (Eds.), *Sex for life: From virginity to Viagra, how sexuality changes throughout our lives* (pp. 198–214). New York: NYU Press.

Browne, J., & Russell, S. (2005). My home, your workplace: people with physical disability negotiate their sexual health without crossing professional boundaries. *Disability & Society, 20*(4), 375–388. doi:10.1080/09687590500086468.

Caldwell, K. (2010). We exist: Intersectional in/visibility in bisexuality & disability. *Disability Studies Quarterly, 30*(3/4). http://dsq-sds.org/article/view/1273/1303. Accessed 19 June 2014.

Crow, L. (1996). Including all of our lives: renewing the social model of disability. http://www.roaring-girl.com/wp-content/uploads/2013/07/Including-All-of-Our-Lives.pdf. Accessed 17 June 2014.

Connell, K. M., Coates, R., & Wood, F. M. (2014). Sexuality following trauma injury: a literature review. *Burns and Trauma, 2*(2), 61–70. doi:10.4103/2321-3868.130189.

Cuskelly, M., & Bryde, R. (2004). Attitudes towards the sexuality of adults with an intellectual disability: Parents, support staff, and a community sample. *Journal of Intellectual and Developmental Disability, 29*(3), 255–264. doi:10.1080/13668250412331285136.

Cuskelly, M., & Gilmore, L. (2007). Attitudes to sexuality questionnaire (Individuals with an intellectual disability): Scale development and community norms.

Journal of Intellectual and Developmental Disability, 32(3), 214–221. doi:10.1080/13668250701549450.

Earle, S. (2001). Disability, facilitated sex and the role of the nurse. *Journal of Advanced Nursing, 36*(3), 433–440. doi:10.1046/j.1365-2648.2001.01991.x.

Esmail, S., Darry, K., Walter, A., & Knupp, H. (2010). Attitudes and perceptions towards disability and sexuality. *Disability & Rehabilitation, 32*(14), 1148–1155. doi:10.3109/09638280903419277.

Gilmore, L., & Chambers, B. (2010). Intellectual disability and sexuality: Attitudes of disability support staff and leisure industry employees. *Journal of Intellectual and Developmental Disability, 35*(1), 22–28. doi:10.3109/13668250903496344.

Gomez, M. T. (2012). The S words: Sexuality, sensuality, sexual expression and people with intellectual disability. *Sexuality and Disability, 30*(2), 237–245. doi:10.1007/s11195-011-9250-4.

Gordon, B. O., & Rosenblum, K. E. (2001). Bringing disability into the sociological frame: A comparison of disability with race, sex, and sexual orientation statuses. *Disability & Society, 16*(1), 5–19. doi:10.1080/713662032.

Greenwell, A., & Hough, S. (2008). Culture and disability in sexuality studies: A methodological and content review of literature. *Sexuality and Disability, 26*(4), 189–196. doi:10.1007/s11195-008-9094-8.

Grönvik, L. (2007). Definitions of disability in social sciences: methodological perspectives. Digital Comprehensive Summaries of Uppsala Dissertations from the Faculty of Social Sciences, ISSN 1652-9030; 29. http://urn.kb.se/resolve?urn=urn:nbn:se:uu:diva-7803. Accessed 18 June 2014.

Lawrence, P., & Swain, J. (1993). Sex education programmes for students with severe learning difficulties in further education and the problem of evaluation. *Disability, Handicap & Society, 8*(4), 405–421. doi:10.1080/02674649366780381.

Lindsay, W., Steptoe, L., & Haut, F. (2012). Brief report: The sexual and physical abuse histories of offenders with intellectual disability. *Journal of Intellectual Disability Research, 56*, 326–331. doi:10.1111/j.1365-2788.2011.01428.x.

McCabe, M. P. (1999). Sexual knowledge, experience and feelings among people with disability. *Sexuality and Disability, 17*(2), 157–170. doi:10.1023/A:1021476418440.

Murphy, G. H., & O'Callaghan, A. L. I. (2004). Capacity of adults with intellectual disabilities to consent to sexual relationships. *Psychological Medicine, 34*(07), 1347–1357. doi:10.1017/S0033291704001941.

Noonan, A., & Taylor Gomez, M. 2011. Who's missing? Awareness of lesbian, gay, bisexual and transgender people with intellectual disability. *Sexuality and Disability, 29*, 175–180. doi:10.1007/s11195-010-9175-2.

O'Toole, C. J. (2000). The view from below: Developing a knowledge base about an unknown population. *Sexuality and Disability, 18*(3), 207–224. doi:10.1023/A:1026421916410.

O'Toole, C. J., & Doe, T. (2002). Sexuality and disabled parents with disabled children. *Sexuality and Disability, 20*(1), 89–101. doi:10.1023/A:1015290522277.

Plummer, S. B., & Findley, P. A. (2012). Women with disabilities' experience with physical and sexual abuse: Review of the literature and implications for the field. *Trauma, Violence, & Abuse, 13*(1), 15–29. doi:10.1177/1524838011426014.

Rembis, M. A. (2010). Beyond the binary: Rethinking the social model of disabled sexuality. *Sexuality and Disability, 28*(1), 51–60. doi:10.1007/s11195-009-9133-0.

Shakespeare, T. (2000). Disabled sexuality: Toward rights and recognition. *Sexuality and Disability, 18*(3), 159–166. doi:10.1023/A:1026409613684.

Shakespeare, T. (2006). The social model of disability. In L. J. Davis (Ed.), *The disability studies reader* (2nd ed., pp. 197–204). New York: Taylor & Francis.

Siebers, T. (2014). A sexual culture for disabled people. In M. Stombler, D. Baunach, W. Simonds, E. Windsor, & E. Burgess (Eds), *Sex matters: The sexuality and society reader* (4th ed., pp. 375–384). New York: W.W. Norton.

Taylor, A., & Gosney, M. A. (2011). Sexuality in older age: Essential considerations for healthcare professionals. *Age and Ageing, 40*(5), 538–543. doi:10.1093/ageing/afr049.

Tepper, M. S. (2000). Sexuality and disability: The missing discourse of pleasure. *Sexuality and Disability, 18*(4), 283–290. doi:10.1023/A:1005698311392.

Tepper, M. S., Whipple, B., Richards, E., & Komisaruk, B. R. (2001). Women with complete spinal cord injury: A phenomenological study of sexual experiences. *Journal of Sex & Marital Therapy, 27*(5), 615–623. doi:10.1080/713846817.

Tremain, S. (2000). Queering disabled sexuality studies. *Sexuality and Disability, 18*(4), 291–299. doi:10.1023/A:1005650428230.

Tilley, C. M. (1996). Sexuality in women with physical disabilities: A social justice or health issue? *Sexuality and Disability, 14*(2), 139–151. doi:10.1007/BF02590607.

Wiegerink, D., Roebroeck, M., Bender, J., Stam, H., & Cohen-Kettenis, P. (2011). Sexuality of young adults with cerebral palsy: Experienced limitations and needs. *Sexuality and Disability, 29*(2), 119–128. doi:10.1007/s11195-010-9180-6.

World Health Organization. (2006). *Defining sexual health: Report of a technical consultation on sexual health, 28–31 January 2002, Geneva*. World Health Organization.

Trans* Sexualities

11

Aaron H. Devor and Kimi Dominic

Evidence suggests that gender-variant people have existed in many societies around the world and throughout time. In some cultures they have well-defined roles and have enjoyed some social acceptance, whereas in others there has been little or no tolerance for significant gender non-conformity (Bullough 2007). While gender has been universally used by societies as a main organizing principle, understandings of the importance of gender, and the criteria used to determine gender conformity and variance, have been diverse. Moreover, sexuality is generally seen as an integral component of what constitutes gender, though this, too, has varied significantly (Jacobs 2014).

Gender-variant people in Western societies include a wide range of people who, for various reasons and to various degrees, feel that the sexes and/or genders to which they were assigned at birth are not consistent with their own identities. Recent estimates of the incidence of trans*-identified people in Western urban societies run between 0.5 % and 1 % (Conron et al. 2012). There are many terms with which such people might describe themselves. While the language of gender variance is in constant flux, we offer explanations of some of the more commonly-used terms to anchor our discussion. We acknowledge that what we offer is only an incomplete and approximate snapshot taken at a particular time and place.

11.1 Introduction to Some Key Terms

In everyday usage, the terms "sex" and "gender" are commonly thought of as having the same meaning. Furthermore, the words "sex" and "sexuality" are frequently used as synonyms. Although a relatively clear understanding can generally be taken from the context in which they are used, when considering gender-variant people, these terms are best treated as having distinct, although related, meanings.

Distinctions between what is signified by "sex" and what is signified by "gender" are key to understanding gender-variant people. In the simplest version, "sex" refers to the biological characteristics of a person, whereas gender refers to social characteristics. Transgender activist

---

Trans* is defined by GATE-Global Action for Trans* Equality as: "Anyone who has a gender identity which differs from the gender they were assigned at birth and who chooses, or prefers, to present themselves differently than what is expected of the gender they were assigned at birth. This includes people who identify as transsexual, transgender, cross dressing, gender variant, gender fluid, genderqueer, agender, and many other identities, and serves as a placeholder term to refer to a wide variety of gender variance without reducing any one identity to characteristics of other identities." (GATE-Global Action for Trans* Equality, n.d.).

Parts of this chapter were previously published in Aaron Devor (2015). Trans* Bodies. In P. Whelehan & A. Bolin (Eds.), *The International Encyclopedia of Human Sexuality*. Malden, Oxford: John Wiley and Sons.

A. H. Devor (✉) · K. Dominic
Sociology Department, University of Victoria, Victoria, BC, Canada
e-mail: ahdevor@uvic.ca

K. Dominic
e-mail: kdominic@uvic.ca

J. DeLamater, R.F. Plante (eds.), *Handbook of the Sociology of Sexualities,* Handbooks of Sociology and Social Research, DOI 10.1007/978-3-319-17341-2_11, © Springer International Publishing Switzerland 2015

Virginia Prince is widely attributed with having quipped "Sex is between the legs. Gender is between the ears".[1] However, things are rarely that simple.

Sexes and genders may be *assigned* to people at birth, may be *identities* that develop and change over time, and may be *attributed* by others on the basis of observed characteristics. *Sex* can be comprised of many variables, such as chromosomes, hormones, internal and external reproductive organs, and secondary sex characteristics, all of which may appear in a myriad of combinations. Furthermore, which characteristics are definitive of the sexes of individuals have been the subject of intense public, legal, legislative and medical debates, with outcomes varying among times and places. The widespread occurrence of such debates highlights that sex statuses are ultimately the result of contingent and socially negotiated agreements, rather than the inevitable results of physiological imperatives.

Sexes are generally assigned at birth on the basis of a quick visual inspection of the genitals of new-born infants. In most common practice, people are assigned as female, male, or intersex.[2] Intersex people are assigned, generally as soon as possible, as either males or females, usually based on an assessment of genital appearance, less often as a result of more extensive testing (Lee et al. 2006). Further investigations into assigned sexes are rare, even for trans* people who express dissatisfaction with their assigned sex.

In addition to their assigned sexes, individuals also have *sex identities*, that is to say that people feel that they belong in particular sex statuses. For most people, their assigned sex is also the sex with which they identify, whereas among gender-variant people, this may not be the case. Other people also make assumptions and draw conclusions about the sexes of people they meet, most frequently on the basis of a cursory visual appraisal of the person's outward appearance and without being privy to detailed physical information. Such sex attributions can contribute positively or negatively to the identities and self-esteem of individuals.

In common parlance, *gender* is thought to be synonymous with sex. The genders of men and women are presumed by many to be natural and inevitable social attributes based on biological imperatives. From this perspective, women and men are thought to look, think, feel, and act the way they do because they have physical sexes which cause them to do so (Davis 2008). Others have argued that genders are entirely the result of the forces of socialization (Carter 2014). The dominant expert opinion is that genders are a result of a mixture of biological and social influences. Genders, like sexes, may be *assigned*, may be *identities*, or may be *attributed*.

Genders are social statuses originally assigned at birth on the basis of the presumed correspondence between sexes and genders. Because it is common that sex and gender are two words which are used interchangeably for the same thing, when a sex is assigned at birth on the basis of genital inspection, the corresponding gender is, in effect, also assigned. Males are assigned as boys, later to become men. Females are assigned as girls, later to become women. People form their gender identities partially as a function of their acceptance of their assigned sexes, and partially on the basis of their comfort with their assigned genders.

When people are accepting of their assigned sexes and genders as correctly representing their inner senses of themselves, the term *cisgender*[3] may be used as a descriptor, either as an identity

---

[1] The exact quotation from 1973 is: "Any kind of carving that you might do on me might change my sex, but it would not change my gender, because my gender, my self-identity, is between my ears, not between my legs" (Prince 2005b, p. 30).

[2] Intersex refers to a wide range of conditions wherein physiological indicators of maleness and femaleness are combined in non-standard ways in a single individual. In earlier literature, intersexed people were often referred to the "hermaphrodites" (Dreger 2000). This is now considered derogatory. Current medical literature will often use the term "DSD," as an abbreviation for Disorders of Sexual Development. Some activists prefer to use DSD to mean Diversity of Sexual Development.

[3] The prefix "cis" comes from the Latin meaning "on this side of" and is used to refer to people whose gender identities are congruent with those to which they were assigned at birth. Variations on the terms cisgender (e.g., cis man, cissexual) have been adopted as parallel terms to transgender-based terms.

or as an attribution. When people feel that their originally-assigned sexes or genders are not appropriate to who they feel themselves to be, they may identify as *transgender* or *trans**.

An increasing number of people find that the traditional division of genders into men and women is not adequate to capture their own gender identities and experiences. They may identify as *gender fluid*, *genderqueer*, or a range of other identities that do not reinforce a binary notion of there being only two genders. Most gender fluid or genderqueer people do not wish to be identified as men/males, women/females, or trans*, although they may incorporate some aspects of these identities into their gender presentations. Often, they will prefer the use of gender neutral pronouns. The gender expression of gender fluid and genderqueer individuals may encompass elements of both standard genders, and although they may be comfortable with sometimes appearing as the standard genders, they want the freedom to move among them, and to other gender expressions, at will. Still others find that their gender identities fall outside of binary conceptions, or outside of gender, altogether. Those who do not identify with any gender may refer to themselves as *agender*, *neutrois*, or *eunuchs*. Those people who were assigned as female at birth and who do not fully identify as females/women, or have adopted another gender identity, are usually referred to as being on the *trans-masculine* spectrum, whereas those who were assigned as males at birth and who do not fully identify as males/men, or have adopted another gender identity, are usually referred to being on the *transfeminine* spectrum.

Attributions made by observers about the genders and sexes of other people are made in daily life almost exclusively on the basis of how observers interpret the gender expressions of the people they are observing (Devor 1989; Kessler and McKenna 1978). People who express a femininity that appears to be natural are attributed with being women as well as female. People who make naturalistic presentations of masculinity are attributed with being men as well as male. Most members of social groups accept that gender expressions are highly socially variable and will not question their attributions of genders and

sexes on the basis of small variations or anomalies of gender expression. Indeed, the presumed correspondences between sexes and genders are so strong in the minds of most people that once they have made gender and sex attributions, few things can cause them to reassess their attributions. Evidence of an originally-assigned sex that does not match a gender presentation will frequently cause the validity of an otherwise-acceptable gender presentation to be overturned (Devor 1987, 1989). These dynamics, which are largely invisible in the lives of cisgender people, are of great importance in the lives of trans* people.

Sexuality concerns patterns of both romantic and erotic interests which may, or may not, involve the presence of other people in actuality, in fantasy, or virtually. People may have their own sexual *identities*, and they may have sexualities *attributed* to them by others. Sexual identities and attributions may be based on fantasies about, or desires for, romantic or sexual activities in the presence, or absence, of actual sexual activities. People may experience sexual fantasies, desires, and practices which are not all equally consistent with their sexual identities, or with the sexualities attributed to them by others. As well, individuals' experiences of their sexuality may change in different contexts. Individuals, and those who are making attributions about them, will therefore differentially weight various aspects of sexuality when constructing their sexual identities, or when making attributions about others.

Sexualities involve both bodies and genders. When only cisgender people are part of the equation, sexual identities and attributions may be relatively uncomplicated: genders and sexes align in the usual fashion, and sexual identities and attributions can be made on the basis of either sexes or genders. However, trans* and genderqueer people often have bodies which exhibit non-standard mixtures of sex characteristics, and which do not align in the usual ways with typical gender categories. The bases for sexual identities and attributions thus become considerably more nuanced (Devor 1993; Page and Peacock 2013; Schilt and Windsor 2014).

11.2 Older Ideas About Gender and Sexuality Persist Along with Newer Ones

While people who appear to contemporary eyes as trans* have always existed, early research on gender-variant people took place as part of more general attempts to understand the interplay of human sex, gender, and sexuality (Bullough 2007). As medicine became accepted during the latter half of the nineteenth century as the legitimate authority over studies of sexual and gender variance, medical researchers increasingly turned their attention to non-heterosexual sexual practices (Cole and Meyer 1998; Reicherzer 2008). This greater medical attention to sexuality and gender took place under an ontological orientation that conflated sex, gender, and sexuality. In this context, human sexual and gender variance came to be labelled as pathological.

This conflation of sex-gender-sexuality[4] was based on a number of common social norms, which largely continue in popular discourse today. In its contemporary form, the conflation of sex-gender-sexuality can be summarized as follows (Devor 1989; 2000):

- Sexes are social statuses believed to be intrinsic biological characteristics. There are thought to be two, and only two sexes, male and female. All humans are believed to be either one sex or the other. Normally, no one can be neither; no one can be both; and no one can change sex without major medical intervention.
- Genders are social statuses that are considered to be the social manifestations of sexes. There are supposed to be two, and only two genders, men and women (boys and girls). All males are expected to be either boys or men; all females are expected to be either girls or women. Normally, everyone is either one gender or the other; no one can be neither; no one can be both. Because of the widespread belief that genders are rooted in biological characteristics,

it is believed that no one can change gender without major medical intervention.
- Gender role styles are viewed as culturally-defined ways of expressing or displaying sex and gender statuses. There are two main gender role styles: masculinity and femininity. Most males are masculine men. Most females are feminine women. Many people do not exactly fit their expected gender roles and it is commonly believed that this is due to poor socialization or psychological pathology.
- While a wide range of sexual practices are commonly recognized, people are normatively expected to be heterosexual as part of their gender expression which, in turn, is presumed to be biologically determined. Because of this conflation of sexuality with sex and gender statuses, gay men are often assumed to be womanly men and lesbian women are assumed to be manly women (Freeman et al. 2010).

Within the context of wide-spread acceptance in the nineteenth century of the idea of causative links between sex, gender and sexuality, Karl Heinrich Ulrichs (1864–1880/1994) linked homosexuality with a discomfort with one's body and with one's sex. Ulrichs postulated that same-sex desires were best explained as being the result of having the mind of one sex in the body of the other (Meyerowitz 2002), describing homosexual men using a conceptualization later widely taken up to describe transsexual people, "*anima muliebris virili corpore inclusa*" (a female psyche confined in a male body) (Ulrichs 1864–1880/1994, p. 289). Posited this way, homosexuality could be seen as a form of heterosexuality inherent in a gender-variant mind, rather than as a challenge to the "natural" alignment of gender and sexuality (Dreger 2000). Similarly, in 1886, psychiatrist Richard von Krafft-Ebing (1886/1998) also linked same-sex desires with gender variance. He conceptualised gender variance as having one's "psychical personality" unduly influenced by sexual feelings.

During this same period, physicians were also attempting to understand intersex conditions, which were then called hermaphroditism. The accepted wisdom of the time was that most

---

[4] To differentiate between contemporary uses of sex, gender and sexuality, and historical uses which conflate the concepts, hyphens are used to denote when any subset of these terms is conflated.

instances were actually "pseudo-hermaphroditism" wherein a "true sex" could be eventually uncovered. However, some people, having had their "true sex" diagnosed at birth, later felt that the sex assigned to them had been incorrect. This opened up the possibility of a person's "true sex" being found in something other than genitalia and gonads, and problematized the accepted link between sex-gender-sexuality (Dreger 2000).

This line of thought was continued by Magnus Hirschfeld who outlined two major challenges to the conflation of gender-sexuality. Firstly, Hirschfeld (1991/1910) proposed a theory of intermediaries, positing that every human is a unique natural combination of maleness and femaleness, and so has a unique sex identity that is neither simply male nor female. Secondly, he argued that transvestism can occur separately from homosexuality; and thirdly, that it is not a priori pathological (Hirschfeld 1991/1910). Havelock Ellis (1913) further extended Hirschfeld's work by delineating two types of people who crossdress: those who wore the clothing of the other sex without feeling like they belonged to the other sex, and those who felt like the other sex–thus presaging the emergence of the concept of transsexualism (Ellis 1913).

In 1949, pop sexologist D.O. Cauldwell named the desire to be the other gender as "transsexuality." Although opinions regarding gender variance were changing, those of Cauldwell were typical of the day. Cauldwell (1949) considered transsexuality to be delusional, psychopathic, and linked with homosexuality (Ekins and King 2001; Sullivan 2008). Cauldwell further considered transsexual people as "an adversary to the ethical, law-abiding citizen" (Irving 2008, p. 43), and suggested that any acquiescence to transsexual people's demands for surgery amounted to collusion with "psychosis" (Cauldwell 1949; Stryker 2008).

In 1966, endocrinologist Harry Benjamin published *The Transsexual Phenomenon* in which he argued that transsexuality was distinct from transvestism and homosexuality, and deserving of hormonal and surgical treatments. Benjamin's most provocative claims were that transsexuality had mixed biological, environmental and psychological causes, that all humans had some characteristics of the other gender (what he termed "bisexuality"), and that the existence of transsexuals challenged the assumptions of binary gender by embodying that "bisexuality" (Benjamin 1966, 1969).

However, his greatest influences on discourses of gender variance come from two other arguments. The first was his contention that all true transsexuals desired—and requested—medical intervention. Although this can be traced to the fact that the only gender-variant people physicians encountered at the time were those seeking medical interventions (Cole and Meyer 1998; Denny 2006; Reicherzer 2008), the idea nevertheless has had a lasting impact on popular understandings of trans* people. Benjamin also considered profound psychological distress to be a defining characteristic of transsexualism, locating the source of that distress in the patient having the "wrong body." Indeed, because Benjamin's work was hugely influential among professionals and trans* people alike, the idea of being in the "wrong body" became deeply embedded in both institutional and personal discourses on transsexuality (Stone 1992).

Around the same time as the publication of Benjamin's book, Johns Hopkins University opened the first hospital-based gender clinic, supported by funding from the Erickson Educational Foundation (Devor and Matte 2007) and with the professional involvement of John Money, Richard Green and Robert Stoller (Ettner 2007; Gherovici 2011; Stryker 2008). Within a few years, a number of gender clinics were set up around the world. These clinics propagated many of the same assumptions about the nature of gender variance, and further reinforced them by providing patient data "proving" the original assumptions (Denny 2006). Most notably, heteronormative gender presentations and attitudes were required of trans* people who wished to qualify for treatment, and treatment was predicated on the assumption that trans* people all desired full medical sex and gender reassignment.[5]

---

[5] See Sect. 4 for a discussion of techniques which may be used to alter one's gender presentation.

One voice in opposition to the model of gender variance promoted by medical authorities was that of Virginia Prince, an early and long-lived advocate for social acceptance of crossdressing among heterosexual males. She did not believe that gender variance was a psychiatric disturbance and made it "her mission to educate the medical profession" that crossdressing need not be a threat to social order, nor an expression of homosexuality (Ekins and King 2005, p. 7; Prince 2005a). Prince argued that it was possible to live as one's chosen gender without genital surgery, what Prince referred to as living as a "transgenderist" (Prince 2005c). While her motivation may have been largely grounded in her reluctance to request medical validation for a life that she did not consider disturbed or abnormal (Ekins and King 2005), her advocacy also furthered the conceptual separation of gender from sex and contributed to an expansion of the boundaries of gender expression.

11.3 Methodological Concerns

Earlier research on trans* people's lives, including trans* sexualities, was almost exclusively done by cisgender people in ways that did not meaningfully credit trans* people with expertise about their own lived experiences (Cromwell 1999; Namaste 2000). This research drew almost entirely on two types of samples: people who came to gender clinics looking for access to medical resources, and people who joined transgender organizations. In practice, this meant that most research samples were limited to transsexually-identified people around the time of their transitions, and members of organizations for socially and politically outgoing male heterosexual crossdressers. Due to the social skills required to successfully access gender clinics, cultural aversions to transition among some groups (Roen 2001), and the financial resources required to transition or to participate in crossdressers' lifestyle and advocacy organizations, this sampling technique also had the effect of biasing samples toward white, urban, middle- and upper-middle-class transfeminine people (Vecolli 2014).

People who attend at gender clinics requesting evaluation and medically-assisted gender transitions represent only a very small slice of the entirety of trans* people. Many trans* people have little or no desire for such services, some are medically or socially unable to transition, or some do not have the social abilities, geographical proximity, or financial resources to access clinics. Furthermore, contemporary research indicates that, for the small slice of the trans* population who do engage in medically-assisted transitions, the time between deciding to transition and completing transition is when trans* people experience distress at levels high enough to significantly increase their likelihood of attempting suicide. Distress, suicidal ideation and attempts decrease significantly once trans* people have been able to accomplish satisfactory transitions (Bauer et al. 2012). The limitations of studying trans* people at the time of transition were often compounded by the fact that few trans* people chose to remain available to clinic-based researchers once they had received the treatments that they had sought (Rachlin 2007). As a result, samples drawn from people attending gender clinics have over-represented the degree of distress and self-harm experienced by the larger trans* population, and have contributed to an over-focus on transition issues to the near exclusion of study of any other aspect of trans* lives. Data gathered from clinics also has a tendency to be skewed by the fact that trans* people wishing to obtain such services commonly educate themselves about the criteria in use by clinics, and ensure that they present themselves in ways that will prove successful in obtaining the results that they seek (Bolin 1987; Denny 2006). As well, especially in the early years of trans* research, most European and North American clinics saw a preponderance of transfeminine people. Therefore, it is not clear that such data ever provided either an accurate picture of trans* people in general or of clinic attenders.

Support and advocacy groups for male crossdressers in the latter half of the twentieth century often specifically defined their membership as excluding female crossdressers and gay men. As well, they often based their arguments for acceptance on claims related to their conservative middle-class "respectability" when dressed as women. People who conveyed any other kind of trans* gender expressions were excluded from these groups (Bullough 2000), and thus also from the research which used group members as research subjects, contributing further to the paucity of early research on transmasculine people.

More recent research has continued to make use of gender clinic samples but has expanded into other areas as well. Trans* people have also begun to be more active in conducting research involving their own communities, reaching out to a wider variety of trans* people, including those who do not make use of the services of gender clinics (Beemyn and Rankin 2011). One particularly useful innovation which is being increasingly taken up in population-based surveys is the use of a two-step process for identifying trans* people wherein step one asks about sex assigned at birth and step two asks about current gender identity (Tale et al. 2013). Nonetheless, sampling biases continue to be common.

Ongoing issues related to using clinic-based sampling are demonstrated well by research into the HIV risks of trans* people. Because many studies have depended on urban HIV testing sites, people who are economically marginalised and people of colour have been overrepresented, whereas those who do not have access to clinics have been missed (Bauer and Scheim 2013; Miner et al. 2012).

Internet sampling has been increasingly used as access to the Internet has grown. This has offered some significant benefits over in-person surveying, such as recruiting participants who do not frequent clinics, reaching people who may not feel comfortable identifying themselves to another person as trans*, reaching people who are using the Internet as a way to explore aspects of themselves that they might otherwise feel unable to explore in the "real world," and access to people spread over more geographically dispersed areas (Kuper et al. 2012; Miner et al. 2012). Internet surveys have also permitted much larger samples to be gathered at considerably less expense.

However, online participants must have access to the Internet and be visiting specific sites or forums, or know someone who does, in order to become aware of research advertisements (Iantaffi and Bockting 2011; Kuper et al. 2012). When using Internet-based sampling, researchers lack of control over data collection settings, are neither able to enforce inclusion and exclusion criteria nor respond to participant questions (Miner et al. 2012). Internet sampling also tends to be biased toward social-media-savvy younger trans* people, as well as those with a college education and a higher socioeconomic status (Schilt and Windsor 2014). Furthermore, sampling via the Internet continues to suffer from a bias toward trans* people who are being surveyed around the time of their greatest gender flux early in their transitions because they are the people most frequently viewing trans*-specific web sites (Iantaffi and Bockting 2011).

11.4 Sexualities Involve Bodies. Sexualities Involve Genders.

Genders and sexualities are related in heteronormative societies in that most people, at least in the early stages of sexual attraction, are attracted to others on the basis of gendered appearances and assumptions. In other words, when most people are attracted to someone, they unthinkingly make stereotypical assumptions, based on gender and sex attributions, about what kinds of bodies those people might bring to sexual encounters (Devor 1993). This, however, is disrupted by people whose bodies do not align with stereotypical assumptions, and often necessitates a reconsideration, and sometimes even a renegotiation, of sexual practices, sexual and/or gender identities on the part of both trans* persons and their intimate partners (Page and Peacock 2013).

Some trans* people actively wish to be easily identified as such; many prefer to appear cisgender but are nonetheless recognizably trans* due to aspects of their physical presence; some trans* people are able to live the majority their everyday lives very comfortably and unrecognizably in their preferred gender. However people may present their genders, sexualities involve bodies (see Chap. 9). Moreover, sexualities are understood through the interactions of the sexed and gendered bodies and identities, which may align in a seemingly limitless array of combinations (Devor 1993; Schleifer 2006).

Some trans* people find that it is not necessary to permanently change their bodies in substantial ways in order to effectively communicate their gender identities. Many trans* people, however, will take steps to transform their secondary or primary sex characteristics so as to better express their gender identities (Factor and Rothblum 2008). Techniques used by trans* people to express their gender identities may include changes to deportment, body, facial- and head-hair styles, clothing, cosmetics, jewellery, fashion accessories, body fat, and muscularity. Trans* people may also strategically employ voice and speech modifications, padding, concealment devices, sex toys, genital or breast prostheses, genital enhancement or diminishment devices, tattooing, or piercings. More permanent changes may be brought about by hormone therapy, gender confirmation surgeries[6], and ancillary masculinising or feminising procedures–any of which can occur in various combinations.

Some trans* people who feel that they are *neither* of the two most commonplace genders, or that they are some mixture of the two, may combine any of the above techniques in unusual and fluid ways which disrupt common assumptions about the usual correspondences between sexes and genders. Some people feel a periodic need to step outside of their quotidian genders to inhabit other forms of gender expression for shorter periods of time. They may make wholehearted attempts to present themselves as the other normative gender, they may make symbolic partial gestures in this direction, or they may make parodic or hyperbolic presentations that nonetheless serve as valid and satisfying forms of gender identity expression for them.

Other trans* people find that they need to alter their bodies in more long-lasting ways.

Such alterations may involve treatment with sex steroid hormones, surgical sex reassignment procedures, and ancillary procedures to feminize or masculinize facial features or body contours. These treatments and procedures are typically combined with at least some of the techniques described above. The range of combinations is as varied as the gender identities of the trans* people who employ them.

The effects of sex steroid hormones (depending on one's specific genetic inheritance) can be quite dramatic. In transmasculine-spectrum people the effects may include: lower pitch to the voice, thickening and increased oiliness of skin, growth of facial and body hair, loss of head hair, increased muscularity, masculine body fat distribution, cessation of menses, and growth of the clitoris. In transfeminine-spectrum people the effects may include: increased softness and decreased oiliness of skin, growth of breasts, slowed growth of facial and body hair, slowed loss of head hair, decreased muscularity, feminine body fat distribution, loss of erectile function, decrease in testicular and penile volume, decrease in fertility.

Surgical interventions for transmasculine-spectrum people include: breast reduction, breast removal (mastectomy), recontouring the chest for a masculine look, removal of the internal reproductive organs (hysterectomy, salpingo-oophorectomy), removal of the vulva (vulvectomy), removal of the vagina (vaginectomy), transformation of the enlarged clitoris into a small penis (metoidioplasty), construction of a penis (phalloplasty), rerouting of the urethra (urethroplasty), construction of scrotum and testicles (scrotoplasty and testicular implants), erectile implants, liposuction (most commonly of hips and thighs), voice-masculinizing surgeries, facial masculinizing surgeries, chest implants, calf implants.

Surgical interventions for transfeminine-spectrum people include: breast augmentation (mammoplasty), removal of the testicles (castration), removal of the penis (penectomy), construction of a vulva (vulvoplasty), clitoris (clitoroplasty) and vagina (vaginoplasty), rerouting of the urethra (urethroplasty), voice-feminizing surgeries, brow, chin, or Adam's apple, recontouring (facial

---

[6] Also frequently referred to as sex reassignment surgeries, or gender reassignment surgeries.

feminization surgery and lipofilling), scalp hair implants, hip and buttocks augmentation (implants and lipofilling).[7]

However, due to individual choices, social realities, and technical limitations, very few trans* people are able to live the entirety of their lives without some disclosure of their trans* identities. This is especially true in sexually intimate situations involving close physical contact with, or observation of, physical bodies. Thus, while the physical changes undertaken by trans* people are usually most deeply motivated by their gender identity needs, in many instances the expression of their own sexuality, and that of their partners, will also be impacted by the bodily alterations they undertake to bring their gender identities and bodies into better alignment.

In day-to-day interactions, some trans* people may strategically deploy stereotypical masculinity or femininity in order to be recognised as their gender and sex identities by making use of the common assumption that people possess bodies that match their gender presentations in normative ways (Devor 1987, 1989; Dozier 2005). However, this becomes more difficult to accomplish in the context of sexuality, particularly in situations that involve either disrobing, or other kinds of physical contact that would expose non-stereotypical bodies. When sex characteristics and gender presentations are known to not align in typical ways—which is much more likely to become known in sexual situations—trans* people become much more vulnerable to a number of indignities and dangers (Lombardi 2009). They may be objectified or fetishized, have their gender identities invalidated, be denied due respect, or be abused, violated, assaulted, or murdered.

Some trans* people choose to brave some of these risks because to do otherwise would be to hide their gender identities. Other trans* people's gender identities are such that, under most non-sexual circumstances, their gender presentations are sufficiently conforming to normative expectations that their risks of adverse outcomes are low. However, every trans* person, even those who most approximate cisgender appearances, remains vulnerable to the entire catalogue of invalidations and dangers should information about their gender identities become known, which will happen in the majority of partnered sexual encounters. Hence, trans* people are continually attempting to strike a balance between true-to-themselves gender and sexual expressions, and their safety.

When trans* people contemplate sexual contact they have to make strategic decisions about how, when, and what to disclose to potential partners about their bodies (Reisner et al. 2010). Such disclosure decisions and acts are often a source of anxiety for trans* people. This adds an extra, and thick, layer of apprehension to the usual acceptance and performance anxieties inherent in most sexual encounters (Iantaffi and Bockting 2011; Kosenko 2011).

Many sexual practices of trans* people and their partners may change when trans* people undergo bodily changes. When trans* people feel that their gender identities are being correctly perceived by others, they often feel invigorated and more firmly situated in their physical selves. This can result in increased sexual confidence and changes in sexual interests (Brown 2010). Among transmasculine people who use hormonal treatments, in addition to a generalised masculinisation of bodies, increased testosterone and decreased estrogens usually result in increased libido, often accompanied by increased sexual adventurousness and decreased emotionality, as well as diminished fertility. Among transfeminine people, in addition to a generalised feminisation of bodies, increased estrogens and decreased testosterone usually have the obverse effect on libido and sexual adventurousness, as well as decreasing erectile functioning and fertility (Coleman et al. 2011). Moreover, both

---

[7] Any surgical procedure will result in scarring which will affect tissue sensitivities, including sexual sensitivities. Post-surgical complications can further reduce tissue sensitivities. However, one of the goals of genital surgeries is to allow gender-congruent use of genitalia, including sexual use. Successful metoidioplasties generally result in increased sexual satisfaction. Phalloplasty techniques vary, as do the resultant sexual sensitivity levels. Successful genital reconstructions for transfeminine-spectrum people result in orgasmic capacity in the majority of cases (Cotton, 2012; Klein and Gorzalka, 2009; Lief and Hubschman, 1993).

hormone-induced and surgical alterations to primary and secondary sex characteristics will necessarily change the sexual practices associated with them.

Sexuality generally involves other people, real, desired, or virtual. When trans* people change their gender identities and/or gendered appearances, the categorisations of relationships involving them may correspondingly change as well (Aramburu Alegría 2013; Devor 1993, 1994). Furthermore, trans* people may also find that their patterns of sexual attractions change as their gender identities change (Coleman et al. 1993; Devor 1993; Dozier 2005). This may cause established sexual relationships to become transformed into other varieties of sexual relationships, into nonsexual relationships, or to end (Brown 2009; Hines 2006). Thus the sexual identities and practices of trans* people, and those of their sexual partners, may be significantly affected by changes both in identities and in bodies.

Because trans*bodies often disrupt the assumed heteronormative understandings of the relationships between sex, gender and sexuality, trans* people, and their sexual/romantic partners, often find that they must consciously negotiate and articulate the meanings of their sexual identities and sexual interactions (Edelman and Zimman 2014; Schilt and Windsor 2014; Devor 1993). Thus, when trans* people engage in sexual practices that are congruent with their gender identities, they can lead the way in creating new understandings of relationships between genders, sexed bodies, sexual practices, and sexual identities. And, because most trans* people have sexual relationships with cisgender people, the ways in which they, and their partners, together understand and practice their sexualities are gradually creating more opportunities for trans* people and cisgender people alike to engage in more diverse and affirming sexualities.

11.5   Stability and Change in Sexualities

In relationships only involving cisgender people, determining accurate descriptions of sexualities may be difficult enough. People may form their own identities, and others may make attributions, based on a variety of criteria. They may consider current, or relatively recent, or lifetime fantasies, desires, or behaviours as being valid bases for determining their own sexual identities, or making attributes about those of other people. However, because people's behaviours, desires, and fantasies are not always consistent over time, nor are they necessarily all consistent with any particular sexual orientation at any one time, some aspects of individuals' sexualities will be given more credence while other aspects may be disregarded as anomalous and unimportant. For cisgender people, the most common sexualities of heterosexual, homosexual, and bisexual are based on binary conceptualizations of the sexes-genders of the individuals involved. Increasingly, those cisgender people who do not feel that these options properly encompass how they see themselves have adopted queer as a sexual identity that allows them more flexibility.

When trans* individuals have gender identities which do not match their bodies in standard sex-gender ways, when individuals have bodies which do not correspond to standard sex configurations, all of the difficulties inherent in situations involving only cisgender people are further compounded, and it becomes more difficult to make use of the standard sexual categories. An approach used primarily by professionals in reference to both cisgender and trans* people is to describe sexualities on the basis of the types of people one finds attractive: *androphilic* and *gynephilic*. However, these terms are generally used with an assumption that attractions are to cisgender people and so leave undefined the question of whether "andro" refers to male bodies, men, or masculinities and whether "gyne" refers to female bodies, women, or femininities.

The further designator of *autogynephilia* has been developed in reference to some trans* people. While there have been sporadic attempts to extend the usage of the term to include cisgender women (Moser 2009) and to define a parallel term, *autoandrophilia* (Bockting et al. 2009; Knudson et al. 2011), the concept has been used almost exclusively in reference to people assigned as males at birth. Autogynephilia has been proposed as a sexual orientation wherein male-bodied persons live much of their lives as masculine heterosexual men while periodically taking sexual pleasure in presenting and seeing themselves as females and/or women. This kind of activity is more commonly referred to as crossdressing. In many cases, this is a clandestine activity. In some cases, it becomes overt on a part-time basis. In a smaller number of cases, usually later in life, it may lead to partial or complete gender and sex reassignment (Blanchard 1989; Lawrence 2013).

Most contemporary researchers accept self-reports concerning trans* people's sexual identities, and among those trans* people whose bodies do not align with their gender identities in stereotypical ways, people tend to claim their sexual identities more on the basis of their gender identities than on the basis of their physical bodies (Devor 1993; Samons 2009). However, in older research it was not uncommon to see trans* people's sexualities attributed to them by researchers on the basis of their sex assigned at birth. For example, androphilic transmen have been variously referred to as "non-homosexual female gender dysphorics" (Olsson and Möller 2006) and "non-homosexual female-to-male transsexuals" (Chivers and Bailey 2000). Underlying differences between older and newer approaches is a question that appears to be one of the willingness of researchers to accept that trans* people's self-identifications provide accurate data.

The majority of transmasculine people report that they are gynephilic both before and after undertaking transition (Dozier 2005; Schilt and Windsor 2014). Prior to identifying as trans*, many transmasculine individuals identify as lesbians, later rejecting that identity in favour of ones which better recognize their gender identities (Devor 1997b; Rubin 2003). Most commonly, after transition transmasculine people identify as heterosexual or as some non-standard sexual identity such as queer or pansexual (Beemyn and Rankin 2011).

While only a small minority of transmasculine people are androphilic prior to transition (Bockting et al. 2009; Coleman et al. 1993), a substantial minority of transmasculine people are androphilic after transition, and sexually active

with cisgender men who identify as gay, bisexual, or queer. Many of the transmen, and their cisgender partners, involved in these encounters and relationships see their relationships and sexual activities as gay (Brown 2009; Devor 1993; Lewins 2002). This is true even in those relationships where sexual activities involve pleasurable use of transmen's non-surgically-altered genitals (Bockting et al. 2009), which the individuals involved may recast in ways consistent with their identities by using terms such as "mangina" or "man hole" (Coleman et al. 1993; Zimman 2014).

Among adult transwomen who report having been trans*-identified from a very young age, most report having been androphilic and highly gender nonconforming throughout their lives (Samons 2009). Some of them spend time in gay men's communities prior to their transitions (Lev 2004). They may identify as gay, queer, straight, or any number of other sexual identities prior to transition, and most commonly identify as bisexual or heterosexual after transition (Beemyn and Rankin 2011).

In addition to the many transwomen who are androphilic before and after transition, a sizeable portion of transfeminine people are gynephilic throughout their lives, some are bi-, omni-, or pansexual, and some are asexual (Blanchard 1985, 1988). Prior to transition, many of those who are gynephilic have fully male heterosexual lives, marrying and fathering children. After transition they may identify as lesbians, bisexual, queer, and a variety of other less common sexual identities (Kuper et al. 2012), including many transwomen who do not undergo sex reassignment surgeries (Samons 2009). Some transwomen who were gynephilic prior to transition engage in androphilic or bisexual activities after transition (Daskalos 1998; Lawrence 2013).

The majority of autogynephilic individuals live overtly heteronormative lives and only engage in autogynephilic sexuality clandestinely. Some autogynephilic individuals supplement their autogynephilic sexual interests with occasional sexual interactions with gynephilic or bisexual males. However, those autogynephilic transfeminine individuals who live full time as women, with or without sex reassignment surgeries, are almost exclusively gynephilic and most often identify as lesbian or queer (Lawrence 2013).

Many trans* people prefer sexual partners who are themselves gender variant. They generally sexually identify on the basis of their own gender identities and those of their partners, rather than the sexes they were assigned at birth. They most often use the common identifiers of straight, gay, lesbian, or bisexual (Bockting et al. 2009; Schleifer 2006; Schrock and Reid 2006). People in relationships which involve one or more gender-variant persons may also describe their relationships as some variant of queer as a way to recognize that they do not, and in many ways cannot, fit into more traditional binary-based conceptualization of sexuality (Kuper et al. 2012).

11.6 Sexualities Involve Other People

As trans* people change their gender expressions and their bodies, their sexual partners often find that they must also recalibrate their own understandings of their mutual sexual activities, and of their own sexual identities. Moreover, such renegotiations can be ongoing, as bodies and understandings evolve, with identities and definitions at first depending more on heteronormative gender sexual scripts and slowly relaxing over time as both partners become more settled and secure in their new realities (Brown 2010; Dozier 2005). In particular, trans* body parts may need to be renamed, whether or not they are physically altered, and certain acts will often be discontinued while others are taken up. Such adjustments can be crucial to achieving successful continuation of relationships originally established under a rubric of hetero- or homosexuality as one or more partner moves from living as one sex and/or gender to another.

When trans* people describe their sexual histories/stories, they tend to do so in ways that validate and align with their current gender identities (Bockting et al. 2009; Schleifer 2006; Schrock and Reid 2006), which may have the effect of obscuring or recasting past relationships and the roles of other people who were in them. While this may be confirming of their present identities, some trans* people, and their partners, can find the resultant invisibility of some parts of their personal history to be distressing (Brown 2009). Among those who describe their relationships in ways that align with heteronormative ideals many report that they simultaneously feel both more understood, accepted, and gender confirmed by mainstream society and, at the same time, some people experience lower levels of self-esteem due to the lack of explicit recognition of their full life histories (Iantaffi and Bockting 2011).

Comparisons of relationship stability among transmen and transwomen indicate that, prior to transition, transmen tend to form more stable relationships than do transwomen (Kockott and Fahrner 1988). Post-transition, transmen and lesbian transwomen have the most stable relationships (Lewins 2002), and cisgender women in relationships with post-transition transmen report relationship satisfaction and stability equivalent to that reported by cisgender women partnered with cisgender men (Fleming et al. 1985; Kins et al. 2008; Kockott and Fahrner 1988).

While a large majority of transmen are gynephilic and active as lesbians prior to transition, a smaller majority continue to be gynephilic and identify as heterosexual or queer after transition (Bockting et al. 2009; Devor 1993, 1997a; Rubin 2003). Feminine cisgendered women partners of transitioning transmen, who initially identify as lesbian women in relationships with masculine women, sometimes find it difficult to relinquish their lesbian identities which they have had to aggressively claim in order to garner accurate sexual attributions from others (Brown 2009; Joslin-Roher and Wheeler 2009). This can be a source of relationship strain which causes many such relationships to dissolve (Brown 2009; Lev 2004).

While some transmen are androphilic prior to identifying as trans* and engage in sexual relationships with men, they often take limited satisfaction from such relationships in which they appear to be women in heterosexual relationships, rather than men in homosexual relationships.

Among those transmen who are androphilic after transition, it is most common for them to realize their trans* identities before they realized that they were androphilic. After transition, gay transmen report feeling increased confirmation of their gender and sexual identities (Bockting et al. 2009; Devor 1997a; Schleifer 2006) and similar levels of relationship satisfaction as do gay cisgender men (Dozier 2005).

Disclosure of trans* identity within already established relationships, and the changes which usually follow, inevitably add strain to relationships. The stress of accepting the changes that a trans* partner may undergo are often very difficult for their partners to navigate (Aramburu Alegría 2010, 2013). In addition, when trans* people in sexual relationships change their identities, their partners may be unable to change their own sexual desires and identities in concert (Alexander 2003; Aramburu Alegría 2010, 2013). One study found that only just over half of the couples studied were still together five years or more after one partner disclosed a trans* identity (Aramburu Alegría 2013).

It is not unusual for wives or long-term partners of male crossdressers to find out that their husbands are part-time crossdressers many years into a relationship. Not infrequently, they find out by discovering women's clothing in their male partners' possession. Many feel betrayed that their partners could have kept such a secret from them for years and trust between them can become undermined. Few female partners are able to enthusiastically share their male partners' passions for crossdressing. Most become anxiously concerned that disclosure will expose the family to unbearable stigma, and most demand that their male partners' crossdressing activities remain private (Erhardt 2007; Weinberg and Bullough 1988).

Factors contributing to couples staying together may include emotional honesty, a willingness to embrace new sexual practices and identities, greater age at disclosure, and longer relationships prior to disclosure (Alexander 2003; Aramburu Alegría 2010, 2013; Hines 2006). Among those who are able to weather the stress of changing gender identities, some find that their sexual lives together improve, and some find that their sexual lives dwindle.

11.7 Sexual and Reproductive Health

Questions of sexual health for trans* people involve three main areas of concern: sexual satisfaction, health of sexual organs, and sexually transmitted infections. In addition to health of sexual organs, reproductive health issues for trans* people include banking of reproductive gametes, and intentional and unintentional pregnancies.

Among those trans* people who engage in medically-assisted gender reassignment procedures, sexual satisfaction generally improves to the extent that the procedures produce the desired results (De Cuypere et al. 2005). However, there have been reports of instances wherein poor functional or cosmetic surgical outcomes have had the opposite effect and, in some cases, ability to orgasm has been diminished or entirely lost (Sohn and Exner 2008). Furthermore, as noted above, although trans* individuals may find increased sexual satisfaction in inhabiting bodies which better reflect their gender identities, their partners may be unable to sexually transition with them, in which cases, trans* people may experience temporary, or more long lasting, diminishment in sexual satisfaction.

Many trans* people experience discomfort and shame concerning sexual parts of their bodies, especially prior to completing whatever gender and sex transitions they desire. Some continue to feel this way throughout their lifetimes, generally because of lack of access to technically satisfactory surgical results. One result of these feelings is that many trans* people are reluctant to access routine medical screening and maintenance procedures such as vaginal exams, pap smears, and breast exams for transmen, and prostate and testicular exams for transwomen. Their reluctance may be further compounded by hesitations due to concerns about the prevalence of ignorant or hostile care providers; by concerns about being required to access care, or being denied access to care, at facilities dedicated to providing services for people of their birth-assigned sex; or being denied needed services on the basis of their current sex or gender (Hartofelis and Gomez 2013; National Center for Transgender Equality 2012; Silverman 2009).

Elevated rates of HIV infection are of particular concern in certain segments of trans* populations, especially among people of colour as well as transfeminine-spectrum people (Hwang and Nuttbrock 2014). A disproportionate number of trans* people live in poverty and suffer from mental health, drug and alcohol abuse problems (National Center for Transgender Equality 2012). One result is that a disproportionate number of transwomen and a small number of transmen engage in survival sex work. For many of those who engage in it, sex work provides the only source of income sufficient to allow them to finance the costs of their transitions (Israel and Tarver 1997; Namaste 2000, 2009; Nemoto et al. 2014) while also increasing their exposure to risky sexual practices.

Risk of HIV infection can also be elevated in non-commercial sexual relationships involving trans* people. Concerns about genital adequacy can also undermine trans* people's sexual confidence, one result of which can be that trans* people may be insufficiently assertive about protecting themselves against risks of sexual infections (Bockting et al. 1998; Nemoto et al. 2004). Trans* people who feel that their relationships with cisgender people may be insecure because of their being trans* may also be more likely to impair their judgement through the use of drugs or alcohol. They may be more willing to risk HIV infection than risk losing their relationships by insisting on proper protection against HIV (Hotton et al. 2013; Nemoto et al. 2004; Sevelius et al. 2009). Those trans* people whose partners are active as gay or bisexual men are at compounded risk of infection due to the higher rates of infection in those sexual communities (Reisner et al. 2010; Rowniak et al. 2011).

Hormone treatments used by many trans* people decrease, or completely block, fertility. Removal of reproductive organs, of course, eliminates most capacity for reproduction. For these reasons, the World Professional Associa-

tion for Transgender Health (WPATH) recommends reproductive counselling for all people considering any of these treatments (Coleman et al. 2011). Trans* people who wish to have children using their own gametes after hormonal or surgical treatments can bank sperm or eggs, prior to transition, for later use (Coleman et al. 2011). Gynephilic transwomen with intact reproductive organs, and who are sexually active, can impregnate. Similarly, androphilic transmen with intact reproductive organs, and who are sexually active, can become pregnant. As well, a small number of transmen, of a variety of sexual orientations, have interrupted their hormonal treatments specifically for the purpose of becoming pregnant either through sexual intercourse, or by way of artificial insemination (Coleman et al. 2011; Murphy 2010). However, the availability of trans-specific reproductive health care is limited (National Center for Transgender Equality 2012).

11.8   Future Directions

Most of the research into trans* sexualities is limited to that which looks at the time around transition and the first few years beyond. As a result, little is known about sexuality in the lives of trans* people in the years before and after transition, or in the lives of those who identify as trans* and do not transition. These would be fruitful areas for future research.

Many trans* people are attracted to opportunities to experiment with alternatives to the limitations that they feel on the basis of their bodies. To that end, many trans* people are active in cybersex, fantasy, and science-fiction arenas where they are not bound by physical bodies and may take on whatever characteristics they wish to explore (Hansbury 2011). Similarly, many trans* people enjoy BDSM sexuality (bondage and discipline, dominance and submission, sadomasochism) for the role-playing opportunities it affords them to try out alternative sexual roles (Bauer 2008). Both of these areas are understudied and would be valuable areas of focus for future research.

The paucity of research about the sexualities of older trans* adults is part of a larger pattern of neglect concerning sexualities of people over the age of 50 years (Jablonski et al. 2013; Kazer et al. 2013; Witten and Eyler 2012; Zeiss and Kasl-Godley 2001). While there is some evidence that many of the same sexual patterns seen in younger trans* adults also hold true as trans* people age (Cook-Daniels and Munson 2010), much more research is needed. As trans* people age they have particular needs in terms of health care and housing which, in turn, further complicate questions about sexuality. Further research is needed in this area as well.

On the other end of the age spectrum, although research about trans* youth is increasing, particularly in the areas of gender identity support and treatment, research concerning trans* youths' sexualities is still very limited. The heteronormative conflation of gender expectations and sexual expectations, and their special intensity for teens and young adults, combine to make sexuality especially fraught for trans* teens and young adults who struggle with additional identity issues beyond those that plague most young people (Grossman and D'Augelli 2006). This conflation also complicates sexuality education, which has yet to address the needs of trans* students (Gowen and Winges-Yanez 2014). It also intersects with various forms of victimization, and together these have a notable effect on rates of relationship violence (Dank et al. 2014) and sexual risk-taking by trans* youth (Robinson and Espelage 2013). This would also be a welcome area for further research.

Finally, although increasing, little work has been done into the experiences of trans* people of colour, and even less into the sexualities of trans* people of colour. Much of the research done to date has over-represented the risks of HIV infection among trans* people of colour in Western societies, or has been about trans* people of colour in other cultures. More research is needed about the sexualities of trans* people of colour.

11.9 Conclusion

The sexuality of trans* people is as varied and complex as human imagination will allow. However, trans* people and their sexual partners, as is the case for cisgender people and their sexual partners, must find ways to make sense of their bodies, their fantasies and desires, and their sexual practices within the context of a social system which still largely confers intelligibility and social acceptance only upon binaries versions of sex, gender, and sexuality. Nonetheless, many trans* people, and their partners, are forced by the realities of their lives to mount challenges to accepted ways of being. Some do this enthusiastically, some reluctantly, some with equanimity. All contribute to the advancement of sexual and gender diversity.

References

Alexander, J. (2003). There are different points in your life where you can go either way: Discussing transsexuality and bisexuality with some women of CrossPort. *Journal of Bisexuality, 3*(3–4), 129–150.

Aramburu Alegría, C. (2010). Relationship challenges and relationship maintenance activities following disclosure of transsexualism. *Journal of Psychiatric and Mental Health Nursing, 17,* 909–916.

Aramburu Alegría, C. (2013). Relational and sexual fluidity in females partnered with male-to-female transsexual persons. *Journal of Psychiatric and Mental Health Nursing, 20,* 142–149.

Bauer, R. (2008). Transgressive and transformative gendered sexual practices and white privileges: The case of the dyke/trans BDSM communities. *Women's Studies Quarterly, 36*(3/4), 233–253.

Bauer, G., Anjali K., Pyne, J., Redman, N., Scanlon, K., & Travers, R. (2012). *Improving the health of trans communities: Findings from the Trans PULSE Project.* Rainbow Health Ontario Conference, Plenary Presentation. Ottawa, ON, Canada. http://transpulseproject.ca/wp-content/uploads/2012/04/Trans-PULSE.-Rainbow-Health-Ontario-Conference.-Plenary-2012-vFINAL.pdf.

Bauer, G., & Scheim, A. (2013). Sampling bias in transgender studies. *Lancet, 13,* 832.

Beemyn, G., & Rankin, S. (2011). *The lives of transgender people.* New York: Columbia University Press.

Benjamin, H. (1966). *The transsexual phenomenon.* New York: Julian Press.

Benjamin, H. (1969). Newer aspects of the transsexual phenomenon. *Journal of Sex Research, 5*(2), 135–144.

Blanchard, R. (1985). Typology of male-to-female transsexualism. *Archives of Sexual Behavior, 14*(3), 247–261.

Blanchard, R. (1988). Nonhomosexual gender dysphoria. *Journal of Sex Research, 24,* 188–193.

Blanchard, R. (1989). The concept of autogynephilia and the typology of male gender dysphorics. *The Journal of Nervous and Mental Disease, 177*(10), 616–623.

Bockting, W., Benner, A., & Coleman, E. (2009). Gay and bisexual identity development among female-to-male transsexuals in North America: Emergence of a transgender sexuality. *Archives of Sexual Behavior, 38,* 688–701.

Bockting, W., Robinson, B., & Rosser, B. (1998). Transgender HIV prevention: A qualitative needs assessment. *AIDS Care: Psychological and Socio-medical Aspects of AIDS/HIV, 10*(4), 505–525.

Bolin, A. (1987). *In search of Eve.* South Hadley: Bergin & Garvey.

Brown, N. (2009). "I'm in transition too:" Sexual identity renegotiation in sexual-minority women's relationships with transsexual men. *International Journal of Sexual Health, 21*(1), 61–77.

Brown, N. (2010). The sexual relationships of sexual-minority women partnered with trans men: A qualitative study. *Archives of Sexual Behavior, 39,* 561–572.

Bullough, V. (2000). Transgenderism and the concept of gender. *International Journal of Transgenderism, 4*(3). http://www.symposion.com/ijt/gilbert/bullough.htm.

Bullough, V. (2007). Legitimatizing transsexualism. *International Journal of Transgenderism, 10*(1), 3–13.

Carter, M. (2014). Gender socialization and identity theory. *Social Sciences, 3,* 242–263.

Cauldwell, D. (1949). Psychopathia transexualis. *International Journal of Transgenderism, 5*(2). http://www.symposion.com/ijt/cauldwell/cauldwell_02.htm.

Chivers, M., & Bailey, M. (2000). Sexual orientation of female-to-male transsexuals: A comparison of homosexual and nonhomosexual types. *Archives of Sexual Behavior, 29,* 259–278.

Cole, C., & Meyer, W., III. (1998). Transgender behaviour and DSM IV. In D. Denny (Ed.), *Current concepts in transgender identity* (pp. 227–236). New York: Garland Publishers.

Coleman, E., Bockting, W., Botzer, M., Cohen-Kettenis, P., DeCuypere, G., Feldman, J., et al. (2011). Standards of care for the health of transsexual, transgender, and gender nonconforming people, version 7. *International Journal of Transgenderism, 13*(4), 165–232.

Coleman, E., Bockting, W., & Gooren, L. (1993). Homosexual and bisexual identity in sex-reassigned female-to-male transsexuals. *Archives of Sexual Behavior, 22*(1), 37–50.

Conron, K. J., Scott, G., Stowell Sterling, G., & Landers, S. J. (2012). Transgender health in Massachusetts: Results from a household probability sample of adults. *American Journal of Public Health, 102*(1), 118–122.

Cook-Daniels, L., & Munson, M. (2010). Sexual violence, elder abuse, and sexuality of transgender adults, age 50+: Results of three surveys. *Journal of GLBT Family Studies, 6*(2), 142–177.

Cotton, T. T. (Ed.). (2012). *Hung jury: Testimonies of genital surgery by transsexual men.* Oakland: Transgress Press.

Cromwell, J. (1999). *Transmen and FTMs: Identities, bodies, genders, and sexualities.* Urbana: University of Illinois Press.

Dank, M., Lachman, P., Zweig, J., & Yahner, J. (2014). Dating violence experiences of lesbian, gay, bisexual and transgender youth. *Journal of Youth and Adolescence, 43,* 846–857.

Daskalos, C. T. (1998). Changes in the sexual orientation of six heterosexual male-to-female transsexuals. *Archives of Sexual Behavior, 27*(6), 605–614.

Davis, E. (2008). Situating "fluidity:" (Trans)gender identification and the regulation of gender diversity. *GLQ: A Journal of Lesbian and Gay Studies, 15*(1), 97–130.

De Cuypere, G., T'Sjoen, G., Beerten, R., Selvaggi, G., De Sutter, P., Hoebeke, P., et al. (2005). Sexual and physical health after sex reassignment surgery. *Archives of Sexual Behavior, 34*(6), 679–690.

Denny, D. (2006). Transgender communities of the United States in the late twentieth century. In P. Currah, R. Juang, & S. Minter (Eds.), *Transgender rights* (pp. 171–191). Minneapolis: University of Minnesota Press.

Devor, A. (2000). How many sexes? How many genders? When two are not enough. http://web.uvic.ca/~ahdevor/HowMany/HowMany.html. Accessed 14 June 2014.

Devor, A., & Matte, N. (2007). Building a better world for transpeople: Reed Erickson and the Erickson Educational Foundation. *International Journal of Transgenderism, 10*(1), 47–68.

Devor, H. (1987). Gender blending females: Women and sometimes men. *American Behavioral Scientist, 31,* 12–40.

Devor, H. (1989). *Gender blending: Confronting the limits of duality.* Bloomington: Indiana University Press.

Devor, H. (1993). Sexual orientation identities, attractions, and practices of female-to-male transsexuals. *Journal of Sex Research, 30*(4), 303–315.

Devor, H. (1994). Toward a taxonomy of gendered sexuality. *Journal of Psychology and Human Sexuality, 6*(1), 23–55.

Devor, H. (1997a). *FTM: Female-to-male transsexuals in society.* Bloomington: Indiana University Press.

Devor, H. (1997b). More than manly women: How female-to-male transsexuals reject lesbian identities. In B. Bullough, V. Bullough, & J. Elias (Eds.), *Gender blending* (pp. 87–102). Amherst: Prometheus.

Dozier, R. (2005). Beards, breasts, and bodies: Doing sex in a gendered world. *Gender & Society, 19*(3), 297–316.

Dreger, A. (2000). *Hermaphrodites and the medical invention of sex.* Cambridge: Harvard University Press.

Edelman, E. A., & Zimman, L. (2014). Boycunts and bonus holes: Trans men's bodies, neoliberalism, and the sexual productivity of genitals. *Journal of Homosexuality, 61*(5), 673–690.

Ekins, R., & King, D. (2001). Pioneers of transgendering: The popular sexology of David O. Cauldwell. *International Journal of Transgenderism, 5*(2). http://www.symposion.com/ijt/cauldwell/cauldwell_01.htm.

Ekins, R., & King, D. (2005). Virginia Prince: Transgender pioneer. *International Journal of Transgenderism, 8*(4), 5–15.

Ellis, H. (1913). Sexo-aesthetic inversion. *Alienist and Neurologist, 34*(3–14), 1–31.

Erhardt, V. (2007). *Head over heels: Wives who stay with cross-dressers and transexuals*. New York: Howarth Press.

Ettner, R. (2007). Transsexual couples: A qualitative evaluation of atypical partner preferences. *International Journal of Transgenderism, 10*(2), 109–116.

Factor, R., & Rothblum, E. (2008). Exploring gender identity and community among three groups of transgender individuals in the United States: MTFs, FTMs, and genderqueers. *Health Sociology Review, 17,* 235–253.

Fleming, M., MacGowan, B., & Costos, B. (1985). The dyadic adjustment of female-to-male transsexuals. *Archives of Sexual Behavior, 14*(1), 47–55.

Freeman, N., Johnson, K., Ambady, N., & Rule, N. (2010). Sexual orientation perception involves gendered facial cues. *Personality and Social Psychology Bulletin, 36*(10), 1318–1331.

GATE-Global Action for Trans Equality. (n.d.). Trans*. Resource Document. http://transactivists.org/trans/. Accessed 7 July 2014.

Gherovici, P. (2011). Psychoanalysis needs a sex change. *Gay & Lesbian Issues and Psychology Review, 7*(1), 3–18.

Gowen, L., & Winges-Yanez, N. (2014). Lesbian, gay, bisexual, transgender, queer and questioning youths' perspectives of inclusive school-based sexuality education. *Journal Sex Research, 51*(7), 788–800.

Grossman, A., & D'Augelli, A. (2006). Transgender youth: Invisible and vulnerable. *Journal of Homosexuality, 51*(1), 111–128.

Hansbury, G. (2011). Trans/virtual: The anxieties of transsexual and electronic embodiments. *Journal of Gay & Lesbian Mental Health, 15,* 308–317.

Hartofelis, E., & Gomez, A. (2013). Trans men's health is a 'women's health' issue: Expanding the boundaries of sexual and reproductive health care. Resource Document. National Women's Health Network. https://nwhn.org/newsletter/node/1533. Accessed 7 July 2014.

Hines, S. (2006). Intimate transitions: Transgender practices of partnering and parenting. *Sociology, 40,* 353–371.

Hirschfeld, M. (1991/1910). *The transvestites: The erotic drive to cross-dress* (Trans: M. A. Lombardi-Nash). Buffalo: Prometheus Books. (Original work published 1910).

Hotton, A., Garofalo, R., Kuhns, L., & Johnson, A. (2013). Substance use as a mediator of the relationship between life stress and sexual risk among young transgender women. *AIDS Education and Prevention, 25*(1), 62–71.

Hwang, S. J., & Nuttbrock, L. (2014). Adolesent gender-related abuse, androphilia, and HIV risk among transfeminine people of color in New York City. *Journal of Homosexuality, 61*(5), 691–713.

Iantaffi, A., & Bockting, W. (2011). Views from both sides of the bridge? Gender, sexual legitimacy and transgender people's experiences of relationships. *Culture, Health & Sexuality: An International Journal for Research Intervention and Care, 13*(3), 355–370.

Irving, D. (2008). Normalized transgressions: Legitimizing the transsexual body as productive. *Radical History Review, 100,* 38–59.

Israel, G., & Tarver, D. (1997). *Transgender care: Recommended guidelines, practical information, and personal accounts*. Philadelphia: Temple University Press.

Jablonski, R., Vance, D., & Beattie, E. (2013). The invisible elderly: Lesbian, gay, bisexual, and transgender older adults. *Journal of Gerontological Nursing, 39*(11), 46–52.

Jacobs, S. K. (2014). Introduction: Special issue on "gender, sexuality and political economy." *International Journal of Politics, Culture and Society, 27*(2), 129–152.

Joslin-Roher, E., & Wheeler, D. (2009). Partners in transition: The transition experiences of lesbian, bisexual, and queer identified partners of transgender men. *Journal of Gay & Lesbian Social Services, 21*(1), 30–48.

Kazer, M., Grossman, S., Kerins, G., Kleis, A., & Tocchi, C. (2013). Validity and reliability of the Geriatric Sexuality Inventory. *Journal of Gerontological Nursing, 39*(11), 38–45.

Kins, E., Hoebeke, P., Heylens, G., Ruben, R., & De Cuypere, G. (2008). The female-to-male transsexual and his female partner versus the traditional couple: A comparison. *Journal of Sex & Marital Therapy, 34,* 429–438.

Kessler, S. J., & McKenna, W. (1978). *Gender: An ethnomethodological approach*. New York: Wiley-Interscience.

Klein, C., & Gorzalka, B. B. (2009). Sexual functioning in transsexuals following hormone therapy and genital surgery: A review. *The Journal of Sexual Medicine, 6*(11), 2922–2939.

Knudson, G., De Cuypere, G., & Bockting, W. (2011). Second response of the World Professional Association for Transgender Health to the proposed revision of the diagnosis of Transvestic Disorder for DSM 5. *International Journal of Transgenderism, 13*(1), 9–12.

Kockott, G., & Fahrner, E.-M. (1988). Male-to-female and female-to-male transsexuals: A comparison. *Archives of Sexual Behavior, 17*(6), 539–546.

Kosenko, K. (2011). The safer sex communication of transgender adults: Processes and problems. *Journal of Communication, 61,* 476–495.

Krafft-Ebing, R. v. (1998). *Psychopathia Sexualis* (Trans: F. S. Klaf) New York: Arcade Publishing. (Original work published 1886).

Kuper, L., Nussbaum, R., & Mustanski, B. (2012). Exploring the diversity of gender and sexual orientation identities in an online sample of transgender individuals. *Journal of Sex Research, 49*(2–3), 244–254.

Lawrence, A. (2013). *Men trapped in men's bodies: Narratives of autogynephilic transsexualism*. New York: Springer.

Lee, P., Houk, C., Faisal Ahmed, S., & Hughes, I. (2006). Consensus statement on management of intersex disorders. *Pediatrics, 118,* e488–e500.

Lev, A. (2004). *Transgender emergence: Therapeutic guidelines for working with gender-variant people and their families*. New York: The Hawthorn Clinical Practice Press.

Lewins, F. (2002). Explaining stable partnerships among FTMs and MTFs: A significant difference? *Journal of Sociology, 38*(1), 76–88.

Lief, H. I., & Hubschman, L. (1993). Orgasm in the postoperative transsexual. *Archives of Sexual Behavior, 22*(2), 145–155.

Lombardi, E. (2009). Varieties of transgender/transsexual lives and their relationship with transphobia. *Journal of Homosexuality, 56*, 977–992.

Meyerowitz, J. (2002). *How sex changed: A history of transsexuality in the United States*. Cambridge: Harvard University Press.

Miner, M., Bockting, W., Swinburne Romine, R., & Raman, S. (2012). Conducting Internet research with the transgender population: Reaching broad samples and collecting valid data. *Social Science Computer Review, 30*(2), 202–211.

Moser, C. (2009). Autogynephilia in women. *Journal of Homosexuality, 56*(5), 539–547.

Murphy, T. (2010). The ethics of helping transgender men and women have children. *Perspectives in biology and medicine, 53*(1), 46–60.

Namaste, V. (2000). *Invisible lives: The erasure of transsexual and transgendered people*. Chicago: University of Chicago Press.

Namaste, V. (2009). Undoing theory: The "transgender question" and the epistemic violence of Anglo-American feminist theory. *Hypatia, 24*(3), 11–21.

National Center for Transgender Equality. (2012). Transgender Sexual and Reproductive Health: Unmet Needs and Barriers to Care. Resource document. http://transequality.org/Resources/Factsheet_TransSexualandReproHealth_April2012.pdf. Accessed 8 January 2014.

Nemoto, T., Bödeker, B., Iwamoto, M., & Sakata, M. (2014). Practices of receptive and insertive anal sex among transgender women in relation to partner types, sociocultural factors, and background variables. *AIDS Care: Psychological and socio-medical aspects of AIDS/HIV, 26*(4), 434–440.

Nemoto, T., Operario, D., Keatley, J., & Villegas, D. (2004). Social context of HIV risk behaviours among male-to-female transgenders of colour. *AIDS Care, 16*(6), 724–735.

Olsson, S.-E., & Möller, A. (2006). Regret after sex reassignment surgery in a male-to-female transsexual: A long-term follow-up. *Archives of Sexual Behavior, 35*(4), 501–506.

Page, A., & Peacock, J. (2013). Negotiating identities in a heteronormative context. *Journal of Homosexuality, 60*(4), 639–654.

Prince, V. (2005a). Homosexuality, transvestism and transsexuality: Reflection on their etiology and differentiation. *International Journal of Transgenderism, 8*(4), 17–20. (Original work published 1957).

Prince, V. (2005b). Sex vs. gender. *International Journal of Transgenderism, 8*(4), 29–32. (Original work published 1973).

Prince, V. (2005c). Transsexuals and pseudotranssexuals. *International Journal of Transgenderism, 8*(4), 33–37. (Original work published 1978).

Rachlin, K. (2007). The questions we ask: Conducting socially conscious research with transgender individuals. In W. Meezan & J. Martin (Eds.), *Handbook of research with lesbian, gay, bisexual and transgender populations* (pp. 261–279). New York: Routledge.

Reicherzer, S. (2008). Evolving language and understanding in the historical development of the Gender Identity Disorder diagnosis. *Journal of LGBT Issues in Counselling, 2*(4), 326–347.

Reisner, S., Perkovich, B., & Mimiaga, M. (2010). A mixed methods study of the sexual health needs of New England transmen who have sex with nontransgender men. *AIDS patient care and STDs, 24*(8), 501–513.

Robinson, J., & Espelage, D. (2013). Peer victimization and sexual risk differences between lesbian, gay, bisexual, transgender, or questioning and heterosexual youths in grades 7–12. *American Journal of Public Health, 103*(10), 1810–1819.

Roen, K. (2001). Transgender theory and embodiment: The risk of racial marginalisation. *Journal of Gender Studies, 10*(3), 253–263.

Rowniak, S., Chesla, C., Rose, C., & Holzemer, W. (2011). Transmen: The HIV risk of gay identity. *AIDS Education and Prevention, 23*(6), 508–520.

Rubin, H. (2003). *Self-made men: Identity and embodiment among transsexual men*. Nashville: Vanderbilt University Press.

Samons, S. (2009). *When the opposite sex isn't: Sexual orientation in male-to-female transgender persons*. New York: Routledge.

Schilt, K., & Windsor, E. (2014). The sexual habitus of transgender men: Negotiating sexuality through gender. *Journal of Homosexuality, 61*(5), 732–748.

Schleifer, D. (2006). Make me feel mighty real: Gay female-to-male transgenderists negotiating sex, gender and sexuality. *Sexualities, 9*, 57–75.

Schrock, D., & Reid, L. (2006). Transsexuals' sexual stories. *Archives of Sexual Behavior, 35*(1), 75–86.

Sevelius, J., Reznick, O., Hart, S., & Schwarcz, S. (2009). Informing interventions: The importance of contextual factors in the prediction of sexual risk behaviors among transgender women. *AIDS Education and Prevention, 21*(2), 113–127.

Silverman, M. (2009). Issues in access to healthcare by transgender individuals. *Women's Rights Law Reporter, 30*(2), 347–351.

Sohn, M., & Exner, K. (2008). Genital reassignment surgery for transsexual people. *Sexologies, 17*, 283–290.

Stone, S. (1992). The empire strikes back: A posttranssexual manifesto. *Camera Obscura, 10* (2 29), 150–176.

Stryker, S. (2008). *Transgender history*. Berkeley: Seal Press.

Sullivan, N. (2008). The role of medicine in the (trans) formation of "wrong" bodies. *Bodies & Society, 14*(1), 105–116.

Tale, C., Ledbetter, J., & Youssef, C. (2013). A two-question method for assessing gender categories in the social and medical sciences. *Journal of Sex Research, 50*(8), 767–776.

Ulrichs, K. H. (1994). *The riddle of "man-manly" love: The pioneering work on male homosexuality*. (Trans: M. Lombardi-Nash) Buffalo: Prometheus Books. (Original work published 1864–1880).

Vecolli, L. (2014). Moving beyond what the founders kept. Moving Trans* History Forward Symposium, Victoria, BC, Canada.

Weinberg, T., & Bullough, V. (1988). Alienation, self-image, and the importance of support groups for the wives of transvestites. *Journal of Sex Research, 24*, 262–268.

Witten, T., & Eyler, A. (2012). Preface. In T. W. Eyler (Ed.), *Gay, lesbian, bisexual & transgender aging* (pp. ix–xiii). Baltimore: The Johns Hopkins University Press.

Zeiss, A., & Kasl-Godley, J. (2001). Sexuality in older adults' relationships. *Generations, 25*(2), 18–25.

Zimman, L. (2014). The discursive construction of sex: Remaking and reclaiming the gendered body in talk about genitals among trans men. In L. Zimman, J. Davis, & J. Raclaw (Eds.), *Queer excursions: Retheorizing binaries in language, gender, and sexuality* (pp. 13–34). New York: Oxford University Press.

Part IV
Sexualities in Social Context

Casual Sex: Integrating Social, Behavioral, and Sexual Health Research

12

Justin R. Garcia, Susan M. Seibold-Simpson,
Sean G. Massey and Ann M. Merriwether

12.1 Introduction

In the last decade there has been an abundance of research on the topic of casual sex, often fueled by debates as to whether the phenomenon represents the "new" state of romantic and sexual experience in the developed world, and often peppered with concerns about sexual "risk." The focus of much of the research on casual sex has been the uncommitted "no-strings-attached" aspects of a sexual encounter between two people not currently in a romantic relationship with each other. The literature has now become voluminous, with different research streams—and different theoretical and methodological traditions—covering various facets of casual sex, ranging from people's attitudes toward behaviors, from one-night stands to friends-with-benefits, and from heterosexual college campus samples to samples of urban men who have sex with men (MSM). This work has been done by a surprisingly wide variety of scholars and scientists, and several recent reviews have attempted to synthesize various aspects of this literature (e.g., Garcia et al. 2012; Hatfield et al. 2012; Heldman and Wade 2010). In the current chapter we try to avoid regurgitation of existing reviews, but rather to connect-the-dots between seemingly disparate aspects of this work to help guide current and future research on the topic of casual sex while incorporating sexual health.

At present, the aspect of casual sex research most in the limelight is sexual "hook-up" behavior among U.S. emerging adults. The public and academic interest in this topic is intensified by debates as to whether there exists a new *hook-up culture* among youth that is interwoven with the strict enforcement of gender and class norms on college campuses, sexual debut and early romantic and sexual experiences during late adolescence and young adulthood, and patterns of alcohol and drug use/experimentation during this time. Adding further emphasis, new attention has been drawn to the topic of college students' (uncommitted) sexual experiences following the 2014 *Not Alone* report of the White House Task Force to Protect Students from Sexual Assault, and subsequent national conversations regarding the disturbingly high rate of sexual assaults carried out on U.S. college campuses each year

J. R. Garcia (✉)
The Kinsey Institute & Department of Gender Studies,
Indiana University, Bloomington, IN 47405, USA
e-mail: jusrgarc@indiana.edu

S. M. Seibold-Simpson
Decker School of Nursing, Binghamton University,
Binghamton, NY 13902, USA
e-mail: ssimpson@binghamton.edu

S. G. Massey
Women, Gender, & Sexuality Studies Program,
Binghamton University, Binghamton, NY 13902, USA
e-mail: smassey@binghamton.edu

A. M. Merriwether
Departments of Psychology and Human Development,
Binghamton University, Binghamton, NY 13902, USA
e-mail: amerriwe@binghamton.edu

J. DeLamater, R.F. Plante (eds.), *Handbook of the Sociology of Sexualities,* Handbooks of Sociology and
Social Research, DOI 10.1007/978-3-319-17341-2_12, © Springer International Publishing Switzerland 2015

(according to the U.S. National Institute of Justice an estimated 1-in-5 women and 1-in-20 men will be victims of attempted or completed sexual assault during their undergraduate career). However, research on sexual hook-ups is just beginning to move beyond primarily descriptive studies. Consequently, it is difficult to make informed applications of this work to the various educational and intervention initiatives, such as reducing casual sex-related sexual violence or improving emerging adults' mental health outcomes. However, as addressed later in this paper, there is a robust literature in sexual health on the topic of casual sex that, when merged with the more sociological literature on sexual hook-ups, has potential for greater intellectual and applied depth in understanding casual sex in the United States.

12.2 Cultural Representations of Sex Without Commitment

Despite research showing that nearly all American adults engage in premarital sex (Finer 2007; Garcia and Kruger 2010; Herbenick et al. 2010), the notion that coupledom and sexual activity occur within exclusive committed relationships is often taken for granted. Yet partnered sexual activity beyond the context of a marital union occurs across a continuum of commitment variations. Within that continuum, the distinguishing feature of **casual sex** is that the interaction lacks explicit commitment vis-à-vis a clearly institutionalized/delineated social status. But even within casual sex there are varieties of arrangements—from friends with benefits, to one night stands, to recurring hook-ups and more—that further distinguish types of casual sex, primarily on the basis of relational commitment (see Wentland and Reissing 2011).

Of the varieties of casual sex, it is "hooking up" that has caught the attention of the American public. Books on casual sex now range from the occasional academic treatise such as Bogle's (2008) *Hooking Up*, to more playful contributions such as self-guided diaries like *Hook-ups & Hangovers* (Chronicle Books 2011), to self-help

handbooks such as *The Happy Hook-up* (Sherman and Tocantins 2004), *The Hook-up Handbook* (Rozler and Lavinthal 2005), and *11 Points Guide to Hooking Up* (Greenspan 2011). Most of these books aim to guide young heterosexual women to get the most out of their uncommitted sexual encounters. Given the sexual double standards and gender imbalances that plague sexual relationships (Allison and Risman 2013; Armstrong et al. 2012; Tolman 2002), this is a welcome development. However, although the U.S. social context is captivated by casual sex, it generally also condemns it. Consequently, the epistemological dissonance between being *able to engage* in casual sex and the social potential and psychological consequences of *actually engaging* in casual sex may occasionally become conflated. It is this very tension, between what *ought* to be and what *is*, particularly as applied to sexuality, that some have argued stifles the integration of feminist scholarship with bio-behavioral sciences (Fisher et al. 2013). On the other hand, the collision of these theoretical foundations has produced and is producing a field of sexuality that some have argued is finally embodying what it means to be interdisciplinary (Tolman and Diamond 2014).

Given this contradictory social backdrop, popular representation of casual sex suggests that it may result in more than the excitement of emotionally unburdened sexual release. Recent movies such as *Knocked Up* and *Juno* that portray pregnancy occurring between casual sex partners offer a romanticized view of unintended pregnancy; they suggest that continuing a relationship and having a child after a relatively uncommitted sexual experience can be enriching. Other blockbuster movies like *No Strings Attached* and *Friends with Benefits* follow the lead characters as they fumble through the ups and downs of practicing uncommitted sex. Important to the plot twist, these films portray attractive young men and women as they enjoy the physical pleasures of sex, and then try to manage the intense romantic feelings that develop for their NSA ("no strings attached") sexual partner. And research seems to support a similar plot line. In a 2013 nationally representative study, *Singles in America*, a sub-sample of 1042 singles were asked whether they had ever had a one-night stand or casual hook-up that turned into a long-term, committed, romantic relationship (Garcia and Fisher 2015). In the survey, 40 % of men and 24 % of women said "yes". And when asked whether they had ever had a friends-with-benefits relationship that turned into a long-term committed partnership, 36 % of men and 23 % of women said "yes". This suggests, again, that one of the more novel aspects of casual sex today is the shifting relationship between dating and courtship practices, including, apparently, that casual sex is sometimes a courtship practice in and of itself.

Countless songs contain allusions to uncommitted sex, either advising the listener to avoid it or advocating the pursuit of it—e.g., *Get Lucky* by Daft Punk, or *Casual Sex* by My Darkest Days, with lyrics like "You'll never meet my mom, strings will never be attached. We'll always get along, 'cause it doesn't have to last". Advertisements for websites and mobile phone apps encourage men and women to realize their 'sexual urges' and find a nearby hook-up partner. Geolocation apps like Grindr, which is primarily a hook-up app for gay men, and Tinder, which is being used across genders and sexual orientations, are well-known examples that allow individuals to find potential romantic or sexual partners who are nearby and interested. Apps like Tinder may help researchers better understand casual sex. Tinder users establish their search settings and then see a series of profiles consisting of photos and a brief description, and any friends/ interests they have in common (based on Facebook profiles). But to start a chat/conversation, both users must indicate that they "like" the other by 'swiping' to one side on their Smartphones. This somewhat levels the gendered, heterosexual playing field, if even momentarily for initial courtship, in that *both* individuals must indicate interest and at any time can terminate a chat connection. The research questions this may raise are also increasingly socially relevant given the popularity of such technology: Tinder recently announced traffic of nearly 1 billion 'swipes' per day, and some 12 million matches made per day.

Magazine editorials ask why people hook-up, or give tips on how to be more successful at it.

A recent *Cosmopolitan* article discusses how dating is broken but the reason may not be casual sex (Lieberman 2014), and the magazine *Seventeen* has an entire section devoted to "Hooking Up Tips". The *New York Times* has featured the topic several times, questioning how concerned America should be for its youth, and asking what has or hasn't changed since the sexual revolution of the 1960s, with titles like "The End of Courtship?", "Sex on Campus—She Can Play That Game, Too", and "Is Hookup Culture Leaving Your Generation Unhappy and Unprepared for Love?". Even the American Psychological Association's flagship magazine, *APA Monitor*, featured the topic as the February 2012 cover story, urging practitioners to know the data on the psychological and health consequences of hooking up. Casual sex is undergoing a cultural shift, and a research agenda aimed at understanding it is now vital.

12.3 Hooking Up

As noted, *hooking up* as a specific form of casual sexual activity has garnered the most research attention to date. This research has primarily focused on white heterosexual college students in North America. Based on studies in the U.S. and Canada, about 65 to 85 % of college students have had a sexual hook-up (Garcia et al. 2012). However, the specific behaviors in these hook-up encounters tends to vary, ranging from kissing and heavy petting to penetrative intercourse, with the ambiguous terminology purposefully employed by some youth. Scholars have proposed a variety of similar, albeit slightly variable, definitions of what constitutes a hook-up. The common element, however, is its *uncommitted* aspect. But if one were to also count other varieties of uncommitted sex (see Claxton and van Dulmen 2013), such as "booty calls" (late night visits for sex) and "friends-with-benefits" (ongoing sexual but supposedly not romantic relationships), the rates of allegedly casual sexual encounters would be considerably greater.

This increase in attention by scholars should not be taken to mean casual sex is an altogether new phenomenon. Indeed, it is not a new

American pastime (Johnson 2008; Reay 2014) and has been studied outside the current hook-up culture frame (Boswell and Spade 1996; Cates 1991; Maticka-Tyndale 1991). However, the contemporary social discourse about casual sex, cultural representations of hooking up in a wide variety of media, and perhaps most notably, the shifting relationship between uncommitted sexual behavior and committed romantic relationships today, is unprecedented. That is, hook-ups are most striking in light of changing patterns of courtship and dating in contemporary industrialized settings (Garcia and Fisher 2015; Stinson 2010). The demographic rules surrounding sexual relationships have changed. Ages of sexual maturity are younger than ever before, while ages of first marriage and first birth are later than ever before. And, all the while, traditions of courtship and sentiments of compulsory early heterosexual marriage have dissipated (Bogle 2008; Garcia and Reiber 2008).

Several historical trends have likely contributed to hooking up as a socially constructed aspect of the sexual landscape. Along with rapidly changing social conventions and patterns of leisure activity, the rise of the automobile and entertainment venues such as cinemas and drive-in movie theatres in the early to mid-twentieth century, familial supervision of dating and traditional patterns of courtship began to diminish (Bailey 1988; Stinson 2010). For centuries, a young man visited the home of a young woman to woo her in the presence of her family. But by the mid-1900s, a courting couple could speed off in a car—where they could get to know each other more fully—even sexually—in private. Then, along with the rise of the feminist movement, mixed-sex parties, the use of alcohol and drugs, increasing access to birth control (condoms and oral contraceptives), and changing attitudes about virginity, marriage, and reproduction in the 1960s and 1970s, American young adults (and late adolescents) became even more sexually liberated, increasing opportunities to experience sexual activity outside of legal marriage.

Sexual behavior in contexts other than committed romantic relationships became a topic of scientific interest beginning in the mid-twentieth century (Ellis 1958; Kinsey et al. 1948, 1953), and especially during the sexual liberation period of the 1960s and 1970s (Altman 1971, 1982). Attention to casual sexual encounters among men who have sex with men (MSM) also increased as an area of study during the 1980s, likely as a direct result of the HIV/AIDS epidemic. Public health research on uncommitted sexual behaviors, focused on preventing the spread of sexually transmitted infections (STIs), extends well beyond heterosexual college students. Note that, in contrast, there is a relatively small literature on such behaviors among women who have sex with women (WSW), as their lower sexually transmitted infection (STI) incidence has not, at least based on epidemiological data, led to the research urgency and funding (and medicalization) as it has among MSM (see Cacchioni, Chap. 24, this volume).

Most of the research to date has focused on the occurrence of sexual hook-ups among *emerging adults*, individuals between the ages of 18 and 25 years, who are in the developmental transition stage between adolescence and young adulthood (Arnett 2000, 2004). Researchers generally have not restricted the specific behaviors that constitute a sexual hook-up, however, possibly including heavy petting, kissing, oral sex (performed or received), vaginal intercourse and/or anal intercourse. But this research has primarily focused on white, heterosexual youth, with samples drawn from North American college campuses. Although these may technically be "convenience" samples, it is worth noting that for those studying sexual cultures during emerging adulthood, specifically in the context of college campuses, this is as much the ideal target sample as it is a convenience sample. Despite many unanswered questions about sexual hook-ups, the collective data have produced some consistent patterns (Bogle 2008; Garcia et al. 2012): a majority of men and women on North American college campuses today have hooked up at least once (with sexual activity in hook-ups ranging from kissing to sexual intercourse); undergraduate students regard hooking up as distinct from romantic dating activities; and both men and women experience a kaleidoscope of negative *and* positive reactions after having casual sex.

A few social and psychological factors may also be key in contributing to the current hook-up phenomenon. Today emerging adults tend to push away from parental figures to test their social and personal boundaries, define their identity, and experiment with sex, romance, alcohol and other drugs (Arnett 2000, 2004). In fact, a developmental approach based on Erikson (1959, 1968) might even characterize this as a typical developmental trajectory—although the social setting of the college campus, with many relatively young individuals with nearly no direct adult supervision and support may also seem unique in this light. Many emerging adults have a deep desire to belong to a peer group, and thus follow social—and sexual—norms (Arnett 2004; Erickson 1968). Most emerging adults in the United States and other post-industrial societies are not yet constrained by marital and parenting responsibilities; and those who attend (residential) colleges are surrounded by others of the same general age. Thus many emerging adults, especially on college campuses, have the time, opportunity, and socially-constructed environments to engage in casual sex. In fact, in one survey of 221 university students, participants reported more sexual hook-ups than first dates over the previous 2 years: women reported an average of 2.31 first dates and 4.34 hook-ups, and men reported an average of 3.11 first dates and 5.71 hook-ups (Bradshaw et al. 2010). But these patterns likely begin at an earlier age. In a study of middle school and high school students, 32 % had experienced sexual intercourse, and 61 % of those who were sexually experienced had had sexual encounters with someone who was not a dating or relationship partner (Martinez et al. 2011). It seems safe to say that engaging in sexual activity, including non-relationship sexual activity (Manning et al. 2006), has become normative among some/many American youth.

12.4 Theoretical Approaches to Casual Sex

We proposed an interdisciplinary biopsychosocial model to attempt a synthesis of traditionally disconnected theoretical perspectives and to provide a more holistic understanding of hook-up culture (Garcia et al. 2012). Several scholars writing on casual sex have advocated and/or employed multifactorial approaches (Eshbaugh and Gute 2008; Fisher et al. 2012; Hatfield et al. 2012). Overall, however, research on casual sex has been generally atheoretical, in terms of generating new theoretical frameworks or shifting existing paradigms, although clearly influenced by three perspectives in particular: sexual scripts (see Wiederman, Chap. 2, this volume), evolutionary psychology, and public health. While no systematic citation analysis has been done, it appears that scholars primarily remain within their own discipline, citing work with the same approach they themselves employ.

Interdisciplinarity may be as driven by the data as much as it is by the theoretical leanings of the researchers. Multiple studies in the casual sex literature have produced findings that cannot be explained by traditional frameworks used to study sexual behavior. For instance, take the finding from one survey study of over 500 college students' self-reporting motivations for hooking up. While around 90 % engaged in sexual hook-ups for physical gratification, approximately 53 % of *both* men and women engaged in sexual hook-ups for emotional gratification, and over half of *both* men and women hooked up in the hope of initiating a traditional romantic relationship (Garcia and Reiber 2008). A strict evolutionary psychological approach relying on sexual strategies theory is insufficient to explain this lack of sex difference or patterns of women engaging in casual sex for the unknown likelihood of relationship outcomes. On the other hand, a strict gender theory approach relying on sexual scripts and hegemonic masculinities is limited in explaining the patterns of men engaging in casual sex hoping to find and maintain romantic intimacy. But this is just one example to suggest there is an interaction of biological, psychological, social, and cultural factors at play that likely influence sexual, and specifically casual sexual behaviors.

These divergent theoretical models also predict parallel patterns and outcomes. Evolutionary and social models often generate similar hypotheses about uncommitted sex, although "each addresses a different level of analysis" (Fisher et al. 2012, p. 47). Using two mid-level theories, Fisher et al. (2012) explained that "parental investment theory is an example of an ultimate level of explanation, while social role theory is an example of a proximate level, although each leads to the same prediction" (p. 47). They argued that evolutionary behavioral sciences may be most helpful in exploring the reproductive motive, and sexual scripts may be most useful in exploring the cultural discourse agenda. That is, while evolutionary principles may influence why emerging adults engage in uncommitted sex (ultimate level explanations), social roles and sexual scripts influence how emerging adults navigate their desires in a particular sociocultural context (proximate level explanations). For instance, religiosity (religious feelings and attendance at religious services) was related to lower frequency of engaging in intercourse during a hook-up encounter (Penhollow et al. 2007) and thus may represent an adaptive sociocultural constraint. High degrees of closeness to peer social networks and peer communication about hook-ups were associated with more sexual hook-ups (Holman and Sillars 2012); this may be considered a facultative response to adaptively react to peer expectations and local norms.

Framing the juxtaposition of emerging adulthood and casual sexual encounters within the life course perspective provides additional insight (see Carpenter, Chap. 5, this volume). The life course perspective suggests that individuals and families transition through different stages as they age, and that these stages are affected by social timing as well as historical influences (Elder and Rockwell 1979). The transition from childhood to adolescence, from adolescence to early adulthood, and then to full adulthood is influenced by early life experiences within the family, society, economics, and the specific time period in history when the transition occurs (Elder et al. 2003; Shanahan 2000). In particular, it is inextricably aligned with sexual scripts and what is perceived as acceptable sexual behavior for men or women within their multiple contexts of race/ethnicity, socioeconomic status, family history, and peer norms. For example, for many university students, engaging in a wide variety of sexual experiences before settling down with adult responsibilities, means they are participating in normative college student developmental phenomena. This isn't the case for all young adults, however, and experiences of casual sex can be very different for women as compared with men, particularly regarding feelings of regret and shame.

Within the public health literature, casual sex is often portrayed from a "disaster model" perspective (Garcia et al. 2012). This approach to human sexuality, as has been critiqued, minimizes the focus on desire and pleasure as positive outcomes, and focuses instead on risk and adverse health outcomes, with an emphasis on the occurrence of sexually transmitted infections (STIs), HIV/AIDS, and unwanted pregnancy. A key theoretical underpinning for the disaster model is Jessor's problem-behavior theory (Jessor 1991). Jessor and Jessor 1977 suggest that the behavior system, which includes problem behaviors as well as conventional behaviors, is impacted by the personality system and the perceived environment system. Variables within the personality system (e.g., values, beliefs, attitudes) and the perceived environmental system (e.g., peer models, social control, support) can contribute to engagement in problem behaviors, with multiple problem behaviors (e.g., alcohol use, smoking, unprotected sexual intercourse) often co-occurring. Problem behavior theory has been used in multiple studies associated with sexual risk behaviors including early sexual initiation (Li et al. 2007), multiple sexual partners (Moilanen 2010), and hooking up (Fielder et al. 2013).

12.5 Methodological Approaches to Casual Sex

A wide variety of research methods have now been employed in the study of casual sex. The work to date has largely been survey-based and descriptive in nature, with more recent researchers relying on the internet for data collection. Most studies have focused on university students on college campuses, and as a result participant demographics generally include primarily white, heterosexual, upper-to-middle class participants (see Paik, Chap. 6, this volume). While most studies have relied on surveys and questionnaires, a few studies on casual sex have also employed qualitative interview based methods to better tease apart what underlies men's and women's self-reported responses (Bogle 2008). A few studies have begun addressing casual sex with other methods, such as social psychological experiments (Conley et al. 2012) and behavioral neurogenetics (Garcia et al. 2010), but these methods are rare in this field of inquiry.

However, in a now classic study that has influenced much research on casual sex, researchers used an experimental ethology approach. Clark and Hatfield (1989), had confederates (5 women, 4 men) of varying attractiveness (attractiveness had no effect on results) randomly approach people on campus (48 men, 48 women) and tell them "I have been noticing you around campus. I find you to be very attractive." The confederate then asked the participants one of three questions: "Would you go out with me tonight?"; "Would you come over to my apartment tonight?"; or "Would you go to bed with me tonight?". Across two trials, while around half of both men and women agreed to going out on a date, 69% of men and 0% (6% in second trial) of women agreed to go over to the person's apartment, and while 75% (69% in second trial) of men agreed to go to bed with the woman that night, 0% of women agreed. This study demonstrated that men were much more likely than women to accept casual sex offers from unknown research confederates. Conley (2011) replicated and extended this finding, however, demonstrating that, under certain conditions of perceived comfort, the gender differences in acceptance of casual sex are diminished. That is, the gender dif-

ference found by Clark and Hatfield should not be entirely attributed to a sex difference in sexual desire or interest in casual sex, but in part related to other gendered issues such as sexual comfort and safety. However, it is worth noting that in meta-analyses of gender differences/similarities (Hyde 2005; Petersen and Hyde 2011), attitudes toward casual sex consistently produce a sizable and significant gender difference, with men more open and accepting than women.

Given the developmental context of sexual activity in general, and uncommitted sex in specific (Haydon et al. 2012), it is also necessary to investigate changes in sexual behaviors and outcomes that occur over the entire lifespan. To this end, some researchers have begun employing longitudinal methods to better understand changes over time. However, these studies primarily follow college students across a semester or an academic year (e.g., Fielder and Carey 2010; Vrangalova 2015), with some recent studies following individuals through developmental trajectories (e.g., Lyons et al. 2015). Uncommitted sexual encounters have become somewhat of a hallmark of early or emerging adulthood (Garcia et al. 2012; Stinson 2010), and can begin in adolescence. Studies of casual sex aligning with sexual debut and occurring before college, and among emerging adults not attending college, are also needed.

There are two major methodological flaws that are common across much of the existing research on casual sex, specifically those that focused on sexual hook-ups: the overuse of convenience samples and failure to integrate variables of sexual orientation, race, and socioeconomic class. More recently, several studies have employed larger and more expansive data sets (e.g., England; Garcia). Perhaps more importantly, several studies have included targeted research questions related to these issues—about issues such as orgasm, dating, mental health, condom use, relationship outcomes—and thus begin to change the research literature landscape in needed ways.

To move beyond hetero-centric questions of casual sex, several researchers have asked questions related to uncommitted sex across sexual orientations. One focus has been on gay men, such as their use of websites or apps for casual sex, or bathhouses or other types of sex clubs catering to gay men, as aspects of a gay culture that is permissive of casual sex (Holmes et al. 2007; Kirby and Thornberg-Dunwell 2014; Prestage et al. 2011). This research has been conceptualized quite differently, in part due to the phenomenon being more mainstream within these communities (compared to heterosexual swingers or sex clubs). In one study using data from the Online College Social Life Survey, meeting venues also varied for opposite-sex compared to same-sex dates and hook-ups (Kuperberg and Padgett 2015). Recent research by Rupp et al. (2014) has focused on the hook-up experiences of "queer" women. They argue that the college hook-up scene provides an opportunity for emerging adults to explore sexuality, along with a context to experience same-sex sexual encounters without questioning one's sexual identity. Indeed Rupp and colleagues suggest that "barsexuals," or women who engage in public displays of same-sex sexual behavior, such as straight women kissing each other in bars, may be engaging in an activity not simply for the male gaze. "Barsexuality" may allow women to experience and enjoy their own sexual interests beyond traditional or exclusive heterosexuality. Similarly, findings from the National Survey of Sexual Health and Behavior (a U.S. nationally representative probability sample) identified a much higher percentage of American men and women who had ever engaged in same-sex sexual behavior compared to the percentage who identify as having a homosexual orientation (Herbenick et al. 2010). Although speculative, it seems most probable that many such encounters are sexual experiments and uncommitted in nature.

Casual sex in emerging adulthood, along with the privilege of engaging in a college party culture and emerging with positive outcomes, may be a particularly classed and raced experience (Armstrong and Hamilton 2013). This is consistent with findings in a recent interview study of 87 undergraduates. College students who lived on campus engaged in hook-ups more regularly than commuter students (Allison and Risman 2013). However, all respondents noted that hooking up is part of what they perceived as the "typical" college experience. Allison and Risman (2013) also established that hooking up was most prevalent among white,

middle-class students who did not hold a job. In an important contribution, they noted, "Working class and racial minority students who lived on campus or in city apartments were less likely to actively participate in either on- or off-campus party and social scenes. Two primary mechanisms emerged to explain these patterns: socioeconomic resources and racial peer group" (p. 112).

Future research on casual sex must address the intersectional variables of race, class, gender and sexual orientation, as well as sociodemographic variables, including where participants live (see Hubbard et al., Chap. 17, this volume; Harris and Bartlow, Chap. 15, this volume). Being a commuter student and possibly living with family, or working when others are engaged in the college party scene, may serve as barriers to having the time and space to engage with casual sex partners. Moreover, it is important to consider the demographic landscape of the larger population. Research has shown that some students, such as Greek fraternity/sorority members and athletes, may have access to more sexual opportunities and partners given elevated subcultural social status (Townsend 1995). However, if a sample is drawn from a campus where a disproportionate number of racial/ethnic minority students fall into a specialized category (Ray and Rosow 2010), such as athletics, it may give the false impression that minority students engage in more casual sex when in fact it is privileged athletes who drive the effect. We specifically note this caution as something we have observed in our own data.

12.6   Affect and Casual Sex

The World Health Organization has stated that "Sexual health requires a positive and respectful approach to sexuality and sexual relationships, as well as the possibility of having pleasurable and safe sexual experiences, free of coercion, discrimination and violence" (WHO 2006). In the United States, this was followed by the 2010 Centers for Disease Control and Prevention's meeting, "A Public Health Approach for Advancing Sexual Health in the United States: Rationale and Options for Implementation" (CDC 2010). Despite a positive start, little has been published regarding healthy, positive outcomes associated with any type of sexual contact, let alone uncommitted sexual experiences. Shifting the paradigm away from a disaster-focused model towards a healthy sexuality model requires a fundamental shift in sexuality education (see Fields et al., Chap. 21, this volume). Nystrom et al. (2013) discussed the shift in Oregon from a risk-focused paradigm to a youth development model that places young people at the center of their sexual health and well-being. Halpern (2010) noted that changing how we "conceptualize and study adolescent sexual health and development is not a new idea" (p. 6) but it appears to have gained little traction.

It is clear from the existing research that uncommitted sexual encounters tend to result in a range of concomitant feelings afterwards, ranging from generally positive affect (Campbell 2008; Garcia and Reiber 2008; Lewis et al. 2012), to regret and negative emotional states (Eshbaugh and Gute 2008; Fisher et al. 2012; Townsend and Wasserman 2011). A number of factors contribute to the positive and/or negative reactions individuals have to hook-ups. In one sample of Canadian university students, Fisher et al. (2012) found that feelings of regret in uncommitted sexual encounters were related to quality of sex, with "good" pleasurable sex associated with less feelings of regret and "bad" unfulfilling sex associated with more feelings of regret.

In an innovative longitudinal study evaluating the putative effect of casual sex on well-being, Vrangalova (2015) followed 528 undergraduate students across an academic year. After controlling for a number of variables, on average those students who reported engaging in sexual hook-ups for "autonomous" reasons (emanating from one's self) reported no negative outcomes, while those who engaged in sexual hook-ups for "non-autonomous" reasons (self-imposed pressures, external forces, lack of intentionality) were more likely to report lower self-esteem, higher depression and anxiety, and more negative health outcomes. Autonomous hook-up motivations were not associated with the mental health outcomes measured.

In a study of 832 college students, 26 % of women and 50 % of men reported a positive emotional reaction following a hook-up, and 49 % of women and 26 % of men reported a negative reaction. The remainders for each sex had a mix of both positive and negative reactions (Owen and Fincham 2011). Similarly, in a survey study of 250 U.S. college students, emotional reactions to hook-ups were generally more positive than negative (Snapp et al. 2015). Further, sexual satisfaction in hook-ups was predicted by intimacy and pleasure motives, and positive emotional reactions were predicted by self-affirming motives. In another study of 6995 adult participants (Mark et al. In Press) sexual satisfaction was rated greater than emotional satisfaction within casual sex relationship contexts (one night stand, first date, sex with a friend, and hookups) than within more committed relationship contexts (married, living together, committed unmarried relationship). Men found all contexts except for sex in a committed unmarried relationship significantly more sexually and emotionally satisfying than women, and gay men reported gaining the most sexual and emotional satisfaction out of casual sex contexts, with lesbian women reporting the least out of casual sexual contexts. While participants generally rated all casual sexual relationship contexts with relatively greater sexual satisfaction than emotional satisfaction, the mean ratings of sexual satisfaction for both men and women were considerably lower in the casual contexts than the committed contexts assessed (Mark et al. In Press).

It is commonly believed that men and women hook-up for sexual pleasure. Yet hooking up is not always as sexually gratifying as tabloids, TV shows, movies, or blogs would lead participants to believe. Data show that both men and women are less likely to achieve orgasm during a hook-up than during sex with a committed partner. Uncommitted sexual hook-ups result in inconsistent rates of perceived sexual quality and sexual pleasure. In a large U.S. convenience sample study of heterosexual undergraduate students that contrasted sexual activity during first time hook-ups with relationship sexual activity, Armstrong et al. (2009) found that 85 % of men and 68 % of women reached orgasm during relationship sex, whereas only 31% of men and 10% of women reached orgasm during hook-ups. However, among both men and women the average rate of orgasm experience increased for repeated hook-up encounters. Women were especially more likely to achieve orgasm if their most recent hook-up encounter was with a partner they had previously hooked up with (Armstrong et al. 2009, 2012). Moreover, qualitative findings suggest that many emerging adult men and women don't necessarily expect women to orgasm in sexual hook-ups, and on average neither sex seemed particularly concerned about women achieving orgasm in uncommitted sexual encounters as compared to in relationships, although, perhaps for different reasons. In a replication and extension of this work (Garcia et al. in review), findings also indicated that both sexes and particularly women expected and desired orgasm much less in the context of an uncommitted sexual encounter, suggesting that contexts and what is wanted in them are qualitatively different in people's imagined and desired sexual repertoires. But we are left to wonder why people (specifically youth and women) engage in casual sexual behavior if indeed the scripted view of it as 'fun and pleasurable' is factually and experientially inaccurate.

Another research question asks what type of sexual behaviors happen during sexual hook-ups, and if these specific behavioral repertoires in turn influence sexual outcomes including pleasure and orgasm. Some researchers have parsed the type of behaviors engaged in, but others have not—for theoretical reasons. Casual sexual encounters include whichever behaviors individuals engage in during those contexts, which very well may be different than in romantic relationships, although systematic comparisons of sexual behavior by sexual context have not been well established, taking into account partner, experience, and other factors.

A variety of factors are likely to contribute to reduced sexual pleasure, or at least to reduced possibility of orgasm during a hook-up. Some people enjoy sex only in the context of a partnership; others enjoy sex in both committed and uncommitted relationships. Thus, a negative at-

titude toward uncommitted sex could limit one's ability to orgasm during an uncommitted sexual encounter, reducing the pleasure of the experience (Armstrong et al. 2012; Garcia et al. in review). Levels of comfort with various sexual behaviors in an uncommitted encounter, and differences in potential risk associated with different specific sexual behaviors, can also impact feelings of pleasure and satisfaction. Several scholars have also noted that college students tend to over-perceive the comfort level of their hook-up partners while engaging in a variety of sexual behaviors (what psychologists call *pluralistic ignorance*); men, in particular, tend to overestimate a woman's comfort with sexual intercourse (Reiber and Garcia 2010; Lambert et al. 2003).

Sexual double standards may also limit the potential for pleasure in casual sex. Some women who engage in casual sex worry about being negatively perceived, harshly judged, and stigmatized (Armstrong et al. 2012; Conley et al. 2012; Vrangalova 2015). Other women feel they have been denied a partner's sexual attentiveness. Still others feel that casual sex jeopardizes their ability to negotiate safer sex via condom use. College women report greater thoughts of worry and vulnerability during sexual hook-ups than do college men (Townsend and Wasserman 2011), indicating a gender difference in attitudes about casual sex.

These worries are perhaps well founded. Research has shown that women who engage in uncommitted sex are judged more negatively and stigmatized by both men and other women (Conley et al. 2012). Even Sigmund Freud noted that heterosexual women and the men who engage in sexual activity with them struggle with a "Madonna-Whore dichotomy," wherein women experience difficulty being culturally labeled or even pigeonholed as either an extremely selective virginal spouse or a potentially promiscuous sexual object, rather than occupying space of an autonomous sexual agent pursuing a healthy sexuality.

Taken together, data on the association of pleasure and hooking up are varied. Some people report feeling sexually aroused, satisfied, happy, and/or proud, while others report feeling disappointed, confused, embarrassed, and/or scared (Paul and Hayes 2002). Some researchers report that a majority of men and women are glad that they have had their hook-up experiences. Still other researchers find that a majority of both men and women have felt regret for engaging in sexual hook-ups. These concomitant positive and negative responses are not altogether different from what is reported after first coitus experiences (Sprecher et al. 1995). Who experiences what, and when they experience either positive, negative, or ambivalent (or all) has not yet been well established, but researchers are beginning to understand that there are a plurality of responses and reactions, and that several factors may serve as barriers to more positive and pleasurable outcomes.

12.7   Casual Sex and Sexual Health

As Fielder et al. (2013) have accurately noted, relatively little is known about the mental and physical health effects of casual or uncommitted sex. In addition to the mental health impact, commonly cited adverse effects include unintended/unwanted pregnancy, sexually transmitted infections, including HIV/AIDS, and sexual victimization (Claxton and van Dulmen 2013; Heldman and Wade 2010; Vasilenko et al. 2012). For those who have casual sex, in addition to potentially experiencing an adverse health effect, there is the added burden of *worrying about* these negative health effects. For example, Vasilenko et al. (2012) found that female college students had almost three times greater odds of worrying about their health when they had sex with an uncommitted partner as compared to a dating partner. This kind of worrying likely results in negative perceptions that probably reduces the possible positive affect of sexual encounters.

Physical health research regarding uncommitted sexual encounters has focused on primary prevention (preventing the adverse health effects from occurring) or secondary prevention (early identification and management of adverse health outcomes) and is generally based on a risk framework. There is a small literature on the positive outcomes associated with casual sex, such as experiencing orgasm and sexual pleasure (Armstrong et al. 2012; Lyons et al. 2014), but these are relatively distinct from the literature in sexual health. This is perhaps because as a field public health is primarily driven by preventing or reducing adverse health outcomes/diseases, with a small emphasis on health promotion. Further, research in public health has historically been influenced by a shifting political climate that has ranged from puritanical condemnation of sexual agency to a tolerance of normative sexuality, as long as it is generally framed with a risk narrative.

The possibility of becoming pregnant is a common fear associated with sexual activity among heterosexually active emerging adults (Vasilenko et al. 2012) and frequently supersedes concern regarding STIs and HIV/AIDS during casual sex (Kalish 2013; Milhausen et al. 2013). According to the National Survey on Family Growth, 57% of adolescent females and 46% of adolescent males reported they would be "very upset" if they were to become pregnant at this point in their life (Martinez et al. 2011). Both adolescent men (Lohan et al. 2010) and adolescent women (Finer et al. 2005) expressed concern about the impact of having a child on future plans as well as on current opportunities. Concern about unintended pregnancy is justified: in 2008 (most recent data available), women 18-to-24-years-old had the highest rates of unintended pregnancy and unintended pregnancy ending in birth when compared with other age groups (Finer and Zolna 2014). In addition to age, these rates varied according to an assortment of other social factors including: relationship status (cohabitating status greater than married or not cohabitating), income level (highest for poor women), education level (highest for women with less than a college degree), and race/ethnicity (minority women having twice the rates for White women). Finer and Zolna noted that even when controlling for income, minority women continued to have the highest unintended pregnancy rates across all income levels. They went on to note that low-income Black women had the highest rates of unintended pregnancies, up to 163 per 1000 women. However, little is known about unintended pregnancy resulting specifically from casual sex. The preponderance of research regarding pregnancy for adolescents and emerging adults considers 'relationship status' as 'being in a committed relationship' (e.g., married versus non-married; cohabiting versus non-cohabiting; current relationship versus no relationship), while not specifically indicating whether the committed relationship resulted from a casual sexual encounter (Guzman et al. 2010). Concern about unintended pregnancy varies according to age (Hayford and Guzzo 2013), race/ethnicity (Guzman et al. 2010; Manlove et al. 2013), and gender (Carter et al. 2012).

A variety of factors contribute to avoiding pregnancy during uncommitted sexual encounters. Hooking up includes a continuum of physical behaviors including kissing and genital stimulation (in addition to oral, anal, and vaginal sexual intercourse), and choosing not to engage in penile-vaginal penetration is perhaps one way to attempt to avoid pregnancy. Research suggests that the most common method of pregnancy prevention during penile-vaginal intercourse during casual sex is condom use (Manlove et al. 2014), but use of highly effective contraception or dual-method use occurs as well (Walsh et al. 2014).

With regard to pregnancy-related concerns that might emerge from casual sex, not much is known about how uncommitted sex partners decide whether to have an abortion or continue with a pregnancy. Not being in a steady, committed relationship can make having a child difficult and could contribute to the decision to have an abortion (Finer et al. 2005; Santelli et al. 2006). Women in their teens and early 20s represented almost half of those who had abortions in 2010; women aged 20–24 accounted for 32.9%, and women 15–19 accounted for 14.6% of all abortions (Pazol et al. 2013). While unintended pregnancy rates have been essentially stable in the U.S., abortion rates have decreased steadily since 1990 (Finer and Zolna 2014).

Not all heterosexual young adults, however, perceive themselves at risk for becoming pregnant and consequently may be less likely to use a form of contraception (Polis and Zabin 2012). Analyzing data from a 2009 nationally representative telephone survey of 1800 unmarried men and women aged 18–29 years, 19% of women and 13% of men believed that they were very likely to be infertile.

Sexually transmitted infections (STIs) are a particular concern in uncommitted sexual relationships, given the potential for concurrent partners and/or the lack of testing between partners. STI rates peak during emerging adulthood (Centers for Disease Control and Prevention 2014). Many adolescents and young adults mistakenly perceive themselves at low risk for STIs during casual sex (Downing-Matibag and Geisinger 2009). Fielder et al.'s (2013) longitudinal study of first year college students suggested that hook-up behavior predicted the acquisition of STIs. Perception of risk of acquiring STIs varies based on the type of casual sex (e.g., hook-up versus FWB) (Manlove et al. 2014; Pollack et al. 2013) and type of physical contact (e.g. oral sex versus vaginal intercourse) (Downing-Matibag and Geisinger 2009; Pollack et al. 2013). Other factors related to perception of risk include gender (Pollack et al. 2013) and race/ethnicity (Carter et al. 2012). While acquisition of an STI or HIV/AIDS generally requires some level of penetrative sexual contact (e.g., anal or vaginal intercourse), *who* an individual has sex with, in addition to the protective measures taken to avoid infection, contribute to varying rates in different sociodemographic groups.

In one qualitative study of U.S. college students (32 men and 30 women), a majority of participants were unconcerned about contracting infections from hook-ups involving oral sex, and only about half of participants were concerned with contracting an STI from anal or vaginal intercourse during a hook-up (Downing-Matibag and Geisinger 2009). For a variety of reasons, students did not consider risks during hook-ups, overestimating their safety primarily due to stereotypes based on contact. They had a high degree of trust in partners who were acquaintances, or partners perceived to have positive personal characteristics. Community trust– the perception that HIV/AIDS was not a real concern among fellow students and local residents–and lack of knowledge about STIs, including confusion about sexually transmitted infection risks, particularly from oral sex, contributed to respondents' low risk estimates. The rise of HIV preventive drugs, such as TRUVADA and PrEP, may also provide interesting new research directions with regard to intimacy, as individuals may feel condom use becomes less necessary if they have otherwise protected themselves despite condom non-use.

Risk of STIs is often considered within the larger context of partner trust, intimacy, and love (Downing-Matibag and Geisinger 2009; Erlandsson et al. 2013; Pollack et al. 2013). Partners who are perceived to be well-known (e.g., friends with benefits) are often considered to be infection-free (Carter et al. 2012; Downing-Matibag and Geisinger 2009). Moreover, young adults voice concern that requesting the use of a condom may interfere with their friendship (Carter et al. 2012; Corbett et al. 2009). Conversely, Lehmiller et al. (2014) identified that compared to romantic partners, friends with benefits relationships involved safe sex practices more frequently and participants communicated more about concurrent partners—things perhaps taken for granted in committed and putatively exclusive relationships.

The question of concurrent relationships or infidelity adds an additional dimension to condom use and trust (Brown et al. 2012; Paik 2010b; Riehman et al. 2006). Concurrency has been defined as having a main sexual partner and at least one current casual sexual partner simultaneously (Waldrop-Valverde et al. 2013). Some work suggests that young adults, particularly women, will sometimes be concerned about requesting that a partner use condoms. It may be seen as an acknowledgment or assumption of indiscretion or infidelity (Brady et al. 2009). Results from Swartzendruber et al.'s (2013) systematic review suggested that partner concurrency, as well as having multiple partners, was associated with being diagnosed with STIs. While concurrency certainly does not always indicate uncommitted sexual encounters (Nelson et al. 2011), concurrent relationships can potentially include several different types of casual sex partners, which can affect risk of condom use and STI acquisition. According to Paik (2010a), in a study of 783 adults aged 18–59, a quarter of both women and men said that either they or their partner had had a concurrent partner, while one in ten of each gender reported mutual nonmonogamy. Men were more likely than women to have had a concurrent partner (17% vs. 5%), and women were more likely than men to report that a partner had had a concurrent partner (17% vs. 8%). With respect to sexual health outcomes, in a study of 2288 young women Boyer et al. (2006) found that perception of a sex partner having other partners was associated with acquiring an STI, while methods of contraception, including condoms and frequency of condom use, were not associated with acquiring an STI. Of course, another strategy for STI secondary prevention is regular STI testing, either for the individual, the partner, or both (Champion and Collins 2013; Singer et al. 2006).

Use of condoms remains the primary way to prevent STIs and HIV/AIDS. Condoms are considered to be a "dual protection" method (Carter et al. 2012) and are more likely to be used as contraception in casual sex than more effective birth control (e.g., oral contraceptives and other hormonal methods or IUDs), due to their ability to protect from both pregnancy and STIs (Reece et al. 2010). Use of condoms or other methods of contraception at first intercourse remains lower than optimal, and varies by gender, race/ethnicity, and type of relationship (Gibbs 2013). Gibbs (2013) found that when examining casual sex as first intercourse, 51% of women and 64% of men indicated that they used condoms only, and 27% of women and 23% of men indicated not using any method. Teens who initiate sex at young ages may take longer to initiate any type of contraceptive use, but once they do, they are often consistent users: contraceptive use at mid-adolescence is similar to late adolescence (Finer and Philbin 2013). This specifically relates to casual sex, as not using condoms with a new partner is related to contracting an STI.

Condoms may not be used by a heterosexually active man if he believes his partner is using an alternative method of contraception or is at low risk of infection. Regarding friends with benefits relationships, Weaver et al. (2011) identified that "participants that reported inconsistent condom use sometimes explained that they relied on the birth control pill for contraception, knew their partner's sexual history, or knew the partner for a long time and therefore trusted them" (p. 51). Reasons for nonuse of condoms are complex and multifaceted (Paterno and Jordan 2012); however not using condoms or contraception can contribute to increased worries about health and feelings of guilt when compared to those who used contraception (Vasilenko et al. 2012).

Condoms have a relatively high failure rate due to the need to use with each and every act of penetrative sex, and are known to have some (real and perceived) negative aspects (Davis et al. 2014; Erlandsson et al. 2013; Higgins and Hirsch 2008). Additionally, condoms are not always available when individuals engage in a sex (Erlandsson et al. 2013) and their use may be affected by alcohol or drug use (Walsh et al. 2014). Not surprisingly, condom use to prevent STIs is higher in casual sex than in committed relationships with steady partners (Champion and Collins 2013; Matson et al. 2011; Nelson et al. 2011). However, while condom use is common during vaginal-penile intercourse, use is relatively uncommon during oral sex (Downing-Matibag and Geisinger 2009).

As noted previously, condoms are common as a method of contraception and STI protection in casual sex when compared to committed relationships. Additionally, there appears to be a hierarchy of condom use related to STI prevention based on the type of uncommitted sexual encounters as well. Weaver et al. (2011) noted that a few participants indicated that condoms were more important for one-night stands or hook-ups than for friends with benefits relationships. Similarly, Manlove et al. (2014), in their study using the National Longitudinal Survey of Youth Rounds 6–9 (2002–2005), established two types of short-term relationships based on levels of intimacy and commitment, short-term casual relationships and short-term rosy outlooks. Couples in casual relationships had higher levels of condom use (33%) and lower levels of hormonal method use (18%) and were less likely to use hormonal methods versus nothing, or to use dual methods rather than a condom alone when compared to the short-term/rosy outlooks group. Similarly, Fielder et al. (2013), in their longitudinal study of 483 college women, found that women were

more likely to report dual method use when their partner was a friend rather than an established romantic partner. They noted that only 14% were consistent dual method users, while 33% used dual methods inconsistently.

12.8 Unwanted Sexual Contact

Unwanted sexual contact can and does occur within uncommitted sexual encounters (Garcia et al. 2012; Heldman and Wade 2010), including hook-ups, booty-calls, one-night stands, and friends-with-benefits relationships (Klipfel et al. 2014). Unwanted sexual contact moves beyond vaginal, anal, and genital-oral contact to also include fondling or touching of the breasts or genitals (Crown and Roberts 2007; Flack et al. 2007) and exists along a continuum from *not desired* to *unwanted and coerced* to *forcible sexual contact* and *rape* (Flack et al. 2007). Unwanted sexual contact is more likely to occur in the context of uncommitted sexual encounters than in committed or exclusive dating relationships (Hill et al. In review; Hall and Knox 2013; Tomsich et al. 2013). Fielder et al. (2013) noted that 24% of women in their longitudinal study reported at least one sexual victimization event during the first year of college and that hook-up behavior increased risk for sexual victimization. The risk of unwanted sexual contact during casual encounters is associated with alcohol use (Abbey et al. 2003; Franklin 2010; Tomsich et al. 2013). In a study of 178 undergraduate students at a small liberal arts university, Flack et al. (2007) reported that 78% of unwanted penetrative sex (including oral, vaginal, and anal) took place while hooking up. These unwanted sexual intercourse experiences resulted in a variety of negative mental health outcomes, including unwanted memories (47%), avoidance and numbing responses (50%), and/or hyperarousal (30%).

Unwanted sexual contact is often preceded by verbal coercion (Wright et al. 2010). In one study of college women (Christopher 1988), 95% reported being pressured into at least one unwanted sexual event, with several forms of coercion experienced prior to an unwanted event: 3.4%

had been pressured by explicit threats, 4.8 % by physical force, 35 % by deceptive promise and statements of affection ("sweet-talked"), and 55 % reported feeling pressured by behaviors that communicated an expectation of having sex (persistent attempts to initiate sexual activity). Others scholars found similar patterns. Based on interviews conducted with 21 participants, Beres (2010) noted that some women were not clear about whether they wanted to have sex and instead, they 'went along' with what was happening. Similarly, in Plante's qualitative interviews of college students, several women noted engaging in unwanted sexual activity because they felt it was expected or in some cases so that they could end the encounter and leave (Plante, personal communication). This is likely heightened in the context of uncommitted encounters, which are more likely than other contexts to involve unarticulated motives as well as unfamiliar people and spaces. This also suggests that recent discussion of U.S. government mandates requiring affirmative sexual consent ("yes means yes") on many college campuses, while contentious, may be particularly warranted. The impact of unwanted sexual contact can include regret, depression, and other types of psychological harm (Crown and Roberts 2007, Flack et al. 2007). Research on casual sex and sexual experiences that are either unwanted or coercive appears to be gaining interest, and we anticipate more research will be forthcoming on this particular poorly understood aspect of casual sex.

12.9 Conclusion

Sexual behavior in uncommitted relationships is now being explored from a variety of disciplinary and theoretical perspectives. Many scholars have argued that casual sex is best understood from an interdisciplinary biopsychosocial perspective that incorporates recent research trends in human biology, reproductive and mental health, as well as sexuality studies. But actually applying such a perspective is perhaps easier said than done. Research suggests that a variety of factors may influence these sexual patterns, including motivation, campus climate, partner pressure and alcohol use. However, research in sexual health highlights the need for further integration and theorizing before casual sex research has a theoretically informed and goal-focused agenda. The findings that a majority of both men and women are motivated to engage in hook-ups, but often experience complex positive and negative outcomes, and often desire (and sometimes develop) a longer-term romantic relationship, reflect social contexts and the cross-cultural and biological centrality of the pair-bond (Fisher 1992; Jankowiak and Fischer 1992; Gray and Garcia 2013). In fact, it is the opposition of casual sex to the human tendency to engage in sexual activity in the context of socially sanctioned romantic relationships that is perhaps most striking to researchers and the public, and although increasingly socially acceptable, practices of casual sex may leave us with many more research questions to come.

Acknowledgements We are extremely grateful to the editors, Rebecca Plante and John DeLamater, for their thoughtful and detailed feedback that helped improve this chapter and integrate it into the larger collection and literature.

References

Abbey, A., Clinton-Sherrod, A. M., McAuslan, P., Zawacki, T., & Buck, P. O. (2003). The relationship between the quantity of alcohol consumed and the severity of sexual assaults committed by college men. *Journal of Interpersonal Violence, 18*(7), 813–833.

Allison, R., & Risman, B. J. (2013). A double standard for "Hooking up": How far have we come toward gender equality? *Social Science Research, 42*(5), 1191–1206.

Altman, D. (1971). *Homosexual: Oppression and liberation.* New York: Outerbridge & Dienstfrey.

Altman, D. (1982). *The homosexualization of America: The Americanization of the homosexual.* New York: St Martin's.

Armstrong, E. A., & Hamilton, L. (2013). *Paying for the party: How college maintains inequality.* Cambridge: Harvard University Press.

Armstrong, E. A., England, P., & Fogarty, A. C. K. (2009). Orgasm in college hookups and relationships. In B. J. Risman (Ed.), *Families as they really are* (pp. 362–377). New York: Norton.

Armstrong, E. A., England, P., & Fogarty, A. C. K. (2012). Accounting for women's orgasm and sexual enjoyment in college hookups and relationships. *American Sociological Review, 77*(3), 435–462.

Arnett, J. J. (2000). Emerging adulthood: A theory of development from the late teens through the twenties. *American Psychologist, 55*, 469–480.

Arnett, J. (2004). *Emerging adulthood: The winding road from the late teens through the twenties.* New York: Oxford University Press.

Bailey, B. L. (1988). *From front porch to back seat: Courtship in twentieth century America.* Baltimore: Johns Hopkins University Press.

Beres, M. (2010). Sexual miscommunication? Untangling assumptions about sexual communication between casual sex partners. *Culture, Health & Sexuality, 12*, 1–14.

Bogle, K. A. (2008). *Hooking up: Sex, dating, and relationships on campus.* New York: New York University Press.

Boyer, C. B., Sebro, N. S., Wibbelsman, C., & Shafer, M. A. (2006). Acquisition of sexually transmitted infections in adolescents attending an urban, general HMO teen clinic. *Journal of Adolescent Health, 39*, 287–90.

Boswell, A. A., & Spade, J. Z. (1996). Fraternities and college rape culture: Why are some fraternities more dangerous places for women. *Gender & Society, 10*(2), 133–147.

Bradshaw, C., Kahn, A. S., & Saville, B. K. (2010). To hook up or date: Which gender benefits? *Sex Roles, 62*, 661–669.

Brady, S., Tschann, J. M., Ellen, J. M., & Flores, E. (2009). Infidelity, trust, and condom use among Latino youth in dating relationships. *Sexually Transmitted Diseases, 36*(4), 227–231.

Brown, J. L., Sales, J. M., DiClemente, R. J., Latham Davis, T. P., & Rose, E. S. (2012). Characteristics of African American adolescent females who perceive their current boyfriends have concurrent sexual partners. *Journal of Adolescent Health, 50*(4), 377–382.

Campbell, A. (2008). The morning after the night before: Affective reactions to one-night stands among mated and unmated women and men. *Human Nature, 19*, 157–173.

Carter, M. W., Hock-Long, L., Marie Kraft, J., Henry-Moss, D., Hatfield-Timajchy, K., & Singer, M. (2012). Strategies for managing the dual risk of sexually transmitted infections and unintended pregnancy among Puerto Rican and African American young adults. *American Journal of Public Health, 102*(3), 449–456.

Cates, W. (1991). Teenagers and sexual risk taking: The best of times and the worst of times. *Journal of Adolescent Health, 12*, 84–94.

Centers for Disease Control and Prevention. (2010). *A public health approach for advancing sexual health in the United States: Rationale and options for implementation, meeting report of an external consultation.* Atlanta: Author.

Centers for Disease Control and Prevention. (2014). *Sexually transmitted disease surveillance 2013.* Atlanta: U.S. Department of Health and Human Services.

Champion, J. D., & Collins, J. L. (2013). Conceptualization of sexual partner relationship steadiness among ethnic minority adolescent women: Implications for evidence-based behavioral sexual risk reduction interventions. *Journal of the Association of Nurses in AIDS Care, 24*(3), 242–255.

Christopher, F. (1988). An initial investigation into a continuum of premarital sexual pressure. *Journal of Sex Research, 25*(2), 255–266.

Chronicle Books. (2011). *Hook-ups & hangovers: A journal.* San Francisco: Chronicle Books.

Clark, R. D., & Hatfield, E. (1989). Gender differences in receptivity to sexual offers. *Journal of Psychology & Human Sexuality, 2*, 39–55.

Claxton, S. E., & van Dullmen, M. H. M. (2013). Casual sexual relationships and experiences in emerging adulthood. *Emerging Adulthood, 1*(2), 138–150.

Conley, T. D. (2011). Perceived proposer personality characteristics and gender differences in acceptance of casual sex offers. *Journal of Personality and Social Psychology, 100*, 309–329.

Conley, T. D., Ziegler, A., & Moors, A. C. (2012). Backlash from the bedroom: Stigma mediates gender differences in acceptance of casual sex offers. *Psychology of Women Quarterly, 37*(3), 392–407.

Corbett, A. M., Dickson-Gomez, J., Hilario, H., & Weeks, M. R. (2009). A little thing called love: Condom use in high-risk primary heterosexual relationships. *Perspectives on Sexual and Reproductive Health, 41*(4), 218–224.

Crown, L., & Roberts, L. J. (2007). Against their will: Young women's nonagentic sexual experiences. *Journal of Social and Personal Relationships, 24*, 385–405.

Davis, K. C., Schraufnagel, T. J., Kajumulo, K. F., Gilmore, A. K., Norris, J., & George, W. H. (2014). A qualitative examination of men's condom use attitudes and resistance: "it's just part of the game." *Archives of Sexual Behavior, 43*(3), 631–643.

Downing-Matibag, T. M., & Geisinger, B. (2009). Hooking up and sexual risk taking among college students: A health belief model perspective. *Qualitative Health Research, 19*(9), 1196–1209.

Elder, G. H., & Rockwell, R. C. (1979). The life-course and human development: An ecological perspective. *International Journal of Behavioral Development, 2*, 1–21.

Elder, G. H., Johnson, M. K., & Crosnoe, R. (2003). The emergence and development of life course theory. In J. T. Mortimer & M. J. Shanahan (Eds.), *Handbook of the Life Course* (pp. 3–19). Springer.

Ellis, A. (1958). *Sex without guilt.* New York: Lyle Stuart.

Erikson, E. H. (1959). *Identity and the life cycle.* New York: International Universities Press.

Erikson, E. H. (1968). *Identity, youth and crisis.* New York: Norton.

Erlandsson, K., Jinghede Nordvall, C., Ohman, A., & Häggström-Nordin, E. (2013). Qualitative interviews with adolescents about "friends-with-benefits" relationships. *Public Health Nursing* (Boston, Mass.), *30*(1), 47–57.

Eshbaugh, E. M., & Gute, G. (2008). Hookups and sexual regret among college women. *The Journal of Social Psychology, 148*, 77–89.

Fielder, R. L., & Carey, M. P. (2010). Prevalence and characteristics of sexual hookups among first-semester female college students. *Journal of Sex & Marital Therapy, 36*, 346–359.

Fielder, R. L., Walsh, J. L., Carey, K. B., & Carey, M. P. (2013). Predictors of sexual hookups: A theory-based, prospective study of first-year college women. *Archives of Sexual Behavior, 42*(8), 1425–1441.

Finer, L. B. (2007). Trends in premarital sex in the United States, 1954–2003. *Public Health Reports, 122*, 73–78.

Finer, L. B., & Philbin, J. M. (2013). Sexual initiation, contraceptive use, and pregnancy among young adolescents. *Pediatrics, 131*(5), 1–6.

Finer, L. B., & Zolna, M. R. (2014). Shifts in intended and unintended pregnancies in the United States, 2001–2008. *American Journal of Public Health, 104*(Suppl 1), S43–S48.

Finer, L. B., Frohwirth, L. F., Dauphinee, L. A., Singh, S., & Moore, A. M. (2005). Reasons U.S. women have abortions: quantitative and qualitative perspectives. *Perspectives on Sexual & Reproductive Health, 37*(3), 110–118.

Fisher, H. E. (1992). *Anatomy of love: The natural history of monogamy, adultery, and divorce.* New York: W. W. Norton & Company.

Fisher, M. L., Worth, K., Garcia, J. R., & Meredith, T. (2012). Feelings of regret following uncommitted sexual encounters in Canadian university students. *Culture, Health & Sexuality, 14*(1), 45–57.

Fisher, M. L., Chang, R. S., & Garcia, J. R. (2013). Introduction to evolution's empress. In M. L. Fisher, J. R. Garcia, & R. S. Chang (Eds.), *Evolution's empress: Darwinian perspectives on the nature of women* (pp. 1–16). New York: Oxford University Press.

Flack, W. R., Daubman, K. A., Caron, M. L., Asadorian, J. A., D'Aureli, N. R., Gigliotti, S. N., Hall, A. T., Kiser, S., & Stine, E. R. (2007). Risk factors and consequences of unwanted sex among university students: Hooking up, alcohol, and stress response. *Journal of Interpersonal Violence, 22*(2), 139–157.

Franklin, C. A. (2010). Physically forced, alcohol-induced, and verbally coerced sexual victimization: Assessing risk factors among university women. *Journal of Criminal Justice, 38*, 149–159.

Garcia, J. R., & Fisher, H. E. (2015). Why we hook up: Searching for sex or looking for love? In S. Tarrant (Ed.), *Gender, sex, and politics: In the streets and between the sheets in the 21st century.* New York: Routledge.

Garcia, J. R., & Kruger, D. J. (2010). Unbuckling in the Bible Belt: Conservative sexual norms lower age at marriage. *The Journal of Social, Evolutionary, and Cultural Psychology, 4*, 206–214.

Garcia, J. R., & Reiber, C. (2008). Hook-up behavior: A biopsychosocial perspective. *The Journal of Social, Evolutionary, and Cultural Psychology, 2*, 192–208.

Garcia, J. R., MacKillop, J., Aller, E. L., Merriwether, A. M., Wilson, D. S., & Lum, J. K. (2010). Associations between dopamine D4 receptor gene variation with both infidelity and sexual promiscuity. *PLoS ONE, 5*, e14162.

Garcia, J. R., Reiber, C., Massey, S. G., & Merriwether, A. M. (2012). Sexual hookup culture: A review. *Review of General Psychology, 16*(2), 161–176.

Garcia, J. R., Lloyd, E. A., Wallen, K., & Fisher, H. E. (2014). Variation in orgasm occurrence by sexual orientation in a sample of U.S. singles. *Journal of Sexual Medicine, 11*(11), 2645–2652.

Garcia, J. R., Massey, S. G., Merriwether, A. M., & Seibold-Simpson, S. M. (In Review). Orgasm experiences among emerging adult men and women: Gender, relationship context, and attitudes toward casual sex.

Gibbs, L. (2013). Gender, relationship type and contraceptive use at first intercourse. *Contraception, 87*(6), 806–812.

Gray, P. B., & Garcia, J. R. (2013). *Evolution and human sexual behavior.* Cambridge: Harvard University Press.

Greenspan, S. (2011). *11 points guide to hooking up: Lists and advice about first dates, hotties, scandals, pickups, threesomes, and booty calls.* New York: Skyhorse Publishing.

Guzman, L., Wildsmith, E., Manlove, J., & Franzetta, K. (2010). Unintended births: Patterns by race and ethnicity and relationship type. *Perspectives on Sexual and Reproductive Health, 42*(3), 176–185.

Hall, S. S., & Knox, D. (2013). A profile of double victims: Sexual coercion by a dating partner and a stranger. *Journal of Agression, Maltreatment & Trauma, 22*, 145–158.

Halpern, C. T. (2010). Reframing research on adolescent sexuality: Healthy sexual development as part of the life course. *Perspectives on Sexual and Reproductive Health, 42*(1), 6–7. doi:10.1363/420610.

Hatfield, E., Hutchison, E. S. S., Bensman, L., Young, D. M., & Rapson, R. L. (2012). Cultural, social, and gender influences on casual sex: New developments. In J. M. Turner & A. D. Mitchell (Eds.), *Social psychology: New developments.* Hauppauge: Nova Science.

Hayford, S. R., & Guzzo, K. B. (2013). Racial and ethnic variation in unmarried young adults' motivation to avoid pregnancy. *Perspectives on Sexual and Reproductive Health, 45*, 41–51.

Haydon, A. A., Herring, A. H., & Halpern, C. T. (2012). Associations between patterns of emerging sexual behavior and young adult reproductive health. *Perspectives on Sexual and Reproductive Health, 44*(4), 218–227.

Heldman, C., & Wade, L. (2010). Hook-up culture: Setting a new research agenda. *Sexuality Research and Social Policy, 7*, 323–333.

Herbenick, D., Reece, M., Schick, V., Sanders, S. A., Dodge, B., & Fortenberry, J. D. (2010). Sexual behavior in the United States: Results from a national probability sample of men and women ages 14–94. *Journal of Sexual Medicine, 7*, 255–265.

Higgins, J. A., & Hirsch, J. S. (2008). Pleasure, power, and inequality: Incorporating sexuality into research on contraceptive use. *American Journal of Public Health, 98*(10), 1803–1813.

Hill, M. S., Garcia, J. R., Musicaro, R. M., & Geher, G. (In review). Casual but not always wanted: Exploring the occurrence of unwanted sexual experiences in the context of sexual hookups.

Holman, A., & Sillars, A. (2012). Talk about "hooking up": The influence of college student social networks on nonrelationship sex. *Health Communication, 27,* 205–216.

Holmes, D., O'Byrne, P., & Gastaldo, D. (2007). Setting the space for sex: Architecture, desire, and health issues in gay bathhouses. *International Journal of Nursing Studies, 44*(2), 273–284.

Hyde, J. S. (2005). The gender similarities hypothesis. *American Psychologist, 60*(6), 581–592.

Jankowiak, W. R., & Fischer, E. F. (1992). A cross-cultural perspective on romantic love. *Ethnology, 31,* 149–155.

Jessor, R. (1991). Risk behavior in adolescence: A psychosocial framework for understanding and action. *Journal of Adolescent Health, 12,* 597–605.

Jessor, R., & Jessor, S. L. (1977). *Problem behavior and psychosocial development: A longitudinal study of youth.* New York: Academic.

Johnson, C. R. (2008). Casual sex: Towards a 'Prehistory' of gay life in Bohemian America. *Interventions: International Journal of Postcolonial Studies, 10*(3), 303–320.

Kalish, R. (2013). Masculinities and hooking Up: Sexual decision-making at college. *Culture, Society & Masculinities, 5*(2), 147–165.

Kinsey, A. C., Pomeroy, W. B., & Martin, C. E. (1948). *Sexual behavior in the human male.* Philadelphia: W. B. Saunders.

Kinsey, A. C., Pomeroy, W. B., Martin, C. E., & Gebhard, P. H. (1953). *Sexual behavior in the human female.* Philadelphia: W. B. Saunders.

Kirby, T., & Thornber-Dunwell, M. (2014). Uptake of PrEP for HIV slow among MSM. *The Lancet, 383,* 399–400.

Klipfel, K. M., Claxton, S. E., & van Dulmen, M. H. M. (2013). Interpersonal aggression victimization within casual sexual relationships and experiences. *Journal of Interpersonal Violence, 29,* 557–569.

Kuperberg, A., & Padgett, J. E. (2015). Dating and hooking up in college: Meeting contexts, sex, and variation by gender, partner's gender, and class standing. *Journal of Sex Research, 52,* 517–531.

Lambert, T. A., Kahn, A. S., & Apple, K. J. (2003). Pluralistic ignorance and hooking up. *Journal of Sex Research, 40,* 129–133.

Lehmiller, J. J., VanderDrift, L. E., & Kelly, J. R. (2014). Sexual communication, satisfaction, and condom use behavior in friends with benefits and romantic partners. *Journal of Sex Research, 51*(1), 74–85.

Lewis, M. A., Granato, H., Blayney, J. A., Lostutter, T. W., & Kilmer, J. R. (2012). Predictors of hooking up

sexual behavior and emotional reactions among U.S. college students. *Archives of Sexual Behavior, 41*(5), 1219–1229.

Li, X., Stanton, B., & Yu, S. (2007). Factorial structure of problem behaviors among urban and rural American adolescents. *Journal of the National Medical Association, 99*(11), 1262–1270.

Lieberman, C. (2014, February 10). Why college sating is so messed up?. COSMOPOLITAN. http://www.cosmopolitan.com/sex-love/advice/a5585/college-dating-screwed-up/.

Lohan, M., Cruise, S., O'Halloran, P., Alderdice, F., & Hyde, A. (2010). Adolescent men's attitudes in relation to pregnancy and pregnancy outcomes: a systematic review of the literature from 1980e2009. *Journal of Adolescent Health, 47,* 327e345.

Lyons, H. A., Manning, W. D., Longmore, M. A., & Giordano, P. C. (2014). Young adult casual sexual behavior: Life-course-specific motivations and consequences. *Sociological Perspectives, 57*(1), 79–101.

Lyons, H. A., Manning, W. D., Longmore, M. A., & Giordano, P. C. (2015). Gender and casual sexual activity from adolescence to emerging adulthood: Social and life course correlates. *Journal of Sex Research, 52,* 543–557.

Manlove, J., Steward-Streng, N., Peterson, K., Scott, M., & Wildsmith, E. (2013). Racial and ethnic differences in the transition to a teenage birth in the United States. *Perspectives on Sexual and Reproductive Health, 45*(2), 89–100.

Manlove, J., Welti, K., Wildsmith, E., & Barry, M. (2014). Relationship types and contraceptive use within young adult dating relationships. *Perspectives on Sexual & Reproductive Health, 46*(1), 41–50.

Manning, W. S., Giordano, P. C., & Longmore, M. A. (2006). Hooking up: The relationship contexts of "nonrelationship" sex. *Journal of Adolescent Research, 21,* 459–483.

Mark, K. P., Garcia, J. R., & Fisher, H. E. (In Press). Emotional and sexual satisfaction across sexual relationship contexts: Gender and sexual orientation differences and similarities. *The Canadian Journal of Human Sexuality.*

Martinez, G., Copen, C. E., & Abma, J. C. (2011). Teenagers in the United States: Sexual activity, contraceptive use, and childbearing, 2006–2010 National Survey of Family Growth. *Vital and Health Statistics, 23*(31).

Maticka-Tyndale, E. (1991). Sexual scripts and AIDS prevention: Variations in adherence to safer-sex guidelines by heterosexual adolescents. *Journal of Sex Research, 28,* 45–66.

Matson, P. A., Adler, N. E., Millstein, S. G., Tschann, J. M., & Ellen, J. M. (2011). Developmental changes in condom use among urban adolescent females: Influence of partner context. *Journal of Adolescent Health, 48,* 386–390.

Milhausen, R. R., McKay, A., Graham, C. A., Crosby, R. A., Yarber, W. L., & Sanders, S. A. (2013). Prevalence and predictors of condom use in a national sample of

Canadian university students. *Canadian Journal of Human Sexuality, 22*(3), 142–151.

Moilanen, K. L., Crockett, L. J., Rafaelli, M., & Jones, B. L. (2010). Trajectories of sexual risk from middle adolescence to early adulthood. *Journal of Research on Adolescence, 20,* 114–139.

Nelson, L. E., Morrison-Beedy, D., Kearney, M. H., & Dozier, A. (2011). Always, never, or sometimes: Examining variation in condom-use decision making among black adolescent mothers. *Research in Nursing & Health, 34*(4), 270–281.

Nystrom, R. J., Duke, J. E. A., & Victor, B. (2013). Shifting the paradigm in Oregon from teen pregnancy prevention to youth sexual health. *Public Health Reports, 128* Suppl (1), 89–95.

Owen, J., & Fincham, F. D. (2011). Young adults' emotional reactions after hooking up encounters. *Archives of Sexual Behavior, 40,* 321–330.

Paik, A. (2010a). "Hookups," dating, and relationship quality: Does the type of sexual involvement matter? *Social Science Research, 39,* 739–753.

Paik, A. (2010b). The contexts of sexual involvement and concurrent sexual partnerships. *Perspectives on Sexual and Reproductive Health, 42,* 33–42.

Paterno, M. T., & Jordan, E. T. (2012). A review of factors associated with unprotected sex among adult women in the United States. *JOGNN: Journal of Obstetric, Gynecologic & Neonatal Nursing, 41*(2), 258–274.

Paul, E. L., & Hayes, K. A. (2002). The casualties of "casual" sex: A qualitative exploration of the phenomenology of college students' hook-ups. *Journal of Social and Personal Relationships, 19,* 639–661.

Pazol, K., Creanga, A. A., Burley, K. D., Hayes, B., & Jamieson, D. J. (2013). Abortion surveillance—United States, 2010. *Morbidity and Mortality Weekly Report Surveillance Summaries, 62*(8), 1–44 (Washington, D.C.: 2002).

Penhollow, T., Young, M., & Bailey, W. (2007). Relationship between religiosity and "hooking up" behavior. *American Journal of Health Education, 38,* 338–345.

Petersen, J. L., & Hyde, J. S. (2011). Gender differences in sexual attitudes and behaviors: A review of meta-analytic results and large datasets. *Journal of Sex Research, 48*(2–3), 149–165.

Polis, C. B., & Zabin, L. S. (2012). Missed conceptions or misconceptions: Perceived infertility among unmarried young adults in the United States. *Perspectives on Sexual and Reproductive Health, 44*(1), 30–38.

Pollack, L. M., Boyer, C. B., & Weinstein, N. D. (2013). Perceived risk for sexually transmitted infections aligns with sexual risk behavior with the exception of condom nonuse: Data from a nonclinical sample of sexually active young adult women. *Sexually Transmitted Diseases, 40*(5), 388–394.

Prestage, G., Jin, F., Grulich, A., de Wit, J., & Zablotska, I. (2011). Gay men are less likely to use condoms with casual sex partners they know "well." *AIDS and Behavior,* 1–5. doi:10.1007/s10461-011-9952-8

Ray, R. & Rosow, J. 2010. Getting off and getting intimate: How normative institutional arrangements

structure black and white fraternity men's approaches towards women. *Men and Masculinities, 12,* 523–546.

Reay, B. (2014). Promiscuous intimacies: Rethinking the history of American casual sex. *Journal of Historical Sociology, 27*(1), 1–24.

Reece, M., Herbenick, D., Schick, V., Sanders, S. A., Dodge, B., & Fortenberry, J. D. (2010). Condom use rates in a national probability sample of males and females ages 14 to 94 in the United States. *Journal of Sexual Medicine, 7*(Supplement 5), 266–276.

Reiber, C., & Garcia, J. R. (2010). Hooking up: Gender differences, evolution, and pluralistic ignorance. *Evolutionary Psychology, 8,* 390–404.

Riehman, K. S., Wechsberg, W. M., Francis, S. A., Moore, M., & Morgan-Lopez, A. (2006). Discordance in monogamy beliefs, sexual concurrency, and condom use among young adult substance-involved couples: Implications for risk of sexually transmitted infections. *Sexually Transmitted Diseases, 33*(11), 677–682.

Rozler, J., & Lavinthal, A. (2005). *The hookup handbook: A single girl's guide to living it up.* New York: Simon Spotlight Entertainment.

Rupp, L. J., Taylor, V., Regev-Messalem, S., Fogarty, A. C. K., & England, P. (2014). Queer women in the hookup scene: Beyond the closet? *Gender & Society, 28*(2), 212–235.

Santelli, J. S., Speizer, I. S., Avery, A., & Kendall, C. (2006). An exploration of the dimensions of pregnancy intentions among women choosing to terminate pregnancy or initiate prenatal care in New Orleans, Louisiana. *American Journal of Public Health, 96*(11), 2009–2015.

Shanahan, M. J. (2000) Pathways to adulthood in changing societies: Variability and mechanisms in life course perspective. *Annual Review of Sociology, 26,* 667–692.

Sherman, A. J., & Tocantins, N. (2004). *The happy hookup: A single girl's guide to casual sex.* Berkeley: Ten Speed Press.

Singer, M. C., Erickson, P. I., Badiane, L., Diaz, R., Ortiz, D., Abraham, T., & Nicolaysen, A. M. (2006). Syndemics, sex and the city: Understanding sexually transmitted diseases in social and cultural context. *Social Science & Medicine, 63*(8), 2010–2021.

Snapp, S., Ryu, E., & Kerr, J. (2015). The upside to hooking up: College students' positive hookup experiences. *International Journal of Sexual Health, 27*(1), 43–56.

Sprecher, S., Barbee, A., & Schwartz, P. (1995). "Was it good for you, too?": Gender differences in first sexual intercourse experiences. *Journal of Sex Research, 32*(1), 3–15.

Stinson, R. D. (2010). Hooking up in young adulthood: A review of factors influencing the sexual behavior of college students. *Journal of College Student Psychotherapy, 24,* 98–115.

Swartzendruber, A., Zenilman, J. M., Niccolai, L. M., Kershaw, T. S., Brown, J. L., DiClemente, R. J., & Sales, J. M. (2013). It takes 2: partner attributes associated with sexually transmitted infections among adolescents. *Sexually Transmitted Diseases, 40*(5), 372–378.

Tolman, D. (2002). *Dilemmas of desire: Teenage girls talk about sexuality*. Cambridge: Harvard University Press.

Tolman, D. T., & Diamond, L. M. (2014). Sexuality theory: A review, a revision, and a recommendation. In D. T. Tolman & L. M. Diamond (Eds.), *APA handbook on sexuality and psychology* (pp. 3–27). Washington, D.C.: APA Press.

Tomsich, E. A., Schaible, L. M., Rennison, C. M., & Gover, A. R. (2013). Violent victimization and hooking up among strangers and acquaintances on an urban campus: An exploratory study. *Criminal Justice Studies: A Critical Journal of Crime, Law and Society, 26*, 433–454.

Townsend, J. M. (1995). Sex without emotional involvement: An evolutionary interpretation of sex differences. *Archives of Sexual Behavior, 24*, 173–206. doi:10.1007/BF01541580.

Townsend, J. M., & Wasserman, T. H. (2011). Sexual hookups among college students: Sex differences in emotional reactions. *Archives of Sexual Behavior, 40*, 1173–1181.

Vasilenko, S. A., Lefkowitz, E. S., & Maggs, J. L. (2012). Short-term positive and negative consequences of sex based on daily reports among college students. *Journal of Sex Research, 49*(6), 558–569.

Vrangalova, Z. (2015). Does casual sex harm college students' well-being? A longitudinal investigation of the role of motivation. *Archives of Sexual Behavior, 44*, 945–959.

Waldrop-Valverde, D. G., Davis, T. L., Sales, J. M., Rose, E. S., Wingood, G. M., & DiClemente, R. J. (2013). Sexual concurrency among young African-American women. *Psychology, Health, & Medicine, 18*(6), 676–686.

Walsh, J. L., Fielder, R. L., Carey, K. B., & Carey, M. P. (2014). Dual method use among a sample of first-year college women. *Perspectives on Sexual & Reproductive Health, 46*(2), 73–81.

Weaver, A. D., MacKeigan, K. L., & MacDonald, H. A. (2011). Experiences and perceptions of young adults in friends with benefits relationships: A qualitative study. *Canadian Journal of Human Sexuality, 20*(1), 41–53.

Wentland, J. J., & Reissing, E.D. (2011). Taking casual sex not too casually: Exploring definitions of casual sexual relationships. *The Canadian Journal of Human Sexuality, 20*(3), 75–91.

World Health Organization. (2006). *Defining sexual health: Report of a technical consultation on sexual health,* 28–31 January 2002, Geneva: Author.

Wright, M. O., Norton, D. L., & Matusek, J. A. (2010). Predicting verbal coercion following sexual refusal during a hookup: Diverging gender patterns. *Sex Roles, 62*, 647–660.

Consensual Non-Monogamies in Industrialized Nations

13

Elisabeth Sheff and Megan M. Tesene

While non-monogamy has been a common form of human relationship across many cultures and eras, it has primarily been in the form of *polygyny*—one husband with multiple wives. Even in cultures in which celebrate monogamy, it is with the knowledge that "boys will be boys," and the entrenched sexual double standard allows married/partnered men to cheat, patronize prostitutes, and pursue multiple lovers with far more freedom than allowed to women. It is a shift towards gender neutrality that demarcates contemporary non-monogamies in industrialized nations from past multiple-partner relationship forms. While the gendered double standard remains in force, women are able to access a degree of sexual freedom previously unknown in more traditional forms of non-monogamy, especially the forms of polygamy (multiple-partner marriage) that prize women's sexual "purity" as proof of her worth and family honor. Swinging, polyamory, open, anarchic, and monogamish relationships—broadly termed *Consensual Non-Monogamy* (CNM)—all provide gender-neutral access to sexual variety, and their growing popularity indicates a profound shift in attitudes towards monogamy and polygamy.

E. Sheff (✉)
Sociology, Oglethorpe University, Atlanta,
GA 30319, USA
e-mail: drelisheff@gmail.com

M. M. Tesene
Sociology Department, Georgia State University, Atlanta,
GA 30302, USA
e-mail: mtesene1@gsu.edu

All forms of CNM are *consensual*, meaning that they are openly conducted rather than cheating or clandestinely having multiple partners while in an ostensibly monogamous relationship. CNM relationships vary in terms of how many rules structure sexual/romantic interactions and how emotionally intimate the relationships are allowed to become. *Open* is a broad category that simply means non-monogamous. *Swingers* emphasize sexual variety outside of the couple and emotional exclusivity within the couple, while *polyamorists* emphasize the loving connections between or among more than two people, with sexual connections optional. *Monogamish* couples agree to various forms of sexual contact outside of the couple's relationship, and *relationship anarchists* refuse all rules and focus on treating people well enough in the moment that they stay together by choice. We will explain each category in greater depth throughout this chapter.

Since the advent of the sexual revolution of the 1960s and 1970s, intimate relationships in the United States have been in a state of flux (Rubin 1993; Stacey 1996; Tolman 2002). That revolution, along with the rise of openly conducted, non-monogamous relationships as a social choice spurred social scientists to study swinging (Bartell 1971; Fang 1976; Henshel 1973) and open or "multilateral" marriages (Constantine and Constantine 1973; Ellis 1970; Smith and Smith 1974). Other societal changes such as movements for gay emancipation (D'Emilio 1983) and women's liberation (Daly 1985; Ferree and Hess 1994), alterations in families such as

J. DeLamater, R.F. Plante (eds.), *Handbook of the Sociology of Sexualities*, Handbooks of Sociology and Social Research, DOI 10.1007/978-3-319-17341-2_13, © Springer International Publishing Switzerland 2015

women's increased participation in the paid work-force and rising divorce rates (Brines and Joyner 1999; Popenoe 1993; Yoder and Nichols 1980), and larger social modifications such as counter-cultural movements have expanded some social roles and transformed elements of society in fits and starts (Bornstein 1994; Butler 1990; Weeks 1985). These and other social influences, particularly the advent of Internet communications, have created a wider range of relationship options than previously available, as well as a larger social conversation around the meaning and utility of monogamy (Conley et al. 2013; Matsick et al. 2013). Even with this wider range of options, non-monogamy remains unconventional and stigmatized. As a result, people with greater social privilege—especially well educated white people with professional jobs—are more able to openly practice non-monogamy (and participate in research) because they have the resources to buffer themselves from the pernicious impacts of social stigma (Sheff and Hammers 2011).

Because women's ability to own property, get degrees and credentials, and work for pay appears to be fundamental to the development of gender-neutral forms of non-monogamy, this chapter focuses on non-monogamies in industrialized nations where women have access to full citizenship. As much of the research we reference was conducted in the United States, this chapter focuses primarily on the U.S. and to a lesser degree other industrialized nations. In this chapter we first introduce types of non-monogamy, distinguish between and among non-monogamies, and then identify some areas of common overlap shared among non-monogamies. Next we explore theories pertaining to non-monogamy and the methods scholars have used to study them. This chapter closes with a discussion of directions for future research regarding non-monogamies.

13.1   Types of Non-Monogamy

In this section we discuss sexualities and sexual relationships as a fluid mix of identity, behavior, and practice, primarily because the research we cite has not yet settled the precise distinctions between and among them. As Plummer (2011) points out in his 40-year retrospective on labeling theory, "the politics of naming and control, and the trouble that labels can cause" (p. 84) have shaped academic and popular culture debates about distinctions between sexual practices, behaviors, and identities (see also Gagnon and Simon 2011). Some of the people we discuss below actively identify with a specific label such as polyamorist, swinger, non-monogamist, or relationship anarchist. Others engage in consensually non-monogamous relationships but do not label themselves.

In addition to label and identity, types of non-monogamy also vary by a number of factors including degrees of transparency, sexual involvement, and emotional intimacy. Cheating and adultery stand out for their lack of transparency and absence of negotiation among the partners involved. The other forms listed below—swinging, polyamory, monogamish, and uncategorized relationships—routinely rely on conversation to establish guidelines that structure dating and safer-sex practices. Even relationship anarchy can rely on negotiation to reject monogamy, if not usually to establish rules that structure relationships. In the absence of a cultural script detailing ways in which people can be relationship anarchists, they must negotiate alternatives in order to avoid falling in to predetermined cultural scripts. While these alternatives might not include rules, they still require negotiation in order to be understood and consensual.

13.1.1   Adultery and Cheating

Monogamous relationships continue to be those most idealized in Western culture (Mint 2014). Consequently, any relationship that is perceived as non-monogamous tends to be valued in a negative manner (Carr 2010; Mint 2014; Treas and Giesen 2000). For some, any non-monogamous relationship is viewed as adulterous, regardless of whether or not both partners have consented to having sexual interactions with persons outside the relationship dyad. Mint (2014) exposes a false duality when it comes to monogamy and cheating in the United States —either relationships are monogamous or they aren't. Such thinking prevents consideration and/or acceptance of those relationships that fall outside of this dichotomous order (Mint 2014). One of the consequences of this ideological framework is that those relationships that are consensually non-monogamous tend to be lumped together by the broader society as immoral and inherently adulterous (Frank 2013), perhaps explaining the widespread disdain for non-monogamies in general. However, there are distinct differences between cheating and relationships that are consensually non-monogamous, as many researchers have noted in their studies of communities practicing CNM. While the majority of this chapter will focus on those relationships that fall under the category of consensual non-monogamy, it is also necessary to highlight some of the key trends in attitudes and practices towards cheating.

Contemporary studies show that more than 90 % of Americans identify cheating as either "always" or "almost always" wrong (Carr 2010; Treas and Giesen 2000). While attitudes towards cheating appear to be increasingly negative over time, actual extramarital practices among married heterosexuals have remained relatively stable since the 1990s with approximately 20–25 % of ever-married men and 10–15 % of ever-married women admitting to having "ever having sex with someone other than their spouse while married," a figure that would include consensual non-monogamy as well (Carr 2010, p. 59). However, it is important to note that statistics on cheating tend to be heterocentric and are not immune to methodological problems, and thus potential inaccuracies. For instance, subjective definitions of sex and cheating vary from person to person, making it difficult to know the actual frequency with which cheating occurs (Moller and Vosser 2014). Another concern is social desirability; respondents may be less likely to report that they have cheated since the behavior continues to be labeled as immoral within the broader culture. Such self-policing in reporting may be more common among women who have historically been subjected to a sexual double standard, causing them to be judged more harshly

for adulterous behavior than are men (Drigotas and Barta 2001).

Despite these potential limitations, recent studies continue to use self-reported data to identify demographic trends of marital cheating—noting that men are more likely than women to report cheating, Blacks more likely than Hispanics who are more likely than Whites to report cheating, and younger cohorts and those with higher levels of education are less likely to view cheating in a negative manner than are older persons or those with lower levels of education (Carr 2010). Paramount to understanding any societal trends, it is also necessary to identify some of the ways that our society is changing. Shifts in the economy, the workplace, the division of labor, the pursuit of higher education, and the ever-increasing role that technology has on our day-to-day lives appear to have an impact on attitudinal and behavioral practices. As Carr (2010) notes "many women have the economic resources to leave a philanderer. And, it's no longer husbands who bear sole responsibility for home-wrecking. As more women work outside the home and earn their own income, there's less at stake for them if they are caught" (p. 60). Also, women who work for pay have more opportunities to meet additional partners at work, as men in paid work traditionally had. Furthermore, as our technological capabilities expand, opportunities for engaging in adultery also proliferate (Carr 2010; Cossman 2006). Texts, emails, social media, personal cell phones, Internet communities, and dating sites have opened an entire new landscape, ripe with opportunities for cheating (Carr 2010; Cossman 2006)—or getting caught.

13.1.2 Monogamish

Popularized within the last few years by Dan Savage (2011), a well-known author and podcaster, monogamish relationships are those in which a couple is primarily monogamous but allows varying degrees of sexual contact with others. Rules structuring these external sexual contacts vary by couple (Grov et al. 2014), ranging from only allowing one-night stands (no second time with the same person) or only specific kinds of sexual activity (i.e., kissing and groping are OK but no intercourse) to time limits (no more than a week) or location limitations (only when people are traveling or not at home).

Most academic research on monogamish relationships has occurred within the last 5 years and tends to focus on men in same-sex relationships. For instance, Parsons et al. (2013) defined monogamish relationships as those in which "both men have agreed that any sexual activities with casual partners must happen when both members of the couple are present and involved (e.g. threeways or group sex)" (p. 303). They (Parsons et al. 2013) found that monogamish men fared better than single men on a variety of measures, from using fewer drugs to having greater relationship satisfaction and better health. When compared to monogamous men, however, monogamish men had higher levels of substance use (Parsons et al. 2013), though other data (Parsons and Starks 2014) indicate similar rates of drug use when monogamish men are compared with monogamous or single men. Monogamish relationships appeared to offer psychological and health benefits on par with monogamous relationships, both of which had higher degrees of satisfaction and lower rates of depression when compared to single men or those in open relationships (DuBois 2013; Parsons et al. 2013). Hosking (2013) measured the relationship between satisfaction and perceived discrepancies in benefit among gay men in open relationships using frequency of casual sex, attractiveness of casual partners, and overall perceived benefit. Findings indicate that men who perceive that they receive less benefit to their open sexual agreement feel less satisfied in their relationships than do men who perceive that they receive equal or greater benefit (Hosking 2013). Andrews (2014) studied factors that influence decision-making regarding "extra-relational sex" and found that the factors that exerted the most influence were similar relational values, the ways in which partners react to specific incidents, and the ability to accept influence from one's partner.

13.1.3　Polyamory

An outgrowth of the free-love movement in the United States in the 1960s and 1970s, polyamory became a distinct relationship form in the 1980s. Most popular in Australia, Canada, the United States, and Western Europe, polyamory tends to be prevalent in places where women can earn their own money and control their reproduction.

Types Polyamory is a relationship style that allows people to openly conduct multiple sexual and/or romantic relationships simultaneously, ideally with the knowledge and consent of all involved in or affected by the relationships. *Polyfidelity* is similar except that it is a closed relationship style that requires sexual and emotional fidelity to an intimate group that is larger than two. *Polyaffective* relationships are emotionally intimate, non-sexual connections among people connected by a polyamorous relationship, such as two heterosexual men who are both in sexual relationships with the same women and have co-spousal or brother-like relationships with each other (Sheff 2005, 2014a).

Hierarchy Some poly people organize their relationships by emotional importance (Labriola 1999; Sheff 2005), with *primary* partners mirroring the cultural conception of a spouse: often cohabiting; making important decisions together; external social recognition as a couple (sometimes including legal marriage); intertwined financially; and sometimes having children together. *Secondary* partners are similar to a boyfriend or girlfriend in that they are less likely to cohabit, tend to remain financially independent, and often are accorded less social power and consideration than primary partners. This relatively disempowered state often creates problems and tensions, and fosters lively community debates in online discussion forums[1] and academic pub-

---

[1] The polyamorous community and academic groups that have discussed secondary status include Polyfamilies, PolyResearchers, Lovingmore, More Than Two, Fetlife, and LiveJournal at the minimum and probably many, many more.

lications (Butterworth 2009; Ho 2006; Labriola 1999). Many of the more experienced polys de-emphasize or even reject hierarchy, focusing instead on practical and pragmatic connections such as residential status to define their relationships as nesting for those who live together and non-nesting for those who live separately (Sheff 2014a).

Size Poly relationships vary by the number of people involved. *Poly singles* or *solo polys* are people who prioritize autonomy of decision-making over primary partnership. A fluid category, solo poly covers a range of relationships, from the youthful "free agent" or recent divorcee who might want to "settle down" some day but for now wants to play the field with casual, brief, no-strings-attached connections, to the seasoned "solo poly" who has deeply committed, intimate, and lasting relationships with one or more people. Like all sexualities, issues of identity complicate solo poly and all poly identities. Some who date multiple people openly might fit the definition of solo poly but not identify as such (Sheff 2005).

Some solo polys have relationships that they consider emotionally and possibly sexually primary, but not primary in a logistical, rank, or rules-based sense. Others don't want the kinds of expectations and limitations that come with a primary romantic/sexual relationship. In many cases solo polys intend to remain "singleish" indefinitely because they are strongly motivated by autonomy, value their freedom, and identify primarily as individuals rather than as parts of a multi-person unity. For others, circumstances (such as ending a primary relationship) converge so that a solo poly person is not in any romantic relationship at the moment, and yet maintains their polyamorous identity (much like a single lesbian might still consider herself a lesbian even if she is not currently in a romantic/sexual relationship) (Sheff 2011, 2014a, b). This is not to say singleish people are all aloof or detached: Solo polys routinely consult with their partners, frequently considering their partners' needs and feelings when making important decisions. Ultimately, though, solo polys are beholden more to themselves (and possibly children or

non-romantic significant others) than to any romantic partner (Sheff 2013).

The *open couple* is the most common form of open relationship (Labriola 1999; Sheff 2014a) and is characteristically composed of a married or long-term committed couple that takes on a third (or sometimes forth or fifth) partner whose involvement and role in the relationship is always secondary (Labriola 1999). A couple practicing this relationship type might engage in sexual activity with the secondary partner together or separate, or they may each have independent outside relationships with different secondary partners—regardless of the specific parameters, the primary couple always remains a priority. Open couples often mirror swinging relationships in that both are emotionally committed dyadic relationships that are open to having sexual relationships with others (Bergstrand and Sinski 2010; Fernandes 2009; Gould 1999).

While the phrase *open relationship* has come to be used as somewhat of an umbrella term for a diverse range of non-monogamous relationship structures such as swinging or polyamory (Block 2008; Munson and Stelboum 1999; Taormino 2008), it most commonly is thought to represent what Labriola (1999) describes as a primary/secondary model previously referenced. Primary partners are those who make joint decisions, prioritize each other emotionally, and often live together and share finances. Secondary partners, in contrast, generally do not cohabit, spend less time together, and have a lower level of emotional priority. This relationship type was initially presented in O'Neill and O'Neill's (1972) book, *Open Marriage*, in which they discussed their research and perspectives about an evolving relationship structure that defied traditional notions of monogamy (O'Neill and O'Neill 1972; Taormino 2008). In it, they described a primary relationship that was open to non-monogamous intimacy, which would lead to the potential growth of both partners, and the relationship as a whole (O'Neill and O'Neill 1972; Taormino 2008).

Vees and *triads,* both relationships involving three people, are generally distinguished by their degree of emotional and sexual intimacy. In a vee there is often more separation, usually with one person in relationships with two others who are not sexually connected with each other and instead may range from acquaintances to close friends or even enemies. Triads tend to be more emotionally intimate and often include some degree of sexual interaction among all three members, though some polyaffective triads have platonic relationships between some of the members. *Quads* are relationships composed of four people. Sometimes quads form when a triad or vee adds a fourth, and other quads coalesce when two couples join to make a larger grouping. *Moresomes* have five or more people in a relationship, and at some point they verge in to intimate networks which are groups of people with interlocking and overlapping relationships. Like vees and triads, quads, moresome, and intimate networks often include nonsexual, polyaffective relationships among some members as well. Finally, *polycules* are the constellation of relationships involved in and affected by a given polyamorous relationship. Polycules are extended chosen families comprised of the adults and children connected by polyamorous and polyaffective relationships, such as a quad with children and several additional partners dating members of the quad and their partners or significant others including children and non-romantic partners.

13.1.4 Polygamy

Alongside (and even predating) monogamy, legal and religious institutions throughout the world have long recognized polygynous relationships as valid. Polygamy—a form of marriage consisting of more than two persons—is most commonly practiced as polygyny, a marriage of one husband and multiple wives who are each sexually exclusive with the husband (Goldfeder and Sheff 2013). Worldwide, Muslims are those who are most likely to be polygynous, with higher concentrations of polygyny in the Middle East and parts of Africa (Dalton and Leung 2014). Polyandry—a marriage of one wife to multiple husbands—is far more rare, as marriages between one woman and multiple men have received less social, political, and cultural support than have

polygynous relationships (Goldfeder and Sheff 2013; Hassinger and Kruger 2013; Trevithick 1997). Just as the endorsement of polygyny over polyandry has much to do with women's social, political, and economic power, those women in polyandrous marriages tend to be subservient to each of their husbands' expectations and desires. In this way, polyandry is not comparable to polygyny in terms of the relational power and prestige of the single man or woman; rather, it is the men who maintain control in each of these relationship forms. However, Mulder (2009) argues that women are the ones who are the most likely to benefit from polygyny in that the men who take on multiple wives tend to be those who have high statuses within their communities.

Researchers have theorized on the disparate frequencies of polygyny versus polyandry throughout history and across different cultures. While polygynous marital structures have been documented by anthropologists in approximately 84 % of human cultures (Ember et al. 2007), only 1–2 % have included polyandry as a legitimate family form. Polyandrous relationships primarily consist of brothers who share the same wife—such practices often result from ecological constraints on population size. For instance, in the mountainous terrain of Tibet, fraternal polyandry prevents scarce farmland from division into parcels that would be too small to support a family (Goldstein 1987). Hassinger and Kruger (2013) offer a socio-biological approach to explaining the frequency of polygyny and polyandry throughout the globe, postulating that,

> high sex ratios, indicating a relative surplus of men, will be associated with a greater extent of polygyny. Although an association between polyandry and a relative surplus of men is numerically intuitive, we base our prediction on the divergence in reproductive strategies between men and women. These sex differences shape how men and women leverage the advantages associated with numerical scarcity for different reproductive goals. (p. 132)

In the United States, the Fundamentalist Latter Day Saints (FLDS or Fundamentalist Mormon) are the best-known polygynists, though the Nation of Islam and other Muslim groups also have multiple-partner marriages. Generally condemned as harmful, exploitative, and abusive towards women and children (Fry 2010; Goldfeder and Sheff 2013)—anti-polygamy statutes have constrained polygynists throughout the United States. For instance, in some FLDS communities, girls are married when they are young and after being denied education or any sense of intellectual or personal development (Fry 2010). Despite the continued stigma associated with polygamy in the United States, polygynous relationships have gained more positive press and mainstream coverage in recent years.

Television shows such as *Sister Wives* and *Big Love* offer an intimate glimpse into the lives of the men, women, and children who make up polygynous families—whether real or fictional. Such exposure brings the experiences of this stigmatized familial structure into the open and into the public discourse (Brown 2012; Goldfeder and Sheff 2013), creating potential avenues for shifting cultural values. For instance, the Browns, who are the family featured in Sister Wives, were the subject of a 2010 investigation due to their exposure through reality television (Nelson 2013). In response, they filed a case with the state of Utah, challenging the constitutionality of the state's current anti-polygamy laws. In December of 2013, a federal judged ruled in their favor, striking down several key parts of the law as unconstitutional—essentially decriminalizing polygamy in Utah (McCombs 2014; Nelson 2013; Politi 2013). While legal marriage to more than one person remains illegal, as does the marriage of an adult to a minor, those relationships that consist of consenting adults, cohabitating with one another, and raising a family together will no longer be subject to criminal sanctions, providing that the new law holds (McCombs 2014; Politi 2013). Similarly, those living separately and those not raising a family are not subject to legal repercussions under the law as the legal issue at hand is multiple marriages. The recent efforts of Utah's attorney general in appealing the court's ruling highlight just how volatile the issue remains; these newfound rights will no doubt continue to be debated both publicly and legally (McCombs 2014).

Members of the general public and media outlets continue to erroneously conflate polygamous marital structures with polyamory, requiring that we clarify some of the ways that these relationship types differ. One of the main differences is that polyamory involves the knowledge and consent of all persons involved; further, both men and women can take part in contemporaneous sexual or romantic relationships with multiple persons (Goldfeder and Sheff 2013; Sheff 2014a). This diverges from traditional polygamy—primarily practiced as polygyny, where the husband has sexual access to each of his wives but they do not have sexual access to anyone other than their husband. Rather, each wife must be sexually available to her husband. Similarly, in polyandrous marriages, the wife must be sexually available to all of her husbands. Note the power dynamics in terms of sexual availability and access as polygamous marriages entail the sexual availability of women to men. Polyamory and swinging, on the other hand, allow for all people involved to have a voice and to consent to the parameters of the relationship—sexual or otherwise. Another important difference is that polyamory allows for same-sex sexual activity whereas traditional polygamous relationships are founded upon heterosexual interactions (Goldfeder and Sheff 2013). While polyamorous relationships no doubt must deal with gender, sexuality, class, and racialized hierarchies prevalent in our society, these differences highlight the ways in which polyamorous individuals attempt to promote egalitarian and progressive principles within their respective relationships.

13.1.5   Rejection of Categorization

Consistent with a growing trend among young people who reject labels of all sorts, there are many who participate in consensual non-monogamy who refuse to categorize their relationships as one of the many labels listed in this chapter. Two of the most common ways to reject categorization around monogamy are engaging in open relationships or relationship anarchy.

Relationship anarchy is a new concept that recently developed out of polyamorous and anarchist communities (Crosswell 2014). The fundamental ideas about relationship anarchy are still being developed within these communities, and as such, there is not yet any identifiable research in this area. However, several blogs and news pieces are beginning to surface—highlighting some of the foundational ideologies and practices of relationship anarchists (Autumn 2014; Crosswell 2014; Nordgren 2006). Given the anarchist nature of this relationship philosophy, just how one engages in relationship anarchy is unique and individualistic—as is generally the case with most non-monogamous relationship forms.

Despite the subjective understandings of what constitutes relationship anarchy, there are some common themes presented in the various discussions and blog postings. The first theme is that relationship anarchists are highly critical of normative tendencies within US culture which prioritize romantic and sex-based relationships over non-sexual or non-romantic relationships (Autumn 2014; Crosswell 2014). Relationship anarchists seek to eliminate specific distinctions between or hierarchical valuations of friendships versus romantic or sexual relationships (Autumn 2014). In other words, sexual relationships are no more valuable than are aromantic friendships. Each relationship is unique and can evolve as needed by those involved; if conflict arises, those involved address it or the relationship comes to an end (Autumn 2014). Furthermore, an individual can have many concurrent meaningful and loving relationships because "love is abundant," it is not limited to a couple, and the love people feel does not diminish when it expands to include another person (Nordgren 2006, p. 3).

Another important theme within relationship anarchy is resistance to placing demands or expectations on the people involved in a relationship (Autumn 2014; Crosswell 2014; Nordgren 2006). Whereas the specific rules and guidelines employed in swinging or polyamorous relationships are often regarded by practitioners as what makes their relationships work, relationship anarchists reject such notions, noting how the implementation of rules or demands highlight the inherent sense of entitlement and denial of others' self-determination (Nordgren 2006). In relationship anarchy, no one need give anything up or compromise in order to sustain a relationship; rather, it is better to amicably separate than to sustain an unhappy and unfulfilling relationship (Autumn 2014). Figure 13.1 is an attempt to portray these distinctions visually.

13.1.6 Swinging

Among recognized or intentional forms of non-monogamy, swinging is the best known and most popular (Bergstrand and Sinski 2010; Frank 2013; NASCA 2014). It is also tremendously diverse, ranging from brief interactions between or among strangers at sex parties or clubs to groups of friends who know each other and socialize for many years (Bergstrand and Williams 2000; Fernandes 2009; Gould 1999). While researchers have yet to agree on a single, comprehensive definition of swinging (Fernandes 2009), many describe it as a practice that occurs when committed couples consensually exchange partners specifically for sexual purposes (Bartell 1970; Denfeld and Gordon 1970). Sometimes couples engage in this sexual activity together, in the presence of their partner, and other times the activity may take place in private, away from each other (Bergstrand and Sinski 2010). Individuals and couples routinely negotiate a range of agreements and rules within their relationships, commonly attempting to ensure that everyone involved is comfortable with those parameters and consents to the activities taking place (Bergstrand and Sinski 2010; Fernandes 2009). Another important aspect of swinging is that the couple frequently remains emotionally monogamous—their love and commitment to one another remains the primary focus of their relationship while sex with others is viewed as recreational (Bergstrand and Sinski 2010; Bergstrand and Williams 2000; Fernandes 2009).

The origins of swinging have been traced back to WWII and a group of Air Force fighter pilots and their wives (Fernandes 2009; Talese 1980). These military couples reportedly attended

Fig. 13.1 Clearly, one size does not fit all

parties (dubbed "key clubs") in which one member of the couple, either the wife or soldier, would place their house keys into a pile or hat. At the end of the evening, keys would be selected randomly, in effect pairing off sexual partners for the evening (Bergstrand and Williams 2000; Fernandes 2009; Gould 1999). During the 1950s, the media designated the practice "wife swapping," a term that has fallen out of favor as sexist since it implied that wives were mere property to be traded by men, rather than active and consensual participants (Denfeld and Gordon 1970; Fernandes 2009). Over time, the term "swinging" also came to be stigmatized, when several articles, both journalistic and academic, framed swingers as deviant and pathological (Butler 1979; Fernandes 2009). During the 1980s, members of this community began to refer to their behavior simply as "the lifestyle" as a way to reject deviant labels and connotations (Fernandes 2009). Today, the North American Swing Club Association (NASCA 2014) proudly uses both terms (swinging and the lifestyle) to describe community members and practices. Touting an international presence and proposing an increased prevalence of swinging, a trend noted by researchers as well (Bergstrand and Williams 2000; Jenks 1998), NASCA provides an online forum where swingers can connect with one another and locate clubs, parties, or events where they can engage in the lifestyle.

Despite claims that rates of swinging continue to increase among members of the general public in the United States (Bergstrand and Williams 2000; Jenks 1998; NASCA 2014), contemporary studies on swinging are surprisingly sparse. Academic studies on swinging flourished in the sexually adventurous 1960s and 1970s, documenting new trends in extra-marital or co-marital sexual involvement (Bartell 1971; Fang 1976; Henshel 1973). Studies examined swingers' race and ethnicity (Bartell 1970; Jenks 1985), social class (Flanigan and Zingdal 1991), education (Gilmartin 1975; Jenks 1985; Levitt 1988), and political perspectives (Bartell 1970). This research created a profile of a swinger as a "White, middle to upper middle class person in his or her late 30s who is fairly conventional in all ways except for her or his lack of religious participa-

tion/identification and participates in swinging" (Jenks 1998, p. 507)—a demographic that has remained relatively stable today, with the exception of a broader representation of political ideology than in the past (Bergstrand and Williams 2000; Fernandes 2009). While NASCA (2014) boasts that swingers come from all walks of life, the recent literature continues to find an overwhelmingly White, married (ostensibly heterosexually), middle to upper middle class, highly educated, and religiously affiliated (although not necessarily active) demographic (Bergstrand and Williams 2000; Fernandes 2009).

13.2 Commonalities Among Non-Monogamies

Non-monogamy is not for everyone—it can be complex, stigmatized, misunderstood, difficult, and emotionally fraught. People who elect to engage in non-monogamy range from religious practitioners of polygyny involved in Islam or the Fundamentalist Latter Day Saints (Mormons) who are often personally and politically conservative, to practitioners of polyamory or relationship anarchy who tend to be personally and politically liberal or progressive. Especially among the more liberal groups, there is significant overlap with other unconventional subcultures such as Pagans, geeks, gamers, science fiction enthusiasts, and practitioners of BDSM (previously known as sadomasochism, also termed kinky sex or kinksters).

13.2.1 (Lack of) Diversity

Studies indicate a lack of racial and class diversity among consensual non-monogamists, with the preponderance of sample members being white, middle or upper middle-class, highly educated people (Noël 2006; Sheff and Hammers 2011; Willey 2006). While the North American Swing Club Association (2014) claims that swingers are highly diverse in terms of demographics, the research indicates otherwise—identifying swingers as overwhelmingly white, middle class, well-educated, and primarily consisting of heterosexuals and bisexual women, as bisexual men are generally discouraged from participating at swinging events (Bergstrand and Sinski 2010; Fernandes 2009; Jenks 1998).

13.2.2 Consent via Negotiation

Ironically we begin the section on commonalities with a distinction that identifies a significant difference between the categories of non-monogamies: cheating and forced polygamy in contrast with consensual non-monogamy. CNM includes the majority of polygynous relationships in the US (Goldfeder and Sheff 2014), swinging, polyamory, and a range of open, monogamish, and anarchic relationships. Those who cheat do so clandestinely, without the consent of their partners, and often in direct violation of marital vows or relationship agreements. Similarly, young girls in arranged polygynous marriages with older men are generally not able to abstain from those marriages, rendering them unable to consent in any meaningful way. In this way, cheating and forced polygyny are fundamentally different from the consensual forms of non-monogamy identified above. The two relationship categories also have distinctly different outcomes for their practitioners, such as greater rates of STI transmission among non-consensual non-monogamists than among consensual non-monogamists (Conley et al. 2012) and greater rates of stigma when compared with cheaters (Conley et al. 2013). This is not to say that all forms of CNM are perfectly consensual—certainly the more subtle and overt forms of coercion, manipulation, and unconscious flailing are evident in consensually non-monogamous relationships, as in many other kinds of romantic and familial relationships.

Many non-monogamists rely on honest communication to negotiate consensual agreements that allow a variety of ways to have multiple partners. Academicians (McLean 2004; Ritchie and Barker 2006; Wosick-Correa 2010) examine communication and honesty, and community members instruct each other on how to best communicate in numerous website chat-rooms, personal and email discussions, and books (Anapol 2010; Easton and Hardy 2011; Veaux and Rickert 2014).

In addition to establishing consent, non-monogamists often use communication as a tool to structure their relationships (McLean 2004; Ritchie and Barker 2006; Wosick-Correa 2010). Absent readily available role models, those seeking to establish consensually non-monogamous relationships are often required to improvise, experiment, and explore in order to find a configuration that suits them. Verbal communication and negotiation facilitate the exploration and help to make sense of the outcomes, further modifying relationship agreements, skills, and strategies through continued conversation (Parsons et al. 2012; Ritchie and Barker 2006).

13.2.3 Focus on Emotions

Much of the communication referenced above revolves around emotions: what people are feeling, why, how they want to deal with the emotions, how others are feeling in response to how the first person was feeling, etc. Scholars identify emotions as crucial to the construction of a polyamorous identify (Deri 2015; Ritchie and Barker 2006; Wosick-Correa 2010), and it figures prominently in community discussions of lived polyamorous experiences. Love, desire, and jealousy take especially important, and related, roles in these academic and community discussions.

Love and Desire Non-monogamous relationships allow and encourage connections among multiple partners. For some—especially common among mainstream swingers—these connections are restricted to sexual desire (rather than emotional connection) and the exploration of sexual variety, with emotions like love reserved for the core dyad/primary partner/spouse (Phillips 2007). Others, like polyamorists, seek love as a key component of their multiple relationships and wait to have sex until they are emotionally involved (Sheff 2005, 2014a). Hidalgo et al. (2008) troubled the "dyadic imaginary" by pointing out that love need not be dyadic; further, they note how our culture's tendency to idealize dyadic love serves to render all non-dyadic intimacy and sexual relationships both invisible and illegitimate. Still others like those in open or anarchic relationships refuse rules and categories, refraining from distinguishing or limiting relationships by categorizing them. Cook (2005) documented levels of commitment in polyamorous relationships, connecting love with willingness to tolerate conflict and sustain poly relationships through transitions, and Sheff's (2014) research confirmed those findings linking love with commitment and relationship durability.

Relationship anarchists on the other hand, refuse to recognize love or sex-based relationships as any more meaningful than aromantic or asexual relationships such as close friendships (Autumn 2014; Crosswell 2014; Nordgren 2006). They place no hierarchy or value on these relationships while also recognizing that love is not limited to romantic coupledom—rather it is abundant and present in many relationship structures (Autumn 2014; Crosswell 2014; Nordgren 2006).

Jealousy One of the main arguments for monogamy is that it abates jealousy because lovers are exclusively relating with each other and refrain from sexual contact with others. In practice, jealousy is common in monogamous relationships as well, because the level of cheating and popularity of serial monogamy mean that even people in theoretically or currently monogamous relationships often doubt each others' actual or future sexual fidelity.

Non-monogamists use a range of techniques to deal with jealousy, with widely varying results. Some (especially the monogamish, swingers, and open relators) employ a "don't ask, don't tell" strategy and thus attempt to avoid jealousy by avoiding knowledge of any outside encounters. Others go to the other extreme in their attempt to avoid jealousy by being present at each sexual encounter together; even if they are interacting separately with other people they always do so in full view and with the approval of their primary partner. Polyamory community lore counsels people to be aware that jealousy will probably

occur, and rather than trying to make their partners do something to make the jealousy go away, polys often try to "work through" their jealousy, identifying the fear, insecurity, or unmet need at the root of the jealousy and addressing that issue rather than the jealousy itself, which is cast as a reflection of the real issue underneath.

Much of the literature on jealousy is directed to therapists who counsel non-monogamous clients through their attempts to deal with their own jealousy, or questions the meaning of or necessity for and alternatives to jealousy (Easton and Hardy 2011; Fierman and Poulsen 2014; Labriola 2013). Deri (2015) focuses on queer women's experiences of jealousy and "polyagony" in polyamorous relationships, finding that respondents were able to use specific norms, etiquette, tools, and strategies to cultivate compersion, which is "the feeling of taking joy in the joy that others you love share among themselves, especially taking joy in the knowledge that you beloveds are expressing love for one another" (p. 32).

13.3 Theories of Non-Monogamy

As with many other studies on sexuality, theories that complement qualitative data are popular among scholars examining non-monogamy, especially Social Constructionism, Feminisms, and Queer Theory. While we present them as distinct categories below, multiple works could appear in more than one category, and indeed many theorists use more than one of these complementary theories.

13.3.1 Social Constructionism

The general tone of much of the published research on non-monogamies has a social constructionist tenor, if not explicitly identifying as social constructionism per se. Many of the research pieces in Barker and Langdridge's (2010) edited volume *Understanding Non-Monogamies* rely on an implicitly social constructionist understanding, though the theory section of that same tome takes a decidedly queer theoretical approach.

Klesse (2005) examines social constructions of bisexual non-monogamous women as promiscuous and worthy of special social stigma, as well as the discourses associated with polyamory (Klesse 2012). Numerous scholars examine the social construction of monogamy, with Conley et al. (2013) critiquing contemporary constructions of monogamy as inconsistent and vague, and suggesting that monogamy is often less beneficial than popular thought would imply. Munson and Stelboum (1999) are similarly critical of monogamy and argue that most lesbian polyamorists are not at any greater risk than monogamous lesbians because of the low rates of woman-to-woman transmission of STIs. Wosick-Correa (2010) examined the ways in which polys "resist the master monogamous template" and constructed relationships based on emotional and sexual intimacy with multiple people.

13.3.2   Feminisms

Early anarchist feminists like Emma Goldman espoused revolutionary love and sexual freedom, rejecting the patriarchal requirement of female sexual fidelity and instead championing women loving whom and how they chose (Marso 2003; Rogness and Foust 2011). Later scholars took up a similar charge, critiquing monogamy and compulsory heterosexuality as crucial elements of a patriarchal ownership model that disadvantages women and benefits men (Robinson 1997), and a political regime that undermines women's freedom and self-determination. Some feminist scholars like Jackson and Scott (2003) wonder if feminism has lost its edge and become co-opted into believing that monogamy could be a good thing for women. Others apply well-recognized feminist concepts to non-monogamies. In her book on polyamorous families in Australia, Pallotta-Chiarolli (2010) uses the Latina feminist concept of the mestizaje (Anzaldua 1987; Moraga 1981) to theorize that polyamorous and bisexual families exist on the borders between monogamy and non-monogamy, heterosexuality and homosexuality.

13.3.3   Queer Theory

Perhaps the most prolific current theoretical trend in non-monogamies literature is queer theory, such as Schippers' (forthcoming) examination of compulsory monogamy and the subversive potential of non-monogamies to queer ostensibly monogamous political and social life. Similarly, Klesse (2012) explores the queer potential for gay and bisexual non-monogamous relationships. Non-monogamies provide rich fodder for queer theory because they have the potential to disturb traditional dichotomies such as fidelity/infidelity or heterosexuality/homosexuality (Barker and Langdridge 2010). Shannon and Willis (2010) suggest that queer theories and non-monogamies can provide anarchism with a more holistic and nuanced understanding of sexual freedom. Barker and Langdridge's (2010) edited volume takes a mostly queer theoretical approach with its section on theorizing non-monogamies that includes chapters focusing on the conditions of freedom in practices of non-monogamies (Finn 2010), "intimate privilege" in the public sphere (Rambukkana 2010), queering non-monogamy (Wilkinson 2010), and compulsory monogamy (Heckert 2010). Trahan (2014) posits "relational literacy" as the ability to sustain intimate relationships outside of accepted dichotomies, and ties non-monogamies to queer identities and the potential to destabilize mononormativity. Hidalgo et al. (2008) challenge the cultural primacy of the "dyadic imaginary" with their queer analysis of love in non-monogamous relationships.

13.4   Methods

Mainstream society in the United States continues to cast non-monogamy and those who practice it as deviant and pathological (Mint 2014). Thus, non-monogamous relationships are not as common as socially sanctioned monogamous relationship structures. Such trends marginalize non-monogamous practitioners, making them part of hidden and hard-to-reach populations and creating methodological barriers for researchers who hope to gain access to members of these communities. As such, researchers have primarily employed participant observation, as well as snowball and respondent-driven sampling methods which have proven the most effective and appropriate in locating populations with these characteristics (Babbie 2013). While these methods have enabled social scientists to locate and conduct research in these communities (Sheff 2007), the findings are not generalizable and tend to paint a somewhat homogenous picture of non-monogamy in terms of race, class, and education inequality—serving as another way to reproduce structural inequalities (Sheff and Hammers 2011).

Research on non-monogamies have had a recent resurgence, proliferating in the era of sexual liberation in the 1960s and 1970s, stagnating under the specter of HIV/AIDS in the 80s and 90s, and flourishing again in more recent decades (Barker and Landridge 2010). Much of the current research has focused on swinging, polyamory, and gay open relationships—offering comparisons of non-monogamy to monogamy, highlighting the ways that non-monogamy is either superior or inferior to monogamy, identifying the specific ways in which non-monogamy forms differ from one another (e.g., how is swinging different from polyamory), using autoethnography to explore non-monogamy (Aoki 2005; Sheff 2007), and examining the rules and boundaries managed by non-monogamous practitioners (Barker and Landridge 2010). Methodologically, the majority of research utilizes survey research and face-to-face interviews (Barker and Landridge 2010) or focus groups (Ritchie and Barker 2005). However, because of societal stigma and hesitancy of those who are members of marginalized communities to engage in face-to-face research (Fernandes 2009; Jenks 1998), there has been a surge of Internet-based research on sexual non-conformist communities (Sheff and Hammers 2011; Weber 2002; Weitzman 2006). These online methods can provide respondents with a sense of anonymity which, in turn, encourages honest and candid participation (Fernandes 2009).

The Internet has proven an effective tool, both for sexual non-conformists and for those who wish to research them (Sheff and Hammers 2011). Sexual non-conformists were once secluded from others like themselves; now, with the click of a button, they can connect, network, and learn the ins-and-outs of their respective communities (Sheff and Hammers 2011; Weinrich 1997). Similarly, researchers are now able to utilize various Internet resources to gain access to these once hidden communities. However, despite the benefits offered by the Internet, it also serves as a means through which inequality can be reproduced in detrimental ways (Sheff and Hammers 2011). For instance, studies show that certain segments of the population are more or less likely to own or use a computer, let alone have Internet access (Mossberger et al. 2008; Ono and Zavodny 2003; Sheff and Hammers 2011). Those who do have Internet access tend to be white, middle-class, and well educated (Sheff and Hammers 2011; Warf and Grimes 1997), though as web technology pervades society this appears to be changing. Even so, racial trends in web use tend not only to foster homogenous online communities of non-monogamous practitioners, but also result in research that reflects these demographic traits and experiences—possibly offering a biased lens into the lives of non-monogamous individuals as a whole. Sheff and Hammers (2011) contend that scholars must take precautions and make efforts to diminish such biases in the research so as to offer a more holistic view into the subjective and complex lives of non-monogamous practitioners as a whole. Additional methodological considerations include the difficulty of knowing the true boundaries of an Internet sample. When researchers recruit "polyamorists," only people who identify as such are likely to respond (Sheff 2014d). These studies miss the entire population of those who eschew identification, are unfamiliar with terminology, or think it does not apply in their case. Finally, researchers have no control over conditions of completion of online surveys, which can produce even higher rates of missing data (see Paik, Chap. 6, this volume).

13.5 Directions for Future Research

As evidenced by this and many other volumes, expanding relational and sexual diversity appear to be hallmarks of this era. This trend has grown to include non-monogamies, which are now becoming an important component of many other kinds of relationships. Future research would do well to examine the numbers and types of non-monogamists, diversity among non-monogamists, and their relationship outcomes.

13.5.1 Numbers and Types

Counting and distinguishing non-monogamists can be deceptively difficult. Even defining identity categories and distinguishing them from other forms of non-monogamy is difficult for academicians and community members alike. Beyond the difficulty of defining identity categories lies the challenge of determining who is authorized to enforce the definition. Does a researcher have the right to determine that someone is in an open relationship because they meet the criteria, even if that person does not self-identify as such? What about a couple who thinks of themselves as swingers, but swings with the same friends for years and years, falling in love with each other and raising children together? They fit the polyamorous ideal, but should they count as poly even though they identify as swingers? Who gets to decide?

Even once researchers decide whom to count, it is a challenge to find them. Like many other sexual minorities, non-monogamists have good reason to hide their relationships from the general public because being exposed as sexually or relationally unconventional can mean loss of employment, housing, relationships with friends and families of origin, or custody of children (Sheff and Hammers 2011). With so much to lose, it is no surprise that non-monogamists and other sexual or relational non-conformists sometimes remain closeted.

There is also no reliable way to count non-monogamists at this point. As of yet, no one has been able to collect data about the prevalence and diversity of non-monogamies on a nationally representative sample of people from any nation. While numerous studies have used representative samples to measure attitudes towards and (to a lesser extent) personal experiences with adultery or cheating, none have measured consensual non-monogamies such as polyamory, polygamy, or swinging. In addition to lack of funding and stigma against sexuality research, another hurdle facing those who want to measure the number of non-monogamists in a representative sample is the youth of the research body. As of yet there is no established standard question or module that has been proven to reliably measure the incidence of and attitudes towards non-monogamy, although the Non-Monogamies Collective from Poly Researchers constructed a module that it is attempting to test online.[2]

Much of the current research on CNM and other marginalized sexualities relies on the Internet or word of mouth to recruit participants—neither of which provide a random sample or access the full range of people in a given category. Even though the Internet is much more widely accessible than it was even 10 years ago, collecting data from online samples will still slant it towards white middle class people who have access to high speed Internet services and the privacy to visit sites that might be blocked by the filters on public library servers.

13.5.2 Diversity Among Practitioners

The previously mentioned paucity of knowledge regarding people of color and working class people (Sheff and Hammers 2011) remains an issue that future research must address. In addition to diversifying the racial and ethnic composition of their respondent samples, researchers should also consider including more diverse people in

---

[2] The GSS Non-Monogamies Collective submitted a module to the General Social Survey for the 2016 survey. While the module was not selected for inclusion in the GSS, researchers are attempting to pilot-test it online and eventually establish its reliability in order to resubmit it to additional surveys. Please contact Elisabeth Sheff at drelisheff@gmail.com for more information.

their studies with a wider range of ages, sexual orientations, (dis)abilities, religions, and nationalities. The free-love generation who sparked non-monogamous communities and practices are now aging into retirement and beyond, with unknown consequences for their lives, families, health, and society at large. Studying aging among non-monogamists could provide useful information to health care providers, family services, and demographers alike. Non-monogamy has been comparatively well-explored among gay men (Andrews 2014; Hosking 2013; Parsons and Starks 2014) and heterosexual couples (Bergstrand and Sinski 2010; Fernandes 2009; Gould 1999), but research on lesbians, bisexuals, and other sexual orientations remains sparse and should be expanded. Research on the intersection of non-monogamy and disability is a burgeoning but still under-researched area. Thus far, studies indicate that non-monogamous families can find multiple partners extremely useful when dealing with issues surrounding family members' disabilities (Sheff 2014a). In sum, research on non-monogamies must expand to include a broader range of practitioners in a wider variety of relationships.

13.6 Relationship Outcomes

Not only should consensual non-monogamies be compared with monogamous relationships, but non-monogamies should be compared with each other in order to determine the utility, health, and durability of non-monogamous relationships. Longitudinal research on how long different kinds of non-monogamous relationships last and in what form, as well as various forms of non-monogamy impact members' health, happiness, parenting, and overall wellbeing would provide valuable insight into both monogamous and non-monogamous relationships. Such research is scant right now (Pallotta-Chiarolli 2010; Sheff 2014a, c), but the critical mass of research practice and interest in non-monogamies is likely to shift that in the coming years. As more studies examine non-monogamies, they will reveal patterns in various relationship forms and indicate

strategies that monogamists can adopt to deal with their own relational complexities.

References

Anapol, D. (2010). *Polyamory in the 21st century: Love and intimacy with multiple partners*. Lanham: Rowman & Littlefield Publishers.

Andrews, P. (2014). How gay men make decisions about the place of extra-relational sex in their committed relationships. *Psychotherapy in Australia, 20*(3), 40.

Anzaldua, G. (1987). *Borderlands/La Frontera: The New Mestiza*. San Francisco: Aunt Lute Books.

Aoki, E. (2005). Coming out as "we 3:" Using personal ethnography and the case study to assess relational identity and parental support of gay male three-partner relationships. *Journal of GLBT Family Studies, 1*(2), 29–48.

Autumn. (2014). Relationship anarchy is not polyamory. Multiple Match: Create Your Open Relationship. http://www.multiplematch.com/2013/12/relationship-anarchy-is-not-polyamory/. Accessed 22 June 2014.

Babbie, E. (2013). *The practice of social research*. Belmont: Wadsworth.

Barker, M., & Landridge, D. (2010). Whatever happened to non-monogamies? Critical reflections on recent research and theory. *Sexualities, 13*(6), 748–772.

Bartell, G. (1970). Group sex among the mid-Americans. *Journal of Sex Research, 6*(2), 113–130.

Bartell, G. (1971). *Group sex: An eyewitness report on the American way of swinging*. New York: Wyden.

Bergstrand, C., & Sinski, J. (2010). *Swinging in America: Love, sex, and marriage in the 21st century*. Santa Barbara: ABC-CLIO LLC.

Bergstrand, C., & Williams, J. (2000). Today's alternative marriage styles: The case of swingers. *Electronic Journal of Human Sexuality, 3*. http://www.ejhs.org/volume3/swing/bo dy.htm. Accessed 28 Dec 2014.

Block, J. (2008). *Open: Love, sex, and life in an open marriage*. Berkeley: Seal Press.

Bornstein, K. (1994). *Gender outlaw: On men, women, and the rest of us*. New York: Vintage.

Brines, J., & Joyner, K. (1999). The ties that bind: Principles of cohesion in cohabitation and marriage. *American Sociological Review, 64*, 333–365.

Brown, K. (2012). *Becoming sister wives: The story of an unconventional marriage*. New York: Gallery Books.

Butler, E. (1979). *Traditional marriage and emerging alternatives*. New York: Harper and Row.

Butler, J. (1990). *Gender trouble: Feminism and the subversion of identity*. New York: Routledge.

Butterworth, M. (2009). *Attachment and polyamory: The attachment hierarchies of adults with multiple romantic partners* (Doctoral dissertation). Salt Lake City: The University of Utah.

Carr, D. (2010). Cheating hearts. *Contexts, 9*(3), 58–60.

Conley, T. D., Moors, A. C., Ziegler, A., & Karathanasis, C. (2012). Unfaithful individuals are less likely to practice safer sex than openly non-monogamous individuals. *Journal of Sexual Medicine, 9*(6), 1559–1565.

Conley, T. D., Moors, A. C., Matsick, J. L., & Ziegler, A. (2013). The fewer the merrier? Assessing stigma surrounding consensually non-monogamous romantic relationships. *Analyses of Social Issues and Public Policy, 13*(1), 1–30.

Constantine, L., & Constantine, J. (1973). *Group marriage: A study of contemporary multilateral marriage.* New York: Macmillan.

Cook, E. S. (2005). *Commitment in polyamorous relationships.* (Doctoral dissertation). Denver: Regis University.

Cossman, B. (2006). The new politics of adultery. *Columbia Journal of Gender and Law, 15,* 274.

Crosswell, M. (2014). Relationship anarchy basics. The Good Men Project. http://goodmenproject.com/gender-sexuality/relationship-anarchy-basics-jvinc/. Accessed 22 June 2014.

Dalton, J., & Leung, T. C. (2014). Why is polygyny more prevalent in Western Africa? An African slave trade perspective. *Economic Development & Cultural Change, 62*(4), 599–632.

Daly, M. (1985). *Beyond God the father: Toward a philosophy of women's liberation.* Boston: Beacon Press.

Denfeld, D., & Gordon, M. (1970). The sociology of mate swapping: Or the family that swings together clings together. *The Journal or Sex Research, 6*(2), 85–100.

Deri, J. (2015). *Love's refraction: Jealousy and compersion in queer women's polyamorous relationships.* Toronto: University of Toronto Press.

Drigotas, S., & Barta, W. (2001). The cheating heart: Scientific explorations of Infidelity. *Current Directions in Psychological Science, 10*(5), 177–180.

Du Bois, S. (2013). *Examining partnership and health in multiple samples of gay and bisexual Men* (Doctoral dissertation). Chicago: University of Illinois at Chicago.

D'Emilio, J. (1983). *Sexual politics, sexual communities: The making of a homosexual minority in the United States, 1940–1970.* Chicago: University of Chicago Press.

Easton, D., & Hardy, J. W. (2011). *The ethical slut: A practical guide to polyamory, open relationships, and other adventures.* Random House, LLC.

Ellis, A. (1970). Group marriage: A possible alternative? In H. A. Otto (Ed.), *The family in search of a future.* New York: Appleton-Century-Crofts.

Ember, M., Ember, C., & Low, B. (2007). Comparing explanations of polygyny. *Cross-Cult Research, 41,* 428–440.

Fang, B. (1976). Swinging: In retrospect. *Journal of Sex Research, 12*(3), 220–237.

Ferree, M., & Hess, B. (1994). *Controversy and coalition: The new feminist movement.* Boston: Twayne-G.K. Hall & Co.

Fernandes, E. (2009). The swinging paradigm: An evaluation of the marital and sexual satisfaction of swingers. *Electronic Journal of Human Sexuality, 12.* http://www.ejhs.org/Volume12/Swinging2.htm. Accessed 28 Dec 2014.

Fierman, D. M., & Poulsen, S. S. (2014). Open relationships: A culturally and clinically sensitive approach. In T. Nelson & H. Winawer (Eds.), *Critical topics in family therapy: AFTA monograph series highlights* (pp. 151–161). Heidelberg: Springer International Publishing.

Finn, M. (2010). Conditions of freedom in practices of non-monogamous commitment. In M. Barker & D. Landridge (Eds.), *Understanding non-monogamies* (pp. 225–236). New York: Routledge.

Flanigan, W., & Zingdale, N. (1991). *Political behavior of the American electorate.* Washington, DC: CQ Press.

Frank, K. (2013). *Plays well in groups: A journey through the world of group sex.* Lanham: Rowman and Littlefield.

Fry, A. (2010). Polygamy in America: How the varying legal standards fail to protect mothers and children from its abuses. *Saint Louis University Law Journal, 54,* 967–1439.

Gagnon, J. H., & Simon, W. (2011). *Sexual Conduct: The Social Sources of Human Sexuality.* Piscataway: Transaction Publishers.

Gilmartin, B. G. (1975). That swinging couple down the block. *Psychology Today, 8,* 54–58.

Goldfeder, M., & Sheff, E. (2013). Children of polyamorous families: A first empirical look. *Journal of Law and Social Deviance, 5,* 150–243.

Goldstein, M. (1987). When brothers share a wife. *Natural History, 96*(3), 109–112.

Gould, T. (1999). *The lifestyle: A look at the erotic rites of swingers.* Buffalo: Firefly.

Grov, C., Starks, T. J., Rendina, H. J., & Parsons, J. (2014). Rules about casual sex partners, relationship satisfaction, and HIV risk in partnered gay and bisexual men. *Journal of Sex & Marital Therapy, 40*(2), 105–122.

Hassinger, B., & Kruger, D. (2013). The polygyny paradox: Several male biased populations exhibit a high prevalence of polygyny. *Journal of the Evolutionary Studies Consortium, 5,* 131–137.

Hidalgo, D. A., Barber, K., & Hunter, E. (2008). The dyadic imaginary: Troubling the perception of love as dyadic. *Journal of Bisexuality, 7*(3-4), 171–189.

Heckert, J. (2010). Love without borders? Intimacy, identity, and the state of compulsory monogamy. In M. Barker & D. Landridge (Eds.), *Understanding non-monogamies* (pp. 255–266). New York: Routledge.

Henshel, A. (1973). Swinging: A study of decision making in marriage. *American Journal of Sociology, 4,* 885–891.

Hosking, W. (2013). Satisfaction with open sexual agreements in Australian gay men's relationships: The role of perceived discrepancies in benefit. *Archives of Sexual Behavior, 42*(7), 1309–1317.

Ho, P. S. Y. (2006). The (charmed) circle game: Reflections on sexual hierarchy through multiple sexual relationships. *Sexualities, 9*(5), 547–564.

Jackson, S., & Scott, S. (2003). Whatever happened to feminist critiques of monogamy? In H. Graham, A. Kaloski, A. Neilson, & E. Robertson (Eds.), *The feminist seventies* (pp. 112–134). York: Raw Nerve Books.

Jenks, R. (1985). Swinging: A replication and test of a theory. *Journal of Sex Research, 21*(2), 199–205.

Jenks, R. (1998). Swinging: A review of the literature. *Archives of Sexual Behavior, 27*(5), 507–521.

Klesse, C. (2005). Bisexual women, non-monogamy and differentialist anti-promiscuity discourses. *Sexualities, 8*(4), 445–464.

Klesse, C. (2012). *The spectre of promiscuity: Gay male and bisexual non-monogamies and polyamories.* England: Ashgate Publishing Limited.

Labriola, K. (1999). Models of open relationships. In M. Munson & J. Stelboum (Eds.), *The lesbian polyamory reader: Open relationships, non-monogamy, and casual sex* (pp. 217–225). New York: Routledge.

Labriola, K. (2013). *The jealousy workbook: Exercises and insights for managing open relationships.* San Francisco: Greenery Press.

Levitt, E. (1988). Alternative lifestyle and marital satisfaction: A brief report. *Annual Review of Sex Research, 1,* 455–461.

Marso, L. J. (2003). A feminist search for love: Emma Goldman on the politics of marriage, love, sexuality and the feminine. *Feminist Theory, 4*(3), 305–320.

Matsick, J. L., Conley, T. D., Ziegler, A., Moors, A. C., & Rubin, J. D. (2013). Love and sex: polyamorous relationships are perceived more favourably than swinging and open relationships. *Psychology & Sexuality*, (ahead-of-print), 1–10.

McCombs, B. (2014). Utah to appeal ruling in 'Sister Wives' case. Washington Times. http://www.washingtontimes.com/news/2014/sep/25/utah-to-appeal-ruling-in-sister-wives-case/ Accessed 1 Jan 2015.

McLean, K. (2004). Negotiating (non) monogamy: Bisexuality and intimate relationships. *Journal of Bisexuality, 4*(1–2), 83–97.

Mint, P. (2014). The power dynamics of cheating: Effects on polyamory and bisexuality. *Journal of Bisexuality, 4*(3-4), 55–76.

Moller, N., & Vossler, A. (2014). Defining infidelity in research and couple counseling: A qualitative study. *Journal of Sex & Marital Therapy, 11,* 1–11.

Moraga, C. (1981). *This bridge called my back: Writings by radical women of color.* New York: Kitchen Table, Women of Color Press.

Mossberger, K., Tolbert, C., & McNeal, R. (2008). *Digital citizenship: The internet, society, and participation.* Cambridge: MIT Press.

Mulder, M. B. (2009). Serial monogamy as polygyny or polyandry? *Human Nature, 20*(2), 130–150.

Munson, M., & Stelboum, J. (1999). *The lesbian polyamory reader: Open relationships, non-monogamy, and casual sex.* New York: Routledge.

North American Swing Club Association. (2014). North American Swing Club Association FAQs. The Lifestyle Organization. http://www.nasca.com. Accessed 27 June 2014.

Nelson, S. (2013). 'Sister Wives' defeat polygamy law in federal court. US News. http://www.usnews.com/news/articles/2013/12/16/sister-wives-defeat-polygamy-law-in-federal-court. Accessed 27 June 2014.

Noël, M. J. (2006). Progressive polyamory: Considering issues of diversity. *Sexualities, 9*(5), 602–620.

Nordgren, A. (2006). The short instructional manifesto for relationship anarchy. The Anarchist Library. http://theanarchistlibrary.org/library/andie-nordgren-the-short-instructional-manifesto-for-relationship-anarchy. Accessed 22 June 2014.

Ono, H., & Zavodny, M. (2003). Race, internet usage and E-commerce." *The Review of Black Political Econmy, 30* (Winter), 7–22.

O'Neill, N., & O'Neill, G. (1972). *Open marriage: A new life style for couples.* New York: M. Evans and Co.

Pallotta-Chiarolli, M. (2010). *Border sexualities, border families in schools.* Lanham: Rowman & Littlefield.

Parsons, J. T., & Starks, T. J. (2014). Drug use and sexual arrangements among gay couples: Frequency, interdependence, and associations with sexual risk. *Archives of Sexual Behavior, 43*(1), 89–98.

Parsons, J. T., Starks, T. J., Gamarel, K. E., & Grov, C. (2012). Non-monogamy and sexual relationship quality among same-sex male couples. *Journal of Family Psychology, 26*(5), 669–677.

Parsons, J. T., Starks, T. J., DuBois, S., Grov, C., & Golub, S. A. (2013). Alternatives to monogamy among gay male couples in a community survey: Implications for mental health and sexual risk. *Archives of Sexual Behavior, 42*(2), 303–312.

Phillips, S. (2007). There were three in bed: Discursive desire and the sex lives of swingers (Doctoral thesis, Memorial University of Newfoundland: New Foundland and Labrador, Canada).

Plummer, K. (2011). The Labeling perspective forty years on. In H. Peters & M. Dellwing (Eds.), *Langweiliges Verbrechen: Warum KriminologInnen den Umgang mit Kriminalität interessanter finden als Kriminalität* (pp. 83–101). Germany: Springer.

Politi, D. (2013). Federal judge effectively decriminalizes polygamy in Utah. *Slate.* http://www.slate.com/blogs/the_slatest/2013/12/15/federal_judge_effectively_decriminalizes_polygamy_in_utah.html. Accessed 27 June 2014.

Popenoe, D. (1993). American family decline, 1960–1990: A review and appraisal. *Journal of Marriage and the Family, 55*(3), 527–542.

Rambukkana, N. (2010). Sex, space and discourse: Non/monogamy and intimate privilege in the public sphere. In M. Barker & D. Landridge (Eds.), *Understanding non-monogamies* (pp. 237–242). New York: Routledge.

Ritchie, A., & Barker. M. (2005). Explorations in feminist participant-led research: Conducting focus group discussion with polyamorous women. *Psychology of Women Section Review, 7*(2), 47–57.

Ritchie, A., & Barker, M. (2006). "There aren't words for what we do or how we feel so we have to make them up:" Constructing polyamorous languages in a culture of compulsory monogamy. *Sexualities, 9*(5), 584–601.

Robinson, V. (1997). My baby just cares for me: Feminism, heterosexuality and non-monogamy. *Journal of Gender Studies, 6*(2), 143–157.

Rogness, K. Z., & Foust, C. R. (2011). Beyond rights and virtues as foundation for women's agency: Emma Goldman's rhetoric of free love. *Western Journal of Communication Studies, 75*(2), 148–167.

Rubin, G. (1993). Thinking sex: Notes for a radical theory of the politics of sexuality. In H. Abelove & M. A. Barale (Eds.), *The lesbian and gay studies reader* (pp. 3–44). New York: Routledge.

Savage, D. (2011). Monogamish. *The Stranger.* http://www.thestranger.com. Accessed 15 Jan 2015.

Schippers, M. (Forthcoming). *PolyQueer: Compulsory monogamy and the queer potential of plural sexualities.* New York: New York University Press.

Shannon, D., & Willis, A. (2010). Theoretical polyamory: Some thoughts on loving, thinking, and queering anarchism. *Sexualities, 13*(4), 433–443.

Sheff, E. (2005). *Gender, family, and sexuality: Exploring polyamorous community* (Doctoral dissertation). Boulder: University of Colorado at Boulder.

Sheff, E. (2007). The reluctant polyamorist: Auto-ethnographic research in a sexualized setting. In M. Stomber, D. Baunach, E. Burgess, D. Donnelly, & W. Simonds (Eds.), *Sex matters: The sexuality and society reader* (2nd ed., pp. 111–118). Boston: Allyn & Bacon.

Sheff, E. (2011). Polyamorous families, same-sex marriage, and the slippery slope. *Journal of Contemporary Ethnography, 40*(5), 487–520.

Sheff, E. (2013). Solo polyamory, singleish, single & poly. Psychology Today. http://www.psychologytoday.com/blog/the-polyamorists-next-door/201310/solo-polyamory-singleish-single-poly. Accessed 6 Jan 2015.

Sheff, E. (2014a). *The polyamorists next door: Inside multiple partner relationships and families.* Lanham: Rowman and Littlefield.

Sheff, E. (2014b). Not necessarily broken: Redefining success when polyamorous relationships end. In S. Newmahr & T. Weinberg (Eds.), *Selves, symbols and sexualities: Contemporary readings* (pp. 201–214). Thousand Oaks: Sage.

Sheff, E. (2014c). The future of (non and serial) monogamy. Psychology Today. http://www.psychologytoday.com/blog/the-polyamorists-next-door/201404/the-future-non-and-serial-monogamy. Accessed 6 Jan 2015.

Sheff, E. (2014d). How many polyamorists are there in the United States? Psychology Today. http://www.psychologytoday.com/blog/the-polyamorists-next-door/201405/how-many-polyamorists-are-there-in-the-us. Accessed 11 Jan 2015.

Sheff, E., & Hammers, C. (2011). The privilege of perversities: Race, class, and education among polyamorists and kinksters. *Psychology & Sexuality, 2*(3), 198–223.

Smith, J., & Smith, L. (1974). *Beyond monogamy: Recent studies of sexual alternatives in marriage.* Baltimore: The Johns Hopkins University Press.

Stacey, J. (1996). *In the name of the family: Rethinking family values in the postmodern age.* Boston: Beacon Press.

Talese, G. (1980). *Thy neighbor's wife.* New York: Dell Publishing.

Taormino, T. (2008). *Opening up: A guide to creating and sustaining open relationships.* San Francisco: Cleis Press Inc.

Trahan, H. A. (2014). Relationship literacy and polyamory: A queer approach. Dissertation, Bowling Green: Bowling Green State University.

Tolman, D. (2002). *Dilemmas of desire: Teenage girls talk about sexuality.* Boston: Harvard University Press.

Treas, J., & Giesen, D. (2000). Sexual infidelity among married and cohabiting Americans. *Journal of Marriage & Family, 62*(1), 48–60.

Trevithick, A. (1997). On a panhuman preference for monandry: Is polyandry an exception? *Journal of Comparative Family Studies, 28*(3), 154–181.

Veaux, F., & Rickert, E. (2014). *More than two: A practical guide to ethical polyamory.* Portland: Thorntree Press.

Warf, B., & Grimes, J. (1997). Counterhegemonic discourses and the internet. *Geographical Review, 87*(2), 259–274.

Weber, A. (2002). Survey results: Who are we? And other interesting impressions. *Loving More Magazine, 30,* 4–6.

Weeks, J. (1985). *Sexuality and its discontents: Meanings, myths, and modern sexualities.* London: Routledge.

Weinrich, J. (1997). Strange bedfellows: Homosexuality, gay liberation, and the internet. *Journal of Sex Education & Therapy, 22*(1), 58–66.

Weitzman, G. (2006). Therapy with clients who are bisexual and polyamorous. *Journal of Bisexuality, 6*(1/2), 137–164.

Wilkinson, E. (2010). What's queer about non-monogamy? In M. Barker & D. Landridge (Eds.), *Understanding non-monogamies* (pp. 243–254). New York: Routledge.

Willey, A. (2006). "Christian nations," "polygamic races" and women's rights: Toward a genealogy of non/monogamy and whiteness. *Sexualities, 9*(5), 530–546.

Wosick-Correa, K. (2010). Agreements, rules and agentic fidelity in polyamorous relationships. *Psychology & Sexuality, 1*(1), 44–61.

Yoder, J. D., & Nichols, R. C. (1980). A life perspective comparison of married and divorced persons. *The Journal of Marriage and Family, 42,* 413–419.

Sexuality in Long-Term Relationships

14

Amy C. Lodge

Sex is a key component of long-term relationships; research consistently links higher levels of sexual frequency (DeLamater et al. 2008; DeLamater and Moorman 2007), sexual satisfaction (DeLamater et al. 2008; Gott and Hinchliff 2003b; Sprecher and Cate 2004), sexual desire (Skultety 2007), and an absence of sexual dysfunction (Laumann et al. 2008) to greater relationship satisfaction and stability (Sprecher and Cate 2004). The causal relationships between these variables are likely bidirectional (Sprecher and Cate 2004). For example, one longitudinal study found that sexual satisfaction positively influences marital quality (Yeh et al. 2006), yet it is just as likely the case that higher levels of relationship satisfaction lead to more satisfying and frequent sexual interactions (Sprecher and Cate 2004). In short, the quality and frequency of sexual experiences are an integral part of long-term relationships.

Most studies on sex in long-term couples, particularly those based on survey research, rely on measures of vaginal intercourse (although sometimes oral and anal sex are measured) (Lodge and Umberson forthcoming; Peplau et al. 2004). This is problematic, however, for a few reasons. First, although some studies suggest that heterosexual couples consider only penetrative, vaginal intercourse to be "real sex" (Lodge and Umberson

2012; Waite and Das 2010), other studies suggest that when vaginal intercourse is either not possible or desired, couples redefine the meaning of sexuality to include other physically intimate experiences (e.g., kissing, holding hands, cuddling) (Gott and Hinchliff 2003a, b; Lodge and Umberson 2012). Second, survey questions that ask about instances of "intercourse" may not adequately measure lesbian sexuality, and as a result estimates of sexual frequency in lesbian couples may be inaccurately low (Peplau et al. 2004). There is therefore a need for future studies to develop more inclusive and expansive measures of sexuality in long-term relationships.

Definitions of long-term relationships also vary, although many studies define long-term relationships as those lasting at least 7 years or more, based on the fact that the median marital duration for heterosexual divorcing couples is 7 years (Elliott and Umberson 2008; Lodge and Umberson 2012). Similar standards have been used to define long-term gay and lesbian cohabiting couples (Umberson et al. 2015b), although given that relationship duration may vary among different couple types (i.e., married versus cohabiting; gay versus lesbian versus heterosexual) (Moore and Stambolis-Ruhstorfer 2013), it is unclear if this is an appropriate benchmark for all types of relationships.

In this chapter, I first summarize the current state of knowledge on sexuality in long-term relationships. Second, I discuss the leading methodological approaches to studying sex in long-term relationships and suggest innovative

A. C. Lodge (✉)
Center for Social Work Research, University of Texas, 1717 W. 6th St. Suite 310 Austin TX 78703, USA
e-mail: AmyLodge@utexas.edu

J. DeLamater, R.F. Plante (eds.), *Handbook of the Sociology of Sexualities,* Handbooks of Sociology and Social Research, DOI 10.1007/978-3-319-17341-2_14, © Springer International Publishing Switzerland 2015

methods for future research. Third, I discuss limitations of existing research on this topic and suggest directions for future research. The majority of research on sex in long-term relationships is descriptive and based on survey measures of sexual frequency, sexual satisfaction, sexual desire, and sexual dysfunction. Further, most research on this topic focuses on individuals in heterosexual marital relationships and as a result little is known about how individuals in other types of long-term relationships experience sex. As I discuss in this chapter, there is a need for more theoretically-informed studies on sex in long-term relationships, qualitative studies, dyadic research (i.e., research that studies both partners in a relationship), research on non-heterosexual relationships, non-marital relationships, and research on how social class and racial/ethnic diversity shape experiences of sex in long-term relationships.

14.1   Literature Review

14.1.1   Why Sex Matters for Relationships

Numerous studies suggest that sex is an integral component of same- and different-sex long-term relationships. Most couples remain sexually active into deep old age (Lindau et al. 2007), and the quantity and quality of sexual activities are linked to several indicators of relationship quality—including relationship satisfaction, feelings of love, commitment, and relationship stability (Sprecher and Cate 2004). Causal direction for these variables has been difficult to determine, although it is likely that these associations are bidirectional—individuals who are happier in their relationships are also more likely to have more frequent and satisfying sexual interactions at the same time that frequent and satisfying sexual interactions reinforce individuals' positive feelings about their partner and relationship (Lodge and Umberson forthcoming; Sprecher and Cate 2004). However, it is important to note that some long-term relationships are characterized by infrequent or nonexistent sexual activity or low levels of sexual satisfaction, but high levels of relationship satisfaction (and vice versa); more

research is needed on these "outlier" couples (Sprecher and Cate 2004).

14.1.2   Descriptive Studies

Kinsey et al. (1948, 1953) pioneered research on human sexuality. As a result, most contemporary social science research reflects this Kinseyian tradition in that is descriptive and survey-based, focusing most often on sexual frequency, levels of sexual satisfaction and sexual desire, sexual attitudes and recently—alongside what has been termed the "medicalization of sex" (Tiefer 1996)—incidence of sexual dysfunctions.

14.1.2.1   Sexual Frequency

Sexual frequency varies considerably in relationships, depending on a number of factors including relationship duration, age, union status (i.e., marital versus cohabiting relationship), and whether the relationship is composed of two men, two women, or a man and a woman. Most studies on sexual frequency in long-term relationships have focused on heterosexual marital relationships. Although estimates vary, studies based on nationally representative samples suggest that heterosexual married couples have sex on average between 6 and 7 times a month (Call et al. 1995; Laumann et al. 1994; Michael et al. 1994).

As previously noted, although most surveys ask about frequency of vaginal intercourse, other studies ask about the frequency of other sexual activities (Laumann et al. 1994). For example, data from the National Health and Social Life Survey (NHSLS) found that although most respondents reported having vaginal sex at the last instance of sex (95 %), 30 % reported having oral sex and 1 to 2 % reported having anal sex the last time they had sex (Laumann et al. 1994). Further, most respondents said they had engaged in oral sex at some point in their lifetime and 10 % reported engaging in anal sex at some point in their lifetime (Laumann et al. 1994). Blumstein and Schwartz (1983) found higher estimates of oral sex; their non-representative data suggested that 50 % of gay couples, 39 % of lesbian couples, and 30 % of heterosexual couples usually or always engage in oral sex. Laumann et al. (1994) also found that young adults, White adults, and adults with higher levels of education were more likely to report engaging in oral and anal sex, compared to older adults, Black and Hispanic adults, and individuals with lower levels of education. More recent data from the National Survey of Sexual Health and Behavior (NSSHB) indicate that more than 50 % of men and women ages 18–49 report having oral sex in the past year, while 20 % of men ages 25–49 and women ages 20–39 report having anal sex in the past year (Herbenick et al. 2010).

Numerous studies suggest that sexual frequency declines over time in all types of long-term relationships (Willetts et al. 2004). Research suggests that the most important reason for this decline is habituation—that is decreased interest in sex resulting from the predictability of sex with a particular partner (Call et al. 1995; Peplau et al. 2004). One study on marital duration and sexual frequency, however, found that the most precipitous decline in sexual frequency occurs during the first year of marriage (Call et al. 1995). This phenomenon is typically referred to as the "honeymoon effect," whereby levels of sexual frequency become more routine and predictable (Call et al. 1995).

In addition to habituation, age is a major reason that sexual frequency declines over time in long-term relationships (DeLamater and Moorman 2007; Kontula and Haavio-Mannila 2009; Lindau et al. 2007). For example, one study, using nationally representative survey data, found that whereas heterosexual married couples had sex on average 6.3 times per month, couples under the age of 24 reported having sex 11.7 times per month and the frequency of sex declined with each subsequent age group to 3 times a month for couples over the age of 65 (Call et al. 1995). However, while age is associated with a decline in vaginal and oral sex, age is not associated with frequency of kissing, hugging, caressing, and sexual touching (AARP 2005). Evidence further suggests that although cohort or generational differences may explain some of the decline in sexual frequency over the course of relationships (because older cohorts tend to engage in less sex in mid and later life than more recent cohorts), age is a more important predictor of sexual frequency

(DeLamater and Moorman 2007; Edwards and Booth 1994). Although some of the age-related decline in sexual frequency in long-term relationships stems from physical health problems experienced by one or both partners that limit sexual activity (DeLamater et al. 2008; DeLamater and Moorman 2007), age remains an independent and significant correlate of lower levels of sexual frequency in long-term relationships (Karraker and DeLamater 2013; Karraker et al. 2011).

Several studies suggest that sexual frequency varies by relationship type and union status. For example, gay male couples and heterosexual cohabiting couples have higher rates of sexual frequency than heterosexual married couples, who in turn have higher rates of sexual frequency than lesbian couples (Peplau et al. 2004; Willetts et al. 2004). It is not clear why these differences exist, although sexual frequency may be higher in cohabiting compared to marital relationships because of the less traditional characteristics of cohabiting relationships. It is also plausible that couples who have higher levels of sexual frequency are also couples who are less likely to marry. As discussed later in this chapter, differences in levels of sexual frequency between lesbian, gay, and heterosexual couples may stem from—in part—different gender compositions within these couples. Greater sexual frequency among gay couples, compared to heterosexual married couples, may also be attributable to the fact that gay couples have traditionally been denied access to the institution of marriage (given that cohabiting couples have higher levels of sexual frequency compared to married couples). In other words, it is plausible that cohabiting gay couples have higher rates of sexual frequency compared to married gay couples and because surveys have most often relied on samples of cohabiting gay couples that this may explain some of the difference in sexual frequency between gay couples and heterosexual married couples, although research has not explored this possibility.

Other factors associated with sexual frequency include relationship satisfaction (as previously discussed) (Sprecher and Cate 2004; Willetts et al. 2004) and gender (Willetts et al. 2004). In terms of gender, data from the NHSLS indicate that heterosexual married men report having sex (partnered or unpartnered) 6.9 times a month, compared to 6.5 times a month for heterosexual married women (Laumann et al. 1994; Michael et al. 1994). These differences may be due to gender differences in reporting (whereby men may overestimate sexual frequency and/or women may underestimate sexual frequency) and the fact that men may be more likely than women to have sex outside of the marital relationship (Willetts et al. 2004). Some studies also suggest that living in a rural area, being Catholic, and having a demanding job are associated with lower levels of sexual frequency, although race, ethnicity, social class, and religion generally do not appear to be correlated with levels of sexual frequency (Willetts et al. 2004).

14.1.2.2 Sexual Satisfaction

As previously noted sexual satisfaction is a key component of relationship satisfaction. Sexual satisfaction is rarely defined in the literature but instead is typically measured with one subjective question: "How satisfied are you with your sex life together?" (Schwartz and Young 2009). Levels of sexual satisfaction are positively related to levels of love, commitment, and relationship quality (Sprecher and Cate 2004). The causal relationship between these variables is not well established, although some longitudinal evidence suggests that changes in sexual satisfaction are linked to changes in relationship satisfaction (Sprecher 2002). Further, longitudinal evidence links lower levels of sexual satisfaction to subsequent relationship dissolution (Sprecher and Cate 2004). Indeed, given evidence that most people in committed relationships are sexually satisfied—Laumann et al. (1994) found that 88 % of heterosexual married respondents report being extremely or very sexually satisfied—it is likely that relationships wherein one or both partners are not sexual satisfied are less likely to last.

Sexual frequency is consistently correlated with levels of sexual satisfaction; individuals who have more frequent sex also report greater levels of sexual satisfaction (Smith et al. 2011; Sprecher and Cate 2004). Again, the causal direction of this relationship is unclear, but likely bidirectional. Individuals who have positive feelings about their sexual encounters are likely to want to have more frequent sex, at the same time that more frequent sex is likely to result in greater frequency of orgasm and in turn, greater sexual satisfaction.

Although sexual frequency predicts sexual satisfaction, and relationship duration and age are negatively related to sexual frequency, numerous studies find that age and relationship duration are not related to sexual satisfaction (McKinlay and Feldman 1994; Sprecher and Cate 2004; Ventegodt 1998). In terms of age, however, research has produced inconsistent results; some studies find that sexual satisfaction increases with age (Gullette 2011; Vares et al. 2007), while still other studies have found that sexual satisfaction declines with age (AARP 2005, 2010). One possibility for these discrepancies may be that cohort and age are confounded in several studies on this topic and that cohort differences—not age—explain declines in sexual satisfaction (Carpenter et al. 2009). Younger or later-born cohorts (i.e., the baby boomer generation) tend to employ a wider range of sexual techniques (e.g., incorporation of oral sex and genital touching) than older or earlier-born cohorts (i.e., the silent generation and the greatest generation) (Edwards and Booth 1994) and later-born cohorts also have higher levels of sexual satisfaction than earlier-born cohorts (Beckman et al. 2008). This may be because greater variation in sexual techniques allows individuals to maintain high levels of sexual satisfaction even as they experience age-related physical changes that interfere with the ability to have (frequent) sex.

Although some studies find no gender differences in levels of satisfaction (e.g., Blumstein and Schwartz 1983), other studies have found such differences. For example, the AARP survey of midlife and older adults (2005) found that partnered men are more likely than partnered women to report that they are dissatisfied or somewhat satisfied with their sexual relationship, whereas partnered women are more likely than partnered men to report that they are extremely satisfied or neutral with respect to their sex life (similar gendered patterns were found among the unpartnered). Further, some evidence suggests that sexual satisfaction is more closely linked to relationship satisfaction for men than it is for women;

one longitudinal study found that low levels of sexual satisfaction predict relationship dissolution for men, but not women (Sprecher 2002).

Research is also unclear on whether sexual satisfaction levels differ for individuals in gay, lesbian, and heterosexual relationships. One study found no differences between gay, lesbian, and heterosexual couples (Kurdek 1991), while the American Couples Study (Blumstein and Schwartz 1983) found that gay men were less likely to report that they were sexually satisfied, compared to individuals in heterosexual and lesbian relationships. Further, research indicates that women in lesbian relationships have more frequent orgasms—which is a predictor of sexual satisfaction (Sprecher and Cate 2004)—compared to women in heterosexual relationships (Peplau et al. 2004). However, for all couples—gay, lesbian, and heterosexual—sexual satisfaction is closely linked to relationship satisfaction (Peplau et al. 2004; Schwartz and Young 2009).

Although limited information exists on racial/ethnic differences in sexual satisfaction, results from the AARP (2005) survey of mid and later life adults suggests that Asian Americans have lower levels of sexual satisfaction than Whites, Blacks, and Hispanics (AARP 2005). Further, partnered Blacks and Hispanics are more likely than Whites and Asian Americans to believe that their partner is very satisfied with their sexual relationship and to discuss sexual satisfaction with their partner (AARP 2005). The AARP survey does not offer any explanations for these racial/ethnic differences; thus, future research should examine if these variations exist in other samples as well as explore explanations for racial/ethnic differences in sexual satisfaction in long-term relationships.

Other factors related to higher levels of sexual satisfaction include higher levels of orgasmic frequency, greater sexual communication, higher levels of accepted sexual initiations, low levels of sexual conflict, similarity between partners in terms of sexual behavior preferences, sexual desire, and sexual attitudes (Sprecher and Cate 2004), better physical health (AARP 2005), higher socioeconomic status (Castellanos-Torres et al. 2005), and higher levels of physical activity (AARP 2005).

14.1.2.3 Sexual Attitudes

Most adults regard sexuality as an important component of relationships. For example, a recent nationally representative survey of adults ages 45 and older found that 60 % believe that sexual activity is critical for relationship quality (AARP 2010). There may be gender differences in sexual attitudes; for example, middle-aged and older men are more likely than middle-aged and older women to report that sex is important for quality of life and relationship satisfaction (AARP 2010). Men's and women's views on sexual activity may converge with age, however; one study found that as men age they place less importance on sexual activity (Wiley and Bortz 1996).

Some research suggests that sex becomes less important for some couples over the course of long-term relationships, as both men and women come to view emotional intimacy as more important than sexual intimacy (Lodge and Umberson 2012; Umberson et al. 2015b). This change in the meaning of sex in relationships may be adaptive given that sexual frequency declines over time in long-term relationships and as one or both partners face physical (e.g., menopause, erectile dysfunction) or social changes (e.g., transition to parenthood) that make sex either less desired or feasible. On the other hand, other research suggests that sex does not decrease in significance for some mid- to later life couples—particularly gay couples—and that a reduction in sexual frequency may be experienced as a threat to a masculine identity for both gay and straight men (Lodge and Umberson 2013; Slevin and Mowery 2012). Cohort differences may also matter for attitudes toward sex; research reveals that younger cohorts of older adults have more positive attitudes toward sexuality than older cohorts (Beckman et al. 2008), which may in part reflect a gradual shift away from cultural discourses that define older adults as asexual to discourses that emphasize the importance of remaining sexually active as a marker of healthy and successful aging (Gott 2005; Katz and Marshall 2003).

14.1.2.4   Sexual Desire

Sexual desire is a complex phenomenon that encompasses biological drives, psychological motivations, and personal and social expectations, beliefs, and values (Kingsberg 2000). Individuals who are partnered report higher levels of sexual desire than individuals who do not have a partner (DeLamater and Sill 2005; Skoog 1996). However, a variety of relationship characteristics appear to be important for levels of sexual desire, perhaps particularly for women—which fits with theory and research that suggests that women's sexual desire is more fluid and sensitive to relational context (Diamond 2009; Peplau 2001). For example, one study found that relationship duration is negatively related to sexual desire for women, but not men (Kontula and Haavio-Mannila 2009). Relationship quality also matters a great deal for sexual desire; research suggests that women who are able to talk to their partners about how to facilitate their sexual desire report having more sexual desire (Wood et al. 2007). A lack of sexual desire is also associated with low expectations about the future viability of their current relationship for women, but not men (Laumann et al. 2005). Other relationship characteristics, such as conflict and partner discrepancies in desire, may also affect levels of sexual desire (that is, individuals may try to match their level of desire to that of their partner) (Skultety 2007).

Aging may also negatively impact sexual desire (DeLamater and Sill 2005; Laumann et al. 2005) in long-term relationships. Some research suggests that the negative relationship between age and sexual desire is stronger for men (DeLamater and Sill 2005) or only holds for men (Laumann et al. 2005). However, women may have lower levels of sexual desire than men: One study of Finnish adults found that at the age of 60 one-half of women reported a somewhat frequent lack of desire, compared to only 15 % of men (Kontula and Haavio-Mannila 2009). Some women also experience a decreased level of desire during the menopausal transition (Basson 2005). However, it remains unclear whether these decreased levels of desire are attributable solely to menopause, as the social context in which women find themselves profoundly shapes how they experience and express desire during menopause (Wood et al. 2007). For example, a loss of reproductive capacities may negatively affect women's sense of femininity and sexual identity, and thus levels of sexual desire (Kingsberg 2000). Moreover, women who believe that the physical signs of aging make them unattractive may experience a reduced level of sexual desire (Kingsberg 2000). Postmenopausal women's relationships with their partners also profoundly shape how they experience and express sexual desire (Wood et al. 2007). Beliefs about age and appropriateness of sexual activity may also be important: for women a lack of interest in sex is associated with the belief that aging reduces sexual desire and activity (Laumann et al. 2005). Additional factors that have a negative effect on sexual desire include poor health (Kontula and Haavio-Mannila 2009; Laumann et al. 2005), high blood pressure (DeLamater and Sill 2005), depression (Laumann et al. 2005), and low socioeconomic status and levels of education (DeLamater and Sill 2005). There is also some evidence that among partnered women in the U.S., White and Hispanic women are more likely than Black women to report low levels of desire (West et al. 2008). Despite research on levels of sexual desire, still little is known about the lived experience of sexual desire in long-term relationships or how these lived experiences differ for different social groups.

14.1.2.5   Sexual Dysfunction

As part of a broader shift of the medicalization of sexuality (Tiefer 1996) (see Cacchioni, Chap. 24, this volume), a great deal of research has focused on sexual dysfunction. Research on sexual dysfunction reflects the Diagnostic and Statistical Manual of Mental Disorders' classification scheme, whereby sexual problems fall into four categories: (1) sexual desire disorders, (2) sexual arousal disorders, (3) orgasmic disorders, and (4) sexual pain disorders. Sexual dysfunction is important because it may cause depression (Araujo et al. 1998) and marital and relationship conflict (Rust et al. 1988), and is associated with an overall diminished quality of life (Laumann et al. 1999). Moreover, one sexual dysfunction may precipitate another dysfunction; for example, men who experience erectile dysfunction (ED) are more likely to later report low levels of sexual desire (Kingsberg 2000).

Being in a long-term, committed relationship is somewhat protective of sexual dysfunction (Laumann et al. 1999, 2005, 2008). For example, among 57 to 85 year-olds, married men are less likely than widowed or never married men to experience a lack of sexual pleasure and less likely to experience performance anxiety in comparison to separated or divorced men (Laumann et al. 2008). Additionally, among 40 to 80 year-old men, being in an uncommitted relationship is associated with a greater likelihood of erectile difficulties (Laumann et al. 2005). Similarly, among women ages 40 to 80, those who believe or worry that their current relationship is unlikely to last are more likely to report an inability to orgasm (Laumann et al. 2005). This resonates with recent research that suggests that college women are more likely to experience orgasms in committed heterosexual relationships than they are in heterosexual casual relationships (i.e., "hookups") (Armstrong et al. 2012). Relationship satisfaction is also predictive of sexual functioning (Laumann et al. 2008). Women who are dissatisfied with their relationship are more likely to experience a lack of sexual pleasure and an inability to orgasm, while men who are dissatisfied with their relationship are more likely to experience a lack of sexual interest (Laumann et al. 2008). Further, leaving an unsatisfactory relationship for a new, satisfying relationship may positively impact sexual functioning for both men and women (Kontula and Haavio-Mannila 2009).

14.1.3 Feminist Studies

14.1.3.1 Performativity Studies

Recent qualitative research has applied feminist theoretical perspectives to the study of sex in long-term relationships. One such perspective is the "doing gender" perspective; this perspective was originally developed by West and Zimmerman (1987) to refer to the performance of

gender—whereby individuals "do" gender in response to culturally constructed notions of masculinity and femininity. In doing so, they reproduce—although sometimes contest—dominant cultural ideologies about gender. Recently, some studies have examined how men and women perform gender in the context of long-term sexual relationships. For example, Lodge and Umberson (2012) found that aging married men and women attempt to perform gender in line with cultural ideals of feminine (i.e., passive, lower levels of sexual desire) and masculine (i.e., active, high levels of sexual desire) sexuality, even as aging presents challenges to these ideals. Specifically, when husbands experience lower levels of desire women often resist initiating sex (even when they desire sex) because it goes against cultural beliefs about feminine sexuality (Lodge and Umberson 2012). Umberson et al. (2015b) also applied a *doing gender* perspective to the topic of sexuality in long-term relationships to show that women in both heterosexual and same-sex relationships were more apt than heterosexual or gay men to view sex and emotional intimacy as integrally linked.

Expanding on West and Zimmerman's (1987) formulation, Laz (1998) developed the concept of the performance of age, whereby individuals "act their age"—that is behave in line with cultural ideas about what is age appropriate. Lodge and Umberson (2012) applied this perspective to explain why later life—but not midlife—couples deemphasize the importance of sex for their relationships. Studies suggest that maintaining an active sex life is increasingly conceptualized as a part of "successful aging," (Gott 2005; Katz and Marshall 2003), but that the targets of these discourses are largely midlife individuals. In contrast, there remains considerable cultural ambivalence about later life adults' sexuality (Frankowski and Clark 2009). Thus, not having sex in later life is more culturally normative than it is for midlife couples, which may be why later life couples deemphasize the importance of sex for their relationships. There is a need for more studies to examine how cultural ideas about age shape the experience of sexuality across the life course as individuals "do" age in their sexual relationships, as well as how cultural ideas around gender, race/ethnicity, and other social statuses intersect with ideas about age to shape the experience of sexuality in unique ways for different groups.

Further expanding on this theoretical tradition, Elliott and Umberson (2008) developed the concept of the "performance of desire," to refer to a process of "managing feelings around one's sexual relationship according to how one thinks desire should be both felt and performed" (p. 394). They find that because cultural discourses emphasize the importance of sex for marital relationships, married women often attempt to feel and be more sexual in an attempt to match their level of desire to their husband's, whereas married men often attempt to feel and be less sexual in an attempt to match their level of desire to their wife's (2008). The recognition of sexual desire as profoundly shaped by social context and meanings and something that one "performs" is important and future research should explore how cultural meanings around sex and desire shape how men and women in a variety of relational contexts "do" desire.

Theoretical work by Jackson and Scott (2007) has also interrogated the ways in which orgasms are interactionally performed in heterosexual relationships. In particular, they note that because masculine sexuality is based on a performance ethic in which men must demonstrate potency and virility, women must in turn convincingly perform orgasms—that is demonstrate that they are experiencing desire and pleasure (2007). Although research suggests that women "fake" orgasms (Jackson and Scott 2007), empirical studies have not examined the interactional work that goes into doing so in long-term relationships nor how this may change over the course of relationships. Future research should thus examine this question among diverse couples.

14.1.3.2 Emotion Work and Sex

A few recent studies working from a feminist perspective have examined emotion work around sex in long-term relationships. Emotion work was originally defined by Hochschild (1979) to refer to labor that involves managing one's emotions to conform to the "feeling rules" of a particular context. A number of studies demonstrate that women do substantially more emotion work than men and that this is particularly true in heterosexual relationships, whereby women undertake emotion work in order to promote relationship quality (Duncombe and Marsden 1993; Erickson 2005; Hochschild 2003). Theoretical work by Jackson and Scott (2007) further suggests that because successful performances of masculine (hetero)sexuality require that men demonstrate an ability to sexually please women, women undertake considerable emotion work to convince their partners that they are experiencing sexual pleasure. Elliott and Umberson (2008) in turn applied these insights to study sex in long-term heterosexual marital relationships and found that because sex tends to be viewed as an integral component of marriage and sex is a frequent source of marital conflict, women undertake emotion work in an attempt to be more desiring of sex—either by initiating sex or by being more receptive to their husband's sexual advances. They further found that husbands expect their wife to perform such emotion work. Although less common, some husbands undertake emotion work to repress their sexual desires to avoid marital conflict.

Another recent study examined emotion work around sex in long-term lesbian, gay, and heterosexual couples and found that the division of emotion work and type of emotion work around sex varies based on both an individual's gender as well as the gender of their partner (Umberson et al. 2015b). For example, both heterosexual and lesbian women described emotion work directed toward being more desiring of sex because they view sex as integral to emotional intimacy and relationship quality, but this was less common for women in lesbian relationships because divergent levels of sexual desire were less common in lesbian relationships compared to heterosexual relationships. Further, the division of emotion work directed toward enhancing sexual desire was more equal in lesbian relationships than heterosexual relationships, because both partners in lesbian relationships often reported undertaking such work. In contrast, men were less likely than women to report that they viewed as sex as linked to emotional intimacy, and this was particularly the case for men in gay relationships. Because of the common view in gay relationships that sex and emotional intimacy are unrelated, emotion work in gay relationships often entailed one partner (who desired monogamy) working to accept their partner's view that sexual nonexclusivity is acceptable as long as it does not involve emotional intimacy. However, all couples reported that over the course of their relationships sexual frequency has declined and in turn they engaged in emotion work to see intimacy as unrelated to sex (Umberson et al. 2015b).

14.1.3.3 Gay and Lesbian Couples

There has been relatively little research on sexuality in long-term gay and lesbian couples; in part this may stem from the fact that researchers are wary of reproducing stereotypes about the hypersexuality of gay men or the sexual deviancy of sexual minorities generally (Peplau et al. 2004). However, research has consistently demonstrated that, like heterosexual long-term relationships, same-sex couples experience declines in sexual frequency with relationship duration. However, men in gay relationships consistently report higher levels of sexual frequency than individuals in other couple types, which stems in part from the fact that a significant amount of gay men in coupled relationships supplement their sex lives with outside partners (Schwartz and Young 2009). Age is also negatively correlated with sexual frequency for gay and lesbian couples, although, as in heterosexual relationships, relationship duration exerts a stronger negative impact on sexual frequency. Research also consistently demonstrates that gay couples have higher levels of sexual frequency than heterosexual couples, who in turn have higher levels of sexual frequency than lesbian couples (Peplau et al. 2004).

Lesbian couples' low levels of sexual frequency, often referred to as "lesbian bed death" may stem from several factors. First, research suggests that because of gender socialization women are less attuned to their sexual desires as well as less likely to initiate sex than men, and this effect may be amplified in a relationship with two women (Peplau and Fingerhut 2007; Peplau et al. 2004). Another possibility is that women simply have lower levels of sexual desire than men, the effect of which is again amplified in a relationship involving two women (Peplau and Fingerhut 2007; Peplau et al. 2004). A third possible explanation is that many surveys fail to accurately capture the realities of lesbian sex; survey questions often ask respondents about instances of "intercourse," thus underestimating the frequency of sexual activity in lesbian relationships (Peplau and Fingerhut 2007; Peplau et al. 2004). Thus, it remains unclear if "lesbian death bed" actually exists or if lower levels of sexual frequency among lesbian couples in survey research reflect the questions that researchers ask and how they ask them. Regardless, recent research suggests that some lesbian couples perceive "lesbian death bed" to be a real phenomenon and actively seek to avoid it in their relationship by attempting to feel or "do" desire and engage in sexual intimacy (Umberson et al. 2015b).

Another theme from previous research is that individuals in gay couples are less likely than individuals in heterosexual and lesbian couples to believe that sexual exclusivity is important as well as less likely to be sexually exclusive (Peplau and Fingerhut 2007; Peplau et al. 2004). However, nonmonogomous gay couples often establish sexual contracts that set rules around extradyadic sex, including rules about safe sex and emotional attachment to other partners (see Sheff and Tesene, Chap. 13, this volume). Importantly sexual exclusivity is not related to levels of relationship satisfaction, commitment, closeness, or relationship satisfaction for gay couples (Peplau et al. 2004).

14.2 Methodologies

The dominant methodological strategy for studying sexuality in long-term relationships has been survey methods, which typically rely on individual outcomes (rather than dyadic outcomes). In the past two decades, several nationally representative surveys (e.g., NHSLS, The National Survey of Sexual Health and Behavior [NSSHB], AARP Sexuality at Midlife and Beyond surveys, National Survey of Families and Households [NSFH], and the National Social Life, Health, and Aging Project [NSHAP]) have included measures on sexual frequency, sexual satisfaction, sexual desire, sexual attitudes, among other variables. Thus, we now have an impressive foundation of cross-sectional knowledge in terms of these outcomes. To advance knowledge in the study of sex in close relationships, more innovative methods are needed, however. In this section, I discuss some of these, including the need for more dyadic research, longitudinal surveys (including daily diary methods), qualitative studies, and the need for nationally representative data on gay and lesbian relationships.

14.2.1 Dyadic Data

An important avenue for future research on sex in long-term relationships is to study dyads (i.e., both partners in a relationship), rather than individuals in relationships (DeLamater and Hyde 2004; Perlman and Campbell 2004). Dyadic data allow researchers to compare partners' perspectives and behaviors, identifying points of overlap and difference (Umberson et al. 2015a). For example, researchers might compare partners' levels of sexual satisfaction to examine how partner similarity and/or discrepancy predict sexual frequency or relationship dissolution. Dyadic data further allow for validity checks— that is, by comparing partners' reports (e.g., reports of sexual frequency or change in sexual frequency over time) (Umberson et al. 2015a). Partner discrepancies can also reveal valuable information about relationships. For example, Mitchell et al. (2012) collected dyadic data to study concordance around sexual agreements or contracts around extradyadic sex among gay couples and found that couples who were more congruent about having and adhering to sexual agreements had higher levels of relationship satisfaction. Another important characteristic of dyadic data is that it can yield relationship-level data; for example researchers might ask whether the division of labor (a relationship-level variable) is related to sexual frequency (another relationship-level variable). It is important that researchers conduct both quantitative and qualitative dyadic research.

14.2.2 Longitudinal Methods

Research on sexuality has historically been plagued by funding issues (Perlman and Campbell 2004). As a result, few nationally representative longitudinal studies have included measures on sexuality. One recent exception to this is NSHAP, which includes numerous questions about sex. However, this survey is limited to adults ages 57 to 85. As I discuss later, however, longitudinal research is particularly important for research that incorporates a life course perspective, given that only longitudinal research can fully address questions around relationship and sexual turning points and histories (see Carpenter, Chap. 5, this volume). Collecting longitudinal qualitative data is also important. Diamond (2009) collected longitudinal data to examine women's transitions between same- and different-sex unions as well as transitions in women's sexual identities. Similarly, researchers could collect qualitative longitudinal data to examine changes in the meanings and importance of sex over time within relationships as well as how meanings around sex change during and after relationship and other life course (e.g., becoming a parent) transitions.

One particularly fruitful avenue for longitudinal research is daily diary studies, in which respondents fill out surveys for several consecutive days (usually over a period of several weeks). Daily diary studies are increasingly common in family research generally, but have less frequently been applied to the study of sex. Such surveys could, however, yield important information about how sexual frequency, satisfaction, desire and other variables related to sex fluctuate daily, as well as how they may fluctuate in response to other relationship variables (which likely also fluctuate daily), such as levels of relationship conflict, perceived emotional support, and the division of labor. Dyadic daily diary studies, whereby both partners (independently) fill out daily questionnaires that ask questions about their sexual relationships are a particularly useful avenue for future research in this regard. For example, Ridley et al. collected daily diary data to reveal that daily fluctuations in positive and negative feelings towards one's partner were associated with fluctuations in sexual thoughts and behaviors, although in different ways for gay, lesbian, and heterosexual couples (Ridley et al. 2008). A more recent daily diary study with heterosexual couples found that daily fluctuations in sexual desire and partner discrepancy in levels of desire were associated with quality of sexual experience (Mark 2014). Dyadic daily diary studies thus provide an opportunity to address a range of questions concerning sex in coupled relationships.

14.2.3 Qualitative Methods

To date, most studies on sex in long-term relationships have been based on survey data. Thus, there is a need for more qualitative studies on this topic, which is also a particularly important endeavor for theoretical development. Qualitative data are particularly well-suited to revealing meanings (e.g., social, cultural, and individual understandings and perceptions) around sex in long-term relationships. This is important because researchers typically assume meanings in designing survey questions, but the particular questions asked may or may not accurately reflect respondents' lived meanings around sex. Further, the fact that so much survey research has focused on sexual frequency may reflect a male perspective, to the extent that women may be more concerned with the quality of sexual interactions, as opposed to the frequency of those interactions (Schwartz 2004). Thus, findings from qualitative research can be used to inform future surveys, by revealing important new insights into the experience of sex in long-term relationships. Recent qualitative studies on sex in long-term relationships have revealed, for example, important insights into emotion work around sex in lesbian, gay, and heterosexual relationships (Elliott and Umberson 2008; Umberson et al. 2015b), the performance of sexual desire in marital relationships (Elliott and Umberson 2008), how the meaning of sex changes over time in long-term relationships (Lodge and Umberson 2012; Umberson et al. 2015b), and how individuals construct meanings around the link between sex and emotional intimacy in lesbian, gay, and het-

erosexual relationships (Umberson et al. 2015b). These findings (which are described above) reveal important theoretical insights that can be used to inform future surveys.

14.2.4 Nationally Representative Data on Gay and Lesbian Couples

Obtaining nationally representative data on gay and lesbian individuals and couples remains a challenge. This is particularly the case in terms of research on sexuality, given that funding agencies have often been reluctant to fund sexuality research. For example, in order to obtain funding for the NHSLS Laumann et al. had to abandon their plans to include adequate subsamples of gay and lesbian respondents (Perlman and Campbell 2004). Thus, most nationally representative surveys that include data on sexuality do not include sufficient numbers of gay and lesbian individuals or couples. As a result, most of what we know about sex in gay and lesbian couples is based on convenience samples (Peplau et al. 2004). Obtaining nationally representative samples of gay and lesbian couples, however, is important for a fuller understanding of the diversity of sex in long-term relationships. Such samples can also reveal important insights into how gender matters not just at the individual-level but at the relationship-level, given that researchers could compare sexual relationships composed of two women, two men, and one woman and one man.

14.3 Future Directions

14.3.1 The Need for Theoretically-Informed Studies

Four broad theoretical perspectives have informed the study of sex in intimate relationships: evolutionary psychology, attachment theory, social exchange theory, and symbolic interactionism (Perlman and Campbell 2004). Of these theories, the only one that it is distinctly sociological is symbolic interactionism and many of the recent theoretically-informed studies on sex in long-term relationships reviewed earlier (e.g., studies that apply a performance perspective) certainly reflect this theoretical tradition. However, many—if not most—studies on this topic are simply descriptive. Thus, one of the most pressing concerns for future research on sex in long-term relationships is the need for theoretical development and theoretically-informed studies. In this section, I suggest that incorporating theoretical insights from the following theories can reveal new insights into the study of sex in long term relationships: (1) a "gendered sexuality over the life course" perspective, (2) a gender-as-relational perspective, (3) critical feminist gerontology, and (4) queer theory. Merging some or all of these different theoretical perspectives into a particular study can reveal new insights into this topic and also responds to calls for the use of more integrative theorizing in the study of sex in relationships (DeLamater and Hyde 2004).

14.3.1.1 Gendered Sexuality Over the Life Course Perspective

Drawing on gender, scripting, and life course theories, Carpenter (2010, Chap. 5) argues that research on sexuality should incorporate a "gendered sexuality over the life course" theoretical perspective. Specifically, from this perspective: "sexual beliefs and behaviors result from individuals' lifelong accumulation of advantageous and disadvantageous experiences, and their adoption and rejection of sexual scripts, within specific socio-historical contexts" (Carpenter 2010, p. 157; Montemurro 2014). Further, these gender-specific experiences and scripts give rise to gendered trajectories of sexuality, which are experienced differently at the intersection of race/ethnicity, social class, and sexual identity. Future research could apply this perspective to the topic of sex in long-term relationships by using longitudinal or retrospective data to examine how earlier life course experiences of gendered sexuality matter for later life experiences of gendered sexuality, and how those experiences are inflected by race/ethnicity, social class, and sexual identity. For example, research suggests that in heterosexual relationships men's sexual pleasure is typically privileged (Armstrong et al. 2012), yet women whose early life course relationships do not conform to this gendered pattern may develop a greater sense of sexual agency and greater expectations of sexual pleasure, which in turn likely shape their experiences of partnered sex throughout the life course—albeit in different ways based on women's various social locations and access to privilege.

A life course perspective further points to the importance of relationship histories (Cooney and Dunne 2001) and how they intersect with sexual histories. Earlier relationship experiences—both in terms of the current relationship and previous relationships—are likely important for understanding how sex is presently experienced within long-term relationships. For example, although the link between relationship satisfaction and sexual satisfaction is well established, it is unclear if or how levels of relationship satisfaction early in the course of relationships may be related to levels of sexual satisfaction later on or vice versa. Further, from a gendered sexuality over the life course perspective, relational experiences likely occur in particularly gendered ways. Thus, future research on sex in long-term relationships should apply these insights. Doing so would undoubtedly reveal new insights into gendered experiences of sex in long-term relationships as well as how those may differ across social groups.

14.3.1.2 Gender as Relational

A gender-as-relational theoretical framework builds on insights from a doing gender perspective (West and Zimmerman 1987) to argue that gender is performed in relation to others and individuals do gender differently based on social context (Springer et al. 2012). Recent research applying this perspective to understand gendered experiences of intimate relationships, for example, suggests that men will perform masculinity differently based on whether they are in a relationship with a man or woman. Umberson et al. (2015b) find that meanings and experiences of sex in long-term relationships reflect an individual's gender in relation to the gender of their partner in that women partnered with women reinforce a view of emotional intimacy and sex as integrally connected, while women partnered with men challenge their partner to adopt this perspective at the same time that their partner challenges this view. In contrast, men partnered with men reinforce one another's view of intimacy and sex as separate. Researchers could adopt this theoretical lens to investigate a variety of gendered sexual phenomenon within same-sex and different-sex long-term relationships.

14.3.1.3 Critical Feminist Gerontology

For a fuller understanding of gendered sexuality over the life course and in particular gendered experiences of sexuality in mid and later life, I further suggest that researchers integrate key theoretical insights from *critical feminist gerontology*. Critical feminist gerontology integrates a feminist perspective (which maintains that gender is a key axis of inequality), with critical gerontology, which emphasizes that ageism—as a cultural and social structural system—is a key axis of inequality (Calasanti 2005). For example, research on sex in long-term relationships applying this perspective has focused on the role of cultural devaluations of the aging body, and in particular the devaluation of the appearance of the aging female body and the devaluation of the functionality of the aging male body, in shaping gendered sexual experiences in long-term relationships (Lodge and Umberson 2012). This perspective is not only useful for understanding gendered experiences of sex in later-life relationships, but gendered sexual experiences in early adulthood and midlife relationships as well, because constructions of age and ageism operate at all points of the life course (albeit in different forms). While previous research has included age and gender as variables in research on sex in long-term relationships, future research can go further to examine how age and gender intersect as cultural and structural systems to shape sexual experiences across the life course. Critical feminist gerontology can also be applied to queer couples: for example, research has applied this perspective to understand why some midlife men in relationships with other men find perceived declines in the attractiveness of their bodies—that is both self-perceptions that their bodies are declining in attractiveness as well as perceptions that others perceive their bodies as declining in attractiveness—as having a negative impact on their sex lives (Lodge and Umberson 2013).

14.3.1.4 Queer Theory

Queer theory disrupts the heteronormative assumptions (i.e., assumptions based on conventional understandings of gender and heterosexuality) upon which much contemporary research and theory is based upon. Queer theory can therefore be merged with any of the above theories to reveal new insights into the study of sex in long-term relationships that disrupt heteronormative assumptions about gender, sex, and relationships. For example, Brown (2009) suggests that merging queer and life course theories is a particularly useful endeavor because queer theory disrupts the heteronormative assumptions upon which life course research is often based on (e.g., assumptions of marriage and parenthood), at the same time that life course theory provides a framework for examining life experiences as shaped by social structures and relational contexts with others.

In terms of sex in long-term relationships, queer theory could be merged with a gendered sexuality over the life course theoretical framework to examine how gendered experiences of sexuality differ for gender queer individuals (i.e., individuals who do not endorse or conform to conventional masculine and feminine identities and presentations) over the life course. These perspectives could also be merged to examine how transitioning from different-sex to same-sex (and vice versa) relationships or from different gendered identities (e.g., from a man to a woman) over the life course shape relational sexual experiences (see Devor and Dominic, Chap. 11, this volume). Similarly, researchers could merge a gender-as-relational framework with queer theory to ask questions about how a woman partnered with a woman might experience sex differently than a woman partnered with a man or a man partnered with a man in order to potentially queer our understandings of gender, sex, and relationships.

14.3.2 The Need for More Research on Diversity in Long-Term Relationships

In addition to the need for more research on sex in LGBT relationships, little research has focused on sex in non-marital relationships. Research is needed to understand if and how sex may be experienced differently in non-traditional long-term relationships—including nonmonogamous and living-apart-together relationships (i.e., those where partners maintain separate residences, but often spend the night at one another's homes). The application of queer and life course theories could be particularly useful for understanding non-traditional long-term relationships.

Additionally, more research is needed on experiences of sex in long-term relationships across different racial-ethnic (DeLamater and Hyde 2004), cultural (Perlman and Campbell 2004) and social class groups, as well as how these experiences may differ based on the racial-spatial and social class organization of specific communities (Laumann et al. 2004). Although previous research suggests that there are differences in sexual experiences for different social groups (Laumann et al. 1999), little is known about *why* these differences exist (DeLamater and Hyde 2004). Although some descriptive studies include racial/ethnic and/or socioeconomic status as variables in their analytical models, the tasks of systematically examining racial/ethnic and socioeconomic status differences, the effect sizes of such differences, and if meanings and lived experiences of sex in long-term relationships differ across groups have not been adequately performed. This likely connects to the dearth of qualitative research: we don't know these things because researchers have failed to ask certain questions and most of what we know on the topic of sex in long-term relationships is based on middle-class white samples. These omissions have occurred not only at the individual-level, but at the dyadic level as well. For example, an interesting avenue for future research could be to examine if and how racial/ethnic or socioeconomic difference *within* a couple shape sexual experiences. In addition to the paltry attention paid to race, ethnicity, and social class, research on this topic has been dominated by a focus on the United States context, virtually ignoring cross-cultural experiences of sex in long-term relationships (Perlman and Campbell 2004). An important exception to the dearth of cross-cultural research is the Global Study of Sexual Attitudes and Behaviors (GSSAB), a survey of 27,500 men and women from 29 different countries (Laumann et al. 2005). However, in addition to survey research that compares different national and cultural groups, we need research that can speak to the links between sexual and relational experiences and specific cultural norms and values (Peplau et al. 2004). These omissions likely stem from the fact that questions of difference in the study of sexuality have overwhelmingly focused on gender (DeLamater and Hyde 2004); thus, questions around race, ethnicity, and culture represent a key area for future research on this topic.

Significant strides have been made in the study of sex in long-term relationships over the past 20 years. Researchers now have access to high quality survey data and we now an impressive foundation of knowledge on topics such as sexual frequency, sexual satisfaction, and the association between these two variables to relationship satisfaction. However, to keep the field moving along at this impressive pace, researchers must pioneer new methodological strategies, move beyond descriptive studies to apply cutting-edge theoretical perspectives to the study of sex in long-term relationships, and shed greater light on the full diversity of sexual experiences in long-term relationships.

References

AARP. (2005). Sexuality at midlife and beyond: 2004 update of attitudes and behaviors. http://assets.aarp.org/rgcenter/general/2004 _sexuality.pdf. Accessed 7 Dec 2013.

AARP. (2010). Sex, romance, and relationships: AARP survey of midlife and older adults. http://assets.aarp.org/rgcenter/general/srr_09.pdf. Accessed 1 Dec 2010.

Araujo, A. B., Durante, R., Feldman, H. A., Goldstein, I., & McKinlay, J. B. (1998). The relationship between depressive symptoms and male erectile dysfunction: Cross-sectional results from the Massachusetts Male Aging Study. *Psychosomatic Medicine, 60*, 458–465.

Armstrong, E. A., England, P., & Fogarty, A. C. K. (2012). Enjoyment in college hookups and relationships. *American Sociological Review, 77*, 435–462.

Basson, R. (2005). Women's sexual dysfunction: Revised and expanded definitions. *Canadian Medical Association Journal, 172*, 1327–1333.

Beckman, N., Waern, M., Gustafson, D., & Skoog, I. (2008). Secular trends in self reported sexual activity and satisfaction in Swedish 70 year olds: Cross-sectional survey of four populations, 1971–2000. *British Medical Journal, 337*, 151–154.

Blumstein, P., & Schwartz, P. (1983). *American couples: Money, work, sex.* New York: Morrow.

Brown, M. T. (2009). LGBT aging and rhetorical silence. *Sexuality Research and Social Policy, 6*, 65–78.

Calasanti, T. (2005). Is feminist gerontology marginal? *Contemporary Gerontology, 11*, 107–111.

Call, V., Sprecher, S., & Schwartz, P. (1995). The incidence and frequency of marital sex in a national sample. *Journal of Marriage and the Family, 57*, 639–652.

Carpenter, L. M. (2010). Gendered sexuality over the life course: A conceptual framework. *Sociological Perspectives, 53*, 155–178.

Carpenter, L. M., Nathanson, C. A., & Kim, Y. J. (2009). Physical women, emotional men: Gender and sexual satisfaction in midlife. *Archives of Sexual Behavior, 38*, 87–107.

Castellanos-Torres, E., Alvarez-Dardet, C., Ruiz-Munoz, D., & Perez, G. (2013). Social determinants of sexual satisfaction in Spain considered from the gender perspective. *Annals of Epidemiology, 23*, 150–156.

Cooney, T. M., & Dunne, K. (2001). Intimate relationships in later life: Current realities, future prospects. *Journal of Family Issues, 22*, 838–858.

DeLamater, J. D., & Hyde, J. (2004). Conceptual and theoretical issues in studying sexuality in close relationships. In J. Harvey, A. Wenzel, & S. Sprecher (Eds.), *The handbook of sexuality in close relationships* (pp. 7–30). Hillsdale: Erlbaum.

DeLamater, J. D., & Moorman, S. (2007). Sexual behavior in later life. *Journal of Aging and Health, 19*, 921–945.

DeLamater, J. D., & Sill, M. (2005). Sexual desire in later life. *Journal of Sex Research, 42*, 138–149.

DeLamater, J. D., Hyde, J., & Fong, M. (2008). Sexual satisfaction in the seventh decade of life. *Journal of Sex and Marital Therapy, 34*, 439–454.

Diamond, L. M. (2009). *Sexual fluidity: Understanding women's love and desire.* Cambridge: Harvard University Press.

Duncombe, J., & Marsden, D. (1993). Love and intimacy: The gender division of emotion and emotion work, a neglected aspect of sociological discussion of heterosexual relationships. *Sociology, 27*, 221–41.

Edwards, J. N. & Booth, A. (1994). Sexuality, marriage, and well-being: The middle years. In A. S. Rossi (Ed.), *Sexuality across the life course* (pp. 233–259). Chicago: University of Chicago Press.

Elliott, S., & Umberson, D. (2008). The performance of desire: Gender and sexual negotiation in long-term marriages. *Journal of Marriage and Family, 70*, 391–406.

Erickson, R. J. (2005). Why emotion work matters: Sex, gender, and the division of household labor. *Journal of Marriage and Family, 67*, 337–351.

Frankowski, A. C., & Clark, L. J. (2009). Sexuality and intimacy in assisted living: Residents' perspectives

and experiences. *Sexuality Research and Social Policy, 6*, 25–37.

Gott, M. (2005). *Sexuality, sexual health, and ageing.* Maidenhead: Open University Press.

Gott, M., & Hinchliff, S. (2003a). How important is sex in later life? The views of older people. *Social Science & Medicine, 56*, 1617–1628.

Gott, M., & Hinchliff, S. (2003b). Sex and ageing: A gendered issue. In S. Arber, K. Davidson, & J. Ginn (Eds.), *Gender and ageing: Changing roles and relationships* (pp. 63–78). Buckingham: Open University Press.

Gullette, M. M. (2011). *Agewise: Fighting the new ageism in America.* Chicago: University of Chicago Press.

Herbenick, D., Reece, M., Schick, V., Sanders, S. A., Dodge, B., & Fortenberry, J. D. (2010). Sexual behavior in the United States: Results from a national probability sample of men and women ages 14–94. *Journal of Sexual Medicine, 7*, 255–265.

Hochschild, A. R. (1979). Emotion work, feeling rules, and social structure. *American Journal of Sociology, 85*, 551–575.

Hochschild, A. R. (2003). *The managed heart: Commercialization of human feeling.* Berkeley: University of California Press.

Jackson, S., & Scott, S. (2007). Faking like a woman? Towards an intepretive theorization of sexual pleasure. *Body & Society, 13*, 95–116.

Karraker, A., & DeLamater, J. (2013). Past-year sexual inactivity among older married persons and their partners. *Journal of Marriage and Family, 75*, 142–163.

Karraker, A., DeLamater, J., & Schwartz, C. R. (2011). Sexual frequency decline from midlife to later life. *The Journals of Gerontology Series B: Psychological Sciences and Social Sciences, 66*(4), 502–512.

Katz, S., & Marshall, M. (2003). New sex for old: Lifestyle, consumerism, and the ethics of aging well. *Journal of Aging Studies, 17*, 3–16.

Kingsberg, S. A. (2000). The psychological impact of aging on sexuality and relationships. *Journal of Women's Health & Gender-Based Medicine, 9*, S33–S38.

Kinsey, A. C., Pomeroy, W. B., & Martin, C. E. (1948). *Sexual behavior in the human male.* Philadelphia: W.B. Saunders.

Kinsey, A. C., Pomeroy, W. B., Martin, C. E., & Gebhard, P. H. (1953). *Sexual Behavior in the human female.* Philadelphia: W.B. Saunders.

Kontula, O., & Haavio-Mannila, E. (2009). The impact of aging on human sexual activity and sexual desire. *Journal of Sex Research, 46*, 46–56.

Kurdek, L. A. (1991). Sexuality in homosexual and heterosexual couples. In K. McKinney & S. Sprecher (Eds.), *Sexuality in close relationships* (pp. 177–191). Hillsdale: Lawrence Erlbaum Associates.

Laumann, E. O., Gagnon, J. H., Michael, R. T., & Michaels, S. (1994). *The social organization of sexuality: Sexual practices in the United States.* Chicago: University of Chicago Press.

Laumann, E. O., Paik, A., & Rosen, R. C. (1999). Sexual dysfunction in the United States: Prevalence and predictors. *Journal of the American Medical Association, 6*, 537–544.

Laumann, E. O., Ellingson, S., Mahay, J., Paik, A., & Youm, Y. (Eds.) (2004). *The sexual organization of the city*. Chicago: University of Chicago Press.

Laumann, E. O., Nicolosi, A., Glasser, D. B., Paik, A., Gingell, C., Moreira, E., & Wang, T. (2005). Sexual problems among women and men aged 40–80 y: prevalence and correlates identified in the Global Study of Sexual Attitudes and Behaviors. *International Journal of Impotence Research, 17*, 39–57.

Laumann, E. O., Das, A., & Waite, L. J. (2008). Sexual dysfunction among older adults: Prevalence and risk factors from a nationally representative probability sample of men and women 57–85 years of age. *Journal of Sex Medicine, 5*, 2300–2311.

Laz, C. (1998). Act your age. *Sociological Forum, 13*, 85–113.

Lindau, S. T., Schumm, L. P., Laumann, E. O., Levinson, W., Muircheartaigh, C. A., & Waite, L. J. (2007). A study of sexuality and health among older adults in the United States. *New England Journal of Medicine, 357*, 762–774.

Lodge, A. C., & Umberson, D. (2012). All shook up: Sexuality of mid- and later life married couples. *Journal of Marriage and Family, 74*, 428–443.

Lodge, A. C., & Umberson, D. (2013). Age and embodied masculinities: Midlife gay and heterosexual men talk about their bodies. *Journal of Aging Studies, 27*, 225–232.

Lodge, A. C., & Umberson, D. (Forthcoming). Mid and late life couples and sexual intimacy. In J. Bookwala (Ed.), *Couple relationships in mid and late life: Current perspectives*. Washington, DC: American Psychological Association.

Mark, K. P. (2014). The impact of daily sexual desire and daily sexual desire discrepancy on the quality of the sexual experience in couples. *The Canadian Journal of Human Sexuality, 23*, 27–33.

McKinlay, J. B., & Feldman, H. A. (1994). Age-related variation in sexual activity and interest in normal men: Results from the Massachusetts Male Aging Study. In A. S. Rossi (Ed.), *Sexuality across the life course* (pp. 261–286). Chicago: University of Chicago Press.

Michael, R. T., Gagnon, J. H., Laumann, E. O., & Kolata, G. (1994). *Sex in America*. Boston: Little, Brown.

Mitchell, J. W., Harvey, S. M., Champeau, D., Moskowitz, D. A., & Seal, D. W. (2012). Relationship factors associated with gay male couples' concordance on aspects of their sexual agreements: Establishment, type, and adherence. *AIDS and Behavior, 16*, 1560–1569.

Montemurro, B. (2014). *Deserving desire: Women's stories of sexual evolution*. New Brunswick: Rutgers University Press.

Moore, M. R., & Stambolis-Ruhstorfer, M. (2013). LGBT sexuality and families at the start of the twenty-first century. *Annual Review of Sociology, 39*, 491–507.

Peplau, L. A. (2001). Rethinking women's sexual orientation: An interdisciplinary, relationship-focused approach. *Personal Relationships, 8*, 1–19.

Peplau, L. A., & Fingerhut, A. (2007). The close relationships of lesbians and gay men. *Annual Review of Psychology, 58*, 405–424.

Peplau, L. A., Fingerhut, A. W., & Beals, K. P. (2004). Sexuality in the relationships of lesbians and gay men. In J. H. Harvey, A. Wenzel, & S. Sprecher (Eds.), *Handbook of sexuality in close relationships* (pp. 349–369). Mahwah: Lawrence Erlbaum Associates.

Perlman, D., & Campbell, S. (2004). Sexuality in close relationships: Concluding commentary. In J. H. Harvey, A. Wenzel, & S. Sprecher (Eds.), *Handbook of sexuality in close relationships* (pp. 613–635). Mahwah: Lawrence Erlbaum Associates.

Ridley, C., Ogolsky, B., Payne, P., Totenhagen, C., & Cate, R. (2008). Sexual expression: Its emotional context in heterosexual, gay, and lesbian couples. *Journal of Sex Research, 45*, 305–314.

Rust, J., Golombok, S., & Collier, J. (1988). Marital problems and sexual dysfunction: How are they related? *The British Journal of Psychiatry, 152*, 629–631.

Schwartz, P. (2004). What we know about sexuality in intimate relationships. In J.H. Harvey, A. Wenzel, & S. Sprecher (Eds.), *Handbook of sexuality in close relationships* (pp. 597–612). Mahwah: Lawrence Erlbaum Associates.

Schwartz, P. & Young, L. (2009). Sexual satisfaction in committed relationships. *Sexuality Research & Social Policy, 6*, 1–17.

Skoog, I. (1996). Sex and Swedish 85-year-olds. *New England Journal of Medicine, 334*, 1140–1141.

Skultety, K. (2007). Addressing issues of sexuality with older couples. *Generations, 3*, 31–37.

Slevin, K. F., & Mowery, C. (2012). Exploring embodied aging and ageism among old lesbians and gay men. In L. Carpenter & J. DeLamater (Eds.), *Sex for life: From virginity to Viagra, how sexuality changes throughout our lives* (pp. 260–277). New York: New York University Press.

Smith, A., Lyons, A., Ferris, J., Richters, J., Pitts, M., Shelley, J., & Simpson, J. M. (2011). Sexual and relationship satisfaction among heterosexual men and women: The importance of desired frequency of sex. *Journal of Sex and Marital Therapy, 37*, 104–115.

Sprecher, S. (2002). Sexual satisfaction in premarital relationships: Associations with satisfaction, love, commitment, and stability. *Journal of Sex Research, 3*, 1–7.

Sprecher, S., & Cate, R. M. (2004). Sexual satisfaction and sexual expression as predictors of relationship satisfaction and stability. In J. H. Harvey, A. Wenzel, & S. Sprecher (Eds.), *Handbook of sexuality in close relationships* (pp. 235–255). Mahwah: Lawrence Erlbaum Associates.

Springer, K. W., Hankivsky, O., & Bates, L. M. (2012). Gender and health: Relational, intersectional, and biosocial approaches. *Social Science & Medicine, 74*, 1661–1666.

Tiefer, L. (1996). The medicalization of sexuality: Conceptual, normative, and professional issues. *Annual Review of Sex Research, 7*, 252–282.

Umberson, D., Thomeer, M. B., Kroeger, R., Lodge, A. C., & Xu, M. (2015a). Challenges and opportunities for research on same-sex relationships. *Journal of Marriage and Family, 77*, 96–111.

Umberson, D., Thomeer, M. B., & Lodge, A. C. (2015b). Intimacy and emotion work in lesbian, gay, and heterosexual relationships. *Journal of Marriage and Family, 77*, 542–556.

Vares, T., Potts, A., Gavey, N., & Grace, V. (2007). Reconceptualizing cultural narratives of mature women's sexuality in the Viagra era. *Journal of Aging Studies, 21*, 153–164.

Ventegodt, S. (1998). Sex and the quality of life in Denmark. *Archives of Sexual Behavior, 27*, 295–307.

Waite, L. J., & Das, A. (2010). Families, social life and well-being at older ages. *Demography, 47*, S87–S109.

West, C., & Zimmerman, D. H. (1987). Doing gender. *Gender & Society, 1*, 125–151.

West, S. L., D'Aloisio, A. A., Agans, R. P., Kalsbeek, W. D., Borisov, N. N., & Thorp, J. M. (2008). Prevalence of low sexual desire and hypoactive sexual desire disorder in a nationally representative sample of U.S. women. *Archives of Internal Medicine, 168*, 1441–1449.

Wiley, D., & Bortz, W. M. (1996). Sexuality and aging—usual and successful. *The Journals of Gerontology Series A: Biological Sciences and Medical Sciences, 51*, M142–M146.

Willetts, M. C., Sprecher, S., & Beck, F. D. (2004). Overview of sexual practices and attitudes within relational contexts. In J. H. Harvey, A. Wenzel, & S. Sprecher (Eds.), *Handbook of sexuality in close relationships* (pp. 57–85). Mahwah: Lawrence Erlbaum Associates.

Wood, J. M., Mansfield, P. K., & Koch, P. B. (2007). Negotiating sexual agency: Postmenopausal women's meaning and experience of sexual desire. *Qualitative Health Research, 17*, 189–200.

Yeh, H., Lorenz, F. O., Wickrama, K. A. S., Conger, R. D., & Elder, G. H., Jr. (2006). Relationships among sexual satisfaction, marital quality, and marital instability at midlife. *Journal of Family Psychology, 29*, 339–343.

Intersectionality: Race, Gender, Sexuality, and Class

15

Angelique Harris and Susannah Bartlow

15.1 Introduction and Definitions

From its origins in the Black feminist legal scholarship of Kimberlé Williams Crenshaw to its contemporary centrality in online activist debates, intersectionality has always signaled both academic insights and activist implications. As a basic definition, *intersectionality* refers to the ways in which race, class, gender, sexual orientation, age, religion, and other locations of social group membership impact lived experiences and social relations. The term emphasizes the mobility of social group identities and locations, not simply of their appearances in individual bodies. As Africana and Women's Studies public intellectual Brittany Cooper (2014) has written, "we have to remember that intersectionality was never put forth as an account of identity but rather an account of power."

Black feminist scholar Nikol Alexander-Floyd (2012) situates the term in its intellectual heritage in her work on the co-optation of Black feminist research and experiences in intersectional scholarship. Borrowing from Linora Salter's revision

of the term "ideograph," Alexander-Floyd (2012) characterizes intersectionality as,

> a catch-all word that stands in for the broad body of scholarship that has sought to examine and redress the oppressive forces that have constrained the lives of [B]lack women in particular and women of color more generally. As an idea or an analytically distinct concept, intersectionality is a moniker, identified with Crenshaw (1989), meant to describe the "intersecting" or co-determinative forces of racism, sexism, and classism in the lives of black women. (p. 4)

The Combahee River Collective, a group of Black women activists who organized starting in 1974 and developed a statement widely circulated as one of the founding documents of intersectional theory (1995), and Kimberle Crenshaw, who coined the term "intersectionality" in her 1989 essay on race and sex in the law and activism, are two of the critical figures in late twentieth century foundations of the term. For the purposes of this handbook, we focus on the use of intersectionality in social science sexuality research, and we address the Combahee River Collective and Crenshaw's originating intersections of race, class, gender, and sexual orientation, with a recognition that the fundamental definition of intersectionality should compel us to examine other intersections (with the presumption that one's ability status, for example, would appreciably impact the experience of class, race, gender and sexuality). With particular respect to sexuality studies, we address how work around these four social group identity categories has shaped or neglected the knowledge base about intersection-

A. Harris (✉)
Social and Cultural Sciences, Marquette University Milwaukee, Milwaukee, WI 53233, USA
e-mail: angelique.harris@marquette.edu

S. Bartlow
Gender and Sexuality Resource Center, Marquette University Milwaukee, Milwaukee, WI 53233, USA
e-mail: susannah.bartlow@marquette.edu

ality and sexuality. We also consider work deriving from many disciplines and methodological approaches, following upon Alexander-Floyd's (2012) observation that

> intersectionality can be defined as the commitment to centering research and analysis on the lived experiences of women of color for the purpose of making visible and addressing their marginalization as well as an ethos of challenging business as usual in mainstream disciplines' habits of knowledge production. (p. 9)

We conclude by recommending future directions that continue with Crenshaw and other feminist scholars' ongoing work to retain the intellectual heritage of the concept while moving forward with its applications.

15.2 History of Thought

Although intersectionality, as a concept, was first "named" by Kimberlé Williams Crenshaw in 1989 (Crenshaw 1989), Black feminist scholars and activists have long emphasized the intersections of their simultaneous and multiple identities, such as race, gender, class, and sexuality, and the ways in which they influence their lived experiences. These Black feminist theories are rooted in the history of Black women in the United States and are deeply embedded in the cultures and everyday lives of Black women (Collins 2000). Understanding intersectionality or the ways in which multiple forms of oppression, in this case, based on race, gender, class, and sexuality all intersect to oppress (Collins 2000), is key in understanding the perspective from which Black women view the world.

During a speech at an 1851 women's rights convention in Akron, Ohio, abolitionist and activist Sojourner Truth is said to have asked, "Ain't I a woman?" as she discussed the challenges unique to African American women at the time, explaining to her audience that her racial and gender oppressions were intertwined. Sojourner Truth also famously bared her breast, in another oratorical demonstration of her humanity, to be met with responses that reinforced how sexuality often meets at the intersection of race

and gender (Washington 1993). Since then, Black feminist scholars and activists have complicated notions of single identity issues that traditional feminists often employed, emphasizing that there was no hierarchy of identity and oppression (Lorde 1984; Hooks 1981).

Various authors, theorists, and activists have contributed to this understanding of the multiple forms of oppression that Black women have experienced. In 1839, Angelina and Sarah Grimké helped to publish a book called *American Slavery As It Is: Testimony of a Thousand Witnesses* (Perry 2001). These sisters were raised in a Southern slave holding family before moving North to participate in the abolitionist movement. They criticized women's anti-slavery groups because they failed to acknowledge the experiences of Black women (Davis 1981) and argued that the two oppressions were similar. The Grimké sisters argued that until Blacks received their freedom, women would never get theirs. Unlike many White women abolitionists, the Grimke Sisters were particularly concerned with the sexual exploitation that Black women experienced at the hands of their masters. Social convention prevented them from speaking frankly and honestly about this sexual exploitation (Hooks 1981). Ida B. Wells, however, directly addressed Black sexuality and oppression in her work.

Born to ex-slaves, Ida B. Wells began her fight for equal rights when she was 22 and sued a railway company for discrimination, however it was the lynching of her three friends by a Memphis mob, which prompted her to begin her lifelong crusade against lynching. Wells suggested that White men once controlled Black bodies through slavery, but they lost that control once the enslaved were freed, thus, they attempted to control the Black body through lynching's, castrations, and rapes (Wells-Barnett 2002). She argued that control of the Black body is yet another oppression Blacks experience (Wells-Barnett 2002).

Though Black (and some White) women recognized the intersecting oppressions that Black women experienced due to race, class, and gender, it was Audre Lorde who was among the first to include sexuality as an important identity and the location of one of the many oppressions that

Black women experience. Emphasizing the importance of identity in her work, Lorde (1984) explains that she writes from the perspective of a "Black woman, lesbian, feminist, mother of two children, daughter of Grenadian immigrants, educator, cancer survivor, [and] activist" (p. 8). Lorde, like Cooper, urged Black women to label and define themselves for themselves, or others will do it for them and use it against them. Lorde also urges Black communities to recognize the oppression they inflict on sexual minorities and for lesbian, gay, bisexual, and transgender (LGBT) communities to recognize and evaluate their treatment of people of color. Lorde was also active in the Black feminist lesbian organization Combahee River Collective (Combahee River Collective 1983).

Patricia Hill Collins (2000) states that intersectionality is the "analysis claiming that systems of race, social class, gender, sexuality, ethnicity, nation, and age form mutually constructing features of social organization which shape Black women's experiences and, in turn, are shaped by Black women" (p. 299). This intersectionality helps to create a system of power, or what she calls, *the matrix of domination*. The matrix of domination is

> the overall organization of hierarchical power relations for any society. Any specific matrix of domination has 1. a particular arrangement of intersecting systems of oppression, e.g. race, social class, gender, sexuality, citizenship status, ethnicity and age; and 2. a particular organization of its domains of power, e.g. structural, disciplinary, hegemonic, and interpersonal. (Collins 2000, p. 299)

15.3 Methodologies

Intersectionality is not just used as a framework to examine the lives and experiences of Black women and other women of color; it is also used to examine the role that intersecting identities and oppressions have on the lives and experiences of other women and men of color (Choo and Ferree 2010). Scholars, Cho et al. (2013) argue that intersectionality has expanded to a field of study to include, "investigation[s] of intersectional dynamics... debates about the scope and content of

intersectionality as a theoretical and methodological paradigm, and ... political interventions employing an intersectional lens" (p. 785).

As a methodological framework, intersectionality allows researchers to examine the multiple ways intersecting identities and oppressions may influence a respondent's identity, and thus, her or his response to various questions or prompts in the data collection process (Choo and Ferree 2010; Simien 2007). An intersectional framework helps the researcher to know what categories to include in data collection and how to analyze the findings (Christensen and Jensen 2012). Christensen and Jensen (2012) argue,

> Basically, intersectionality raises the fundamental methodological question of how to analyze such mutually constitutive processes. Some authors have discussed these complexities in terms of the status of the social categories... emphasizing that different social categories produce different types of knowledge. (p. 111)

These scholars focus on what categories of identity should exist and the differences between categories and within categories (Christensen and Jensen 2012). The two general categories of social science research are qualitative and quantitative research.

15.3.1 Intersectionality in Qualitative Research

Qualitative research is an in-depth analysis of a population or issue and is more likely to focus on small sample sizes in an effort to provide a more detailed account of a group or individual's experiences (Harris and Tyner-Mullings 2013). Researcher Gemma Hunting (2014) explains, "[b]oth intersectionality and qualitative methodology share assumptions about the context-bound nature of research, the importance of foregrounding voices of differently situated individuals, and the need to address power imbalances between researchers and those with whom research is conducted" (p. 1). Qualitative methodologies include interviews, focus groups, and ethnographies. As small groups and populations are studied within qualitative research, intersectional frameworks are often used to help researchers understand notions of identity in data analysis for qualitative studies. "Intersectionality cautions against thinking in categories" (Hunting 2014, p. 3), and as such, qualitative methodologies are well suited for an intersectional framework as it can be applied to help increase understandings of issues and experiences such as in criminal justice and health.

For instance, Adam Trahan (2011) argues that in examining the criminal justice system, intersectional frameworks help researchers better take into account the ways in race, gender, and class influence experiences with the criminal justice system. Carmen H. Logie et al. (2011) conducted a series of focus groups to study coping mechanisms and experiences of discrimination among HIV positive women. Their (2011) sample consisted of 69% women of color, 23% lesbian/bisexual, and 22% were transgender. They explain that,

> [e]ach focus group explored the following topics: research priorities (e.g., important issues in the lives of HIV-positive women); challenges and strengths in daily life; medical issues and needs; community and academic partnerships (e.g., relationships between participants and university researchers); and issues that were silenced in one's community. (Logie et al. 2011, p. 4)

Logie et al. (2011) were able to take into account the different experiences of the study participants in designing focus groups and questions. However, some of the challenges associated with qualitative research, in general, often is obtaining a sample size large enough to make generalizations concerning study findings. For example, Logie et al. 2011, found that

> despite numerous attempts and rescheduling, only one woman participated in the Latina focus group and five participated in the Asian/South Asian group. This situation could be reflective of the lack of services geared for Latina, Asian, and South Asian HIV-positive women—the culturally specific [AIDS Service Organizations] predominately serve men. (p. 4)

Nonetheless, qualitative research is widely regarded as the best methodology in which to apply intersectional frameworks in study design, data collection, and analysis.

15.3.2 Intersectionality in Quantitative Research

Quantitative, or survey-based, research examines the, "relationship between variables or understand how certain characteristics have an effect on others" (Harris and Tyner-Mullings 2013, p. 141). In examining an issue quantitatively, researchers typically begin by developing one or more hypothesis or research questions concerning the relationship between variables or measureable characteristics. Harris and Tyner-Mullings explain that "[s]ince quantitative research consists of placing individuals and their responses into certain predetermined categories and relies on statistical analysis, the samples are often much larger than those which would be collected through qualitative methods" (2013, p. 141). As such, researchers often create a series of questions in their surveys with a list of categories depending on the purpose of the survey and the anticipated sample population. Capturing the anticipated responses of people and taking into account intersectionality and the impact of social and cultural factors on perceptions and experiences is often a challenge for quantitative researchers. Categories are often perceived as being mutually exclusive, such as "female/male" or "Black/White," research rarely takes into account the intersections of these identities and the unique experiences people would have as a result of these experiences. In quantitative research and data collection, intersectionality can help researchers determine what categories to include and what statistical analyses to perform in order to interpret the data. Quantitative researcher Catherine E. Harnois (2010) explained that intersectional frameworks in research design

> takes into consideration the potential racial and ethnic biases described by multiracial feminist theories. In brief, by comparing the relationship among multiple observed variables, multiple group analysis allows us to determine whether it is reasonable to use the same measurement instrument for people in different groups (e.g., women who are [B]lack, [W]hite, and Latina). (p. 161)

This is particularly the case in research that examines women and "minorities," such as racial and ethnic minorities and sexual minorities. Lisa

Bowleg (2012) explains that "[t]he problem with the 'women and minorities' statement… is the implied mutual exclusivity of these populations. Missing is the notion that these two categories could intersect, as they do in the lives of racial/ethnic minority women" (p. 1267). The question for quantitative researchers then becomes, how does one take into account multiple identities, perceptions, and experiences in their studies?

Within quantitative research, applying intersectional analysis can be rather challenging as intersectionality takes into account multiple identities. Quantitative data sets often contain large numbers of subjects, which add a level of complexity for those who intend to apply an intersectional framework in their research. Additionally, even if an intersectional framework is applied, there are challenges in how to interpret the data. For example, the *Black Lesbians Stress and Resilience Study* (BLSR) uses a mixed qualitative and quantitative approach to examine Black lesbians. As the study participants are marginalized based on race, gender, and sexual orientation, researchers worked to apply an intersectional framework in the survey and faced difficulty in interpreting the data.

> For example, only 9% and 21% of the BLSR sample disagreed or were neutral respectively about the statement, "Racism, sexism, and homophobia are all serious issues in my life" (p. 234). By contrast, more than half of the sample (67%) agreed with the statement that racism, sexism and heterosexism were all serious issues in their lives. The question: how to interpret the 30% who disagreed or were neutral about these issues? (Bowleg 2008, pp. 320–321)

However, Bowleg (2008) contends that the challenges to both quantitative and qualitative intersectional studies include,

> (1) how to make sense of quantitative findings about intersectionality; and (2) how to interpret narratives in which interviewees talk about some, but not all of their major intersections of social inequality; for example, the intersections of racism and heterosexism, but not sexism. (p. 320)

Nonetheless, regardless of the many challenges of applying intersectional frameworks to quantitative research, quantitative methodologies need to better take into account the variety of issues and concerns in which people with multiple identities experience (McCall 2005).

15.4 Sexualities Research

Following the intellectual history of the term, scholars in Africana, History, and Women's Studies have taken up the charge with work such as Danielle L. McGuire's *At the Dark End of the Street* (2011) (about Black women's work to end sexual and domestic violence as a foundational necessity for the mid-twentieth century African American civil rights movement) and extensive research on the sexualization of African American and diaspora women in antebellum, Reconstruction, and twentieth century American culture. Texts such as Siobhan Somerville's *Queering the Color Line* adopt a historical-cultural studies lens to investigate the interlocking oppressions of race and gender in the development of sexuality research; foundational texts in research on medicalization of sexuality illustrate the gendered, though not the raced and classed, dimensions of medical sex assignment (Fausto-Sterling 2000). In their 2011 text, *Theorizing Intersectionality and Sexuality*, Taylor, Hines and Casey offer a broad view of the adoption and contestation of "intersectionality," citing a persistent if "uneasy" tendency for feminist scholars to rely on binaries or discrete categories, and the "complicated relationship… between queer theory and intersectionality." *Theorizing* attempts an anthologized intervention into "the under-development of sexuality in the application of intersectionality" (Taylor et al. 2011, p. 3) and incorporates an unproven assertion that intersectionality may even be seen as "'outmoded' and 'outdated'" within feminist research, thus attempting a move within and through a term that has yet to be truly thoroughly explored. This resource may be of particular relevance for those interested in UK debates and scholarship; it incorporates memoir, qualitative and quantitative social science, and discussions of criminology, transgender identity, ability, and youth well-being at the intersection of sexual identity and social class.

As a field, U.S. Sexuality Studies most often incorporates analysis of sexual identity and sexual politics, as in research by American Studies scholar C.J. Pascoe (2011) on race, gender, class and sexuality in a California high school that emphasizes the interlocking privileges informing violence against women and feminine-presenting men (Pascoe's ethnography identifies that racial, sexual, and class bias are often at the root of these gendered behaviors). Elizabeth Armstrong and Laura T. Hamilton's *Paying for the Party* (2013) and other research on college student sexual behavior indicates that "sexuality and romance" are "central mechanisms through which the college experience reinforce[s] preexisting class hierarchies" such as professional attainment (p. 103). In the study, Armstrong and Hamilton classified (2013) women by "pathway" (coursework and professional track) and "fit" (resources, temperament, and social connections), delineating how the university's structures and resources intersected with students' entering status and experiences to build "distinctive combinations of major, GPA, extracurricular activities, and network ties that, depending on their class background, were more or less transferable into economic security" (p. 647). In particular, in a chapter on party culture, Armstrong and Hamilton analyze how students strive for "erotic status" using the many tools of wealth and class status to "gain rank within peer cultures;" among college-aged White women, jockeying for erotic status often relies upon "the skill and ease with which they navigated the fine line between 'sexy' and 'slutty'" (p. 1902), compacting the complex negotiations for educational and professional attainment into a single word—"slut." In short, much of the research on sexualities—whether behavior, identity, desire or sexual politics—has focused on how sexual identity and/or sexual behavior may reproduce additional social hierarchies. This approach addresses intersectionality's structural analysis, yet fails to incorporate its insights on multiple, interlocking oppressions and to extend its intellectual heritage as a Black feminist theoretical innovation.

In studies of sexual behavior, intersectional acknowledgement is often limited to what Crenshaw and Fine in Berger (2010) name as a "flattening" approach that does not account for the term's usefulness in identifying structural dynamics. Political scientist Julia Jordan-Zachery (2007), and Catherine Harnois (2010), demonstrate that lists of identities that are not operationalized to intersect may be merely "descriptive… [and] ignores the liberation/political framework of intersectionality" (p. 261). This cultural studies/cultural theory and social research divide has led to some limitations in intersectional work on sexual behavior. LGBT Studies, Transgender Studies, and other related fields tend to use the discourses of identity to investigate sexuality. The literature on identity is vast and complex; on behavior and desire, growing; yet the three dimensions of sexuality are rarely engaged in connection with one another and even less frequently in connection with research on social power.

In higher education/student affairs literature, which often employs social science methods, research emphasizes the experiences of LGB and T-identified students and faculty (to a lesser extent staff). Sue Rankin's 2010 report on the State of LGBT People in Higher Education demonstrates strong emphasis and analysis of intersectionality, reflecting data about the varied experiences of Lesbian, Gay, Bisexual, Transgender, and other sexual minority-identified individuals from White first-generation transgender men to cisgender, lesbian identified, trans women of color (Rankin et al. 2010). Transfeminine, transmasculine, and gender non-conforming people were significantly more likely to experience harassment; multiple minoritized identities—that is, study participants with targeted social group identities in multiple categories—are at much greater risk for experiencing multiple and intersecting forms of harassment (for instance, respondents of color were 10 % more likely than White respondents to have experienced racial profiling or harassment) (Rankin et al. 2010, pp. 10–11). Yet this intersectional research does not often cross disciplinary boundaries and is typically deployed as research supporting practical modifications in student affairs or other educational practice, rather than as social science research in its own right.

With increasing acceptance of lesbian, gay, and (to a lesser extent) transgender and bisexual individuals, queer scholars and activists, such as Jasbir Puar, Sara Ahmed, Kenyon Farrow, Janet Mock, and political scientist Dara Z. Strolovitch, have adopted intersectional analysis to interrogate the political agenda of same-sex marriage. Strolovitch (2012) writes:

> The rights and respectability made possible through marriage serve also to silence, exploit, and reinforce other lines of marginalization and exclusion, and those who continue to engage in such practices are now doubly marginalized—first, by the stigma associated with homosexuality among members of the general public, and again by the internal policing and secondary marginalization on the part of an LGBT community that views such practices as unevolved. (Cohen 1999, p. 394)

In performance studies, E. Patrick Johnson's ethnographic and performative work *Sweet Tea* (2008), on the lives of queer Black men in the southern U.S., co-exists as a text of oral histories and as a performance piece. The oral histories, which Johnson conducted over a ten-year period, weave tales of church, school, family, sexual activity, gender presentation, and racial history, emphasizing the intersecting experiences of sexual identity and behavior with culturally and regionally grounded analysis of race, class, gender, and sexual orientation. In the performance piece, Johnson presents vocal and visual enactments and recordings of the interviews themselves. In an interview with scholar Marc Anthony Neal (2014), Johnson explicitly cites the narratives as emerging from an intellectual question about Black gay identity that also engages personal narrative, research ethics, and social history. Researchers and scholar-activists like the editorial collective of *The Feminist Wire* (www.thefeministwire.com) adopt a similarly "grounded theory" approach that takes into account the primacy of material effects of intersecting oppressions and the necessity of a mobile and engaged scholarly practice that regularly interrogates its methods and engages with research subjects as equals who speak back to the research process and product (Berger and Guidroz 2010). This integrative scholar-activist approach to studying sexuality is one of the most promising directions

that aligns with the intellectual and political history of intersectionality.

15.5 Intersectionality, Social Science Research, and Social Locations

15.5.1 Intersectionality and Religion

As Black feminist theorists have emphasized, religion and spirituality play a major role in notions of identity for many individuals. Increasingly, researchers have examined the roles that religion and spirituality play in influencing identity formation. This is especially the case when it comes to issues of sexuality (Rodriguez et al. 2013). For many people of color, religion and spirituality offer a sense of acceptance and hope. When examined from an intersectional framework, religion can take on an identity that influences how one experiences their culture and identity, and how it empowers them. For example, intersectionality has been used to explore religion as an aspect of identity among queer Muslims (Rahman 2010).

Intersectionality and Interdisciplinary Studies:

Multiple interdisciplinary fields apply intersectionality to research on sexuality, including Sexuality Studies, Performance Studies, LGBT Studies, Africana Studies, Latino/a Studies, Asian American Studies, Transgender Studies, Women's Studies, and Ethnic Studies (to name a few). As Taylor et al. (2011) note, much of this research emphasizes the difficulty of exploring identity and sexuality as both identities and lived practices, especially given that many of the interdisciplinary fields listed above are awash in the knowledge and discourse of queer theory. Interdisciplinary social science research on sexuality within interdisciplinary studies, then, has adopted each discipline's interpretation of the postmodern turn, while incorporating intersectional methods and considerations in its methodologies.

Even geography has adopted the lens of intersectionality, though with some limit to investigating gender and race. Michael Brown (2012) notes with regard to geography, "Beyond gender and race, however, other axes of identity and structures of oppression have received far less attention" (p. 544).

15.5.2 Intersectionality and the Body:

15.5.2.1 Sexual Violence and Gender-Based Violence

Research on sexual and gender-based violence, has mixed visibility of intersectional approaches. Uniquely valuable in this respect is the work of Andrea Smith, particularly *Conquest*; her historical and theoretical account of sexual violence in Native American communities and Indian Country utilizes both the identity and power dimensions of intersectionality. Ching-In Chen, Leah Piepzna-Samarasinha, Jai Dulani, and Andrea Smith's *The Revolution Starts at Home* (2011) is an essential text investigating intersectional gender-based violence work both in activist practice and in social science theory and research. The text is a multi-genre collection that incorporates political analysis, poetry, and practical resources for addressing the intersecting forms of violence in activist communities in ways that account for intersecting power dynamics and attempt to create alternatives to oppressive accountability systems. This text, now out of print, originally appeared as a zine (self-published resource) emerging from multiple intersecting social movements that were seeking responses and analysis of gender-based violence that moved beyond prison or other state systems. The zine became a book published by Boston's South End Press that blended personal narrative with structural critiques. Ana Lara's "there is another way," for instance, provides reflections, strategies, and analysis alongside personal narrative and includes a Survivor's Rights and Responsibilities list incorporating a balance of individual and social tactics, from naming the right to a "safe and secure home" to assuming responsibility to "form healthy relationships that nourish [themselves]" (p. 15). Another chapter, "Taking Risks: Implementing Grassroots Accountability Strategies," written by a collective of community workers and activists, outlines guidelines and approaches for initiating community (rather than system-based) responses

to intimate partner violence. The personal stories, critical analysis, and social welfare tactics in *The Revolution Starts at Home* explicitly address both structural and individual intersections of gender-based violence.

15.5.2.2 Intersectionality and Health

Intersectionality has been used as a framework to also examine issues of health and illness. Health disparities and inequalities are a matter of life and death. In an article entitled, "The Problem With the Phrase Women and Minorities: Intersectionality—an Important Theoretical Framework for Public Health," Lisa Bowleg (2012) writes,

> Acknowledging the existence of multiple intersecting identities is an initial step in understanding the complexities of health disparities for populations from multiple historically oppressed groups. The other critical step is recognizing how systems of privilege and oppression that result in multiple social inequalities (e.g., racism, hetero- sexism, sexism, classism) intersect at the macro social-structural level to maintain health disparities. (p. 1267)

Previous research blamed health disparities on biological, genetic, cultural, or lifestyle choice differences between racial groups. The representation of underrepresented and marginalized individuals and groups, how they are viewed and stereotyped, as well as the dominant group's behavior, practices, and expectations have implications for health. Public health and medical researchers have increasingly focused on the ways in which discrimination influences health. For example, researchers working to examine the pathways through which racism impacts health status argue that racial discrimination increase stress levels, which eventually wear down the body. Understanding the multiple facets of inequality is key to understanding how inequality impacts health.

Critical intersectional analysis provides the framework for analyzing the health effects of gendered, racial/ethnic, and class-based inequalities in the U.S. This framework also provides the theoretical foundation for claiming health as a human right. According to Amy J. Schulz and Leith Mullings (2005), intersectionality helps researchers to consider how sociocultural, historical, and contemporary contexts shape knowledge and how health, illness, and inequality are understood. Intersectionality allows researchers to consider the ways in which inequalities are produced within particular social contexts and helps to gain a better understanding of the commonalities as well as differences in these patterns as they emerge in various locations, particularly as they apply to health care. It shows how institutions structure health care access across race, gender, and class lines. Importantly, Schulz and Mullings (2005) argue that intersectional frameworks provide for the potential reduction and/or elimination of health inequalities through resistance, interventions, and health social movements.

Loretta J. Ross (2009) builds upon Black feminist scholarship to identify the unique need for an intersectional analysis with respect to women's reproductive health. The intersecting systems of White supremacy and the mechanisms of population control in the U.S. and abroad create unique conditions of peril for African American, Latino/a, Asian American, Native American, and other women of color in accessing and maintaining human rights. Sociologist Laura Briggs' *Reproducing Empire* (2002) investigates colonialism and reproductive health in Puerto Rico, asserting that "forms of sexuality are crucial to colonialism" in both "the work of racialization" and the economic and political colonial project (p. 4). In a chapter on the politics of sterilization, Briggs notes the complex intersections of race, gender, and class through a critique of the position of mainstream U.S. socialist feminists, whose pro-nationalist position inadvertently supported a dimension of nationalist Puerto Rican politics that was explicitly pro-natalist (opposed to birth control and sterilization) and anti-feminist. The complexity of these politics, and their immersion in the multiple social movements for autonomy around race, class, gender, and nationalist politics, exemplify intersectional research. This work, and other activist and social science research, indicate a scholarly perspective that both centers the experiences of women of color (especially Black women) and that considers research and activism from a framework of both structural and individual experiences.

15.6   Future Directions

In 1996, Steven Seidman argued that "sociologists will need to listen to what feminists, queer theorists, or poststructuralists are saying"—and indeed, this insight is doubly relevant today, as social science researchers trained in intersectional and Black feminist theoretical perspectives emerge into a field that continues to marginalize intersectionality to its "flattened" lists of identities. A few directions to stem this tide suggest themselves.

One of the key emergent discussions would be to strengthen the quantitative methodologies for measuring sexuality, race, gender, and class in the social sciences. At present, limited resources are available for researchers wishing to investigate how (for example) LGBT+activists navigate health care access outside of state systems like marriage, civil union, or domestic partnership. How are those choices and opportunities structured by divergent racial/ethnic and cultural understandings of sexual identity for people seeking (for example) reproductive health care? Beyond direct theorizing, and activist interventions such as the Callan-Lorde Health Care Center in New York City, there are limited proven models for better understanding these intersections. The Fenway Institute in Boston conducts research at multiple identity intersections; yet few models exist for appropriately measuring the relationship between or among categories which, for now, are treated in isolation.

Studies of sexual behavior would also benefit from much deeper understanding of intersectional experiences of sexual fluidity. Existing research on sexual fluidity among women, for example, does not incorporate substantial investigation of how race, class, and cisgendered experiences may contribute to fluidity of desire, behavior, or identity (such as Diamond 2009).

One of the critical future directions—from both the activist/political and theoretical perspective of intersectionality—would be to incorporate existing research on social identity into research on sexual behavior. How are individuals' experiences of sexual attraction structured by their racial or class identity development? What is the relevance of campus institutional heterosexism (e.g., binary gender housing or gender-divided student activities) on college students' experiences of racial diversity? What could Critical Whiteness Studies contribute to the findings that a majority of people who self-identify as polyamorous are also White and middle- to upper-middle class? Dominant identity categories, rather than simply being noted, must be meaningfully investigated in their dominance for intersectionality to thrive. Any number of insights could be gained by merging the insights of intersectional humanities research with social science approaches.

This general call for interdisciplinary work can also be understood as another larger direction—working with intersectionality requires working at the intersections, not only of identities and social locations/systems, but of academic disciplines. As Alexander-Floyd (2012) suggests, intersectionality poses a challenge to existing systems of knowledge production, and to meaningfully incorporate intersectional analysis, researchers must be willing to engage their theoretical and methodological intersections as well. The constraints of contemporary university politics may limit immediate interventions in this respect, but we urge researchers and research associations to think through structural and institutional interventions to advance this direction.

Finally, researchers in sexuality would be well served to consider what Dean Spade (2013) calls "intersectional resistance"—"practices aimed at dismantling population control [that] take as their targets systems of legal and administrative governance such as criminal punishment, immigration enforcement, environmental regulation, child welfare and public benefits" (p. 1031). The projects and activism discussed in this chapter—like the Sylvia Rivera Law Project, the Callan-Lorde Health Center, FIERCE and Queers for Economic Justice, and more—"see[k] out the root causes of despair and violence facing intersectionally targeted populations and in doing so engag[e] with the law differently than rights-seeking projects do" (Spade 2013, p. 1032). Spade's argument—that individually-focused social movement advocacy is fundamentally different than rights-based advocacy and must be better understood to re-

dress significant human rights concerns—applies equally to rights and individually based research.

It also extends the originating perspective of intersectional work. Whether taking up projects that partner with intersectional resistance movements (such as the UndocuQueer movement to recognize the needs of LGBTQ + undocumented people); to ask relevant research questions, considering the differences between individually structured and intersectionally constituted research methodologies, or conducting research that interrogates the relationship of individual sexual behavior, identity, and desire to the state systems that constitute it, we encourage the next generations to extend intersectional sexuality studies by taking seriously both intersectional theories and the resistance from which, and in which, those intersections rise.

References

Alexander-Floyd, N (2012). Disappearing acts: Reclaiming intersectionality in a Post-Black Feminist era. *Feminist Formations, 24*(1), 1–25.

Armstrong, E., & Hamilton, L. T. (2013). *Paying for the Party: How college maintains Inequality*. Harvard: Boston.

Berger, M. T., & Guidroz, K. (Eds.). (2010). *Intersectional approach: Transforming the academy through race, class, and gender: Transforming the academy through race, class, and gender*. Chapel Hill: University of North Carolina Press.

Bowleg, L. (2008). When Black + Lesbian + Woman ≠ Black Lesbian Woman: The Methodological challenges of qualitative sex roles and quantitative intersectionality research. Sex *Roles, 59*, 312–325.

Briggs, L. (2002). *Reproducing Empire: race, sex, science and U.S. imperialism in Puerto Rico*. Berkeley: University of California Press.

Bowleg, L. (2012). "The problem with the phrase women and minorities: intersectionalty—an important theoretical framework for public health". *American Journal of Public Health 102*(7), 1267–1273.

Brown, M. (2012). Gender and sexuality 1: Intersectional anxieties. *Progress in Human Geography, 36*(4), 541–550.

Chen, C., Dulani J., Piepzna Samarasinha, L., & Smith, A. (2011). *The revolution starts at home: confronting intimate violence in activist communities*. Boston: South End Press.

Cho, S., Crenshaw, K. W., & McCall, L. (2013). Toward a field of intersectionality studies: Theory, applications, and praxis. *Signs, 38*, 785–810.

Choo, H. Y., & Ferree, M. M. (2010). Practicing intersectionality in sociological research: A critical analysis of inclusions interactions and institutions in the study of inequalities. *Sociological Theory, 2*(2), 129–140.

Christensen, A., & Jensen, S. Q. (2012). Doing intersectional analysis: Methodological implications for qualitative research. *NORA—Nordic Journal of Feminist and Gender Research, 20*(2), 109–125.

Cohen, C. J. (1999). *The boundaries of blackness: AIDS and the breakdown of black politics.* Chicago, IL: The University of Chicago Press.

Collins, P. H. (2000). *Black feminist thought: Knowledge, consciousness, and the politics of empowerment.* New York: Routledge.

Combabee River Collective. (1983). *Combabee river collective statement: Black feminist organizations in the 70s and 80s.* Kitchen Table/Women of Color, New York, NY.

Cooper, B. (2014). On bell, Beyoncé and Bullshit. *Crunk Feminist Collective.* http://www.crunkfeministcollective.com/2014/05/20/on-bell-beyonce-and-bullshit/. Accessed 18 July 2014.

Crenshaw, K. W. (1989). Demarginalizing the intersection of race and sex: A Black feminist critique of antidiscrimination doctrine, feminist theory and anti-racist politics. *University of Chicago Legal Forum*, 138–167.

Davis, A. Y. (1981). *Women, race, and class.* New York: Vintage Books.

Diamond, L. (2009). *Sexual fluidity: Understanding women's love and desire.* Boston: Harvard University Press.

Fausto-Sterling, A (2000). *Sexing the body.* New York: Basic Books.

Harnois, C. E. (2010). Imagining a "Feminist Revolution": Can multiracial feminism revolutionize quantitative social science research? In M. T. Berger, & K. Guidroz (Eds.), *The intersectional approach: Transforming the academy through race, class* (pp. 157–172). Chapel Hill: The University of North Carolina Press.

Harris, A, & Tyner-Mullings, A. R. (2013). *Writing for emerging sociologists.* Thousand Oaks: Sage.

Hooks, B. (1981). *"Ain't I A Woman": Black women and feminism.* Boston: South End Press.

Hunting, G. (2014). Intersectionality-informed qualitative research: A premier. Institute for Intersectional Research and Policy, SFU: Burnaby, British Columbia, Canada.

Johnson, E. P. (2008). *Sweet Tea: black gay men of the South.* Chapel Hill: The University of North Carolina Press.

Johnson, E. P. (2014). Left of black S4: E23: Staging black gay men of the South. Interview with Marc Anthony Neal. http://newblackman.blogspot.com/2014/03/left-of-black-s4e23-staging-black-gay.html. Accessed 26 Dec. 2014.

Jordan-Zachery, J. (2007). Am I a Black Woman or a Woman Who Is Black?: A few thoughts on the meaning of intersectionality. *Politics & Gender, 3*(2), 254–263.

Lorde, A. (1984). *Sister outsider: Essays and speeches by Audre Lorde.* Freedom: The Crossing Press.

Logie, C. H., James L., Tharao W., & Loutfy, M. R. (2011). HIV, gender, race, sexual orientation, and sex work: A qualitative study of intersectional stigma experienced by hiv-positive women in Ontario, Canada. *PLOS Medicine, 8*(11), 1–12. doi:10.1371/journal.pmed.1001124.

McCall L. (2005). The complexity of intersectionality. *Signs, 30*(3), 1771–1800.

McGuire, D (2011). *At the dark end of the street.* New York: Vintage.

Pascoe, C. J. (2011). *Dude, You're a Fag!* Berkeley: University of California Press.

Perry, M. (2001). *Lift up thy voice: The Sarah and Angelina Grimké family's journey from slaveholders to civil rights leaders.* New York: Penguin Books.

Rankin, S., Blumenfeld, W. J., Weber, G. N., & Frazer, S. (2010). *State of higher education for LGBT people.* Charlotte: Campus Pride.

Ross, L. (2009). The color of choice. In INCITE! Women of Color against Violence (Eds.), *The revolution will not be funded: beyond the non-profit industrial complex.* Boston: South End Press.

Schulz, A. J., & Mullings, L. (Eds.). (2005). *Gender, race, class, and health: Intersectional approaches.* Hoboken: Jossey-Bass.

Seidman, S. (1996). *Queer theory/sociology.* Cambridge: Blackwell Publishers.

Simien, E. M. (2007). "Doing intersectionality research: from conceptual issues to practical examples". *Politics & Gender 3*(2), 264–271.

Spade, D. (2013). Intersectional resistance and law reform. *Signs, 38*(4), 1031–1055 (Intersectionality: Theorizing Power, Empowering Theory).

Strolovich, D. (2012). Intersectionality in time: Sexuality and the shifting boundaries of intersectional marginalization. *Politics & Gender, 8*(3), 386–396.

Taylor, Y., Hines, S., & Casey, M. E. (2011). *Theorizing intersectionality and sexuality.* New York: Palgrave Macmillan.

Trahan, A. (2011). Qualitative research and intersectionality. *Critical Criminology, 19*, 1–14.

Washington, M. (Ed.). (1993). *Narrative of sojourner truth.* New York: Vintage Classics.

Wells-Barnett, I. B. (2002). *On lynchings.* Amherst: Humanity Books.

Asexualities: Socio-Cultural Perspectives

16

Carol Haefner and Rebecca F. Plante

16.1 Introduction

Not everyone who uses the term asexual seems to be aware that asexuals do exist. Jesuit priests David Nantais and Scott Opperman (2002), trying to debunk myths about religious life, asserted on a website:

> Myth 8: Religious are asexual
>   Question: What do you call a person who is asexual? Answer: Not a person. Asexual people do not exist. Sexuality is a gift from God and thus a fundamental part of our human identity. Those who repress their sexuality are not living as God created them to be: fully alive and well. As such, they're most likely unhappy

Was the use of "asexual" an unfortunate mistake by two men who were unaware of the existence of people who are indeed asexual? Or was this statement an uncritical recitation of a culturally normative fixation on sexuality and the central position that sexuality holds in United States society?

Imagine being in a world where your lived experience is denied because it is contrary to cultural norms, where the desire for sex and/or

sexual activity is a foreign concept, where friends and family members tell you there is something wrong with you, where doctors try to fix you, a world where your innermost self needs to remain hidden, a world that you are *in* but not *of*. This may seem like the beginning of a fairytale or the story of a space creature who crash-lands on earth. But it may be telling the story of your asexual neighbor, close friend, sibling or child.

Historically the term *asexual* has been used by scientists to refer to plants and animals that "manage to reproduce without sex" (Roughgarden 2004, p. 16). More recently, especially since the first more contemporary social scientific study of asexuality in humans was published, researchers and the public have been introduced to the term as it may apply to humans. There is a possibly small and growing community of individuals who identify as *asexual* (though numbers are not fully known) and who profess to have little or no sexual desire or attraction for another person of any sex or gender (Bogaert 2004; Brotto et al. 2010; Scherrer 2008). The study of asexuality is important because the very concept calls into question what we as a society take to be "normal." As Katz (2007) put it: "examination of... formerly unquestioned, socially institutionalized norms and systems may provide a startling new view of a previously invisible, taken-for-granted, 'normal' social universe [and] perhaps even unsettle forever our idea of norm and deviance" (pp. 16–17). We also believe it is important to recognize and value the experience of asexuals not only because they can teach us

C. Haefner (✉)
Psychology Department, Sofia University, Palo Alto, CA 94303, USA
e-mail: carol.haefner@sofia.edu

R. F. Plante
Department of Sociology, Ithaca College, Ithaca, NY 14850, USA
e-mail: rplante@ithaca.edu

J. DeLamater, R.F. Plante (eds.), *Handbook of the Sociology of Sexualities,* Handbooks of Sociology and Social Research, DOI 10.1007/978-3-319-17341-2_16, © Springer International Publishing Switzerland 2015

something about society at large, but because their experience deserves to be recognized and valued for itself.

We start with a brief history of the term *asexual*, and then differentiate asexuality from the pathologized diagnoses of Male Hypoactive Sexual Desire Disorder and Female Sexual Interest/ Arousal Disorder. Asexuality is often conflated with *celibacy*; however, self-labeled asexuals and researchers alike distinguish asexuality from celibacy. We will also address asexuality's place within a spectrum of LGTBQ identities, along with a discussion of the diversity within the asexual community and the implications of that diversity for research. Finally, we will contextualize asexuality within a socio-cultural context.

16.2 Studying Asexualities

Research about asexuality has been ambiguous, simultaneously defining it as a lack of sexual *attraction* (being drawn to others; Bogaert 2004) and a lack of sexual *desire* (wanting to be sexual in some way; Prause and Graham 2007); current researchers seem to have settled on the *lack of attraction* as the defining feature of asexuality (DeLuzio Chasin 2011). For example, participants in Scherrer's 2008 study mentioned lack of attraction as the key feature of their experiences. She speculated that this may be attributable to the Asexual Visibility and Education Network (AVEN 2014), the largest online, global community of asexuals, which suggests that "someone who does not experience sexual attraction" (www.aven.org) as the defining feature of an asexual *identity*. Researchers have not agreed on whether asexuality is defined by identity, behavior, or desire, or some combination of these (Poston and Baumle 2010).

Uncertainty extends to the question of whether asexuality should claim a place in the alphabet soup of *sexual orientations*, or as Bogaert (2006) suggests, represent a unique orientation—not a *sexual* orientation at all. This would seem to support Stein's (1999) view that, at least from a behavioral perspective, an asexual has "no sexual orientation" (p. 43). Bogaert hypothesizes that

perhaps asexuality is a *lack* of orientation, or at least should not be assumed to be in the same category as the "mainstream" sexual orientations, such as heterosexual, bisexual, or homosexual. Other research suggests that asexuality may be better described as a *romantic* orientation rather than a more traditionally conceived sexual orientation (Brotto et al. 2010; Scherrer 2008). These researchers found that some participants preferred to identify by their romantic orientation (i.e., heteroromantic, homoromantic, biromantic) rather than by a sexual orientation. That only some participants chose to identify by their romantic orientation suggests that this is one area of diversity (among several) within the asexual community that warrants further examination.

Until recently asexuality has been a little-studied phenomenon. Why is it important to study it now if, as some research suggests, perhaps only one percent of the population identifies as asexual (Bogaert 2004)? It is nonetheless important to honor the experiences of that one percent. Further understanding and study of asexuality will also shed much-needed light on other assumptions made every day about human sexualities. Eli Coleman clarified one: "Asexuality defies one of the basic tenets of sexuality: That we are all sexual beings" (Melby 2005, p. 4). Coleman does not elaborate on what he means by *sexual beings*, but he seems to reduce 'sexual beings' to people with "sexual drive" (p. 4). Is he suggesting that sexual drive or sexual desire is an essential part of human nature? If so, this is not a new idea. As far back as the second century CE, Christian churches argued that the one thing all human beings shared was a sexual nature, and that this common human condition was defined by sexual desire (Brown 1988). Sexual desire was, and still is, seen as a "natural drive" (Sipe 2007, p. 545) that is presumably constant and universal in all humans (Bay-Cheng 2006).

There are notable historical (and current) exceptions to the expectations that sexual desire is and should be natural, constant, and universal. Critical African American and Whiteness studies reveal the complicated, laden history of desire in the U.S (Owen 2014). "Asexuality-as-ideal" was a mistaken, misinterpreted application of racial, sexual, and social hegemonic values, where 'asexual' white women were vaunted as ideal examples of those who could restrain their desires. 'Asexual' black women were seen as "less threatening" than their stereotyped, caricatured, and feared "hypersexual counterpart" (p. 122). Owen is clear: conceptualizations of asexuality are and were inextricably linked to conceptualizations of *hypersexuality*. Presumably some sort of vague Goldilocks notion of sexuality (i.e., the "just right" amount or type) is also implicated in these historical prescriptions for the way people were expected to be sexual (Plante 2006).

16.3   Asexuality as Orientation: Some Historical Perspectives

We have already mentioned one way in which the definition of asexual could be ambiguous—as a lack of sexual *attraction* or as a lack of sexual *desire*—without full clarity about how these experiences or sensations may differ. A brief look at the historical use of the term will demonstrate that this ambiguity is not new. Johnson and Johnson (1963) presented one of the earliest definitions of *asexual*, which they used to describe the second of what they argued were four developmental stages of sexual behavior. The first stage was called *nonsexual* and lasted until puberty. During the nonsexual stage people were presumed "innocent [and] sexless except for classification purposes" (p. 52). After puberty, when sex could no longer be "ignored or denied" (p. 52), individuals were labeled *asexual*. At this stage asexual was defined as a "state of unexpressed sexuality which [was] presumed to last for the remainder of life among those who do not marry" (p. 52) or those whose "mates" (p. 52) become sexually incapacitated or uninterested. The third stage was the *sexual* stage. Those who "enter into a monogamous marriage are the exclusive possessors of a 'sex life'" (p. 52). Finally, the elderly, whether married or unmarried, were expected to revert to the nonsexual stage. The use of asexual in this model seems to suggest that sexual desire is present but not acted upon, which is the basic definition of *celibacy* (Terry 2012), and that sex-

ual desire should never be acted upon outside of (heterosexual) marriage. The description of the asexual phase in this model has moralistic overtones, with an implicit message that partnered sexual activity is for reproduction.

Johnson (1977) used *asexual* as a default term to describe women who "regardless of physical or emotional condition, actual sexual history, and marital status or ideological orientation, seem to *prefer* not to engage in sexual activity" (p. 97). Johnson suggested that in early Christianity, women drawn to an asexual life often chose the life of religious asceticism, where their asexuality was admired; continence was valued as a form of "physical heroism" (Brown 1988, p. 60). Historical changes in attitudes transformed these asexual women from "self-disciplined ascetic[s], to be awed, into the repressed neurotic[s] to be 'cured'" (Johnson 1977, p. 98). Nonetheless, it is vital to clarify that historical versions of asexuality may not be the same as the asexuality/asexualities we see today. Contemporary social contexts and individual self-definitions are implicated in what we currently understand to be asexuality. One scholar goes as far as arguing that

> asexuality, like most sexualities, is in significant and intricate ways carved into existence by science. This is not to say that science alone is inventing asexuality but that science, in collusion with other social forces, is defining what asexuality is and how it functions. (Przybylo 2013, p. 225)

One of the first theories of sexual orientation that included asexuality appeared in 1980 (Storms). The author tested two assumptions in his study: that sexual orientation was related to a person's "sex role" (gender role) orientation, and that sexual orientation was related to a person's erotic orientation. Though Storms found no evidence for the first assumption, he did find evidence for the second.

Based on his findings, Storms (1980) created a two-dimensional map of sexual orientation with four orientation categories: asexual, bisexual, heterosexual, and homosexual. "Asexuals" were described as low in both homo- and heteroerotic fantasies. By comparison, "bisexuals" were described as having a high incidence of both homo- and heteroerotic fantasies. Predictably, homosexuals had significantly more fantasies involving the same sex and significantly fewer involving the opposite sex than did heterosexuals. Besides occupying a quadrant in the two-dimensional model, asexuals were only mentioned one other time in the article. Storms said his model allowed for the distinction between bisexual and asexual, absent in other models (i.e., Kinsey's and Masters and Johnson's). Significantly, the term *asexual* did not appear in any of the data analysis. It is unclear whether Storms had any asexuals in his study or how he arrived at his assertion that asexuals have a low incidence of erotic fantasies.

Unlike Storms (1980), who seems to have created an asexual orientation almost by default, Nurius (1983) analyzed data from 685 participants who volunteered to answer a detailed questionnaire regarding their sexual activities. She used the standard typology of sexual orientation (i.e., heterosexual, homosexual, bisexual, and asexual) but based her classifications on participant responses to the Sexual Activity and Preference Scale (SAPS). Groups were defined according to their stated preferences on measures of heterosexuality or homosexuality; asexuals were defined as those who scored less than 10.0 on both measures. Of the 685 respondents, 5% of the men and 10% of the women (total of 56), were classified as asexual, those who preferred "not to be involved in any sexual activities" (p. 122). This is approximately 8.2% of the sample, higher than Bogaert's (2004) finding of 1% and Prause and Graham's (2007) estimate of 3.5% of the population. It is difficult to know if these findings vary so widely because of sampling error, measurement error, or other methodological issues, or if the findings reflect real incidences of asexualities.

Berkey et al. (1990) created the Multidimensional Scale of Sexuality (MSS) specifically to "validate and to contrast six proposed categories of bisexuality" (p. 67). The 45-item scale also included categories related to homosexuality, heterosexuality, and asexuality. The scale included four items specific to asexuality:

(a) I have never been aroused by erotic material which features members of either my *same* or *opposite* sex, (b) I have never felt in love with members of either my *same* or *opposite* sex, (c) I am not sexually attracted to members of either my *same* or *opposite* sex, (d) I have never engaged in sexual activity with members of my *same* or *opposite* sex. (pp. 73–76)

To be categorized asexual, participants would have had to answer affirmatively to all four statements. It is worth noting that, in this scale, asexuality was defined, in part, by not feeling "in love" with the same or other sex. This conceptualization of asexuality would seem to preclude some asexuals' desires for romantic and/or affectional bonding, interactions, and relationships. Given more recent studies of asexuality, which show that some asexuals will engage in sexual activity and do desire romantic relationships (Bogaert 2006; Brotto et al. 2010; Scherrer 2008), it is not surprising that Berkey et al. (1990) found that "no subject described his or her sexual orientation as 'asexual'" (p. 77). Respondents may not have been able to classify themselves as absolutely as the scale seemed to assume. Another researcher attempted to categorize the sexual orientation of transsexuals (note: *transsexual* was the term of art at the time) using sexual fantasy and behavior questionnaires (Green 1990). He defined asexual as a "dearth of sexual attractions or behaviors" (p. 791).

Rothblum and Brehony (1993) wanted to describe lesbians "who were a couple in every way except that they were not currently sexually involved with each other" (p. 5) and so used the term *asexual* to describe these nonsexual but romantic relationships. They expected that these women would keep their asexuality hidden from their lesbian communities. The authors argued that lesbian couples (along with gay men and cohabiting heterosexuals) were "defined by the presence of sexual activity" (p. 6) whereas heterosexual married couples were considered to be "coupled" even in the absence of sexual activity.

To address some of the limitations of previous measures of sexual orientation, Sell (1996, 2006) developed the Sell Assessment of Sexual Orientation. Sell argued that those who wanted to measure sexual orientation had four choices—dichotomous measures, the Kinsey Scale, the Klein Scale, or the Shively and DeCecco Scale.

Sell listed many limitations for each of these measures, too numerous to be described here. He concluded that in order to successfully measure sexual orientation, homosexuality and hetero-sexuality should be considered separately and measured on a continuum. The Sell Assessment contained "12 items, 6 of which assess sexual at-tractions, 4 of which assess sexual behavior, and 2 of which assess sexual identity" (p. 302). He defined sexual orientation as the "extent of sexu-al attractions toward members of the other, same, both sexes, or neither" (p. 302), and contended that the 12 assessment items measure homosexu-ality, heterosexuality, bisexuality *and* asexuality.

Carlat et al. (1997) speculated that among a group of anorexic males, asexuality—defined as having no sexual interest—was caused by the ef-fects of low protein intake combined with "active repression of sexual desire" (p. 1131) (Note that this speculation does not reflect the definition of asexuality in current research). None of the con-ceptualizations of asexuality we have discussed were based on research conducted with *self-identified* asexuals; the models seem to assume that asexuality is a default for anyone who may not experience sexual desire/attraction and/or for people who are not engaging in sexual activity by choice. The models also leave no room to ac-commodate the complicated, shifting terrains of desire, attraction, and activity, which cannot ever be as absolute as Berkey et al.'s (1990) construc-tion. However, the current literature is clear that *choosing* not to have sex or repressing sexual de-sire is not defined as asexuality, nor is a lack of sexual desire always deemed pathological.

16.4   Contemporary Myths

There are several cultural myths about asexuality. One is that people with disabilities are expected to be (or just "are") nonsexual or asexual –in this case meaning not engaging in sexual activ-ity regardless of whether there is a desire for sex (Milligan and Neufeldt 2001; Tepper 2000; Treischmann 1988). This idea has often been imposed on disabled people (see Jungels and Bender, Chap. 10, this volume). It precludes the

possibility that a disabled person could *choose* to identify as asexual (Kim 2011). Eunjung Kim (2011) analyzes the entangled history of asexual-ity and disability:

> Disability scholars rightfully challenge the per-vasive and harmful perception that asexuality is inevitable for (sexual) people with disabilities. Disability activists in sex-positive movements often attack the stereotype of disabled people as asexual and claim that 'we are sexual, we enjoy sex, and we have to be able to have sex'. However, the universalizing claim that all disabled people are sexual denies that asexuality can be positively experienced by any subjects with a disability, thus displaying the tendency to negatively generalize about asexuality as unnatural and indeed impos-sible. The insistence that sexual desire is natural for disabled people makes those people who do not feel sexual desire seem 'abnormal'. Kaz, a blogger who describes herself as being on the autistic spec-trum and asexual, illustrates the difficulty in find-ing acceptance in the disability community: '[M]y saying I am asexual in the disabled community can be interpreted as my affirming and reinforc-ing those stereotypes, which tends to make people rather angry' (2009). (Kim 2011, p. 482)

Another assumption is that older adults are asexual (Esmail et al. 2010; Brock and Jennings 2007; Lau-mann et al. 2006). As with disabled people, this im-poses socially-constructed sexual norms on older adults. When society reveres youth and uncritically reproduces the idea that heterosex is primarily for reproduction, the expectation that older adults are or should be asexual gains traction (Deacon et al. 1995). The sexual expression of older adults may be governed, at least in part, by societal beliefs about sex lives of the aging (Sandberg 2013) and so they "think they should act asexually or risk being labeled deviant" (Deacon et al. 1995, p. 499).

Celibacy is defined as "abstinence from sexu-al activity…the voluntary sacrifice of all sexual pleasure" (Sipe 2007, p. 545). This definition implies that sexual desire is *present* but may not be *acted upon*. Celibate individuals "actively choose to go against their sexual desires" (Bo-gaert 2006, p. 248). AVEN (2014) clarifies on their web page that, "Unlike celibacy, which people choose, asexuality is an intrinsic part of who we are" (Overview, para 1). Celibacy is con-structed as seemingly temporary or time-bound sexual abstinence although desire and attraction may otherwise be present. AVEN seems to argue that asexuality is not just an orientation, similar to bisexuality or heterosexuality, but is also not chosen.

16.5 The Impact of the Diagnostic and Statistical Manual of Mental Disorders

It is impossible to fully discern the impact that the *Diagnostic and Statistical Manual of Mental Disorders (DSM)* has had on the conceptualization of asexuality as an orientation and on self-identified asexuals. The third edition of the *DSM* (*DSM-III*, American Psychiatric Association [APA] 1980), included the diagnostic category *inhibited sexual desire disorder* (ISDD), which was defined as "persistent and pervasive inhibition of sexual desire" (p. 278). Later ISDD was renamed to *Hypoactive Sexual Desire Disorder* (HSDD; *DSM-III-R*, APA 1987) and was defined as "persistent or recurrently deficient or absent sexual fantasies and desire for sexual activity" (p. 293), reminiscent of Storms' 1980 definition. It was left to clinicians to decide what a "normal" level of desire was. Several researchers have critiqued the *DSM* definition, arguing that sexual desire was poorly defined (Beck 1995; McNab and Henry 2006). The one thing that seems to be consistent across *DSM* editions is the "assumption that *some* level of sexual desire is normative" (Prause and Graham 2007, pp. 341–342).

Since sexual desire has been conceptualized as a universal human experience for centuries (Brown 1988), the presumption of a normal level of desire probably did not originate with the *DSM*. The codification of a specific diagnosis concerning sexual desire may have contributed to the inclination to pathologize all instances of disinterest in sex, and has contributed to the "pejorative flavor of the word 'asexual'" (Cerankowski and Milks 2010, p. 653). No doubt there are some instances when the absence of sexual desire should be taken seriously, especially when it causes distress for an individual. But research shows that most asexuals *do not* feel distress about their lack of sexual desire (Brotto et al. 2010; Brotto and Yule 2011; Poston and Baumle 2010). Even de-

scribing asexuality as something *lacking* is misrepresentative and assumes that *possessing* sexual desire is the norm; see DeLuzio Chasin (2013) for a discussion of the impact of an essentialist view of asexuality on asexuals and those who might be defined as *sexuals* (e.g., heterosexuals, bisexuals, etc.).

Most of the current literature on asexuality was published before the *DSM-5* (APA 2013) was released and so refers to *hypoactive sexual desire disorder* (HSDD) in general (i.e., including both male and female) and sexual aversion disorder, one of several types of sexual dysfunction that has been linked to asexuality. In the *DSM-IV-TR* (APA 2000) *sexual aversion disorder* was defined as "the aversion to and active avoidance of genital sexual contact with a sexual partner" (p. 54). Prause and Graham (2007) found that "asexuals were not well-described as motivated by avoidance, as relevant in social phobias and sexual aversion difficulties" (p. 352), meaning that asexuals do not avoid or fear sex. The researchers used several scales (Sexual Inhibition scale, Dyadic Sexual Desire, Sexual Excitation, and Sexual Arousability Inventory questionnaires) and determined that the asexuals in their study did not avoid sex out of fear, but they did show lower excitatory drive than non-asexuals.

The *DSM-5* (APA 2013) no longer includes sexual aversion disorder as a diagnostic criterion. It does include two new gendered or sexed categories of sexual dysfunction that are important to the discussion of asexuality: *female sexual interest/arousal disorder* (FSI/AD), which combines sexual desire and sexual arousal disorders, and *male hypoactive sexual desire disorder* (MHSDD). The diagnostic criteria for FSI/AD focuses on the absence of or reduced interest in sexual activity and sexual thoughts or fantasies; little or no interest in initiating sexual activity; no or reduced pleasure, arousal, and/or reduced or absent sensations (genital or nongenital) during sexual activity—all lasting a minimum of 6 months. As with other sexual dysfunction disorders, the symptoms must cause distress in the individual and symptoms may not be caused by some other condition (i.e., medical, environmental, or interpersonal). The *DSM-5* has added the caveat that "'desire discrepancy,' in which a woman has lower desire for sexual activity than her partner, is not sufficient to diagnose female sexual interest/arousal disorder" (p. 433). This statement may begin to address the problems that have arisen from the process of norming sexual desire.

There was a push within the asexual community to update the *DSM-5* (APA 2013), hoping for a more asexual-friendly definition of HSDD (Jay and Hinderliter 2008). Curiously, there is a statement associated with FSI/AD that says: "If a lifelong lack of sexual desire is better explained by one's self-identification as 'asexual' then a diagnosis of female sexual interest/arousal disorder would not be made" (p. 434). There is no such statement or acknowledgment of asexuality associated with *male hypoactive sexual desire disorder* (MHSDD) which, in the *DSM-5*, uses the same definition that appeared in the *DSM-IV-TR*. The criterion for diagnosis with either FSI/AD or MHSDD is that the lack of desire causes an individual distress. For the most part, asexuals do not report feeling distress (as defined by researchers and clinicians) about their lack of interest in sexual activity (partnered and/or solo).

16.6 Asexuality in the Popular Press

Asexuality has received increased attention in mass or popular media; newspaper and magazine articles are a rich source of useful information about the real-life stories of asexuality (Cox 2008; Gadette 2004; Pereira 2007). But some mass media accounts display disbelief and skepticism (Nantais and Opperman 2002; Sammon 2005). Many writers do not present asexuality in a neutral, knowledgeable, or open-minded way. Some, after giving a definition of asexuality, go on to use phrases such as "aversion to sex," "voluntary asexuality," or "sexless lonely hearts" (Gadette 2004). John Sammon (2005), who unabashedly proclaimed that he rarely thinks of anything but sex, suggested that:

> If you're in favor of denying yourself the intense pleasure of sex, you could also deny yourself career fulfillment, travel and adventure, good health, a whole host of life-reaffirming situations. A new cottage industry will take root catering to the needs of people who have decided that it was desirable to die never having lived. (pp. 25–26)

Sammon seemed to be suggesting that sex is the only way people feel alive. Social science researchers dispute this, finding that asexuals are mentally healthy people, some of whom look for and have satisfying, emotionally connected relationships (Brotto et al. 2010).

Sex therapist Joy Davidson argued that asexuality can be explained by endocrine imbalances, a reaction to punishment for sexual feelings, sexual abuse, or a "shameful arousal pattern that the individual does not want to have triggered" (Melby 2005, p. 4). Davidson also expressed her opinion on "20/20" (a television news program), saying that to self-identify as asexual "you might as well label yourself not curious, unadventurous, narrow-minded, blind to possibilities. That's what happens when you label yourself as sexually neutered" (Pereira 2007, p. 61). She was plugging her new book *Fearless Sex*. Davidson and others like her have a vested interest in encouraging people to buy into sex-normative paradigms. After all, in the United States, "Sex is hot. Sex is power. Sex is money" (Pereira 2007, p. 63). Pereira stated that acknowledging some individuals' disinterest in sex would affect the bottom line of almost every industry. For example, with the "sex hook" less relevant, advertising as it is today could also become obsolete; why use sex to sell if not everyone responds to this message? In fact, Schwartz (2007), writing specifically about heterosexuality, suggested that one reason advertisers spend so much money to use sex to sell products is because being a "sexual being" (p. 83) is not natural and is instead "*seen as an act of will*" (p. 83; emphasis in original) that advertisers must continuously reinforce. Asexuality seems to challenge the basic, taken-for-granted assumptions of those who subscribe to a sex-normative model of human sexualities.

16.7 Asexual Voices and Perspectives

Asexuals tell a different story. To generalize, many asexuals seem to be happy for and respond positively to both research and mass media attention (Brotto et al. 2010; Westphal 2004). Some popular press outlets have given space for asexuals to tell their own stories. Weisberg (2007) recounts the life of Cijay Morgan, who, like so many asexuals, watched as her junior high and high school friends developed attractions to and crushes on boys. Later, she followed her friends to bars and tried to play the dating game. While waiting for her "prince" to arrive she realized that she was attracted to women—not in a sexual way, but as her preference for intimate relationships. Her ideal relationship would include "living happily ever after and being exclusive and going on holidays and really, really enjoying each other's company. But it never ends up in bed" (Weisberg 2007).

In 2006, Joan, in her mid-30s, saw a television program on asexuality and her life has never been the same. She finally came to understand herself better, yet feels that she cannot come out to friends or family because she feels they would think something is wrong with her and she does not want to carry the "stigma" of asexuality (Weisberg 2007). Many asexuals have a difficult time "coming out" about their asexuality to friends and family—some live for years with the secret (Pacho 2013).

At the age of 34, Erick had already spent 15 years trying to explain his lack of sexual desire. When finally he came out to his family the reaction was "You should see a shrink. That can't be normal" (Van De Mark 2007). Erick's experience would seem to make Joan's fear understandable. Joan's apprehensions about revealing herself to friends and family and the reaction Erick received from his family reveal culture's deeply embedded notions of "normal" sexuality.

Paul and Amanda, both asexual, were married in 2007, having met two years earlier. The celebration in their honeymoon suite consisted of Scrabble games with their friends. Their friends were invited to bring sleeping bags and spend the night. Paul and Amanda had never had sex and did not intend to start on their honeymoon. As of September, 2008 Paul and Amanda were happily married, wanting to adopt children (Cox 2008).

David Jay, the founder of AVEN, pointed out that much of the mass media coverage of asexuality focuses on the "sex asexuals aren't having, rather than on the real story: 'the different ways that asexual people are doing all of the thousands of things in our culture based on sexuality'" (Pereira 2007, p. 62). Jay is clear: he feels that asexuality *is* a sexual identity and not *a lack* of sexual identity (Melby 2005). He also asserts that he feels no distress or interpersonal difficulty. Melby also profiled Julie Decker, another asexual who knew she was different from her friends from an early age. Julie, 27, a bookstore employee and writer of fantasy fiction, has no interest in sex, does not date, does not masturbate, has never experienced oral sex or intercourse, and says she is not missing anything. She is not interested in a long-term relationship, but has lots of friends and does not feel lonely. Julie, like David Jay, says she has no interpersonal difficulty because of being asexual nor does she feel distress about her asexual identity or her life.

Compared to the historical literature about classification, where researchers defined asexuality without, apparently, consulting any asexuals, asexual voices are now more widely heard (Carrigan 2012). Many people are actively making the space to describe their own lived experiences, via self-published essays, comic strips, and websites (for example, www.asexualityarchive.com, rotten-zucchinis.tumblr.com, asexualpocsunite.tumblr.com). Some address the myths we have described earlier (i.e., asexuality is not a sexual dysfunction), and argue that asexuality is a sexual orientation (see also Bogaert 2006). Many asexuals tried to fit into the traditional and narrowing conceptualizations of sexuality (i.e., heterosexuality, homosexuality, and/or bisexuality)—which are largely based on the desire to interact sexually with another person—before realizing they were different. They would then begin to explore nontraditional identities (Haefner 2012). Brotto et al.'s (2008) study noted that many asexuals experienced confusion about sexual identity, and experimented with heterosexual orientations before discovering the online asexual community called AVEN.

At the moment there is no diagnostic test for asexuality, so all asexuals are self-identified (and perhaps should be?). Internet communities like AVEN strive to accept anyone, even if an asexual identity might ultimately be a temporary stop along the way in the search for an orientation or identity that might better align with personal experience. Asexuality does not require that a person identify as a life-long asexual who will never change this identity, although most people on AVEN do self-identify in precisely this manner. As AVEN's (2014) website states:

> Most people on AVEN have been asexual for our entire lives…. There is no litmus test to determine if someone is asexual. Asexuality is like any other identity-at its core, it's just a word that people use to help figure themselves out. If at any point someone finds the word asexual useful to describe themselves, we encourage them to use it for as long as it makes sense to do so ("Identity," www.aven.org).

16.8 Diversity among Asexuals

Contemporary researchers who recruit via AVEN, which boasts that it "hosts the world's largest online asexual community" (AVEN 2014), report some cultural and ethnic diversity in their participants. For example in Scherrer's 2008 study, the majority of respondents self-identified as Caucasian, but some also identified as Native American, Asian and Asian American, Latino, and multiracial (not all participants could be categorized based on the information they supplied). Scherrer also reported an international participant pool: "One participant each from France, Israel, Moldova, Russia, Scotland, Hungary, Sweden, Italy, New Zealand, European Union, two from Turkey, four from Germany, six from Australia, 10 from Canada, 11 from England, and the remaining 52 from the USA" (p. 625). These numbers may suggest that asexuality is more prevalent in the U.S., or perhaps that self-definition, awareness, or participation in something like AVEN is more prevalent in the U.S. They may also reflect that fact that U.S. researchers who recruit from AVEN often require the potential participant be fluent in English. Respondent pools may thus be skewed toward the U.S. and other English-speaking countries. Most studies of asexuality have been done by researchers in the U.S. (e.g., Brotto et al. 2010; Brotto and Yule 2011; Poston and Baumle 2010) or the United Kingdom (e.g., Carrigan 2011; Aicken et al. 2013).

"Diversity among asexuals" usually refers to the diverse ways self-identified asexuals express their asexualities in everyday life, their relationship preferences, and/or their comfort with sexual activities. Some asexuals will have sexual intercourse of various forms and some will masturbate, but some will feel repulsed by the idea of most (or all) forms of sexual activity. Some consider holding hands a sexual activity; others will sleep naked next to their partners. Some asexuals entertain the idea of polyamorous (romantic) relationships where the partner, often a "sexual" person, has sexual needs met by other partners (see Sheff and Tesene, Chap. 13, for general discussion of polyamory). Others have no desire for intimate or romantic relationships, identifying instead as *aromantic* (see Haefner 2012; Prause and Graham 2007; Scherrer 2008).

"Diversity" also encompasses the creative use of language asexuals have adopted to name and explain their experiences. For example, some asexuals prefer to identify with their romantic inclinations (i.e., heteroromantic, homoromantic, biromantic, etc.), if they have them. Many asexuals also have a diverse language for identifying their genders (e.g., agender, pangender, genderqueer, transgender etc.), along with unique ways of talking about the ways in which they conceptualize sex (e.g., Ace/ace, sex-positive, sex-neutral, demi-sexual, grey-A/grace, anti-sex, A-fluid) (Carrigan 2011; Emens 2014). Definitions differ, but each term addresses a nuanced aspect of sexuality and relationships. For example, grey-A refers to a person who may have brief, fleeting, or infrequent *possible* sexual attraction or desire. Demi-sexual refers to a person whose sexuality is strongly organized around deep knowledge of and love for a very specific person; a demi-sexual would only experience attraction after the development of this relational intimacy. Terms have also been developed to refer to people who are *not* asexual—*sexual/s* and *allosexual*.

16.9 Future Research

Research on asexuality among humans is fairly new and clearly fraught with a range of concerns and caveats. Thus there are many avenues for research that could yield important findings and new theories.

16.9.1 Longitudinal Study

Though some research has suggested that asexuality may be life-long (Brotto et al. 2010), there have been no longitudinal or long-term studies on asexuality across the life-course (see Carpenter, Chap. 5, this volume, for a discussion of this perspective). How do asexualities change, adapt, grow, and evolve through the life-course? How do asexuals come to understand the paths of their identities, orientations, and selves? One research team *has* conducted a 14-day diary study of asexuality, coming out, and intimacy (Scott et al. 2014). Participants were asked to record instances and occasions in everyday life when asexuality was 'relevant'; researchers were interested in a key question: "How do people experience asexuality themselves, and how does it affect their social lives?" (Scott et al. 2014). This exploratory research suggests that asexuality is experienced as a series of diverse and wide-ranging events that create an individual's sense of identity. More truly longitudinal or long-term studies could help further describe the trajectory of individuals' self-development and understanding (Carrigan et al. 2013).

16.9.2 Models of Asexual Identity/ Orientation Development

Is it useful to conceptualize asexuality as an identity or an orientation? Why are the classifications and distinctions seen as necessary, clarifying, or productive? If there were to be any models or typologies, who would develop them and how? To serve what functions or purposes? The *collective identity* model, synthesized by David Jay (2014), suggests that:

> Asexual people have something in common because they have all chosen to actively disidentify with sexuality, a socially dominant framework for thinking about everything from pleasure to attractiveness to intimacy.
>
> Under this model an asexual person is anyone who uses the term "asexual" to describe themselves. The label can only be applied internally, no one has the power to create a set of criteria which determine who "is" and "is not" asexual. The

desire to identify as asexual comes from occupying a particular social position relative to culturally dominant ideas about sexuality. This common social position is the one thing which unifies all asexual people.

An interpretation like this is both useful *and* incomplete, a problem that would beset perhaps any attempt to model something as diverse as asexualities.

Models of and for asexual development might progress similarly to models suggested for other aspects of human sexualities (e.g., Diamond 2009; Troiden 1988). Diamond's (2009) longitudinal multi-decade qualitative study of women (initially interviewed just after coming out as bisexual or lesbian), suggests that identity development is not linear, straightforward, or fixed. We can infer from her research that, in general, a key variable in identity/orientation development is relevance: which aspects of sexualities are relevant to individuals at various points in their lives? How do social, contextual, life-course, and psychological experiences connect to help an asexual individual map out a sense of self, identity, and salience? A truly useful model of asexuality development would encompass cognitive, behavioral, and interactional aspects of self.

16.9.3 The Process of "Coming Out"

Are asexualities unique, different, singular? Comparisons and connections with other presumed coming out models suggest that asexualities researchers can learn from the errors and fallacies embedded within those models (see Savin-Williams 2014). Assumptions about how individuals come out—that it is a "process;" that it is linear; that it is orderly; that it is individual, social, and contextual—may not apply to asexualities (or to any sexual identities or orientations). Coming out may differ depending upon all aspects of an individual's asexual identity, taking into account romantic orientation (does a person wish to find a romantic asexual relationship, and if so, what sort?), gender identity, and intersectional variables such as race, class, nationality, and religion.

16.9.4 How to Improve Research on Asexualities

Generally, social science sexualities research of all kinds can suffer from fundamental flaws—researcher bias, respondent bias, sample bias, and poor or inadequate theorizing, to name a few. A lack of understanding of the issues particular to asexualities hampers some researchers, and improvements may be easier to discuss than implement. Perhaps the most important would be to develop research methods free of and cognizant of latent underlying sexual-normative assumptions. Awareness of the hegemony inherent in the assumption that humans "are" sexual (or are otherwise choosing celibacy) is fundamental.

Clarifying the role of intersectional variables—gender, race, ethnicity, class, age, and national origins—will be vital for future research to be taken seriously. For example, middle-class asexual white men may face particular challenges due to cultural assumptions about the highly prescribed and hegemonic ways in which men are expected to be sexual. Przybylo (2014), citing Hollway's "male sex drive imperative," summarizes other researchers' discussions of the sexual scripting that many white, middle-class men are subject to: compulsory heterosexuality and coupling, along with the ejaculation, orgasm, and coital imperatives (Przybylo 2014). Research designed to capture the importance of and role of intersectional variables should acknowledge the culturally and socially constructed ways in which asexuality can be understood differently depending on race, class, ethnicity, gender, national origin, and so forth. People with class, race, ethnicity, and nationality privilege may be able to "do" or perform their asexualities with more resources and less stigma than people with less privilege.

Some progress has been made recently, with scholarship by authors acknowledging their points of view as "aces" (asexuals) and privileging more nuanced frames of reference and participant-observer (or insider) methods and arguments (e.g., Milks and Cerankowski 2014; Haefner 2012). We can see progress institutionally—the National Women's Studies Association (NWSA) now includes the Asexuality Interest Group, which hosted its first set of panels in 2012 (personal communication, 2014); presenters addressed activism, awareness, embodiment, religion, humanities perspectives, and social sciences perspectives, among other topics. The Interest Group formed because audience members in the first NWSA panel on asexuality (in 2011) suggested it and then worked to make it happen.

Blogs covering personal, political, activist, social, historical, and scholarly work abound (e.g., asexualsexologist.com, asexualagenda. wordpress.com, asexualexplorations.net). Siggy, a contributor to the collaborative, community-building asexualagenda.wordpress.com, has interviewed activists and scholars commenting on everything from asexualities in Russia to race and racism within some online communities. Other blogs or compilation sites reveal the complicated relationships between and among race, class, and "being ace" (e.g., asexualpocsunite.tumblr.com; thethinkingasexual.wordpress.com).

Researchers need to better conceptualize the relationships between and among:

a. sexual desire and sexual attraction
b. love and sex
c. love and sexual desire
d. romantic attraction and love
e. intimacy and romance

Careful consideration of the ways in which sexualities researchers have elided these key and abstract concepts should reveal fruitful lines of study. Given their focus on respondent-centered, meaning-making practices, symbolic interactionist approaches particularly (and other qualitative research approaches more generally), may have much to add (Waskul and Plante 2010). Expanding our awareness of the ways in which asexuals define and understand themselves is crucial to developing a more nuanced picture of the diversity of asexualities.

References

Aicken, C. R. H., Mercer, C. H., Cassell, J. A. (2013). Who reports absences of sexual attraction in Britain? Evidence from national probability surveys. *Psychology & Sexuality, 4*(2), 121–135. doi:10.1080/1941989 9.2013.774161.

American Psychiatric Association. (1980). *Diagnostic and statistical manual of mental disorders* (3rd ed.). Washington, DC: Author.

American Psychiatric Association. (1987). *Diagnostic and statistical manual of mental disorders* (revision, 3rd ed.). Washington, DC: Author.

American Psychiatric Association. (2000). *Diagnostic and statistical manual of mental disorders* (text revision, 4th ed.). Washington, DC: Author.

American Psychiatric Association. (2013). *Diagnostic and statistical manual of mental disorders* (5 ed.). Washington, DC: Author.

AVEN. (2014). Asexual visibility & education network. http://www.asexuality.org. Accessed 1 June 2014.

Bay-Cheng, L. Y. (2006). The social construction of sexuality: Religion, medicine, media, schools, family. In R. D. McAnulty & M. M. Burnette (Eds.), *Sex and sexuality: Vol. 1. Sexuality today: Trends and controversies* (pp. 203–228). Westport: Praeger.

Beck, J. G. (1995). Hypoactive sexual desire disorder: An overview. *Journal of Consulting and Clinical Psychology, 63*(6), 919–927.

Berkey, B. R., Perelman-Hall, T., & Kurdek, L. A. (1990). The multidimensional scale of sexuality. *Journal of Homosexuality, 19*(4), 67–87.

Bogaert, A. F. (2004). Asexuality: Prevalence and associated factors in a national probability sample. *Journal of Sex Research, 41*(3), 279–286.

Bogaert, A. F. (2006). Toward a conceptual understanding of asexuality. *Review of General Psychology, 10*(3), 241–250.

Brock, L. J., & Jennings, G. (2007). Sexuality and intimacy. In J. A. Blackburn & C. N. Dulmus (Eds.), *Handbook of gerontology: Evidence-based approaches to theory, practice, and policy* (pp. 244–268). Hoboken: Wiley.

Brotto, L., & Yule, M. A. (2011). Physiological and subjective sexual arousal in self-identified asexual women. *Archives of Sexual Behavior, 40,* 699–712. doi:10.1007/s10508-010-9671-7.

Brotto, L., Knudson, G., Inskip, J., Rhodes, K., & Erskine, Y. (2010). Asexuality: A mixed-methods approach. *Archives of Sexual Behavior, 39,* 599–618. doi:10.1007/s10508-008-9434-x.

Brown, P. (1988). *The body and society: Men, women and sexual renunciation in early Christianity*. New York: Columbia University Press.

Carlat, D. J., Camargo, C. A., Jr., & Herzog, D. B. (1997). Eating disorders in males: A report on 135 patients. *American Journal of Psychiatry, 154*(8), 1127–1132.

Carrigan, M. (2011). There's more to life than sex? Difference and commonality within the asexual community. *Sexualities, 14*(4), 462–478. doi:10.1177/1363460711406462

Carrigan, M. (2012). "How do you know you don't like it if you haven't tried it?" Asexual agency and the sexual assumption. In T. G. Morrison, M. A. Morrison, M. A. Carrigan, & D. T. McDermott (Eds.), *Sexual minority research in the new millennium* (pp. 3–20). New York: Nova Science.

Carrigan, M., Gupta, K., & Morrison, T. G. (2013). Asexuality special theme issue editorial. *Psychology & Sexuality, 4*(2), 111–120.

Cerankowski, K. J., & Milks, M. (2010). New orientations: Asexuality and its implications for theory and practice. *Feminist Studies, 36*(3), 650–664.

Cox, P. (2008). We're married, we just don't have sex. http://www.apositive.org/?s=some+like+it+hot. Accessed 3 Jan 2009.

Deacon, S., Minichiello, V., & Plummer, D. (1995). Sexuality and older people: Revisiting the assumptions. *Educational Gerontology. Special Issue: Learning to live at all ages, 21*(5), 497–513.

DeLuzio Chasin, C. J. (2011). Theoretical issues in the study of asexuality. *Archives of Sexual Behavior, 40,* 713–723.

DeLuzio Chasin, C. J. (2013). Reconsidering asexuality and its radical potential. *Feminist Studies, 39*(2), 405–426.

Diamond, L. M. (2009). *Sexual fluidity: Understanding women's love and desire*. Cambridge: Harvard University Press.

Emen, E. (2014). Compulsory sexuality. *Stanford Law Review, 66,* 303–386.

Esmail, S., Darry, K., Walter, A., & Knupp, H. (2010). Attitudes and perceptions towards disability and sexuality. *Disability and Rehabilitation, 32*(14), 1148–1155. doi:10.3109/09638280903419277.

Gadette, J. (2004). Asexual underground: Gay passe? Straight sedate? Get ready for the nerdy underbelly of no sex. http://www.slweekly.com/index.cfm?do=article.details&id=1CA812CA-2BF4-55D0-F1F09D9BE9B80EB9. Accessed 21 Sept 2009.

Green, R. & Fleming, D. T. (1990). Transsexual surgery follow-up: Status in the 1990s. *Annual Review of Sex Research 1*(1), 163–174.

Haefner, C. (2012). *Asexual scripts: A grounded theory inquiry into the intrapsychic scripts asexuals use to negotiate romantic relationships*. (Doctoral dissertation), Retrieved from ProQuest Dissertation and Theses database. (Order No. AAI3457969).

Jay, D. (2014). Collective identity model. In AVEN Wiki. http://www.asexuality.org/wiki/index.php?title=Collective_identity_model. Accessed 7 Aug 2014.

Jay, D., & Hinderliter, A. C. (2008). DMS fireside chat. https://www.youtube.com/watch?v=4z3u0DyUe6U. Accessed 14 Aug 2009.

Johnson, W. R., & Johnson, J. A. (1963). *Human sex and sex education*. Philadelphia: Lea & Febiger.

Johnson, M. T. (1977). Asexual and autoerotic women: Two invisible groups. In H. L. Gochros & J. S. Gochros (Eds.), *The sexually oppressed* (pp. 96–109). New York: Association Press.

Katz, J. N. (2007). *The invention of heterosexuality*. Chicago: The University of Chicago Press.

Kim, E. (2011). Asexuality in disability narratives. *Sexualities, 14*(4), 479–493.

Laumann, E. O., Paik, A., Glasser, D. B., Kang, J.-H., Wang, T., Levinson, B., Gingell, C., et al. (2006).

A cross-national study of subjective sexual well-being among older women and men: Findings from the global study of sexual attitudes and behaviors. *Archives of Sexual Behavior, 35*(2), 145–161.

McNab, W. L., & Henry, J. (2006). Human sexual desire disorder: Do we have a problem? *The Health Educator, 38*(2), 45–52.

Melby, T. (2005). Asexuality gets more attention, but is it a sexual orientation? *Contemporary Sexuality: The International Resource for Educators, Researchers and Therapists, 39*(11), 1–5.

Milligan, M. S., & Neufeldt, A. H. (2001). The myth of asexuality: A survey of social and empirical evidence. *Sexuality and Disability, 19*(2), 91–109.

Milks, M. & Cerankowski, K. J. (2014). Introduction: Why asexuality? Why now? In K. J. Cerankowski & M. Milks (Eds.), *Asexualities: Feminist and queer perspectives* (pp. 1–14). New York: Routledge.

Nantais, D., & Opperman, S. (2002). Eight myths of religious life. http://vocation-network.org/articles/show/49. Accessed 3 Jan 2009.

Nurius, P. S. (1983). Mental health implications of sexual orientation. *Journal of Sex Research, 19*(2), 119–136.

Owen, I. H. (2014). On the racialization of asexuality. In K. J. Cerankowski & M. Milks (Eds.), *Asexuality: Feminist and Queer perspectives* (pp. 119–135). New York: Routledge.

Pacho, A. (2013). Establishing asexual identity: The Essential, the imaginary, and the collective. *Graduate Journal of Social Science, 10*(1), 13–35.

Pereira, K. (2007). Do not want: The asexual revolution gets organized. *Bitch: Feminist Response to Pop Culture, 37,* 58–63.

Plante, R. F. (2006). *Sexualities in context: A social perspective.* Boulder: Westview Press.

Poston, D. L., & Baumle, A. K. (2010). Patterns of asexuality in the United Satees. *Demographics Research, 23*(18), 509–530. doi:10.4054/DemRes.2010.23.18.

Prause, N., & Graham, C. A. (2007). Asexuality: Classification and characterization. *Archives of Sexual Behavior, 36*(3), 341–356.

Przybylo, E. (2013). Producing facts: Empirical asexuality and the scientific study of sex. *Feminism & Psychology, 23*(4), 224–242.

Przybylo, E. (2014). Masculine doubt and sexual wonder: Asexaully-identified men talk about their (A) sexualities [sic]. In K. J. Cerankowski & M. Milks (Eds.), *Asexualities: Feminist and queer perspectives* (pp. 225–246). New York: Routledge.

Rothblum, E. D., & Brehony, K. A. (1993). Introduction: Why focus on romantic but asexual relationships among lesbians? In E. D. Rothblum & K. A. Brehony (Eds.), *Boston marriages: Romantic but asexual relationships among contemporary lesbians.* Amherst: University of Massachusetts Press.

Roughgarden, J. (2004). *Evolution's rainbow: Diversity, gender, and sexuality in nature and people.* Berkeley: University of California Press.

Sammon, J. (2005). Asexuality: No sex as good as sex? http://sammonsays.com/artman/publish/Asexuality-No-Sex-as-good-as-Sex-column.shtml. Accessed 2 Jan 2009.

Sandberg, L. (2013). Just feeling a naked body close to you: Men, sexuality and intimacy in later life. *Sexualities, 16*(3/4), 261–282. doi:10.1177/1363460713481726.

Savin-Williams, R. C. (2014). The new sexual-minority teenager. In D. A. Powell & J. S. Kaufman (Eds.), *The meaning of sexual identity in the 21st century* (pp. 5–20). New York: Cambridge Scholars Publishing.

Scherrer, K. S. (2008). Coming to an asexual identity: Negotiating identity, negotiating desire. *Sexualities, 11*(5), 621–641. doi:10.1177/1363460708094269.

Schwartz, P. (2007). The social construction of heterosexuality. In M. S. Kimmel (Ed.), *The sexual self: The construction of sexual scripts* (pp. 80–92). Nashville: Vanderbilt University Press.

Scott, S., McDonnell, L., & Dawson, M. (2014). Asexuals live: Social relationships and intimate encounters. http://www.discoversociety.org/2014/06/03/asexual-lives-social-relationships-and-intimate-encounters/. Accessed 23 June 2014.

Sell, R. L. (1996). The sell assessment of sexual orientation: Background and scoring. *Journal of Gay, Lesbian, & Bisexual Identity, 1*(4), 295–310.

Sell, R. L. (2006). Defining and measuring sexual orientation for research. In A. M. Omoto & H. S. Kurtzman (Eds.), *Sexual orientation and mental health: Examining identity and development in lesbian, gay, and bisexual people* (pp. 355–374). Washington, DC: American Psychological Association.

Sipe, A. W. R. (2007). Celibacy today: Mystery, myth, and miasma. *Cross Currents, 57*(4), 545–562.

Stein, E. (1999). *The mismeasure of desire: The science, theory, and ethics of sexual orientation.* New York: Oxford University Press.

Storms, M. D. (1980). Theories of sexual orientation. *Journal of Personality and Social Psychology,* (5), 783–792.

Tepper, M. S. (2000). Sexuality and disability: The missing discourse of pleasure. *Sexuality and Disability, 18*(4), 283–290.

Terry, G. (2012). "I'm putting a lid on that desire:" Celibacy, choice and control. *Sexualities, 15*(7), 871–889.

Treischmann, R. B. (1988). *Spinal cord injuries: Psychological, social, and vocational rehabilitation.* New York: Demos.

Troiden, R. R. (1988). *Gay and lesbian identity: A sociological analysis. Dix Hills.* New York: General Hall.

Van De Mark, B. (2007). Asexuality: Beyond the acronyms. http://www.gaylesbiantimes.com/?id=10304. Accessed 24 Dec 2008.

Waskul, D. D., & Plante, R. F. (2010). Sex(ualities) and symbolic interaction. *Symbolic Interaction, 33*(2), 148–162.

Weisberg, J. (2007). Asexuals want out. http://www.xtra.ca/public/viewstory.aspx?AFF_TYPE=1&STORY_ID=2959&PUB_TEMPLATE_ID=3. Accessed 27 Dec 2008.

Westphal, S. P. (2004). Glad to be asexual. New Scientist. http://www.newscientist.com/article/dn6533-feature-glad-to-be-asexual.html?full=true. Accessed 27 Dec 2008.

Cities and Sexualities

Phil Hubbard, Andrew Gorman-Murray
and Catherine J. Nash

17.1 Introduction

Urban studies was somewhat slow to recognise that sexuality is as foundational to the making of social and spatial orders as the categories of class, race or gender. Initial insights into the place of sexuality in the city were hence restricted to consideration of the distributions of "zones of vice" and studies of prostitution (e.g. Kneeland 1913; Reckless 1926; Symanski 1974). However, the increased visibility of lesbian and gay life in a range of Western cities in the 1970s and 1980s (e.g. San Francisco, New York, Amsterdam, Berlin and Paris) saw pioneering studies emerge, highlighting the importance of particular neighbourhoods in the social, economic and political life of those whose lives fell outside the heterosexual "norm" (e.g. Harry 1974; Levine 1979;

Castells and Murphy 1982). The realization that some "gay neighbourhoods" were spaces of incipient gentrification helped to bring the investigation of sexuality into dialogue with unfolding debates in urban studies about the important role of culture and lifestyle in driving processes of capital accumulation through property development (e.g. Lauria and Knopp 1985). Such themes have subsequently become important within a body of work concerned more broadly with the relations of "sexuality and space" (Bell and Valentine 1995), the majority of which has an urban focus. This nascent sub-discipline—which draws on perspectives from geography, sociology and planning about the "placed" and "spaced" construction of sexuality—has become arguably more important in twenty-first century by shifting its focus beyond a fixation with the location of "zones of vice" or "gay neighbourhoods" to consider the broader ways that urbanization shapes sexual practice, performance and identity (Brown et al. 2007; Doan 2011; Hubbard 2012).

Such studies of sexuality in the twenty-first century city seem more necessary than ever given the rising rates of divorce in the urban West, a seeming normalisation of serial monogamy and the increasing rate of single living. Such changing sexual norms have important consequences for housing and domestic reproduction, which demand to be investigated further, while the legalisation of civil partnership and gay marriage in some jurisdictions suggests the emergence of new homonormative lifestyles, spaces and households. Indeed, in a context where many societies

P. Hubbard (✉)
School of Social Policy, Sociology and Social Research,
University of Kent, Canterbury CT2 7NZ, UK
e-mail: P.Hubbard@kent.ac.uk

A. Gorman-Murray
School of Social Sciences and Psychology, University of
Western Sydney, Locked Bag 1797, Penrith, NSW 2751,
Australia
e-mail: a.gorman-murray@uws.edu.au

C. J. Nash
Department of Geography, Brock University,
St. Catharines, ON L2S 3A5, Canada
e-mail: cnash@brocku.ca

J. DeLamater, R.F. Plante (eds.), *Handbook of the Sociology of Sexualities,* Handbooks of Sociology and
Social Research, DOI 10.1007/978-3-319-17341-2_17, © Springer International Publishing Switzerland 2015

are more open about sexuality, and more accepting of sexual diversity, the opportunities for investors, developers and retailers to profit through the promotion of sexual consumption and "queer diversity" appear more pronounced than ever (Bell and Binnie 2004; Kanai 2014). In the wake of the 2008 Global Financial Crisis these observations are particularly significant given some conventional tactics of urban property development have been found lacking: not only does "sex sell," it appears recession-proof (Brents and Sanders 2010).

One of the main contributions of sexuality and space studies is to show that transformations in the nature of intimate and sexual life occur in particular cities, albeit these are often slow and painful: moral crusades against various manifestations of the sex industry abound, for example, while the acceptance of LGBT (lesbian, gay, bisexual, trans-) residents in many cities has been gradual and grudging. In this sense, the changing sexual landscape of cities reflects shifting social norms and moral sentiments: the city can be seen as a battleground where those with non-normative sexual orientation or proclivities seek to territorialise space, producing neighbourhoods which normalise and promote their identities. Yet this process is subject to intense regulation, and policy-makers often respond in irrational ways to the apparent dismantling of traditional sexual mores by "over-regulating" spaces associated with non-conventional and "deviant" sexualities (Maginn and Steinmitz 2014). The "sexscapes" of the city accordingly appear stubbornly recalcitrant and strangely conservative: the city is not always as "soft" or pliable as it might be, and is often a space of intensive surveillance where sexual norms are monitored through diverse practices of policing, family planning, health regulation, environmental planning, licensing and "municipal law" (Valverde and Cirak 2003; Hubbard 2013; Prior and Gorman-Murray 2014).

This chapter accordingly reviews key themes and emergent issues in the study of sex in the city, and demonstrates that the field has moved beyond a consideration of well-known "gay villages" to encompass an examination of sexuality in "ordinary" cities as well as the global tourist centres often understood as a focus for sexual encounter, commerce and trade. At the same time, the chapter incorporates scholarship that analyses how "gay villages" have changed over recent decades, with many such neighbourhoods in the West now in a state of flux (and even decline) (Nash and Gorman-Murray 2014). The chapter begins by considering shifting theoretical frameworks that have guided studies of the sexual organisation of the city before examining how such ideas have been worked through in considerations of both LGBT residence and the landscapes associated with heterosexuality in the city. The chapter concludes by alighting onto some key—and emerging—debates around the changing relations of sexuality and the city in an era of heightened global migration, and considers the challenges this poses in terms of the methods we use to interrogate the relationships of sexuality and space.

17.2 The Sexual Organisation of the City

One of the obvious starting points for considering the relationship of sex and the city is to observe the palpable disparities in the sexual lives of those who live in different parts of the city. While there is merit in simply describing the diverse ways sexuality is expressed in cities, and how this varies between different neighbourhoods, the majority of scholarship in this tradition is more concerned with theorising why such variation occurs, relating this to wider social processes. Here, a number of different perspectives have proved valuable: in this section we consider four key theoretical traditions, which we refer to as the ecological tradition, the deployment of ideas from social interactionism, Marxist perspectives and, finally, a developing approach based on the adoption of "queer" theories.

17.2.1 Ecological Perspectives

Mapping of specific "deviant" behaviours—such as alcoholism, suicide and criminality—has long been a stock in trade of urban studies, revealing the concentration of urban 'problems' in particular neighbourhoods. Sexual deviance is no exception: repeated empirical observation of morbidity from sexually transmitted diseases, for example, demonstrates there are distinctive clusters of higher sexual partnering, risk and infection within specific urban neighbourhoods (Adimora and Schoenbach 2005). Given the fact that people tend to form sexual relationships with people in the neighbourhoods where they live (Zenilman et al. 1999), the existence of such clusters—typically in inner-city districts—may be thought of as indicating distinctive geographies of urban sexual life, with higher rates of infection being displayed in areas where there are higher rates of concurrency (sexual relationships with multiple partners that overlap in time) and where non-monogamous sexual activity appears the norm rather than the exception. Here, we can invoke the perspective of "moral geography" and consider the development of different social and sexual norms in specific urban neighbourhoods (Hubbard 2000): questions of whether certain acts blend into or transgress the character of specific urban districts are, in turn, informed by assumptions about the type of places that they are, whether "high" or "low," "central" or "peripheral," "core" or "marginal."

Some of the ecological ideas proposed by the Chicago School of Sociology remain remarkably useful here, albeit they are couched in a language of "invasion" and "succession" that seems somewhat archaic today. Indeed, a key idea emerging from the pioneering urban studies of Park, Burgess, Reckless and others was that the city's structure could be understood as reflecting a battle for resources (particularly that most precious of resources in the city: land). The ensuing patterning of the city was seen to reflect varied degrees of social power, with the most successful locating in the more spacious outer suburbs, whereas the least affluent and mobile tended to cluster in inner cities. Here, the observation that prostitution tended to occur in marginal or "twilight" areas of cities led to the conclusion that prostitution was one of the pathologies associated with suburbs where residents had not

assimilated into the dominant social and moral order. In Ernest Burgess's classic zonal model, sex work was thus located in the inner-city "zone in transition"—a relatively deprived area typified by high numbers of immigrants and multi-family residences (see also Maginn and Steinmitz 2014 on urban/suburban sexscapes).

In one sense, the concentration of sex work in marginal and deprived urban districts should not be surprising, as sex work has proved a vital urban survival strategy for many existing on the edge of poverty (not least migrant women who may be poorly served by social security systems). While subsequent accounts have suggested neither the workers or the clients who frequent red-light landscapes necessarily reside in these deprived areas, a key contribution of such initial mappings of urban morality was to point out that forms of "scary sex"—that is, sex that falls outside the moral conventions of monogamy, coupledom and "vanilla" reproductive sex (Rubin 1984)—are often located away from the spaces claimed by the more affluent (i.e. the cleansed "family" spaces of suburbia). This can be viewed as a product of historically layered moral codes, legal strictures and policing practices that have combined to encourage the containment of "vice" in inner-city areas away from the more affluent suburbs; simultaneously, it can also be viewed in the context of the social and political power wielded by the most established, articulate and powerful citizens. Such ideas are borne out by studies of the NIMBYism that has been levelled at particular land uses associated with non-conforming sexual identities, including bars, clubs and community spaces developed by LGBT residents (see Doan 2011).

17.2.2 Social Constructionism and "Sexual Fields"

Within the wider debates about the social construction of sexuality, the work of Gagnon and Simon (1973) is recognised as offering a rich theoretical context for the understanding of human sexual conduct. While the Chicago School's theorisation suggested that those in the inner city had yet to be sufficiently socialised into dominant norms of behaviour, and in effect lived in liminal areas, Gagnon and Simon's work offers the basis for a more critical account in which people's sexuality is shaped by sexual "scripts." By highlighting the importance of cultural, interpersonal and intra-personal scenarios of sexual conduct, their work provides a basis for thinking about sexual norms as shaped by social norms that are inevitably emplaced. An example is the existence of areas that come to be known as spaces of LGBT residence: these can be scripted positively as spaces of sexual freedom and liberation (hence: gay villages) or negatively as spaces of constraint and deviance (hence: gay ghettos). This identification of spaces as either normal or deviant can provide a basis for people to make sense of their own action, with emotion and desire accordingly shaped by the sexual scripts and social norms existing in different times and spaces.

Such notions have been developed via engagement with symbolic interactionist ideas, which regard the city as made up of distinct "sexual fields" that provide the context for dating and mating (see Green, Chap. 3, this volume): here, it is stressed that neighbourhoods shape sexual identities at same time as they are shaped by them. Sexual fields emerge "when a subset of actors with potential romantic or sexual interest orient themselves toward one another according to a logic of desirability imminent to their collective relations" (Green 2014, p. 27). While such fields should not necessarily be thought in spatial terms, in the words of Laumann et al. (2005), "different combinations of sexual culture, institutional and social-network support (or the lack thereof), and social space create different sex markets or scenes." This infers there are locally shared ideas and images about appropriate sexual objects, aims and activities that shape how individuals value sexual relationships, partner preferences and behavioural repertoires.

Green (2008) argues that this type of perspective introduces "an additional layer of complexity" to studies fixated on sexual behaviour at the micro level by shifting attention to the "meso level" of "erotic worlds." Such worlds reflect the socially constituted desires of erotic participants in an aggregated form, anchoring these to physical sites, "such as bars, nightclubs, bathhouses, and chat rooms." Under this framework, gay identity can be regarded as formed out of shared community space where homosexual conduct and romantic relationships are regarded as the normal and accepted behaviour. There is a strong link here to Bourdieusian notions of erotic habitus, given the hypothesised linkage between individual fantasy and wider social and sexual structures, leading to the idea that these worlds are segregated and stratified. This implies that an urban perspective can allow for reflection on the unequal access that individuals have to different sexual fields in the city, these being striated by divisions of class, gender and race (see also Ellingson et al. 2004).

17.2.3 Marxist Urbanism and the Place of Sex in the City

Deferring from this social interactionist perspective, some interpretations of the urban experience as fundamentally shaped by capitalist processes offer a different take on sex, sexuality and the city. For example, Castells' (1983) pioneering work on "the urban question" theorised the city as a space of conflict where certain groups can mobilise to acquire collective resources, enabling them to maintain a certain standard of living within cities that are profoundly iniquitous and generally organised in favour of the capitalist class. In this regard, Castells argued that the emergence of gay residential spaces in the city had both a 'defensive' and 'progressive' function, being spaces where homosexual identities could be mobilised and politicised, albeit these were often regarded as spaces of condoned "deviance." Later accounts developed this in terms of thinking about how the visibility of "gay villages" made a case for LGBT populations to enjoy a fuller right to the city (and equal citizenship rights to the heterosexual populations whose interests had tended to dominate urban politics) (Forest 1995; Nash 2006). In the terms deployed by Marxist urbanist Henri Lefebvre, this enables gay populations to carve out ontological representations of space that shape their own lifeworlds through a "tria-lectics" which relates urban practice to identity and imagination (Miller 2005).

However, these perspectives on the resistances which are possible for "sexual dissidents" to enact in the everyday city need to be held in tension with the idea that the construction of gay (and, to an extent, lesbian) social spaces has very often facilitated real-estate speculation in previously underdeveloped areas (Castells 1983). This is most notable in accounts that consider the place of "gay communities" within the city in terms of the dynamics of investment and disinvestment that produce the uneven rental values which allow for constant circulation of capital as it seeks more profitable sites for its own realisation. So while many important studies of the formation of gay and lesbian "villages" postulate that the incipient gentrification associated with gay and lesbian inner-city residency resulted from childless single and partnered individuals seeking affordable apartments and flats (rather than houses) in inner-city locations (Lauria and Knopp 1985; Adler and Brenner 1992), there is also an important sense in which this process triggered the conditions for a gentrification that benefitted property developers and corporations rather than LGBT populations:

> Many of these once-derelict neighborhoods, such as the Castro in San Francisco, West Hollywood in Los Angeles, Boys Town in Chicago, the South End in Boston, Chelsea in New York, the Gayborhood in Philadelphia, and Midtown in Atlanta, have developed reputations as desirable places for LGBT people to live and recreate. At the same time, their renovation has made them more attractive to non-LGBT individuals in search of in-town living. Higher demand for property in these neighborhoods has resulted in steep rises in rents, frequent conversion of rental properties to condominiums, and competition for commercial space, which make it difficult for less affluent LGBT people and businesses targeted to the community to remain in the neighborhoods (Doan and Higgins 2011, p. 6).

Thus, Marxist perspectives on the sexuality of the city show that the organisation of space into distinct neighbourhoods can reproduce capitalist values both through the reproduction of labour (via the privileging of the family norm in the suburbs) as well as the creation of urban spaces in which alternative forms of desire can be contained and enhanced. This is a "restricted" urban economy in which desire is channelled to corporate, capitalist ends. The city plays an active role in perpetuating this economy via the spatial identification and isolation of spaces of "sexual risk." In this sense, the licensing or granting of planning permission for brothels (Hubbard et al. 2013), lap dance clubs (Hubbard and Colosi 2014), gay saunas (Prior 2008) or sex shops (Coulmont and Hubbard 2010) might all be read as symbolic of the liberalisation of sex and the city, but each can be interpreted as an attempt to survey, contain and enhance the value of commercial sex in the city.

17.2.4 Queer Urban Theory

Marxist ideas focus on the reproduction of capitalism rather than the maintenance of heteronormative values in the city, but both are clearly important in contemporary writing on the relation of sexuality and space, much of which is informed by queer theory. Herein, the idea that city normalises sexual values based on futurity, social reproduction and the family via place attachments, performativity and "geographies of affect" is important in much contemporary writing on the sexual organisation of the city (see especially Brown 2009). Here, consideration of the way that the built forms of schools, shopping malls, hotels, housing and so on works to normalise particular sexualities, putting some things into view, and others out of reach, provides valuable insight into how space and place normalize particular sexual performances. Such examples stress that vision is crucial in the sex life of the city and the making of urban sexual subjectivities (Hubbard 2011). Yet the "erotics of looking" (Bell and Binnie 1998) must be considered alongside other sensations and experiences of the urban—for example, the ways cities sound, smell, taste and feel—and the ways these haptic and sensory sensations are connected to the movements of bodies, the rhythms of streetlife, the appearance of buildings, urban microclimates, the design of public spaces and so on (Andersson 2012; Oswin 2013). Combined, it is these that effectively sexualise space:

> Space and place work together in the formation of sexual space, inspiring and circumscribing the range of possible erotic forms and practices within a given setting. The atmospheric qualities of a given locale are thus both hard and soft, immediate and (potentially) diffuse: location … architecture, décor, history and site-generated official and popular discourses merge into a singular entity (though there may be multiple interpretations of it). The immediate properties of a given space's atmosphere suggest to participants the state of mind to adopt, the kinds of sociality to expect and the forms of appropriate conduct. They also facilitate or discourage types of conduct and encounter (Green 2008, pp. 5–6).

A queer perspective on such issues, informed by accounts that stress the embodied experience of urban life, hence helps us to question established spatial ontologies, including the distinctions made between public/private (Knopp 2007; Gorman-Murray 2012) and rural/urban spaces (Gandy 2012; Gorman-Murray et al. 2012a; Patrick 2014). Working through such ideas, geographers have argued that repetitive embodied performances of heterosexuality make us mistake urban public space as inherently heterosexual, whereas this is actually a regulatory fiction whose power is punctured through visible performances of homosexual identity such as those associated with Gay Pride (Browne 2007).

17.3   Gay Villages and LGBT Identities

The historical emergence and contemporary status of so-called LGBT or gay villages in major cities in North American, the UK, Europe and Australia has been the subject of a vast body of research. Most of this argues that the foundations of such villages began in the West in the period after WWII, when gay men and lesbians flocked to the downtown or inner-city neighbourhoods of large cities, seeking other like-minded individuals for support and community (Castells 1983; Wotherspoon 1991; Weston 1995). In many such cities during 1970s and 1980s, de-industrialisa-

tion and decentralisation meant that inner-city neighbourhoods were somewhat marginal and rundown, providing a location where those "alternative" lifestyles could co-exist with other marginal groups—e.g. sex workers, drug addicts and the chronically unemployed (Knopp 1995; Knopp 1998; Lauria and Knopp 1985). Despite the somewhat seedy and destitute nature of such districts, gay men and lesbians were able to find relatively safe locations to escape the largely homophobic nature of public urban spaces.

The development of the gay rights movement and related HIV/AIDS activism in the early 1980s, coincided with and was supported by the consolidation of gay-oriented commercial and residential territories. Gay political activism took advantage of this concentrated economic and social capital to further political and social objectives, including initiatives at the local level such as pushing back against police harassment, to national campaigns for human rights. As gay men and lesbians increasingly benefited from anti-discrimination legislation and growing, albeit uneven, acceptance in mainstream society in the 1990s, cities increasingly incorporated gay districts—or what were becoming known as gay "villages"—into tourism and marketing strategies, largely driven by neoliberal impulses to compete for the favours of a new "creative class" seeking a certain kind of cosmopolitan urban experience (Florida 2002). This mainstreaming of LGBT spaces and experiences has generated pointed arguments about the commodification of gay life and the development of an identity-based politics grounded in consumerist practices. Some scholarship also argues that gay villages are dominated by white middle-class, gay male interests, and are thus perceived as marginalising and exclusionary to lesbians, LGBT people of colour, older LGBT people and those of lower socioeconomic means (Duggan 2002; Richardson 2004, 2005). Indeed, while lesbians have always made use of gay villages they tend to have established distinct social networks and enclaves of their own, although never achieving the political and economic strength of gay villages (Podmore 2013; Rothenberg 1995; Valentine 1993).

Hence, while contemporary gay villages are now completely interwoven into the fabric of inner-city life and touted as evidence of a city's tolerance and diversity, some critiques argue that only some LGBT people have gained acceptance through an assimilationist politic that "privileges a middle-class aesthetics and monogamous, consumerist coupledom" (Nash and Gorman-Murray 2014). This arguably constitutes a form of "homonormativity" that privileges some gays and lesbians over others as they are able to freely participate in commodified, consumerist gay village spaces (Duggan 2002; Rushbrook 2002; Binnie 2004). It is important to note that the possibilities for such inclusion are experienced unevenly, differently and with a geographical specificity: the gay village cannot be understood as monolithically homonormative (Brown 2009).

Many contemporary gay villages are in a state of flux (Brown 2013), losing their gay owned and/or operated businesses as well as their residential gay populations as rents and taxes rise and consumer spending decreases (Collins 2004; Ruting 2008). Some claim that with social, political and legal inclusions, LGBT people no longer need gay villages and are more comfortable moving beyond LGBT spaces. Nevertheless, this new freedom LGBT have to experience the city more widely is arguably limited to those homonormative LGBT people embodying middle-class and normatively gendered demeanours (Visser 2008). Those individuals who do not fit homonormative LGBT identities, those identifying as queer, post-gay, heteroflexible or trans-, have never found the gay village a comfortable location and may still not have the "rights to the city" enjoyed by homonormative gay men and women (Nash 2011, 2013a; Nash and Bain 2007). Others claim that gay villages might, in part, be victims of their own success, where, as commodified, consumeristic spaces, they are increasingly inhabited by heterosexuals looking for exciting nightlife or downtown living in relatively safe neighbourhoods (Binnie and Skeggs 2004; Casey 2004). Finally, a new generation of gay men and lesbians are connecting with others through new social media in ways that render the gay village superfluous (Mowlabocus 2010; Usher and

Morrison 2010). A new generation of gay men and lesbians may also be finding traditional gay villages limiting, regarding them as an historical and political area that is no longer of relevance (to them) (Sullivan 2005; Nash 2013a; Vaccaro 2009).

Whether gay villages will disappear is a matter of some debate and arguably depends on any number of factors, including a village's history, geography, and political, economic and social circumstances. Toronto's gay village, for example, has considerable support from the City of Toronto through its tourism and marketing initiatives, and has a strong Business Improvement Association (BIA) devoted to maintaining the strength and relevance of the gay village to current and future generations of LGBT people. The Church and Wellesley BIA has raised funds to support a planning study of the area, make street improvements (parklets, street signage, commemorative statues) and support of gay village businesses (Nash and Gorman-Murray 2015b). The district also benefits from the advocacy of its openly lesbian city councillor, Kristen Wong-Tam, and is home to major LGBT institutions, including the LGBT community centre, 519 Church Street. By contrast, Oxford Street, Sydney's "traditional" LGBT village, has been experiencing decline for some time (Reynolds 2009). Its daytime economy is struggling while the night-time economy is becoming increasingly problematic with numerous clubs and bars frequented by young heterosexuals. Another inner-city neighbourhood—Newtown—is arguably becoming the new "queer" district, offering a community feeling, vibrant street-life, and diverse and welcoming spaces, including a range of LGBT-specific and LGBT-friendly organisations and services (Gorman-Murray 2006; Gorman-Murray and Waitt 2009; Gorman-Murray and Nash 2014).

What is becoming clear is that the experiences of LGBT people in cities in the Global North are currently undergoing transformation, although it is difficult to tell what the ultimate outcome will be. Scholarship has certainly shown that some LGBT people are able to move into other areas of the city, more freely experiencing an openly visible gay or lesbian identity (Nash 2013a; Nash

2013b). While these new transformations might suggest the decline of the gay village in favour of other neighbourhoods, it might be more useful to think about gay villages and new LGBT districts in terms of mobile and relational geographies, linked through expanding networks constituted by flows of people goods and ideas. The increasingly mobile lives of some LGBT people, achieved through shifting social positioning as much as new technologies, are creating relationships both in and between historically important gay villages and the new nodes and pathways open to LGBT people (Nash and Gorman-Murray 2014; Gorman-Murray and Nash 2014).

17.4   Heterosexual Landscapes of the City

Given the normalisation and assimilation of LGBT values in many Western cities, it is tempting to argue that the city is becoming "softer" as traditional sexual moralities and norms are challenged. The seeming diminution of the traditional family, the rise of divorce, and the legal recognition of same-sex civil unions all suggest something fundamental has happened to sexuality in recent decades, with the idealisation of the nuclear family being superseded by a wider range of possible household types and lifestyle choices. In its "plastic" incarnation, sex has become recreational, with the trade in sperm and human embryos, in vitro fertilization and reproductive technologies meaning that sex itself is no longer even required for procreation. The implication is, seemingly, that people are more able to choose sexual lifestyles and identities beyond the taken-for-granted norm of the married, co-resident, heterosexual couple with children. Giddens' (1993) identification of the dominance of "confluent" love based on mutual satisfaction rather than life-long commitment highlights this putative shift in sexual ethics, something registered in the increased purchase of sexual services, the consumption of pornography, the use of online dating sites and pursuit of hetero-flexible lifestyles (Attwood 2007).

But it is clear that this sexual "diversification and dispersion" (Sigusch 1998) remains geographically uneven. Clearly, not all cities are equally open to sexual diversity, and even in the urban West there are still clear limits to sexual citizenship. The contemporary Western city remains highly normative, reproducing certain assumptions about the importance of an emotionally-mature sexuality that takes as its object of desire a consenting adult partner (and certainly not a coerced or exploited person, a child, or an animal, nor anyone whose consent is not explicable to the state and law). Singleness also remains suspect, whether people live alone by choice or appear unable to form relationships (Wilkinson 2014). This implies we should not aim to simply contrast the homosexual and heterosexual experience of the city, but adopt a queer perspective that considers the plurality of sexual identities that exist in the city:

> The reservations about focusing excessively on dualistic thinking … imply that it may be particularly important to encourage non-heteronormative constructions of heterosexual identity, rather than seeing heterosexual identity categories as inevitably producing their 'other', namely, subordinated lesbian and gay identities and vice versa. Non-heteronormative heterosexuality would be based on not privileging heterosexual identity over other categories such as gay, lesbian or transgendered identity (Johnson 2002, p. 301).

Literatures on the regulation of deviant or "Other" heterosexualities within the city make this clear, particularly those that focus on the historical regulation of single mothers, prostitutes and "hysterical" female sexualities (Hubbard 2011). In contrast, less has been said about the ways that dominant heterosexualities have marginalised particular masculine identities and practices, though the way that contemporary moral panics are whipped up around figures including bigamists, perpetrators of domestic violence, errant fathers, paedophiles and sex tourists suggests dominant notions of heterosex cannot accommodate many expressions of male desire (see especially the literatures on the spatial restrictions placed on sexual offenders in the US city, for example, Grubesic 2010; Berenson and Applebaum 2011).

There is then a strong case for further opening up the "black box" of heterosexuality to explore the many possible articulations of heterosexual desire that are included or excluded within the city. Considering the emergence of "panic figures" and the measures used to regulate excessive, perverse or immoral forms of heterosex has been one route into mapping the shifting contours of sexuality in the city (Hubbard 2000). Literatures on prostitution in particular help to clarify how heternormativity is reproduced spatially through the exclusion and containment of commercial sex work away from "family spaces" (the subtext here being that prostitution and pornography threatens to seduce the innocent into immoral sexual practices) (see Laing and Cook 2014). Overt policies of zoning and licensing hence exclude brothels and sex shops from the proximity of educational establishments, religious establishments and suburban "family" areas (Hubbard et al. 2013), as well as central urban areas earmarked for gentrification (Papayanis 2000).

Yet there is much variation here: adult entertainment in the form of female striptease is apparently accepted at the heart of many successful urban economies in the form of "gentleman's clubs" (Maginn and Steinmitz 2014) albeit some towns and cities appear to accommodate such sexualised rituals more comfortably than others. For example, McGrath (2015) notes Portland's growing reputation as "Pornland," reputedly with more strip clubs per head of population than any other US city:

> The high visibility of strip clubs and their spatial integration within residential and commercial districts has made strip clubs a mundane part of the Portland's urban landscape and culture. Strip clubs have come to be inextricably linked with the city's civic image, appearing in both local and national media about the city …the retro neon marquee of downtown Portland's Mary's Club, which claims to be "Portland's first topless bar" is a landmark for residents and tourists alike … The club's iconic cocktail-waitress logo is a familiar sight on jackets and t-shirts around the city … Portland is [also] proud of its famous strippers, such as rock musician Courtney Love, who worked at Mary's, and Viva Las Vegas, who immortalized the local scene in her memoir Magic Gardens (2009). The strip club industry is a visible … participant in civic life through activities such as a fundraiser for breast cancer research and one club's annual bikini dog wash, proceeds of which go to the local humane society. Some club owners are also professionalizing, joining forces, and assertively engaging with neighbors and government agencies (McGrath 2015, p. 65).

McGrath shows that though there has never been an explicit urban strategy promoting commercial sex as an engine of economic growth, a combination of factors conspired to create the cultural and market conditions in which sex businesses could prosper. The same is arguably true in UK cities including Newcastle, Blackpool and Brighton, which act as centres of a stag and hen tourism (Hubbard 2011). Within such youth-dominated night-time economies, visits to sites of adult entertainment and lap dance clubs are customary, and sexualised display commonplace: sex toys are openly paraded, bodies are exposed, cross-dressing is de riguer. In such spaces, "playful deviance" (Redmon 2003) shifts centre-stage, and the definition of sexual transgression rendered problematic.

In recounting such arguments it is important to remember that there are others who regard the presence of sexualised images in the cityscape—especially those of women—as offensive and intimidating, perpetuating ideas that women are always 'on display' as sexual objects (Lim and Fanghanel 2013). Feminist groups regularly oppose the opening of lap dance premises (see Hubbard and Colosi 2014), and many other business and resident groups typically portray sex businesses as bad neighbors (Hubbard et al. 2013). Even in Portland, McGrath (2015) indicates that such clubs are not necessarily embraced by all people who live and work nearby. Opposition to these businesses periodically rears its head at neighborhood association meetings, in editorial pages, ballot measures, or city ordinances. Such opposition feeds upon negative portrayals of sexual entertainment as normalising retrogressive, male attitudes towards women. It is also informed by the assumption that the presence of clubs is associated with increased rates of both violent and non-violent crime (see Paul et al. 2001; Linz et al. 2000; Hanna 2005). Working through these debates, it seems that the identities and spaces that can be accommodated within normative heterosexuality are constantly changing. This reminds us that heteronormativity is not a monolithic or unbending structure, but a concept that shifts to encompass different masculine and feminine performances over time.

17.5 Virtualisation, Mobility and Globalisation

One of the starting points for any exploration of sex and the city is the observation that cities—and especially big cities—are sites where disconnected people, perhaps drawn from different cultural and geographical backgrounds, are drawn into sexual relationships bound by the rules of attraction (Hubbard 2011). While the assumption that people tend to partner with people within their own neighbourhood provides a launching pad for many studies of the sexual organisation of the city, these ideas must be held in tension with an awareness of the shifting mobilities ushered in by the technological changes associated with globalisation. Two trends are notable here: firstly, the rise of e-communication and Internet technologies that allow individuals to maintain social and sexual relationships at a distance; and, secondly, the improvement of transport technologies that allow many individuals to maintain transnational lifestyles.

In relation to the former, it is evident that message boards and social networking sites like Facebook and Twitter are used by LGBT groups to communicate, make contact with others, organise events, create communities, and tell the stories of their lives (Pullen and Cooper 2010), encouraging the movement of those of LGBT identification to specific cities and neighbourhoods which they imagine may be more conducive to meeting others like them. This may of course simply exacerbate the tendency for LGBT populations to gravitate towards the biggest cities, and the marketing of certain cities as spaces for "gay tourism" is clearly a factor here. However, Binnie (2014) argues that "given the intensification of networked links and resources within queer cyberspace, it is hard to retain the tenability of assertions of queer cultural life within one local-

ity remaining uninformed by events, practices and values from elsewhere" (p. 595). Here the suggestion appears that changing communication is enabling the globalisation of the gay lifestyles most vividly associated with metropolitan centres of the West. This implies that a persistent focus on the largest cities which are the "hubs of a global network of sexual commerce around which images, bodies and desires circulate voraciously" (Hubbard 2012, p. 176) is perhaps misplaced: as Myrdahl (2013) has argued, gay and lesbian lives are of course led in cities both small and large, with e-communication making it easier to feel part of a "queer" community even if one is living in a small or remote town.

More widely, Internet technologies allow for the production of intimacies-at-a-distance in all manner of ways, being tied into practices of coupling, partnership and sex itself (Valentine 2008). This means that distance does not necessarily bring intimacy to an end, with growing numbers of individuals "living apart together" (Duncan and Phillips 2010), including commuter couples where one partner works away from home during the week, dual career couples who live apart maintaining individual residences in separate locations, and diasporic families whose members may be scattered across the globe (Constable 2009). At a more local level, websites and phone apps appear significant in reshaping the parameters of dating and relationships, and it is widely assumed that they are providing a means for individuals to meet, and mate with, others from a wider range of social backgrounds and communities (Brickell 2012). While dating sites such as Match and "hook up apps" like Tinder are widely used by a variety of audiences, others are more specifically designed with those with particular tastes in mind, sometimes tied in to the promotion of fetish and kink pornography sites (Attwood 2007; Mowlabocus 2012). Again, this means that residence in the larger towns and cities traditionally associated with fetish clubs or swinging scenes is no longer necessary for individuals to become part of BDSM networks: in an important sense, such networks and communities have gone virtual.

This virtualisation of sexual relations poses important questions about the city as the primary site for sexual encounter, particularly in the realm of commercialised or paid-for sex (Cunningham and Kendell 2011). But this should not distract from the fact that most sexual encounters are embodied and proximate rather than virtual or at-a-distance, and that cities remain key meeting grounds where global business people, tourists, immigrant workers and hosts circulate and mix to varied degrees. Mai and King (2009, p. 297) remind us that "beyond their common function as mobile workers within the global capitalist economy … migrants and other 'people on the move' are sexual beings expressing, wanting to express, or denied the means to express, their sexual identities": cities characterised by high rates of in-and out-migration tend to be characterised by highly diversified sexual scenes and "hybrid" sexual cultures (Oswin 2013).

As numerous historical accounts have made clear, the sexual mixing evident in postcolonial cities can often create deep anxieties, with myths concerning the sexual Otherness of migrants sometimes used to make a case for increasing surveillance of the spaces associated with racial Others (see, for example, Brown and Knopp 2010, on the venereal politics of wartime Seattle). In the contemporary era, policy discourses equating trafficking and prostitution have become widespread, with concern about the erosion of national sovereignty becoming condensed in the figure of the trafficked female prostitute (Mai 2013). The fact that such policy preoccupations do not allow for other possible subject positions and practices (e.g. men who sell sex to men, non-migrant sex workers and instances of uncoerced prostitution) does not diminish their importance in framing recent legal reform. Indeed, the conflation of prostitution and trafficking has taken on particular significance in an era when migration is regarded as a source of anxiety: the enactment of new prostitution legislation intended to protect "vulnerable women" from sexual exploitation can thus be read as one means by which European states are seeking to reduce anxiety about the globalised

future (Hubbard 2011). Ironically, moments of global hospitality such as the Olympics, when cities are supposed to extend a welcome to the world, appear to be associated with increased efforts to regulate and discipline the forms of sexuality permissible in "world cities," as Matheson and Finkel (2013) show in the context of Vancouver's Winter Olympics of 2010 and Hubbard and Wilkinson (2014) demonstrate in relation to London 2012. Indeed, while Gandy (2012) notes that the geography of sexual subcultures in London is highly variegated, including anonymous (gay) sex in public spaces and cruising grounds, such forms of sex stand at odds with sexually normative, neoliberal notions of hospitality which are based on white, middle class, domesticated consumer norms.

Recent urban scholarship on cities under conditions of contemporary globalisation, informed by increasingly sophisticated understandings of the ways that cities exist as "unbounded places" may then be increasingly valuable in considering the intersection of nationalism, ethnicity and sexuality. Here, relational understandings of space (Massey 2007) hence provide a way of approaching the city as a series of relatively disconnected and dispersed, activities, made in and through many different kinds of networks. This type of perspective has important implications for studies of sex in the city given it suggests that cities cannot be understood solely through reference to the nation-state in which they are located: it also challenges the idea that the city-state is a coherent actor by insisting it is a set of actors with different and often competing intentions, with policies being constructed and mobilised in a multiplicity of sites, both near and far. As Ward (2010) succinctly argues, this means we need not only to study cities, but also the relations that bind them together and push them apart. However, research has as yet said little about sexuality as something that binds particular cities together, despite the evidential importance of sex to the economies of cities and, conversely, the importance of cities in articulating flows of migration in which love and sex can be a significant motive for movement (King and Mai 2009; Morrison et al. 2013).

17.6 Methodological Challenges

These musings on the "worlding" of urban space have some important implications for methods of studying the sexuality of cities. One traditional way in which it has been possible to consider the sexual organisation of the city is through mapping exercises which, with varying levels of precision and via different technologies (e.g. see Brown and Knopp 2006), allow us to "see" the emplacement of sex in the landscape. This important tradition introduces a "spatial epistemology" into the study of sexuality, albeit such cartographic traditions have clear limits. Here, it is possible to think about using different forms of data which might allow us to register the sexuality of the city: one can map places of significance in the development of LGBT scenes, for example, or examine the distribution of arrests for street soliciting or kerb-crawling in jurisdictions where public prostitution remains illegal (Ashworth et al. 1988). Moreover, the inclusion of questions on sexuality, same-sex households, civil unions and gay marriages in many national census exercises, provides the basis for innovative studies in which the centrality of the city in gay life can be explored and questioned (e.g. Gorman-Murray and Brennan-Horley 2010; Wimark and Östh 2014). However, to date, there has yet to be any significant use of online data to map shifting networks of sex and sociality despite the rise of dating apps which use global positioning data to locate potential sexual partners in the vicinity (see Brubaker et al. 2014).

Yet mappings of how different sexual groups or identities come to be associated with particular neighbourhoods are just the beginning for many studies of sexuality and space: maps are often intuitively suggestive of the processes that might result in the emergence of distinctive sexual landscapes, but they support a "pointillist" view of the world in which identities are 'fixed' in places. As much work on the sexuality of the city insists, the sex life of the city is much more fluid and "messy" than this implies. This is thought to be especially the case for LGBT populations, something Knopp (2007) underlines when he argues that "queers' lived experiences" entails a radically different relationship to notions like place and space than that of "more sedentary non-queers" (p. 35). As he notes, "the visibility that placement brings" can make LGBT populations vulnerable to violence, meaning that queers are "frequently suspicious, fearful and unable to relate easily to the fixity and certainty inhering in most dominant ontologies of 'place'" (p. 35).

Grasping the fluidity and messiness of queer urban life-worlds can therefore be challenging given the transient and semi-anonymous nature of the experiences central in reproducing both the erotic and social lives of LGBT-identified individuals living in cities, noting that for some people such identifications are themselves deeply problematic: Kanai (2014) states that being "gay" "seems to be a privilege of the urban middle-class affiliated to the central city's Eurocentric worldliness and benefiting from economic globalization" (p. 4). In his view, sexual dissidents from disadvantaged metropolitan outskirts cannot afford the luxury of dissociating identity politics from more pressing concerns related to basic material needs and clear threats in their everyday lives. This suggests that methods need to be aware of the specific languages used to describe sexual identification and practice in different parts of the world, and the use of ethnographic methods capable of grasping the "elisions, inequalities and erasures that trouble and disrupt" Eurocentric mappings of gay modernity in the city (Manalansan 2014).

Such observations highlight what is perhaps the most significant challenge to the current literature on sexuality and space, namely the need for its practitioners to escape the confines of Eurocentric world-view that typically privileges white, middle-class males, to the exclusion of trans-people, the lower class, and people of colour. The failure of much of the literature to adequately acknowledge intersectionality remains notable, particularly in the post-colonial contexts (see Harris & Bartlow, Chap. 15, this volume). Even a cursory overview suggests many of the discussions concerning sex in the city remain within a "homonormative" frame that re-centres the position of the most privileged LGBT individuals (Puar 2006), often marginalising queers of colour. As Haritaworn (2008) shows, this often involves the analogising of race and sexuality: by isolating and comparing the experiences of "gays" (white) and "blacks" (heterosexual), these writers obliterate racialised queer subjectivities and the multiple allegiances that they potentially give rise to. Likewise, Spurlin (2000) argues that "with its narrow Eurocentric, and therefore imperialistic gaze, queer studies has not seriously engaged how queer identities and cultural formations have taken shape and operate outside of large metropolitan locations" (p. 183), suggesting the need for studies of sexuality to move beyond engagement with the "proud, Prada-wearing, marriage-bound, tax-paying, legitimate citizens of the 'queer global city'"(Manalansan 2014, p. 12) to encompass other citizens and other cities (see also Gorman-Murray et al. 2012b). Kanai's (2014) suggestion that future research will need to take stock of the heterogeneity and contingency of urban sexuality in Latin America and elsewhere implies a need for comparative work which is not merely aware of difference, but which evinces the intersections of sex, class, gender, age and ethnicity which produce localized manifestations of sexual life in different cities (see also Brown 2008; Browne and Bakshi 2011 on "ordinary cities").

17.7 Conclusions

The literature on the relationship of sexuality and the city is now significant, having grown from a relative "niche" study of sites of "deviant sex" to a more encompassing consideration of the role of urbanisation in shifting the parameters of sexual life. As has been shown here, at least three key conclusions can be drawn from this literature. The first is that while cities in general are seen as spaces of sexual diversity and experimentation, this liberalism is more associated with the urban than the suburban, and has often been limited to the neighbourhoods that have been labelled as "gay villages" and/or red light zones (Ryder 2004). A second key conclusion is that this patterning reflects both choice and constraint within cities that are overwhelmingly heterosexual and heteronormative, and where regulatory mechanisms serve to police the boundaries between "queer" urban spaces and suburban landscapes that often appear exclusionary to those failing to conform to dominant sexual norms (Hubbard 2011). However, a third conclusion is that shifting morality, coupled with a selective commodification of queer sex, is encouraging an assimilation of gay villages, the emergence of more "mixed" queer-friendly neighbourhoods, and a revision of the sexual landscape in which commercial sex is visible and apparently accepted (Brown 2013; Gorman-Murray and Nash 2014). Here, the alignment of middle-class aesthetics, capital accumulation strategies and sexual normativity is also allowing sexual diversity to be mobilised as a marketing tool in the global battle for investment and tourist consumption across a range of urban spaces (Bell and Binnie 2004).

Such conclusions point to an increasingly sophisticated understanding of the ways urban life mediates the "sexual scripts" available to us as we live our sexual lives. Here, moving beyond dominant understandings of urban/suburban has been significant (Tongson 2011), as has the recognition that some heterosexualities are "queered" through processes of spatial exclusion (Hubbard 2000). For all of this, it is clear that literatures on the relations of sexuality and space still fail to address a number of important questions concerning the intersection of class, race and gender with sexuality. For instance, much of the writing on sex in the city remains fixated on the global cities of the West, failing to consider the different inflections of sexuality in non-metropolitan, non-Western and more "ordinary" cities (Brown 2008). Here, queer writing on homonationalism adds new perspectives on the ways that capital accumulation aligns with sexual, racial and class norms to produce particular representations of the sex life of cities (Puar 2006). It is clear from such queer critiques that many of our "mappings" of sex in the city fail to grasp matters of desire and corporeality through methods that are sufficiently alert to the diverse gendered, classed and racialised experiences of sexual space. This implies that much remains to be done in unpicking existing assumptions about sex in the city, providing fuller and more nuanced understandings of how urbanisation is implicated in broader processes of sexual change.

References

Adimora, A. A., & Schoenbach, V. J. (2005). Social context, sexual networks, and racial disparities in rates of sexually transmitted infections. *Journal of Infectious Diseases, 191*(Suppl. 1), S115–S122.

Adler, S., & Brenner, J. (1992). Gender and space: Lesbians and gay men in the city. *International Journal of Urban and Regional Research, 16*(1), 24–34.

Andersson, J. (2012). Heritage discourse and the desexualisation of public space: The "historical restorations" of Bloomsbury's squares. *Antipode, 44*(4), 1081–1098.

Ashworth, G. J., White, P. E., & Winchester, H. P. (1988). The red-light district in the west European city: A neglected aspect of the urban landscape. *Geoforum, 19*(2), 201–212.

Attwood, F. (2007). No money shot? Commerce, pornography and new sex taste cultures. *Sexualities, 10*(4), 441–456.

Bell, D., & Binnie, J. (1998). Theatres of cruelty, rivers of desire. In N. Fyfe (Ed.), *Images of the street: Planning, identity, and control in public space* (pp. 129–140). London: Routledge.

Bell, D., & Binnie, J. (2004). Authenticating queer space: Citizenship, urbanism and governance. *Urban Studies, 41*(9), 1807–1820.

Bell, D., & Valentine, G. (1995). *Mapping desire: Geographies of sexualities*. London: Routledge.

Berenson, J. A., & Appelbaum, P. S. (2011). A geospatial analysis of the impact of sex offender residency restrictions in two New York counties. *Law and Human Behavior, 35*(3), 235.

Binnie, J. (2004). *The globalization of sexuality*. London: Sage.

Binnie, J. (2014). Relational comparison, queer urbanism and worlding cities. *Geography Compass, 8*(3), 590–599.

Binnie, J., & Skeggs, B. (2004). Cosmopolitan knowledge and the production and consumption of sexualized space: Manchester's gay village. *The Sociological Review, 51*(1), 39–61.

Bouthillette, A.-M. (1994). Gentrification by gay male communities: A case study of Torontos Cabbagetown. In S. Whittle (Ed.), *The margins of the city: Gay mens urban lives* (pp 65–84). Aldershot: Ashgate.

Brents, B.G., & Sanders, T. (2010). Mainstreaming the sex industry: Economic inclusion and social ambivalence. *Journal of Law and Society, 37*(1), 40–60.

Brickell, C. (2012). Sexuality, power and the sociology of the internet. *Current Sociology, 60*(1), 28–44.

Brown, G. (2004). Cosmopolitan camouflage: (Post-)gay space in Spitalfields, east London. In J. Binnie, S. Holloway, S. Millington, & C. Young (Eds.), *Cosmopolitan urbanism* (pp. 130–145). New York: Routledge.

Brown, G. (2008). Urban (homo)sexualities: Ordinary cities and ordinary sexualities. *Geography Compass, 2*(4), 1215–1231.

Brown, G. (2009). Thinking beyond homonormativity: Performative explorations of diverse gay economies. *Environment and Planning A: Society and Space, 41*(6), 1496–1510.

Brown, M., & Knopp, L. (2006). Places or polygons? Governmentality, scale, and the census in the Gay and Lesbian Atlas. *Population, Space and Place, 12*(4), 223–242.

Brown, M. (2013). Gender and sexuality II: There goes the gayborhood? *Progress in Human Geography*. doi:10.1177/0309132513484215.

Brown, M., & Knopp, L. (2010). Between anatamo-and bio-politics: Geographies of sexual health in wartime Seattle. *Political Geography, 29*(7), 392–403.

Brown, G., Browne, K., & Lim, J. (Eds.) (2007). *Geographies of sexualities: Theory practices and politics*. Chichester: Ashgate.

Browne, K. (2007). A party with politics? (Re) making LGBTQ pride spaces in Dublin and Brighton. *Social & Cultural Geography, 8*(1), 63–87.

Browne, K., & Bakshi, L. (2011). We are here to party? Lesbian, gay, bisexual and trans leisurescapes beyond commercial gay scenes. *Leisure Studies, 30*(2), 179–196.

Brubaker, J. R., Ananny, M., & Crawford, K. (2014). Departing glances: A sociotechnical account of leaving Grindr. *New Media & Society*. doi:1461444814542311.

Casey, M. (2004). De-dyking queer space(s): Heterosexual female visibility in gay and lesbian spaces. *Sexualities, 7*(4), 446–461.

Castells, M., & Murphy, K. (1982). Cultural identity and urban structure: The spatial organization of San Francisco's gay community. *Urban policy under capitalism Beverley Hills, Sage*, 237–259.

Castells, M. (1983). *The city and the grassroots: a cross-cultural theory of urban social movements*. Berkeley: University of California Press.

Collins, A. (2004). Sexual dissidence, enterprise and assimilation: Bedfellows in urban regenderation. *Urban Studies, 41*, 1789–1806.

Constable, N. (2009). The commodification of intimacy: Marriage, sex, and reproductive labor. *Annual Review of Anthropology, 38*, 9–64.

Coulmont, B., & Hubbard, P. (2010). Consuming sex: Socio-legal shifts in the space and place of sex shops. *Journal of Law and Society, 37*(1), 189–209.

Cunningham, S., & Kendall, T. D. (2011). Prostitution 2.0: The changing face of sex work. *Journal of Urban Economics, 69*(3), 273–287.

Doan, P. L. (Ed.). (2011). *Queerying planning: Challenging heteronormative assumptions and reframing planning practice*. Chichester: Ashgate Publishing.

Doan, P. L., & Higgins, H. (2011). The demise of queer space? Resurgent gentrification and the assimilation of LGBT neighborhoods. *Journal of Planning Education and Research, 31*(1), 6–25.

Duggan, L. (2002). The new homonormativity: the sexual politics of neoliberalism. In: R. Castronovo & D. D. Nelson (Eds.), *Materializing democracy: Towards a revitalized cultural politics* (pp. 175–194). Durham: Duke University Press.

Duncan, S., & Phillips, M. (2010). People who live apart together (LATs)–how different are they? *The Sociological Review, 58*(1), 112–134.

Ellingson, S. E., Laumann, E. O., Paik, A., & Mahay, J. (2004). The theory of sex markets. In E. O. Laumann, S. Ellingson, J. Mahay, A. Paik, & Y. Youm (Eds.), *The sexual organization of the city* (pp. 1–23). Chicago: University of Chicago Press.

Florida, R. L. (2002). *The rise of the creative class: and how it's transforming work, leisure, community and everyday life*. New York: Basic books.

Forest, B. (1995). West Hollywood as symbol: the significance of place in the construction of a gay identity. *Environment and Planning D, 13*, 133–133.

Gagnon, J. H., & Simon, W. (1973). *Sexual conduct: The social sources of human sexuality*. Chicago: Aldine Transaction Publishers.

Gandy, M. (2012). Queer ecology: Nature, sexuality, and heterotopic alliances. *Environment and Planning—Society and Space, 30*(4), 727.

Giddens, A. (1993). *The transformation of intimacy: Sexuality, love and eroticism in modern societies*. Chichester: Wiley.

Gorman-Murray, A. (2006). Imagining King Street in the gay/lesbian media. *M/C Journal, 9*, 3.

Gorman-Murray, A. (2012). Queer politics at home: Gay mens management of the public/private boundary. *New Zealand Geographer, 68*(2), 111–120.

Gorman-Murray, A., & Brennan-Horley, C. (2010). The geography of same-sex families in Australia: Implications for regulatory regimes. *Law in Context, 28*(1), 43–64.

Gorman-Murray, A., & Nash, C.J. (2014). Mobile places, relational spaces: Conceptualizing an historical geography of Sydney's LGBTQ neighbourhoods. *Environment and Planning D: Society and Space, 32*(4), 622–641.

Gorman-Murray, A., & Waitt, G. (2009). Queer-friendly neighbourhoods: Interrogating social cohesion across sexual difference in two Australian neighbourhoods. *Environment and Planning A, 41*(12), 2855–2873.

Gorman-Murray, A., Brennan-Horley, C., McLean, K., Waitt G., & Gibson, C. (2010). Mapping same-sex couple family households in Australia. *Journal of Maps, 6*(1), 382–392.

Gorman-Murray, A., Pini, B., & Bryant, L. (Eds.). (2012a). *Sexuality, rurality, and geography*. Lanham: Lexington.

Gorman-Murray, A., Waitt G., & Gibson, C. (2012). Chilling out in cosmopolitan country: Urban/rural hybridity and the construction of Daylesford as a lesbian and gay rural idyll. *Journal of Rural Studies, 28*(1), 69–79.

Green, A. I. (2008). The social organization of desire: The sexual fields approach. *Sociological Theory, 26*(1), 25–50.

Green, A. I. (2014). *Sexual Fields: Toward a Sociology of Collective Sexual Life*. Chicago: University of Chicago Press.

Green, A. I., Follert, M., Osterlund, K., & Paquin, J. (2010). Space, place and sexual sociality: Towards an atmospheric analysis. *Gender, Work & Organization, 17*(1), 7–27.

Grubesic, T. H. (2010). Sex offender clusters. *Applied Geography, 30*(1), 2–18.

Hanna, J. (2005). Exotic dance and adult entertainment: A guide for planners and policy makers. *Journal of Planning Literature, 20*(2), 116–133.

Haritaworn, J. (2008). Shifting positionalities: Empirical reflections on a queer/trans of colour methodology. *Sociological Research Online, 13*(1), 13–26.

Harry, J. (1974). Urbanization and the gay life. *Journal of Sex Research, 10*(3), 238–247.

Hubbard, P. (2000). Desire/disgust: Mapping the moral contours of heterosexuality. *Progress in Human Geography, 24*(2), 191–217.

Hubbard, P. (2012). *Cities and sexualities*. New York: Routledge.

Hubbard, P. (2013). Kissing is not a universal right: Sexuality, law and the scales of citizenship. *Geoforum, 49*, 224–232.

Hubbard, P., & Colosi, R. (2015). Taking back the night? *Gender and the Contestation of Sexual Entertainment in England and Wales Urban Studies, 52*(3), 589–605.

Hubbard, P., & Wilkinson, E. (2014). Welcoming the world? *Hospitality, Homonationalism, and the London 2012 Olympics Antipode*. doi:10.1111/anti.12082.

Hubbard, P., Boydell, S., Crofts, P., Prior, J., & Searle, G. (2013). Noxious neighbours? Interrogating the impacts of sex premises in residential areas. *Environment and Planning A, 45*(1), 126–141.

Johnson, C. (2002). Heteronormal citizenship and the politics of passing. *Sexualities, 5*(2), 317–331.

Kanai, J. M. (2014). Buenos aires beyond (homo) sexualized urban entrepreneurialism: The geographies of queered tango. *Antipode*. doi:10.1111/anti.12120.

Kneeland, G. (1913). *Commercialized vice in New York*. New York: Garland.

Knopp, L. (1995). Sexuality and urban space: gay male identity politics in the United States, the United Kingdom and Australia. In R. Fincher & J. Jacobs (Eds.), *Cities of difference* (pp. 149–178). New York: Guilford.

Knopp, L. (1998). Exploiting the rent gap: The theoretical significance of using illegal appraisal schemes to encourage gentrification in New Orleans. *Urban Geography, 11*(1), 48–64.

Knopp, L. (2007). From lesbian to gay to queer geographies: Pasts, prospects and possibilities. In G.L. Brown, K. Browne, & J. Lim (Eds.) *Geographies of sexualities: Theory practices and politics* (pp. 171–191). Farnham: Ashgate.

Laing, M., & Cook, I. (2014). Governing sex work in the city. *Geography Compass, 8*(8), 505–515.

Lauria, M., & Knopp, L. (1985). Toward an analysis of the role of gay communities in the urban renaissance. *Urban Geography, 6*(2), 152–169.

Levine, M. P. (1979). Gay ghetto. *Journal of Homosexuality, 4*(4), 363–377.

Liepe-Levinson, K. (2002). *Strip show: Performances of gender and desire*. New York: Routledge.

Lim, J., & Fanghanel, A. (2013). Hijabs, hoodies and hot-pants; negotiating the Slutin SlutWalk. *Geoforum, 48,* 207–215.

Linz, D., Blumenthal E., Donnerstein, E., Kunkel, D., Shafer, B., & Lichtenstein, A. (2000). Testing legal assumptions regarding the effects of dancer nudity and proximity to patron on erotic expression. *Law and Human Behaviour, 24*(5), 507–533.

Maginn, P., & Steinmitz, C (2014). Spatial and regulatory contours of the (sub)urban sexscape. In P. Maginn & C. Steinmitz (Eds.), *(Sub)urban sexscapes* (pp. 1–17). London: Routledge.

Mai, N., & King, R. (2009). Love, sexuality and migration: mapping the issue (s). Mobilities, 4(3), 295–307.

Mai, N. (2013). Embodied cosmopolitanisms: the subjective mobility of migrants working in the global sex industry. *Gender, Place & Culture, 20*(1) 107–124.

Mai, N., & King, R. (2009). Love, sexuality and migration: mapping the issue(s). *Mobilities, 4*(3), 295–307.

Manalansan, M. F. (2014). Queer worldings: The messy art of being global in Manila and New York. *Antipode.* doi:10.1111/anti.12061.

Masey, D. (2007). *For space.* London: Sage.

Matheson, C. M., & Finkel, R. (2013). Sex trafficking and the Vancouver Winter Olympic Games: Perceptions and preventative measures. *Tourism Management, 36,* 613–628.

McGrath, M. M. (2015). Conflict and co-existence? Strip clubs and neighbours in Pornland Oregon. In P. Maginn & C. Steinmitz (Eds.), *(Sub)urban sexscapes* (pp. 140–156). London: Routledge.

McKee, A., McNair, B., & Watson, A. F. (2014). Sex and the virtual suburbs: The pornosphere and community standards. In P. Maginn & C. Steinmitz (Eds.) *(Sub) urban sexscapes* (pp 171–190). London: Routledge.

Miller, V. (2005). Intertextuality, the referential illusion and the production of a gay ghetto. *Social & Cultural Geography, 6*(1), 61–79.

Morrison, C.A., Johnston, L., & Longhurst, R. (2013). Critical geographies of love as spatial, relational and political. *Progress in Human Geography, 37*(4), 505–521.

Mowlabocus, S. (2010). *Gaydar culture.* Farnham: Ashgate.

Mowlabocus, S. (2012). *Gaydar culture: Gay men, technology and embodiment in the digital age.* Farnham: Ashgate.

Myrdahl, T. M. (2013). Ordinary (small) cities and LGBQ lives. *ACME, 12*(2), 279–304.

Nash, C. J. (2006). Toronto's gay village (1969–1982): Plotting the politics of gay identity. *The Canadian Geographer/Le Géographe canadien, 50*(1), 1–16.

Nash, C. J. (2011). Trans experiences in lesbian and queer space. *The Canadian Geographer/La Geographe Canadien, 55*(2), 192–207.

Nash, C. J. (2013a). The age of the post-mo? Torontos changing gendered and sexual landscapes. *Geoforum, 49,* 243–252.

Nash, C. J. (2013b). Queering neighbourhoods: Politics and practice in Toronto. *Acme: International E-Journal for Critical Geographies, 12,* 193–219.

Nash, C. J., & Bain, A. (2007). 'Reclaiming raunch'? Spatializing queer identities at Toronto women's bathhouse events. *Social & Cultural Geography, 8*(1), 47–62.

Nash, C. J., & Gorman-Murray, A. (2014). LGBT neighborhoods and new mobilities: Towards understanding transformations in sexual and gendered urban landscapes. *International Journal of Urban and Regional Research, 38*(3), 356–372.

Nash C. J., & Gorman-Murray, A. (2015a). Lesbians in the city: Mobilities and relational geographies. *Journal of Lesbian Studies, 19*(2), 173–191.

Nash C. J. & Gorman-Murray, A. (2015b). Recovering the gay village: A comparative historical geography of urban change and planning in Toronto and Sydney. *Historical Geography, 43,* in press.

Oswin, N. (2013). Geographies of sexualities: The cultural turn and after. In N. Johnson, R. Schein, & J. Winders (Eds.), *The Wiley companion to cultural geography* (pp. 105–116). Chichester: Wiley.

Papayanis, M. A. (2000). Sex and the revanchist city: Zoning out pornography in New York. *Environment and Planning D, 18*(3), 341–354.

Patrick, D. J. (2014). The matter of displacement: A queer urban ecology of New York Citys High Line. *Social & Cultural Geography, 15*(8), 920–941.

Paul, B., Linz, D., & Shafer, B. (2001). Government regulation of adult businesses through zoning and anti-nudity ordinances: Debunking the legal myth of negative secondary effects. *Communication Law and Policy, 6*(2), 355–391.

Podmore, J. (2013). Lesbians as village queers: The transformation of Montréal's lesbian nightlife in the 1990s. *Acme: International E-Journal for Critical Geographies, 12*(2), 220–249.

Prior, J. (2008). Planning for sex in the city: Urban governance, planning and the placement of sex industry premises in inner Sydney. *Australian Geographer, 39*(3), 339–352.

Prior, J., & Gorman-Murray, A. (2014). Housing sex within the city: the placement of sex services beyond respectable domesticity? In P. Maginn & C. Steinmitz (Eds.), *(Sub)urban sexscapes* (pp. 101–116). London: Routledge.

Puar, J. K. (2006). Mapping US homonormativities. *Gender, Place and Culture, 13*(1), 67–88.

Pullen, C., & Cooper, M. (Eds.). (2010). *LGBT identity and online new media.* New York: Routledge.

Reckless, W. C. (1926). The distribution of commercialized vice in the city: A sociological analysis. *Publications of the American Sociological Society, 20,* 164–76.

Redmon, D. (2003). Playful deviance as an urban leisure activity: Secret selves, self-validation, and entertaining performances. *Deviant Behavior, 24*(1), 27–51.

Richardson, D. (2004). Locating sexualities: From here to normality. *Sexualities, 7*(4), 391–411.

Reynolds, R. (2009). Endangered territory, endangered identity: Oxford Street and the dissipation of gay life 1. *Journal of Australian Studies, 33*(1), 79–92.

Richardson, D. (2005). Desiring sameness? The rise of a neoliberal politics of normalization. *Antipode, 37*(3), 515–535.

Rothenberg, T. (1995). And she told two friends: Lesbians creating urban social space. In D. Bell & G. Valentine (Eds.) *Mapping desire: Geographies of sexualities* (pp. 165–181). London: Routledge.

Rubin, G. (1984). Thinking sex: Notes for a radical theory of the politics of sexuality. In C. Vance (Ed.), *Pleasure and danger* (pp. 71–90). London: Routledge.

Rushbrook, D. (2002). Cities, queer space and the cosmopolitan tourist. *GLQ: A Journal of Lesbian and Gay Studies, 8,* 183–206.

Ruting, B. (2008). Economic transformations of gay urban spaces: Revisiting Collins evolution gay district model. *Australian Geographer, 39,* 259–269.

Ryder, A. (2004). The changing nature of adult entertainment districts: Between a rock and a hard place or going from strength to strength? *Urban Studies, 41*(9), 1659–1686.

Sigusch, V. (1998). The neosexual revolution. *Archives of Sexual Behavior, 27*(4), 331–359.

Spurlin, W. J. (2000). Remapping same-sex desire: Queer writing and culture in the American heartland. In D. Shuttleton, D. Watt, & R. Phillips (Eds.), *De-centring sexualities: Politics and representations beyond the metropolis* (pp. 182–198). London: Routledge.

Symanski, R. (1974). Prostitution in Nevada. *Annals of the Association of American Geographers, 64*(3), 357–377.

Tongson, K. (2011). *Relocations: Queer suburban imaginaries.* New York: NYU Press.

Usher, N., & Morrison, E. (2010). The demise of the gay enclave, communication infrastructure theory and the transformation of gay public space. In C. Pullen & M. Cooper (Eds.), *LGBT Identity and Online New Media* (pp. 271–287). London: Routledge.

Vaccaro, A. (2009). Intergenerational perceptions, similarities and differences: A comparative analysis of lesbian, gay bisexual millennial youth with generation X and baby boomers. *Journal of LGBT Youth, 6,* 113–134.

Valentine, G. (1993). (Hetero)sexing space: Lesbian perceptions and experiences of everyday spaces. *Environment and Planning D: Space and Society, 11,* 395–413.

Valentine, G. (2008). The ties that bind: towards geographies of intimacy. Geography Compass, 2(6), 2097–2110.

Valverde, M., & Cirak, M. (2003). Governing bodies, creating gay spaces. Policing and security issues in gay downtown Toronto. *British Journal of Criminology, 43*(1), 102–121.

Visser, G. (2008). The homonormalization of white heterosexual leisure spaces In Bleomfontein, South Africa. *Geoforum, 39,* 1344–1358.

Ward, K. (2010). Towards a relational comparative approach to the study of cities. *Progress in Human Geography, 34*(4), 471–487.

Weston, K. (1995). Get thee to a big city: sexual imaginary and the great gay migration. *GLQ: A Journal of Lesbian and Gay Studies, 2,* 253–277.

Wilkinson, E. (2014). Single peoples geographies of home: Intimacy and friendship beyond "the family." *Environment and Planning A, 46*(10), 2452–2468.

Wimark T. and Östh J. (2014). The city as a single gay male magnet? Gay and lesbian geographical concentration in Sweden. *Population, Space and Place.* doi:10.1002/psp.1825.

Wotherspoon, G. (1991). *City of the plain: History of a gay sub-culture.* St. Leonards: Allen and Unwin.

Zenilman, J. M., Ellish, N., Fresia, A., & Glass, G. (1999). The geography of sexual partnerships in Baltimore: Applications of core theory dynamics using a geographic information system. *Sexually Transmitted Diseases, 26*(2), 75–81.

The Queer Metropolis

Amin Ghaziani

Sexuality and the city are longtime and global bedfellows. "Bangkok, Singapore, Hanoi and Delhi are culturally and politically disparate places, distant from the gay capitals of America, Europe or Australia," notes Aldrich (2004, p. 1731), as he takes us on a quick tour. "Each nevertheless demonstrates the city as a catalyst for homosexual activity." This alliance has taken many forms. "The city has shaped the homosexual from molly-houses in early modern London to the culture of 'fairies' and 'wolves' in working-class New York in the early twentieth century, from the carnivalesque tradition in Rio to the 'multicentered geography' of Los Angeles and the cohabitation of traditions in Thailand and Vietnam" (p. 1731).[1]

American sociologists entered the conversation in the early twentieth century by way of the Chicago School of Urban Sociology. "The city was as much a sexual laboratory as a social one,"

Heap (2003, p. 458) remarks in his review. In fact, "by 1938, Chicago sociologists' association of homosexuality with particular urban spaces was so complete that Professor Burgess could expect students…to provide an affirmative answer to the true-false exam question, 'In large cities, homosexual individuals tend to congregate rather than remain separate from each other'" (p. 467).

Sexuality does not have a singular spatial expression—nor has it ever. The quotidian decisions of people who are going about their daily lives cohere, with and without intentions, into diverse trends that scholars have tried to identify. Our objective in this chapter is to review how geographies of sexuality in the United States have fluctuated in form and meaning across three periods of sexual history—what I call the closet, coming out, and post-gay eras.

18.1 The Closet Era (1870—World War II): "Scattered Gay Places"

The homosexual as a "species," to borrow an analogy from Foucault (1978), was born around 1870. Sex between men and sex between women occurred prior to then, of course, since sexual behavior itself is timeless. But an association between bodily acts and an identity—in the way we think about it today—did not always exist. "As defined by the ancient civil or canonical codes, sodomy was a category of forbidden acts; their perpetrator was nothing more than the juridical subject of them" (p. 43). It was in the

---

[1] There are cross-national differences in how sexuality and the city are linked. See Knopp (1998) for a comparative study of Minneapolis, Edinburgh, London, and Sydney. Other examples include Cape Town, South Africa (Tucker 2009); a twenty-city comparison within Germany (Drever 2004); London, England (Houlbrook 2005); a comparison of London and Birmingham, UK (Collins 2004); Newcastle, UK (Casey 2004); Paris, France (Sibalis 2004); Sydney, Australia (Markwell 2002; Faro and Wotherspoon 2000); Toronto, Canada (Murray 1979); and Vancouver, Canada (Lo and Healy 2000).

A. Ghaziani (✉)
Department of Sociology, University of British Columbia, Vancouver, BC V6T 1Z1, Canada
e-mail: amin.ghaziani@ubc.ca

nineteenth-century that the "homosexual became a personage, a past, a case history, and a childhood" (p. 43). Medical officials began to use sexuality to summarize a person's entire profile: "Nothing that went into his total composition was unaffected by his sexuality." This gave the modern homosexual a "soul": "Homosexuality appeared as one of the forms of sexuality when it was transposed from the practice of sodomy onto a kind of interior androgyny, a hermaphrodism of the soul. The sodomite had been a temporary aberration; the homosexual was now a species" (p. 43).

Capitalism conspired in the transition from sex to sexuality. Seventeenth century colonial white families were self-sufficient economies, and their households contained all production-related activities that they needed to farm the land. Sex at this time furthered the goals of procreation, and while homosexual *behavior* existed, a gay or lesbian *identity* did not. Gay men and lesbians as distinct types of people are "a product of history" (D'Emilio 1993, p. 468). This economic system began to decline in the mid-1800s as wage labor gained traction and altered social norms of sex away from "the 'imperative' to procreate" (p. 470). A capitalist logic "created conditions that allowed some men and women to organize a personal life around their erotic/emotional attraction to their own sex" (p. 470). By the late twentieth century, large numbers of men and women were able "to call themselves gay, to see themselves as part of a community of similar men and women, and to organize politically on the basis of that identity" (p. 468). During these years, especially from 1860–1892, "heterosexuality" and "homosexuality" emerged as distinct concepts in sexology, psychology, and the medical sciences as practitioners sorted people into sexual categories (Dean 2014).

These arguments are fairly familiar, but how they connect to the city is not as well known. Enter geographer Larry Knopp, who argues that the industrial revolution and market enterprise were the engines of an urban gay identity. "Industrialism, through the separation of home from workplace and the creation of separate, gendered spheres of production, reproduction, and male-female experiences, created the 'personal' space within which it became possible for human beings to imagine themselves as 'private' creatures with 'individual' sexual identities" (Knopp 1992, pp. 663–664). A strict division of labor at home and in the workplace "left little room for nonheterosexual arrangements" (p. 664). The "assumption of universal heterosexuality" remained mostly unchallenged, since "sexual dissidents" feared sanctions like social stigma and physical violence (p. 663).

I say "most unchallenged" deliberately. Industrial capitalism contained contradictions that allowed individuals who desired others of the same sex to find one another. Knopp (1992) continues, "One strategy for surviving the contradiction between private experience [imagining yourself as gay or lesbian] and public demands for conformity [the pressure to live your life as a married heterosexual person] was the construction, very discreetly, of social spaces in which dominant gender and sexual codings were suspended" (p. 664). Men formed underground networks to pursue their same-sex desires in commodity form (anonymous public places like bars and baths), while women organized their interactions in the domestic sphere, along with a limited number of work and educational arenas. "Over time," Knopp concludes, "some of these spaces became permanent, and provided the material basis for more complex personal interactions and the creation of fully developed alternative communities and identities" (p. 664). In this way, gay identity was fashioned as struggles over space, and its expression varied by gender and along a continuum from public to private.

Consider New York as an example. A remarkably complex gay male world emerged in this city between 1890 and the start of the Second World War as bohemian rebellions inspired men to develop their own commercial establishments. Chauncey (1994, p. 23) characterizes the city at this time as a "topography of gay meeting places"—or "scattered 'gay places,'" to borrow another visual image from urban planner Forsyth (2001, p. 343). These bars, cabarets, theaters, public parks and other cruising areas, restrooms, and even the streets themselves were located in progressive parts of the city, like Greenwich Village for white gay men or Harlem for blacks, which had reputations for "flouting bourgeois convention" (p. 227). Men exploited the anonymity of urban life as they explored their same-sex desires. Even "normal" men were permitted to have sex with other men—especially those who were seen as "fairies"—without any moral condemnation, provided that they "maintained a masculine demeanor and played (or claimed to play) only the 'masculine,' or insertive, role in the sexual encounter—so long, that is, as they…did not allow their bodies to be sexually penetrated." If they met these conditions, then "neither they, the fairies, nor the working-class public considered *them* [the normal men] to be queer" (p. 66).[2] None of these individuals "set the tone" (p. 228) of the neighborhood, however, which is why it would be a mistake to say that the scattered gay places of the closet era were based in gay neighborhoods as we think about that idea today.

Urban histories of women's "romantic friendships," (Rupp 2001) as they were called, are harder to find. Literacy rates for women lagged behind those for men (Faderman 1999, p. 56), and this has resulted in fewer written records to study. In addition, nineteenth century women had restricted access "to both wage-earning jobs and public spaces where they could form same-sex subcultures parallel to those among men" (Dean 2014, p. 58). Even existing are not always easy to interpret. It is difficult to distinguish "women's affectionate companionship from sexual, specifically genital, relations," especially since women's romantic friendships "ran the gamut from friendship and companionship to erotic sexual relationships" (p. 58). For these reasons, it is "historically complicated" (p. 58) to neatly align sexual labels, behaviors, and identities. That said, nineteenth century romantic friendships were "fundamental to the proto-lesbian identities and subcultures that would emerge in the twentieth century" (p. 58). Labels such as "fiery man-eaters" (Friedan 1963, p. 80), "the lesbian" (p. 18), and "the mannish lesbian/congenital invert" (Newton 1993b, p. 291) were circulating by the 1920s, and they all denoted "the presence of a menacing female monster" (p. 18). These charges were designed "to enforce heterosexuality and traditional gender roles among women" (p. 69). But some individuals re-appropriated these terms "to create spaces, discourses, and identities for consciously lesbian women" (p. 69). In doing so, they helped "to form lesbian subcultures in American culture at this time" (p. 69). Kennedy and Davis (1993) document one such working-class and racially diverse community that thrived in Buffalo, New York. Here, women cultivated social networks in private house parties, which became hotbeds of lesbian life. Many women used these social gatherings to craft "cultures of resistance" (p. 2) and find relief from the well of loneliness (Hall 1928) that burdened so many of their lives. The results were often transformative. "I wasn't concentrating on my school work, 'cause I was so enthused and so happy," one women recalled, while another added:

> We wound up at this bar. Now previous to this I had never been to a gay bar. I didn't even know they existed. It was a Friday night and that was the big night…And we walked in and I thought, my God, this is really something. I couldn't believe it…[I] don't think there were any straight people in that bar that night. (quoted in Ghaziani 2014b, p. 14)[3]

As this discussion shows, I do not use the imagery of the closet to suggest that there was an *absence* of queer life in the prewar years. Three popular myths compel many of us to mistakenly

---

[2] Fairies were the ones who were stigmatized in this social world, although they were "publicly tolerated [as] womanlike men" (p. 60). Terms like "normal men" and "fairies," along with strict specifications for sexual roles, suggest the primacy of gender in this historical context. Note as well that "'normal' men, who are also called 'trade' by their fairy…sexual partners, of this period are not to be thought of as 'heterosexual,' at least not yet, as these 'normal' men could engage in sexual activity with other men without the cultural opprobrium of the heterosexual/homosexual system" (p. 60).

[3] Similar to the fairies, homosexual women were also seen as "'female inverts,' as 'inversion' of the female character into that of a male is what it took in sexology's discourse for a woman to pursue another woman, as supposedly only a man would" (p. 59).

believe that this was the case: the myth of isolation (anti-gay bigotry compelled queer people to live solitary lives); invisibility (even if a queer world existed, it was impossible for anyone to find it); and internalization (queer people internalized societal views of homosexuality as a sickness and sin). "All three myths about prewar gay history are represented in the image of the closet," Chauncey (1994, p. 6) writes. "Before Stonewall (let alone before World War II), it is often said, gay people lived in a closet that kept them isolated, invisible, and vulnerable to anti-gay ideology" (p. 6). But this is not true. Like Chauncey, I use the "closet era" as a way to think about queer social and spatial expressions during the years prior to World War II. Gay men and women "appropriated public spaces not identified as gay…in order to construct a gay city in the midst of (and often invisible to) to normative city" (p. 23). Institutional growth of queer subcultures unfolded slowly in these years. The year 1931, however, produced a pivot when a New York-based newspaper featured an exposé on "gay meeting places" (p. 23). A year later, the movie *Call Her Savage* showcased Greenwich's gay scene. By this time, "the Village became noted as the home of 'pansies' and 'lesbians'" (p. 235). But "gay men and women [still] had to fight for space, even in the Village" (p. 227). In 1936, a medical journal published the "Degenerates of Greenwich Village," an article that announced the Village was "now the Mecca for… perverts" (p. 234). Amid these and other sensational headlines, a world-altering event unfolded that, in its wake, would stamp an indelible imprint across the queer metropolis.

18.2 The Coming Out Era (World War II—1997): Gayborhoods Form (1940s) and Flourish (1970s)

World War II was "a nationwide 'coming out' experience" (D'Emilio and Freedman 1997, p. 289), and it ushered in a new sexual era. The war deposited young men and women into cities with major military bases, places like Chicago,

Washington DC, Seattle, San Francisco, San Diego, Philadelphia, New York, Miami, and New Orleans. These areas swelled with servicemen and women who were discharged on the grounds of their real or perceived homosexuality. The war and its discharges "led directly to dawning realization by homosexuals of their numbers, which in turn led to the formation of the postwar self-conception of gays as a quasi-ethnic minority" (Wright 1999, p. 173). The population of San Francisco, for example, had declined during the 1930s—but it grew by more than 125,000 between 1940 and 1950. Census data from 1950 to 1960 show that the number of single-person households in the city doubled following the war and accounted for 38 % of the total residential units (D'Emilio 1989, p. 459).

The concentration of young gay men and lesbians in urban centers altered their spatial imagination. Bars that catered to them opened in larger numbers, and over time, the first formal gay neighborhoods, or gayborhoods, emerged. The men and women who engineered this "society within a society" (Castells 1983, p. 157) did so deliberately. "Not only did they have a sexual network to preserve, they had also to win their right to exist as citizens, they had to engage in political battles, change laws, fight the police, and influence government" (p. 157). This was not an easy task. To succeed, "they [first] had to organize themselves spatially," which enabled them "to transform their oppression into the organizational setting of political power" (p. 157). This is why the emergence of the Castro gayborhood, like so many others, "was inseparable from the development of the gay community as a social movement" and its "control of a given territory" (p. 157).

Before the war, it was against the law in many states for gays and lesbians to gather in public places, even in those bars that they called their own. However, a landmark California Supreme Court decision in 1951 ruled that "it was illegal to close down a bar simply because homosexuals were the usual customers. The first right to a public space had been won" (p. 141). The California case catapulted a national movement to safeguard queer spaces, and it politicized the bars in particular. Activists founded the Tavern Guild in 1962 to protect themselves from police raids and organize voter registration drives in and around the bars (D'Emilio 1983, p. 189). The Guild proved pivotal for the formation of "a more stable gay neighborhood" which, in the same spirit as the politicized bar culture, attracted mostly gay men who sought "to liberate territory where a new culture and political power could be concentrated" (Doan and Higgins 2011, p. 8).

Winning the legal right to gather in public places and forming the Tavern Guild did not provide full immunity from police harassment—either in San Francisco or anywhere else in the United States. On June 28, 1969 in New York, for example, the local police raided the Stonewall Inn, a gay bar located at 53 Christopher Street in Greenwich Village. Compliance during these raids was often as routine as the raids themselves, but this time the bar goers and a growing crowd outside fought back, resulting in 5 days of rioting that changed the face of queer life in America. Bar owners and patrons had defended themselves at other raids in New York and elsewhere, but activists and academics remember Stonewall singularly as having "sparked the beginning of the gay liberation movement" (Bérubé 1990, p. 271); as "*the* emblematic event in modern lesbian and gay history" (Duberman 1993, p. xvii); as "that moment in time when gays and lesbians recognized all at once their mistreatment and their solidarity" (p. xvii); and as "a symbol of a new era of gay politics" (Adam 1995, p. 81).[4]

Stonewall inspired gays and lesbians to come out of the closet en masse and relocate to cities where they hoped to find similar others. This national demographic movement was called the "Great Gay Migration" (Weston 1995, p. 255), and it occurred throughout the 1970s and into the

early 1980s.[5] San Francisco held a special place in it, but the ripple effects stretched to many other areas, including Cherry Grove, a small resort town on Fire Island; Northampton, Massachusetts; Buffalo, New York; Columbia, South Carolina; and Des Moines, Iowa.[6] The great gay migration and gayborhoods were mutually reinforcing: gays and lesbians selected specific areas to which they relocated, and their emergent clusters affirmed a "sexual imaginary" (p. 274)—or a perception that they comprised a people and a tribe, culturally distinct from heterosexuals.

This discussion should prompt us to ask important follow up questions. Why did so many gays and lesbians move to a relatively small number of cities during the great gay migration? And once they arrived, why did they live in the same exact neighborhood? Existing research offers six classes of explanation, each of which tells us about gays as urban actors and the emergence of gayborhoods as urban forms (Table 18.1).

18.2.1   Ecology Arguments

According to ecology arguments, gay neighborhoods, like other urban districts, are "natural areas," which Chicago School sociologists defined as "social spaces created through the 'natural' ecological growth of the city, rather than its planned commercial development" (Park 1926, p. 8; quoted in Heap 2003, p. 465). The size, density, and heterogeneity (Wirth 1938) of urban life incites competition over land use, and people decide where to live based on factors such as the

[4] Another famous episode of resistance to a bar raid occurred at the Black Cat in San Francisco. See Armstrong and Crage (2006) for a discussion about why other events "failed to achieve the mythic stature of Stonewall" (p. 725).

[5] Esther Newton describes an earlier "gay outward migration" that occurred in New York between the war and the 1960s. In this episode, "gays congregated at specific spots on the public beaches from Coney Island to Point Lookout, Riis Park, and Jones Beach," all of which were "a string of beaches running from New York City eastward to the Hamptons, a hundred miles away on the tip of Long Island" (Newton 1993a, p. 44).

[6] Many scholars focus on the Castro district of San Francisco as a "gay mecca" (Stryker and Van Buskirk 1996; Boyd 2005; Stryker 2002). For more on gay life in smaller cities and non-urban areas, see (p. 472).

Table 18.1 The queer metropolis in the coming out era

Explanation	Gays as Urban Actors	Gay Neighborhoods as Urban Forms
Ecology	Gays and straights compete over land use, and they seek access to public transportation and jobs	Gay neighborhoods form as natural areas through processes of invasion and succession
History	Gays respond to unfolding historical conditions and contingencies	Gay neighborhoods form as historical accidents
Community	Gays seek solidarity and fellowship with others who are like them, and they want access to specific institutions	Gay neighborhoods form as more institutions concentrate in an area
Sexuality	Gays seek opportunities for sex, dating, love, and romance	Gay neighborhoods form to ease transactions in a sexual marketplace
Economics	Gays revitalize the city as they seek economic opportunities, affordable housing, and amenities	Gay neighborhoods are the outcome of urban gentrification
Politics	Gays are moral refugees who seek shelter from bigotry and bias	Gay neighborhoods form to provide a safe space from heterosexual hostilities

availability of public transportation and jobs. The city grows as spatially separated territories that form through the "invasion" and "succession" (Park and Burgess 1925; Park 1915; McKenzie 1924; Zorbaugh 1929) of various groups. In a famous diagram,

> [Ernest] Burgess depicted urban growth and social organization as a set of five concentric zones, spreading outward from the Central Business District (Zone I) to the Zone in Transition (II), the Zone of Independent Workingmen's Homes (III), the Zone of Better Residences (IV), and the Commuters' Zone (V)…For Burgess, these zones defined an outward progression of increasing social and moral organization, in which non-normative sexualities were confined principally to the natural areas—the hobohemias, Chinatowns, vice districts, racialized ghettos, bohemian enclaves and the 'the world of furnished rooms'—of the inner city transitional zone. Beginning from this core of sexual abnormality, Burgess implied that the further one moved away from the city's geographic center, the closer the zone's inhabitants approached the ideal of middle-class sexual normativity. (p. 468)

The city of Chicago inspired ecology arguments, which makes it unclear what they can teach us about a place like Los Angeles, for example, that has grown without concentric zones (Kenney 2001; Halle 2003). Furthermore, natural areas focus on race, ethnicity, and social class. When Chicago sociologists addressed sexuality, they used frameworks of "sexual abnormality" or "vice districts," and they seldom theorized the epistemological distinctiveness of sexuality (see Sedgwick 1990, pp. 75–82).

18.2.2   Historical Arguments

Proponents of historical arguments see gays as actors who respond to external conditions and contingencies that they cannot always predict in advance. These "historical accidents" (Collins 2004, p. 1792) incite gayborhoods to form, provided that they inspire similar responses among different individuals. World War II and the Stonewall riots were examples of such triggering events in the US, while the decriminalization of homosexuality in 1967 helped gayborhoods to form in cities like London, Brighton, Manchester, and Newcastle (p. 1800). Typifying this tradition is the "writing of community histories" (D'Emilio 1989, p. 456) where scholars identify the idiosyncrasies of particular places at certain moments in time.[7]

18.2.3   Community Arguments

Others assert that building a gay neighborhood is "inseparable from the development of the gay community" (Castells and Murphy 1982, p. 256). To defend this community argument, Murray (1992) debates Robert Bellah and his colleagues who, in their widely-cited book *Habits of the Heart* (Bellah et al. 1985), seek "to preserve the sacred term 'community' from application

---

[7] Additional examples of historical arguments include (Duggins 2002; Stryker 2002; Stryker and Van Buskirk 1996; Heap 2009).

to what they term 'lifestyle enclaves'" (p. 114). Murray objects on the grounds that their alternate category is "based on the 'narcissism of similarity' in patterns of leisure and consumption" (p. 114). He applies each of Bellah et al.'s three criteria for a "real community" (pp. 153–54; Murray 1996, p. 197)—institutional completeness; commitments among geographically clustered people that carry them beyond their private life into public investments; and a collective memory that preserves the past by recounting stories of shared suffering—to gays and lesbians and concludes, "North American gay communities fit all the criteria suggested by sociologists to define 'community' as well as or better than urban ethnic communities do" (p. 108).

Queer territories nurture the "institutional elaboration of a quasi-ethnic community" (Murray 1979, p. 165; Epstein 1987) by promoting a unique worldview, one that resists restrictive heterosexual norms. Participating in ritual events such as pride parades (Herrell 1993; Armstrong 2002; Bruce 2013), dyke marches (Ghaziani and Fine 2008; Brown-Saracino and Ghaziani 2009), and street festivals that are based in gayborhoods inspires collective effervescence (Durkheim 1912) and solidarity among those who gather for it. In one study of fifty gay white men between the ages of 23 and 48 who lived in DuPont Circle in Washington, D.C., more than 80-percent expressed "a desire to be among other gay men" (Myslik 1996, p. 166) as their major reason for neighborhood selection. The wisdom is worth stating in general terms: gays migrate to their "homeland" (Weston 1995, p. 265) as a "path to membership" (Murray 1992, p. 107) in the community.[8]

The presence of particular institutions is the most prominent part of the community argument. In fact, "the existence of distinctive institutions is more salient to the identification of a community—for both insiders and outsiders—than residential segregation or concentration" (Murray 1992, p. 109). Gayborhoods are home to gay-owned and gay-friendly bookstores, hair salons, churches, travel agencies, realtors, medical facilities, retail stores, periodicals, non-profit organizations, and political groups. This is why academics and laymen alike use phrases like "gay mecca" (Chauncey 1994, p. 245; Beemyn 1997, p. 2), "gay capital" (Browne and Bakshi 2011, p. 180) "gay village" (Binnie and Skeggs 2004, p. 49; Bell and Binnie 2004, p. 1807), and "gay ghetto" (Levine 1979; Sibalis 2004, p. 1739), among others, when they talk about gayborhoods (for review see Brown 2013). Imagine for a moment that you are an urban planner, and you want to build a gay district since they allegedly boost local economic vitality (Florida 2002) and rates of civic engagement (Usher and Morrison 2010). Would you encourage landlords to rent to gay people as a way to increase residential concentration? Or open a gay bar? Those who work in this tradition would advise you to opt for the latter.

18.2.4 Sexuality Arguments

As gays and lesbians fled to gayborhoods across the country, they discovered a treasure trove of possibilities. Sex and love were the most immediate. Building a sexual subculture has been a formative part of queer history. "Pleasure seekers" were gay male activists in the 1950s and 1960s "who felt that the well-being of homosexuals would be ensured by…quietly building and protecting spaces for homosexual socializing" (Armstrong 2002, pp. 42–43). This is an example of the sexuality argument. Proponents advance the view that "gay collective life should be primarily about the pursuit of pleasure" (p. 185). Because homosexuality is not visible on the body like race or gender, sexual minorities encounter a special challenge in finding one another—whether for a night or lifetime. Gayborhoods offer a solution to this problem. The density of gays and lesbians in specific parts of the city helps them to find each other as they pursue matters of the heart and libido.

Sociologist Edward Laumann is a well-known researcher who writes in this tradition. In 2004, he and his colleagues marshalled a wealth of

---

[8] Additional examples of community arguments include (Escoffier 1975; Herrell 1993; Castells and Murphy 1982).

data—a probability sample of households from four Chicago neighborhoods, which resulted in 2114 face-to-face interviews, and a purposive sample of 160 interviews—to investigate "the set of meanings that organize sexual identities, sexual relationships, and participation in a sex market" (Laumann et al. 2004, p. 350). They advance metaphors of sex markets and sexual marketplaces to argue that "meeting and mating are fundamentally local processes" (p. 40) that are organized in distinct neighborhoods. A sex market is a broad spatial milieu within which individuals can organize their general strategy (e.g., a gayborhood), whereas a sexual marketplace is a specific venue where you can meet someone (e.g., a bar). Laumann and his colleagues conclude that sexuality is "firmly embedded within concrete spaces, cultures, social relations, and institutions" (p. 357). The results have been replicated in more recent studies which have found that "sexual desire can be a driving force in neighborhood formation" (Doan and Higgins 2011, p. 15). Even as gay bars close or relocate, sexual minorities still "visit traditional gay commercial centers" to "go the gym, get a drink, buy a book or magazine, and well, for sex" (p. 15).

18.2.5 Economic Arguments

The biggest debate in this conversation is whether economic rationalities or freedom from discrimination provides a more compelling account for why gayborhoods first formed. Those who favor the former offer three types of economic arguments: urban comforts and amenities, critical gay population size, and investment potential. These factors can steer the decisions that gays and lesbians make about where to live. For example, research shows strong correlations between the location of same-sex households and high-amenities in cities like Austin, Atlanta, Fort Lauderdale, Los Angeles, New York, Oakland, San Francisco, San Diego, Seattle, and Washington (Black et al. 2002). If we assume that some of these cities emerged as magnets during the great

migration (which we must do to approximate the past; we do not have census data on same-sex households for the coming out era), then one lesson we can draw is that urban comforts matter in queer residential decision-making. Within a given city, we also know that there are correlations between the number of same-sex residences in a neighborhood and its housing stock, especially that which is older and higher in value (Anacker and Morrow-Jones 2005, p. 390, 406). Why do same-sex households settle in areas with greater cultural offerings, amenities, and desirable housing stock? This happens because "gay households face constraints that make having or adopting children more costly than for otherwise similar heterosexuals" (p. 55). This frees up resources that they can allocate elsewhere, such as moving to a city with a beautiful natural environment, a mild climate, a neighborhood with attractive housing stock, a diverse array of restaurants, and a vibrant local arts and entertainment scene. Those who endorse such an amenities perspective "do not view gay men as special, with idiosyncratic preferences that uniquely determine their location decisions" (p. 56). On the contrary, "other wealthy households or households with low demand for housing will also locate in high amenity areas" (p. 56).[9]

A second subtype of economic arguments—"critical gay population size" (Collins 2004, p. 1791)—explains why queer districts emerge in areas that *lack* amenities: cities that do not have a remarkable climate, or neighborhoods that lack appreciable aesthetic qualities and have an inland location away from the downtown core. These traits would lead us to predict that a gayborhood will *not* form. Yet this happened with the Birmingham Gay Village in England. Once a minimum queer population density was established there, it provided a "virtuous circle" (p. 1791) which motivated more migration to the area. A

---

[9] Additional examples of economic arguments include (Knopp 1990, p. 347; Florida 2002; Collins 2004, p. 1790; Cooke and Rapiano 2007, p. 296).

critical gay population offered a "high amenity value in its own right" (p. 1791).

Gentrification is the final subtype of economic arguments, and it is the most common explanation that scholars propose for why gayborhoods first formed. Marxist urban geographer Ruth Glass (1964) coined the term, and in a widely-cited review essay, sociologist Sharon Zukin (1987, p. 129) defined it as "the conversion of socially marginal and working-class areas of the central city to middle-class residential use" by "private-market investment capital in downtown districts [sometimes called 'central business districts' or CBDs]." In the United States, federal interventions fueled a first wave of urban renewal efforts, which were a response to inner-city decline that white flight caused in the 1960s (Wilson 1987). During this wave, a group of "risk-oblivious" (Gale 1980, pp. 105–106; Kasinitz 1988, p. 175) artists, students, and design professionals, many of whom were gay (Brown-Saracino 2009; Zukin 1987; Knopp 1990, 1997), invested in "islands of renewal in seas of decay" (Berry 1985). These individuals imagined themselves as pioneers who were "taming the urban wilderness" (Smith 1986; Spain 1993, p. 158) as they searched for affordable places to live and "a residential environment where they would not encounter an atmosphere of social alienation" (Pattison 1983, pp. 88–89). Gays and other first wavers were less motivated by the promise of economic gain than by cheap housing, freedom of self-expression with impunity, a search for community, and protection from discrimination.

18.2.6   Political Arguments

The "political and social acceptance of gay individuals" (Black et al. 2002, p. 65) and access to "gay cultural and institutional life" (Knopp 1997, p. 46) interact with economic considerations as gays and lesbians decide where in the metropolis they want to live. For them, "gentrification is not only an economic response to a discriminatory housing market but also a political reaction involving the formation of a collective spatial identity" (Ruting 2008, p. 262). The residential decisions that gay people make are informed by an area's "reputation for tolerating non-conformity" (Chauncey 1994, p. 229). During the coming out era, gays and lesbians invested in these areas "at a financial and social *cost* that only 'moral refugees' are ready to pay" (Castells 1983, p. 161, emphasis added). This observation challenges a reductive view of gays and lesbians as rational, economic actors, and it brings us to the "emancipatory city thesis" (Lees 2000, p. 392; Collins 2004, p. 1799)—or political argument. One activist shared his reverie at the Berkeley gay liberation conference in 1969:

> I have a recurring daydream. I imagine a place where gay people can be free. A place where there is no job discrimination, police harassment or prejudice…A place where a gay government can build the base for a flourishing gay counter-culture and city…It would mean gay territory. It would mean a gay government, a gay civil service, a county welfare department which made public assistance payments to the refugees from persecution and prejudice. (Armstrong 2002, p. 89)

Gayborhoods flourished following the Stonewall riots of 1969 as gays and lesbians from across the United States moved to them and romanticized the possibilities for freedom that they dreamed existed in these areas. Books, magazines, newspapers, television, movies, and personal contacts spread the word about these budding gay territories (Meeker 2006). "Every friend who sends a letter back from San Francisco filled with tales of city streets covered with queers builds the city's reputation as a safe harbor for 'gay people'" (Weston 1995, p. 262). This created a distinct "sexual geography" within the city, one in which gayborhoods shone as "a beacon of tolerance" (Weston 1995, p. 262) in a sea of heterosexual hostility. This brings us to a critical insight: gay neighborhoods are "a spatial response to a historically specific form of oppression" (Lauria and Knopp 1985, p. 152).

Proponents of political arguments see gayborhoods as a type of free space or safe space. A widely-cited passage defines these areas as particular sorts of public places in the community [that] are the environments in which people are able to learn a new self-respect, a deeper and more assertive group identity, public skills, and values of cooperation and civic virtue. Put simply, free spaces are settings between private lives and large-scale institutions where ordinary citizens can act with dignity, independence, and vision. (Evans and Boyte [1986] 1992, p. 17)[10]

Gay social thinkers were active in this conversation. For example, in 1969, Carl Wittman drafted *A Gay Manifesto* in which he described his San Francisco home as a "refugee camp for homosexuals." Gays and lesbians "formed a ghetto, out of self-protection," in his assessment, since "straight cops patrol us, straight legislators govern us, straight employers keep us in line, straight money exploits us." This is why so many gay and lesbian moral refugees of the era invested in the Castro. "We want to make ourselves clear: our first job is to free ourselves; that means clearing our head of the garbage that's been poured into them" (Wittman 1970, pp. 67–68).

Over the years, scholars have often invoked the image of a safe space when discussing gay neighborhoods. Castells and Murphy (1982, p. 237), for example, assert that gays seek to "build up autonomous social institutions and a political organization powerful enough to establish a 'free commune' beyond prejudice." In a later piece, Castells (1983, p. 139, 168) defines gayborhoods as "liberated zones" and "free villages" where gays can "be safe together." Similarly, in his study of the West Hollywood cityhood campaign, Forest (1995) remarks on "the emancipatory and empowering potential" of the queer metropolis: "Public spaces created by gays provide for relative safety, for the perpetuation of gay subcultures," he says. They "provide symbols around which gay identity is centered" and enable sexual minorities "to resist [heterosexual] domination" (p. 137). During the coming out era, gayborhoods provided "a safe harbor" (Weston 1995, p. 262) and "homeland" (p. 269) for its residents. Simple personal acts like "stroll[ing] hand-in-hand or kiss[ing] in the street without embarrassment or risk of harassment" (Sibalis 2004, p. 1748) became deeply political. In fact, when we review the history of the gay and lesbian "fight against violence," we find that "the ideal of 'safe space'" is "fundamental to the emergent forms of LGBT identity," and grass-roots activism in defense of safe spaces has been "one means by which neighborhoods have been claimed" (Hanhardt 2008, p. 63).

18.2.7   Are Gayborhoods Ghettos?

Before we conclude this section, we should ask whether it is appropriate to use the word "ghetto," the way Wittman and others do, when speaking of the queer metropolis. The term originated in sixteenth-century Venice, where it described an area of the city in which authorities forced Jews to live. American sociologists of the Chicago School (e.g., Wirth 1928) began to use the word in the 1920s "to designate urban districts inhabited predominately by racial, ethnic or social minorities, whether by compulsion or by choice" (Sibalis 2004, p. 1739). Within 50 years, scholars were "applying the term 'gay ghetto' to neighborhoods characterized by the presence of gay institutions in number, a conspicuous and locally dominant subculture that is socially isolated from the larger community, and a residential population that is

---

[10] Pamela Allen first used this idea to explain how to build an autonomous women's movement. She advocated working in small groups—which she called "free spaces"—where women could "think about our lives, our society and our potential for being creative individuals" (Allen 1970, p. 6). Free spaces were a solution to Betty Friedan's "problem that had no name" (p. 19); they allowed individual women to realize that they were not alone in how they experienced their life. Sharing stories in free spaces inspired the famous slogan "the personal is political," and it affirmed women's collective reality in a safe space that was not occupied by men. Scholars have described these sites in numerous ways, including abeyance structures (Taylor 1989), cultural laboratories (Mueller 1994), cultures of solidarity (Fantasia 1988), movement half way houses (Morris 1984), havens (Hirsch 1990), independent spaces (Needleman 1994), protected spaces (Tétreault 1993), safe spaces (Gamson 1996), sequestered social sites (Scott 1990), and liberated zones (Fantasia and Hirsch 1995). For a review and critique of research on safe spaces, see (Polletta 1999).

substantially gay" (Levine 1979; p. 1739). Ghettos, in other words, have four defining features: institutional concentration, a locally dominant subculture, social isolation from the surrounding city, and residential segregation typically created by compulsion rather than by choice. Therefore, an urban area is a "gay ghetto" or "lavender ghetto" (Levine 1979, p. 182) if it has large numbers of gay institutions, a visible and dominant gay subculture that is socially isolated from the rest of the city, and a concentrated residential population. Based on these four features, the term gay ghetto is an apt synonym for a gayborhood—but only in the coming out era, as we will see more clearly in the next section.

In summary, ecological, historical, community, sexuality, economic, and political arguments all explain why gay neighborhoods formed and flourished in the coming out era. If we pay attention to the overlaps and intersections among these six factors, we will be able to offer a more holistic assessment not just for the initial emergence of gay neighborhoods but also why they are changing as we embark into a new post-gay world.

18.3 The Post-Gay Era (1998—Present): Gayborhoods Change

In 2007 the *New York Times* published a front-page story with a foreboding headline: "Gay enclaves face prospect of being passé." The journalist elaborated, "These are wrenching times for San Francisco's historic gay village, with population shifts, booming development, and a waning sense of belonging that is also being felt in gay enclaves across the nation" (Brown 2007). The two trends that motivated Brown's story—gays moving out from urban areas that have been culturally-associated with them while more straights move into them—have created anxieties in districts across the country. For instance, on November 28, 2006, the GLBT Historical Society of Northern California hosted three standing-room only roundtable sessions around the theme "Queers in the City: GLBT Neighborhoods

and Urban Planning." The series opened with a poignant question: "Are Gay Neighborhoods Worth Saving?" During the heated debate, board member Don Romesburg disabused the dubious assumptions of some audience members about the stability of queer spaces: "Our neighborhoods get built within particular economic, political, and cultural circumstances. When those change, so do our neighborhoods."

In recent years, journalists, scholars, and everyday people alike have begun to wonder whether gay neighborhoods are disappearing (Doan and Higgins 2011; Usher and Morrison 2010; Nash and Gorman-Murray 2014; Brown 2013). Unique commercial spaces like bars and bookstores are closing up shop, more heterosexuals are moving in, and gays and lesbians are choosing to live in other parts of the city. Demographers who analyze the US census confirm that zip codes associated with traditional gay neighborhoods are "de-concentrating" (Spring 2012, 2013): fewer same-sex households lived in them in 2010 than they did in 2000. Same-sex partner households now reside in 93 % of all counties in the country (Gates and Cooke 2011), and gay life increasingly "blends with other aspects of the city" (Aldrich 2004, p. 1732). Why do so many gay and lesbian households today think outside the gayborhood box?

The answer has to do with seismic shifts in how we think about sexuality. Gay life exists "beyond the closet" (Seidman 2002, p. 6) in places like Canada (Nash 2012), the United Kingdom (Collard 1998a, b), and the United States (Ghaziani 2011)—despite the persistence of heteronormative biases in the state, societal institutions, and popular culture. This prompted British journalist Paul Burston to coin the phrase "post-gay" in 1994. It found an American audience 4 years later in 1998 when *Out* magazine editor James Collard used the term in the *New York Times* to argue,

> We should no longer define ourselves solely in terms of our sexuality—even if our opponents do. Post-gay isn't 'un-gay.' It's about taking a critical look at gay life and no longer thinking solely in terms of struggle. It's going to a gay bar and wishing there were girls there to talk to.

He clarified the urban implications of this idea 2 months later in a separate *Newsweek* feature:

> First for protection and later with understandable pride, gays have come to colonize whole neighborhoods, like West Hollywood in L.A. and Chelsea in New York City. It seems to me that the new Jerusalem gay people have been striving for all these years won't be found in a gay-only ghetto, but in a world where we are free, equal and safe to live our lives.

A similar term arrived in Canada in 2011 when Paul Aguirre-Livingston, writing for Toronto-based magazine *The Grid*, published an article entitled, "Dawn of a New Gay." He described the emergence of "a new type of gay," which he called "the post-mo," short for postmodern homosexual. What we name this new period— "beyond the closet" (Seidman 2002), "new gay" (Savin-Williams 2005; Aguirre-Livingston 2011), "post-closeted cultural context" (Dean 2014), or "post-gay" (Ghaziani 2011, 2014a, b)—matters less than our efforts to grapple with how changing meanings of sexuality affect queer geographies.[11]

The defining and differentiating features of the post-gay era come into greater focus when we compare it with the two prior periods. The heyday of the closet was characterized by concealment (hiding who you are from your family and friends); isolation (being disconnected from networks of other gay people); feelings of shame, guilt, and fear (which stemmed from internalizing societal views about homosexuality); and duplicity (living a double life) (Seidman 2002, pp. 29–30; see also Chauncey 1994; D'Emilio 1983). The coming out era, in contrast, was typified by being open about your sexuality; by constructing a world with almost exclusively

gay social networks; and by believing that "gay is good," to allude to a culturally resonant phrase that activist Franklin Kameny coined in 1968 in an effort to mirror Stokley Carmichael's "black is beautiful" (Valocchi 1999b; Armstrong 2002). Finally, the primary feature of the post-gay era is a dramatic acceptance and ensuing assimilation (Sullivan 2007) of some segments of sexual minorities into the mainstream of American society (Ghaziani 2011). Although an impulse toward "cultural sameness" (Ghaziani 2014b) with straights has arisen several times in the history of queer politics (Armstrong 2002; D'Emilio 1983; Ghaziani 2008), the current iteration is distinct. "Gay life today *is* very different than it was just a decade or two ago" because queer people now have more options for how to live their lives and because "their lives often look more like those of conventional heterosexuals than those of the closeted homosexuals of the recent past" (Seidman 2002, p. 6). In both prior sexual eras, "individuals confronted stark choices: stay in or step out of the closet" (p. 86). Identity choices were also oppositional: "to deny or champion being gay as a core identity" (p. 86). But things are much less stark today. "As individuals live outside the closet, they have more latitude in defining themselves and the place of homosexuality in their lives" (p. 88).[12]

Public opinion that shows liberalizing attitudes toward homosexuality provides one indicator that we have arrived at the doorsteps of a new sexual era. A 2010 Gallup Poll found that "Americans' support for the moral acceptability of gay and lesbian relations crossed the symbolic 50 % threshold in 2010. At the same time, the percentage calling these relations 'morally wrong' dropped to 43 %, the lowest in Gallup's decade-long trend" (Saad 2010). A 2012 Pew Research

---

[11] In his *Newsweek* piece, Collard credits Burston with coining the term post-gay. The term "post-queer" has also recently entered the English lexicon, although it has a very different meaning. Anchored in queer theory (e.g., Seidman 1996), some scholars use it to argue that queer theory neglects the "institutional organization of sexuality" and the "complex developmental processes attendant to sexual identification" (Green 2002, p. 523). Others use it to critique queer theory's binary conception of the world as either queer or heteronormative (Cohen 2001; Ruffolo 2009).

[12] "Assimilation" characterizes the post-gay era—it is a social force—while "integration" is its outcome and thus a material effect. I also use assimilation instead of integration (Brown-Saracino 2011) because the latter implies a broad incorporation of sexual minorities. In a post-gay era, assimilation is sometimes "virtual" (Vaid 1995; Bullough et al. 2006), since it neglects the intersectional realities of many non-heterosexuals (Warner 1999; Duggan 2002; Valocchi 1999a).

Center poll found evidence for this acceptance in all regions of the United States and in urban and rural areas alike (Behind Gay Marriage Momentum 2012). Finally, a 2013 Washington Post-ABC News poll showed that "public support for gay marriage has hit a new high" (Cohen 2013). Fifty-eight percent of Americans now believe that it should be legal for lesbians and gay men to marry, while 36 % say it should be illegal. The pollsters noticed that "public attitudes toward gay marriage are a mirror image of what they were a decade ago: in 2003, 37 % favored gay nuptials, and 55 % opposed them" (Cohen 2013).

These and other opinion polls are in close conversation with the legal landscape, which offers a second indicator for an ongoing post-gay shift. Some researchers use national surveys that ask about same-sex marriage, adoption rights for same-sex couples, employment non-discrimination laws, and beliefs that homosexuality is a sin to generate an "LGB Social and Political Climate Index." They find that states with protective laws "have a much warmer climate towards LGB people" than those states without such laws (Hasenbush et al. 2014). The 2012 elections were historic in this regard.

> A majority of voters in three states—51.5 % in Maine, 52.4 % in Maryland, and 53.7 % in Washington—supported legalizing marriage for same-sex couples in statewide ballot initiatives. These electoral outcomes represent the first examples of popular majorities voting to endorse same-sex marriage in statewide initiatives. (Flores and Barclay 2013)

In addition, the year 2014 saw an "unstoppable momentum for full LGBT equality," in the words of the Human Rights Campaign (2014). This sensibility has been gaining force throughout the post-gay era. We have witnessed the legalization of same-sex marriage in thirty-five states and the District of Columbia, the legalization of same-sex marriage in Scotland, Luxembourg, and Finland (for a total of twenty countries with marriage equality), the elimination by the US Supreme Court of a portion of the Defense of Marriage Act in 2013, and President Obama signing an executive order to protect LGBT federal employees from workplace discrimination.

A third indicator that we are embarking onto a new sexual era comes from changes in social networks. A 2014 survey by the Public Religion Research Institute (PRRI) of 4509 randomly sampled adults 18 years of age or older across the United States found that "the number of Americans who have a close friend or family member who is gay or lesbian has increased by a factor of three over the last two decades, from 22 % in 1993 to 65 % today" (Coffey 2014; Jones et al. 2013). Another 2014 survey by McClatchy-Marist of 1035 randomly sampled adults 18 years of age or older across the United States found that "by 71–27 %, American adults say they know someone who's gay. That's a dramatic change from a generation ago, when a 1999 Pew poll found that Americans said by 60–39 % that they didn't know anyone who was gay" (Kumar 2014). These changes in the composition of social networks may also account for the development of an allies movement of "politically gay" (Meyers 2008) heterosexuals.

A fourth and final indicator comes from the onset of same-sex attractions and coming out of the closet. One U.S. study found, "The average age that gay and bisexual boys had their first same-sex attractions was just before 8, while for girls it was 9, and in many cases the same-sex attractions started several years earlier" (Goodman 2013). In addition, lesbian, gay, and bisexual people are coming out earlier than ever before. The same study also found, "The average coming-out age has declined from 20-something in the 1980s to somewhere around 16 today" (Goodman 2013). According to a study conducted in the U.K., the average age of coming out has fallen by more than 20 years in Britain. "The poll, which had 1536 respondents, found that lesbian, gay and bisexual people aged 60 and over came out at 37 on average. People aged 18 and under are coming out at 15 on average" (Stonewall n. d.). All of this cross-national research shows that the average age of coming out is decreasing as society becomes more accepting of LGB individuals.

It is in this dynamic context that the term post-gay acquires its many meanings. It can express a style of self-identification, describe the tone of a specific space or an entire neighborhood, and it can capture the zeitgeist of a historical moment. Individuals who see themselves as post-gay embrace an identity that subordinates the centrality of their sexual orientation—"I'm more than just gay," they might say. They also disentangle it from a sense of militancy and struggle, feel free from persecution despite awareness that inequalities persist in the world, and prefer sexually integrated company—hence Collard's call for more straight girls in gay bars. Queer social networks today are much more mixed, include more straight people, and their interactions are driven by common aesthetic tastes and interests rather than a sense that they share an oppressed, minority group status with other gays and lesbians (Brown-Saracino 2011). This explains why some individuals see their identity as "fluid, open, or flexible," while others actively resist existing labels like "gay," "lesbian," and "bisexual" (Russell et al. 2009, p. 888). A post-gay space like a bar, meanwhile, is one in which "the need to clearly define and delineate our sexualities is largely deemed unnecessary" (Brown 2006, p. 136, 140), while gayborhoods no longer demand "the assertion of one identity or another. Most times they contain a majority of heterosexuals" (p. 140; Nash 2012). This is possible because "'gay' identities have outlived their usefulness" (p. 140) Think of it this way: During the coming out era, gay villages were "akin to what Rome is for Catholics: a lot of us live there and many more make the pilgrimage" (Myslik 1996,

pp. 167–168). But in a post-gay era, they are "more akin to what Jerusalem is for Jews: most of us live somewhere else, fewer of us make the pilgrimage than in the past, [and] our political power has moved elsewhere" (pp. 167–168).

None of this is to say that people no longer claim a gay or lesbian identity for themselves—they most certainly do—because sexual orientation is still a part of who we are, after all, because heterosexuality is still culturally compulsory (Rich 1980), and because sexual inequalities persist. Post-gays do not pretend that the world is a perfect place. However, with public acceptance of homosexuality and same-sex relationships at an all-time high, it is much easier for some sexual minorities to move into the mainstream and blend into its prized, multicultural mosaic in a way that renders them no different than heterosexuals. This, in turn, has consequences for the decisions they make about where to live. Gay neighborhoods historically provided sexual minorities with a safe space in an often unsafe world. But now, the world itself is becoming much safer. This is an important part of the story for why gayborhoods are de-gaying (gays and lesbians are moving out) and straightening (heterosexuals are moving in) across the United States and in many other parts of the western world. What can we predict will ultimately happen to them? In what follows, we will revisit the same explanations for why gayborhoods first formed as a way to grapple with how and why they are changing in today's post-gay era (Table 18.2).

Table 18.2 The queer metropolis in a post-gay era

Explanation	Prediction
Ecology	Gay neighborhoods will change as a result of invasions and successions
History	Gay neighborhoods will change as a result of historical accidents
Community	Gay neighborhoods will change as existing institutions close, or if new ones open in other parts of the city
	Gay neighborhoods will change as a function of generational cohorts, along with new individual preferences for sexually mixed social networks
Sexuality	Gay neighborhoods will change if residents no longer need them to organize their sexual and romantic transactions
Economics	Gay neighborhoods will change as a result of resurgent gentrification, municipal marketing, mayoral efforts to boost local economic growth, and tourism campaigns
Politics	Gay neighborhoods will change if non-heterosexuals no longer need them to feel safe

18.3.1 Ecology Arguments

All neighborhoods change. This is a simple fact of city life, and it is the premise of ecology arguments. Gay neighborhoods are not an exception to this most basic urban insight. "One group succeed[s] another group in a particular place in the city, just as one group of animals might succeed another on some plains" (p. 29). The process is called "invasion"–of straights into queer spaces–and "succession," as the character and composition of a gayborhood becomes increasingly heterosexual. The conditions that incite invasions are "legion" (p. 29): they include the location of jobs, new construction projects, physical deterioration, market and real estate trends, tourism and other municipal promotion campaigns, and the building of new transportation lines. The inevitability of invasions and successions does not mean that they will transpire without conflict. Resistance is common, but its success depends on "the degree of solidarity of the present occupant" (McKenzie 1924, p. 298). The integration of gays and lesbians into the mainstream implies a decline in their solidarity, given the weakening assumption of a shared minority group identity, as we saw earlier. If this is true, then it will negatively affect the desire among sexual minorities to resist straight invasions.

18.3.2 Historical Arguments

The nascence of the post-gay era makes it tricky to offer historical arguments. One contender is the decline of manufacturing and industrial jobs and a corresponding rise of a service-sector, global economy. We know that this altered the organization of race (Wilson 1987), and it also created a new class geography (Sassen 1998, 2001). But how will it affect sexuality? To compete with a small number of powerful global cities and as manufacturing declined, secondary cities like Chicago, Miami, Manchester, Vancouver, Seattle, and Sydney have re-branded themselves as "places of culture and consumption" (Rushbrook 2002, p. 188). They now show off their stock of ethnic spaces, which "present an 'authentic' other" that can be commodified and consumed. City officials use queer spaces in much the same way—as "a marker of cosmopolitanism, tolerance, and diversity for the urban tourist" (p. 188). In today's post-gay era, "queer and ethnic spaces are offered as equivalent venues for consumption at a cosmopolitan buffet" (p. 188). This is a culturally destructive move, since it "erases their individual histories and functions" (p. 188).

18.3.3 Community Arguments

Gay and lesbian businesses and organizations "anchor" (Ghaziani 2014a) certain neighborhoods in the minds of city residents, and they can bestow upon them a stable identity, despite residential fluctuations. Recall Murray's (1992, p. 109) argument: "the existence of distinctive institutions is more salient to the identification of a community—for both insiders and outsiders—than residential segregation or concentration." This brings us to the community argument, which predicts that gayborhoods will attenuate if existing institutions close or if new ones open in another neighborhood. For example, there were 16 gay bars in Boston and Cambridge between 1993 and 1994, but by 2007 less than half remained. This has a domino effect. "As gay bars vanish, so go bookstores, diners, and all kinds of spaces that once allowed 'blissful public congregation,' as sociologist Ray Oldenburg described their function in his 1989 book 'The Great Good Place'" (Sullivan 2005). When gay and lesbian businesses leave, they "sever ties that link residents to an integrated sense of neighborhood" (Usher and Morrison 2010, p. 277).

The community argument is also sensitive to generational shifts. Post-gays are "twentysomethings" that are part of "a new generation of young gay people" who prefer "sexually mixed company." They are skeptical about whether the "new Jerusalem" exists in a "gay-only ghetto," and so they reject them. Younger gays and lesbians often feel that their sexual orientation is "merely secondary to our place in life"—a life that "in most ways, is not about being gay at all."

In fact, they say that they "do not have that much in common with gay culture." If life is not about being gay, then gayborhoods will not resonate for the next generation (Aguirre-Livingston 2011).

18.3.4 Sexuality Arguments

The sexuality argument is next, and it identifies disturbances in the function of gayborhoods as marketplaces for sexual and romantic transactions. The Internet is a big part of this story. "People still meet romantic partners in [the traditional forums of family, workplace, and neighborhoods], but it seems to be less common," says Michael Rosenfeld. "The Internet is displacing those classic venues" as brokers of sex and romance. It is now easy to find resources about being gay on-line, which disenfranchises the gayborhood for younger individuals or those who come out later in life. Similarly, the Internet allows closeted gays and lesbians to find electronically mediated friendships and sex partners either "for virtual pleasure" or "for real-world fun" (Usher and Morrison 2010, p. 279). In fact, the Internet exerts a dominant influence in how same-sex couples have met one another since the year 2000—over 60 % of couples first met in this way, prompting researchers to conclude that "the Internet seems to be displacing all other ways of meeting for same-sex couples" (Rosenfeld and Thomas 2012, p. 532). On the ground, this creates a "'community' that is unbounded by geography," and it negates the need "to feel physically connected to the community they call their own" (p. 279). One study of 17 international cities asked if gay communities were "dying or just in transition" (Rosser et al. 2008, p. 588). The researchers found that in every one of them, "the virtual gay community was larger than the offline physical community" (p. 588). As a result, some condemn the Internet for creating a "diaspora of gays from traditional urban enclaves."

18.3.5 Economic Arguments

We now arrive at economic and political explanations, the two most common explanations for both gayborhood formation and change. Economic arguments include two subtypes: resurgent gentrification and municipal promotion campaigns. Urban redevelopment efforts in the United States proceeded in two waves. Federal renewal efforts fueled the first, as we saw earlier, and this was a response to inner-city decline that white flight caused in the 1960s. Gentrification resurged in the late 1990s in a second wave that corresponded with rising home prices. Changes in the financing system, increased privatization, and the demolition of public housing caused this second surge (Doan and Higgins 2011). Ironically, while gays and lesbians used the first-wave to build many of their urban districts, the "super-gentrifiers" (p. 7) of the second wave tend to be straights who transform gayborhoods into "visible niche markets for retail commerce and realty speculation" (Hanhardt 2008, p. 65) This process is called "resurgent gentrification," and it prompts the "assimilation of LGBT neighborhoods" into the wider city environment (p. 6). Some gays and lesbians perceive the sexual integration that results as "the pillaging of gay culture" (p. 15) by economically-motivated straights who have little to no commitments to queer causes. In assessing the effects of resurgent gentrification in Atlanta, for example, one study found evidence of residential diffusion without an accompanied increase in support for gay rights: "Rising housing values have dispersed the LGBT population, and former LGBT neighborhoods have become less tolerant of LGBT people and the businesses that anchor the LGBT community" (p. 6). As more straights move in, gay people and their businesses report lower levels of perceived tolerance. In addition, financers and straight newcomers prefer large chain stores which threaten "the cultural icons of queer neighborhoods" (p. 16). Although this frays the fabric of the gayborhood, the desire for a feeling of belonging to a gay community persists, and many former residents say that they would rather live in the area if they could afford it.

The second type of economic argument emphasizes municipal promotion, mayoral efforts to boost local economic growth, and citywide tourism campaigns. In the late 1990s, a group of demographers and economists created a "Gay Index" that ranks regions in the United States based on their concentration of same-sex households. Florida (2002) has publicly championed it, and city agencies routinely use it "because of its highly touted claim to predict economic competitiveness in a global marketplace" (Hanhardt 2008, p. 63). Defining gayborhoods as "entertainment districts" (Lloyd and Clark 2001; Lloyd 2006) signals a shift in how the state perceives these areas: from a "regulatory problem" that required repression and containment in the 1970s and 1980s to a "marketing asset" in recent years (Rushbrook 2002, p. 193). Cities like Chicago, Philadelphia, and Manchester have a municipally marked gayborhood. They have become "the chic social and cultural centres of the city—the place to be seen,…regardless of one's sexual preferences" (p. 1793, 1798). Motivated by neoliberal economic policies (Duggan 2003), such commodification of gayborhoods (Skeggs 1999; Binnie and Skeggs 2004) robs them of their cultural distinctions, leading residents and visitors to perceive them today as "locations to be experienced by the noveau cosmopolitan citizen" (Nash and Gorman-Murray 2014, p. 759)—an urban area unhinged from any particular sexual orientation.

The consumption of queer spaces is part of a "geography of cool" (Rushbrook 2002, p. 183). From the point of view of heterosexuals, this branding of gayborhoods as chic allows them "to overcome their discomfort with being 'out of place' in gay space" (Brown 2006, p. 133; Binnie and Skeggs 2004, p. 40). This is especially true for straight women who sometimes exploit gay men to claim a modern, cosmopolitan identity. Consider an observation that comes from the UK: "The 'pretty gay boy' is increasingly *the* ideal friend to take—or to be taken out by—on the scene, he is the coolest and least threatening accessory a straight girl can have" (Casey 2004, p. 454). Because straights will always outnumber gays and lesbians, queer spaces are not sustainable "unless gay households rarely moved and never sold their property to non-gay households" (Collins 2004, p. 1794). Neither is plausible, of course, and so it is only a matter of time that residential shifts and secondary business growth threaten to erase the colorful character and complexion of gay neighborhoods.

18.3.6 Political Arguments

As the above discussion implies, "gentrification and changing preferences can only provide partial explanations" for why gayborhoods are transforming; "reduced discrimination" also matters (Ruting 2008, p. 266). This brings us to the political argument. Acceptance and assimilation have expanded the queer residential imagination "beyond the gayborhood," (Ghaziani 2014b), and greater equality has "eroded the premium that many gay men and lesbians were once willing to pay" (p. 266) to live there.

In taking a critical view of economic approaches, it is not my objective to refute their validity but rather to bring them into conversation with other forces. Consider, for example, that the same increase in tolerance that allows gays and lesbians to feel comfortable beyond the borders of gay districts also contributes to straight residents feeling more at ease living and socializing in them. Gayborhoods now are a "safe zone for heterosexual women" (Collins 2004, p. 1794), a place where they can "escape the heterosexual male gaze that sexualizes their bodies" (Casey 2004, p. 454) everywhere else in the city. They see the presence of gay people as a sign that "the city or neighborhood is relatively safe" (Florida 2002, p. xvii). Straight men are on board as well. Charles Blow captured their new sense of cool in the title of his 2010 essay in the *New York Times*: "Gay? Whatever, Dude." Blow interviewed Michael Kimmel for his essay, who told him, "Men have gotten increasingly comfortable with the presence of, and relative equality of, 'the other.'" This is why a gayborhood is no longer out-of-bounds for them. Furthermore, the ratio of single straight women to men in these spaces makes them especially attractive—minus all the baggage that comes with homophobia.

Straights have always lived and shopped in gayborhoods, of course, but they have become "a common site on the streets" in recent years, Dan Levy (1996) notes in his story for the *San Francisco Chronicle*. "Two decades of struggle for equal rights have translated into real economic and emotional progress for homosexuals—and many heterosexuals," he explains. "If lesbians and gays no longer feel confined to a homosexual

Table 18.3 The queer metropolis across the closet, coming out, and post-gay eras

Sexual Era	Historical time	Defining features	Location patterns
Closet Era	1870—World War II	Concealment; isolation; feelings of shame, guilt, and fear; living a double life	"Scattered gay places"
Coming Out Era	World War II—1997	Being open and out about sexuality; having almost exclusively gay social networks; believing that "gay is good"	Gayborhoods form (postwar) and flourish (post-Stonewall)
Post-Gay Era	1998—Present	Acceptance of gays and lesbians by main-stream society and their assimilation into it	Existing gayborhoods de-gay and straighten

safe zone, straights are increasingly less likely to be threatened by same-sex attention. Relaxed attitudes about sexual identity have led to a greater permeability" (Levy 1996).

In summary, the relationship between sexuality and the city has evolved in subtle and striking ways as we have moved from the closet to the coming out and post-gay sexual eras (Table 18.3).

18.4 Critiques and Caveats

18.4.1 A Queer Pluralization

While some scholars cite evidence that gayborhoods are changing, others, especially geographers, have discovered the development of new types of urban formations, such as "queer-friendly districts" (Nash and Gorman-Murray 2014, p. 760). These areas are post-gay in the sense that straights are in the majority both residentially and commercially, yet "a significant presence of gay and lesbian residents, businesses, and organizations are welcome nonetheless" (p. 760). The defining feature of queer-friendly spaces is the mutual interaction among gays and straights and their attempts to "foster understanding across sexual difference" (Gorman-Murray and Waitt 2009, p. 2855). One important lesson in this body of work is that we cannot characterize the metropolis as an artificial binary of gayborhoods versus all other "straight spaces" (Browne and Bakshi 2011, p. 181; Frisch 2002; Brown 2008). A "queer pluralization of sexuality" (Brown 2013, p. 1) is a more apt description, since new residential and leisure spaces are continuing to form (see p. 1216).

Not only are "queer geographies" (Browne 2006; Podmore 2013) diversifying within the city, they are also spreading beyond it. A considerable amount of research assumes a migration away from closeted small towns to liberated big cities. To presume that sexual minorities *only* live in cities–and that non-urban contexts are deserts of queer cultures and lives—is an example of a "compulsion to urbanism," one that "codifies the metropolitan as the terminus of queer world making" (Herring 2010). Here we see a challenge to another binary—urban versus rural—that demands "migration [away] from wicked little towns" to the city, which becomes "the sole locus for queer community, refuge, and security" (Herring 2010). Herring calls this "metronormativity." As an alternative, he offers a "queer anti-urbanism," or the ways in which rural gays and lesbians challenge this homogenizing impulse.[13]

18.4.2 The Gendered Metropolis

Another caveat to consider is the ways in which queer spaces include some while excluding others. Gender is one such example and a key differentiator in the spatial expressions of sexuality. There is an astonishing diversity of queer spaces, urban and rural alike, yet our public conversations about them emphasize the experiences of gay men. In doing so, we erase the lives of lesbians. Castells (1983, p. 140) set the terms of debate. "Lesbians, unlike gay men, tend not to concentrate in a given territory," he claimed, and so they "do not acquire a geographical basis."

---

[13] For additional research on queer communities in the country, see (Gray 2009; Forsyth 1997; Bell and Valentine 1995; Phillips et al. 2000). See also research on queer communities in the suburbs: (Brekhus 2003; Lynch 1992; Tongson 2011; Langford 2000; Hodge 1995).

The culprit was a key difference in how men and women relate to space. "Men have sought to dominate, and one expression of this domination has been spatial." Women, on the other hand, have "rarely had these territorial aspirations." When gay men struggle "to liberate themselves from cultural and sexual oppression, they need a physical space from which to strike out." This is because gay men are men. "The same desire for spatial superiority has driven male-dominated cultures to send astronauts to the moon and to explore the galaxy." The situation is different for women. Lesbians "tend to create their own rich, inner world," one that "attaches more importance to relationships." Mapping these biologically deterministic signposts onto the streets of a city, Castells concludes that lesbians are "placeless," that "we can hardly speak of lesbian territory," and that "there is little influence by lesbians on the space of the city."

Although gender accounts for patterns that sweep from gayborhoods to entire galaxies, Castells paints a curiously barren landscape for lesbians. A number of scholars have rejected the "simplistic assumptions" (Binnie and Valentine 1999, p. 176) and "the lie" (Mitchell 2000, p. 193) that lesbians are placeless, that they lack a geographical basis, or that they are without territorial aspirations. Distinct "lesbian geographies" (Valentine 2000) exist—and apart from the more visible, gay male dominated districts. Consider first the Park Slope neighborhood of Brooklyn, where a local lesbian resident said, "Being a dyke and living in the Slope is like being a gay man and living in the Village" (Rothenberg 1995, p. 179). Consider next the tiny town of Northampton, Massachusetts. With its population of roughly 30,000, many consider it the most famous "lesbian mecca" and "haven" in the United States, to borrow descriptions from a 1993 *Newsweek* story: "Lesbians have a mecca, too. It's Northampton, Mass. a.k.a. Lesbianville, U.S.A....Northampton has been a lesbian haven since the late 1970s. 'If you're looking for lesbians, they're everywhere,' said Diane Morgan," who coordinates an annual summer festival. The town even had an openly lesbian mayor, Mary Clare Higgins, who held a near-record tenure of the political office

(six terms of 2 years each, 1999–2011). Gender clearly affects location decisions, and it gives rise to distinct "lesbian spaces" (p. 8) (Table 18.4).[14]

Lesbians are spatially concentrated. They share some areas with men (Provincetown, Rehoboth Beach, and the Castro), but they more often live in less urbanized places. In addition, all of their zip codes are less concentrated overall than those of gay men. Cooke and Rapiano (2007) call this the "Gay and Lesbian Exceptionalism Hypothesis": "Lesbian migration differs from gay migration in that lesbian migration is biased toward less urbanized areas" and those that already have "a sizable partnered lesbian community" (p. 288, 296).

Why do gay men and lesbians sometimes make different residential decisions? Some scholars argue that men and women have different needs to control space, as we have already heard from Castells, while others stress women's lack of economic power (Badgett 2001; p. 69; Adler and Brenner 1992; Taylor 2008). Although the gender wage gap (women's earnings as a percentage of men's) has narrowed, according to the US Labor Department's Bureau of Labor Statistics (2013), women still earn, on average, less than men—81 % of what men earned in 2012. This persistent economic inequality explains why lesbian households are located in lower-income areas. Subcultural differences also matter. Men are more influenced by sexual marketplaces and institution building and women by feminism, countercultures, and informal businesses (Brown-Saracino 2011). Then there are those scholars who emphasize family formation. Female same-sex partner households are more likely to have children, and so they have different needs for housing (Bouthillette 1997). Lesbians are also more likely to live in "less populous regions" (Cooke and Rapiano 2011, p. 295) like rural areas (Kazyak 2011, 2012; Wolfe 1979), while gay men are more likely to select bigger cities. And finally, lesbians often reject existing

---

[14] "'Lesbianville USA' is racially critiqued the same as gay male counterparts. Northampton isn't a utopia for all lesbians, either. It's mostly a white community, with few minorities" (Kantrowitz 1993).

Table 18.4 Highest zip code concentrations of same-sex male and female couples. (Source: 2010 U.S. Census, analyzed by Jed Kolko, *Trulia Trends*)

Same-sex male couples				Same-sex female couples			
Zip Code	Location	% of All Households (%)	Median Price per Sq. Foot	Zip Code	Location	% of All Households (%)	Median Price Per Sq. Foot
94114	Castro, San Francisco, CA	14.2	671	02657	Provincetown, Cape Cod, MA	5.1	532
92264	Palm Springs, CA	12.4	146	01062	Northampton, MA	3.3	187
02657	Provincetown, Cape Cod, MA	11.5	532	01060	Northampton, MA	2.6	189
92262	Palm Springs, CA	11.3	136	02130	Jamaica Plain, Boston, MA	2.4	304
33305	Wilton Manors, Fort Lauderdale, FL	10.6	206	19971	Rehoboth Beach, DE	2.4	187
90069	West Hollywood, Los Angeles, CA	8.9	481	95446	Guerneville, north of San Francisco, CA	2.2	197
94131	Noe Valley/Glen Park/Diamond Heights, San Francisco, CA	7.4	564	02667	Wellfleet, Cape Cod, MA	2.2	340
75219	Oak Lawn, Dallas, TX	7.1	160	94619	Redwood Heights/ Skyline, Oakland, CA	2.1	230
19971	Rehoboth Beach, DE	7.0	187	30002	Avondale Estates, suburban Atlanta, GA	1.9	97
48069	Pleasant Ridge, suburban Detroit, MI	6.8	107	94114	Castro, San Francisco, CA	1.9	671

gayborhoods due to perceptions that they do "not particularly welcome women" (Pritchard et al. 2002, p. 105; Valentine 1993) or that "they are rarely made to feel welcome there" (Sibalis 2004, p. 1747). All of these reasons constrain lesbian territoriality, but they do not negate it. Instead, these factors give outsiders the false impression that lesbians are "hidden" or that they have a "quasi-underground character" (Adler and Brenner 1992, p. 31).[15]

18.4.3 Inclusions and Exclusions

Finally, let us think critically about race and issues of intersectionality. Although sexual identity is multiracial, gayborhoods tend to be overwhelmingly white. This compelled Charles Nero to ask, "Why are the gay ghettoes white?" He suggests that "racialization operates in the gay world as a 'fundamental organizing principle,'" one that residents and realtors deploy to ensure the whiteness of gay enclaves (Nero 2005, p. 229; see also Hunter 2010; Bérubé 2001).

Scholars have documented other exclusions as well. Although "quasi-utopian spaces" (p. 8), gay villages "fall short of their claimed inclusivity" (Nast 2002; Rushbrook 2002) since they exclude working-class gays and lesbians (Barrett and Pollack 2005; Valocchi 1999a), bisexuals (Hemmings 2002), transgender individuals (Doan 2007; Namaste 2000; Nash 2011; Browne 2006), gender non-conformists (Whittle 1996), and anyone who more generally is not homonormative (Duggan 2002, 2003). Thus, while buzzwords like assimilation, acceptance, inclusion, and integration may characterize national public discourse about what it means to be post-gay—and these cultural meanings are impacting the queer metropolis—the critiques and caveats that we have just considered suggest that a limited range of diversity may be valorized in the end:

---

[15] For classic statements on gender and the city, see (Wolfe 1979; Ettorre 1978). Notable community histories include (Newton 1993a; Kennedy and Davis 1993). For additional work see (Browne 2007; Valentine 2000; Podmore 2006; Rothenberg 1995).

a thin slice of racial, gender, and class expression that is displayed within the already-narrow parameters of the "normal" (Warner 1999) and that is palatable to heterosexuals, some of whom merely "tolerate" the gay people (Walters 2014; Jakobsen and Pellegrini 2003) with whom they happen to share an urban space.

To end this chapter on a note of such dire limitations is not a condemnation of any particular people or place. Rather, it is an invitation for future researchers to give voice to the incredible diversity of human sexuality and its geospatial expressions. It is also an appeal, in the same breath, for those of us who call the queer metropolis our home to work together on the ground to realize a vision of full and authentic equality.

References

Adam, B. D. (1995). *The rise of the gay and lesbian movement*. New York: Twayne Publishers.

Adler, S., & Brenner, J. (1992). Gender and space: Lesbians and gay men in the city. *International Journal of Urban and Regional Research, 16*(1), 24–34.

Aguirre-Livingston, P. (2011, June). Dawn of a New Gay. *The Grid.* http://www.thegridto.com/city/sexuality/dawn-of-a-new-gay/. Accessed 1 May 2015.

Aldrich, R. (2004). Homosexuality and the city: An historical overview. *Urban Studies, 41*(9), 1719–1737.

Allen, P. (1970). *Free space: A perspective on the small group in women's liberation*. New York: Times Change Press.

Anacker, K. B., & Morrow-Jones, H. A. (2005). Neighborhood factors associated with same-sex households in U.S. cities. *Urban Geography, 26*(5), 385–409.

Armstrong, E. A. (2002). *Forging gay identities: Organizing sexuality in San Francisco, 1950–1994*. Chicago: University of Chicago Press.

Armstrong, E. A., & Crage, S. M. (2006). Movements and memory: The making of the Stonewall Myth. *American Sociological Review, 71*(5), 724–751.

Badgett, M. V. L. (2001). *Money, myths, and change: The economic lives of lesbians and gay men*. Chicago: University of Chicago Press.

Barrett, D. C., & Pollack, L. M. (2005). Whose gay community? Social class, sexual self-expression, and gay community involvement. *The Sociological Quarterly, 46*(3), 437–456.

Beemyn, B. (Ed.). (1997). *Creating a place for ourselves: Lesbian, gay, and bisexual community histories*. New York: Routledge.

Behind Gay Marriage Momentum, Regional Gaps Persist. (2012, November). *Pew Research Center*. www.people-press.org/2012/11/09/behind-gay-marriage-momentum-regional-gaps-persist/. Accessed 1 May 2015.

Bell, D., & Binnie, J. (2004). Authenticating queer space: Citizenship, urbanism, and governance. *Urban Studies, 41*(9), 1807–1820.

Bell, D., & Valentine, G. (1995). Queer country: Rural lesbian and gay lives. *Journal of Rural Studies, 11*(2), 113–122.

Bellah, R. N., Madsen, R., Sullivan, W. M., Swidler, A., & Tipton, S. T. (1985). *Habits of the heart*. Berkeley: University of California Press.

Berry, B. J. L. (1985). Islands of Renewal in Seas of Decay. In P. E. Peterson (Ed.), *The New Urban Reality* (pp. 69–96). Washington, D.C.: Brookings Institution.

Bérubé, A. (1990). *Coming out under fire: The history of gay men and women in World War Two*. New York: Plume.

Bérubé, A. (2001). How gay stays white and what kind of white it stays. In B. B. Rasmussen, E. Klinenberg, I. J. Nexica, & M. Wray (Eds.), *The making and unmaking of whiteness* (pp. 234–265). Durham: Duke University Press.

Binnie, J., & Skeggs, B. (2004). Cosmopolitan knowledge and the production and consumption of sexualized space: Manchester's gay village. *Sociological Review, 52*(1), 39–61.

Binnie, J., & Valentine, G. (1999). Geographies of sexualities: A review of progress. *Progress in Human Geography, 23*(2), 175–187.

Black, D., Gates, G., Sanders, S., & Taylor, L. (2002). Why do gay men live in San Francisco? *Journal of Urban Economics, 51*(1), 54–76.

Blow, C. M. (2010, June). "Gay? Whatever Dude." *New York Times*. http://www.nytimes.com/2010/06/05/opinion/05blow.html. Accessed 1 May 2015.

Bouthillette, A.-M. (1997). Queer and gendered housing: A Tale of two neighborhoods in Vancouver. In G. B. Ingram, A.-M. Bouthillette, & Y. Retter (Eds.), *Queers in space: Communities, public places, sites of resistance* (pp. 213–232). Seattle: Bay Press.

Boyd, N. A. (2005). *Wide-open town: A history of queer San Francisco to 1965*. Berkeley: University of California Press.

Brekhus, W. (2003). *Peacocks, chameleons, centaurs: Gay Suburbia and the grammar of social identity*. Chicago: University of Chicago Press.

Brown-Saracino, J. (2009). *A neighborhood that never changes: Gentrification, social preservation, and the search for authenticity*. Chicago: University of Chicago Press.

Brown-Saracino, J. (2011). From the lesbian ghetto to ambient community: The perceived costs and benefits of integration for community. *Social Problems, 58*(3), 361–388.

Brown-Saracino, J., & Ghaziani, A. (2009). The constraints of culture: Evidence from the Chicago dyke march. *Cultural Sociology, 3*(1), 51–75.

Brown, G. (2006). Cosmopolitan camouflage: (Post-)gay space in Spitalfields, East London. In J. Binnie, J. Holloway, S. Millington, & C. Young (Eds.), *Cosmopolitan urbanism* (pp. 130–145). New York: Routledge.

Brown, Patricia Leigh. (2007, October). Gay enclaves face prospect of being passé. *The New York Times*. http://www.nytimes.com/2007/10/30/us/30gay.html.

Brown, G. (2008). Urban (homo)sexualities: Ordinary cities and ordinary sexualities. *Geography Compass, 2*(4), 1215–1231.

Brown, M. (2013). Gender and sexuality II: There goes the gayborhood? *Progress in Human Geography.* doi:10.1177/0309132513484215.

Browne, K. (2006). Challenging queer geographies. *Antipode, 38*(5), 885–893.

Browne, K. (2007). Lesbian geographies. *Social and Cultural Geography, 8*(1), 1–7.

Browne, K., & Bakshi, L. (2011). We are here to party? Lesbian, gay, bisexual, and trans leisurescapes beyond commercial gay scenes. *Leisure Studies, 30*(2), 179–196.

Bruce, K. M. (2013). LGBT Pride as a cultural protest tactic in a southern city. *Journal of Contemporary Ethnography, 42*(5), 608–635.

Bullough, V. L., Eaklor, V., & Meek, R. R. (Eds.). (2006). *Bringing lesbian and gay rights into the mainstream: Twenty years of progress.* New York: Routledge.

Casey, M. (2004). De-dyking queer spaces: Heterosexual female visibility in gay and lesbian spaces. *Sexualities, 7*(4), 446–461.

Castells, M. (1983). *The city and the grassroots: A cross-cultural theory of urban social movements.* Berkeley: University of California Press.

Castells, M., & Murphy, K. (1982). Cultural identity and urban structure: The spatial organization of San Francisco's gay community. In N. I. Fainstein & S. F. Fainstein (Eds.), *Urban policy under capitalism* (pp. 237–259). London: Sage.

Chauncey, G. (1994). *Gay New York: Gender, urban culture, and the making of the gay male world, 1890–1940.* New York: Basic Books.

Coffey, M. (2014, February). As more people know someone who is gay, support for gay marriage leaps [Web log post]. http://blogs.marketwatch.com/the-margin/2014/02/26/support-for-gay-marriage-has-increased-over-past-decade-survey/. Accessed 1 May 2015.

Cohen, C. J. (2001). Punks, Bulldaggers, and Welfare Queens: The radical potential of queer politics? In M. Blasius (Ed.), *Sexual identities, queer politics.* Princeton: Princeton University Press.

Cohen, J. (2013, March). Gay marriage support hits high in Post-ABC poll. *The Washington Post.* http://www.washingtonpost.com/blogs/the-fix/wp/2013/03/18/gay-marriage-support-hits-new-high-in-post-abc-poll/. Accessed 1 May 2015.

Collard, J. (1998a, June). A new way of being. *New York Times.* http://www.nytimes.com/1998/06/21/magazine/sunday-june-21-1998-sexual-politics-new-way-of-being.html. Accessed 1 May 2015.

Collard, J. (1998b, August). Leaving the gay ghetto. *Newsweek.*

Collins, A. (2004). Sexual dissidence, enterprise and assimilation: Bedfellows in urban regeneration. *Urban Studies, 41*(9), 1789–1806.

Cooke, T. J., & Rapiano, M. (2007). The migration of partnered gays and lesbians between 1995 and 2000. *Professional Geographer, 59*(3), 285–297.

D'Emilio, J. (1983). *Sexual politics, sexual communities: The making of a homosexual minority in the United States, 1940–1970.* Chicago: University of Chicago Press.

D'Emilio, J. (1989). Gay politics and community in San Francisco since World War II. In M. Duberman, M. Vicinus, & G. Chauncey (Eds.), *Hidden from history: Reclaiming the gay and lesbian past* (pp. 456–473). New York: New American Library Books.

D'Emilio, J. (1993). Capitalism and gay identity. In H. Abelove, M. A. Barale, & D. M. Halperin (Eds.), *The lesbian and gay studies reader* (pp. 467–476). New York: Routledge.

D'Emilio, J., & Freedman, E. B. (1997). *Intimate matters: A history of sexuality in America.* Chicago: University of Chicago Press.

Dean, J. J. (2014). *Straights: Heterosexuality in a post-closeted culture.* New York: New York University Press.

Doan, P. L. (2007). Queers in the American city: Transgendered perceptions of urban spaces. *Gender, Place, and Culture, 14*(1), 57–74.

Doan, P. L., & Higgins, H. (2011). The demise of queer space? Resurgent gentrification and the assimilation of LGBT neighborhoods. *Journal of Planning Education and Research, 31*(1), 6–25.

Drever, A. I. (2004). Separate spaces, separate outcomes? Neighborhood impacts on minorities in Germany. *Urban Studies, 41*(8), 1423–1439.

Duberman, M. (1993). *Stonewall.* New York: Penguin Books Ltd.

Duggan, L. (2002). The new homonormativity: the sexual politics of neoliberalism. In R. Castronovo & D. D. Nelson (Eds.), *Materializing democracy: Toward a revitalized cultural politics* (pp. 175–194). Durham: Duke University Press.

Duggan, L. (2003). *The twilight of equality? Neoliberalism, cultural politics, and the attack on democracy.* Boston: Beacon.

Duggins, J. (2002). Out in the Castro: Creating a gay subculture, 1947–1969. In W. Leyland (Ed.), *Out in the Castro: Desire, promise, activism* (pp. 17–28). San Francisco: Leyland Publications.

Durkheim, E. (1912). *The elementary forms of religious life.* New York: Free Press.

Epstein, S. (1987). Gay politics, ethnic identity: The limits of social constructionism. *Socialist Review, 17*(3–4), 9–54.

Escoffier, J. (1975). Stigmas, work environment and economic discrimination against homosexuals. *Homosexual Counseling Journal, 2*(1), 8–17.

Ettorre, E. M. (1978). Women, urban social movements and the lesbian ghetto. *International Journal of Urban and Regional Research, 2*(1–4), 499–520.

Evans, S. M., & Boyte, H. C. ([1986] 1992). *Free spaces: The sources of democratic change in America.* Chicago: University of Chicago Press.

Faderman, L. (1999). A Worm in the bud: The Early Sexologists and love between women. In L. Gross & J. D. Woods (Eds.), *The Columbia reader on lesbians and gay men in media, society, and politics* (pp. 56–67). New York: Columbia University Press.

Fantasia, R. (1988). *Cultures of solidarity: Consciousness, action, and contemporary American workers*. Berkeley: University of California Press.

Fantasia, R., & Hirsch, E. L. (1995). Culture in rebellion: The appropriation and transformation of the veil in the Algerian revolution. In H. Johnston & B. Klandermans (Eds.), *Social movements and culture* (pp. 144–159). Minneapolis: University of Minnesota Press.

Faro, C., & Wotherspoon, G. (2000). *Street seen: A history of Oxford Street*. Carlton South: Melbourne University Press.

Flores, A. R., & Barclay, S. (2013). *Public support for marriage for same-sex couples by state*. Los Angeles: The Williams Institute.

Florida, R. (2002). *The rise of the creative class*. New York: Basic Books.

Forest, B. (1995). West Hollywood as symbol: The significance of place in the construction of a gay identity. *Environment and Planning D: Society and Space, 13*(2), 133–157.

Forsyth, A. (1997). 'Out' in the Valley. *International Journal of Urban and Regional Research, 21*(1), 36–60.

Forsyth, A. (2001). Sexuality and space: Nonconformist populations and planning practice. *Journal of Planning Literature, 15*(3), 339–358.

Foucault, M. (1978). *The history of sexuality* (Vol. 1). New York: Vintage Books.

Friedan, B. (1963). *The feminine mystique*. New York: Dell Publishing.

Frisch, M. (2002). Planning as a heterosexist project. *Journal of Planning Education and Research, 21*(3), 254–266.

Gale, D. E. (1980). Neighborhood resettlement: Washington, D.C. In S. B. Laska & D. Spain (Eds.), *Back to the city: Issues in neighborhood renovation* (pp. 95–115). New York: Pergamon Press.

Gamson, W. A. (1996). Safe spaces and social movements. *Perspectives on Social Problems, 8*, 27–38.

Gates, G. J., & Cooke, A. M. (2011). *United States census snapshot: 2010*. Los Angeles: The Williams Institute.

Ghaziani, A. (2008). *The dividends of dissent: How conflict and culture work in lesbian and gay marches on Washington*. Chicago: University of Chicago Press.

Ghaziani, A. (2011). Post-gay collective identity construction. *Social Problems, 58*(1), 99–125.

Ghaziani, A. (2014a). Measuring urban sexual cultures. *Theory and Society, 43*(3–4), 371–393.

Ghaziani, A. (2014b). *There goes the gayborhood?* Princeton: Princeton University Press.

Ghaziani, A., & Fine, G. A. (2008). Infighting and ideology: How conflict informs the local culture of the Chicago dyke march. *International Journal of Politics, Culture, and Society, 20*, 51–67.

Glass, R. (1964). *London: Aspects of change*. London: Centre for Urban Studies.

Goodman, J. A. (2013, January). Preparing for a generation that comes out younger. *The Huffington Post*. http://www.huffingtonpost.com/josh-a-goodman/preparing-for-a-generation-that-comes-out-younger_b_2556346.html. Accessed 1 May 2015.

Gorman-Murray, A., & Waitt, G. (2009). Queer-friendly neighbourhoods: Interrogating social cohesion across sexual difference in two Australian neighbourhoods. *Environment and Planning A, 41*, 2855–2873.

Gray, M. L. (2009). *Out in the country: Youth, media, and queer visibility in rural America*. New York: New York University Press.

Green, A. I. (2002). Gay but not queer: Toward a post-queer study of sexuality. *Theory and Society, 31*(4), 521–545.

Hall, R. (1928). *The well of loneliness*. London: Wadsworth.

Halle, D. (Ed.). (2003). *New York and Los Angeles*. Chicago: University of Chicago Press.

Hanhardt, C. B. (2008). Butterflies, whistles, and fists: Gay safe street patrols and the new gay ghetto, 1976–1981. *Radical History Review, Winter, 100*, 60–85.

Hasenbush, A., Flores, A. R., Kastanis, A., Sears, B., & Gates, G. J. (2014). *The LGBT divide: A data portrait of LGBT people in the Midwestern, Mountain, and Southern states*. Los Angeles: The Williams Institute.

Heap, C. (2003). The city as a sexual laboratory: The queer heritage of the Chicago School. *Qualitative Sociology, 26*(4), 457–487.

Heap, C. (2009). *Slumming: Sexual and racial encounters in American nightlife, 1885–1940*. Chicago: University of Chicago Press.

Hemmings, C. (2002). *Bisexual spaces: A geography of sexuality and gender*. New York: Routledge.

Herrell, R. (1993). The symbolic strategies of Chicago's gay and lesbian pride day parade. In G. Herdt (Ed.), *Gay culture in America* (pp. 225–252). Boston: Beacon Press.

Herring, S. (2010). *Another country: Queer anti-urbanism*. New York: New York University Press.

Hirsch, E. L. (1990). *Urban revolt: Ethnic politics in the nineteenth century labor movement*. Berkeley: University of California Press.

Hodge, S. (1995). "No fags out there:" Gay men, identity and suburbia. *Journal of Interdisciplinary Gender Studies, 1*(1), 41–48.

Houlbrook, M. (2005). *Queer London: Perils and pleasures in the sexual metropolis, 1918–1957*. Chicago: University of Chicago Press.

Human Rights Campaign. (2014). Best of 2014 [Web log post]. http://www.hrc.org/bestof2014. Accessed 1 May 2015.

Hunter, M. (2010). All the gays are white and all the blacks are straight: Black gay men, identity, and community. *Sexuality Research and Social Policy, 7*(2), 81–92.

Jakobsen, J. R., & Pellegrini, A. (2003). *Love the sin: Sexual regulation and the limits of religious tolerance*. New York: New York University Press.

Jones, R. P., Cox, D., & Navarro-Rivera, J. (2013). *A shifting landscape: A decade of change in American attitudes about same-sex marriage and LGBT issues*. http://publicreligion.org/site/wp-content/uploads/2014/02/2014.LGBT_REPORT.pdf. Accessed 1 May 2015.

Kantrowitz, B. (1993, July). A town like no other. *Newsweek*. http://www.newsweek.com/town-no-other-193714.

Kasinitz, P. (1988). The gentrification of "Boerum Hill:" Neighborhood change and conflicts over definitions. *Qualitative Sociology, 11*(3), 163–182.

Katz, J. N. (1990). The invention of heterosexuality. *Socialist Review, 20*(1), 7–33.

Kazyak, E. (2011). Disrupting cultural selves: Constructing gay and lesbian identities in rural locations. *Qualitative Sociology, 34*(4), 561–581.

Kazyak, E. (2012). Midwest or lesbian? Gender, rurality, and sexuality. *Gender & Society, 26*(6), 825–848.

Kennedy, E. L., & Davis, M. D. (1993). *Boots of leather, slippers of gold: The history of a lesbian community*. New York: Routledge.

Kenney, M. R. (2001). *Mapping gay L.A.: The intersection of place and politics*. Philadelphia: Temple University Press.

Knopp, L. (1990). Some theoretical implications of gay involvement in an urban land market. *Political Geography Quarterly, 9*(4), 337–352.

Knopp, L. (1992). Sexuality and the spatial dynamics of capitalism. *Environment and Planning D: Society and Space, 10*(6), 651–669.

Knopp, L. (1997). Gentrification and gay neighborhood formation in New Orleans: A case study. In A. Gluckman & B. Reed (Eds.), *Homo economics: Capitalism, community, and lesbian and gay life* (pp. 45–64). New York: Routledge.

Knopp, L. (1998). Sexuality and urban space: Gay male identity politics in the United States, the United Kingdom, and Australia. In R. Fincher & J. M. Jacobs (Eds.), *Cities of difference* (pp. 149–176). New York: Guilford Press.

Kumar, A. (2014, August). Sea change: Americans revising opinions on gays, poll finds. *McClatchy Washington Bureau*. http://www.mcclatchydc.com/2014/08/14/236539_sea-change-americans-revising.html. Accessed 1 May 2015.

Langford, B. (2000). Margins of the city: Towards a dialectic of suburban desire. In R. Phillips, D. Watt, & D. Shuttleton (Eds.), *De-centering sexualities: Politics and representations beyond the metropolis* (pp. 63–78). New York: Routledge.

Laumann, E. O., Ellingson, S., Mahay, J., Paik, A., & Youm, Y. (Eds.). (2004). *The sexual organization of the city*. Chicago: University of Chicago Press.

Lauria, M., & Knopp, L. (1985). Toward an analysis of the role of gay communities in the urban renaissance. *Urban Geography, 6*(2), 152–169.

Lees, L. (2000). A reappraisal of gentrification: Towards a "geography of gentrification." *Progress in Human Geography, 24*(3), 389–408.

Levine, M. P. (1979). Gay ghetto. In M. P. Levine (Ed.), *Gay men: The sociology of male homosexuality* (pp. 182–204). New York: Harper and Row.

Levy, D. (1996, May). There goes the neighborhood. *San Francisco Chronicle*. http://www.sfgate.com/news/article/There-Goes-the-Neighborhood-After-25-years-at-3773959.php.

Lloyd, R. (2006). *Neo-Bohemia: Art and commerce in the postindustrial city*. New York: Routledge.

Lloyd, R., & Clark, T. N. (2001). The city as an entertainment machine. *Critical Perspectives on Urban Redevelopment, 6*, 357–378.

Lo, J., & Healy, T. (2000). Flagrantly flaunting it? Contesting perceptions of locational identity among urban Vancouver lesbians. In G. Valentine (Ed.), *From nowhere to everywhere: Lesbian geographies* (pp. 29–44). New York: Harrington Park Press.

Lynch, F. R. (1992). Nonghetto gays: An ethnography of suburban homosexuals. In G. Herdt (Ed.), *Gay culture in America: Essays from the field* (pp. 165–201). Boston: Beacon Press.

Markwell, K. (2002). Mardi Gras tourism and the construction of Sydney as an international gay and lesbian city. *GLQ: A Journal of Lesbian and Gay Studies, 8*(1–2), 81–99.

McKenzie, R. D. (1924). The ecological approach to the study of the human community. In R. E. Park & E. W. Burgess (Eds.), *The city: Suggestions for investigation of human behavior in the urban environment* (pp. 63–79). Chicago: University of Chicago Press.

Meeker, M. (2006). *Contacts desired: Gay and lesbian communications and community, 1940s–1970s*. Chicago: University of Chicago Press.

Meyers, D. J. (2008). Ally identity: The politically gay. In J. Reger, D. J. Myers, & R. L. Einwohner (Eds.), *Identity work in social movements* (pp. 167–187). Minneapolis: University of Minnesota Press.

Mitchell, D. (2000). *Cultural geography*. Malden: Blackwell.

Morris, A. (1984). *The origins of the civil rights movement: Black communities organizing for change*. New York: Free Press.

Mueller, C. (1994). Conflict networks and the origins of women's liberation. In E. Larana, H. Johnston, & J. R. Gusfield (Eds.), *New social movements: From ideology to identity* (pp. 234–263). Philadelphia: Temple University Press.

Murray, S. O. (1979). Institutional elaboration of a quasi-ethnic community. *International Review of Modern Sociology, 9*(2), 165–178.

Murray, S. O. (1992). Components of gay community in San Francisco. In G. Herdt (Ed.), *Gay culture in America* (pp. 107–146). Boston: Beacon Press.

Murray, S. O. (1996). *American gay*. Chicago: University of Chicago Press.

Myslik, W. (1996). Renegotiating the social/sexual identities of places: Gay communities as safe havens or sites of resistance? In N. Duncan (Ed.), *Bodyspace: Destabilizing geographies of gender and sexuality* (pp. 156–169). New York: Routledge.

Namaste, V. (2000). *Invisible lives: The erasure of transsexual and transgendered people*. Chicago: University of Chicago Press.

Nash, C. J. (2011). Trans experiences in lesbian and queer space. *Canadian Geographer, 55*(2), 192–207.

Nash, C. J. (2012). The age of the "post-mo?" Toronto's gay village and a new generation. *Geoforum*, http://dx.doi.org/10.1016/j.geoforum.2012.11.023. Accessed 1 May 2015.

Nash, C. J., & Gorman-Murray, A. (2014). LGBT neighbourhoods and "New Mobilities:" Towards understanding transformations in sexual and gendered landscapes. *International Journal of Urban and Regional Research, 38*(3), 756–772.

Nast, H. J. (2002). Queer patriarchies, queer racisms, international. *Antipode, 34*(5), 874–909.

Needleman, R. (1994). Space and opportunities. *Labor Research Review, 20*, 5–20.

Nero, C. (2005). Why are the gay ghettos white? In E. P. Johnson & M. G. Henderson (Eds.), *Black queer studies* (pp. 228–245). Durham: Duke University Press.

Newton, E. (1993a). *Cherry Grove, Fire Island: Sixty years in America's first gay and lesbian town.* Boston: Beacon Press.

Newton, E. (1993b). The Mythic mannish lesbian: Radclyffe Hall and the New Woman. In M. Duberman, M. Vicinus, & G. Chauncey (Eds.), *Hidden from history* (pp. 281–293). New York: Meridian.

Orum, A. M., & Chen, X. (2003). *The world of cities: Places in comparative and historical perspective.* Oxford: Blackwell.

Park, R. E. (1915). The city: Suggestions for the investigation of human behavior in the city environment. *American Journal of Sociology, 20*(5), 577–612.

Park, R. E. (1926). The urban community as a spatial pattern and a moral order. In E. W. Burgess (Ed.), *The urban community: Selected papers from the proceedings of the American Sociological Society 1925* (pp. 3–18). Chicago: University of Chicago Press.

Park, R. E., & Burgess, E. W. (Eds.). (1925). *The city: Suggestions for investigation of human behavior in the urban environment.* Chicago: University of Chicago Press.

Pattison, T. (1983). The stages of gentrification: The case of Bay Village. In P. L. Clay & R. M. Hollister (Eds.), *Neighborhood policy and planning* (pp. 77–92). Lexington: Lexington Books.

Phillips, R., Watt, D., & Shuttleton, D. (Eds.). (2000). *De-centering sexualities: Politics and representations beyond the metropolis.* New York: Routledge.

Podmore, J. A. (2006). Gone "underground?" Lesbian visibility and the consolidation of queer space in montreal. *Social and Cultural Geography, 7*(4), 595–625.

Podmore, J. A. (2013). Critical commentary: Sexualities landscapes beyond homonormativity. *Geoforum, 49*, 263–267.

Polletta, F. (1999). "Free spaces" in collective action. *Theory and Society, 28*(1), 1–38.

Pritchard, A., Morgan, N., & Sedgley, D. (2002). In search of lesbian space? The experience of Manchester's gay village. *Leisure Studies, 21*(2), 105–123.

Rich, A. (1980). Compulsory heterosexuality and lesbian existence. *Signs, 5*(4), 631–660.

Rosenfeld, M. J., & Thomas, R. J. (2012). Searching for a mate: The rise of the internet as a social intermediary. *American Sociological Review, 77*(4), 523–547.

Rosser, B. R. S., West, W., & Weinmeyer, R. (2008). Are gay communities dying or just in transition? Results from an international consultation examining possible structural change in gay communities. *AIDS Care, 20*(5), 588–595.

Rothenberg, T. (1995). "And she told two friends:" Lesbians creating urban social space. In D. Bell & G. Valentine (Eds.), *Mapping desire: Geographies of sexualities* (pp. 165–181). London: Routledge.

Ruffolo, D. (2009). *Post-queer politics.* London: Ashgate.

Rupp, L. J. (2001). Romantic friendship. In A. M. Black (Ed.), *Modern American queer history* (pp. 13–23). Philadelphia: Temple University Press.

Rushbrook, D. (2002). Cities, queer space, and the cosmopolitan tourist. *GLQ: A Journal of Lesbian and Gay Studies, 8*(1–2), 183–206.

Russell, S. T., Clarke, T. J., & Clary, J. (2009). Are teens "post-gay?" contemporary adolescents' sexual identity labels. *Journal of Youth and Adolescence, 38*(7), 884–890.

Ruting, B. (2008). Economic transformations of gay urban spaces: Revisiting Collins' evolutionary gay district model. *Australian Geographer, 39*(3), 259–269.

Saad, L. (2010, May). Americans' acceptance of gay relations crosses 50 % Threshold. *Gallup.* www.gallup.com/poll/135764/Americans-Acceptance-Gay-Relations-Crosses-Threshold.aspx. Accessed 1 May 2015.

Sassen, S. (1998). *Globalization and its discontents.* New York: The New Press.

Sassen, S. (2001). *The global city.* Princeton: Princeton University Press.

Savin-Williams, R. C. (2005). *The new gay teenager.* Cambridge: Harvard University Press.

Savin-Williams, R. C., & Diamond, L. (2000). Sexual identity trajectories among sexual-minority youths: Gender comparisons. *Archives of Sexual Behavior, 29*(6), 607–627.

Scott, J. C. (1990). *Domination and the arts of resistance: Hidden transcripts.* New Haven: Yale University Press.

Sedgwick, E. K. (1990). *Epistemology of the closet.* Berkeley: University of California Press.

Seidman, S. (Ed.). (1996). *Queer theory/sociology.* Cambridge: Blackwell Publishers.

Seidman, S. (2002). *Beyond the closet: The transformation of gay and lesbian life.* New York: Routledge.

Sibalis, M. (2004). Urban space and homosexuality: The example of the Marais, Paris' "gay ghetto." *Urban Studies, 41*(9), 1739–1758.

Skeggs, B. (1999). Matter out of place: Visibility and sexualities in leisure spaces. *Leisure Studies, 18*(3), 213–232.

Smith, N. (1986). Gentrification, the frontier, and the restructuring of urban space. In N. Smith & P. Williams (Eds.), *Gentrification of the city.* Winchester: Allen and Unwin.

Spain, D. (1993). Been-heres versus come-heres: Negotiating conflicting community identities. *Journal of the American Planning Association, 59*(2), 156–171.

Spring, A. L. (2012). *Deconcentration of urban gay enclaves: Evidence from the 2000 and 2010 U.S. Censuses.* Denver: Paper presented at the Annual Meetings of the American Sociological Association.

Spring, A. L. (2013). Declining segregation of same-sex partners: Evidence from Census 2000 and 2010. *Population Research and Policy Review, 32*(5), 687–716.

Stonewall by over 20 years. (n. d.). [Web log]. https://www.stonewall.org.uk/media/current_releases/4867.asp.

Stryker, S. (2002). How the Castro became San Francisco's gay neighborhood. In W. Leyland (Ed.), *Out in the Castro: Desire, promise, activism* (pp. 29–34). San Francisco: Leyland Publications.

Stryker, S., & Van Buskirk, J. (1996). *Gay by the Bay: A history of queer culture in the San Francisco Bay Area*. San Francisco: Chronicle Books.

Sullivan, A. (2005, October). The end of gay culture: Assimilation and its meaning. *New Republic*. http://www.newrepublic.com/article/politics/theend-gay-culture.

Sullivan, R. D. (2007, December). Last call: Why the gay bars of Boston are disappearing, and what it says about the future of city life. *Boston Globe*. http://www.boston.com/bostonglobe/ideas/articles/2007/12/02/last_call/.

The End of Gay Culture: Assimilation and Its Meanings. (2005, October 24). *The New Republic*.

Taylor, V. (1989). Social movement continuity: The women's movement in abeyance. *American Sociological Review, 54*, 761–775.

Taylor, Y. (2008). That's not really my scene: Working-class lesbians in (and out of) place. *Sexualities, 11*(5), 523–546.

Tétreault, M. A. (1993). Civil society in Kuwait: Protected spaces and women's rights. *Middle East Journal, 47*(2), 275–291.

Tongson, K. (2011). *Relocations: Queer suburban imaginaries*. New York: New York University Press.

Tucker, A. (2009). *Queer visibilities: Space, identity and interaction in Cape Town*. Malden: Wiley-Blackwell.

U.S. Bureau of Labor Statistics. (2013). *Highlight of women's earnings in 2012* (Report 1045). http://www.bls.gov/cps/cpswom2012.pdf. Accessed 1 May 2015.

Usher, N., & Morrison, E. (2010). The demise of the gay enclave, communication infrastructure theory, and the transformation of gay public space. In C. Pullen & M. Cooper (Eds.), *LGBT identity and online new media* (pp. 271–287). New York: Routledge.

Vaid, U. (1995). *Virtual equality: The mainstreaming of gay and lesbian liberation*. New York: Anchor Books.

Valentine, G. (1993). (Hetero)sexing space: Lesbian perceptions and experiences of everyday spaces. *Environment and Planning D: Society and Space, 11*, 395–413.

Valentine, G. (Ed.). (2000). *From nowhere to everywhere: Lesbian geographies*. Binghamton: Harrington Press.

Valocchi, S. (1999a). The class-inflected nature of gay identity. *Social Problems, 46*(2), 207–224.

Valocchi, S. (1999b). Riding the crest of a protest wave? Collective action frames in the gay liberation movement, 1969–1973. *Mobilization, 4*(1), 59–73.

Walters, S. D. (2014). *The tolerance trap*. New York: New York University Press.

Warner, M. (1999). *The trouble with normal*. New York: The Free Press.

Weston, K. (1995). Get thee to a big city: Sexual imaginary and the great gay migration. *GLQ: A Journal of Lesbian and Gay Studies, 2*(3), 253–277.

Whittle, S. (1996). Gender fucking or fucking gender: Current cultural contributions to the theories of gender blending. In R. Ekins & D. King (Eds.), *Blending genders: Social aspects of cross-dressing and sex-changing* (pp. 196–214). New York: Routledge.

Wilson, W. J. (1987). *The truly disadvantaged: The inner city, the underclass, and public policy*. Chicago: University of Chicago Press.

Wirth, L. (1928). *The ghetto*. Chicago: University of Chicago Press.

Wirth, L. (1938). Urbanism as a way of life. *American Journal of Sociology, 44*(1), 1–24.

Wittman, C. (1970). *A gay manifesto*. New York: Red Butterfly Publication.

Wolfe, D. (1979). *The lesbian community*. Berkeley: University of California Press.

Wright, L. (1999). San Francisco. In D. Higgs (Ed.), *Queer Sites: Gay Urban Histories since 1600* (pp. 164–189). New York: Routledge.

Zorbaugh, H. W. (1929). *The gold coast and the slum: A sociological study of Chicago's Near North Side*. Chicago: University of Chicago Press.

Zukin, S. (1987). Gentrification: Culture and capital in the urban core. *Annual Review of Sociology, 13*, 129–147.

Part V
Sexualities in Institutional Context

The Family in Flux: Changing Sexual and Reproductive Practices

The Family in Flux: Changing Sexual and Reproductive Practices

19

Lauren Jade Martin

Sociologists and anthropologists who study the family as an institution have long recognized the essential role that sexuality plays. In the mid-twentieth century, when the heterosexual nuclear family structure was at its peak in the United States, functionalist sociologists and anthropologists argued that reproduction and the regulation of sexuality were important functions of the family. As other family structures have become more prominent demographically and become objects of study, scholars of the family have debated the relationship between the institution of family, reproduction, and sexuality, and have had to account for changing norms in which sex and childbearing increasingly take place outside the bounds of formalized legal marriage. With the decline of the nuclear family, the growing acceptance of LGBT families, the rise of nonmarital childbearing, and increasing access to reproductive technologies, the idea that a primary function of the family is procreative sexuality has been disrupted. Further, the changing demographics of the family raise questions about the impact of various family structures on sexual identities and behaviors.

19.1 Theoretical Perspectives

Families and reproduction can be studied from a number of theoretical perspectives. The most prominent perspectives include functionalism,

L. J. Martin (✉)
Sociology Department, Pennsylvania State University Berks, Tulpehocken Rd, PO Box 7009, Reading, PA 19610 USA
e-mail: ljm37@psu.edu

social constructionism, and queer and feminist interpretations. Once dominant in family studies, functionalist perspectives have today largely given way to those that take into account constructionist and intersectional analyses more inclusive of race, class, gender, and sexual diversity.

Functionalism Functionalists view the institution of the family as one of society's essential parts, necessary for social reproduction and the regulation of sexuality. They also see a relationship between the structure of the family, its function in society, and the function and roles of individuals within the family. The functionalist perspective, exemplified by anthropologist George Murdock and sociologist Talcott Parsons, dominated studies of the family in the middle of the twentieth century. Murdock and Parsons, both American social scientists, describe the heterosexual nuclear family (that is, a household consisting of a married man and woman and their children) as a universal family model best suited to fulfill its role and function within society.

Murdock, for example, maintains that the nuclear family is a cultural universal, and writes that even polygamous and extended families are combinations and extensions of nuclear family units (Murdock 1965, pp. 1–2). He argues that the nuclear family provides "four functions fundamental to human social life—the sexual, the economic, the reproductive, and the educational" (Murdock 1965, p. 10). The sexual and reproductive functions of the family are linked, but not exclusively. The family provides an arena in which sexual relations are typically legitimized and organized, staking out what is normative sexuality within a given society. For example, some societies may find extramarital sexual relations to be taboo or forbidden, whereas sex with a nonmarital partner in other societies may be permitted or expected. Regardless, the family acts as a regulating force, determining the norms, expectations and characteristics of rules over sexual behavior and expression. It also, essentially, provides the means of reproducing the population through childbearing and socialization.

Parsons, like Murdock, focuses on the nuclear family as an independent social unit, recognizing that this "conjugal family" has a dual role as both a unit of kinship and as a household or place of residence (Parsons 1951, p. 188). He notes the tendency of scholars to emphasize the functions of procreation, child care, sexual relations, and economic and religious functions (Parsons and Bales 1955, p. 8), but, in examining the heterosexual nuclear American family in the mid-twentieth century, sees that many of those functions may be fulfilled outside of the family. Instead, he identifies the most important functions of the nuclear family unit as primary socialization of children, and personality stabilization of adults (Parsons and Bales 1955, pp. 16–17). Within this structure are sets of complementary roles based on age (children and adults) and sex (husband-fathers and wife-mothers). In his interpretation, both erotic relations between heterosexual marital partners and social roles of adult men and women in the family stem from a combination of biological, psychological, and social factors. While his focus was mostly on the American context, his descriptions of the structure and function of family as an institution left him open to critiques that he normalized and universalized one particular *type* of family—that of the heterosexual American middle-class white nuclear family.

Murdock, Parsons, and other structural-functionalists have been critiqued for offering narrow interpretations and explanations of the family, particularly for their emphasis on the heterosexual nuclear family (and, in the American context, largely white and middle-class) as the primary social unit. Although functionalists may acknowledge the existence of other kinship structures, social constructionist, feminist, and queer theoretical perspectives are critical of functionalists' overvaluation of the nuclear family and their standpoint that some types of family structures are universal.

Social Constructionism The second major theoretical perspective used in studies of sexuality in the family is social constructionism. Like structural-functionalist analyses, social constructionist perspectives also understand the family to be an *institution*, but instead of recognizing universal structural patterns and roles, this perspective sees the role of the family as contingent and contextual. Social constructionists point to the ways in which family structures and relationships vary from culture to culture and also across time; therefore the "functions" that families fulfill are not universal or permanent (Coontz 2000; Skolnick 1981). Sociologist Diana Gittins, for example, writes

> Thinking in terms of 'the' family leads to a static vision of how people actually live and age together and what effects this process has on others within the household in which they live. Moreover, the environment and conditions in which any household is situated are always changing, and these changes can and often do have important repercussions on individuals and households. (Gittins 2011, p. 8)

Likewise, Gittins points out that the functions of sexuality and reproduction that are often assumed to be universal and generalized are in fact socially, culturally, and historically contingent. Norms, practices and definitions regarding marriage, same-sex relations, incest, and even biological understandings of parentage and relatedness may vary from culture to culture.

Feminist, Multiracial, and Queer Theory Related to the social constructionist perspective are analyses and histories by feminist, multiracial, and queer theorists in the study of family. Feminist family scholars challenge the roles and functions articulated by models of the heterosexual nuclear family as the normative family type, viewing the prescribed breadwinner-homemaker roles attributed to men and women as reinforcing patriarchal and oppressive power relations (Zinn 2000). Sexual relations within the family may indeed be *dysfunctional* when it is colored by unequal power relations or, further, marked by control, abuse, and violence.

Another constructionist critique made by multiracial feminists is that functionalist perspectives, by focusing on the heterosexual nuclear family, implicitly set up white middle-class heterosexual nuclear families as the ideal, framing working-class, immigrant households, and of color households, and those headed by single parents, as deviant, since their family structures and roles frequently differed from the traditional breadwinner-homemaker structure (Collins 2000; Dill 1988; Zinn 2000). Similarly critiques can be made about the elision of families of lesbian, gay, bisexual, transgender, queer, and polyamorous individuals (Stacey 2011; Stein 1993; Weston 1991). These perspectives move beyond the notion of the family as necessarily consisting of individuals related by marriage or blood residing in the same household, expanding ideas of kinship to "fictive" cooperative and intimate relations of choice among people who provide emotional, physical, and financial support, regardless of consanguinity, common residence, or legal ties (Collins 2000; Stack 1974; Weston 1991). The functions deemed essential to "the family," such as socialization, reproduction, and regulation of sexuality, shift and transform as other family forms are recognized and studied. In Weston's (1991) study of gay kinship, for example, the author describes families as fluid networks with a core of mutual love and support formed by individuals on the basis of affective, rather than biological, ties. In some cases, these families of choice substitute for or replace families of origin, but they may also be considered an expansive family network consisting of lovers, ex-lovers, friends, children, and relatives.

19.2   Methods for Studying Sexuality and Sexual Expression Within Family Studies

A number of methods, both quantitative and qualitative, may be employed to study sexuality in the context of the institution of the family. These include the use of statistics and survey research, longitudinal studies, ethnography and participant observation, interviews, and comparative and historical methods. Each method has its benefits and its drawbacks.

Quantitative Methods Scholars using statistical methods may rely upon large datasets, such as the U.S. Census, American Community Survey (ACS), Vital Statistics compiled by the Centers for Disease Control and Prevention (CDC), the National Survey of Family Growth (NSFG), and the National Survey of American Families (NSAF), in order to identify differences between discrete populations, or to track changes over time. Researchers using national-level data may compare patterns in family structure between different countries, or they may focus on populations within nations. With very large sample sizes in the thousands or even higher, researchers may identify trends within populations such as changes in average age at first birth or marriage, the numbers of individuals per household, or rates of birth outside of marriage. In addition to descriptive data, large sample sizes enable researchers to perform multivariate statistics to compare populations or find correlations between variables, such as the effect of family structure on the sexuality of adolescent girls (Davis and Friel 2001).

There are some drawbacks to statistical analyses of families and households. One issue is definitional—surveys may define terms in ways that do not necessarily match with respondents' own personal understandings of those concepts. For example, as Gittins (2011) and Zinn (2000) both point out, early family scholars frequently conflated "family" with "household," which does not take into account the lived realities of individual family members who do not reside in the same quarters, such as people in the armed forces, or young adults in college. Additionally, tracking families headed by same-sex partners or heterosexual cohabiting couples is sometimes difficult because surveys have not always recognized unmarried partners as family members, or ask questions about household members inconsistently or inadequately (Seltzer 2000). In 2011, the U.S.

Census had to revise its estimates of same-sex married couples, which had inflated numbers because of inaccurately captured data collected in door-to-door surveys (Cohn 2011; US Census Bureau Public Information 2011). Another problem is faced by quantitative researchers who rely on self-reported data: because questions involving sexuality, sexual behavior, and familial relationships involve sensitive or stigmatizing topics, surveys that include self-reports may have inaccuracies if respondents are not truthful. Finally, data about populations with small numbers, such as families and households consisting of Asian American and Native American members, are frequently omitted from statistics (Islam et al. 2010).

Qualitative and Ethnographic Methods Sexuality and family scholars frequently use qualitative methods in their research. Ethnographic projects may involve long-term studies in which researchers embed themselves within a group in order to produce thick, descriptive data about patterned behaviors. Kathryn Edin and Maria Kefalas (2011), for example, spent years interviewing and living among poor single mothers in Philadelphia, PA and Camden, NJ to better understand and draw conclusions about why they seemed to put motherhood ahead of marriage. Ethnographies may also be comparative in nature, such as the work of Judith Stacey (2011), in which the author studies families in Los Angeles, South Africa, and China that veer far from the "traditional" heterosexual nuclear family.

The benefit of ethnographic methods is that researchers gain a deep understanding of their topics. By embedding themselves within a community, some ethnographers aim to gain insider status, building enough trust with respondents that they are able to observe patterns of behavior that are typically hidden or unavailable. Unlike close-ended survey questions, in-depth open-ended interviews give space for respondents to use their own words to describe their attitudes, beliefs, and experiences.

A drawback to ethnographic methods is that participant observation and interviews typically focus on much smaller groups than are studied by statistical analysis. This means that the data may

only be particular to the groups that were studied, and are not generalizable to the population at large. Another drawback is that because the data is collected within a particular place at a particular point in time, and has been informed by interactions between the researcher and his or her participants, the studies are difficult to replicate.

Longitudinal Panel Studies Longitudinal panel studies may be quantitative or qualitative. They rely on cohorts of individuals who are surveyed, interviewed, or observed at various points over time, or "waves." Such studies may be used to identify correlations between different variables over time. For example, the Fragile Families and Child Wellbeing Study focuses on the outcomes of children born to unmarried parents. The study tracks 5000 children born between 1998 and 2000, and involves interviewing parents at the time of their child's birth, and at ages one, three, and five (Center for Research on Child Wellbeing n.d.). The first edition of Annette Lareau's (2003) ethnography of black and white middle-class, working-class, and poor families was not initially conceived as a longitudinal study. In the second edition, Lareau (2011) has followed up with the families a decade later, creating a second wave of interviews and observations to support her earlier analysis.

The advantages to longitudinal studies are that they may capture long-term effects that are not evident in cross-sectional data collected at one point in time, and they also enable scholars to track any measurable changes between waves. A disadvantage, aside from those that accrue to quantitative or qualitative studies as articulated above, is that with each subsequent wave, cohort members may be lost because researchers lose contact with them, or because participants choose to drop out of the study.

19.3 Changing Patterns in Families and Childbearing

Contemporary studies of the family frequently remark upon new and changing patterns of family structure, behaviors, and norms within the

United States and other countries. Many of these changes deal directly with the family and its relationship to sexual expression and reproduction, including new norms regarding premarital sex, same sex relations, delayed marriage and childbearing, cohabitation, divorce, contraception, and reproductive technologies. This section will focus specifically on the changing relationship between marriage/partnership, sex, and procreation.

As discussed earlier, sex and reproduction have frequently been viewed as two of the primary functions of the family, with the particular norms organizing sexual behavior and structures of kinship varying cross-culturally and historically. Thus although one may assume that the typical stages of the life course for heterosexual young men and women have always been to court or date with increasing sexual intimacy, formalize relationships through marriage, and have children, in that precise order, these steps are highly dependent on sociocultural context. Behaviors and practices such as emotional intimacy, premarital sex, sex with nonmarital partners, cohabitation, and nonmarital childbearing have been regarded alternatively as deviant or legitimate in different historical eras and across cultures. Notions about the proper way to form families, or about what a family "should" look like, are not universal. As Coontz (1992) has thoroughly researched and written, people's ideas about "traditional" families have mythologized family forms, viewing them through nostalgic and frequently inaccurate lenses. For example, the heterosexual nuclear breadwinner-homemaker family popularly idealized as the "traditional" family was, according to Coontz (1992), only typical for a brief period of time post-World War II.

Even the relationship between love and marriage has not been a constant historically, nor is love necessarily a prerequisite for marriage cross-culturally, as exemplified by arranged marriages, marriages forged to unite or ally tribes and families, or by the trading of women between men as commodities (Coontz 2006). Although one might assume a linear trajectory in which sexual norms have only become more and more permissive, they have in fact fluctuated. For example,

throughout American history have been periods of time where homoromantic friendships, premarital intimacy, extramarital relationships, and nonmarital childbearing have all been common and accepted—even if not widely lauded—followed by more sexually conservative periods, including the Victorian era and post-WWII (Coontz 1992).

Changing Ideologies of Marriage Norms, attitudes, and ideologies regarding marriage are in flux, leading to debates about whether the family is in decline, or if marriage has become deinstitutionalized (Amato 2007; Cherlin 2004; Coontz 2006). These changes have had great implications for the relationship of marriage to sex and childbearing, not to mention the division of labor and gender roles, but transformation in the organization and ideology of family is not a recent phenomenon. Families in early America were large, extended, and served as sites for production, with each member, including women and children, contributing to the family's subsistence. As this productive function shifted out of the domestic sphere and into the marketplace with the growth of industrial capitalism, the nature of families also shifted, becoming more isolated and nuclear (Cherlin 2009; Coontz 1992; Parsons 1955). By the turn of the twentieth century, stricter boundaries were placed between parents and children, gender roles rigidified, and greater emotional intimacy and romantic compatibility was now expected between husband and wife in "companionate" marriages (Cherlin 2009; Coontz 1992, 2006). Norms regarding gender roles and the function of love in familial relationships have continued to transform.

Scholars of the family have noted a shift in the ideology of love, marriage, family, and sexuality. Giddens (1992), for example, writes of how intimacy has been "restructured," so that heterosexual marriage is no longer the only normative relational expression of love and sexuality. The "pure relationship" has become a new ideal, in which "a social relation is entered into for its own sake, for what can be derived by each person from a sustained association with another; and which is continued only in so far as it is thought by both parties to deliver enough satisfaction for each individual to stay within it" (Giddens 1992, p. 58). This has implications for marital disruption because, as Amato (2007) puts it, "as people's expectations for marriage increased, and as the barriers to divorce declined, the proportion of marriages that did not live up to people's expectations—and hence ended in divorce—also increased" (Amato 2007, p. 9). The shift towards individual and personal satisfaction in relationships happened alongside shifts towards more egalitarian gender roles, loosening of sexual norms, the entry of women into the workforce, no-fault divorce, and other cultural and structural changes in American society (Cherlin 2009; Coontz 2006). As the institution of marriage, its functions, and the roles of family members have changed, so have norms regarding sex prior to, within, and outside of marriage.

The prominence of marriage within American culture persists, however, expanding beyond normative heterosexuality to include struggles for the legal recognition of same sex marriages. As Cherlin writes,

> although the practical importance of marriage has declined, its symbolic importance has increased. In the mid-twentieth century, being married was almost a requirement for being a respectable adult. Having children outside of marriage was stigmatizing, and a person who remained single through adulthood was morally suspect. … Whereas marriage used to be the foundation of adult family life, now it is often the capstone. (Cherlin 2009, p. 139)

The high symbolic value placed on marriage may ironically result in decreased rates of marriage among poor and low-income women. As Edin and Kefalas (2011) concluded upon conducting an ethnography of poor women in Philadelphia, the women did not have children without being married because they devalued marriage. Rather, they valued it so much that they would prefer to wait until their relationships lived up to the financial and emotional conditions that would make a marriage last.

Although heterosexual marriage is valued in the United States, and it is still held up as the ideal institution and site for sexual expression and reproduction, there are greater opportunities and greater acceptance of sex and childbearing that occur outside of the marital relationship, as well as for same-sex marriage. Instead of following precise steps in the life course (e.g., dating, marriage, procreation) that were prevalent in the middle of the 20th century, people now have a wealth of possibilities in terms of how they live their lives, form relationships, and create families (Pew Research Center 2010; Smock and Greenland 2010; Stacey 2011). With the de-institutionalization of marriage (Cherlin 2004), expressions of sexuality inevitably occur outside of marital relationships, weakening "the family" as the primary site for sexual behavior and regulation. The ties between marriage, sex, and procreation have been thoroughly modified. The institution of marriage, its functions, and the roles of family members have changed, along with norms regarding sex prior to, within, and outside of marriage. Demographic trends over time point to dramatic shifts in the sexual, marital, and childbearing behavior of individuals in the United States.

Demographic Trends Today, only 20% of households consist of married couples with children under the age of 18, down from 40% in 1980 (Vespa et al. 2013). Cherlin's (2010) review of family studies literature cites several contemporary trends, including the rise in age at first marriage, divergent rates of marriage and divorce by education and income, rise in proportion of births to unmarried women, more individuals having children with multiple partners, and cohabitation as a precursor to or alternative to marriage (see also Teachman et al. 2000). The Centers for Disease Control and Prevention (CDC) report that 38% of women aged 15–44 surveyed in 2006–2010 have never married, up from 34% in 1982 (Copen et al. 2012, p. 5). More women are also cohabiting with a partner outside of marriage, up from 3% in 1982 to 11% in 2006–2010 (Copen et al. 2012, p. 5).

Individuals are waiting longer to get married. The average age at first marriage in 2006–2010 is 25.8 for women and 28.3 for men (Copen et al. 2012, p. 5). They are having fewer children, and at later ages. The only cohort of women for whom the birth rate has increased is that of women aged

30–44 years, whereas the birth rate for teenagers and women under 30 are on the decline (Martin et al. 2013, pp. 1–2). The average age of women at first birth is now 25.8 years (Martin et al. 2013, p. 2). The probability of marital dissolution is still relatively high, but data from 2006 to 2010 indicate that divorce rates have basically plateaued since the 1970s: the probability of a woman's first marriage lasting 20 years is 52%, and for men 56% (Copen et al. 2012, p. 7). The most dramatic change in marriage and birth statistics is perhaps the increasing proportion of children born to unmarried women. In 2012, 40.7% of births were to unmarried women, up from 18.4% in 1980; almost two thirds (64.8%) of births to women between the ages of 20 and 24 in 2012 were outside of marriage (Martin et al. 2013, p. 9).

Changing Attitudes These demographic shifts in behavior parallel changes in attitudes. Using large-scale national data sets, Thornton and Young-DeMarco (2001) found that in the four decades after 1960, stigma against divorce, premarital sex, cohabitation, and nonmarital childbearing have all declined, particularly among young adults. A 2010 survey by the Pew Research Center found that

> the public is quite open to the idea that marriage need not be the only path to family formation. An overwhelming majority says a single parent and a child constitute a family (86%), nearly as many (80%) say an unmarried couple living together with a child is a family, and 63% say a gay couple raising a child is a family. (Pew Research Center 2010, p. 4)

Interestingly, the same survey indicates that the American public maintains more conservative views about the consequences of nonmarital childbearing: 69% of those surveyed expressed that it was bad for society that more unmarried women were having children (Pew Research Center 2010, p. 4).

Attitudes have also dramatically changed regarding lesbian, gay, bisexual, transgender, and queer individuals, and towards same-sex marriage. The Pew Research Center finds that as of 2013, a clear majority of Americans surveyed

(60%) believe that homosexuality should be accepted by society, up from 47% in 2003 (2013, p. 2). Furthermore, 51% of Americans expressed that they are in favor of same-sex marriage, and a remarkable 72% find it "inevitable" that same sex marriage will be legally recognized (Pew Research Center 2013, p. 1). As statewide gay marriage bans continue to be challenged and declared unconstitutional, the legal status of same-sex partnerships is rapidly shifting to legitimize this family structure.

Role of Medicine and Technology The above demographic changes and shifts in attitude regarding such phenomena as premarital sex, divorce, same-sex relationships, cohabitation, and nonmarital childbearing cement the idea that the family is no longer the only legitimate institution in which sexual expression and procreation must take place. Medicine and technology have severed the biological tie between sex and reproduction, and have contributed to this shift in which sex is no longer considered to be acceptable only within the context of marriage. The legalization of and increased access to abortion and hormonal contraception ("the Pill" and other forms such as contraceptive patches and implants), have been cited by numerous scholars as leading to a sea change in sexual relations (Goldin and Katz 2002; Gordon and Gordon 2002; May 2010). By reducing the incidence and consequences of unplanned pregnancy, individuals—women, especially—have gained more freedom to engage in sexual intimacy prior to and outside of marriage, and to have more control over the timing of pregnancy and childbearing.

Assisted reproductive technologies (ARTs) have also revolutionized the relationship between sex and reproduction (Rothman 2000; Smock and Greenland 2010; Stacey 2011). Whereas contraception and abortion helped non-procreative sexuality flourish, reproductive technologies such as artificial insemination, in vitro fertilization, and surrogacy have produced forms of nonsexual procreation. Infertile couples, lesbians, gay men, and single individuals who may have previously remained childless or adopted have now been able to use medicine and technology in order to have biological children (Mamo 2007; Rothman 2000; Stacey 2011). Use of technology and medicine to achieve pregnancy subverts traditional notions of how families are created (e.g. one man and one woman in the privacy of their home), and who constitutes a family. With the use of in vitro fertilization, for example, both members of a lesbian couple can claim biological ties to children produced through the transfer of one woman's fertilized egg into the other woman's uterus. As Stacey (2011) described in her study of gay men in Los Angeles, she encountered families consisting of gay male couples, their children, as well as the egg donors and surrogates (and their partners and children) who helped them achieve fatherhood.

At the same time, ARTs reinforce the function of reproduction within a family as a normative practice, perhaps creating or adding to stigma faced by those who remain childless or who adopt. By expanding the ability of people to have biologically-related children, ARTs reify the biological and genetic connection of the normative family (Martin 2010). Furthermore, social inequalities among families are reinforced since the expense of treatments such as in vitro fertilization and surrogacy are out of reach for many (Bell 2009).

19.4   Impact of Family Structure on Sexuality and Sexual Behavior of Adults

With the proliferation of and growing tolerance of differing family structures, the question arises: how do sexuality and sexual behavior differ alongside those various structures? This section will briefly cover some of the research regarding sexuality within four family structures: heterosexual marriage, same-sex partnerships, cohabiting relationships, and open relationships. How do gender and the legal status of one's partner impact sexuality and sexual behavior?

Sex and Heterosexual Marriage Sex within heterosexual marital relationships may still be regarded as the behavior that is most recognized as a legitimate expression of sexuality. As Call, Sprecher and Schwartz write, marriage "is the

only context for sexual intercourse that is universally approved" (1995, p. 639). They and other scholars (e.g. Christopher and Sprecher 2000) note the irony that because it is not seen as a "social problem" to be resolved, there have not been as many studies on sexual behavior within marriage as there have been of so-called "deviant" sexuality. Even so, attempts have been made to quantify the frequency of sexual intercourse within heterosexual marriage in the United States and other countries. Using data from the National Survey of Families and Households (NSFH), Call, Sprecher and Schwartz (1995) find that the incidence and frequency of sex declines over time in marital relationships due to factors of aging and habituation. A study of Chinese heterosexual married couples in Hong Kong found a similar correlation between age and declining frequency of sex (Cheung et al. 2008). Other factors that negatively affect sexual frequency include pregnancy and the presence of young children, but sexual frequency increases with marital happiness and sterilization (Call et al. 1995, p. 650). In their review of sexuality literature of the 1990s, Christopher and Sprecher (2000) write that sexual satisfaction tends to decline in marital relationships over time, but at a slower rate than the decline in frequency (p. 1003). Recent data from the National Survey of Sexual Health and Behavior (NSSHB), a large cross-sectional survey of women between 18 and 92 years old, indicates that married and partnered women of all ages report greater frequency of vaginal intercourse than single women (Herbenick et al. 2010, p. 288). Among men surveyed by the NSSHB, vaginal intercourse is also most common among those with relationship partners, but this was particularly true for those between 18 and 24 years old (Reece et al. 2010, p. 298).

Sexual satisfaction is correlated with relationship satisfaction (Schwartz and Young 2009). Stanik and Bryant's (2012) study of 470 newlywed African American couples supports this association between relationship quality and sexual satisfaction. Furthermore, they find "the more [sexually] satisfied husbands and wives were, the less likely they thought they would be to find acceptable alternative partners, which was, in turn, negatively related to their reports of marital quality" (Stanik and Bryant 2012, p. 405).

In addition to the quantitative studies cited above, scholars have also performed qualitative studies to examine sexuality within heterosexual married relationships. Elliott and Umberson (2008), for example, interviewed 31 couples married at least seven years about their sex lives and individual satisfaction; they conducted separate interviews with husbands and wives. The authors found that in the majority of the couples (29 out of 31), at least one spouse saw sex as an essential part of a successful marriage and "describe[d] sex as a barometer of the health of their own marriage" (Elliott and Umberson 2008, p. 396). Further, they found that their respondents believed in stark differences in male and female sexual desire, frequently describing men (in general) as having a greater sex drive than women, even when some respondents reported that in their own relationships the women were just as, if not more, desirous of sex than their husbands (Elliott and Umberson 2008, p. 397). Regardless of any purported biological differences in sex drive between men and women, differences in *expectations* regarding male and female sexuality are clearly gendered, even when they don't match individuals' lived realities.

Sex and Same-Sex Partnerships Studies have also been made regarding sexual behavior within same-sex partnerships. In a review study, Christopher and Sprecher (2000) found a lack of research about long-term committed same-sex relationships, particularly using large national probability samples. Of the existing literature, they found that researchers reported that, similar to heterosexual married relationships, lesbian and gay couples also experience a decline in sexual frequency and satisfaction (Christopher and Sprecher 2000, pp. 1007–1008). Another line of research looks into stereotypes of long-term lesbian relationships compared with both long-term heterosexual and long-term gay male relationships. A number of studies have been made to explore the so-called issue of "lesbian bed death," in which lesbian couples are charged with facing even more steep declines of sexual frequency and satisfaction than their heterosexual counterparts

(Blumstein and Schwartz 1983; Iasenza 2008; van Rosmalen-Nooijens et al. 2008). Iasenza describes lesbian bed death as "the Grandmommy of all lesbian sex myths," arguing that this myth overgeneralizes the experiences of lesbian women (Iasenza 2008, p. 112). She and others critique the work of Blumstein & Schwartz (and those who rely on their 1983 study) for using "male-defined sexuality" as the model of sexuality, overlooking the variety of ways that two women may experience sexual intimacy with each other (Iasenza 2008, pp. 114–115).

Whereas research has focused on exploring and/or debunking "lesbian bed death," studies of gay men's sexual behavior within relationships frequently touches upon instances of nonmonogamous, open, and "monogamish" relationships (Coelho 2011; Hoff and Beougher 2010; Parsons et al. 2013). Operating outside of the boundaries of strict monogamy to various degrees, negotiated agreements of nonexclusivity contradict assumptions about extramarital (or extrarelational) intimacy. In their qualitative study of 39 gay male couples, for example, Hoff and Beougher (2010) found that agreements of nonexclusivity benefit the relationship by helping them to deepen trust and emotional bonds and establish boundaries.

Sex and Cohabitation The sexual behavior of cohabiting heterosexual couples has been studied, often in comparison with married heterosexual couples. Cohabiters report higher frequency of sexual intercourse than their married counterparts (Call et al. 1995, pp. 650–651; Christopher and Sprecher 2000, p. 1002). Cohabiters may also have a higher rate of nonmonogamy and may be more likely to have sexual affairs outside of the relationship than married couples (Christopher and Sprecher 2000, p. 1006; Treas and Giesen 2000, p. 59). In their study of women who serially cohabit, Cohen and Manning (2010) find that women who cohabit with a succession of partners tend to have more non-cohabiting sexual partners than women who marry without cohabiting, as well as women who cohabit with one person (Cohen and Manning 2010, p. 774). Sassler et al. (2012) conducted a study of relationship progression and quality using a nationally representative sample of low- to moderate-income heterosexual couples with minor children in the home. They find an association between early onset of sexual activity, premarital cohabitation, and less satisfying marriages.

Sex and Open Relationships Finally, an understudied family structure is nonmonogamy, which can take the form of open, polyamorous, and swinging relationships. As indicated above, agreements of nonexclusivity are not infrequent within gay male relationships, and may also be found among heterosexual, bisexual, and lesbian romantic and sexual partners (Barker and Langdridge 2010). De Visser and McDonald (2007) find in their qualitative study of four heterosexual swinging couples in England that jealousy may occur quite naturally and frequently, but it is recognized by the couples as something that can be managed through negotiation of rules and boundary setting. Sheff's (2006) ethnographic research on polyamorous communities in the United States reveals how norms and standards of hegemonic masculinity get both undermined and reinforced by poly men as they navigate multiple relationships.

19.5 Impact of Family Structure on Sexuality of Offspring

The role of the family in organizing sexuality and sexual expression is not limited to adults, but also serves to regulate and socialize the sexuality of children. Scholars have debated to what extent family structure influences the outcome of offspring in regard to their sexual behavior, sexual orientation, and patterns of early childbearing. In particular, the relationship and marital status of parents have been studied as independent variables that may affect children's emerging sexuality.

Unmarried, Cohabiting, Divorced, and Remarried Parents Much research has been conducted on the economic and emotional effects of single-parent and unmarried heterosexual cohabiting households, including a series of projects conducted as part of the Fragile Families

and Child Wellbeing Study out of Princeton and Columbia University (E.g. Osborne and McLanahan 2007). Although many of these studies focus on the effects of correlational poverty and household disruption, increasingly scholars have begun to focus on how parents' relationship and living status affects the sexual behavior of offspring. Bulunda and Manning (2008), for example, studied the influence of cohabiting status on the well-being of adolescent girls, including age of first sexual intercourse and teenage pregnancy. Using NSFG data, the authors find that being born to a cohabiting couple makes children 128 % more likely to have sex before the age of 15 than if their parents were married at birth, similar to rates of early sexual activity for the children of single mothers (Bulanda and Manning 2008, p. 606). Children of unmarried cohabiters and single mothers are also much more likely to give birth as teenagers than the children of married parents (Bulanda and Manning 2008, p. 606). Similarly, studies have found increased risks of nonmarital childbearing (Wu 1996) and cohabitation (Teachman 2003) among women who experienced changes in family structure and living arrangements as children and adolescents.

In terms of remarriage, Teachman (2003) finds that women who lived with a stepfather in their household growing up are more likely to marry than to initially cohabit with a partner, but research by Amato and Kane (2011) finds that daughters whose parents divorce or remarry have an increased likelihood of having a cohabiting relationship or a nonmarital birth. It is unclear to what extent these effects of growing up in households with single parents, cohabiting adults, and stepparents result from relative economic deprivation, self-selection, differing patterns of socialization, or the stress and upheavals involved with families in transition.

Lesbian and Gay Parents The effect of growing up with lesbian, gay, and bisexual parents has taken on increasing relevance with contemporary debates about same-sex marriage. According to a brief from the U.S. Census using 2010 American Community Survey data, 84 % of same-sex households included children (compared to 94 %

of opposite-sex married couple households) (Lofquist 2011). Numerous studies, including those by Golombok and Tasker (1996), Allen and Burrell (1997), Jellinek et al. (2008), and Goldberg et al. (2012) have attempted to answer questions about the effects on children of being raised by a lesbian or gay parent and/or within a same-sex household, including on their well-being, sexual orientation, and gender-typed play behavior. Most reputable studies debunk the idea that being raised by lesbian and gay parents has negative effects on children, but Stacey and Bilbarz (2001) raise the concern that researchers may have overcompensated by minimizing differences between heterosexual and homosexual parents. Differences, the authors maintain, do not need to indicate deficits (Stacey and Biblarz 2001, p. 162; Hicks 2005). For example, Stacey and Biblarz (2001) make note of studies that reveal that children of lesbian mothers exhibit less gender-typed roles and behaviors.

Recently, controversy arose with the publication—and use in support of bans against same sex marriage—of an article by sociologist Mark Regnerus (2012a) that claimed negative outcomes for children raised by parents who have had same-sex relationships (see also Cohen 2012; Regnerus 2012b). The American Sociological Association (ASA) released an amicus brief to the United States Court of Appeals in support of overturning gay marriage bans, explicitly disavowing the conclusions of Regnerus's study (American Sociological Association 2014). In preparation for the amicus brief, the ASA requested that sociologists Manning et al. (2014) perform a literature review regarding the well-being of children raised by lesbian and gay parents. The authors find that no significant differences exist between teenagers in households headed by lesbian couples and teenagers residing in households headed by different-sex couples in terms of their probability of being in a romantic or sexual relationship, having an STI, getting pregnant, or getting somebody pregnant (Manning et al. 2014, p. 493).

In addition to the sexual activity of youth raised by lesbian or gay parents, scholars make competing claims about whether the sexual orientation of individuals is affected by being raised by lesbian or gay parents. Golombok and Tasker (1996) looked at longitudinal data collected from childhood through adulthood about young people raised in lesbian households. They found that although those growing up in a lesbian household were more likely to consider the possibility of forming same-sex relationships, there was no significant difference in their sexual orientation compared to individuals raised in heterosexual households, or differences in their reports of being attracted to people of the same gender (Golombok and Tasker 1996, p. 8). They conclude that

> Whereas there is no evidence from the present investigation to suggest that parents have a determining influence on the sexual orientation of their children, the findings do indicate that by creating a climate of acceptance or rejection of homosexuality within the family, parents may have some impact on their children's sexual experimentation as heterosexual, lesbian, or gay. (Golombok and Tasker 1996, p. 10)

A more recent study of adolescents living with same-sex couples found no significant differences compared with adolescents living with heterosexual parents in terms of psychological adjustment, romantic relationships, and sexual orientation (Wainwright et al. 2004). Although several studies have been made of children raised in lesbian households, not as much research has been conducted on the wellbeing and sexuality of children raised by gay men, transgender people, and bisexuals (Biblarz and Savci 2010).

19.6   Emerging Areas in Family and Sexuality Studies

The intersection of family studies with sexuality studies (alongside studies of sex and gender) continues. Three emerging areas that students of the family and sexuality may wish to pay attention to include the changing sexual scripts involved with courtship and dating rituals, the implications of the changing legal status of same-sex marriage, and the rising numbers of "boomerang" and multigenerational households.

Dating and Intimate Friendships There is a growing body of research on contemporary dating practices, particularly among adolescents and young adults who engage in so-called "friends with benefits" or "hook-up" culture, that adds to prior literature on premarital sex (Bogle 2008; England and Ronen 2013; Heldman and Wade 2010). Grouping these practices under the heading "premarital sex" does not necessarily make sense given the trends of delayed marriage and overall decline in marriage, particularly among low-income women and racial minorities (Edin and Kefalas 2011; Pew Research Center 2010). What these studies have in common is the focus on relationships that occur without long-term commitment or cohabitation, if not monogamy. Yet even though previous rites of courtship and dating may have been viewed as testing grounds and precursors to marriage, these fleeting relationships are still relevant to family and sexuality scholarship because they are sites for sexual exploration and experimentation. Furthermore, given that the average age of first marriage and birth of first child has been rising, the time before individuals "settle down" with a partner or children has become an extended stage of the life course.

Same-Sex Marriage As of this writing (2014), same-sex marriage is legal in 35 states plus Washington, D.C., and positive rulings have been issued in an additional 10 states (Freedom to Marry 2014a). Internationally, 18 countries permit same-sex couples to marry, including Spain, France, Brazil, and South Africa (Freedom to Marry 2014b). With the sweeping tide of legal decisions made in favor of same-sex marriage in the United States and other countries come opportunities for further research on the impact of family structure on sexual behavior and satisfaction and how the institution of marriage effects the sexual expression of same-sex relationships. Research may now distinguish same-sex married households from same-sex cohabiting households in order to establish patterns of difference. Additionally, unconventional arrangements of queer households, families, and networks, and alternative pathways to parenthood

continue to be areas ripe for further study. For example, Stacey (2011)'s ethnography of gay families in Los Angeles include descriptions of co-parenting relationships between lesbian and gay male couples. The possibility of three-parent babies is also becoming more of a reality with scientific developments in which mitochondrial DNA is transferred from one woman's egg into another. Parliament in the United Kingdom will soon vote on legislation allowing for such a procedure (Knapton 2014).

Boomerang and Multigenerational Families The economic downturn beginning in 2008, the multi-year housing crisis that followed, and ballooning student debt have converged to cause increasing numbers of families to double or triple up in households (Fry and Passel 2014; Lofquist 2012). According to the Pew Research Center, 18.1 % of Americans lived in households including at least two generations of adults ages 25 or older, and the study's authors largely attribute this phenomenon to young adults (sometimes referred to as the "boomerang generation") between 25 and 34 years old (Fry and Passel 2014, p. 4; Newman 2012; Parker 2012). Extended family households are not limited to adult children living with their parents. 47 % of Americans live in a household with three or more generations of adults (Fry and Passel 2014, p. 15). These extended family households may not be unlike earlier family structures, but because cultural norms regarding sex, dating, and marriage have changed in the meantime, it is of interest to understand how multigenerational households organize and regulate sexual expression and sexuality. How do parents and their adult children negotiate rules and boundaries regarding sexual activity within and without the home, including intimacy with extramarital partners, interracial relationships, same-sex relations, or polyamory?

19.7 Conclusion

When the heterosexual nuclear family was most dominant in the United States, a linear life progression of dating, marriage, and childbearing, in that order, was expected of most individuals, particularly the white middle-class. Even though the very diverse structures of families today look very different from the heterosexual nuclear family analyzed by functionalists Murdock and Parsons in the middle of the 20th century, the two primary functions of the family that they described—sexuality and reproduction—continue to be fruitful areas of study for contemporary family and sexuality scholars. Sexuality and reproduction are still essential aspects of family, but what has changed are definitions and understandings of what family means and how sexuality and reproduction are expressed and realized.

Scholars today study how much the modern family differs from prior iterations, citing statistics relating to delayed marriage and childbearing, cohabitation, same-sex marriage, reproductive technologies, single parents, divorce, remarriage, and nonmarital childbearing. They look at the changing relationships between family, sex, and procreation, noting that the links among them have been disrupted by changes in attitudes, cultural norms, laws, and technology. With the proliferation of diverse family forms, they also study the effects of different family structures on such behaviors and patterns as sexual frequency and satisfaction and effects on adolescent sexuality. Today, we understand that families can take on many different forms, and the paths to creating and sustaining family demand new interpretations of the organization of sexuality and reproduction.

References

Allen, M., & Burrell, N. (1997). Comparing the impact of homosexual and heterosexual parents on children: Meta-Analysis of existing research. *Journal of Homosexuality, 32*(2), 19–35.

Amato, P. R. (2007). *Alone together: How marriage in America is changing*. Cambridge: Harvard University Press.

Amato, P. R., & Kane, J. B. (2011). Parents' marital distress, divorce, and remarriage: Links with daughters' early family formation transitions. *Journal of Family Issues, 32*(8), 1073–1103. doi:10.1177/0192513 × 11404363.

American Sociological Association. (2014). ASA Amicus Brief Supports Suits to Overturn Utah, Oklahoma Gay Marriage Bans: Association Won't Allow Gay Marriage Opponents to Misrepresent Research. http://www.asanet.org/press/amicus_brief_supports_overturn_gay_marriage_bans.cfm. Accessed 11 Aug 2014.

Barker, M., & Langdridge, D. (2010). Whatever happened to non-monogamies? Critical reflections on recent research and theory. *Sexualities, 13*(6), 748–772. doi:10.1177/1363460710384645.

Bell, A. V. (2009). 'It's Way out of my League': Low-income women's experiences of medicalized infertility. *Gender & Society, 23*(5), 688–709.

Biblarz, T. J., & Savci, E. (2010). Lesbian, gay, bisexual, and transgender families. *Journal of Marriage and Family, 72*(3), 480–497.

Blumstein, P., & Schwartz, P. (1983). *American couples: Money, work, sex*. New York: Morrow.

Bogle, K. A. (2008). *Hooking up: Sex, dating, and relationships on campus*. New York: New York University Press.

Bulanda, R. E., & Manning, W. D. (2008). Parental cohabitation experiences and adolescent behavioral outcomes. *Population Research and Policy Review, 27*(5), 593–618. doi:10.1007/s11113-008-9083-8.

Call, V. R. A., Sprecher, S., & Schwartz, P. (1995). The incidence and frequency of marital sex in a national sample. *Journal of Marriage and Family [H.W. Wilson—SSA], 57*, 639.

Center for Research on Child Wellbeing. (n.d.). About the fragile families and child wellbeing study. http://www.fragilefamilies.princeton.edu/about.asp. Accessed 13 August 2014.

Cherlin, A. J. (2004). The deinstitutionalization of American marriage. *Journal of Marriage and Family, 66*(4), 848–861.

Cherlin, A. J. (2009). *The marriage-go-round: The state of marriage and the family in America today*. New York: Alfred A. Knopf.

Cherlin, A. J. (2010). Demographic trends in the United States: A review of research in the 2000s. *Journal of Marriage and Family, 72*(3), 403–419. doi:10.1111/j.1741–3737.2010.00710.x.

Cheung, M. W.-L., Wong, P. W.-C., Liu, K. Y., Fan, S. Y., & Lam, T. (2008). A study of sexual satisfaction and frequency of sex among Hong Kong Chinese couples. *Journal of Sex Research, 45*(2), 129–139.

Christopher, F. S., & Sprecher, S. (2000). Sexuality in marriage, dating, and other relationships: A decade review. *Journal of Marriage and Family, 62*(4), 999–1017.

Coelho, T. (2011). Hearts, groins and the intricacies of gay male open relationships: Sexual desire and liberation revisited. *Sexualities, 14*(6), 653–668. doi:10.1177/1363460711422306.

Cohen, P. N. (2012). Regnerus study controversy guide. http://familyinequality.wordpress.com/2012/08/15/regnerus-study-controversy-guide/. Accessed 11 Aug 2014.

Cohen, J., & Manning, W. (2010). The relationship context of premarital serial cohabitation. *Social Science Research, 39*(5), 766–776. doi:10.1016/j.ssresearch.2010.04.011.

Cohn, D. (2011). Census bureau: Flaws in same-sex couple data. http://www.pewsocialtrends.org/2011/09/27/census-bureau-flaws-in-same-sex-couple-data/. Accessed 8 Aug 2014.

Collins, P. H. (2000). *Black feminist thought: Knowledge, consciousness, and the politics of empowerment*. New York: Routledge.

Coontz, S. (1992). *The way we never were: American families and the nostalgia trap*. New York: BasicBooks.

Coontz, S. (2000). Historical Perspectives on Family Studies. *Journal of Marriage and Family, 62*(2), 283–297.

Coontz, S. (2006). *Marriage, a history: How love conquered marriage*. New York: Penguin.

Copen, C. E., Daniels, K., Vespa, J., & Mosher, W. D. (2012). *First marriages in the United States: Data from the 2006–2010 national survey of family growth* (No. 49). Hyattsville: National Center for Health Statistics.

Davis, E. C., & Friel, L. V. (2001). Adolescent sexuality: Disentangling the effects of family structure and family context. *Journal of Marriage and Family, 63*(3), 669–681.

De Visser, R., & McDonald, D. (2007). Swings and roundabouts: Management of jealousy in heterosexual "swinging" couples. *British Journal of Social Psychology, 46*(2), 459–476.

Dill, B. T. (1988). OUR MOTHERS' GRIEF: Racial ethnic women and the maintenance of families. *Journal of Family History, 13*(1), 415–431. doi:10.1177/036319908801300125.

Edin, K., & Kefalas, M. (2011). *Promises I can keep*. Berkeley: University of California Press.

Elliott, S., & Umberson, D. (2008). The performance of desire: Gender and sexual negotiation in long-term marriages. *Journal of Marriage and Family, 70*(2), 391–406.

England, P., & Ronen, S. (2013). Sex and relationships among youth an intersectional gender lens. *Contemporary Sociology: A Journal of Reviews, 42*(4), 503–513. doi:10.1177/0094306113491547.

Freedom to Marry. (2014a). Freedom to Marry: States [Text]. http://www.freedomtomarry.org/states/. Accessed 9 December 2014.

Freedom to Marry. (2014b). The Freedom to Marry Internationally [Text]. http://www.freedomtomarry.org/landscape/entry/c/international. Accessed 10 December 2014.

Fry, R., & Passel, J. S. (2014). *In post-recession era, young adults drive continuing rise in multi-generational living*. Washington: Pew Research Center's Social and Demographic Trends project. http://www.pewsocialtrends.org/2014/07/17/in-post-recession-era-young-adults-drive-continuing-rise-in-multi-generational-living/. Accessed 17 July 2014.

Giddens, A. (1992). *The transformation of intimacy: Sexuality, love, and eroticism in modern societies*. Stanford: Stanford University Press.

Gittins, D. (2011). The family in question: What is the family? Is it universal? In S. J. Ferguson (Ed.), *Shifting the center: Understanding contemporary families* (Fourth.). New York: McGraw-Hill.

Goldberg, A. E., Kashy, D. A., & Smith, J. Z. (2012). Gender-typed play behavior in early childhood: Adopted children with lesbian, gay, and heterosexual parents. *Sex Roles, 67*(9–10), 503–515. doi:http://dx.doi.org.ezaccess.libraries.psu.edu/10.1007/s11199-012-0198-3.

Goldin, C., & Katz, L. F. (2002). The power of the pill: Contraceptives and women's career and marriage decisions. *Journal of Political Economy, 110*(4), 730–770.

Golombok, S., & Tasker, F. (1996). Do parents influence the sexual orientation of their children? Findings from a longitudinal study of lesbian families. *Developmental Psychology, 32*(1), 3–11.

Gordon, L., & Gordon, L. (2002). *The moral property of women: A history of birth control politics in America*. Urbana and Chicago: University of Illinois Press.

Heldman, C., & Wade, L. (2010). Hook-up culture: Setting a new research agenda. *Sexuality Research and Social Policy, 7*(4), 323–333. doi:10.1007/s13178-010-0024-z.

Herbenick, D., Reece, M., Schick, V., Sanders, S. A., Dodge, B., & Fortenberry, J. D. (2010). Sexual behaviors, relationships, and perceived health status among adult women in the United States: Results from a national probability sample. *The Journal of Sexual Medicine, 7*, 277–290. doi:10.1111/j.1743–6109.2010.02010.x.

Hicks, S. (2005). Is gay parenting bad for kids? Responding to the "Very Idea of Difference" in research on lesbian and gay parents. *Sexualities, 8*(2), 153–168. doi:10.1177/1363460705050852.

Hoff, C. C., & Beougher, S. C. (2010). Sexual agreements among gay male couples. *Archives of Sexual Behavior, 39*(3), 774–787. doi:10.1007/s10508-008-9393-2.

Iasenza, S. (2008). Beyond "Lesbian Bed Death." *Journal of Lesbian Studies, 6*(1), 111–120. doi:10.1300/J155v06n01_10.

Islam, N. S., Khan, S., Kwon, S., Jang, D., Ro, M., & Trinh-Shevrin, C. (2010). Methodological issues in the collection, analysis, and reporting of granular data in Asian American populations: Historical challenges and potential solutions. *Journal of Health Care for the Poor and Underserved, 21*(4), 1354–1381. doi:10.1353/hpu.2010.0939.

Jellinek, M. S., Henderson, S. W., Telingator, C. J., & Patterson, C. J. (2008). Children and adolescents of lesbian and gay parents. *Journal of the American Academy of Child & Adolescent Psychiatry, 47*(12), 1364–1368.

Knapton, S. (2014). Three parent babies given green light by government. http://www.telegraph.co.uk/news/science/science-news/11299513/Three-parent-babies-given-green-light-by-government.html. Accessed 23 December 2014.

Lareau, A. (2003). *Unequal childhoods: Class, race, and family life* (1st ed.). Berkeley: University of California Press.

Lareau, A. (2011). *Unequal childhoods: Class, race, and family life* (2nd ed.). Berkeley: University of California Press.

Lofquist, D. (2011). *Same-sex couple households.* (No. ACSBR/10-03). Washington, D.C.: U.S. Census Bureau. https://www.census.gov/prod/2011pubs/acsbr10-03.pdf. Accessed 11 Aug 2014.

Lofquist, D. (2012). *Multigenerational households: 2009–2011* (No. ACSBR/11-03). Washington, D.C.: U.S. Census Bureau. https://www.census.gov/prod/2012pubs/acsbr11-03.pdf. Accessed 12 August 2014.

Mamo, L. (2007). *Queering reproduction: Achieving pregnancy in the age of technoscience.* Durham: Duke University Press.

Manning, W. D., Fettro, M. N., & Lamidi, E. (2014). Child well-being in same-sex parent families: Review of research prepared for American sociological association amicus brief. *Population Research and Policy Review, 33*(4), 485–502. doi:10.1007/s11113-014-9329-6.

Martin, L. J. (2010). Anticipating infertility: Egg freezing, genetic preservation, and risk. *Gender & Society, 24*(4), 526–545.

Martin, J., Hamilton, B., & Osterman, J. (2013). *Births: Final data for 2012* (National vital statistics reports No. Vol 62 No 9). Hyattsville: National Center for Health Statistics.

May, E. T. (2010). *America and the pill: A history of promise, peril, and liberation.* New York: Basic Books.

Murdock, G. P. (1965). *Social structure.* New York: Free Press.

Newman, K. S. (2012). *The accordion family: Boomerang kids, anxious parents, and the private toll of global competition.* Boston: Beacon Press.

Osborne, C., & McLanahan, S. (2007). Partnership instability and child well-being. *Journal of Marriage and Family, 69*(4), 1065–1083.

Parker, K. (2012). *The boomerang generation: Feeling ok about living with mom and dad.* Washington: Pew Research Center. http://www.pewsocialtrends.org/2012/03/15/the-boomerang-generation/. Accessed 12 Aug 2014

Parsons, T. (1951). *The social system.* Glencoe: Free Press.

Parsons, T. (1955). The American family: Its relations to personality and to the social structure. In T. Parsons, & R. F. Bales (Eds.), *Family, socialization and interaction process.* New York: The Free Press.

Parsons, T., & Bales, R. F. (1955). *Family, socialization and interaction process.* New York: The Free Press.

Parsons, J. T., Starks, T. J., DuBois, S., Grov, C., & Golub, S. A. (2013). Alternatives to monogamy among gay male couples in a community survey: Implications for mental health and sexual risk. *Archives of Sexual Behavior, 42*(2), 303–312. doi:10.1007/s10508-011-9885-3.

Pew Research Center. (2010). *The decline of marriage and rise of new families.* Washington: Pew Research Center.

Pew Research Center. (2013). *In gay marriage debate, both supporters and opponents see legal recognition as "Inevitable."* Washington: Pew Research Center.

Reece, M., Herbenick, D., Schick, V., Sanders, S. A., Dodge, B., & Fortenberry, J. D. (2010). Sexual behaviors, relationships, and perceived health among adult men in the United States: Results from a National probability sample. *The Journal of Sexual Medicine, 7,* 291–304. doi:10.1111/j.1743–6109.2010.02009.x.

Regnerus, M. (2012a). How different are the adult children of parents who have same-sex relationships? Findings from the new family structures study. *Social Science Research, 41*(4), 752–770.

Regnerus, M. (2012b). Parental same-sex relationships, family instability, and subsequent life outcomes for adult children: Answering critics of the new family structures study with additional analyses. *Social Science Research, 41*(6), 1367–1377.

Rothman, B. K. (2000). *Recreating motherhood.* New Brunswick: Rutgers University Press.

Sassler, S., Addo, F. R., & Lichter, D. T. (2012). The tempo of sexual activity and later relationship quality. *Journal of Marriage and Family, 74*(4), 708–725.

Schwartz, P., & Young, L. (2009). Sexual satisfaction in committed relationships. *Sexuality Research and Social Policy: Journal of NSRC, 6*(1), 1–17. doi:10.1525/srsp.2009.6.1.1.

Seltzer, J. A. (2000). Families formed outside of marriage. *Journal of Marriage and the Family, 62*(4), 1247–1268.

Sheff, E. (2006). Poly-Hegemonic masculinities. *Sexualities, 9*(5), 621–642. doi:10.1177/1363460706070004.

Skolnick, A. (1981). The family and its discontents. *Society, 18*(2), 42–47. doi:10.1007/BF02694668.

Smock, P. J., & Greenland, F. R. (2010). Diversity in pathways to parenthood: Patterns, implications, and emerging research directions. *Journal of Marriage and Family, 72*(3), 576–593.

Stacey, J. (2011). *Unhitched: Love, marriage, and family values from West Hollywood to Western China.* New York: NYU Press.

Stacey, J., & Biblarz, T. J. (2001). (How) does the sexual orientation of parents matter? *American Sociological Review, 66*(2), 159–183.

Stack, C. B. (1974). *All our kin: Strategies for survival in a Black* New York: Harper & Row.

Stanik, C. E., & Bryant, C. M. (2012). Sexual satisfaction, perceived availability of alternative partners, and marital quality in newlywed African American couples. *Journal of Sex Research, 49*(4), 400–407.

Stein, A. (1993). *Sisters, sexperts, queers.* New York: Plume.

Teachman, J. (2003). Childhood living arrangements and the formation of coresidential unions. *Journal of Marriage and Family, 65*(3), 507–524.

Teachman, J. D., Tedrow, L. M., & Crowder, K. D. (2000). The changing demography of America's families. *Journal of Marriage and the Family, 62*(4), 1234–1246.

Thornton, A., & Young-DeMarco, L. (2001). Four decades of trends in attitudes toward family issues in the United States: The 1960s through the 1990s. *Journal of Marriage and Family, 63*(4), 1009–1037.

Treas, J., & Giesen, D. (2000). Sexual infidelity among married and cohabiting Americans. *Journal of Marriage and the Family, 62*(1), 48–60.

US Census Bureau Public Information. (2011). Census Bureau releases estimates of same-sex married couples. http://www.census.gov/newsroom/releases/archives/2010_census/cb11-cn181.html. Accessed 13 August 2014.

Van Rosmalen-Nooijens, K., Vergeer, C. M., & Lagro-Janssen, A. L. M. (2008). Bed death and other lesbian sexual problems unraveled: A qualitative study of the sexual health of lesbian women involved in a relationship. *Women & Health, 48*(3), 339–362. doi:10.1080/03630240802463343.

Vespa, J., Lewis, J. M., & Kreider, R. M. (2013). *America's families and living arrangements: 2012* (No. P20-570). U.S. Census Bureau.

Wainwright, J. L., Russell, S. T., & Patterson, C. J. (2004). Psychosocial adjustment, school outcomes, and romantic relationships of adolescents with same-sex parents. *Child Development, 75*(6), 1886–1898.

Weston, K. (1991). *Families we choose*. Columbia: Columbia University Press.

Wu, L. L. (1996). Effects of family instability, income, and income instability on the risk of a premarital birth. *American Sociological Review, 61*(3), 386–406.

Zinn, B. M. B. (2000). Feminism and family studies for a new century. *Annals of the American Academy of Political and Social Science, 571*, 42–183.

Understanding Religious Variations in Sexuality and Sexual Health

20

Amy M. Burdette, Terrence D. Hill and Kyl Myers

20.1 Introduction

Religious involvement—indicated by observable feelings, beliefs, activities, and experiences in relation to spiritual, divine, or supernatural entities—is a prevalent and powerful socio-cultural force in the lives of many Americans. According to national estimates from a recent Gallup poll (2013), a large percentage of U.S. adults continue to affiliate with a religious group (83%). Approximately eight-in-ten U.S. adults report affiliating with a Christian religious organization, while about 5% belong to other faiths. Roughly one-in-six are not affiliated with a religious group. Within Christianity, about half (51.8%) of the U.S. population is Protestant. U.S. Protestants can be divided into three distinct traditions: conservative or evangelical Protestants (roughly one-half of all Protestants, or 26% of the adult population), mainline Protestants (18% of the population), and members of historically African

American Protestant churches (approximately 7% of the population). Catholics comprise almost one-quarter (23.9%) of the U.S. population. Other Christian denominations are much smaller. For example, the Church of Jesus Christ of Latter-day Saints and other Mormon groups make up less than 2% of the adult population (Pew Forum on Religion and Public Life 2008).

These patterns are remarkable on their own, but they also all raise numerous questions concerning the outcomes of religious involvement in everyday life. In this chapter, we provide an overview and critical examination of published research concerning the impact of religious involvement on the outcomes of sexuality and sexual health across the life course. In the pages that follow, we take a broad approach, focusing on a variety of important topics, including sexual behavior, sexual health education, abortion attitudes and behavior, HIV/AIDS, attitudes toward gays and lesbians, and the lived experiences of sexual minorities. Although we draw heavily from research conducted by sociologists, we note several significant contributions by scholars in religious studies, public health, psychology, and child development. We also primarily focus on the U.S. context, but we describe important research conducted in other countries when appropriate. Given the religious make-up of the United States, most of the studies discussed in this review focus on the influence of Christianity on sexuality and sexual health.

A. M. Burdette (✉)
Department of Sociology, Florida State University, Tallahassee, FL 32306, USA
e-mail: aburdette@fsu.edu

T. D. Hill
School of Sociology, University of Arizona, Tucson, AZ 85721, USA
e-mail: tdhill@email.arizona.edu

K. Myers
Department of Sociology, University of Utah, Salt Lake City, UT 84112, USA
e-mail: kyl.myers@soc.utah.edu

J. DeLamater, R.F. Plante (eds.), *Handbook of the Sociology of Sexualities,* Handbooks of Sociology and Social Research, DOI 10.1007/978-3-319-17341-2_20, © Springer International Publishing Switzerland 2015

20.2 Religion and Sexual Behavior

Researchers have linked various indicators of religious involvement and a range of sexual behaviors across the life course, from adolescence (Burdette and Hill 2009; Regnerus 2007; Rostosky et al. 2004) and young adulthood (Adamczyk and Felson 2008; Davidson et al. 2004; Vazsonyi and Jenkins 2010) to adulthood (Barkan 2006; Gillum and Holt 2010) and late life (McFarland et al. 2011). Religion appears to influence both attitudes toward sexual activity and sexual behavior.

Scholars have long noted that U.S. residents who are members of conservative religious communities (e.g., Southern Baptists, Jehovah's Witnesses, and Mormons) (Gay et al. 1996; Petersen and Donnenwerth 1997), those who hold a literalist interpretation of the Bible (Ogland and Bartkowski 2014), and those who display higher levels of religious involvement (Cochran and Beeghley 1991; Ellison et al. 2013) tend to have more conservative sex-related attitudes (e.g., toward premarital sex, extramarital sexual behavior, and homosexuality) than other individuals in the United States. Cross-national studies show that Muslims and Hindus tend to hold more conservative attitudes toward sex than do Christians (Finke and Adamczyk 2008). Evidence also suggests that Jews tend to have more liberal sex-related attitudes than Christians (Regnerus and Uecker 2007). Research examining the sex-related attitudes of Buddhists has yielded inconsistent results (Adamczyk and Pitt 2009; Finke and Adamczyk 2008; De Visser et al. 2007).

20.2.1 Religion and Adolescent Sexual Behavior

Of all of the research on the connection between religion and sexual behavior, perhaps the most scholarly attention has been devoted to understanding the relationship between religious involvement and heterosexual adolescent sexual activity. Research consistently shows that religious involvement, often conceptualized as church attendance, is associated with delayed initiation of sexual intercourse (Regnerus 2007; Meier 2003; Rostosky et al. 2004) and fewer sexual partners (Miller and Gur 2002; Thornton and Camburn 1989) in adolescence. More limited evidence suggests that religiosity is associated with postponement of other types of sexual activity as well, including oral sexual behavior and genital touching (Burdette and Hill 2009; Hull et al. 2011; Regnerus 2007).

Researchers have also noted important variations in adolescent sexual behavior by religious affiliation. Some studies show that adolescents who are affiliated with conservative religious groups (e.g. Mormons, evangelicals, and fundamentalists) are more likely to delay sexual intercourse than their mainline or unaffiliated peers (Beck et al. 1991; Brewster et al. 1998). Other research suggests that adolescents who identify with evangelical Protestant denominations (e.g., Southern Baptists, Pentecostal, and Church of God) are actually less likely to delay sexual intercourse than are mainline and Jewish adolescents (Regnerus 2007). In general, the effects of religious affiliation on sexual behavior are weaker than those of religious involvement. This suggests that degree of involvement matters more than simply identifying with a particular religious group.

Why might religious involvement be associated with delayed sexual activity in adolescence? Various aspects of religiosity may influence teen sexual activity in different, but reinforcing, ways. Church attendance might reduce or delay sexual activity by exposing adolescents to messages and norms concerning sexual morality. Indeed, studies indicate that attitudes about sexual behavior are an important mechanism linking religion and sexual activity (Meier 2003; Rostosky et al. 2003). Religious attendance may also embed adolescents within sexually conservative contexts, where parental monitoring is high (Smith 2003a, b) and informal social sanctions are regularly enforced against persons suspected of non-marital sexual activity (Thornton and Camburn 1989; Adamczyk and Felson 2006). While frequency of church attendance indicates exposure to moral messages, religious salience, or how important religion is to the individual, may indicate the degree to which these messages have been internalized (Rohrbaugh and Jessor 1975). Like church attendance, private religiosity indicates exposure to religious doctrines and reinforces religious teachings in the areas of obedience, self-control, and sexual morality (Smith 2003b).

In addition to personal religiosity, research suggests that both parental religiosity and peer religiosity can influence adolescent sexual behavior. Evidence suggests that parental religiosity is associated with delayed sexual initiation (Manlove et al. 2006) and reduced sexual risk taking (Landor et al. 2011). Similarly, Adamczyk and Felson (2006) find that friends' religiosity has an independent influence on adolescent sexual behavior that is similar in magnitude to personal religiosity. They argue that friends' religious involvement reduces adolescent sexual activity through opportunity limitations, reputational costs, and pro-virginity normative influences. Teens with more religious friends may have more difficulty finding a partner who is or could be sexually active than adolescents embedded in more secular social networks. Losing one's virginity may be a status gain among secular friends, but adolescents with religious friends may lose status by having sexual intercourse (Adamczyk and Felson 2006). More recent work by Adamczyk (2009a) suggests that selection effects may explain part of the link between friends' religiosity and adolescent sexual debut, as teens who delay first intercourse tend to switch to more religious friends while those who have had sexual intercourse tend to switch to less religious friends.

20.2.2 Religion and Adolescent Contraceptive Use

While religious involvement is generally protective of adolescent sexual behavior, associations with contraceptive use are more precarious and sometimes counterproductive. Some evidence indicates that those adolescents who are most likely to delay sexual intercourse (i.e., fundamentalist Protestants) are the least likely to use contraception when they do transition to first sex (Cooksey

et al. 1996; Kramer et al. 2007); however, other research finds no association between religious affiliation and contraceptive use (Brewster et al. 1998). There is little evidence that religious attendance (Brewster et al. 1998; Kramer et al. 2007) or religious salience (Kramer and Dunlop 2012) impact adolescent contraceptive use. Parental religiosity may also negatively impact adolescent contraceptive use by limiting information about birth control. Evidence suggests that both parental public religious involvement and parental religious salience reduce the frequency of conversations with adolescent children about sex and birth control. When religiously devout parents do talk to their teen children about sexual behavior, they often focus on morality, not on conveying information about contraception (Regnerus 2005).

20.2.3 The Virginity Pledge Movement

Beginning in 1993, the Southern Baptist Church sponsored a movement to encourage adolescents to take public virginity pledges in which they vow to abstain from sex until marriage. Since this time, other conservative Christian organizations have spearheaded efforts to promote sexual abstinence among unmarried adolescents and young adults (Carpenter 2011). Research suggests that pledging is most common among evangelical and Mormon youth and rare among Jewish and non-religious teens. Pledging is also more common among adolescents who attend church frequently than among those who attend less often (Regnerus 2007). In their seminal work on the pledge movement, Bearman and Brückner (2001) find that pledgers are much more likely to delay sexual intercourse than adolescents who do not pledge. However, those pledgers who break their promise of abstinence are less likely to use contraception at first intercourse, a finding that is consistent with more recent research on this topic (Manlove et al. 2003; Rosenbaum 2009). Bearman and Brückner explain that pledgers are less likely to be prepared for an experience that they have promised to avoid. The authors argue that being "contraceptively prepared" may be psychologically distressing for teens who have publicly vowed to abstain from sexual intercourse until marriage. In follow up work, these scholars show that the rate of sexually transmitted infections is similar for pledgers and non-pledgers (Brückner and Bearman 2005).

20.2.4 Subgroup Variations in the Relationship Between Religion and Sexual Behavior

Is the association between religious involvement and sexual activity the same for all adolescents? Studies consistently show that religious involvement is more strongly associated with the sexual behavior of females than males (Burdette et al. 2005; Regnerus 2007; Rostosky et al. 2004). Although boys and girls may be encouraged to refrain from sexual activities, virginity status may be especially important for girls. For example, the sexual status of females is often noted within Biblical texts, yet is rarely mentioned for male figures (e.g. Lev. 21:7; Luke 1:34; John 4:17–19).

Some evidence suggests that the association between religious involvement and delayed sexual activity is weaker for African American adolescents than among Whites adolescents (Bearman and Brückner 2001); however, other research finds consistent effects across racial groups (Rostosky et al. 2004). Scholars speculate that Black churches may be more forgiving of sexual transgressions than are predominately White churches (Hertel and Hughes 1987; Lincoln and Mamiya 1990). To this point, it is unclear in the literature how the association between religion and adolescent sexual behavior might vary between non-Hispanic White and Hispanic adolescents. Limited evidence suggests that religiosity reduces sexual activity among Latinas, particularly those of Mexican origin (Edwards et al. 2011).

Few scholars have examined variations in the impact of religiosity on adolescent sexual behavior by sexual identity. In fact, little research has examined the influence of religion on adolescent sexual activity among sexual minority youths. In one important exception to this general trend, Hatzenbuehler et al. (2012) show that living in a county with a religious climate that is supportive of homosexuality is associated with fewer sexual partners for teens identifying as lesbian, gay, or bisexual. Although their results also suggest that the impact of religious climate on sexual behavior is stronger among sexual minority youth than heterosexual teens, additional research is needed to confirm these findings.

20.2.5 Religion and Young Adult Sexual Behavior

While scholars have devoted more attention to examining the relationship between religion and sexual behavior in adolescence than any other stage in the life course, a modest amount of research has examined this association in young adulthood, especially among college students. Understanding the influence of religion on sexual health among emerging adults is important because many Americans exhibit a decline in religious involvement (principally religious attendance) during this stage of life. Although scholars have speculated that this religious decline is due to the secularizing effects of higher education, evidence suggests that emerging adults who do not attend college exhibit the most extensive patterns of religious decline, thus contradicting the conventional wisdom (Uecker et al. 2007).

In general, religion continues to be protective in delaying or reducing sexual activity during young adulthood, including sexual risk taking. Scholarship suggests that religious young adults are more likely to delay (Adamczyk and Felson 2008; Davidson et al. 2004; Vazsonyi and Jenkins 2010) or forgo (Uecker 2008) premarital sex than their non-religious peers. Findings on the impact of religious involvement on the number of sexual partners are more mixed. While some research suggests that religiosity is associated with fewer sexual partners among female undergraduates (Davidson et al. 2004), other work finds no effects for either religious affiliation or participation among young women (Jones et al. 2005).

As changing norms in the dating and sexual behaviors of college students have captured scholarly and media attention (Haley et al. 2001; England et al. 2007), a relatively new line of research explores the connection between religion and "hooking up" among college students. Although somewhat ambiguous in meaning, students generally use the term "hooking up" to refer to a physical encounter between two people who are largely unfamiliar with one another or otherwise briefly acquainted (Glenn and Marquardt 2001). A typical hook-up involves moderate to heavy alcohol consumption (a median of four drinks for women and six for men) and carries no anticipation of a future relationship (England et al. 2007).

Research suggests that church attendance is associated with reduced odds of hooking up (Burdette and Hill 2009) and fewer hook-ups (Brimeyer and Smith 2012) while in college. Limited scholarship also suggests that Catholics display higher rates of hooking up compared to conservative Protestants (Brimeyer and Smith 2012) and those students with no religious affiliation (Burdette and Hill 2009). Burdette et al. (2009) also find that women who attend colleges and universities with a Catholic affiliation are more likely to have hooked up while at school than women who attend academic institutions with no religious affiliation, net of individual-level religious involvement. Other work by Freitas (2008) shows that the influence of religion on casual sexual behavior is limited to those attending evangelical colleges and universities.

While research on hooking up suggests that religious involvement may be a protective force in the lives of young adults, research on contraceptive use among this age group suggests otherwise. In their study of unmarried young adults, Burdette et al. (2014) show that evangelical Protestants are more likely to exhibit inconsistent contraception use than those with no religious affiliation. These scholars also show that conservative Protestants are more likely to hold misconceptions about their own fertility than non-affiliates, suggesting that this group may have limited access to accurate information concerning sexual health. Other research suggests that young women who frequently attend religious services are less likely to use sexual and reproductive health services (i.e., routine gynecologic examination care, sexually transmitted infection testing/treatment, and services for contraception) than young women who attend church less frequently, despite sexual experience (Hall et al. 2012). Taken together, findings from these studies suggest an unmet need for sexual and reproductive health care among religiously active women, particularly those who identify with conservative religious faiths.

20.2.6 Religion and Sexual Behavior in Adulthood

While a number of studies have examined the association between religion and sex-related attitudes among U.S. adults, fewer studies have investigated the relationship between religion and sexual behavior in adulthood. Using pooled data from the General Social Survey (1993–2002), Barkan (2006) shows an inverse association between religiosity and number of sexual partners among never-married adults. Further analysis of subgroup variations shows similar effects for both men and women, but differing effects by race. While religiosity is inversely related to number of partners among Whites, it is unrelated to number of sexual partners among African Americans. Other research examining sexual risk-taking behaviors (e.g., women with male partners who have had sex with other males and having a sexual partner who is an intravenous drug user) suggests that church attendance is protective against sexual risk-taking for women. Among men, members of fundamentalist, non-denominational Protestant and other non-Christian denominations tend to exhibit more sexual risk factors than members of mainline Christian denominations (Gillum and Holt 2010).

A few studies have examined the link between religion and adult sexual behavior among non-Christian groups. This research suggests that Muslims are less likely than Christians to have had premarital sex (Addai 2000; Agha 2009). Using cross-national data, Adamczyk and Hayes (2012) investigate how identifying with one of the major world religions (i.e., Islam, Hinduism, Christianity, Buddhism, or Judaism) and living in a nation with a Muslim culture can impact sexual behavior outside of marriage. Their results show that ever married Hindus and Muslims are less likely to report having had premarital sex than are ever married Jews and Christians. Furthermore, the percentage of Muslims within a nation is associated with fewer reports of premarital sex.

In addition to research examining the link between religion and premarital sexual behavior in adulthood, several studies have examined the relationship between religious involvement and marital infidelity. In these studies, marital infidelity is typically defined as having had sexual intercourse with someone other than one's spouse during the course of the marriage. This definition is somewhat limited—excluding other forms of infidelity—but including couples who have an "open" relationship which includes a negotiated agreement to allow nonmonogamy. This line of research suggests that frequent religious attendance reduces the odds of marital infidelity among U.S. adults (Burdette et al. 2007; Atkins and Kessel 2008). Public religious participation is a potential source of control over marital sexuality because connections to friends and family forged through regular interactions in religious settings may reduce opportunities for extramarital sex and raise the likelihood and costs of detection. There is also some evidence of variations in marital infidelity by religious affiliation. Burdette et al. (2007) find that with the exception of two religious groups (nontraditional conservatives and non-Christian faiths), holding any religious affiliation is associated with reduced odds of marital infidelity compared to those with no religious affiliation. This work also suggests that holding more conservative Biblical beliefs is associated with reduced odds of infidelity. Crossnational research suggests that Muslims are less likely than Hindus, Christians, and Jews to engage in marital infidelity (Adamczyk and Hayes 2012).

The few studies that have examined the relationship between religion and contraceptive use among adults suggest modest differences in contraception decision making by religious affiliation. Drawing on data from the 2006–2008 National Survey of Family Growth (NSFG), Jones

and Dreweke (2011) find that among women who have been sexually active, 99 % have used a contraceptive method other than natural family planning. This figure is virtually identical for sexually experienced Catholic women (98 %), despite opposition from Catholic hierarchy, who only approve of "natural" family planning methods for married couples (e.g., periodic abstinence, temperature and cervical mucus tests). In contrast, evidence suggests that most evangelical Protestant leaders and church members approve of the use of contraception, including sterilization, for married women (Barrick 2010). Findings also show that Protestants are more likely than Catholics to use highly effective contraceptive methods, such as sterilization, hormonal methods, or intrauterine devices (IUDs). Attendance at religious services and religious salience appear to be unrelated to choice of contraceptive method (Jones and Dreweke 2011).

Along with studying the influence of religiosity on personal contraceptive use, scholars have explored other interesting connections between religion and contraception. While few U.S. obstetrician-gynecologists have moral or ethical problems with modern contraceptive methods (only 5 % report objecting to one or more methods), doctors who report high levels of religious salience and those with frequent religious participation are more likely than their less religious counterparts to refuse to offer specific contraceptives (Rosenberg 2011). Similarly, religion is an important predictor of pharmacists' willingness to dispense emergency contraception and medical abortifacients. In their study of Nevada pharmacists, Davidson et al. (2010) show that evangelical Protestants and Catholics are significantly more likely to refuse to dispense at least one medication in comparison to pharmacists with no religious affiliation. Work by these scholars illuminates the influence of religion on healthcare workers who may be given leeway to consider morality and value systems when making clinical decisions about care. Policymakers should consider policies that balance the rights of patients, physicians, and pharmacists alike (Davidson et al. 2010).

20.2.7 Religion and Sexual Behavior in Later Life

The relationship between religion and sexual behavior in later life is virtually unexamined. In one important exception to this general trend, McFarland et al. (2011) investigate the influence of religion on the sex lives of married and unmarried community dwelling older adults (ages 57–85). Using nationally representative data from the National Social Life, Health, and Aging Project, they find that religion is largely unrelated to sexual frequency and satisfaction among married older adults. However, among unmarried adults, religious integration in daily life exhibits a negative association with having had sex in the last year among women, but not among men.

20.3 Religion and Sexual Health Education

Social scientists are interested in the connection between religion and sexual health education primarily due to the success of religious conservatives in implementing abstinence-only sex education in public schools. According to Williams (2011), "the role of evangelical Christianity in the abstinence movement cannot be overstated." Throughout the movement, conservative Christian organizations have been key players in the passage of abstinence education policy and continue to defend abstinence-only education at the local, state, and federal level. While health officials generally view sexual abstinence as a behavioral issue, the majority of advocates of abstinence-only education programs are focused on issues of morality (Santelli et al. 2006). Sexual health education programs continue to define abstinence within the context of Christianity, often referencing Biblical notions of purity and heterosexual marriage (Williams 2011).

Before discussing current connections, it is important to provide a brief history of the connection between the Christian Right and sexual health education. Sex education emerged as an important issue to religious conservatives during the 1970s as part of an overall agenda to combat what they viewed as a decline in sexual morality (Williams 2011). During this time period, the primary goal of the movement was to remove any form of sex education from public schools, as the Christian Right viewed sex education as an attempt by liberals to undermine parental authority and Christian mortality by promoting liberal sexual mores like premarital sexual behavior, abortion, homosexuality, and pornography (McKeegan 1992). By the 1980s, it became clear to religious conservatives that removing any discussion of sexual health from public schools was a losing battle. Rather than accept defeat, conservative Christian groups changed strategies, focusing on restructuring the content of sex education. Grass-roots support was provided by groups like the Eagle Forum, Concerned Women for America, Focus on the Family, and Citizens for Excellence in Education, all of whom devoted major resources to promoting abstinence-only programs as an alternative to comprehensive sexual health education (Rose 2005; Williams 2011).

During the 1990s, the campaign led by religious conservatives to promote abstinence-only education began to achieve considerable political success, and funding for these programs grew exponentially under the George W. Bush administration. From 1996 to 2005, over 1 billion state and federal dollars were allocated to abstinence only sex education programs (Rose 2005). In 1996, the US Congress passed the Personal Responsibility and Work Opportunity Reconciliation Act (PRWORA), the high profile welfare reform bill. PRWORA included a $ 250 million grant for abstinence-only programs (referred to as Title V funding), ushering in the heyday of this form of sex education (Williams 2011; Arsneault 2001). The passage of Title V included a formal definition of abstinence—the A-H criteria—that all federally funded abstinence programs were required to follow. Under Sect. 510 of the 1996 Social Security Act, abstinence education is defined as an educational or motivational program which teaches (A) the social, psychological, and health gains to be realized by abstaining from sexual activity; (B) abstinence from sexual activity outside marriage as the expected standard for all school-age children; (C) that abstinence from sexual activity is the only certain way to avoid out-of-wedlock pregnancy, sexually transmitted diseases, and other associated health problems; (D) that a mutually faithful monogamous relationship in the context of marriage is the expected standard of human sexual activity; (E) that sexual activity outside of the context of marriage is likely to have harmful psychological and physical effects; (F) that bearing children out-of-wedlock is likely to have harmful consequences for the child, the child's parents, and society; (G) young people how to reject sexual advances and how alcohol and drug use increases vulnerability to sexual advances; (H) the importance of attaining self-sufficiency before engaging in sexual activity (Santelli et al. 2006). Title V authorized $ 50 million annually from 1998 through 2002 for abstinence-only education. Regular extensions from 2002 maintained funding levels until 2010, when program funding was incorporated into the health care reform law in an effort to promote bipartisan support for the bill (Williams 2011; Doan and McFarlane 2012). However, federal funding for abstinence-only education has declined significantly. The Obama administration provides federal funds supporting both comprehensive sex education and abstinence-only education. States have the option of applying for either program or both programs (SIECUS 2012).

It is important to note that even during the time period when abstinence-only sexual health education was widespread, with roughly one-third of public school districts teaching an abstinence-only curriculum (Landry et al. 2003), a number of states declined federal funding for these programs. Initially, only California declined the funding provided by Title V after determining abstinence-only programs were ineffective (Raymond et al., 2008). However, by 2009, 24 additional states had rejected funds for abstinence-only education. Evidence suggests that a change in governor partisanship from a Republican to a Democrat, a high percentage of politically liberal residents, and a higher per capita state income are all associated with increased odds of declining federal funding for abstinence-only education (Doan and McFarlane 2012).

Researchers and public health officials have raised several concerns with abstinence-only sexual health curricula. First, the overwhelming majority of Americans do not remain sexually abstinent until marriage. Most individuals will have sexual intercourse for the first time during their teens (Martinez et al. 2011); however, the current average age at first marriage is roughly 26-years-old for women and 28-years-old for men in the United States (U.S. Census Bureau 2010). This suggests that the majority of heterosexual individuals are sexually active for almost a decade before getting married. Further, roughly half of all pregnancies in the United States are unplanned, a rate that is higher for young adults than for any other age group (Finer and Henshaw 2006). Taken together, these facts suggest that teens and young adults benefit from information about effective methods of contraception (Finer and Philbin forthcoming).

Second, there is little evidence that abstinence-only education delays teen sexual activity, and some research indicates that it may deter contraceptive use among sexually active teens (Santelli et al. 2006; Boonstra 2010). Findings from a 2004 congressional report indicate that 11 out of the 13 abstinence-only programs evaluated contained inaccurate information about contraceptive effectiveness and the risks of abortion. These curricula also tended to treat stereotypes about girls and boys as scientific fact and blur religious and scientific information (United States House of Representatives 2004). Santelli et al. (2006) note that governmental failure to provide accurate information about contraception raises serious ethical concerns given that access to complete and accurate sexual health information has been recognized as a basic human right. Abstinence-only education is likely to be particularly detrimental to the well-being of gay, lesbian, bisexual, and transgender youths given that classes are unlikely to meet their health needs and often stigmatize homosexuality as deviant behavior (Santelli et al. 2006).

Finally, scholars have noted that abstinence-only education policies are generally unsupported by U.S. adults. Using a random sample of U.S. adults, Bleakley et al. (2006) show that approximately 82 % of respondents support programs that include abstinence and other methods of preventing pregnancy and sexually transmitted infections. In contrast, abstinence-only education received the lowest levels of support (36 %) and the highest levels of opposition. Evidence suggests that comprehensive sex education is supported by even the most religiously involved Americans, albeit at lower levels than their less religious counterparts (Bleakley et al. 2006; Luker 2006).

20.4 Religion and Abortion

20.4.1 Religion and Abortion Attitudes

A long line of research has consistently linked religion with opinions about the morality and legality of abortion. In their review of the literature, Jelen and Wilcox (2003) determined that religion is one of the strongest predictors of abortion attitudes. Overall, studies suggest that conservative Protestants are more likely than other individuals to hold pro-life attitudes, followed by Catholics and mainline Protestants. Conversely, pro-choice views are most prevalent among Jews and those with no religious affiliation (Cook et al. 1992; Ellison et al. 2005; Hertel and Hughes 1987). Evidence also suggests that there is little variability in attitudes toward abortion among conservative Protestants when compared to members of other religious groups (Hoffmann and Johnson 2005; Hoffmann and Miller 1997, 1998). Further, abortion is one of the few sex-related attitudes for which there is little indication of liberalization among younger generations (Farrell 2011; Smith and Johnson 2010). Drawing on national data, Farrell (2011) finds that younger evangelicals hold more liberal attitudes on same-sex marriage, premarital sex, cohabitating, and pornography, but not abortion, than their older evangelical counterparts.

Why are conservative Protestants distinctive in their pro-life attitudes when compared to members of other faith traditions? As Hoffman and Johnson note (2005), abortion is the pivotal issue that brought conservative Protestants into the political arena in the 1970s, following Roe v. Wade and leading to the founding of the Moral Majority. As such, there has been a consistent message from church leadership that abortion is commensurate to murder, which has likely contributed to reduced heterogeneity on this topic among evangelicals. Given that conservative Protestantism is defined by its commitment to the authority of the Bible, which is viewed as the literal word of God, evangelical leadership often draws on Biblical texts to support their opposition to abortion. Predictably, scholars have consistently found an association between Biblical literalism and conservative outcomes on a range of social issues, including antiabortion orientations (Emerson 1996; Ogland and Bartkowski 2014; Ellison et al. 2005).

Although the Bible has little to say about abortion per se, conservative Protestants focus on passages that describe God as having intentionally "formed" human beings "in the womb" (e.g., Psalm 139:13–16; Isaiah 44:2, 24), which are interpreted as evidence that life begins at conception (Bartkowski et al. 2012). Such interpretations of Biblical texts are consistent with the pro-family worldview of conservative Protestantism, which centers on gender traditionalism, pro-natalism, and the sanctification of family life (Emerson 1996). Furthermore, some conservative Protestants believe that a woman's increased control over her own fertility could undermine divinely ordained gender roles and increase the tendency of women to focus on careers to the detriment of family life (Ellison et al. 2005).

Like evangelical leadership, the Catholic Church has long opposed legalized abortion, often equating the practice to murder (Luker 1985). The official position of the Church on abortion is clearly articulated in the Catechism of the Catholic Church:

> Human life must be respected and protected absolutely from the moment of conception. From the first moment of existence, a human being must be recognized as having the rights of a person— among which is the inviolable right of every innocent being to life (U.S. Catholic Conference 1994, p. 2273).

Despite clear statements from Church leadership condemning abortion, Catholics tend to hold more moderate views on this issue than their evangelical Protestant counterparts. Scholars have noted that American Catholics have long questioned papal authority and selectively appropriate Vatican doctrines on matters of sexuality (Greeley 1990; D'Antonio et al. 2007).

In addition to variations in abortion attitudes by religious affiliation, scholars have noted significant differences by religious practice. Individuals who attend church frequently, report high levels of religious salience, and pray often tend to hold more conservative abortion attitudes than those who attend church infrequently, report lower levels of religious salience, and pray less often (Emerson 1996; Bartkowski et al. 2012; Cook et al. 1992). These indicators of religious involvement may reflect strength of religious belief and commitment to religious principles. For example, attendance at religious services may increase familiarity with official church doctrines and offer a context for socialization on abortion and other social issues via sermons, classes, and informal social contacts with other church members. In their work on U.S. Hispanics, Ellison et al. (2005) show that it is important to consider the combination of religious affiliation and involvement. They find that Hispanic Protestants who attend church frequently are more strongly pro-life than any other segment of the Latino population. Committed Catholics also tend to hold pro-life views, but they are more likely to endorse an abortion ban that includes exceptions for rape, incest, and threats to the mother's life. Finally, their work shows that Latino Protestants and Catholics who rarely attend religious services generally do not differ from religiously unaffiliated Hispanics in their abortion views.

20.4.2 Religion and Abortion Behaviors

While numerous studies have examined the relationship between religion and abortion attitudes, far fewer studies have focused on the effect of religion on abortion behavior. Early studies investigating the influence of religion on abortion behavior were largely based on comparisons between surveys of women at abortion clinics and surveys of the general population (Henshaw and Silverman 1987; Henshaw and Kost 1996). Employing a national survey of 9985 abortion patients, Henshaw and Kost (1996) revealed that while Catholic women were as likely as women in the general population to have an abortion, evangelical Protestant women were much less likely to do so. While informative, studies like these do not allow us to determine whether conservative Protestantism reduces the risk of abortion among pregnant women because evangelicals may be underrepresented at abortion clinics due to their lower likelihood of becoming pregnant out of wedlock. Studies of women at abortion clinics are also limited in their ability to assess causality given that information about personal religiosity is collected after the decision to abort has been made.

More recent scholarship by Amy Adamczyk on the connection between religion and abortion behaviors addresses many of the shortcomings of previous work in this area. Using data from the National Longitudinal Study of Adolescent Health (Add Health), Adamczyk and Felson (2008) reveal that religiosity (i.e., frequency of prayer, service attendance, participation in youth group activities, and subjective religious importance) indirectly reduces the likelihood that a woman will have an abortion by reducing the probability that she will have an out-of-wedlock pregnancy. Among those who become pregnant before marriage, religious women are more likely than secular women to marry the father of the child rather than get an abortion or carry the pregnancy to term outside of marriage. However, for those women who become pregnant and do not marry before the birth, religiosity is unrelated to the probability of having an abortion. Adamczyk and Felson (2008) also note several variations in the likelihood of having an abortion by religious affiliation. They find that women who identify as Catholic, mainline Protestant, and Jewish are more likely than conservative Protestant women to abort an out-of-wedlock pregnancy than carry it to term outside of marriage. Adamczyk and Felson (2008) suggest that conservative Protestants are less likely to have an abortion than mainline Protestants and Catholics due to cultural norms prioritizing motherhood and de-emphasizing educational achievement (Darnell and Sherkat 1997; Lehrer 1999). In follow-up work on the topic, Adamczyk highlights religious contextual variations in abortion behaviors. While living in a county with a higher proportion of conservative Protestants does not appear to influence abortion decisions (Adamczyk 2008), having attended a high school with a high proportion of conservative Protestants appears to discourage abortion (Adamczyk 2009b).

20.5 Religion and HIV/AIDS

Although previous sections of this chapter focus on research conducted on populations within the United States, much of the recent research on the connection between religion and HIV/AIDS has emphasized non-U.S. contexts, particularly Sub-Saharan Africa (SSA). We begin this section by noting important research on the relationship between religion and HIV within the United States and then shift to research centered abroad.

20.5.1 Religion and HIV/AIDS in the United States

Scholarship on religious involvement and HIV/AIDS focusing on the U.S. context has concentrated on three themes: sexual risk taking, service provision by religious organizations (primarily churches), and religious coping among individuals living with HIV and their caregivers. Given that we have devoted the beginning of this chapter to examining the connection between religion and sexual behavior more generally, we only briefly discuss sexual risk-taking and focus primarily on the other two topics. A review of the literature on religion and sexual risk behaviors associated with HIV status (e.g., commercial sex and multiple partners) suggests that religiosity tends to reduce HIV risk (Shaw and El-Bassel 2014). The protective nature of religion appears

to also extend to HIV positive individuals. Employing a nationally representative sample of 1421 people in care for HIV, Galvan et al. (2007) find that religiosity is associated with fewer sexual partners and a lower likelihood of engaging in unprotected sex.

Research examining care provided to individuals living with HIV by religious institutions suggests that churches play a limited, but potentially important, role in service provision for those who are HIV positive. Although faith-based organizations (FBOs) have provided a number of services- including organizing HIV testing (Whiters et al. 2010), prevention education (Agate et al. 2005; Lindley et al. 2010), and housing for HIV positive individuals (Derose et al. 2011)- involvement in HIV care and prevention is uncommon for religious congregations. Using data from a nationally representative sample of U.S. congregations, Frenk and Trinitapoli (2013) find that only 5.6% provide programs or activities that serve people living with HIV/AIDS. Expectedly, congregational attitudes about HIV, homosexuality, and substance abuse are related to the type and intensity of events or programs focused on individuals with HIV (Bluthenthal et al. 2012). Other congregational characteristics appear to be associated with having programs directed at individuals living with HIV including: the presence of openly HIV positive people in the congregation, having a group within the church that assesses community needs, and religious tradition (Frenk and Trinitapoli 2013).

Finally, a number of U.S. studies have investigated the role of religion in coping with HIV. People living with HIV/AIDS often draw on religious resources to help reframe their lives, to overcome feelings of guilt and shame, and to bring a sense of meaning and purpose to their experience (Cotton et al. 2006; Siegel and Schrimshaw 2002; Pargament et al. 2004). Limited evidence suggests that greater engagement in spiritual activities is linked to positive mental health outcomes among HIV positive individuals, including lower levels of depression and distress and higher levels of optimism (Pargament et al. 2004; Simoni and Ortiz 2003; Biggar et al. 1999). Other research suggests that religion is protective against physical decline among individuals with HIV/AIDS. For example, Ironson et al. show that specific dimensions of spirituality (e.g., sense of peace, faith in God) are associated with better immune function (Ironson et al. 2002). More recent work by Ironson et al. (2011) finds that a positive view of God is associated with slower disease progression.

Although the tenor of research on religion and coping among individuals living with HIV is generally positive, a smaller body of research highlights the potentially negative effects of religion for this population. Drawing on a sample of 141 HIV positive African American women, Hickman et al. (2013) show that negative religious coping (e.g., viewing HIV as a punishment from God) is associated with poorer mental health and greater perceptions of stigma and discrimination. Other work shows that men with HIV who report more spiritual struggles (e.g., anger at God) display more depressive symptoms (Jenkins 1995). Finally, evidence suggests that holding a negative view of God (i.e., viewing God as harsh or punishing) is associated with faster disease progression among HIV positive individuals (Ironson et al. 2011).

20.5.2 Religion and HIV/AIDS in Africa

Recent research on the connection between religion and HIV/AIDs has focused on Africa, specifically Sub-Saharan Africa, for three key reasons. First, Africa is characterized by very high levels of religious involvement and a very diverse religious marketplace. In terms of religious make-up, Africa is roughly 50% Christian and 42% Muslim, with smaller numbers identifying with traditional African religions (Trinitapoli and Weinreb 2012). The area between the southern border of the Sahara and the tip of South Africa has been labeled "the most religious place on Earth" (Pew Forum on Religion and Public Life 2010). Second, and perhaps most importantly, SSA is the center of the AIDS pandemic. In 2012, 70% of all new cases of HIV were in the region, and AIDS accounted for 1.2 million deaths. It is important to note, however, that there is extreme-

ly high variation in HIV prevalence across the continent and within African countries (UNAIDS 2013). Finally, social scientists, particularly those in public health, have been interested in the connection between religion and HIV in Africa due to changes in the structure of international aid. Rather than working through governments, international assistance is primarily channeled through non-governmental agencies (NGOs), including faith-based organizations (FBOs). Public health officials have expressed concern that FBOs have increased the overtly religious tone of prevention messages and "moralized" the battle against AIDS. However, Trinitapoli and Weinreb (2012) argue that the incorporation of religion into the fight against AIDS, by loosening restrictions on funding, mirrors the trust of religious leaders in the region. Given that religious leaders are the most trusted authority figures in SSA (much more so than NGO officials or teachers), ignoring religious institutions as service providers potentially cuts off an important resource in the fight against HIV.

Much of the research on religion and HIV in Africa has examined religious variations in HIV risk and status. Evidence from Malawi (Trinitapoli and Regnerus 2006), South Africa (Garner 2000), Zimbabwe (Gregson et al. 1999), and Zambia (Agha et al. 2006) suggests that individuals who are members of more conservative religious denominations (i.e., Pentecostal and certain African Independent Churches) exhibit lower risk of HIV infection as compared to members of other religious faiths, perhaps due to their reduced likelihood of having extramarital partners. There is also limited evidence that Muslims in Africa display lower levels of HIV infection in comparison to other individuals (Gray 2004). Trinitapoli and Weinreb (2012) examine religious variations in HIV status, drawing on biomarker data from 3000 rural respondents in Malawi. Their results reveal few differences in HIV status across religious affiliations with the important exception that HIV is lower among New Mission Protestants (e.g., Church of Christ and Jehovah's Witness) than among members of other religious affiliations. Evidence from their study suggests that individuals with higher levels of religious involvement are less likely to be HIV positive, leading Trinitapoli and Weinreb (2012) to conclude that religious affiliation or identity matters much less than being highly involved within one's religious community.

In addition to studies examining religious variations in HIV risk and status, several studies have explored how religious congregations in Africa communicate information about HIV/AIDS to their congregants. A number of scholars have focused on religious opposition to condom use as a primary barrier to HIV prevention in SSA (Preston-Whyte 1999; Rankin et al. 2005; Epstein 2007). Yet evidence suggests that religious opposition to condom use varies considerably both across and within religious traditions. Similar to research conducted in the United States (Ellingson et al. 2001), findings from these studies suggest that many religious leaders understand the reality of nonmarital sex within their congregations; realizing that messages of sexual abstinence are not sufficient prevention efforts against HIV (Garner 2000; Trinitapoli and Weinreb 2012). Other evidence from a study of religious services in two districts of rural Malawi suggests that while condoms are often explicitly prohibited by church doctrine, some religious leaders encourage members who cannot abstain from sex to use a condom to avoid contracting HIV (Trinitapoli 2006).

20.6   Religion and the GLBT Community

The final substantive section of this chapter focuses on the connection between religion and the gay, lesbian, bisexual, and transgendered (GLBT) community. Scholars interested in this connection have tended to pursue two distinct lines of research. The first line of inquiry centers on religious variations in attitudes toward GLBT individuals among the U.S. public, focusing on issues such as the morality of homosexual relationships, civil liberties, and gay marriage. The second line of scholarship focuses on how religion impacts the lives of members of the GLBT community. Scholarship in this area focuses on

issues such as the level of involvement within religious organizations by gay individuals, the impact of religion on the identity of gay persons, and the connection between religion and mental health outcomes among GLBT individuals.

20.6.1   Attitudes Toward Gays and Lesbians

Several decades of scholarship have investigated the connection between religion and attitudes towards gays and lesbians. The liberalization of attitudes toward homosexuality in the United States over the past 30 years is well documented, with an accelerated rate of acceptance of GLBT rights in recent years. For example, between 2009 and 2014 the percent of U.S. adults who oppose gay marriage shifted from the majority (54 %) to a minority (39 %) (Pew Forum on Religion and Public Life 2014).

Oppositional attitudes towards gays and lesbians have long been associated with certain religious affiliations, beliefs and practices. Disapproval of same-sex marriage is increasingly concentrated among a few religious groups, namely evangelical Protestants, Black Protestants and other religious conservatives (Pew Forum on Religion and Public Life 2014; Public Religion Research Institute 2014). Conservative Protestants typically hold the least accepting attitudes towards: homosexuality (Gay et al. 1996; Hill et al. 2004; Bean and Martinez forthcoming), extending basic civil liberties to gays and lesbians (Petersen and Donnenwerth 1998; Burdette et al. 2005), and gay marriage (Sherkat et al. 2011; Olson et al. 2006). Conversely, members of Jewish and mainline Protestant groups are typically the most liberal, followed by Catholics. Although there is limited research on Muslims, Hindus, and Buddhists in the United States, evidence suggests that Muslims hold more disapproving views of homosexuality relative to those of other religious faiths (Adamczyk and Pitt 2009). Negative attitudes toward gays and lesbians among evangelical Protestants are explained in part by higher levels of church attendance, religious importance, beliefs in Biblical inerrancy (i.e., believing that the Bible is the literal word of God), and conservative political views, all of which are associated with oppositional attitudes towards gays and lesbians (Adamczyk and Pitt 2009; Whitehead 2010; Sherkat et al. 2011).

Beliefs in the doctrine of biblical literalism are directly connected to conservative Protestant opposition to homosexuality, as many conservative Protestants see the Bible as the ultimate source of authority, providing necessary and sufficient information about the conduct of human affairs and the answers to routine problems (Ellison et al. 1996). One of the most widely cited passages from the Old Testament is the account of Sodom in Genesis 19, involving the destruction of the city by God. This passage has been cited as evidence of the threat of sexual immorality, particularly homosexuality, although numerous biblical scholars have offered alternative interpretations (e.g., Boswell 1980; Helminiak 2000). Conservative Protestants more commonly cite New Testament passages as support of the harmful nature of homosexuality. Romans 1:26–27 is often quoted as evidence that homosexuality is both unnatural and perverse. In addition, 1st Corinthians 6:9–10 is often cited as supporting the idea that homosexuals will not be admitted to heaven unless they reform their behavior (Dobson 2000). Drawing on Biblical texts relating to appropriate relationships between husbands and wives (Ephesians 5:22–23, 1 Peter 3:1), or procreation (Genesis 1:27–28), evangelicals also advocate traditional views of marriage which stress sexual purity, gender complementarianism, and authoritative parenting (Regnerus 2007; Wilcox et al. 2004). As Bean and Martinez (forthcoming) note, same-sex unions violate the "biblical" family model because they do not draw on separate roles for men and women, namely the interdependence between male headship and female nurturance (Kenneavy 2012). Evangelicals are also more likely than members of other faiths to believe that gays and lesbians choose their orientation, rather than considering same-sex attraction an inborn trait (Whitehead 2010).

Despite long held opposition to same-sex relationships among evangelicals in the United Sates, there is some evidence of increasing tolerance toward the GLBT community among religious conservatives. Content analysis of popular evangelical literature (Thomas and Olson 2012), as well as public statements from powerful evangelical leaders like Pastor Rick Warren and Richard Cizik (former spokesperson for the National Association of Evangelicals), suggest that conservative Protestant leadership is liberalizing on GLBT rights. Bean and Martinez (forthcoming) argue that increasing ambivalence toward gays and lesbians extends to evangelical laity, as heterosexual evangelicals have become more aware of fellow Christians who "struggle" with same-sex attraction. Evangelicals draw on these personal experiences to form their attitudes towards the GLBT community. Yet competing scripts about homosexuality create practical dilemmas about how to "do" religion in particular social settings. Evidence suggests that younger evangelicals are more accepting of gay rights than previous cohorts, despite the increased attention to preserving "traditional" marriage among some religious conservatives (Farrell 2011; Putnam and Campbell 2012).

20.6.2 Religion in the Lives of Gays and Lesbians

Although there is a dearth of research focusing on levels of religious involvement among sexual minorities, evidence suggests that religion plays an important role in the lives many gays and lesbians in the United States (Cutts and Parks 2009; Sherkat, 2002; Rostosky et al. 2008). Drawing on nationally representative data, Sherkat (2002) finds that while sexual minorities are more likely to become apostates than female heterosexuals, they are no more likely to do so than heterosexual men. Additional findings from this study suggest that gay men are significantly more religiously active than male heterosexuals and other sexual minorities, displaying similar levels of religious activity to female heterosexuals. Other work confirms relatively high levels of religious involvement, particularly private religious behaviors, among gays and lesbians (Rostosky et al. 2008; Cutts and Parks 2009).

A much larger body of research, almost exclusively qualitative in nature, has investigated the conflict between religious and queer identities. Given the level of diversely among religious faiths in attitudes towards the GBLT community, it is no surprise that the potential clash between sexual and religious identity varies greatly by religious tradition. Research suggests that identifying as gay or lesbian is most difficult for those raised in conservative religious environments, such as evangelical Protestant churches (Mahaffy 1996). The conflict between religious identity and GLBT identity also appears to be greater among those with high levels of religious salience (Kubicek et al. 2009). Direct experiences with homophobia found in conservative Protestant churches have been associated with a number of harmful outcomes, including fear of eternal damnation, depression, low self-esteem, and feelings of worthlessness (Barton 2010, 2012).

Research focusing on the African American church paints a more nuanced picture of the relationship between religion and homosexual identity. Scholars note that homosexuality is generally rejected in Black churches, with most places of worship advocating a "don't ask, don't tell" approach to sexuality (Pitt 2010; Harris 2010). However, Fullilove and Fullilove (1999) note that gay men are given a special status within many churches because "they provide the creative energy necessary to the African American religious experience. Just as church women are responsible for nurturing and feeding the congregation, gays in the church are responsible for creating the music and other emotional moments that bring worshippers closer to God." In his research focusing on religiously active gay Black men, Pitt (2010) shows that although most respondents have accepted both their gay and Christian identities, the majority vacillate on whether God approves of their sexual orientation, highlighting the underlying incompatibility between conservative religious doctrine and homosexuality.

Finally, several studies have focused on the experiences of gays and lesbians within gay-affirming churches, and the potential benefits of religious involvement for GLBT identity. Yip (2002) argues that religion provides a framework for practicing sexual inclusion, while scholars like Melissa Wilcox (2003) note that gays and lesbians are creating more inclusive Christian churches. In their research on the Metropolitan Community Church, Rodriguez and Ouellette (2000) find that higher levels of religious involvement correlate with successful integration of religious and sexual identities, arguing that the church plays a key role in identity integration. However, other work suggests that even gay-affirming churches may be limited in their inclusiveness. In her study of two gay affirming Protestant churches, McQueeney (2009) outlines a number of strategies that congregates use to accommodate-but not assimilate-to heteronormative conceptions of the "good Christian." Strategies included minimizing one's sexual identity and normalizing one's sexuality by enacting Christian principles of monogamy, manhood, and motherhood. As a result, these churches create a space for gay and lesbian Christians to view their sexuality as natural, normal, and moral; yet these churches tend to be less welcoming to those individuals who do not conform to the notions of a "good Christian," such as trangendered people and gender/sexual nonconformists.

20.7 Research Limitations and Future Directions

The research reviewed in this chapter is characterized by several limitations. In this section, we review these shortcomings. We also several highlight important directions for future research.

20.7.1 Measurement Issues

Although religion is a multidimensional phenomenon (Idler et al. 2003), most studies employ only one or two indicators of religious involvement (typically religious affiliation, church attendance, or religious salience). Single items tend to have lower validity and reliability than multi-item indicators. Scholars have also questioned the usefulness of traditional measures of religious involvement, especially denominational affiliation

(Alwin et al. 2006). Sociologists of religion have encouraged researchers to consider alternative forms of religious involvement, such as the use of online media and more individualized forms of religious expression, to adequately capture the current religious landscape (Roberts and Yamane 2011). Incorporating a broader array of measures of religion may deepen our understanding of the connections among religion, sexuality, and sexual health. Future research should also devote more attention to religious context (e.g., county-level religious climate and school-level religious context), rather than solely concentrating on individual-level religiosity.

20.7.2   Sexuality and Sexual Health Outcomes

Although previous research has examined a wide range of sexual health outcomes, this body of literature is heavily focused on adolescent sexual activity, especially the transition to first sex. Future research should consider a broader range of sexual health outcomes (e.g., contraceptive decision making, sexually transmitted infections, sexual satisfaction, and sexting) at different stages of the life course. With regard to sexuality, research should continue to consider how religious involvement impacts mental and physical health outcomes among GBLT individuals.

20.7.3   Indirect Effects

Previous research is also limited by theoretical models that overemphasize the direct effects of religion on sexuality and sexual health outcomes. While many studies speculate as to why religious involvement should impact sexuality and sexual health, few studies offer empirical support for these explanations. It is important for future research to examine understudied mechanisms linking religion and sexual health, including social networks, specific religious doctrines, psychological resources, and access to sexual health information and services. It is important to begin by establishing individual mechanisms. Then re-

searchers should consider testing more elaborate theoretical models with complex casual chains.

20.7.4   Subgroup Variations

It is often unclear whether the association between religious involvement and sexual health varies according to theoretically relevant subgroups including gender, race, ethnicity, socioeconomic status, and sexuality. Although some research has explored Black-White differences in the impact of religion on sexual health, there is a dearth of scholarship focused on how religion may impact sexuality or sexual health among Latinos and Asians. Research on how religion impacts the sexual activity of GLBT youths is also virtually non-existent. Furthermore, scholars should consider how the impact of religion on sexual health varies according to socioeconomic indicators like level of education. One question is whether education in some way counteracts the effects of religious involvement.

20.7.5   Alternative Explanations: Personality Traits and Social Desirability

Some scholars have suggested that the protective effects of religious involvement on sexual health outcomes may be explained by certain personality traits that select individuals into religious institutions. The most convincing arguments focus on traits like risk aversion, avoidance of thrill seeking, and self-control. Some evidence suggests that individuals with these characteristics are more likely to display both higher levels of religiosity and healthier lifestyles (Regnerus and Smith 2005). Because studies of religion and sexual health do not adjust for personality, there is little evidence for personality selection. However, it is reasonable to suggest that such personality traits could select certain individuals into risky sexual activities and out of religious institutions. Thus personality selection may account for at least some of the protective effects of religious involvement on certain sexual health outcomes.

Because the majority of research on religion, sexuality, and sexual health necessarily relies on self-reports of sexual behavior, there is some skepticism concerning the reliability of these data. To this point, however, there is little evidence to suggest any consistent association between religiosity and the tendency to give biased, socially desirable responses. At least one study of this issue among young adults argues strongly against such a view (Regnerus and Smith 2005). Nevertheless, it would be helpful for future studies to rule out obvious sources of response bias in work on religion and sexual health.

20.8 Conclusion

In this chapter, we provide an overview and critical examination of published research concerning the impact of religious involvement on the outcomes of sexuality and sexual health across the life course. We take a broad approach, focusing on a variety of important topics, including sexual behavior, sexual health education, abortion attitudes and behavior, HIV/AIDS, attitudes toward gays and lesbians, and the lived experiences of sexual minorities. In the future, researchers should (1) employ more comprehensive measures of religious involvement, (2) investigate understudied outcomes related to sexuality and sexual health, (3) explore mechanisms linking religion, sexuality, and sexual health, (4) establish subgroup variations in the impact of religious involvement, and (5) formally test alternative explanations like personality selection and social desirability. Research along these lines would certainly contribute to a more comprehensive understanding of religious variations in sexuality and sexual health across the life course.

References

Adamczyk, A. (2008). The effects of religious contextual norms, structural constraints, and personal religiosity on abortion decisions. *Social Science Research, 37*(2), 657–672.

Adamczyk, A. (2009a). Socialization and selection in the link between friends' religiosity and the transition to sexual intercourse. *Sociology of Religion, 70*(1), 5–27.

Adamczyk, A. (2009b). Understanding the effects of personal and school religiosity on the decision to abort a premarital pregnancy. *Journal of Health & Social Behavior, 50*(2), 180–195.

Adamczyk, A., & Felson, J. (2006). Friends' religiosity and first sex. *Social Science Research, 35*(4), 924–947.

Adamczyk, A., & Felson, J. (2008). Fetal positions: Unraveling the influence of religion on premarital pregnancy resolution. *Social Science Quarterly, 89*(1), 17–38.

Adamczyk, A., & Hayes, B. E. (2012). Religion and sexual behaviors: Understanding the influence of Islamic cultures and religious affiliation for explaining sex outside of marriage. *American Sociological Review, 77*(5), 723–746.

Adamczyk, A., & Pitt, C. (2009). Shaping attitudes about homosexuality: The role of religion and cultural context. *Social Science Research, 38*(2), 338–351.

Addai, I. (2000). Religious affiliation and sexual initiation among Ghanaian women. *Review of Religious Research, 41*, 328–343.

Agate, L. L., Cato-Watson, D., Mullins, J. M., Scott, G. S., Rolle, V., Markland, M., & Roach, D. L. (2005). Churches United to Stop HIV (CUSH): a faith-based HIV prevention initiative. *Journal of the National Medical Association, 97*(Suppl. 7), 60.

Agha, S. (2009). Changes in the timing of sexual initiation among young Muslim and Christian women in Nigeria. *Archives of Sexual Behavior, 38*(6), 899–908.

Agha, S., Hutchinson, P., & Kusanthan, T. (2006). The effects of religious affiliation on sexual initiation and condom use in Zambia. *Journal of Adolescent Health, 38*(5), 550–555.

Alwin, D. F., Felson, J. L., Walker, E. T., & Tufiş, P. A. (2006). Measuring religious identities in surveys. *Public Opinion Quarterly, 70*(4), 530–564.

Arsneault, S. (2001). Values and virtue: The politics of abstinence-only sex education. *The American Review of Public Administration, 31*(4), 436–454.

Atkins, D. C., & Kessel, D. E. (2008). Religiousness and infidelity: Attendance, but not faith and prayer, predict marital fidelity. *Journal of Marriage & Family, 70*(2), 407–418.

Barkan, S. E. (2006). Religiosity and premarital sex in adulthood. *Journal for the Scientific Study of Religion, 45*(3), 407–417.

Barrick, A. (2010). Most Evangelical leaders OK with birth control. http://www.christianpost.com/news/most-evangelical-leaders-okwith-birth-control-45493/. Accessed 3 June 2014.

Bartkowski, J. P., Ramos-Wada, A. I., Ellison, C. G., & Acevedo, G. A. (2012). Faith, race-ethnicity, and public policy preferences: Religious schemas and abortion attitudes among U.S. Latinos. *Journal for the Scientific Study of Religion, 51*(2), 343–358.

Barton, B. (2010). "Abomination"—life as a bible belt gay. *Journal of Homosexuality, 57*(4), 465–484.

Barton, B. (2012). *Pray the gay away: The extraordinary lives of Bible Belt Gays*. New York: New York University Press.

Bean, L., & Martinez, B. C. (forthcoming). Evangelical ambivalence toward gays and lesbians. *Sociology of Religion*.

Bearman, P. S., & Brückner, H. (2001). Promising the future: Virginity pledges and first intercourse. *American Journal of Sociology, 106*(4), 859–912.

Beck, S. H., Cole, B. S., & Hammond, J. A. (1991). Religious heritage and premarital sex: Evidence from a national sample of young adults. *Journal for the Scientific Study of Religion, 30*(2), 173–180.

Biggar, H., Forehand, R., Devine, D., Brody, G., Armistead, L., Morse, E., & Simon, P. (1999). Women who are HIV infected: The role of religious activity in psychosocial adjustment. *Aids Care, 11*(2), 195–199.

Bleakley, A., Hennessy, M., & Fishbein, M. (2006). Public opinion on sex education in US schools. *Archives Of Pediatrics & Adolescent Medicine, 160*(11), 1151–1156.

Bluthenthal, R. N., Palar, K., Mendel, P., Kanouse, D. E., Corbin, D. E., & Pitkin Derose, P. (2012). Attitudes and beliefs related to HIV/AIDS in urban religious congregations: Barriers and opportunities for HIV-related interventions. *Social Science & Medicine, 74*(10), 1520–1527.

Boonstra, H. (2010). Sex education: another big step forward—and a step back. *The Guttmacher Policy Review, 13*, 27–28.

Boswell, J. (1980). *Christianity, social tolerance, and homosexuality*. Chicago: University of Chicago Press.

Brewster, K. L., Cooksey, E. C., Gulkey, D. K., & Rindfuss, R. R. (1998). The changing impact of religion on the sexual and contraceptive behavior of adolescent women in the United States. *Journal of Marriage & Family, 60*(2), 493–504.

Brimeyer, T. M., & Smith, W. L. (2012). Religion, race, social class, and gender Differences in dating and hooking up among college students. *Sociological Spectrum, 32*(5), 462–473.

Brückner, H., & Bearman, P. (2005). After the promise: The STD consequences of adolescent virginity pledges. *Journal of Adolescent Health, 36*(4), 271–278.

Burdette, A. M., & Hill, T. D. (2009). Religious involvement and transitions into adolescent sexual activities. *Sociology of Religion, 70*(1), 28–48.

Burdette, A. M., Ellison, C. G., & Hill, T. D. (2005). Conservative Protestantism and tolerance toward homosexuals: An examination of potential mechanisms. *Sociological Inquiry, 75*, 177–196.

Burdette, A. M., Ellison, C. G., Sherkat, D. E., & Gore, K. A. (2007). Are there religious variations in marital infidelity? *Journal of Family Issues, 28*, 1553–1581.

Burdette, A. M., Ellison, C. G., Hill, T. D., & Glenn, N. D. (2009). "Hooking up" at college: Does religion make a difference? *Journal for the Scientific Study of Religion, 48*(3), 535–551.

Burdette, A. M., Haynes, S. H., Hill, T. D., & Bartkowski, J. P. (2014.) Religious variations in perceived infertility and inconsistent contraceptive use among unmarried young adults in the United States. *Journal of Adolescent Health, 54*(6), 704–709.

Carpenter, L. M. (2011). Like a virgin...again?: Secondary virginity as an ongoing gendered social construction. *Sexuality & Culture, 15*(2), 115–140.

Cochran, J. K., & Beeghley, L. (1991). The influence of religion on attitudes toward nonmarital sexuality: A preliminary assessment of reference group theory. *Journal for the Scientific Study of Religion, 30*(1), 45–62.

Cook, E. A., Jelen, T. G., & Wilcox, C. (1992). *Between two absolutes: Public opinion and the politics of abortion*. Boulder: Westview.

Cooksey, E. C., Rindfuss, R. R., & Guilkey, D. K. (1996). The initiation of adolescent sexual and contraceptive behavior during changing times. *Journal of Health & Social Behavior, 37*(1), 59–74.

Cotton, S., Puchalski, C. M., Sherman, S. N., Mrus, J. M., Peterman, A. H., Feinberg, J., Pargament, K. I., Justice, A. C., Leonard, A. C., & Tsevat, J. (2006). Spirituality and religion in patients with HIV/AIDS. *Journal Of General Internal Medicine, 21*(S5), S5–S13.

Cutts, R. N., & Parks, C. W. (2009). Religious involvement among black men self-labeling as gay. *Journal of Gay & Lesbian Social Services, 21*(2–3), 232–246.

D'Antonio, W. V., Davidson, J. D., Hoge, D. R., & Gautier, M. L. (2007). *American Catholics today: New realities of their faith and their church*. Lanham: Rowman and Littlefield Publishers.

Darnell, A., & Sherkat, D. E. (1997). The impact of Protestant fundamentalism on educational attainment. *American Sociological Review, 62*, 306–315.

Davidson, J. L., Moore, N. B., & Ullstrup, K. M. (2004). Religiosity and sexual responsibility: Relationships of choice. *American Journal of Health Behavior, 28*(4), 335–346.

Davidson, L. A., Pettis, C. T., Joiner, A. J., Cook, D. M., & Klugman, C. M. (2010). Religion and conscientious objection: A survey of pharmacists' willingness to medications. *Social Science & Medicine, 71*(1),161–165.

Derose, K. P., Mendel, P. J., Palar, K., Kanouse, D. E., Bluthenthal, R. N., Castaneda, L. W., Corbin, D. E., Domínguez, B. X., Hawes-Dawson, J., & Mata, M. A. (2011). Religious congregations' involvement in HIV: A case study approach. *AIDS and Behavior, 15*(6),1220–1232.

De Visser, R. O., Smith, A. M. A., Richters, J., & Rissel, C. E. (2007). Associations between religiosity and sexuality in a representative sample of Australian adults. *Archives of sexual behavior, 36*(1), 33–46.

Doan, A. E., & McFarlane, D. R. (2012). Saying no to abstinence-only education: An analysis of state decision-making. *Publius: The Journal of Federalism, 42*(4),613–635.

Dobson, J. (2000). *Complete marriage and family home reference guide*. Wheaton: Tyndale House Publishers.

Edwards, L. M., Haglund, K., Fehring, R. J., & Pruszynski, J. (2011). Religiosity and sexual risk behaviors among Latina adolescents: Trends from 1995 to 2008. *Journal of Women's Health, 20*(6), 871–877.

Ellingson, S., Tebbe, N., Van Haitsma, M., & Laumann, E. O. (2001). Religion and the politics of sexuality. *Journal of Contemporary Ethnography, 30*, 3–55.

Ellison, C. G., Bartkowski, J. P., & Segal, M. L. (1996). Conservative Protestantism and the parental use of corporal punishment. *Social Forces, 74*, 1003–1028.

Ellison, C. G., Echevarría, S., & Smith, B. (2005). Religion and abortion attitudes among U.S. Hispanics: Findings from the 1990 Latino National Political Survey. *Social Science Quarterly (Wiley-Blackwell), 86*(1), 192–208.

Ellison, C. G., Wolfinger, N. H., & Ramos-Wada, A. I. (2013). Attitudes toward marriage, divorce, cohabitation, and casual sex among working-age Latinos does religion matter? *Journal of Family Issues, 34*(3), 295–322.

Emerson, M. O. (1996). Through tinted glasses: Religion, worldviews, and abortion attitudes. *Journal for the Scientific Study of Religion, 35*(1), 41.

England, P., Fitzgibbons Shafer, E., & Fogarty, A. C. K. (2007). Hooking up and forming romantic relationships on today's college campuses. In M. S. Kimmel & A. Aronson (Eds.), *The gendered society reader*. New York: Oxford University Press.

Epstein, H. (2007). *The invisible cure: Africa, the West, and the fight against AIDS*. New York: Macmillan.

Farrell, J. (2011). The young and the restless? The liberalization of young evangelicals. *Journal for the Scientific Study of Religion, 50*(3), 517–532.

Finer, L. B., & Henshaw, S. K. (2006). Disparities in rates of unintended pregnancy in the United States, 1994 and 2001. *Perspectives on Sexual and Reproductive Health, 38*(2), 90–96.

Finer, L. B., & Philbin, J. M. (forthcoming). Trends in ages at key reproductive transitions in the United States, 1951–2010. *Women's Health Issues*.

Finke, R., & Adamczyk, A. (2008). Explaining morality: Using international data to reestablish the macro/micro link. *Sociological Quarterly, 49*(4), 617–652.

Freitas, D. (2008). *Sex and the soul: Juggling sexuality, spirituality, romance, and religion on America's college campuses*. New York: Oxford University Press.

Frenk, S. M., & Trinitapoli, J. (2013). US Congregations' provision of programs or activities for people living with HIV/AIDS. *AIDS and Behavior, 17*(5), 1829–1838.

Fullilove, M. T., & Fullilove, R. E. (1999). Stigma as an obstacle to AIDS action: The case of the African American community. *American Behavioral Scientist, 42*(7), 1117–1129.

Gallup Poll. (2013). Graph illustration of results from the 2012 Gallup Poll on religion. http://www.gallup.com/poll/1690/Religion.aspx. Accessed 15 Dec 2013.

Galvan, F. H., Collins, R. L., Kanouse, D. E., Pantoja, P., & Golinelli, D. (2007). Religiosity, denominational affiliation, and sexual behaviors among people with HIV in the United States. *Journal of Sex Research, 44*(1), 49–58.

Garner, R. C. (2000). Safe sects? Dynamic religion and AIDS in South Africa. *The Journal of Modern African Studies, 38*(1), 41–69.

Gay, D. A., Ellison, C. G., & Powers, D. A. (1996). In search of denominational subcultures: Religious affiliation and "pro-family" issues revisited. *Review of Religious Research, 38*(1), 3–17.

Gillum, R. F., & Holt, C. L. (2010). Associations between religious involvement and behavioral risk factors for HIV/AIDS in American women and men in a national health survey. *Annals of Behavioral Medicine, 40*(3), 284–293.

Glenn, N., & Marquardt, E. (2001). *Hooking up, hanging out, and hoping for Mr. Right: College women on dating and mating today*. New York: Council on Families.

Gray, P. B. (2004). HIV and Islam: Is HIV prevalence lower among Muslims? *Social Science & Medicine, 58*(9), 1751–1756.

Greeley, A. M. (1990). *The Catholic myth: The behavior and beliefs of American Catholics*. New York: Touchstone.

Gregson, S., Zhuwau, T., Anderson, R. M., & Chandiwana, S. K. (1999). Apostles and Zionists: The influence of religion on demographic change in rural Zimbabwe. *Population Studies, 53*(2), 179–193.

Haley, K. C., Koenig, H. G., & Bruchett, B. M. (2001). Relationship between private religious activity and physical functioning in older adults. *Journal of Religion & Health, 40*(2), 305–312.

Hall, K. S., Moreau, C., & Trussell, J. (2012). Lower use of sexual and reproductive health services among women with frequent religious participation, regardless of sexual experience. *Journal of Women's Health, 21*(7), 739–747.

Harris, A. C. (2010). Sex, stigma, and the Holy Ghost: The Black church and the construction of AIDS in New York City. *Journal of African American Studies, 14*(1), 21–43.

Hatzenbuehler, M. L., Pachankis, J. E., & Wolff, J. (2012). Religious climate and health risk behaviors in sexual minority youths: A population-based study. *American Journal of Public Health, 102*(4), 657–663.

Helminiak, D. A. (2000). *What the Bible really says about homosexuality*. New Mexico: Alamo Square.

Henshaw, S. K., & Kost, K. (1996). Abortion patients in 1994–1995: Characteristics and contraceptive use. *Family Planning Perspectives, 28*, 140–147.

Henshaw, S. K., & Silverman, J. (1987). The characteristics and prior contraceptive use of US abortion patients. *Family Planning Perspectives, 20*(4), 158–168.

Hertel, B. R., & Hughes, M. (1987). Religious affiliation, attendance, and support for "pro-family" issues in the United States. *Social Forces, 37*, 59–70.

Hickman, E. E., Glass, C. R., Arnkoff, D. B., & Fallot, R. D. (2013). Religious coping, stigma, and psychological functioning among HIV-positive African American women. *Mental Health, Religion & Culture, 16*(8), 832–851.

Hill, T. D., Moulton, B. E., & Burdette, A. M. (2004). Conservative protestantism and attitudes toward homosexuality: Does political orientation mediate this relationship? *Sociological Focus, 37*, 59–70.

Hoffmann, J. P., & Johnson, S. M. (2005). Attitudes toward abortion among religious traditions in the United States: Change or continuity? *Sociology of Religion, 66*(2), 161–182.

Hoffmann, J. P., & Miller, A. S. (1997). Social and political attitudes among religious groups: Convergence and divergence over time. *Journal for the Scientific Study of Religion, 36*, 52–70.

Hoffmann, J. P., & Miller, A. S. (1998). Denominational influences on socially divisive issues: Polarization or continuity? *Journal for the Scientific Study of Religion, 37*(3), 528–546.

Hull, S. J., Hennessy, M., Bleakley, A., Fishbein, M., & Jordan, A. (2011). Identifying the causal pathways from religiosity to delayed adolescent sexual behavior. *Journal of Sex Research, 48*(6), 543–553.

Idler, E. L., Musick, M. A., Ellison, C. G., George, L. K., Krause, N., Ory, M. G., Pargament, K. I., Powell, L. H., Underwood, L. G., & Williams, D. R. (2003). Measuring multiple dimensions of religion and spirituality for health research. *Research on Aging, 25*(4), 327.

Ironson, G., Solomon, G. F., Balbin, E. G., O'Cleirigh, C., George, A., Kumar, M., Larson, D., & Woods, T. E. (2002). The Ironson-woods spirituality/religiousness index is associated with long survival, health behaviors, less distress, and low cortisol in people with HIV/AIDS. *Annals of Behavioral Medicine, 24*(1), 34–48.

Ironson, G., Stuetzle, R., Ironson, D., Balbin, E., Kremer, H., George, A., Schneiderman, N., & Fletcher, M. A. (2011). View of God as benevolent and forgiving or punishing and judgmental predicts HIV disease progression. *Journal of behavioral medicine, 34*(6), 414–425.

Jelen, T. G., & Wilcox, C. (2003). Causes and consequences of public attitudes toward abortion: A review and research agenda. *Political Research Quarterly, 56*(4), 489–500.

Jenkins, R. A. (1995). Religion and HIV: Implications for research and intervention. *Journal of Social Issues, 51*(2), 131–144.

Jones, R. K., & Dreweke, J. (2011). *Countering conventional wisdom: New evidence on religion and contraceptive use*. New York: Guttmacher Institute.

Jones, R. K., Darroch, J. E., & Singh, S. (2005). Religious differentials in the sexual and reproductive behaviors of young women in the United States. *Journal of Adolescent Health, 36*(4), 279–288.

Kenneavy, K. (2012). Support for homosexuals' civil liberties: The influence of familial gender role attitudes across religious denominations. *Social Forces, 90*, 1347–1375.

Kramer, M., & Dunlop, A. (2012). Inter-state variation in human papilloma virus vaccine coverage among adolescent girls in the 50 US States, 2007. *Maternal & Child Health Journal, 16*, 102–110.

Kramer, M. R., Hogue, C. J. R., & Gaydos, L. M. D. (2007). Noncontracepting behavior in women at risk for unintended pregnancy: What's religion got to do with it? *Annals of Epidemiology, 17*(5), 327–334.

Kubicek, K., McDavitt, B., Carpineto, J., Weiss, G., Iverson, E., & Kipke, M. D. (2009). "God made me gay for a reason": Young men who have sex with men's resiliency in resolving internalized homophobia from religious sources. *Journal of Adolescent Research, 24*(5), 601–633.

Landor, A., Simons, L. G., Simons, R. L., Brody, G. H., & Gibbons, F. X. (2011). The role of religiosity in the relationship between parents, peers, and adolescent risky sexual behavior. *Journal of Youth and Adolescence, 40*(3), 296–309.

Landry, D. J., Darroch, J. E., Singh, S., Higgins, J. (2003). Factors associated with the content of sex education in U.S. public secondary schools. *Perspectives on Sexual and Reproductive Health, 35*(6), 261–269.

Lehrer, E. L. (1999). Religion as a determinant of educational attainment: An economic perspective. *Social Science Research, 28*(4), 358–379.

Lincoln, E. C., & Mamiya, L. (1990). *The black church in the African American experience* Durham: Duke University Press.

Lindley, L. L., Coleman, J. D., Gaddist, B. W., & White, J. (2010). Informing faith-based HIV/AIDS interventions: HIV-related knowledge and stigmatizing attitudes at project FAITH churches in south Carolina. *Public Health Reports, 125*(Suppl. 1), 12.

Luker, K. (1985). *Abortion and the politics of motherhood*. Berkeley: University of California Press.

Luker, K. (2006). *When sex goes to school*. New York: W.W. Norton & Company.

Mahaffy, K. A. (1996). Cognitive dissonance and its resolution: A study of lesbian Christians. *Journal for the Scientific Study of Religion, 35*(4), 392.

Manlove, J., Ryan, S., & Franzetta, K. (2003). Patterns of contraceptive use within teenagers' first sexual relationships. *Perspectives on Sexual and Reproductive Health, 35*(6), 246–255.

Manlove, J., Terry-Humen, E., Ikramullah, E. N., & Moore, K. A. (2006). The role of parent religiosity in teens' transitions to sex and contraception. *Journal of Adolescent Health, 39*(4), 578–587.

Martinez G., Copen, C. E., & Abma, J. C. (2011). Teenagers in the United States: Sexual activity, contraceptive use, and childbearing, 2006–2010 National Survey of Family Growth. National Center for Health Statistics. *Vital Health Statistics, 23*(31), 1–35.

McFarland, M. J., Uecker, J. E., & Regnerus, M. D. (2011). The role of religion in shaping sexual frequency and satisfaction: Evidence from married and unmarried older adults. *Journal of Sex Research, 48*(2/3), 297–308.

McKeegan, M. (1992). *Abortion politics: Mutiny in the ranks of the right*. New York: The Free Press.

McQueeney, K. (2009). "We are God's children, y'all:" Race, gender, and sexuality in lesbian- and gay-affirming congregations. *Social Problems, 56*(1), 151–173.

Meier, A. M. (2003). Adolescents' transition to first intercourse, religiosity, and attitudes about sex. *Social Forces, 81*(3), 1031–1052.

Miller, L., & Gur, M. (2002). Religiousness and sexual responsibility in adolescent girls. *Journal of Adolescent Health, 31*(5), 401–406.

Ogland, C. P., & Bartkowski, J. P. (2014). Biblical literalism and sexual morality in comparative perspective: Testing the transposability of a conservative religious schema. *Sociology of Religion, 75*(1), 3–24.

Olson, L. R., Cadge, W., & Harrison, J. T. (2006). Religion and public opinion about same-sex marriage. *Social Science Quarterly, 87*(2), 340–360.

Pargament, K. I., McCarthy, S., Shah, P., Ano, G., Tarakeshwar, N., Wachholtz, A., Sirrine, N., Vasconcelles, E., Murray-Swank, N., & Locher, A. (2004). Religion and HIV: A review of the literature and clinical implications. *Southern Medical Journal, 97*(12), 1201–1209.

Petersen, L. R., & Donnenwerth, G. V. (1997). Secularization and the influence of religion on beliefs about premarital sex. *Social Forces, 75*(3), 1071–1088.

Petersen, L. R., & Donnenwerth, G. V. (1998). Religion and declining support for traditional beliefs about gender roles and homosexual rights. *Sociology of Religion, 59*(4), 353–371.

Pew Forum on Religion and Public Life. (2008). U.S. Religious Landscape Survey. http://religions.pewforum.org/pdf/report-religious-landscape-study-full.pdf. Accessed 27 May 2014.

Pew Forum on Religion and Public Life. (2010).Tolerance and tension: Islam and Christianity in Sub-Saharan Africa. http://www.pewforum.org/files/2010/04/sub-saharan-africa-full-report.pdf. Accessed 19 July 2014

Pew Forum on Religion and Public Life. (2014). "March for Marriage" rally reflects steadfast opposition to gay marriage among evangelical Christians. http://www.pewresearch.org/fact-tank/2014/06/19/march-for-marriage-rally-reflects-steadfast-opposition-to-gay-marriage-among-evangelical-christians/. Accessed 19 June 2014.

Pitt, R. N. (2010). "Still looking for my Jonathan:" Gay black men's management of religious and sexual identity conflicts. *Journal of Homosexuality, 57*(1), 39–53.

Preston-Whyte, E. (1999). Reproductive health and the condom dilemma: Identifying situational barriers to HIV protection in South Africa. In J. C. Caldwell (Ed.), *Resistance to behavioral change to reduce HIV/ AIDS infection in predominantly heterosexual epidemics in third world countries* (pp. 139–155). Canberra: Health Transition Center.

Public Religion Research Institute, LGBT Issues & Trends Survey. (2014). http://publicreligion.org/research/2014/02/2014-lgbt-survey/. Accessed 19 June 2014.

Putnam, R. D., & Campbell, D. E. (2012). *American grace: How religion divides and unites us*. New York: Simon and Schuster.

Rankin, S. H., Lindgren, T., Rankin, W. W., & Ng'oma, J. (2005). Donkey work: Women, religion, and HIV/ AIDS in Malawi. *Health Care for Women International, 26*(1), 4–16.

Raymond, M., Bogdanovich, L., Brahmi, D., Cardinal, L. J., Leonard Fager, G., Frattarelli, L. C., Hecker, G., Jarpe, E. A., Viera, A., & Kantor, L. M. (2008). State refusal of federal funding for abstinence-only programs. *Sexuality Research & Social Policy, 5*(3), 44–55.

Regnerus, M. D. (2005). Talking about sex: Religion and patterns of parent-child communication about sex and contraception. *Sociological Quarterly, 46*(1), 79–105.

Regnerus, M. D. (2007). *Forbidden fruit: sex and religion in the lives of American teenagers*. New York: Oxford University Press.

Regnerus, M. D., & Smith, C. (2005). Selection effects in studies of religious influence. *Review of Religious Research, 47*(1), 23–50.

Regnerus, M. D., & Uecker, J. E. (2007). Religious influences on sensitive self-reported behaviors: The product of social desirability, deceit, or embarrassment? *Sociology of Religion, 68*(2), 145–163.

Roberts, K. A, & Yamane, D. (2011). *Religion in sociological perspective*. Thousand Oaks: Sage Publications.

Rodriguez, E. M., & Ouellette, S. C. (2000). Gay and lesbian Christians: Homosexual and religious identity integration in the members and participants of a gay-positive church. *Journal for the Scientific Study of Religion, 39*(3), 333.

Rohrbaugh, J., & Jessor, R. (1975). Religiosity in youth: A personal control against deviant behavior. *Journal of Personality, 43*, 136–155.

Rose, S. (2005). Going too far? Sex, sin and social policy. *Social Forces, 84*(2), 1207–1232.

Rosenbaum, J. E. (2009). Patient teenagers? A comparison of the sexual behavior of virginity pledgers and matched nonpledgers. *Pediatrics, 123*(1), e110–e120.

Rosenberg, J. (2011). Modern contraceptives are supported by almost all US obstetrician-gynecologists. *Perspectives on Sexual and Reproductive Health, 43*(2), 131–132.

Rostosky, S. S., Regnerus, M. D., & Wright, M. L. C. (2003). Coital debut: The role of religiosity and sex attitudes in the Add Health Survey. *Journal of Sex Research, 40*, 358–367.

Rostosky, S. S., Wilcox, B. L., Wright, M. L. C., & Randall, B. A. (2004). The impact of religiosity on adolescent sexual behavior: A review of the evidence. *Journal of Adolescent Research, 19*(6), 677–697.

Rostosky, S. S., Otis, M. D., Riggle, E. D., Kelly, S., & Brodnicki, C. (2008). An exploratory study of religiosity and same-sex couple relationships. *Journal of GLBT Family Studies, 4*(1), 17–36.

Santelli, J., Ott, M. A., Lyon, M., Rogers, J., Summers, D., & Schleifer, R. (2006). Abstinence and abstinence-only education: A review of US policies and programs. *Journal of Adolescent Health, 38*(1), 72–81.

Shaw, S. A., & El-Bassel, N. (2014). The Influence of Religion on Sexual HIV Risk. *AIDS and Behavior, 18*(8), 1569–1594.

Sherkat, D. E. (2002). Sexuality and religious commitment in the United States: An empirical examination. *Journal for the Scientific Study of Religion, 41*(2), 313–323.

Sherkat, D. E., Powell-Williams, M., Maddox, G., & Mattias de Vries, K. (2011). Religion, politics, and support for same-sex marriage in the United States, 1988–2008. *Social Science Research, 40*(1), 167–180.

SIECUS (Sexuality Information and Education Council of the United States). (2012). State profiles: A portrait of sexuality education and abstinence-only-until-marriage programs in the states (Fiscal Year 2012 Edition). http://www.siecus.org/document/docWindow.cfm?fuseaction=document.viewDocument&documentid=205&documentFormatId=264. Accessed 6 June 2014.

Siegel, K., & Schrimshaw, E. W. (2002). The perceived benefits of religious and spiritual coping among older adults living with HIV/AIDS. *Journal for the Scientific Study of Religion, 41*(1), 91–102.

Simoni, J. M., & Ortiz, M. Z. (2003). Mediational models of spirituality and depressive symptomatology among HIV-positive Puerto Rican women. *Cultural Diversity and Ethnic Minority Psychology, 9*(1), 3.

Smith, C. (2003a). Religious participation and network closure among American adolescents. *Journal for the Scientific Study of Religion, 42*, 259–267.

Smith, C. (2003b). Theorizing religious effects Among American adolescents. *Journal for the Scientific Study of Religion, 42*, 17–30.

Smith, B. G., & Johnson, B. (2010). The liberalization of young Evangelicals: A research note. *Journal for the Scientific Study of Religion, 49*(2), 351–360.

Thomas, J. N., & Olson, D. V. (2012). Evangelical elites' changing responses to homosexuality 1960–2009. *Sociology of Religion, 73*, 239–272.

Thornton, A., & Camburn, D. (1989). Religious participation and adolescent sexual behavior and attitudes. *Journal of Marriage and Family, 51*(3), 641–653.

Trinitapoli, J. (2006). Religious responses to AIDS in sub-Saharan Africa: An examination of religious congregations in rural Malawi. *Review of Religious Research, 47*, 253–270.

Trinitapoli, J., & Regnerus, M. D. (2006). Religion and HIV risk behaviors among married men: Initial results from a study in rural Sub-Saharan Africa. *Journal for the Scientific Study of Religion, 45*(4), 505–528.

Trinitapoli, J., & Weinreb, A. (2012). *Religion and Aids in Africa*. New York: Oxford University Press.

Uecker, J. E. (2008). Religion, pledging, and the premarital sexual behavior of married young adults. *Journal of Marriage & Family, 70*(3), 728–744.

Uecker, J. E., Regnerus, M. D., & Vaaler, M. L. (2007). Losing my religion: The social sources of religious decline in early adulthood. *Social Forces, 85,* 1667–1692.

UNAIDS. (2013). UNAIDS Report on the global AIDS epidemic, 2013. Geneva: UNAIDS. http://www.unaids.org/en/resources/publications/2013/name,85053,en.asp. Accessed 13 June 2014.

United States House of Representatives. Committee on Government Reform—Minority Staff. (2004). The content of federally funded abstinence only education programs. http://democrats.reform.house.gov. Accessed 6 June 2014.

U.S. Catholic Conference/Libreria Editrice Vaticana. (1994). *Catechism of the Catholic Church* (2nd ed.) Liguori: Liguori Publications.

U.S. Census Bureau. (2010). America's families and living arrangements: 2010. http://www.census.gov/population/www/socdemo/hh-fam/cps2010.html. Accessed 6 June 2014.

Vazsonyi, A. T., & Jenkins, D. D. (2010). Religiosity, self-Control, and virginity status in college students from the "Bible Belt:" A research note. *Journal for the Scientific Study of Religion, 49*(3), 561–568.

Whitehead, A. L. (2010). Sacred rites and civil rights: Religion's effect on attitudes toward same-sex unions and the perceived cause of homosexuality. *Social Science Quarterly, 91*(1), 63–79.

Whiters, D. L., Santibanez, S., Dennison, D., & Westley Clark, H. (2010). A case study in collaborating with Atlanta-based African-American churches: A promising means for reaching inner-city substance users with rapid HIV testing. *Journal of Evidence-Based Social Work, 7*(1–2), 103–114.

Wilcox, M. M. (2003). *Coming out in Christianity: Religion, identity, and community*. Bloomington: Indiana University Press.

Wilcox, W. B., Chaves, M., & Franz, D. (2004). Focused on the family? Religious traditions, family discourse, and pastoral practice. *Journal for the Scientific Study of Religion, 43*(4), 491–504.

Williams, J. C. (2011). Battling a "sex-saturated society:" The abstinence movement and the politics of sex education. *Sexualities, 14*(4), 416–443.

Yip, A. K. T. (2002). The persistence of faith among non-heterosexual Christians: Evidence for the neosecularization thesis of religious transformation. *Journal for the Scientific Study of Religion, 41*(2), 199–212.

Sexuality and Education: Toward the Promise of Ambiguity

21

Jessica Fields, Jen Gilbert, and Michelle Miller

"Sex ed." For many of us, the term conjures images of painful lectures delivered by poorly trained and visibly uncomfortable physical education teachers, angry parents protesting their school's distribution of condoms, anachronistic films documenting the journey of sperm up the fallopian tubes, and pubescent teens giggling at mentions of menstruation and secondary sex characteristics. Or perhaps the more optimistic among us imagine workshops facilitated by charismatic educators who exalt the importance of birth control, deftly slip condoms onto demonstration bananas, and remain unflappable and empathetic as they demystify puberty for bewildered youth. These admittedly stereotypical portraits of "sex ed" parody the highly contested landscape of sexuality education. The values and assumptions they reflect also make it difficult for educators and researchers to reach beyond conventional ideas about modesty, reproduction, coupling, and health to a more expansive vision of what it could mean to teach and learn about sexuality.

In the discussion that follows, we work from a definition of sexuality education that recognizes all the lessons that young people receive about bodies, relationships, desires, and sex, in formal and informal instruction, and in and out of schools. We understand that an education in sexuality occurs across the lifespan, across institutions and contexts, and in planned and intentional lessons as well as hidden or implicit moments of learning. The complicated terrain of sexuality education is, in part, an effect of the volatility of these two terms: sexuality and education. Like many of our colleagues and peers, we use "sexuality education" to open up the narrow casting of "sex ed" beyond the classroom-based lessons offered as part of an official curriculum. However, we do not presume to have eased the conflicts inherent to sexuality education with this shift in terminology.

Instead, we believe that bringing these contested concepts together, each dense with histories of conflict over their reach and meanings, exposes the underside of "sex ed." Even as we recognize that sexuality is learned across a range of institutions, relationships and structures, we also cast doubt on the confidence that we can predict the learning that goes under the name of "sexuality education." Can sex be educated (Britzman 1998)? This question requires an expansive understanding of both sexuality and education, and while those of us who think about sexuality education are accustomed to recognizing the expansiveness of sexuality, we are less used to seeing education as similarly varied, conflicted and contextual. "Sexuality education" is an awkward soldering together of theories of sexuality with theories of teaching and learning. Critical

J. Fields (✉)
Sociology, San Francisco State University,
San Francisco, CA 94132, USA
e-mail: jfields@sfsu.edu

J. Gilbert
York University, Toronto, ON M3J 1P3, Canada

M. Miller
York University, Toronto, ON M6K 2W1, Canada

research on sexuality education requires not only reaching beyond readily available definitions of sexuality but also rethinking the usual theories of teaching and learning. Sexuality education of all kinds must, first, move beyond an instrumentalist approach to teaching that veers close to behavior modification and, second, move toward learning that promotes ethical and democratic exploration and development (Fields 2008; Gilbert 2014; Lamb 2010).

Moving toward an expansive definition of sexuality education encourages heightened consideration of "the stakes" of teaching and learning about sexuality in and out of schools and the constrained set of worries that drives policy and instruction for young people. These worries are varied: for example, that the sexuality education youth receive does not help them navigate an increasingly sexualized and dangerous world and that the lessons are themselves damaging, exacerbating the risks children and youth already face. Sexuality education has long been a response to adults' concerns about the well-being of young people and the integrity of the family and society. At the very least, sexuality education must address itself to the contemporary terrain of young people's sexual lives: from panics over young people "sexting" to adults' continuing calls for young people to be abstinent, from the development of national sexuality education standards to rising concerns over the safety of lesbian, gay, bisexual, transgender and queer (LGBT/Q) youth in schools. And yet, even as sexuality education encompasses all these issues, its project is greater and more complicated than these worries, lessons, and occurrences suggest. Experiences of sexuality education are never straightforward. Instead, they are informed by and modify larger discourses of race, class, gender, ability, sexual orientation, religion, and other social differences. Sexuality education is similarly not confined to specially designated classes in primary and secondary schools, including health and family studies. Instead teaching and learning happen in hallways, playgrounds, shopping malls, churches, homes, popular culture, and on social media.

In this chapter, as we trace the historical and contemporary debates about the status of sexuality education in schools, we mine these debates for the underlying and enduring assumptions about sexuality and education that invoke conflict and controversy. In particular, we pay attention to how changing ideas about sexuality and education modulate the kinds of programs and interventions offered to young people and the tenor of scholarly conversation. One aim is to survey what we know about sexuality education and how this knowledge has shaped and constrained policy and practice landscapes. Another task is to ask how our confidence in "knowledge," embodied by the turn to discourses of science and health, defends against the uncertainty of teaching and learning. We conclude the chapter by focusing on the ambiguity and uncertainty that is part of the work of teaching and learning about sexuality. We restrict our attention to teaching and learning about puberty, sexuality, and relationships in schools. Readers interested in families, the Internet, and other sources of sexuality education should consult other chapters (see Martin, Chap. 19, this volume).

21.1 A History of Educating Sexuality

Debates about sexuality education can seem utterly contemporary. Sexting, LGBT/Q issues, the sexualization of girls—each emerging controversy is cast as new and unprecedented. Each seemingly new issue, however, gestures toward and often repeats a history linking sexuality to worries about the moral, psychological, and physical well-being of young people (Carlson 2012). And education, for its part, is repeatedly called upon as the cure for these worries. At the turn of the twentieth century, public officials in the United States grew concerned the nation was ill-prepared to contend with the sexual temptations associated with increasing urbanization (Carter 2001; Moran 2000). Over the course of the next century, many policy makers and educators came to believe that public health would be well served by "social hygiene," "family life," and "puberty" education in the schools (Moran 2000). Change was not unidirectional. Schools would be tasked with responding to these "contemporary" worries and maintaining the status quo, affirming the importance of family life, and educating young people out of sexual deviance. Even as these advocates called for schools to take up the task of teaching children and youth about sexual wellbeing, young people's education about sexual health and relationships continued to be primarily the parents' responsibility in the early twentieth century (Kendall 2008), and the education they did receive at school affirmed heteronormative ideals about students' sexual lives.

Sexuality education was reimagined in the wake of the social movements of the 1960s, and the public health focus of the earlier twentieth century was augmented by a new focus on the rights of girls and women. The best time and place to teach and learn about sexuality continued to be debated in the second half of the century as the feminist, youth, and gay rights movements wrought significant changes in U.S. sexual values (Luker 2006; Moran 2000). Though the sexual and gender revolutions of the 1960s, 1970s, and 1980s were neither uninterrupted nor uncontested, the widespread availability of contraception, legalized abortion, liberalization of divorce laws, and new sexual harassment laws helped make greater freedom and agency in private and public relationships seem possible for women and girls. As same-sex desire and expression became increasingly visible, LGBT/Q people also made new claims to a right to live free of discrimination. In the 1980s and 1990s, HIV/AIDS represented a significant public health crisis. Many sexuality educators responded with disciplining lessons that affirmed sexual conformity and punished sexual difference (Patton 1996), but the epidemic also reinvigorated the link between sexuality education and human rights and introduced into schools conversations that challenged homophobia and affirmed LGBT/Q youth.

Contemporary conflicts over sexuality education inherit the effects of these broader "culture wars" that arose in the wake of the sexual, youth and civil rights revolutions of the 1960s, "when it seemed as if all of American society might implode" (Luker 2006, p. 68; see also Hunter 1992). In a two-decade study, Kristin Luker conducted more than 100 interviews with adults living in U.S. communities embroiled in sexuality education debates. She argues these debates are ultimately "about how men and women relate to each other in all realms of their lives" (2006, p. 69) and, like other post-1960s battles, the conflict over sexuality education is caught in a clash between two poles—sexual conservatism and sexual liberalism. In the 1990s, in the United States, this conflict pitted conservative advocates of abstinence-only sex education against the more liberal supporters of comprehensive sex education.

Social conservatives entered late-twentieth-century school-based sex education debates insisting that the only way to keep young people safe from the physical, social, and emotional consequences of sex is to insist that they abstain from having sex beyond the confines of heterosexual marriage. Abstinence-only education thus centers the "traditional" male-headed heterosexual nuclear family and positions other models of sexual relations as a threat to the individual and the community. For supporters, abstinence-only education is a logical response to concerns over teen pregnancies, HIV, and other sexually transmitted infections (STIs) and an overall assault on conventional understandings of gender, family, and sexual expression. Reflecting what C. J. Pascoe refers to as the "twin assumptions that American teens are too innocent to know about sex and too sexual to be trusted with information" (2007, p. 29), abstinence-only programs posit that young people equipped with sexual knowledge are more likely to participate in sexual activities.

Socially liberal educators, advocates, and policy makers responded to arguments for abstinence-only education by promoting school-based comprehensive sexuality education, where teachers would emphasize abstinence as one strategy among others—condoms and contraceptives, for example—that students could adopt to protect their health and wellbeing. While comprehensive educators routinely assert that sexual abstinence is the best choice for youth (Fields 2008; Santelli 2006), comprehensive sexuality education might also include lessons on masturbation and abortion as well as information about gender norms and identities and lesbian, gay, and bisexual sexualities. Comprehensive programs are often organized around a hope that "accurate knowledge, received in a timely fashion, will prepare youth to enter into the world of sexual activity" (Sandlos 2011, p. 307). This belief holds that, when equipped with proper and correct knowledge about sexuality, young people will make better sexual decisions, including decisions to postpone sexual behavior and to practice safe sex.

This fight between abstinence-only and comprehensive sex education has indelibly affected the landscape of sex education across the United States by defining what counts as sex education and establishing the terms for debate about sexuality in schools. In a recent report on the status of sexuality and HIV education programs in each of the states, the Guttmacher Institute reports that 25 states require sexuality education programs to stress abstinence. In a further 12 states, educators must cover abstinence as one option among many of protecting youth from sexual risks and dangers, while 30 states require educators to inform students as to the perceived negative outcomes of teen sex. In 19 states, educators must stress the importance of having sex only within the confines of marriage. Within sexuality education programs, only 19 states require educators to discuss contraception. Twenty states require sexuality education classes to counsel teens about healthy decision-making. The numbers are even more dismal for conversations about sexual orientation—just 13 states require inclusive approaches to considering LGBT/Q issues, while three require that educators offer negative instruction about LGBT/Q sexualities.

21.2 A Sense of Danger

The abstinence-vs.-comprehensive account of contemporary sexuality education debates offers a fair rendering of the political landscape. However, researchers' access to school-based sexuality education is increasingly limited (Fields and Tolman 2006; Kendall 2012, p. 20, 21), making it difficult to observe the relationship between, on the one hand, policy and debate and, on the

other, classroom practice. The limited research available suggests teachers resist formal sexuality education policies and agendas with which they feel uncomfortable (Fields 2008; Hess 2010; Kendall 2012). Thus, knowing a school is formally an "abstinence-only school" does not mean we know the classroom instruction is in practice abstinence-only.

The two-camp account of the sexuality debate also obscures the reality that divisions in the battle over school-based abstinence and comprehensive sexuality programs are not absolute. Interrelated ideas, values, and norms undergird these programs (Fields 2008; Irvine 2002; Kendall 2012). Many educators and policymakers are left feeling that they must choose between these two seemingly-polarized discourses, while critical education theorists have noticed that the discourses that characterize these debates are themselves a product and condition of the conflicts, "traditions and resolutions [that] incorporate one another" (Lesko 2010, p. 281).

Indeed, abstinence-only and comprehensive sexuality education "rely on their opposition" to each other (Lesko 2010, p. 281). Policies and curricula may suggest discrete curricular options, but abstinence-only and comprehensive sexuality education programs share assumptions about youth, sexuality, and learning: that teen sexuality is a site of danger and risk; that such danger and risk is a site of profound worry among adults; and that sexuality education is a necessary, rational, and corrective response to that danger, risk and, worry (Fields 2008; Fields and Tolman 2006; Kendall 2012).

Comprehensive and abstinence-only curricula also share ideas about youth. The cultural, political and social shifts of late-twentieth-century social movements may have been welcome to many, but they have also exacerbated a sense—even among many supporters—that both sexuality and adolescence are sites of risk and danger and that education's role is to ease the risks young people face in their sexual lives (Bay-Cheng 2013; Levine 2002; Robinson 2013). Not surprisingly, then, much contemporary policy-making, public debate, and research on sexuality education focuses on offering children and youth lessons about avoiding sexual danger: will young people learn what they need to avert risk? Invoking concerns with health and prevention, adults organize policy and instruction for young people around the conventional worry that the sexuality education youth encounter in schools may not help them navigate an increasingly sexualized and dangerous world.

Policy and instruction are also motivated by another worry: that sexuality education's lessons are themselves damaging, exacerbating the sexual risks youth and children already face (Fields 2008; Heins 2001; Levine 2002). These worries, so trenchant that they have come to define what counts as sexuality education, span political positions. Sexual liberals and sexual conservatives, to borrow Kristin Luker's (2006) terms, worry that sexuality education puts young people in danger—though the dangers liberals and conservatives perceive may differ. And both camps also see education as a prophylactic against those dangers. Education is both a cause of and cure for danger.

These shared ideas are evident in policy offered across the U.S. political spectrum. Since the 1980s, the U.S. government has supported educational programs that emphasize chastity, self-discipline, and abstinence as strategies for stemming the problems understood to arise from teen sexual activity. The 1996 Personal Responsibility and Work Opportunity Reconciliation Act, enacted by the Democratic administration of Bill Clinton, increased federal support (and required state grantees to provide matching funds) for "abstinence education." Qualified programs would instruct students in the "social, psychological, and health gains" that come with confining sexual expression to heterosexual marriage and the "harmful psychological and physical effects" of sexual activity and parenting outside marriage (Waxman 2004).

More recently, Democratic President Barack Obama came through on an early election promise and eliminated much direct funding for abstinence-only education and instead funded an Office of Adolescent Health (OAH) to administer over $ 100 million in new support for evidence-based teen pregnancy prevention approaches

(Wagoner 2009). OAH funding effectively reversed the second Bush administration's consistent and increasing support for abstinence-only programming. Ironically, the OAH commitment to teen pregnancy prevention also affirms a long-established and conventional approach to sexuality education as a grudging response to vexing social problems. OAH-sponsored teen pregnancy prevention programming might take the form of "comprehensive sexuality education," much to the dismay of those advocating abstinence-only education. Nevertheless, the OAH focus on sexual behaviors–and heterosexual intercourse in particular–threatens to come at the expense of discussing a range of sexual identities, desires, and institutions. The concern with teen pregnancy highlights harmful consequences of heterosexual behaviors for self and society and once again commits education to the conservative aim of promoting the personal and social regulation of young people's sexuality.

These controversies and conflicts draw on an inclination Amy Schalet (2004) argues is characteristic of U.S. adults: parents, educators, and policy makers "dramatize adolescent sexuality" by highlighting conflict between parents and children, antagonism between girls and boys, and the threat of youth being overwhelmed by new sexual feelings and experiences. Schalet's comparative interviews with Dutch parents highlight the distinctiveness of the dramatizing model that animates sexuality education policy in the United States. Few U.S. girls "are assumed capable of the feelings and relationships that legitimate sexual activity," leaving them vulnerable to charge of "slut" (Schalet 2011, p. 325). Dutch girls, on the other hand, living within a normalizing paradigm of sexuality, "are assumed to be able to fall in love and form steady sexual relationships." This assumption defends against an equation of sexual activity with "sluttiness," though the assumption may also "obscure the challenges of negotiating differences" in sexual relationships (Schalet 2011, p. 325). In the United States, notions of good parenting conflict with the possibility of parents and guardians recognizing and supporting their children's sexual development, desires, and agency (Bay-Cheng 2013; Elliott

2012). Together, these images and tropes reflect and buttress ideals of youth as free of sexual experience and knowledge and therefore reliant upon adults' guidance and protection.

These idealized and dramatizing images generate not only ideals to which youth and parents are held but also means of sorting young people into a range of categories: the innocent and the guilty, the vulnerable and the predatory, the pure and the corrupting, those who are "fully participating and valued members of their classrooms and broader communities and those who are not" (Fields and Hirschman 2007, p. 11; see also Angelides 2004). Both conservative and liberal advocates need made-up and archetypal children on which to base their compelling arguments for school-based sexuality education. Images of virgins, pregnant teens, promiscuous girls, predatory boys, suicidal gay students, doomed teens, and confused youth help to clarify and heighten the stakes in debates over curricular goals and social agendas (Connell and Elliott 2009; Fields 2008; Irvine 2002). Will schools help to protect at-risk lesbian, gay, and bisexual youth from bullying, depression, and suicide? Will teachers help vulnerable girls and boys navigate a sexual world that threatens to be undone by a relaxing of gender norms, even among youth? Will communities help baffled teens get the information they need, even if their parents fail to provide the necessary guidance at home? All young people seem "at risk" of being tainted by sexuality—their own or others—and this is a risk against which, advocates claim, education can best mitigate.

21.3 Sexuality Education's Risky Lessons: Formal and Informal

The history of conflict over sexuality and youth permeates the formal and informal lessons young people receive in school. The early progressive hope that education could help young people build healthy, pro-social, sexual lives becomes, in schools, a litany of lessons about sexual morality that "socialize children into systems of inequality" (Connell and Elliott 2009, p. 84; see also Fields 2008). These lessons may claim neu-

trality and lean on a false sense of certainty; however, research consistently shows that sexuality education, from all political perspectives, routinely affirms oppressive values and norms about gender, race, and sexuality, even when presenting what appears to be rational, medically accurate information about bodies, disease and pregnancy prevention, and puberty (McClelland and Fine 2008; Santelli et al. 2006a; Waxman 2004).

At the center of school-based sexuality education stands the white, middle-class, Christian girl whose purity must be protected from predatory sexualities, embodied most dramatically by boys of color and queerness. All the lessons sexuality education offers seem to support this script. Lessons on menstruation and conception reinforce girls' and women's vulnerability and men's virility (Diorio and Munro 2000; Martin 2001). Youth and families of color appear in textbooks and other instructional material primarily in discussions of risk and disease prevention (Fields 2008; García 2009; Whatley 1988). Much instruction and many curricular materials suggest that boys of all races are potential sexual predators. In a heteronormative sexuality education, this discourse prepares students for antagonistic sexual relationships between men and women. Even in sexuality education classrooms formally designated "comprehensive," girls hear little talk from their teachers about female sexual desire (Fine 1988). Instead they hear that, as girls and women, they bear the responsibility of deflecting the inevitable, aggressive sexual advances of their male peers (Fields 2008; Fine 1988; Tolman 2002). Conversations about ethics, desire, and pleasure find little room in the sexuality education curriculum (Allen et al. 2013; Allen and Carmody 2012; Rasmussen 2004). Sharon Lamb's [2013] curriculum for teaching sexuality education in grade nine through a study of secular ethics represents one important exception—an imaginative response to the stagnant terms of the culture wars.

In its current forms, no matter its formal designation—comprehensive or abstinence-only—sexuality education routinely reproduces social inequalities (Connell and Elliott 2009). Rooted in 1996 welfare reform, contemporary abstinence-only education is touted by proponents as a response to poverty and other social ills; thus conventional norms of heterosexual sexual modesty and coupling are presented as vital to not only individual but also social well-being (Fine and McClelland 2006). The sexual expression of poor people—including low-income youth—is subject to greater surveillance and intervention. The implications of this link between young people's sexual activity and social decline extend into educational policy and practice. Jessica Fields (2008) found that in lower-income public schools students were more likely to encounter teachers beholden to the cultural authority of abstinence. Public school sexuality educators faced greater scrutiny and less support than their private school colleagues, and the least advantaged students received the most restrictive sexuality instruction. Only the relatively privileged private school students in Fields' study heard in their sexuality education a call to sexual pleasure, agency, and knowledge. The public school students, by contrast, consistently heard they should mute their desires and equip themselves for the sexual world routinely imagined by abstinence-only instruction—a world marked by violence, risk and consequence.

Sexuality education's lessons are also racialized. Ethnographic studies (Elliott 2012; Fields 2008; Kendall 2012) indicate policy makers, educators, and parents frequently cast some people's sexuality as particularly conflictual and antagonistic. And, while white children and youth are often taken to be sexually innocent in risk-based discourses, African American girls and boys are routinely "adultified"—cast as "sinister, intentional, fully conscious [and] stripped of any element of childish naiveté" (Ferguson 2001, p. 83). Lorena García's (2009) ethnographic research with Latina youth demonstrates the ways schools' racialized structures further marginalize students already facing multiple oppressions by presuming white heterosexuality as a norm. White, middle-class sexuality gets positioned as the ideal of sexuality education as teachers monitor and discipline racialized students' sexuality (Garcia 2009, p. 522; see also Fields 2008 and Pascoe 2007).

Normative notions of family also infuse sexuality education. Nancy Kendall found sexuality educators across the United States present "a particular mode of sex and sexuality that privilege[s] white, middle-class, straight, adult conceptualizations of 'good' and 'bad' sexual decision-making, behaviors and outcomes" (2012, p. 82). When their well-meaning teacher asked students to go home to talk about sex with their parents, Pacific Islander students resisted, explaining they feared their parents would disapprove and punish them for broaching the subject (p. 114). Kendall (2012) observed white sexuality educators who were confused and concerned about the way Native American elders treated pregnant teens in their communities. Having children young and out of wedlock did not garner the same kinds of stigma in Native American communities as it did in the white, middle-class communities in which the educators had grown up. And, while some Native teen mothers might want to return to school after giving birth, the school lacked parenting support programs and other in-school resources that would meet their needs as newly parenting teens. Such assumptions are difficult to dislodge. Even educators who, in the name of cultural sensitivity, alter their programming to address students of different cultural backgrounds are likely to try to bring students and families in line with white, middle-class values (Kendall 2012).

This narrow view of family informs the heteronormative ideas about sexuality and intimacy at the core of much sexuality education. Educators often shy away from lessons about lesbian, gay, bisexual, and queer sexuality and about transgender experiences, casting such lessons as provocative and controversial. Heteronormative school-based sexuality education systematically denies sexually active young people access to educational resources and adult support that would promote their well-being and health: for example, at the turn of the twenty-first century, students report receiving less information about birth control than they would like (Darroch et al. 2000), and teachers reported offering lessons on contraception later and less frequently than they reported a decade earlier (Kaiser Family Foundation 1999). In addition, those youth who identify as lesbian, gay, bisexual, and queer contend with sexuality education that emphasizes heterosexual behaviors, desires, and relationships and that, through its refusal to address lesbian, gay, bisexual, and queer sexuality as anything other than sites of risk and deviance, denies nonconforming youth recognition as fully participating and valued members of their communities who are capable of creating and enjoying meaningful relationships with same-sex partners (Fields 2008; Gilbert 2006; Russell 2003). Under such a curricular and pedagogical regime, all students contend with stunted relational and affective possibilities—even in classrooms that are purportedly neutral (Fields 2005; Fields and Hirschman 2007).

Young people's education in sexuality is not confined to the official classes and curriculum; across the school, young people encounter and engage with a "hidden," "informal," or "evaded" curricula (Apple 2004; Fields 2008). Lessons about sexuality and gender circulate, often unnoticed, throughout the school as policies, practices, curricula, and programs about sexuality meet and intersect with the everyday lives of students and teachers. These lessons take the form of implicit norms governing relationships between students and teachers; youths' management of their own and others' bodies; the social makeup of the school as well as broader community; and students, and teachers, responses to eruptions of homophobia, sexism, or racism in the classroom, lunchroom, and hallway.

School dress codes illustrate how sexuality is schooled through informal practices. Rules around dress—a particularly institutionalized site of extra-curricular sexuality education–assume heterosexual relations among students and suggest heterosexuality is itself a site of tension and conflict. Girls' bodies and sexualities are regulated as potential distractions for male students: distractions must be minimized in order to protect schools' "moral climate." Dress codes thus reinforce sexuality education's suggestion that boys cannot control themselves and must rely on girls' greater capacity to control their own and others' impulses (Raby 2012). Once again, girls are re-

sponsible for delaying sexual activity and ensuring everyone's safety, health, and well-being.

Tensions between discipline and resistance are also evident. Students are subject to these rules, but they also enforce them–and young people's participation lends the hidden, evaded, and informal curricula their power. Students resent rules and their enforcement even as they simultaneously scorn the behavior the rules are intended to curtail. The young women in Rebecca Raby's study recognized the sexism undergirding their being assigned responsibility for the "moral climate" of their school; they also criticized the "frequency, inconsistency and inequality" of rule enforcement. However, they also valued these rules' capacity to regulate the behavior and dress of "other" girls (p. 340). Students' relationship to restrictive regimes becomes ambiguous as they enforce and endorse the very rules that constrain their self-expression.

Ultimately, sexuality education inside and outside the classroom and delivered by teachers and students affirms a "heterosexual imaginary" (Best 2000, p. 195). At times the lessons are embedded in the formal curriculum. Abstinence-only programs locate healthy and moral sexuality inside heterosexual marriage, denying LGBT/Q teens a sexual future (Fisher 2009). Other times the lessons are informal. Lesbian, gay, bisexual, and queer students and teachers often experience schools as unfriendly and even dangerous places marked by bullying and harassment at the hands of administrators, teachers and students. The violence ranges from sexual to physical, from verbal to emotional, and may be as overt as purposeful gender and sexual assault or as insidious as homophobic joking and taunting of students, ignoring verbal and physical harassment when it is witnessed (García 2009, p. 523; Pascoe 2007, pp. 96, 114).

In hopes of creating more open and tolerant spaces for LGBT/Q sexuality and lives, many schools are adopting "safe space" policies and establishing gay-straight alliances. Such spaces simultaneously stand inside and outside the school—claiming meeting space, featured on bulletin boards and websites, touted as signs of school communities' tolerance, even as they also critique school practices and policies and point to the violence and homophobia often characterizing normative school cultures (see for example dePalma and Atkinson 2006; Elia and Eliason 2010; Mayo 2013). Education scholars remind readers that, while schools can be difficult places for LGBT/Q students and teachers, this is only part of the story of what it means to be queer in schools. Even as LGBT/Q students, teachers, and families deserve to live free of harassment and discrimination in schools, they also live ordinary lives (Fields et al. 2014; Marshall 2010; Talburt 2004). Research rarely represents the quotidian aspects of teaching and learning as an LGBT/Q person in school (Gilbert 2014; Talburt 2004). Instead, dramatizing notions of young people's sexuality are left to prevail.

21.4 Sexual Speech, Knowledge, and Innocence

A claim to sexuality's ordinary place in young people's lives is, ironically, controversial. The debate between abstinence-only and comprehensive sexuality education was forever caught within the narrow terms of the culture wars; within these terms, a gradual acceptance of comprehensive sexuality education represented a victory for progressive politics. While research consistently demonstrates that comprehensive sexuality education promotes sexual well-being and offers healthier lessons about gender, sexuality, and decision making (Kirby 2008; Kirby and Laris 2009; Santelli et al. 2006a and 2006b), Nancy Lesko (2010) reminds us to think beyond the dichotomy between abstinence-only and comprehensive curricula and their shared equation of sexuality with danger and education with intervention (see also Fields 2008).

Depravity narratives pervade U.S. debates about sex and sexuality education and reflect the conflation of, on the one hand, sexual behavior and sexual risk and, on the other, education and intervention. Abstinence-only advocates offer stories about teachers who seduce, corrupt, or otherwise sexually endanger their students. In these narratives, sexual speech becomes tantamount to sexu-

al activity and educators who participate in sexual speech leave themselves vulnerable to charges of inappropriate intervention. Even classroom talk of normative heterosexuality can constitute an assault in which adults "persuade, incite, or otherwise arouse youth to later engage in the very acts spoken about" (Irvine 2000, p. 63) and talk about homosexuality becomes an inherently predatory act in which adults initiate children or youth into a host of sexual perversions, including same-sex behaviors and desires (Irvine 2000, 2002; Levine 2002). In these narratives, talking with children and youth about sex is a reckless act, comparable to engaging in sexual activity with children and youth. According to this logic, "[s]exual speech ... provokes and stimulates. It transforms the so-called natural modesty of children into inflamed desires that may be outside the child's control and thus prompt sexual activity" (Irvine 2000, p. 62; see also Heins 2007; Irvine 2002). This framing renders sexuality education a suspect task: a violation of children and youth's sexual innocence and yet another assault on the embattled and idealized child-victim.

This perceived threat mobilized some conservative parents to resist sexuality education in their children's schools; other parents, along with policy makers and educators, are reluctant to publicly endorse sexuality education that promotes anything other than sexual abstinence, normative family structures, and conventional gender expression (Irvine 2002). In this climate, the conflation of sexual speech and sexual acts and the companion panic surrounding sexuality education and the threat of sexual molestation help to naturalize conventional sexual hierarchies in the name of protecting youth. Strategies for mitigating these apparent risks might include, for example, employing only highly trained sexuality educators or instituting peer education programs in which young people, not adults, deliver the instruction. Ultimately, however, protecting youth comes to mean protecting them *from* sexuality education.

The conflation of sexual speech and acts shapes not only public debate but also teaching and learning in the classroom. Looming charges of depravity leave all sexuality education advocates, policy makers, and instructors in a nearly impossible situation: how can they convince parents and community members that their course of instruction does not put young people at risk, let alone that their instruction might ease the risks that young people face? In response, participants in sexuality education debates and policy-making acknowledge that the curriculum they advocate—whether abstinence-only, abstinence-based, or comprehensive—necessarily includes talk of sex; however, they argue, that speech is factually sound and medically accurate and thus the logical and rational choice for any adult committed to promoting the health of children and youth (Fields 2008; Fine 1988; Fine and McClelland 2006). To stave off charges that sexuality education is a depraved activity, teachers, parents, and advocates must invoke sexuality education's potential to save vulnerable children and youth.

Depravity narratives and suspicion of sexuality educators rest on a historically available discourse about the corruptible child; they also help to imagine and constitute a world in which the threat of sexual molestation looms everywhere, every teacher is potentially a pedophile, and learning happens when "the omnipotent, all-controlling adult" meets "the powerless, passive child" (Angelides 2004, p. 160). Sexuality education, resting as it does on talking with youth about sexuality, threatens to become a crime in which "any teacher is a suspect" (Irvine 2000, p. 70). In this political climate, those who advance a vision of sexuality as dangerous and corrupting gain political and social legitimacy. Suspicion and distrust await those who might otherwise resist this normative vision of sexuality and youth by advancing an expansive and nuanced understanding of sexuality and youth.

21.5   The Promise of Rationality

Against the charge that their version of sexuality education injures children and youth, advocates of comprehensive sexuality education turn to the safety of science. In a series of single- and co-authored articles, John Santelli (2006) has been

particularly active in the call for greater attention from citizens, policymakers, and advocates to the science surrounding sexuality education. Ideological positions, like those we have detailed in this chapter, have driven policymaking and practice; science should drive decision making instead. As Santelli and others argue, science points repeatedly to the failure of abstinence-only education to promote sexual health and wellbeing (DeLamater 2007; Santelli et al. 2006a; Schalet et al. 2014)

Consistently, evaluation and social science research indicates that comprehensive sexuality and STI/HIV education has the capacity to decrease rates of unwanted pregnancy, disease and infection and to promote overall sexual health and well-being (Kirby and Laris 2009). Programs that emphasize abstinence at the expense of information about, for example, pregnancy prevention, safer sex, and sexual communication fail to have a positive impact on young people's sexual well-being (Kirby 2008), and they may even threaten human rights (DeLamater 2007; Santelli et al. 2006a). On the other hand, programs that offer comprehensive instruction more effectively delay young people's initiation of consensual sexual behavior and reduce their number of sexual partners (Kirby and Laris 2009).

Biomedical approaches to sexual health and well-being are not enough (Rotheram-Borus et al. 2009). Researchers with the UK project, Sexual Health And Relationships—Safe, Happy And Responsible (SHARE) have launched a series of articles that argue sexuality education curricula "must be carefully embedded in lessons [that] are informed by an awareness of classroom culture, and the needs and skills of teachers" (Wight and Abraham 2000, p. 25; see also Buston et al. 2002). Even with such sensitivity to the context of teaching and learning, a well-designed, theoretically-informed curricula may improve the quality of young people's sexual and emotional lives but have little impact on sexual behaviors, included unprotected sex, contraceptive use, teen pregnancies, or abortions (Henderson et al. 2007; Wight et al. 2002).

Others have expressed concern that even favorably evaluated curricula and programs fail to address issues of pleasure, agency, and ethics—concerns that fill the pages of social science publications on sexuality education (McClelland and Fine 2008). McClelland and Fine (2008) also remind readers that the research science on sexuality education is often "embedded" in existing public policy. And, as Schalet et al. note, "The current policy does not require programs to be engaged with the breadth of current scientific thinking about adolescents and their sexual health" (2014, p. 1605).

The turn to science to justify progressive educational programs is an important, and familiar, political strategy—with science on its side, comprehensive sexuality education seems poised to prevail in the waning days of the culture wars. The rise of language of "evidence-based" curricula and "outcomes" in sexuality education marks this change. What is lost in this political move is an attention to the intimate scenes of teaching and learning that most sexuality education involves. Education scholars have long cast suspicion on the easy relation between knowledge and behavior and cautioned us not to conflate curriculum with learning (Gilbert 2014). For instance, in a study of controversies surrounding the introduction of a gay-positive curriculum in New York City schools, Cris Mayo (2007) insists that the homophobic backlash to the rainbow curriculum has the potential to open up new conversations about LGBT/Q life in schools. Knowledge in this case goes astray and students learn an unexpected lesson about tolerance and love. Abstinence-only and comprehensive sexuality education too often rely on a linear understanding of education: provide students the requisite knowledge so they will adopt the behaviors—for example, sexual abstinence or contraceptive use—that teachers advocate (Lesko 2010). Comprehensive sexuality education and abstinence-only education build on each other and on a shared cultural moment and, as such, "touch in many ways" (Lesko 2010, p. 290). In prevailing comprehensive models of sexuality education, knowledge is presumed to be "positive and accurate," part of a broad definition of freedom as the product of scientific knowledge and empowerment. Abstinence-only models similarly indulge in this "pan-optimism"

(2010, p. 290), in which knowledge produces desired outcomes—discouraging sexual behavior and promoting compliance with gender and sexual norms.

Such optimism is possible only with a notion of knowledge as stable—a notion that empirical research repeatedly indicates is at odds with meaningful sexuality education that would embrace a subjective, relational and holistic view of sexuality itself. No matter whether activists and movements advance abstinence-only or comprehensive curricula, the instruction they advocate promotes or defends against change in cultural ideas about sexuality as evident in thinking about gender, sexual expression and identity, or family (Bay-Cheng 2013; Irvine 2002; Levine 2002; Stein 2006). Despite abstinence-only education's persistent failure to convince youth to remain abstinent or to stem disease and unwanted pregnancies among youth (Kirby 2008), the tenet of sexual abstinence has since the end of the twentieth century asserted "a kind of natural cultural authority, in schools and out" (Fine and McClelland 2006, p. 299). Comprehensive sexuality education advocates who might have otherwise promoted more liberal, progressive, or even radical curriculum and pedagogy have been increasingly accountable to this cultural authority. Young people abstaining from sexual behaviors and exploration has become more desirable than their examining and experiencing sexuality's complexities (Gilbert 2014).

A recourse to science and the discourse of rationality may be an effective political tool and the ground of sound decision making. They are also discursive tools. Science promises to tame the unruliness of sexuality. In their ethnographic studies, both Kendall (2012) and Fields (2008) found this framing affected the ways teachers could engage with sexual information in their classrooms. In a school where controversy about sexual speech led to harassment and censure of some sex educators, teachers—and particularly female teachers—adopted lessons that focused on the biological aspects of puberty and reproduction. This sort of "no nonsense" adherence to science, which neutralizes personal opinion, protects teachers from charges of sexual provocation.

This confidence in the neutrality of science veils a theory of education. A stable, rational, and unambiguous relationship between knowledge and behavior is at the heart of sexuality education debates and practice and, in turn, sexuality education research. Sexuality education that couches itself in the promise of scientific rationality rests on a belief that knowledge replaces ignorance and that behavior change is an effect of rational persuasion. This pedagogical wish—that there could be a direct line between teaching and learning; curriculum and behavior—undergirds all sides of the sexuality education debates. Mainstream curricular positions continue to try to recapture an imagined and predictable relationship between knowledge and behavior: teach young people to abstain, and they will; compromise young people with knowledge of sexual behaviors and desires, and they will be endangered; and present information about risk, prevention, and responsible behavior, and you will promote healthy decision-making in youth.

There are, at least, two limitations to this approach. First, sexuality education risks being conflated with behavior modification. Across studies of sexuality education, researchers attempt to tie particular lessons, programs, policies, and activities to behavior change: delay of sexual intercourse, reductions in STIs and pregnancies, reduction in number of sexual partners, and shifts in attitudes towards LGBT/Q people. These "outcomes," measurable with the logics of scientific rationality, have come to play a significant role in research funding, curriculum development and policy advocacy. And yet, rather than simply being an effect of sexuality education, these conventionally understood outcomes have come to define the purposes and aims of sexuality education. What if, instead of orienting itself around behavioral and attitudinal change, sexuality education focused on the development of thoughtfulness, interpretive practices, or analyses of social inequalities? HIV education might include an exploration of gender scripts and stereotypes (Díaz 1998; Laub et al. 1999), assert a critical understanding of pleasure's role in decisions about safe and unsafe sex (Naisteter and Sitron 2010),

and invite children and youth into conversations about sexuality and loss (Silin 1995).

Second, if sexuality education were to make thoughtfulness a desired outcome—if we connected sexuality to a more holistic notion of a development of a sense of personhood and relationality—sexuality education might be located somewhere besides health and physical education. Many researchers, frustrated by the limitations inherent in legitimized school-based sexuality education programs (such as their duration, the curricular demands, and teacher anxiety over controversy), argue that sex education may be productively folded into other subject matter areas. For example, Rogow and Haberland (2005) argue that social studies classrooms offer ideal sites for critical sexuality education. Because social studies courses are interdisciplinary, they can incorporate lessons on many aspects of sexuality often left untackled in official sex education courses: social construction of gender differences and discrimination, differential access to sexual and reproductive choice, rape and other aspects of sexuality that are "fundamentally social matters" (p. 338). Similarly, Brian Casemore et al. suggest that sex education could adopt the interpretive practices of reading literature where what is at stake is not just "the facts" about sexuality but how our engagements with knowledge are shaped by our desires (2011; see also Casemore 2010; Sandlos 2011). Alyssa Niccolini notices that a missing discourse of female desire (Fine 1988) in an "old fashioned" high school sexuality education lead some young racialized women to engage with black lesbian erotica in "free reading" sessions in English class. Niccolini defends the texts as allowing young women to "imagine themselves as sexual beings capable of pleasure and cautions about danger without carrying the undue burden of social, medical and reproductive consequences" (2013, p. 3). In a similar vein, Catherine Ashcraft (2012) explores critical literacy education as a site of teaching and learning about sexuality. In these versions of sexuality education, danger is not just a risk to be avoided either by banning talk about sex, neutralizing it through discourses of science, or modifying young people's behaviors; instead, the dangerousness of sexuality becomes an occasion for thinking.

At stake in these re-imaginings of sexuality education is the importance of what Michelle Fine and Sara McClelland (2006) call "thick desire." A theory of thick desire does not collapse sexuality into danger and instead understands that

> "young people are entitled to a broad range of desires for meaningful intellectual, political, and social engagement, the possibility of financial independence, sexual and reproductive freedom, protection from racialized and sexualized violence, and a way to imagine living in the future tense" (p. 300).

In this theory, the danger of sexuality comes largely from trying to exercise sexual agency in an unjust world. To make sexuality less risky means addressing the pervasive social inequalities that structure young people's relationships and protecting young people's rights to an education, self-expression, and healthy futures (Biegel 2010; Levesque 2000; Mayo 2013). And a sexuality education that looks beyond notions of risk toward thick desire might also support a more ambitious vision of education as responsible to a sense of secular ethics, citizenship, and personhood.

21.6 The Ambiguity of Risk

Articulating a vision of education that promotes well-being through a more expansive and less instrumentalist approach to risk, sexuality, and education involves both a rethinking of young people's sexuality as comprising more than risk *and* an acknowledgement that many of the risks young people face reflect adult-made social conditions (Schaffner 2005). Jessica Fields and Deborah Tolman redefine risk

> as a necessary part of life, as something that sometimes turns out well, as something that people sometimes willingly take on in order to push forward and grow[, and] as a function not of individual decision making but instead as a function of social conditions that put some young people at much greater risk of violence and exploitation than others (2006, p. 72).

We must, as Steven Angelides (2004) insists, distinguish risk from a sense of inevitable danger *and* couple risk with the possibility of pleasure. By linking risk with a sense of pleasure and insisting that the equation of youth with "riskiness" is itself dangerous, some researchers have begun to make a claim for the generative capacities of risk. Risk, in these formulations, is marked by ambivalence and ambiguity. It is not an objective assessment of a situation but an interpretation.

And yet, there are those who worry that this ambiguity threatens to undermine young people's well-being. Without a definition of what it means to abstain, for instance, adolescents appear to be at risk of stumbling into a world characterized by the dangers of pregnancy and sexual behavior (see, for example, Sawyer et al. 2007). According to this instrumental argument, if "misconceptions and ambiguities" about abstinence are allowed to stand (Goodson et al. 2003, p. 91), educators and researchers will be unable to offer effective sexuality education, evaluate sexuality education programs, and equip young people to recognize when they are being sexually active and when their behaviors constitute a sexual risk (Haglund 2003). In response, many social science researchers, like policy makers, have sought an appropriate, clear definition that would help "provide adolescents with the information and decision-making skills to assess and maintain well-being" (Ott et al. 2006, p. 197).

An alternative lies in the work of researchers who, rather than positing these "highly personalized and often contradictory" definitions as problems to stamp out, approach the ambiguity of terms like "abstinence" and "sexuality" as problems to engage, as conditions of learning and of sexual life. Young people's lack of clarity about abstinence and virginity reflects a broader lack of consensus in our society (Bersamin et al. 2007). And, like the category "abstinence," what counts as "sexual intercourse" is not immune from ambiguity and uncertainty. In the Toronto Teen Survey, a large-scale survey of young people's experiences of sexuality, 4% of respondents reported being unsure whether they had had sexual intercourse. Among that group, 21% had reported having vaginal intercourse, 28% reported having oral sex and 9% reported having anal sex (Flicker et al. 2010). Resistance to clear-cut definitions suggests that young people's experiences of sexuality and of learning about sexuality exceed the normative cultural messages about risk, responsibility, and disease that characterize most abstinence-only and comprehensive sexuality education. As Jen Gilbert (2010) argues, advocates of comprehensive sex education have tried to evacuate sexuality of ambiguity by appealing to the language of health:

> In the effort to stave off the incursions of abstinence into sex education, we have, in comprehensive sex education, made sex a problem of and for 'health.' Here, 'health' stands in for the adhesive and prosocial qualities of sexuality. 'Healthy sexuality,' 'healthy relationships,' 'healthy body image,' 'healthy self-esteem:' youth drown in admonitions that they should feel positive about any and all aspects of their bodies, selves, and identities. In comprehensive sex education, a proper, 'healthy' sexuality leads to relationships, intimacy, maturity, and pleasure (p. 233).

Such an approach to education casts sexual decision making as wholly rational and denies "affect as a central part of what knowledge does" (Lesko 2010, p. 282). The affective experiences of learning about sexuality exceed the bounds of rational and predictable knowledge—we do not always make healthy choices, even as adults. This excess animates young people's experiences of sexuality and persists in classroom practice. It also pervades local and national sexuality education debates. Consistently, sexuality education evokes a range of fraught social concerns about, for example, which family formations communities will accept and celebrate in their midst; how best to respond to increasing numbers of—and tolerance of—LGBT/Q youth; the relative responsibility of families and schools to provide for young people's sexual well-being and moral character; and how educators, families, service providers, and other community members will respond to the incidence and risk of teen pregnancies and STIs.

Ambiguity and ambivalence in sexuality education policy and practice represent a call to move beyond the polarized debate between abstinence-only and comprehensive sexuality educa-

tion and allow instead for an expansive approach to learning and knowing that opens with and sustains questions. Indeed, in this chapter we argue for teaching and learning in which "not knowing and feeling confused [might become] the basis of learning about sexuality" and not something to be corrected (Gilbert 2010, p. 5). In this vision of sexuality education, the ambivalence, pleasure, worry, and other sexual experiences and associations that are currently interpreted as intruding upon effective teaching, learning, and policy would be recognized and contended with as the cultural conditions in which communities debate sexuality education policy and practice and, ultimately, the stuff of sexuality education itself.

References

Allen, L., & Carmody, M. (2012). "Pleasure has no passport": Re-visiting the potential of pleasure in sexuality education. *Sex Education: Sexuality, Society and Learning, 12*(4), 455–468.

Allen, L., Rasmussen, M. L., Quinlivan, K. (Eds.). (2013). *Interrogating the politics of pleasure in sexuality education: Pleasure bound.* New York: Routledge.

Angelides, S. (2004). Feminism, child sexual abuse, and the erasure of child sexuality. *GLQ: A Journal of Lesbian and Gay Studies, 10*(2), 141–177.

Apple, M. W. (2004). *Ideology and curriculum.* London: Routledge.

Ashcraft, C. (2012). But how do we talk about it? Critical literacy practices for addressing sexuality with youth. *Curriculum Inquiry, 42*(5), 597–628.

Bay-Cheng, L. Y. (2001). SexEd.com: Values and norms in web-based sexuality education. *Journal of Sex Research, 38*(3), 241–251.

Bay-Cheng, L. Y. (2013). Ethical parenting of sexually active youth: Ensuring safety while enabling development. *Sex Education: Sexuality, Society and Learning, 13*(2), 133–145.

Bersamin, M. M., Fisher, D. A., Walker, S., Hill, D. L., & Grube, J. W. (2007). Defining virginity and abstinence: Adolescents' interpretations of sexual behaviors. *Journal of Adolescent Health, 41*(2), 182–188.

Best, A. L. (2000). *Prom night: Youth, schools, and popular culture.* New York: Routledge.

Biegel, S. (2010). *The right to be out: Sexual orientation and gender identity in America's public schools.* Minneapolis: University of Minnesota Press.

Britzman, D. P. (1998). *Lost subjects, contested objects: Toward a psychoanalytic inquiry of learning.* Albany: State University of New York Press.

Buston, K., Wight, D., Hart, G., & Scott, S. (2002). Implementation of a teacher-delivered sex education programme: Obstacles and facilitating factors. *Health Education Research, 17*(1), 59–72.

Carlson, D. (2012). *The education of eros: A history of education and the problem of adolescent sexuality. Studies in Curriculum Theory Series*. Florence: Routledge, Taylor & Francis Group.

Carter, J. B. (2001). Birds, bees, and venereal disease: Toward an intellectual history of sex education. *Journal of the History of Sexuality, 10*(2), 213–250.

Casemore, B. (2010). Free association in sex education: Understanding sexuality as the flow of thought in conversation and curriculum. *Sex Education: Sexuality, Society and Learning, 10*(3), 309–324.

Casemore, B., Sandlos, K., & Gilbert, J. (2011). On taking an interpretive risk in sex education. *Teachers College Record*. http://www.tcrecord.org ID Number: 16383, Accessed 5 May 2015.

Connell, C., & Elliott, S. (2009). Beyond the birds and the bees: Learning inequality through sexuality education. *American Journal of Sexuality Education, 4*(2), 83–102.

Darroch, J. E., Landry, D. J., & Singh, S. (2000). Changing emphases in sexuality education in U.S. public secondary schools, 1988–1999. *Family Planning Perspectives, 32*(5): 204–211.

DeLamater, J. (2007). Gender equity in formal sexuality education. In S. S. Klein, B. Richardson, D. A. Grayson, L. H. Fox, C. Kramarae, D. S. Pollard, & C. A. Dwyer (Eds.), *Handbook for achieving gender equity through education* (2nd ed., pp. 411–420). New York: Routledge.

dePalma, R., & Atkinson, E. (2006). The sound of silence: Talking about sexual orientation and schooling. *Sex Education: Sexuality, Society and Learning, 6*(4), 333–349.

Díaz, R. M. (1998). *Latino gay men and HIV: Culture, sexuality, and risk behavior*. New York: Routledge.

Diorio, J. A., & Munro, J. A. (2000). Doing harm in the name of protection: Menstruation as a topic for sex education. *Gender and Education, 12*(3), 347–365.

Duggan, L., & Hunter, N. D. (2006). *Sex wars: Sexual dissent and political culture*. New York: Routledge.

Elia, J. P. (2000). Democratic sexuality education: A departure from sexual ideologies and traditional schooling. *Journal of Sex Education and Therapy, 25*(2–3), 122–129.

Elia, J. P., & Eliason, M. J. (2010). Dangerous omissions: Abstinence-only-until-marriage school based sexuality education and the betrayal of LGBTQ youth. *American Journal of Sexuality Education, 5*(1), 17–35.

Elliott, S. (2012). *Not my kid: What parents believe about the sex lives of their teenagers*. New York: New York University Press.

Ferguson, A. A. (2001). *Bad boys: Public schools in the making of black masculinity*. Ann Arbor: University of Michigan Press.

Fields, J. (2005). "Children having children": Race, innocence, and sexuality education. *Social Problems, 52*(4), 549–571.

Fields, J. (2008). *Risky lessons: Sex education and social inequality*. New Brunswick, NJ: Rutgers University Press.

Fields, J., & Hirschman, C. (2007). Citizenship lessons in abstinence-only sexuality education. *American Journal of Sexuality Education, 2*(2), 3–25.

Fields, J., & Tolman, D. L. (2006). Risky business: Sexuality education and research in US schools. *Sexuality Research and Social Policy, 3*(4), 63–76.

Fields, J., Mamo, L., Gilbert, J., & Lesko, N. (2014). Beyond bullying. *Contexts, 13*(4), 80–83.

Fine, M. (1988). Sexuality, schooling, and adolescent females: The missing discourse of desire. *Harvard Educational Review, 58*(1), 29–54.

Fine, M., & McClelland, S. I. (2006). Sexuality education and desire: Still missing after all these years. *Harvard Educational Review, 76*(3), 297–338.

Fisher, C. M. (2009). Queer youth experiences with abstinence-only-until-marriage sexuality education: "I can't get married so where does that leave me?" *Journal of LGBT Youth, 6*(1), 61–79.

Flicker, S., Travers, R., Flynn, S., Larkin, J., Guta, A., Salehi, R., Pole, J.D., & Layne, C. (2010). Sexual health research for and with urban youth: The Toronto Teen Survey story. *The Canadian Journal of Human Sexuality, 19*(4), 133–144.

Francis, D. A., & DePalma, R. (2014). Teacher perspectives on abstinence and safe sex education in South Africa. *Sex Education: Sexuality, Society and Learning, 14*(1), 81–94.

Freeman, S. K. (2008). *Sex goes to school: Girls and sex education before the 1960s*. Champaign: University of Illinois Press.

García, L. (2009). "Now why do you want to know about that?" Heteronormativity, sexism, and racism in the sexual (mis)education of Latina ydouth. *Gender & Society, 23*(4), 520–541.

Gilbert, J. (2006). "Let us say yes to what turns up": Education as hospitality. *Journal of the Canadian Association for Curriculum Studies, 4*(1), 25–34.

Gilbert, J. (2010). Ambivalence only? Sex education in the age of abstinence. *Sex Education: Sexuality, Society and Learning, 10*(3), 233–237.

Gilbert, J. (2014). *Sexuality in school: The limits of education*. Minneapolis: University of Minnesota Press.

Goldman, J. D., & Bradley, G. L. (2001). Sexuality education across the lifecycle in the new millennium. *Sex Education: Sexuality, Society and Learning, 1*(3), 197–217.

Goodson, P., Suther, S., Pruitt, B. E., & Wilson, K. (2003). Defining abstinence: Views of directors, instructors, and participants in abstinence-only-until-marriage programs in Texas. *Journal of School Health, 73*(3), 91–96.

Griffin, P., & Ouellett, M. (2003). From silence to safety and beyond: Historical trends in addressing lesbian, gay, bisexual, transgender issues in K-12 schools. *Equity & Excellence in Education, 36*(2), 106–114.

Guttmacher Institute. (2014). State policies in brief: Sex and HIV education. http://www.guttmacher.org/statecenter/spibs/spib_SE.pdf. Accessed 4 Nov 2014.

Haffner, D. W. (2011). Dearly beloved: Sexuality education in faith communities. *American Journal of Sexuality Education, 6*(1), 1–6.

Haglund, K. (2003). Sexually abstinent African American adolescent females' descriptions of abstinence. *Journal of Nursing Scholarship, 35*(3), 231–236.

Heins, M. (2007). *Not in front of the children: 'Indecency,' censorship, and the innocence of youth.* New Brunswick, NJ: Rutgers University Press.

Henderson, M., Wight, D., Raab, G. M., Abraham, C., Parkes, A., Scott, S., & Hart, G. (2007). Impact of a theoretically based sex education programme (SHARE) delivered by teachers on NHS registered conceptions and terminations: Final results of cluster randomised trial. *Britsh Medical Journal, 334*(7585), 133.

Hess, A. (2010). Hold the sex, please: The discursive politics between national and local abstinence education providers. *Sex Education: Sexuality, Society and Learning, 10*(3), 251–266.

Hindin, M. J., & Fatusi, A. O. (2009). Adolescent sexual and reproductive health in developing countries: An overview of trends and interventions. *International Perspectives on Sexual and Reproductive Health, 35*(2), 58–62.

Hunter, J. D. (1992). *Culture wars: The struggle to control the family, art, education, law, and politics in America.* New York: Basic Books.

International Sexuality and HIV Curriculum Working Group. (2009, 2011). *It's all one curriculum: Guidelines and activities for a unified approach to sexuality, gender, HIV, and human rights education.* New York, NY: Population Council.

Irvine, J. M. (2000). Doing it with words: Discourse and the sex education culture wars. *Critical Inquiry, 27*(1), 58–76.

Irvine, J. M. (2002). *Talk about sex: The battles over sex education in the United States.* Berkeley: University of California Press.

Kaiser Family Foundation. (1999). *Sex education in America: A view from inside the nation's classrooms.* Menlo Park, CA: Kaiser Family Foundation.

Kendall, N. (2008). Sexuality education in an abstinence-only era: A comparative case study of two US states. *Sexuality Research and Social Policy, 5*(2), 23–44.

Kendall, N. (2012). *The sex education debates.* Chicago: University of Chicago Press.

Kirby, D. B. (2008). The impact of abstinence and comprehensive sex and STD/HIV education programs on adolescent sexual behavior. *Sexuality Research and Social Policy, 5*(3), 18–27.

Kirby, D. B, & Laris, B. A. (2009). Effective curriculum-based sex and STD/HIV education programs for adolescents. *Child Development Perspectives, 3*(1), 21–29.

Lamb, S. (1997). Sex education as moral education: Teaching for pleasure, about fantasy, and against abuse. *Journal of Moral Education, 26*(3), 301–315.

Lamb, S. (2010). Toward a sexual ethics curriculum: Bringing philosophy and society to bear on individual development. *Harvard Educational Review, 80*(1), 81–106.

Lamb, S. (2013). *Sex ed for caring schools: Creating an ethics-based curriculum.* New York: Teachers College Press.

Laub, C., Somera, D.M., Gown K., & Diaz, R. (1999). Targeting 'risky' gender ideologies: Constructing a community-driven, theory-based HIV prevention intervention for youth. *Health Education and Behavior, 26*(2), 185–199.

Lesko, N. (2010). Feeling abstinent? Feeling comprehensive? Touching the affects of sexuality curricula. *Sex Education: Sexuality, Society and Learning, 10*(3), 281–297.

Levesque, R. J. (2000). Sexuality education: What adolescents' educational rights require. *Psychology, Public Policy, and Law, 6*(4), 953.

Levine, J. (2002). *Harmful to minors: The perils of protecting children from sex.* Minneapolis: University of Minnesota Press.

Levine, D. (2011). Using technology, new media, and mobile for sexual and reproductive health. *Sexuality Research and Social Policy, 8*(1), 18–26.

Lou, C. H., Zhao, Q., Gao, E. S., & Shah, I. H. (2006). Can the Internet be used effectively to provide sex education to young people in China? *Journal of Adolescent Health, 39*(5), 720–728.

Luker, K. (1996). *Dubious conceptions: The politics of teenage pregnancy.* Cambridge: Harvard University Press.

Luker, K. (2006). *When sex goes to school: Warring views on sex—And sex education—Since the sixties.* New York: WW Norton & Company.

Marshall, D. (2010). Popular culture, the 'victim' trope and queer youth analytics. *International Journal of Qualitative Studies in Education, 23*(1), 65–85.

Martin, E. (2001). *The woman in the body: A cultural analysis of reproduction.* Boston: Beacon Press.

Mayo, C. (2007). *Disputing the subject of sex: Sexuality and public school controversies.* Lanham, MD: Rowman & Littlefield.

Mayo, C. (2013). *LGBTQ youth and education: Policies and practices.* New York: Teachers College Press.

McClelland, S. I., & Fine, M. (2008). Embedded science: Critical analysis of abstinence-only evaluation research. *Cultural Studies ↔ Critical Methodologies, 8*(1), 50–81.

Moran, J. P. (2000). *Teaching sex: The shaping of adolescence in the 20th century.* Cambridge: Harvard University Press.

Naisteter, M. A., & Sitron, J. A. (2010). Minimizing harm and maximizing pleasure: Considering the harm reduction paradigm for sexuality education. *American Journal of Sexuality Education, 5*(2), 101–115.

Niccolini, A. D. (2013). Straight talk and thick desire in erotica noir: Reworking the textures of sex education in and out of the classroom. *Sex Education: Sexuality, Society and Learning, 13*(suppl. 1), S7–S19.

Ott, M. A., Pfeiffer, E. J., & Fortenberry, J. D. (2006). Perceptions of sexual abstinence among high-risk early and middle adolescents. *Journal of Adolescent Health, 39*(2), 192–198.

Pascoe, C. J. (2007). *Dude, you're a fag: Masculinity and sexuality in high school.* Berkeley: University of California Press.

Patton, C. (1996). *Fatal advice: How safe-sex education went wrong*. Durham, NC: Duke University Press.

Raby, R. (2012). *School rules: Obedience, discipline, and elusive democracy*. Toronto: University of Toronto Press.

Rasmussen, M. L. (2004). Wounded identities, sex and pleasure: "Doing it" at school. NOT!. *Discourse, 25*(4), 445–458.

Rasmussen, M. L. (2010). Secularism, religion and "progressive" sex education. *Sexualities, 13*(6), 699–712.

Robinson, K. H. (2013). *Innocence, knowledge and the construction of childhood: The contradictory nature of sexuality and censorship in children's contemporary lives*. New York: Routledge.

Rogow, D., & Haberland, N. (2005). Sexuality and relationships education: Toward a social studies approach. *Sex Education: Sexuality, Society and Learning, 5*(4), 333–344.

Rotheram-Borus, M. J., Swendeman, D., & Chovnick, G. (2009). The past, present, and future of HIV prevention: Integrating behavioral, biomedical, and structural intervention strategies for the next generation of HIV prevention. *Annual Review of Clinical Psychology, 5*, 143.

Russell, S. T. (2003). Sexual minority youth and suicide risk. *American Behavioral Scientist, 46*(9), 1241–1257.

Ryan, C., Russell, S. T., Huebner, D., Díaz, R., & Sanchez, J. (2010). Family acceptance in adolescence and the health of LGBT young adults. *Journal of Child and Adolescent Psychiatric Nursing, 23*(4), 205–213.

Sandlos, K. (2011). The enigmatic messages of sexuality education: Julie Gustafson's *Desire. Sexuality Research and Social Policy, 8*(1), 58–66.

Santelli, J. S. (2006). Abstinence-only education: Politics, science, and ethics. *Social Research: An International Quarterly, 73*(3), 835–858.

Santelli, J., Ott, M. A., Lyon, M., Rogers, J., & Summers, D. (2006a). Abstinence-only education policies and programs: A position paper of the Society for Adolescent Medicine. *Journal of Adolescent Health, 38*(1), 83–87.

Santelli, J., Ott, M., Lyon, M., Rogers, J., Summers, D., & Schleifer, R. (2006b). Abstinence and abstinence-only education: A review of U.S. policies and programs. *Journal of Adolescent Health, 38*(1), 72–81.

Sawyer, R. G., Howard, D. E., Brewster-Jordan, J., Gavin, M., & Sherman, M. (2007). "We didn't have sex… did we?" College students' perceptions of abstinence. *American Journal of Health Studies, 22*(1), 46–55.

Schaffner, L. (2005). *So called girl-on-girl violence is actually adult-on-girl violence*. Great Cities Institute Working Paper No. GCP-05-03. Chicago: Author.

Schalet, A. (2004). Must we fear adolescent sexuality? *Medscape General Medicine, 6*(4), 44.

Schalet, A. T. (2011). *Not under my roof: Parents, teens, and the culture of sex*. Chicago: University of Chicago Press.

Schalet, A. T., Santelli, J. S., Russell, S. T., Halpern, C. T., Miller, S. A., Pickering, S. S., Goldberg S. K., & Hoe-

nig, J. M. (2014). Invited Commentary: Broadening the Evidence for Adolescent Sexual and Reproductive Health and Education in the United States. *Journal of Youth and Adolescence, 43*(10), 1595–1610.

Schwartz, P. (2007). *Prime: Advice and adventures on sex, love and the sensuous years*. New York: Collins.

Silin, J. G. (1995). *Sex, death, and the education of children: Our passion for ignorance in the age of AIDS*. New York: Teacher's College Press.

Smith, G., Kippax, S., Aggleton, P., & Tyrer, P. (2003). HIV/AIDS school-based education in selected Asia-Pacific countries. *Sex Education: Sexuality, Society and Learning, 3*(1), 3–21.

Stein, A. (2006). *Shameless: Sexual dissidence in American culture*. New York: New York University Press.

Talburt, S. (2004). Constructions of LGBT youth: Opening up subject positions. *Theory into Practice, 43*(2), 116–121.

Tolman, D. L. (2002). *Dilemmas of desire: Teenage girls talk about sexuality*. Cambridge: Harvard University Press.

Trudell, B. N. (1993). *Doing sex education: Gender politics and schooling*. New York: Routledge.

Trudell, B., & Whatley, M. (1991). Sex Respect: A problematic public school sexuality curriculum. *Journal of Sex Education & Therapy, 17*(2), 125–140.

Wagoner, J. (2009). Appropriations bill marks victory for sexual health: Advocates need to remain vigilant. *Advocates for Youth Blog*. http://www.advocatesforyouth. org/blogs-main/advocates-blog/1544-appropriations-bill-marks-victory-for-sexual-health-advocates-need-to-remainvigilant. Accessed 2 Jan 2015.

Waxman, H. (2004). The content of federally funded abstinence-only education programs. Washington, DC: US House of Representatives Committee on Government Reform—Minority Staff Special Investigations Division. http://oversight. house. gov/documents/20041201102153-50247.pdf.

Weaver, H., Smith, G., & Kippax, S. (2005). School-based sex education policies and indicators of sexual health among young people: A comparison of the Netherlands, France, Australia and the United States. *Sex Education: Sexuality, Society and Learning, 5*(2), 171–188.

Whatley, M. H. (1988). Raging hormones and powerful cars: The construction of men's sexuality in school sex education and popular adolescent films. *Journal of Education, 170*(3), 100–121.

Whatley, M. H., & Trudell, B. K. (1993). Teen-Aid: Another problematic sexuality curriculum. *Journal of Sex Education & Therapy, 19*(4), 251–271.

Wight, D., & Abraham, C. (2000). From psycho-social theory to sustainable classroom practice: Developing a research-based teacher-delivered sex education programme. *Health Education Research, 15*(1), 25–38.

Wight, D., Raab, G. M., Henderson, M., Abraham, C., Buston, K., Hart, G., & Scott, S. (2002). Limits of teacher delivered sex education: Interim behavioural outcomes from randomised trial. *British Medical Journal, 324*(7351), 1430.

Sex Work

Susan Dewey

22.1 Defining Sex Work

Activist Carol Leigh coined the term "sex work" in the 1970s to refer to the exchange of intimacy for money or something of value. In so doing, she acknowledged transactional sexual exchange as worthy of the same respect accorded to other income-generating occupations (Leigh 1997). *Sex work* has become a widely accepted descriptive phrase that readily translates to other languages as well as the human rights frameworks integral to many international organizations and social justice activist groups. Examples of the term's common use in other languages include *trabajador sexual* in Spanish, *travailleuse du sexe* in French, and *professional do sexo* in Portuguese. Some speakers of languages that do not include a non-pejorative word for those who engage in sexual labor have embraced the English language term as part of a rights-based approach to the issue; hence it is as common to hear the English "sex worker" used by speakers of South Asian languages as it is to hear it at United Nations or other international gatherings.

Sex work encompasses a rather diffuse constellation of behaviors and associated beliefs that revolve around the exchange of sex or sexualized intimacy for money or something of value. Hence someone described as "a sex worker" can be a highly educated woman who charges thousands of dollars for a discreet hour in an equally expensive hotel room, or a man experiencing homelessness who quickly performs oral sex on another man in exchange for $ 20 or a place to sleep. Sex workers include people who self-identify with a variety of sexual orientations and gender identities, although these preferences are not always congruent with the type of sex work they perform. For instance, a heterosexually identified man, lesbian identified woman or transgender person may provide compensated sexual services to men, who constitute the majority of consumers, irrespective of their own sexual preferences.

The size and scope of the commercial sexual economy is extremely difficult to quantify due to a number of factors, including criminalization, the clandestine nature of most transactional sexual exchanges, and, of course, considerable variability in definitions of the behaviors that constitute sex work. Efforts at such quantification speak to these difficulties; for instance, one widely read report observed that income generated from what its authors termed "the underground commercial sexual economy" ranged from 39.9 to 290 million dollars (Dank et al. 2014, p. 2). Part of the problem with quantification stems from a tendency to collapse distinctions between different types of sex work, such that findings reported in popular publications on one specific type of sex work may be inappropriately generalized to all types of sex work. For instance, a highly respected newspaper analyzed 190,000 sex workers' online advertisements, and reported

S. Dewey (✉)
Department of Gender and Women's Studies, University of Wyoming, Laramie, WY, USA
e-mail: sdewey3@uwyo.edu

J. DeLamater, R.F. Plante (eds.), *Handbook of the Sociology of Sexualities,* Handbooks of Sociology and Social Research, DOI 10.1007/978-3-319-17341-2_22, © Springer International Publishing Switzerland 2015

a drop of almost $ 100 in hourly earnings for sex workers following the financial crisis ("Prostitution and the internet," 2014). While this is certainly an important finding with respect to the lives of relatively privileged female sex workers (the study ignored men and made no mention of transgender individuals), it is quite problematic that it featured under the rather authoritative title "Prostitution and the Internet" ("Prostitution and the internet," 2014).

As with research that attempts to quantify the commercial sexual economy, prevailing popular cultural representations focus upon transactional sexual exchanges that take place between male clients and female providers. Yet sex workers also include men, women, and transgender individuals providing services to clients who identify their own gender and sexual orientations in equally complex ways. Sex work also takes place in venues that vary tremendously in cost, services provided, levels of emotional intimacy, and risks posed. So while this catchall term helps to forge both theoretical and activist connections between various forms of sexual labor and those who perform it, such inclusivity belies considerable controversy among those engaged in transactional sex as well as the individuals, organizations, and governments concerned with its regulation.

22.2 Controversies Surrounding Sex Work

Although widely accepted among researchers, activists, and international organizations alike, the term "sex work" remains contentious among those who oppose sex work on moral, legal, or other ideological grounds. Affirming sexual labor as legitimate work deserving of state protections and endorsement proves problematic for those who believe that transactional sex, particularly prostitution, endorses male privilege and encourages violence against women. Ideological approaches to this issue are many and varied but can be characterized by three general positions, each with its own unique strengths and weaknesses, predominating contemporary debates: *sex workers' rights advocacy*, *abolitionism*, and *harm reduction*.

22.2.1 Sex Workers' Rights Advocacy

Sex workers' rights advocates contend that consenting adults should have the freedom to engage in paid sexual activities without fear of arrest or other forms of government intervention. Proponents of this position argue that legislation and policy related to this predominantly feminized form of work has historically been informed by religious, moral, or political beliefs that view the exchange of sex or sexualized intimacy for money as immoral, deviant, and harmful to society. With a rallying cry of "no bad women, just bad laws," this position dates from the 1970s, when sex workers such as Margo St. James and Carol Leigh combined second wave feminist demands for women's equal sexual rights with the sex positive movement that embraced sexuality as healthy and empowering. Examples of contemporary sex workers' rights groups include the national groups COYOTE (an acronym for Call off Your Old Tired Ethics), the Sex Workers Outreach Project (SWOP), as well as local urban groups such as the New York City-based Sex Workers Project of the Urban Justice Center, or the Calcutta-based Durbar Mahila Samanwaya Committee.

One of the greatest strengths of the sex workers' rights approach is its encouragement of labor organizing among an otherwise relatively disparate group of individuals in order to engage in collective action (Gall 2011; Chateauvert 2014). Weaknesses of the sex workers' rights position include its dominance by relatively privileged, well-educated, and predominantly white women, as well as its tendency to ignore the frequency of violence and trauma prevalent in less privileged forms of sex work often performed by women of color. Less privileged individuals engaged in transactional sex often do not self-identify as sex workers due to the stigma associated with these activities or acknowledgment that their engagement in them constitutes a survival behavior rather than a professional trajectory. Hence sex workers' rights advocates tend to neglect women of color and less class privileged women in their arguments that criminalization and social stigma, rather than the transactional sexual encounter itself, cause the greatest number of harms to individuals engaged in sex work.

22.2.2 Abolitionism

Abolitionists argue that transactional sex is an essentially violent, sexist act warranting moral, legal, and political condemnation. Contemporary abolitionists, who appropriate their name from the anti-slavery movement of the 1700s, draw parallels between conditions faced by women in prostitution today and persons enslaved as plantation laborers centuries earlier (Bernstein 2007a). Abolitionists argue that women cannot consent to prostitution or other forms of transactional sex due to the high frequency of violence, trauma, and addiction they believe to be inherent in exchanging sex for money. Examples of self-identified abolitionist organizations include the evangelical Christian International Justice Mission and the feminist Coalition against the Traffic in Women.

The abolitionist movement has been extraordinarily successful in its strategy of classifying all transactional sexual exchanges as "modern day slavery." For instance, the U.S. government's subscription to this ethos explicitly forbids the use of the term "sex work" in federal funding applications from scholars or practitioners (U.S. Department of State 2006). What abolitionists term an "end demand" approach, which has enjoyed global implementation, explicitly connects the commercial sex industry with the coercion involved in sex trafficking. Despite its successes, abolitionism takes a problematically heteronormative approach in its exclusive focus on women as sex workers and their male clients as violent abusers, completely neglecting the experiences of men and transgender individuals involved in sex work, as well as their non-violent clients. Scholars, such as sociologist Ronald Weitzer, have heavily criticized the abolitionist movement's use of unsubstantiated claims regarding the number of women forced into prostitution, as well as its highly emotionalized depiction of the issue (Weitzer 2010). Abolitionism's conflation of all forms of transactional sex with traf-

ficking also ignores the considerable diversity of experiences between, for instance, a woman dancing topless to pay for college and a person who engages in survival sex to mitigate their experiences with homelessness and addiction.

22.2.3 Harm Reduction

Harm reduction comprises a set of risk minimization practices first named in the 1980s as a response to the HIV-induced public health crisis that first, and most destructively, impacted individuals engaged in sex work and intravenous drug use (Cusick 2006). Recognizing that numerous sociostructural factors contribute to individuals' decisions to engage in stigmatized and criminalized sex work and drug use activities, harm reduction provides an achievable means to reduce health and safety risks among those who cannot, or do not wish to, stop. Examples of harm reduction might include providing condoms or clean syringes to sex workers who cannot afford or access them, or sharing strategies for lower contact, less invasive sexual practices (Overs and Longo 1996). Harm reduction groups tend to be community-based and rely on a peer-to-peer approach in which individuals, some of whom have direct life experiences with sex work and problematic drug use, engage in street or other forms of outreach to educate others about ways to protect themselves in behavioral environments that present health and safety risks.

Harm reduction's greatest strengths lie in its non-judgmental approach to stigmatized behaviors, such that an empathic outreach volunteer might be a vulnerable sex worker's only point of entry into necessary medical treatment or social support. By reaching out to some of the most marginalized individuals, harm reduction proponents argue that they directly facilitate healthier and safer communities as a whole by reducing disease transmission and incidences of unsafe sex and drug use. Yet this approach draws criticism from some criminal justice professionals and abolitionists who contend that harm reductionists' distribution of safer sex and drug use paraphernalia at best offers a superficial solution and, at worst, indirectly endorses these practices. One leader in the abolitionist movement succinctly states that harm reduction fails because "the world's sex slaves need liberation, not condoms" (Hughes 2003).

The specific cultural and historical context in which these debates take place, of course, heavily informs their content and direction. Historically, antagonistic debates about transactional sex have typically revolved around public health, community order, and the role of the state in regulating sexual conduct. Many scholars, for instance, have noted similarities between contemporary abolitionism and Progressive Era campaigns against "white slavery," both of which followed unprecedentedly high levels of migration and consequent shifts in sociosexual norms, and focused heavily upon the purported innocence of white women forced into prostitution by predatory immigrant, or non-white, Others (Doezema 2000; Donovan and Barnes-Brus 2011). Debates regarding sex work, including the appropriate terminology to describe the behavior itself, reveal much about broader cultural anxieties surrounding gendered sexual norms and related privileges.

22.3   Types of Sex Work

The cultural construction of sexuality, with its accompanying gender norms, standards of beauty, and beliefs, directly informs the diverse behaviors, practices, and beliefs comprising sex work. Yet even within a single cultural context, different types of sex work vary considerably in terms of labor conditions, legal status, risks, stigma, and the type of physical contact and emotional labor provided. Sex work constitutes a continuum of income generation activities ranging from performers who have limited contact with clients while dancing partially clothed or nude in a bar or other entertainment venue, to "full service" providers who independently advertise their sexual services on the Internet. While the former faces no risk of arrest, disease transmission, and faces relatively low levels of stigma, these are major concerns for the latter.

Sex work resembles most other forms of work in that privileges accorded on the basis of race, class, citizenship status, and other factors directly correlate with higher income, safer working conditions, greater negotiating powers with clients, and decreased likelihood of experiencing stigma or arrest. Hence conventionally attractive white women with higher education levels predominate at the upper echelons of the sex work continuum, while minorities, men who have sex with men, and transgender individuals face additional risks, lower earnings, and other limiting factors that, unfortunately, mirror the discriminatory forces that such individuals face in other social sectors of the society in which they live. In the United States, for instance, evidence suggests that women of color enter sex work at younger ages, face higher levels of violence (Clarke et al. 2012), receive less money for their work (Brooks 2010a), and face high levels of arrest, especially when combined with problematic substance use (Miller and Neaigus 2002).

This has been an issue in the sex workers' rights movement, such that a high-earning escort and a street-based worker who trades oral sex for small amounts of money share little in common (Dewey and Zheng 2013). A person who engages in a legal, often low-contact, form of transactional sex in the relative privacy of an indoor venue has an entirely different set of concerns than one facing homelessness, addiction, and police harassment while illegally soliciting clients on the street. For instance, New Zealand brothel workers enjoy government protections, including pensions and an occupational safety handbook (New Zealand Department of Labor 2004), whereas U.S. street workers face rates of violent death estimated at nearly 100 times their female counterparts who do not engage in this form of sex work (Quinet 2011).

Individuals may move between different types of sex work as they age, seek greater freedom in their work, migrate to another country, or work only occasionally due to an unusually high offer of money or rapport with a prospective client. For instance, research among U.S. exotic dancers, who work legally, suggests that the offer of additional money, combined with the fluid body boundaries while performing for clients, may encourage some women to occasionally engage in prostitution (Wesely 2003). Likewise, Chinese women working in hostess bars, where women sing karaoke with (and sometimes provide illegal sexual services for) their male clients, may follow a downward career trajectory from more lucrative, higher status venues to riskier, less well-paid forms of sex work as they age (Zheng 2009). Individuals who migrate to a new country seeking economic opportunities may engage in sex work when faced with poor wages and the anonymity offered in their new environment, which limits the possibility that friends and family in their place of origin will find out about their activities (Agustín 2007).

Despite such fluidity and variation among types of sexual labor and those who engage in it, this chapter delineates seven major types of sex work: live stage shows, pornography, massage and sauna, escorting, brothel or establishment-based, tourism-related, and street-based. Prevailing cultural norms, legislative and regulatory approaches, and, of course, individual characteristics of sex worker and client, all inform the particularities that characterize each type of work, including behavioral variation, cost, labor practices, safety, as well as the gender and sexual identity of sex worker and client.

Forms of sex work that are either legal, such as municipally-regulated live stage shows, or highly visible, such as street-based sex work, tend to predominate in the literature due to the comparative ease with which researchers can contact individuals working in these venues. Much less research exists on those forms of sex work that operate in a more clandestine manner because of criminalization, management concerns about alienating clients or drawing public attention to stigmatized or illegal activities that take place there, or, among those who work independently, individual desires to keep their work a secret.

22.3.1 Live Stage Shows

Stage shows generally take place in an indoor venue (typically a club or bar) designed specifically for this purpose and feature individuals who remove their clothing during the course of a song, perform topless or nude, or who model lingerie for an audience or single client. This form of sex work can also take place more privately, such as at bachelor parties or other events that take place at a location of the client's choice, such as a private home; clients generally organize such events by contacting the provider(s) or establishment directly. Cost of entry into such clubs range in price from, at the low end, the price of a beer and small tips distributed to dancers to several $ 100 in cover charges, tips, and high-priced alcohol or, in the case of a peep show, quarters inserted into a machine in front a window.

A lower end strip club will often feature an exhausted woman holding onto a pole mounted onstage as she shakes her thong-clad hips, scanning the audience of working class men to determine who she will solicit for a $20 private dance, her sole source of income, for which she will gyrate on the customer's lap (sometimes to the point of ejaculation) for the duration of a song (Bradley-Engen 2009). A higher cost establishment will likely have multiple stages where dancers have paid "stage fees" of up to $ 100 to perform (due to their classification, under U.S. labor law, as independent contractors) and feature numerous private rooms where dancers can solicit larger amounts of money from more privileged clients (Barton 2006). Somewhat paradoxically, higher cost venues have stricter rules regarding sexual contact, such that a client could much more realistically expect sexual contact at a lower cost venue (Dewey 2010). Stage shows may also feature elaborate acts designed to shock, such as in Thailand, where a performer may use her vagina to smoke a cigarette, eject ping pong balls at the audience, or as a receptacle from which she will remove a string of razor blades (Wilson 2010). They may also feature, as in Amsterdam, couples engaged in sexual intercourse on stage.

Erotic dancers may call themselves dancers, strippers, lingerie models or, less frequently, burlesque artists. In recent years these types of performances have become a greater part of popular culture in the United States and Western Europe, such that women who have no intention of engaging in sex work pay to take "stripper-cize" classes (Donaghue et al. 2011). Yet despite such popularity, erotic dance establishments in the U.S. frequently face restrictive zoning requirements, accusations of causing neighborhood decline, and other hostile community reactions (Hanna 2012). Such controversy speaks to their tenuous position as legal establishments operating in a cultural environment that generally stigmatizes the sex industry as harmful to society.

As with other forms of sex work, women are the majority of live stage show performers and men comprise the majority of clients. Yet sex workers who perform live stage shows also include, albeit in fewer numbers, muscular men who perform for heterosexually-identified women (Montemurro et al. 2003), or couples. Go-go dancing, which svelte young men perform at gay clubs (DeMarco 2002), transgender beauty or singing competitions (Hwahng and Nuttbrock 2007), and other live stage shows performed in queer communities can go far beyond a simple income generation strategy to constitute important forms of sexualized self-expression for some individuals.

22.3.2 Pornography

Pornography comprises sexually explicit acts or poses recorded as still images, visual recordings of varying duration, and live performances via streaming video (see Wosick, this volume). The rapid expansion of the Internet revolutionized the pornography industry such that a dizzying array of sexually explicit materials catering to extremely specialized markets have proliferated. Indeed, a team of neuroscientists who undertook the largest-ever study of online pornography use estimate that a full 14 % of total Internet searches and 4 % of websites are devoted to sexually explicit materials (Ogas and Gaddam 2012). According to technology industry specialists, the largest pornographic websites have 4.4. billion page views per month and are three times larger than CNN or ESPN (Anthony 2012). Contemporary pornography contains even more variance than other types of sex work due to the speed

with which images can be produced and disseminated via various online portals. For analytical purpose, pornography may be grouped into the three broad categories of *softcore*, *hardcore*, and, more recently, *gonzo*, all of which feature preference-based specializations regarding body type, sex acts performed, gender identity, ethnicity or race, partner combinations, and fetish, a broad category comprising behaviors often related to materials (such as shoes or latex) or behavioral practices (such as body modification or bondage).

Softcore pornography includes print media, such as well-known magazines like *Playboy* and *Hustler*, as well as video, and typically features non-penetrative sexual activity that may involve a single person, two persons of the same or opposite sex, or many individuals. Hardcore pornography can also involve multiple media formats but distinguishes itself in its display of full vaginal or anal penetration with an object or other body part. Gonzo pornography, which takes its name from Hunter S. Thompson's "gonzo journalism," in which the reporter directly participates in events being chronicled, is a more extreme form of hardcore pornography that frequently features extreme and often lengthy close-ups of penetrative sex acts, some of which may be filmed by the participants themselves (Hardy 2008). Amateur aspirants to pornographic fame who do not feature in third party-produced images and videos may post their own on the websites, such as Xtube, which offer them a percentage of the profits.

Researchers have explored the question of whether pornography simply mirrors broader socio-sexual norms or actually encourages harmful practices, particularly violence against women (Boyle 2011) and women of color's sexualization in problematic ways that perpetuate racism (Brooks 2010b; Miller-Young 2014). Overlap between pornography and other sex industry sectors can pose increased risks to sex workers, especially when clients request or demand particular acts involving aggression, body fluids, or other potentially harmful practices they have viewed onscreen. This is not a new phenomenon, as evidence suggests that the advent of 1980s VHS technology, which allowed individuals to watch pornography at home rather than visiting an adult theater, directly contributed to increased body contact during lap dances at strip clubs seeking to compete with lower costs forms of adult entertainment that could be viewed privately (Shteir 2005, pp. 317–325).

These debates began in the 1970s, when feminist scholars began to argue that pornography objectifies and reduces women to things, commodities, and sexual body parts for men's sexual enjoyment (Dworkin 1981). More contemporary feminists build upon these critiques by arguing that pornography's highly sexualized images of women has saturated U.S. popular culture and consequently negatively impacted sexual relationships between men and women, sometimes to the point of addicting viewers (Dines 2011). Individuals who take this position point to the mainstream adoption of garments, such as women's thong underwear, or other bodily adornments which were once only visible in pornography.

Yet others argue that pornography can be an important educational tool with the potential to expand sexual horizons (Albury 2014; Weinberg et al. 2010). Research suggests that pornography plays an important role in queer communities by providing positive images gender and sexual identities (Thomas 2010). Transgender activist and pornography performer Buck Angel, for instance, considers the use of his hyper-masculine muscular physique and vagina in pornography a political act in its subversion of heteronormative gender stereotypes (Hunt 2011). There are also genres of feminist pornography that cater specifically to lesbians, heterosexually-identified women, and couples (Bakehorn 2010).

Research with women who perform in pornography does not support claims that the industry is inherently abusive. For instance, such actresses reported enjoying sex more and had higher self-esteem than their female counterparts who did not perform in pornography (Griffith et al. 2013). In a counterpart study, only a small minority (14 %) of male performers entered the industry for the money, with most citing lifestyle factors as the main motivators for entry (Griffith et al. 2012).

Pornography tends to be filmed and distributed quickly, with men generally paid less than their female counterparts (Escoffier 2007), although they may also have more room for advancement as directors or editors (Abbott 2010). Well-known or very popular performers earn a quarter million dollars per year (Grudzen et al. 2009), and may occasionally contract as "features" at live stage show venues where their popularity ensures a large audience and, quite often, disdain from the dancers who regard them as engaged in a lower status form of sex work (Dewey 2010). They also make appearances at professional conventions, such as the Adult Video News (AVN) Expo, where they meet their fans, showcase their work, and raise their popularity (Voss 2012).

Such interaction between pornography performers and their fans also takes place in webcam modeling, in which a (typically male) customer, uses a personal computer to access a website that takes his credit card information in exchange for a set period of interactive time with a performer, who is usually a seductively dressed or nude female (Attwood 2011). The customer can request the webcam model to perform particular sexual acts, which she does from a location that remains undisclosed to the customer (Bleakley 2014). Pornography performers and producers, who work in a global industry with multiple hubs, operate at the edges of the law due to considerable variations in national legislation and shifting perspectives on the subject.

22.3.3 Massage and Sauna

Massage parlors, saunas, and, in some Asian contexts, barbershops and beauty salons, are all venues that can serve as locations for transactional sexual exchanges under the guise of providing or receiving other, generally less socially stigmatized services, such as a body rub or haircut. Such establishments may advertise the sexual activities possible there explicitly or through client word of mouth regarding sexual services contracted there during or after a massage (Soothill 2004). As with other forms of sex work, the degree of openness with which these services are advertised and provided depend largely on the legislative and cultural climate in which such businesses operates.

Massage parlor-related sex work can involve a quick, clandestine encounter following a massage, or a long, involved and emotionalized exchange between sex worker and client. Saunas and related establishments, likewise, may advertise body-related pleasures and relaxation, which are not explicitly sexual in and of themselves, in ways that make it clear to potential clients that sex is for sale on site. These advertisements vary based upon local laws; for instance, prostitution between two consenting adult partners is legal in Brazil yet profiting from such an exchange is not. Hence the sexual acts that take place in exchange for money between consenting adults in a massage parlor or sauna are not illegal, but the establishment's cut into the sex workers' profits are, in fact, against the law (Blanchette and da Silva 2011).

Massage and sauna venues almost always employ sex workers of a specific gender identity and service clients of a particular sexual orientation. Such establishments in Brazil can range from those staffed by conventionally attractive young women who offer older men sex for money, or others where men, who may or may not self-identify as gay or bisexual, provide sexual services to men, some of whom travel from North America or Western Europe for this purpose (Mitchell 2010). Venues may also include establishments that do not explicitly advertise sex for sale for legal or other reasons, such as those at Japan's Soaplands, where female sex workers provide male clients with a warm bubble bath as well as sexual services (Miyazaki et al. 2002). Barbershops and beauty salons in China, South Korea, and elsewhere in East Asia sometimes function as sex work venues due to the ease with which such establishments can clandestinely carry out prostitution-related activities under the guide of providing legal services (Chin and Finckenauer 2012).

A number of North American massage parlor workers are migrant women from Asia, particularly China, Vietnam, and Thailand, who sometimes work with limited English proficiency and knowledge about their legal rights (Nemoto et al. 2003). One study in Vancouver, for instance, found that Canada-born massage parlor workers perceived their work as more violent and dangerous than their migrant counterparts, who faced significant social and legal barriers to finding safer working conditions (Bungay et al. 2012). The legal status of massage parlor-based sex work likewise plays a critical role in workers' well-being; one Norway-based study, for instance, found that policymakers willful disregard of the perspectives of women employed in such establishments worsened their working conditions and overall well-being (Skilbrei 2001). These findings underscore that, as with other forms of labor, an individual's experience of sex industry participation directly intersects with numerous other structural inequalities, including the right to be heard. Hence some sex workers may find it preferable to work more independently as an escort who advertises her or his own sexual services or pays a third party to deal with clients.

22.3.4   Escorting

Escort work, like pornography, changed dramatically following the proliferation of web hosting services that make it easy for a person to advertise her or his sexual services online, complete with seductive photographs and select amounts of personal information. An escort may also do this through an agency, which invariably requires a percentage of the sex workers' profits in return. North American individuals engaged in escort work may advertise independently on low-cost websites such as backpage or craigslist, where descriptions are short and often designed to evade law enforcement's scrutiny while also piquing client interest.

Escorts may also have their own websites that, depending upon the laws governing prostitution in the area where they work, describe the sexual services they offer. For those working in places where prostitution is illegal, many explicitly state that the client will pay to spend time with her (or him), with no guarantee of sexual services provided. Such websites rarely show the face of the individual whose services are advertised, which serves the dual function of protecting their privacy through relative anonymity and, in criminalized environments, evading identification by police.

Those escorts who advertise independently enjoy a level of autonomy, discretion, and an ability to selectively choose clients that is rather unique among sex workers. These escorts, however, tend to have higher levels of education and associated class and racial privileges that, in turn, make them appealing to affluent clients who may regard them as peers in some respects (Bernstein 2007b). Research that has more specifically explored the role of race in escorting observes that sex workers of color may encounter clients who want to engage in demeaning acts of racialized dominance; people of color employed by escort agencies noted that they received less money and were advertised in ways that depicted them as uneducated or hyper-sexualized (Koken et al. 2009).

Escorts who offer in-call services have the client come to a location of the sex worker's choice, such as a rented apartment or condominium unit, or, less frequently, their own home. Those who do out-call work, which is more common due to the high costs of in-call work and, for those who work illegally, risks of police detection, travel to the client's choice of location for the sexual encounter. Even researchers who explicitly oppose the legalization or decriminalization of sex work acknowledge that independent escorts, most of whom use the Internet as their preferred communication tool, work without regulation and are very difficult for law enforcement to detect and monitor (Jeffreys 2010).

Escorts may also offer clients a girlfriend or boyfriend experience, which involves the sort of affective labor that an intimate partner might provide. Such arrangements may mirror relationships that do not involve the explicit exchange of such for money, leading one researcher, based upon her research in Cambodia to characterize this role as "professional girlfriend" (Hoefinger 2013). Research with clients indicate that this form of sex work may even be preferred among men who buy sex due to the heightened levels

of intimacy and affective bonds involved (Milrod and Monto 2012).

Escorts' relative anonymity and increased control over their working conditions and client choice do not, unfortunately, seem to reduce the amount of stigma they experience. Both female and male escorts in one U.S. study reported facing social isolation and anxiety regarding when, and to whom, they could fully disclose the true nature of their income-generating activities (Koken 2012; Koken et al. 2004). Male escorts additionally seem to report more positive experiences, including heightened self-esteem and pleasure taken in having multiple sex partners (Uy et al. 2004).

Escorts' client recruitment methods may partially account for the work's positive impacts, particularly among those who solicit clients from public locations, such as bars or hotels, where less explicitly transactional forms of sexual exchange also transpire. Studies of this form of sex work are quite limited, due perhaps in part to clandestine working circumstances, but existing research indicates that its associated discretionary practices can considerably increase sex worker control of the exchange. These practices can include extended periods in a social setting, most often a bar or other convivial environment with others present, where a sex worker may scrutinize a client's behavior while engaging in flirtatious banter that helps to create an affective bond, prior to deciding whether to engage in sex (Hoang 2011; Trotter 2007). Sex workers may cede some of this control, albeit while receiving additional protections, when working in a fixed site establishment, such as a brothel or other building that provides sexual services.

22.3.5 Brothel or Establishment-Based

Brothel or establishment-based sex work generally involves a number of sex worker colleagues congregating in a single indoor location designed for that purpose, such as a hotel-like structure with multiple bedrooms, a hostess bar, or a more clandestine site that may appear to be a private residence in order to avoid police detection.

Establishment-based sex workers operate in an environment that is both highly independent, in terms of sex worker's individual responsibilities to solicit clients, and also subject to surveillance in that workers must provide owners and managers with a percentage of their income and follow rules regarding behavior and comportment. Individuals may reside and engage in sex work in the same location for an extended period of time in order to save money on accommodation or, as a public health regulation (Brents and Hausbeck 2005; Kelly 2008).

Legal forms of establishment-based sex work typically feature government oversight in some form, usually in terms of licensing, mandatory health checks, and registration of individual sex workers. For instance, women who advertise themselves to potential clients through windows in the red light districts of Amsterdam and Antwerp pay to rent the windowed room where prostitution takes place, and face oversight by municipal authorities (Weitzer 2012). In the U.S., establishments that provide sexual services are illegal and their owners, managers, and employees subject to arrest, with the exception of 11 counties in the state of Nevada, where county governments tightly regulate brothels. These establishments charge workers rent in addition to taking a percentage of their profits, making them lucrative legal business ventures (Brents et al. 2010).

Offering sexual services for money is also illegal in China and Japan, two countries featuring large numbers of hostess bars, establishments that offer groups of male patrons female companionship through shared karaoke singing and alcohol consumption (Kamise 2013). While some hostess bars feature rooms for sex and make no secret of the services on offer, not all such establishments offer illegal sexual services. Many hostess bar workers are female migrants from rural areas (Zheng 2009) or from other, less affluent countries (Parreñas 2011) whose economic vulnerability may lead them to engage in transactional sex with clients. There are also "host bar" establishments staffed by men paid to drink alcohol and sing karaoke with women clients (Takeyama 2010).

The intermediary status of the brothel or other sexualized venue as a fixed site establishment facilitating the act of prostitution renders it in a liminal category that can make research access difficult even when brothel work is completely legal. This stems partially from the reality that brothels and related establishments generally face regulatory requirements exceeding those of businesses unrelated to sexual commerce, which may make managers and owners wary of researchers (Crofts 2010). Establishments that researchers have been able to document range in size from apartments (O'Connell Davidson 1998) to Germany's "mega-brothels," large-scale and often multi-story buildings employing many sex workers (Isgro et al. 2013).

The fixed site nature of brothel or other forms of establishment-based sex work sharply distinguishes it from more opportunity-based varieties that arise, by and large, from socioeconomic disparities, such as those that occur between tourists and locals. In sharp contrast to the business model that informs brothel or other establishment-based sex work, tourism-based sexual encounters or, in some cases, relationships, can arise when neither party expects it and can be difficult to differentiate from other forms of consensual sexual behavior.

22.3.6 Tourism-Related

The prominent intersections between sex work and the dynamics of race, class, gender, and citizenship privilege emerge with stark clarity in sex tourism, in which those with the relative privilege of leisure time and disposable income travel to another country and engage in sex with local people. While not all tourist-local sex constitutes an intentional exploitation of preexisting socioeconomic and racial inequalities, such sexual encounters can be complicated by the stark differences in access to privilege. This is exemplified by the frequency with which tourists experience freedom of mobility and locals struggle with difficulties in making ends meet.

Locales known throughout Western Europe and North America as popular destinations for (predominantly) older white males to travel in search of sex primarily with younger women of African or Asian descent, often have histories of domination by colonial empires, including the U.S. military. Some sex tourism destinations in Asia, for instance, emerged due to their close proximity to U.S. military bases (Cheng 2010; Kovner 2012). Many locales where sex tourism takes place are popular destinations for visitors due to scenic beaches and year-round warm temperatures, which some scholars have argued contributes to perceptions among tourists that the rules of home, including social norms governing sexual conduct and appropriate partner choice, do not apply (Padilla 2007).

Neocolonial stereotypes dating from the era of the Caribbean plantation economy, which relied almost exclusively on labor performed by enslaved persons of African descent, inform some North American and Western European tourists' perceptions of Caribbean and Latin American people as hyper-sexualized (Cabezas 2009; Williams 2013). Yet not all sex tourism fits a problematic, and often racialized, sexual stereotype of aging white men seeking sex with much younger women. Gay men also travel to destinations in search of sexual encounters with local men, sometimes situating their choices as part of a sexually liberating human rights framework that imagines local men as imprisoned by homophobic cultural norms that otherwise prohibit them from expressing their true sexual orientation (Mitchell 2011). In the Caribbean, North American and Western European women draw upon the same set of racialized gender stereotypes as their male counterparts in seeking out Afro-Caribbeans, who supposedly possess greater sexual prowess and other masculinized traits than men in their home country (Sanchez Taylor 2006).

Forming a sexual or long-term affective bond with a tourist represents one of the few means by which some women may achieve their dreams of migrating to another country or having a financially self-sufficient household. Women in the Dominican Republic who become involved in sexual relationships with tourists, many of whom come from Germany, may simultaneously juggle several men, who likely do not know about each other, with the knowledge that few are likely to send remittances or maintain contact once they leave the island, let alone provide a sought-after means to migrate abroad (Brennan 2004). Similar affective or sexual strategies have been reported in numerous countries, including lesser-frequented destinations such as Madagascar (Cole 2010), and highlight the socioeconomic disparities between visitors and locals. Yet these strategies also represent a powerful tool of resistance, in which local people refuse to accept the structural conditions that limit their mobility and, in some ways, tourists seek liberation from the constraints of home.

22.3.7 Street-Based

Street-based prostitution takes distinct forms specific to the cultural and community context in which it occurs. Generally, this form of sex work is unregulated and conducted in public spaces with varying degrees of discretion that depend upon the legal and social environment. These can range from an ordinarily dressed single woman who sits at a bus stop, appearing to wait for public transportation in a neighborhood where prostitution frequently occurs and is highly policed, to, in areas where street-based solicitation is tolerated, a sexily dressed transgender individual in elaborate makeup and stiletto heels openly and flirtatiously hailing prospective clients.

In North America, this form of sex work is illegal and often directly correlates with addiction, homelessness, and other marginalizing life circumstances that make it a highly dangerous and poorly paid activity, and yet this is not the case everywhere in the world. Street-based sex work generally take place in outdoor locations frequented by large numbers of transient men, such as truck stops or ports (Trotter 2011), or urban neighborhoods either zoned for that purpose by a municipal authority, as in the "drive-in sex" facilities of Amsterdam and Zurich (Foulkes 2013), or characterized by urban blight and the drug economy (Hubbard and Sanders 2003).

North American street-based sex workers experience high levels of researcher scrutiny from the fields of public health, with its focus on addiction and disease transmission, criminal justice, with a concern about prostitution's connection to other forms of illegal activity, and feminist research, which tends to highlight the abuses women face in this form of work. Indeed, research consistently emphasizes that North American street-based sex workers frequently experience higher rates of violence than others who do not engage in this form of sex work (Dalla et al. 2003). Often, such violence is a by-product of criminalized environments characterized by multiple forms of structural and interpersonal violence that also exist outside the context of the paid sexual encounter (Romero-Daza et al. 2005).

Street-based sex work can be independent, in which a woman works entirely on her own to solicit clients, or with a pimp who takes a percentage (or, in some cases, all) of her income (Norton-Hawk 2004; Williamson and Cluse-Tolar 2002). Pimp control has become the focus of increased scrutiny in North America due to criminal justice professionals' and activists' anti-trafficking efforts, which assert that the relationship between a sex worker and a pimp is akin to the trauma bond established in a domestic violence relationship. As such, a "trauma-informed approach" informs most North American court-mandated prostitution diversion programming, which usually involves a woman arrested for prostitution being sentenced to attend a therapeutic group in which social services providers encourage women to "work on" examining life events that supposedly led to their engagement in street-based sex work (Peiss 2005).

Street-based sex work may also be a survival strategy for transgender individuals, particularly those who face multiple forms of structural violence when they cannot "pass" as conventionally masculine or feminine. This can make it difficult to find employment, housing, or shelter accommodation, the latter of which tends to be segregated by heteronormative sex categories. Young transgender people who have run away from abusive homes or have been thrown out by transphobic or unsupportive parents, also can face limited options for income generation such that

street-based sex work can be an appealing option. This form of sex work can also potentially provide an affirming statement of sexual attractiveness for a person with a history of stigmatization because of his or her gender identity (Sausa et al. 2007).

Street-based sex work can also be conceived as a tool of resistance in communities that face systematic exclusion from socioeconomic opportunities. Anthropologists Claire Sterk (1999) and Lisa Maher (2000) conducted ethnographic studies in Atlanta and New York City, respectively, with primarily African-American women engaged in street-based sex work to support a crack cocaine addiction. Their findings highlighted how some women found liberation in crack and street-based sex work as it allowed them to eschew the significant constraints that otherwise shaped the alternatives open to them, including low-wage work and extensive parenting responsibilities while living in poverty. For such women, these freedoms outweighed the indisputably high personal costs of violence, arrest, and other forms of state surveillance.

22.4 Theoretical Approaches and Associated Regulatory Frameworks

Contemporary regulatory frameworks that focus upon sex work tend to cluster into three distinct types, all of which draw upon particular ideological stances toward sex work: *criminalization, legalization,* and *decriminalization.* These legislative and policy approaches tend to reflect prevailing cultural norms regarding sexuality and gender as well as entrenched beliefs about privacy and the appropriate role of the state in regulating individual behavior deemed unseemly or problematic by powerful groups. Some governments and municipalities, as in the case of decriminalization in New Zealand or health policy in Brazil, consult directly with sex workers to formulate evidence-based approaches to these enduring issues. Others, as in the United States, completely ignore sex workers as a constituent group and implement policies and laws developed using a criminal justice approach that relies almost exclusively on incarceration and court-mandated diversion programming.

22.4.1 Criminalization

The *criminalization* approach tends to frame sex work as a deviant behavior linked to other illegal or socially harmful activities, such as the illicit drug economy, sex trafficking, and the spread of sexually transmitted infections. This approach takes a zero tolerance position which tasks the criminal justice system with the oversight of sex workers through their arrest in undercover operations, street "sweeps," and subsequent incarceration or mandated drug and therapeutic treatment. Abolitionist ideology, which views all sex work as a form of violence against women, also supports criminalization, with a special focus on the arrest and punishment of sex workers' clients, who abolitionists believe to be engaging in abusive and pathological behavior (Lederer 2010).

This legislative approach is rarely clear-cut, as it may make some forms of sex work, or some behaviors associated with sex work, illegal while others remain legal or entirely outside the purview of state regulation. Topless or nude dancers in the U.S., who perform legally, must adhere to complex rules regarding their distance from clients, types of touching allowed, and degrees of nudity; failure to follow these rules can result in a prostitution arrest (Dewey 2010). Likewise, the Canadian province of Ontario enforces legal statutes surrounding nearly all the conditions and behaviors necessary for prostitution to take place, including communicating for the purposes of prostitution (van der Meulen 2010).

Proponents of criminalization subscribe to a model of deterrence and intervention whereby arrest can remove from the general population and potentially rehabilitate individuals engaged in behaviors deemed morally problematic by the state. Due to their high visibility in public, North American street-based sex workers face very high rates of arrest. Potential benefits of criminalization, accordingly, include court-mandated addictions or therapeutic treatment for a population that faces high rates of problematic substance abuse and past histories of trauma (Shdaimah and Wiechelt 2012). In the U.S., street-based sex work typically takes place in poor communities predominated by the drug economy, subjecting all neighborhood women to solicitation by men, which criminalization attempts to deter. Additional benefits of criminalization include the potential identification of women and girls forced into prostitution, and community disavowal of male sexual privilege.

Criminalization's negative consequences for sex workers and, less frequently, their clients, include arrest, incarceration, and lifelong criminal records that can make it difficult to find legal employment, housing, or government benefits. Evidence suggests that criminalization increases health and safety risks for sex workers, particularly those who work outdoors, due to high rates of policing which can force women to work in isolated areas and limit their ability to negotiate condom use (Shannon et al. 2009). In the U.S., police may use condoms as evidence in support of a prostitution conviction, which discourages sex workers from carrying them. Until relatively recently in the U.S. state of Louisiana, sex workers could face felony charges and mandatory sex offender registration for engaging in oral or anal sex for money; many states likewise make prostituting with HIV, irrespective of the act performed or whether the parties used a condom, a felony offense (Dewey and St. Germain 2014). Criminalization is also very costly to taxpayers due to the law enforcement activities it necessitates.

With a few exceptions, the criminalization approach to sex work prevails in the United States, China, Sweden, and Iran; in the latter sex workers may receive a sentence of death by stoning ("Applications of Islamic Law," 2005). Sex workers in China face incarceration as well as mandatory internment in facilities designed to rehabilitate them (Jacobs 2014); these are not categorically different from the court-mandated prostitution diversion programs (some of which are residential) U.S. sex workers can find themselves living in following their arrest (Wahab and Panichelli 2013). The "Swedish model," a form of criminalization highly praised by abolitionists, focuses on ending consumer demand for transactional sexual services by arresting sex workers' clients, rather than the sex workers themselves (Berger 2012).

22.4.2 Legalization

The *legalization* approach tends to position sex work as an enduring human reality that warrants state oversight as a means to minimize public health and safety risks for sex workers, their clients, and the communities in which they live. Municipal authorities typically oversee this regulatory mechanism by requiring sex industry establishments, individuals who work in them, or both, to register with a government-appointed authority, submit to mandatory health screenings, pay taxes, and comply with health, safety, and other workplace standards established by a government entity. In this approach, government's appropriate role in regulating individual transactional sexual behavior involves oversight that, in some respects, resembles other forms of legal business.

As with criminalization, the legalization approach typically focuses its attentions upon particular types of sex work and sex workers, such that some face more state scrutiny than others. Sex workers in the U.S.-Mexico border city of Tijuana, for instance, may register with a municipal authority and receive a permit to legally practice their trade, yet individuals who are not citizens of Mexico are ineligible to do so and consequently face police harassment and numerous other risks while working illegally (Katsulis 2010). Nairobi, Kenya-based sex workers, likewise, frequently face police harassment, client violence, and other negative work-related outcomes because many remain unaware that prostitution is not illegal under Nairobi municipal by-laws (Izugbara 2011).

Proponents of legalization contend that this approach has numerous benefits for the state and its citizens by generating tax revenue, ensuring public health through increased condom use and mandatory health screenings for sex workers, and

reducing stigma. Legalization can also increase sex workers' safety by ensuring a non-adversarial police presence in neighborhoods or establishments in which they work, as well as by encouraging sex workers to report abuse without fear of arrest (Office of Police Integrity 2008). Further, legalization could deter men who, in criminalized systems, capitalize on sex workers' fears of police to commit violent acts with impunity, or serial murderers who target sex workers because investigation of their deaths often do not receive the same scrutiny as other homicide cases (Salfati et al. 2008).

Critics of legalization argue that legalizing any form of sex work effectively puts the state in the pimping business by regulating and profiting, via tax revenue, from the ultimate expression of male sexual privilege (Jeffreys 2008). Opponents also contend that mandatory health checks for sex workers only reinforce this privilege and may, in fact, be meaningless given that sex workers' clients are not subject to health screenings in any form. Others feel that legalization is inherently morally objectionable on religious grounds, which may prohibit sexual expression outside of marriage.

Municipalities or other forms of local government may choose to legalize certain forms of sex work, even in countries where these practices are otherwise illegal. Eleven counties in the U.S. state of Nevada, for instance, have legalized brothel-based prostitution with the provision that such establishments must meet stringent standards regarding taxation and health screenings, among others (Brents et al. 2010). Such establishments have faced criticism regarding the practice of forcing sex workers to sign a contract that does not permit them to leave the facility for the weeks or months in which they are working there, and mandates high percentages of money sex workers must give to the establishment (Farley 2007). Legalization can also be intimately tied to broader state projects, as in the Mexican state of Chiapas, where politicians aimed to modernize sexual commerce by opening and regulating a legal brothel known as The Galactic Zone (Kelly 2008).

22.4.3 Decriminalization

The *decriminalization* approach to sex work involves the removal of laws related to transactional sexual exchange between consenting adults. This approach generally stems from the belief that state intervention in such exchanges incurs high criminal justice or regulatory costs to the state that, in turn, offer relatively low benefits to society at large. In some instances, this approach may also be informed by the philosophy of harm reduction and culturally entrenched beliefs about adults' rights to sexual privacy. Sex workers' rights activists often support decriminalization, which does not subject their income generating activities to taxation, mandatory health screenings, or other forms of government oversight.

While decriminalization necessitates the removal of laws related to the exchange of sex for money between consenting adults, laws forbidding potentially abusive practices remain in place. These can include statutes regarding pimping, trafficking, or otherwise profiting from the sexual labor of others, as well as laws against minor participation in sex work. Likewise, sex workers involved in the drug economy or other illegal activities still face criminal sanctions for these activities in systems where sex work is decriminalized.

Advocates of decriminalization argue that research consistently shows that criminalizing sex work and its practice limits women's choices and forces them to work on the margins of society, thereby increasing their risk of physical and sexual violence. Studies clearly show that decriminalization is generally associated with better health status, reduced stigma, and access to services for sex workers (Abel et al. 2010; Harcourt et al. 2010). Still others argue that the state should not intervene in adult's sexual decision-making practices, including by profiting from these practices via taxation, and accordingly support decriminalization.

Decriminalization's opponents contend that the state has a moral responsibility to regulate public health threats and other negative ancillary elements sometimes thought to accompany transactional sexual exchange. In so doing, opponents of this policy may employ dominant moral discourses regarding the risks that sex work poses to society, themselves, and the wider socio-moral order. Other opponents may fear that eschewing all regulation of sex work creates an environment of lawlessness and disorder that may, in fact, increase the risks for parties involved in transactional sexual exchange as well as society at large.

Perhaps the most famous instance of decriminalization is New Zealand, where law and policy employed evidence-based knowledge to advocate for harm reduction (Abel et al. 2010). De facto decriminalization may also exist when police, whether due to corruption or lack of resources, decide not to enforce existing laws due to prevailing acceptance of sex work in particular neighborhoods, such as the Patpong area of Bangkok, where sex work constitutes the major industry despite its illegality (Khruakham and Lawton 2012). While the legal intentions underlying each of these situations is different, the effect is the same.

22.5 Methodologies Employed in Sex Work Research

Sex work research methodologies tend to be specific to both the parameters of researchers' home disciplines as well as the cultural and legal context surrounding the type of sexual labor under study. Anthropologists and some other social scientists, for instance, must spend long periods of time developing strong bonds of rapport with research participants and often do so through active participation in the sex work environment under study (see Perez-y-Perez, Chap. 7, this volume). The goal of such ethnographic work is to uncover the nuances of sex workers' everyday lives and the worldviews which inform their decision-making. Conversely, public health, social epidemiology, and related biomedical fields often require researchers to collect large amounts of information, sometimes in a short period of time, about many different research participants in order to assert the scientific validity of their claims.

These different methodological approaches each have particular strengths in the ways that they highlight specific aspects of sex workers' experiences. Large-scale public health studies, for instance, emphasize the higher rates of violence and drug-related vulnerabilities that many street-based sex workers face (Shannon et al. 2007), while ethnographies of their everyday lives and work practices illuminate how street-involved individuals may conceive of their sex work and drug use activities as a form of resistance to gendered and racialized constraints on their life choices (Sterk 1999). Likewise, ethnographies of topless dancers may stress the women's emotional labor and stigma-related toll this work takes on their relationships (Price-Glynn 2010), whereas public health research with this group of women may focus on their drug use or sexual exchange practices (Reuben et al. 2011).

Researchers generally recruit sex worker participants in one of three ways: through the establishments where they work, chain referral strategies that rely upon established trust networks between sex worker colleagues, or through institutional facilities that incarcerate or provide court-mandated therapeutic treatment for sex workers. Workplace recruitment works well when the type of sex work under study enjoys legal status, and published research reflects this in the large number of publications on strip clubs, most of which has been conducted by women, some of whom performed as dancers during the course of their research (Egan 2006; Frank 2002). Female researchers have also worked at hostess bars in China and Japan as a means to participate directly in the women's lives (Parreñas 2011; Zheng 2009).

Chain referral strategies may be the only option for researchers who want to engage with sex workers who solicit clients outside of fixed venues, or who face the threat of criminal sanctions for their activities and may understandably be resistant to outsiders. Research with escorts relies typically relies upon chain referral, as some individuals who perform this type of sex work may not publically disclose their activities (Wahab 2004). Those who carry out work in sex worker communities may be fortunate enough to participate in everyday life events that highlight

the nuances of cultural elements that frame their lives (Day 2007; Kelly 2008).

Part of the reason that street-based sex workers have been studied so extensively is that they are more readily accessibly due to the ease with which researchers can locate such individuals in jail, homeless shelters, addiction treatment facilities, or in urban neighborhoods that function as informal prostitution tolerance zones. Public health and criminal justice interests in street-based sex work, at least in North America, stem from its connections to addiction, as research demonstrates that some, but by no means all, sex workers engage in drug abuse, and that addiction strongly correlates with street-based sex work in many urban locales (Edwards et al. 2006).

Potentially problematic ethical issues arise in all methodological approaches due to the social and/or criminal sanctions sex workers face in almost all societies. Researchers, most of whom are social scientists, have only relatively recently begun to explore these issues in published works (Dewey and Zheng 2013). One of the most challenging ethical dilemmas presented by this type of research stems from the reality that sex work, particularly many forms of street-based sex work, often takes place in low income, minority, or otherwise disadvantaged neighborhoods with a history of negative interactions with dominant institutions. Hence researchers may find themselves in a position where their work may further stigmatize and sustain social prejudices against historically oppressed groups, including sex workers themselves. Likewise, public health and criminal justice research risks reifying stereotypes about sex workers as deviants deserving of state medical and criminal justice interventions.

Researchers must carefully balance their empirical agenda with the knowledge that they are working in a political minefield and may be subject to attacks from powerful abolitionist forces that "regard the sex industry as a despicable institution and who are active in campaigns to abolish it" (Weitzer 2005, p. 934). Self-identified abolitionist researchers may confine their survey instruments to questions about violence and abuse while deliberately seeking out women who have had negative experiences with sex work and reside in shelter or other facilities designed to assist them in leaving the trade. Research designed upon the premise that sex work-related behavior is inherently violent and damaging will likely result in findings that corroborate this philosophical perspective, resulting in a disturbingly cyclical pattern of preexisting belief informing methodology which, in turn, produces results that confirm the research's underlying ideological premise.

22.6   Future Research Directions

Sex work research is a burgeoning field with many potentially fertile areas for further exploration, particularly with respect to clients, race and racism, the impacts of politicization on research and public policy, and ethnographies of sex workers' full personhood. Researchers aiming to make truly innovative contributions to this ever-growing body of interdisciplinary work might consider aligning the respective goals and methodologies of public health and ethnographic work much more consistently than has been done to date. Sex work research could benefit tremendously from a truly interdisciplinary large-scale mixed methods study that employs the quantitative strengths of the biomedically-informed fields with the ethnographic power of the qualitative social sciences. Such an empirically careful study would have great potential to offer evidence-based recommendations for law and policy.

22.6.1   Clients

Research with sex workers predominate in the literature with a conspicuous and puzzling lack of work regarding their clients. The result is a rather frustrating situation in which much is known about only half of the people who participate in transactional sexual exchange practices. Existing work focuses on men who pay women for sex, situating their behavior in the context of male privilege as well as changing sociocultural perceptions of relationships and work more generally (Bernstein 2007c). Other researchers have found that men who pay for sex do not dif-

fer significantly from men who do not (Monto 2009), and that paying for sex or sexualized services involves complex processes related to the social construction and reification of masculinity (Frank 2002; Sanders 2008).

This under-researched area could benefit from inquiry into numerous areas already well-studied among female sex workers. For instance, little is known about how the characteristics of sex workers' clients vary based on type of sex work, or the factors that motivate individuals to pay for sex. Future research could move beyond assumptions that may reinforce stereotypes about men as hypersexual, or even as sexual aggressors, to explore the role played by clients' perceptions of risk in the transactional sexual encounter. Researchers might also consider exploring pornography's role in influencing sex work, including acts popularly requested, thereby potentially illuminating overlap that takes place between otherwise disparate sex industry sectors. Finally, analyzing men's experiences with "end demand" initiatives such as John Schools and arrest would provide valuable evidence-based recommendations for law and public policy.

22.6.2   Race and Racism

Existing sex work research features a conspicuous lack of critical race analysis, which is quite striking given the pervasive inequalities related to race and ethnicity that characterize most forms of transactional sexual exchange. While the literature on sex tourism is particularly attuned to how ideas about race among both tourists and locals inform how individuals may contract and participate in such relationships, U.S.-based research rarely focuses explicitly on these issues. Race tends to feature as ancillary in such studies, even when the majority of research participants are women of color, such as is often the case in street-based sex work.

Future research may explore the enduring question of whether pornography, like other media forms, just provides an audience with desired imagery or, in fact, actually helps to create particular standards of beauty and desirability.

Studies could also tackle the reality that women of color's overrepresentation in lower paid and higher risk forms of sex work mirrors broader forms of socioeconomic exclusion the women face in other areas of life. Likewise, researchers would do well to consider the overrepresentation of African-American men in pimping or pandering arrests, eerily mirroring the somewhat surreal popular cultural representations of pimps as violent conspicuous consumers who profit from their hypnotic impact on vulnerable women. It is quite paradoxical that street-based sex work studies with women who work with men who could be described as pimps have addressed this form of labor as a tool of resistance, and yet studies of their male counterparts have not pursued this avenue of inquiry. Researchers could also engage with the interpersonal dynamics of race in queer communities, such that transgender persons of color face particularly densely coagulated challenges which they may respond to very creatively, both in terms of artistic expression and in strategies for self-actualization.

22.6.3   Politicization of Research

Sex work researchers, irrespective of what they study and their perspective on it, operate in a political minefield subject to the vicissitudes of government funding, public opinion, and highly polarized debates on the subject. Researchers often share stories about how gatekeeping practices among federal funders, journal editors, and other powerful figures aligned with the abolitionist movement may prevent the development of empirical inquiry into sex work, and yet the full impact of these practices has yet to feature in a full-length study. This is particularly significant given that the vast majority of sex work researchers are female and engaged in research by and about women.

It is critical to empirically determine if and how academic gatekeepers, including funders, impede innovations in public health and legal policy on sex work through their alignment with particular ideological stances. Sex work researchers in search of funding often find that they must

either highlight the public health aspects of their research, which potentially reinforces prevailing assumptions about sex workers as pathological deviants, or focus upon trafficking, thereby minimizing the clear agency that sex workers demonstrate in their lives and decision-making practices. Taken together, these two prevailing approaches to sex work research not only reinforce stereotypes about sex workers as diseased criminals, but almost assures that future funded research will continue to do so. This occurs as part of a cycle whereby a great deal of sex work-related knowledge is highly emotive and characterized by false statistics that gain acceptance through repetition, lending spurious authority to many reports (UNESCO 2011).

22.6.4   Ethnographies of Sex Workers' Full Personhood

Ethnographic explorations of sex workers' full personhood have featured in anthropological accounts of sex workers' lives and subjectivities outside North American contexts, while U.S. and Canadian ethnographies on the subject are quite limited. Conversely, such explorations tend to be the norm in sex work research outside North America, which almost as a matter of course explores the sophisticated interplay between cultural context and individual experiences in sex workers' everyday lived experiences (Dewey and Kelly 2011). Anthropologists such as Denise Brennan, Don Kulick, and Tiantian Zheng have masterfully integrated their analyses of the broader structural and institutional factors, as well as individual choices, that combine to shape sex workers' lives (Brennan 2004; Kulick 1998; Zheng 2009).

Such an ethnography of full personhood might also be critically attuned to sex workers' career trajectories, including the motivations underlying movement between different forms of sex work. This area of inquiry deserves special attention in research focused upon individual sexual identity and queer community membership, particularly in terms of how stigmatized sexual preferences combine with stigmatized forms of sex work. To this end, researchers should consider encouraging sex worker-authored (or co-authored) pieces that emphasize first person accounts of these experiences. Life history-centered texts authored by sex workers themselves tend to be limited to those with higher levels of education and related forms of privilege (Almodovar 1993; Kuczynski 2001), whereas the few book-length life history works about street-involved individuals either focus predominantly on violence and abuse (Raphael 2004) or, while outstanding, are a bit dated (Pettiway 1997; Pettiway 1996). Overall, researchers would do well to consider innovative strategies by which they can facilitate greater audiences for sex workers' voices to be heard in their full, and sometimes even contradictory, complexity.

22.7 Concluding Thoughts

Analysis presented here demonstrates that sex work is not categorically distinct from other forms of gendered social interaction and, in most cases, relies heavily upon the sophisticated cultural referents that inform sexuality, gender roles, and notions of transgression surrounding both. Those engaged in this fascinating area of study enjoy the freedom to explore numerous intersections between the considerable variations in human sexual desires and practices as well as social, legal and moral regulatory frameworks designed to restrict, oversee, or even outright curtail them. Indeed, the study of sex work often resembles a mirror which reflects, albeit in a somewhat distorted form, some of the most labyrinthine facets of the social world.

References

Abel, G., Fitzgerald, L., Healy, C., & Taylor, A. (2010). *Taking the crime out of sex work: New Zealand sex workers' fight for decriminalization*. Bristol: The Policy Press.

Abbott, S. (2010). Motivations for pursuing a career in pornography. In R. Weitzer (Ed.), *Sex for sale: Prostitution, pornography, and the sex industry* (2nd ed., pp. 47–66). New York: Routledge.

Albury, K. (2014). Porn and sex education, porn as sex education. *Porn Studies, 1*(1–2), 172–181.

Almodovar, N. (1993). *Cop to call girl: Why I quit the LAPD to make an honest living as a Beverly Hills prostitute*. New York: Simon & Schuster.

Anthony, S. (2012). Just how big are porn sites? Extreme-Tech. http://www.extremetech.com/computing/123929-just-how-big-are-porn-sites. Accessed 4 April 2014.

Applications of Islamic law. (2005). The New York Times. http://www.nytimes.com/2005/03/12/weekinreview/rohdtext.html. Accessed 12 March 2005.

Attwood, F. (2011). Through the looking glass? Sexual agency and subjectification online. In R. Gill & C. Scharff (Eds.), *New femininities* (pp. 203–214). Melbourne: Palgrave Macmillan.

Augustín, L. (2007). *Sex at the margins: Migration, labor markets and the rescue industry*. London: Zed Books.

Bakehorn, J. (2010). Women-made pornography. In R. Weitzer (Ed.), *Sex for sale: Prostitution, pornography, and the sex industry* (2nd ed., pp. 99–150). New York: Routledge.

Barton, B. (2006). *Stripped: Inside the lives of exotic dancers*. New York: New York University Press.

Berger, S. (2012). No end in sight: Why the "end demand" movement is the wrong focus for efforts to eliminate human trafficking. *Harvard Journal of Law & Gender, 35*, 523–570.

Bernstein, E. (2007a). The sexual politics of the 'new abolitionism. *Differences: Journal of Feminist Cultural Studies, 18*(3), 128–151.

Bernstein, E. (2007b). Sex work for the middle classes. *Sexualities, 10*(4), 473–488.

Bernstein, E. (2007c). *Temporarily yours: Intimacy, authenticity, and the commerce of sex*. Chicago: University of Chicago Press.

Blanchette, T., & da Silva, A. (2011). Prostitution in contemporary Rio de Janeiro. In S. Dewey & P. Kelly (Eds.), *Policing pleasure: Sex work, policy, and the state in global perspective* (pp. 130–145). New York: New York University Press.

Bleakley, P. (2014). "500 tokens to go private": Camgirls, cybersex and feminist entrepreneurship. *Sexuality & Culture, 18*(4), 892–910.

Boyle, K. (2011). Producing abuse: Selling the harms of pornography. *Women's Studies International Forum, 34*(6), 593–602.

Bradley-Engen, M. (2009). *Naked lives: Inside the worlds of exotic dance*. Albany: State University of New York Press.

Brennan, D. (2004). *What's love got to do with it? Transnational desires and sex tourism in the Dominican Republic*. Durham: Duke University Press.

Brents, B., & Hausbeck, K. (2005). Violence and legalized brothel prostitution in Nevada: Examining safety, risk, and prostitution policy. *Journal of Interpersonal Violence, 20*(3), 270–295.

Brents, B., Jackson, C., & Hausbeck, K. (2010). *The state of sex: Tourism, sex, and sin in the new American heartland*. New York: Routledge.

Brooks, S. (2010a). Hypersexualization and the dark body: Race and inequality among black and Latina women in the exotic dance industry. *Sexuality Research & Social Policy, 7*(2), 70–80.

Brooks, S. (2010b). *Unequal desires: Race and erotic capital in the stripping industry*. Albany: SUNY Press.

Bungay, V., Halpin, M., Halpin, P., Johnston, C., & Patrick, D. (2012). Violence in the massage parlor industry: Experiences of Canadian-born and immigrant women. *Health Care for Women International, 33,* 262–284.

Cabezas, A. (2009). *Economies of desire: Sex and tourism in Cuba and the Dominican Republic*. Philadelphia: University of Pennsylvania Press.

Chateauvert, M. (2014). *Sex workers unite: A history of the sex workers' rights movement from Stonewall to Slutwalk*. Boston: Beacon.

Cheng, S. (2010). *On the move for love: Migrant entertainers and the U.S. military in South Korea*. Philadelphia: University of Pennsylvania Press.

Chin, K., & Finckenauer, J. (2012). *Selling sex overseas: Chinese women and the realities of prostitution and global sex trafficking*. New York: New York University Press.

Clarke, R. J., Clarke, E. A., Roe-Sepowitz, D., & Fey, R. (2012). Age at entry into prostitution: Relationship to drug use, race, suicide, education level, childhood abuse, and family experiences. *Journal Of Human Behavior In The Social Environment, 22*(3), 270–289.

Cole, J. (2010). *Sex and salvation: Imagining the future in Madagascar*. Chicago: University of Chicago Press.

Crofts, P. (2010). Brothels: Outlaws or citizens? *International Journal of Law in Context, 6*(2), 151–166.

Cusick, L. (2006). Widening the harm reduction agenda: From drug use to sex work. *International Journal of Drug Policy, 17,* 3–11.

Dalla, R., Xia, Y., & Kennedy, H. (2003). "You just give them what they want and pray they don't kill you:" Street-level sex workers' reports of victimization, personal resources and coping strategies. *Violence against Women, 9*(11), 1367–1394.

Dank, M., Khan, B., Downey, P., Kotonias, C., Mayer, D., Owens, C., Pacifici, L., Yu, L. (2014). *Estimating the size and structure of the underground commercial sex economy in eight major US cities*. Washington, D.C.: The Urban Institute.

Day, S. (2007). *On the game: Women and sex work*. London: Pluto.

DeMarco, J. (2002). The world of gay strippers. *The Gay & Lesbian Review, 9*(2), 12–14.

Dewey, S. (2010). *Neon wasteland: On love, motherhood, and sex work in a Rust Belt town*. Berkeley: University of California Press.

Dewey, S., & Kelly, P. (Eds.). (2011). *Policing pleasure: Sex work, policy, and the state in global perspective*. New York: New York University Press.

Dewey, S., & St. Germain, T. (2014). Sex workers/sex offenders: Exclusionary criminal justice practices in New Orleans. *Feminist Criminology*. doi:10.1177/1557085114541141

Dewey, S., & Zheng, T. (2013). *Ethical research with sex workers: Anthropological approaches*. New York: Springer (SpringerBriefs in Anthropology and Ethics)

Dines, G. (2011). *Pornland: How porn has hijacked our sexuality*. Boston: Beacon Press.

Doezema, J. (2000). Loose women or lost women?: The re-emergence of the myth of white slavery in contemporary discourses of trafficking in women. *Gender Issues, 18*(1), 23–50.

Donaghue, N., Kurz, T., & Whitehead, K. (2011) Spinning the pole: A discursive analysis of the websites of recreational pole dancing studios. *Feminism & Psychology, 21*(4), 443–457.

Donovan, B., & Barnes-Brus, T. (2011). Narratives of sexual consent and coercion: Forced prostitution trials in Progressive-Era New York City. *Law & Social Inquiry, 36*(3), 597–619.

Dworkin, A. (1981). *Pornography: Men possessing women*. London: The Women's Press.

Edwards, J., Halpern, C., & Wechsberg, W. (2006). Correlates of exchanging sex for drugs or money among women who use crack cocaine. *AIDS Education and Prevention, 18*(5), 420–429.

Egan, D. (2006). *Dancing for dollars and paying for love and paying for love: The relationships between exotic dancers and their regulars*. New York: Palgrave MacMillan.

Escoffier, J. (2007). Porn star/stripper/escort: Economic and sexual dynamics in a sex work career. *Journal of Homosexuality, 53*(1/2), 173–200.

Farley, M. (2007). *Prostitution and trafficking in Nevada: Making the connections*. San Francisco: Prostitution Research & Education.

Foulkes, I. (2013). Zurich introduces "drive-in" sex boxes. *BBC News*. http://www.bbc.com/news/world-europe-23839358. Accessed 26 Aug. 2014.

Frank, K. (2002). *G-strings and sympathy: Strip club regulars and male desire*. Durham: Duke University Press.

Gall, G. (2011). *An agency of their own: Sex worker union organising*. Winchester: Zero Books.

Griffith, J., Adams, L., Hart, C., Mitchell, S., & Kruger, A. (2012). Pornography actors: A qualitative analysis of motivations and dislikes. *North American Journal of Psychology, 14*(2), 245–256.

Griffith, J., Mitchell, S., Hart, C., Adams, L., & Gu, L. (2013). Pornography actresses: An assessment of the damaged goods hypothesis. *Journal of Sex Research, 50*(7), 621–632.

Grudzen, C., Ryan, G., Margold, W., Torres, J., & Gelberg, L. (2009). Pathways to health risk exposure in adult film performers. *Journal of Urban Health, 86*(1), 67–78.

Hanna, J. L. (2012). *Naked truth: Strip clubs, democracy, and a Christian right*. Austin: University of Texas Press.

Harcourt, C., O'Connor, J., Fairley, C., Wand, H., Chen, M., Marshall, L., Egger, S., Kaldor, J. M., & Donovan, B. (2010). The decriminalization of prostitution is associated with better coverage of health promotion programs for sex workers. *Australian and New Zealand Journal of Public Health, 34*(5), 482–486.

Hardy, S. (2008). The pornography of reality. *Sexualities, 11*(1/2), 60–63.

Hoang, K. (2011). "She's not a low class dirty girl!": Sex work in Ho Chi Minh City, Vietnam. *Journal of Contemporary Ethnography, 40*(4), 367–96.

Hoefinger, H. (2013). *Sex, love and money in Cambodia: Professional girlfriends and transactional relationships.* New York: Routledge.

Hubbard, P., & Sanders, T. (2003). Making space for sex work: Female street prostitution and the production of urban space. *International Journal of Urban and Regional Research, 27*(1), 75–89.

Hughes, D. (2003). Humanitarian sexploitation: The world's sex slaves need liberation, not condoms. *The Weekly Standard, 8*(23). http://www.uri.edu/artsci/wms/hughes/condoms_sex_slaves. Accessed 14 Aug. 2014.

Hunt, D. (2011). *Mr. Angel.* Monroe: Pearl Wolf Productions, LLC.

Hwahng, S., & Nuttbrock, L. (2007). Sex workers, fem queens, and cross-dressers: Differential marginalizations and HIV vulnerabilities among three ethnocultural male-to-female communities in New York City. *Sexuality Research & Social Policy, 4*(4), 36–59.

Isgro, K., Stehle, M., & Weber, B. (2013). From sex shacks to mega-brothels: The politics of anti-trafficking and the 2006 soccer World Cup. *European Journal of Cultural Studies, 16,* 171–193.

Izugbara, C. (2011). Hata watufanyeje, kazi itaendelea: Everyday negotiations of state regulations among female sex workers in Nairobi, Kenya. In S. Dewey & P. Kelly (Eds.), *Policing pleasure: Sex work, policy and the state in global perspective* (pp. 115–129). New York: New York University Press,.

Jacobs, A. (2014). For prostitutes jailed in China, forced labor with no recourse. *The New York Times.* http://www.nytimes.com/2014/01/02/world/asia/for-prostitutes-in-china-jail-with-no-recourse.html. Accessed 1 Jan. 2014.

Jeffreys, S. (2008). *The industrial vagina: The political economy of the global sex trade.* New York: Routledge.

Jeffreys, S. (2010). "Brothels without walls:" The escort sector as a problem for the legalization of prostitution. *Social Politics, 17*(2), 210–234.

Kamise, Y. (2013). Occupational stigma and coping strategies for women engaged in the commercial sex industry: A study on the perceptions of "kyaba-cula hostesses" in Japan. *Sex Roles, 69*(1–2), 42–57.

Katsulis, Y. (2010). *Sex work and the city: The social geography of health and safety in Tijuana, Mexico.* Austin: University of Texas Press.

Kelly, P. (2008). *Lydia's open door: Inside Mexico's most modern brothel.* Berkeley: University of California Press.

Khruakham, S., & Lawton, B. (2012). Assessing the impact of the 1996 Thai prostitution law: A study of police arrest data. *Asian Journal of Criminology, 7*(1), 23–36.

Koken, J. (2012). Independent female escort's strategies for coping with sex work related stigma. *Sexuality & Culture, 16*(3), 209–229.

Koken, J., Bimbi D., Parsons, J., & Halkitis, P. (2004). The experience of stigma in the lives of male internet escorts. *Journal of Psychology and Human Sexuality, 16,* 13–32.

Koken, J., Bimbi, D., & Parsons, J. (2009). Male and female escorts: A comparative analysis. In R. Weitzer (Ed.), *Sex for sale: Prostitution, pornography, and the sex industry* (2nd ed., pp. 205–232). New York: Routledge.

Kovner, S. (2012). *Occupying power: Sex workers and servicemen in postwar Japan.* Palo Alto: Stanford University Press.

Kuczynski, A. (2001). The sex-worker literati. The New York Times. http://www.nytimes.com/2001/11/04/style/the-sex-worker-literati.html. Accessed 15 Aug. 2014.

Kulick, D. (1998). *Travesti: Sex, gender, and culture among Brazilian transgendered prostitutes.* Chicago: University of Chicago Press.

Lederer, L. (2010). Addressing demand: Why and how policymakers should utilize law and law enforcement to target customers of commercial sexual exploitation. *Regent University Law Review, 23,* 297–309.

Leigh, C. (1997). Inventing sex work. In J. Nagel (Ed.), *Whores and other feminists* (pp. 226–231). New York: Routledge.

Maher, L. (2000). *Gender, race, and resistance in a Brooklyn drug market.* Oxford: Oxford University Press.

Milrod, C., & Monto, M. (2012). The hobbyist and the girlfriend experience: Behaviors and preferences of male customers of Internet sexual service providers. *Deviant Behavior, 33*(10), 792–810.

Miller-Young, M. (2014). *A taste for brown sugar: Black women in pornography.* Durham: Duke University Press.

Miller, M., & Neaigus, A. (2002). An economy of risk: Resource acquisition strategies of inner city women who use drugs. *International Journal of Drug Policy, 13,* 409–418.

Mitchell, G. (2010). Fare tales and fairy tails: How gay sex tourism is shaping the Brazilian dream. *Wagadu: A Journal of Transnational Women's & Gender Studies, 8,* 93–114.

Mitchell, G. (2011). Turbo consumers in paradise: Tourism, civil rights, and Brazil's gay sex industry. *American Ethnologist, 38,* 666–682.

Miyazaki, M., Takagi, S., Kato, M., & Une, H. (2002). Prevalences of and risk factors for sexually transmitted diseases among Japanese female commercial sex workers in middle- and high-class soaplands in Japan. *STD & AIDS, 13*(12), 833–838.

Montemurro, B., Bloom, C., & Madell, K. (2003). Ladies night out: A typology of women patrons of a male strip club. *Deviant Behavior, 24*(4), 333–352.

Monto, M. (2009). Prostitutes' customers: Motives and misconceptions. In R. Weitzer (Ed.) *Sex for sale: Prostitution, pornography, and the sex industry* (2nd ed., pp. 233–254) New York: Routledge.

Nemoto, T., Operario, D., Takenaka, M., Iwamoto, M., & Nhung Le, M. (2003). HIV risk among Asian women working at massage parlors in San Francisco. *AIDS Education & Prevention, 15,* 245–256.

New Zealand Department of Labor. (2004). A guide to occupational health and safety in the New Zealand sex industry. Wellington, New Zealand. http://www.heart-intl. net/HEART/082504/NewZealandHealth&Safetyse. pdf. Accessed 10 Aug. 2014.

Norton-Hawk, M. (2004). A comparison of pimp- and non-pimp-controlled women. *Violence against Women, 10,* 189–194.

O'Connell Davidson, J. (1998). *Prostitution, power, and freedom.* Ann Arbor: University of Michigan Press.

Office of Police Integrity. (2008). *Interacting with sex workers: A good practice guide and self-check.* Melbourne: Victoria, Australia. http://www.ibac.vic.gov. au/docs/default-source/opi-prevention-and-education/interacting-with-sex-workers-a-good-practice-guide-and-self-check-november-2008.pdf?sfvrsn=2. Accessed 14 Aug. 2014.

Ogas, O., & Gaddam, S. (2012). *A billion wicked thoughts: What the internet tells us about sexual relationships.* New York: Plume.

Overs, C., & Longo, P. (1996). *Making sex work safe: A practical guide for programme managers, policymakers and field workers.* Edinburgh: Network of Sex Work Projects.

Padilla, M. (2007). *Caribbean pleasure industry: Tourism, sexuality and AIDS in the Dominican Republic.* Chicago: University of Chicago Press.

Parreñas, R. (2011). *Illicit flirtations: Labor, migration, and sex trafficking in Tokyo.* Palo Alto: Stanford University Press.

Peiss, K. (2005). Navigating meaty theory projects: Lessons from a qualitative evaluation of Salt Lake City's prostitution diversion project. *Affilia, 20*(2), 203–221.

Pettiway, L. (1996). *Honey, honey, Miss Thang: Being Black, gay, and on the streets.* Philadelphia: Temple University Press.

Pettiway, L. (1997). *Workin' it: Women living through drugs and crime.* Philadelphia: Temple University Press.

Price-Glynn, K. (2010). *Strip club: Gender, power, and sex work.* New York: New York University Press.

Prostitution and the internet: How new technology is shaking up the world's oldest profession. (2014). The Economist. http://www.economist.com/news/briefing/21611074-how-new-technology-shaking-up-oldest-business-more-bang-your-buck. Accessed 14 Aug. 2014.

Quinet, K. (2011). Prostitutes as victims of serial homicide: Trends and case characteristics, 1970–2009. *Homicide Studies, 15,* 74–100.

Raphael, J. (2004). *Listening to Olivia: Violence, poverty, and prostitution.* Boston: Northeastern University Press.

Reuben, J., Serio-Chapman, C., Welsh, C., Matens, R., & Sherman, S. (2011). Correlates of current transactional sex among a sample of female exotic dancers in Baltimore, MD. *Journal of Urban Health, 88*(2), 342–351.

Romero-Daza, N., Weeks, M., & Singer, M. (2005). Conceptualizing the impact of indirect violence on HIV risk among women involved in street prostitution. *Aggression and Violent Behavior, 10,* 153–170.

Salfati, G., James, A., & Ferguson, L. (2008). Prostitute homicides: A descriptive study. *Journal of Interpersonal Violence, 23,* 505–543.

Sanchez Taylor, J. (2006). Female sex tourism: A contradiction in terms? *Feminist Review, 83*(1), 42–59.

Sanders, T. (2008). *Paying for pleasure: Men who buy sex.* London: Willan.

Sausa, L., Keatley, J., & Operario, D. (2007). Perceived risks and benefits of sex work among transgender women of color in San Francisco. *Archives of Sexual Behavior, 36,* 768–777.

Shannon, K., Bright, V., Gibson, K., & Tyndall, M. (2007). Sexual and drug-related vulnerabilities for HIV infection among women engaged in survival sex work in Vancouver, Canada. *Canadian Journal of Public Health, 98,* 465–469.

Shannon, K., Strathdee, S., Shoveller, J., Rusch, M., & Tyndall, M. (2009) Structural and environmental barriers to condom use negotiation with clients among female sex workers: Implications for HIV-prevention strategies and policies. *American Journal of Public Health, 99,* 659–665.

Shdaimah, C., & Wiechelt, S. (2012). Converging on empathy: Perspectives on Baltimore City's specialized prostitution diversion program. *Women & Criminal Justice, 22*(2), 156–173.

Shteir, R. (2005). *Striptease: The untold history of the girlie show.* Oxford: Oxford University Press.

Skilbrei, M. (2001). The rise and fall of the Norwegian massage parlours: Changes in the Norwegian prostitution setting in the 1990s. *Feminist Review, 67,* 63–77.

Soothill, K. (2004). Parlour games: The value of an Internet site providing punters' views of massage parlors. *The Police Journal, 77*(1), 43–53.

Sterk, C. (1999). *Fast lives: Women who use crack cocaine.* Philadelphia: Temple University Press.

Takeyama, A. (2010). Intimacy for sale: Masculinity, entrepreneurship, and commodity self in Japan's neoliberal situation. *Japanese Studies, 30*(2), 231–246.

Thomas, J. (2010). Gay male pornography since Stonewall. In R. Weitzer (Ed.), *Sex for sale: Prostitution, pornography, and the sex industry* (2nd ed., pp. 67–90). New York: Routledge.

Trotter, H. (2007). Navigating risk: Lessons from the dockside sex trade for reducing violence in South Africa's prostitution industry. *Sexuality Research & Social Policy, 4*(4), 106–119.

Trotter, H. (2011). *Sugar girls and seamen: A journey into the world of dockside prostitution in South Africa.* Athens: Ohio University Press.

United Nations Educational, Scientific and Cultural Organization/UNESCO. (2011). Trafficking and HIV/AIDS statistics project. Bangkok: UNESCO. http://www.unescobkk.org/culture/diversity/trafficking-hiv/ Accessed 14 Aug. 2014.

U.S./United States Department of State. (2006). A statement on human trafficking-related language. Washington, D.C.: U.S. Department of State. http://2001-2009. state.gov/g/tip/rls/rm/78383.htm Accessed 14 Aug. 2014.

Uy, J., Parsons, J., Bimbi, D., Koken, J., & Halkitis, P. (2004). Gay and bisexual male escorts who advertise on the Internet: Understanding reasons for and effects of involvement in commercial sex. *International Journal of Men's Health, 3,* 11–26.

van der Meulen, E. (2010). Illegal lives, loves, and work: How the criminalization of procuring affects sex workers in Canada. *Wagadu: A Journal of Transnational Women's & Gender Studies, 8,* 217–233.

Voss, G. (2012). "Treating it as a normal business:" Researching the pornography industry. *Sexualities, 15*(3/4), 391–410.

Wahab, S. (2004). Tricks of the trade: What social workers can learn about female sex workers through dialogue. *Qualitative Social Work, 3*(2), 139–160.

Wahab, S., & Panichelli, M. (2013). Ethical and human rights issues in coercive interventions with sex workers. *Affilia: Journal of Women & Social Work, 28*(4), 344–349.

Weinberg, M., Williams, C., Kleiner, S., & Irizarry, Y. (2010). Pornography, normalization, and empowerment. *Archives of Sexual Behavior, 39,* 1389–1401.

Weitzer, R. (2005). *Flawed theory and method in studies of prostitution, violence against women, 11*(7), 934–949.

Weitzer, R. (2010). The mythology of prostitution: Advocacy research and public policy. *Sexuality Research & Social Policy, 7,* 5–29.

Weitzer, R. (2012). *Legalizing prostitution: From illicit vice to lawful business.* New York: New York University Press.

Wesely, J. (2003). "Where am I going to stop?" Exotic dancing, fluid body boundaries, and effects on identity. *Deviant Behavior, 24,* 483–503.

Williams, E. (2013). *Sex tourism in Bahia: Ambiguous entanglements.* Urbana-Champaign: University of Illinois Press.

Williamson, C., & Cluse-Tolar, T. (2002). Pimp-controlled prostitution: Still an integral part of street life. *Violence Against Women, 8,* 1074–1092.

Wilson, A. (2010). Post-Fordist desires: The commodity aesthetics of Bangkok sex shows. *Feminist Legal Studies, 18*(1), 53–67.

Zheng, T. (2009). *Red lights: The lives of sex workers in postsocialist China.* Minneapolis: University of Minnesota Press.

Pornography

23

Kassia R. Wosick

23.1 Introduction

The sex industry is built upon the commodification of sexuality, which involves the sale and purchase of sexual services and products. Ronald Weitzer aptly describes the industry as "the workers, managers, owners, agencies, clubs, trade associations, and marketing involved in sexual commerce, both legal and illegal varieties" (2010, p. 1). Revenue is typically generated through lap dances, stripping, telephone sex, live sex shows, prostitution, sex toys, and, most prominently, pornography.

The majority of academic work on the sex industry over the past 40 years has occurred primarily in humanities (cultural, film, media, gender, and queer studies), and to a lesser extent, the social sciences (namely psychology and sociology). Notable publications include a range of books, articles, and also anthologies that join scholarly work and anecdotal reflections from industry insiders offer critical perspectives on the existence, history, development, debates, innovations, impact and significance of pornography (see Hines and Kerr 2012; Nagle 1997; Williams 2004). McKee (2009) suggests that humanities scholars

have less difficulty researching pornography than do social scientists for theoretical, empirical, and discipline-driven reasons. However, social scientists are increasingly contributing to literatures and dialogues on the entire sex industry, although most have focused primarily on pornography's social and psychological effects (Hardy 2004).

This chapter presents a synopsis of pornography as it relates to sexualities in an institutional context. While some have suggested that pornography itself exists as an institution, the chapter places pornography in the larger social context of the economy through its integral role in the sex industry. The economic dimensions of the sex industry, especially pornography, are routinely used as justification for academic research and critique (Voss 2012). Several scholars suggest this is problematic given a lack of accurate data (Roberts 2006), precise comprehensive statistics (Tibbals 2014), industry self-reporting (Tanner 2005), reporting on only legal commercial sex profit (Weitzer 2010), and porn's involvement with major corporations in the media economy (Paasonen et al. 2007). A range of commonly cited domestic and global sex industry revenues estimate the United States industry alone to be a \$3 to 10 billion business annually, and the global industry ranges from \$50 to 60 billion dollars a year (Comella 2010; Paasonen et al. 2007; Weitzer 2010).

While the sex industry has traditionally been controlled by and primarily intended for satisfying the somewhat normative sexual desires of heterosexual men, recent social shifts have di-

An erratum to this chapter can be found at
DOI 10.1007/978-3-319-17341-2_26

K. R. Wosick (✉)
Department of Sociology, New Mexico State University,
Las Cruces, NM, 88003, USA
e-mail: kassiaw@nmsu.edu

versified sexual commerce, especially in terms of pornography's production, content, and consumption (Wosick-Correa and Joseph 2008). Heterosexual pornography continues to dominate domestic and global markets, and remains a major focus of inquiry and debate in both academic and mainstream contexts. However, gay men's pornography, lesbian pornographic production, trans and genderqueer erotica, and bisexual porn represent an important expansion for the industry. Further, while men are more likely to report consuming pornographic material, women do access a wide array of pornography for their own purposes (Laumann et al. 1994; Paul 2009). Women-made and female-friendly porn are increasingly popular genres. New and different sexualities, desires, and interests are continually expanding porn's content, production, and availability. And as technology progresses, so too does pornography in form and function.

The consumption of pornography (viewing, purchasing, experiencing) is pervasive across cultures (Attwood 2005), although it has and continues to be widely contested for a variety of reasons that include exploitation, degradation, and violence primarily against women, people of color, youth, and sexual identities. Concurrently, pornography has also been credited with providing sexual information, opportunities for sexual dialogues, sexual validation, and possibilities for pleasure to individuals and society at large. This chapter offers a general overview of pornography that highlights its parameters, relevance, impact, and empirical significance. The chapter begins with defining and categorizing pornography before presenting the main dialogues and approaches surrounding porn's cultural and empirical relevance. The chapter highlights traditional and emergent pornographic genres reflecting a range of gender and sexual identities, especially in terms of niche production. The relationship between technology and pornography, as well as the business of pornography are briefly discussed. The chapter concludes with suggestions for continued research on pornography.

23.2 Defining Pornography

There is no universally agreed upon definition of pornography. Paasonen et al. (2007) refer to pornography as an "issue of genre, industry and regulation" that has been "defined in terms of content (sexually explicit depictions of genitalia and sexual acts), lack thereof (materials without any redeeming artistic, cultural or social value), intention (texts intended to arouse their consumers) and effect (texts arousing their consumers)" (p. 1). Brian McNair (2013) similarly argues that pornography is a "cultural form defined by its context (sex), its intention (to sexually arouse), and its transgressive relationship to prevailing codes of sexual display and representation" (p. 18). Indeed, entire publications have been devoted to teasing out definition(s) of the pornographic, documenting the historical shifts in defining pornography, and problematizing the necessity of its definition.

Academics sometimes refer to pornography as sexually explicit material (SEM), which on the one hand helps to avoid stigma and problematic definitional processes, but on the other emphasizes the explicit qualities that are often controversial with regard to porn. The etymological origin of pornography comes from the Greek *pornographos* (*porne* prostitute and *graphein* to write) (merriam-webster.com). The word pornography first appeared in the Oxford English Dictionary in 1857, the same year that England passed a law banning the sale and distribution of sexual materials considered "obscene" (Nathan 2007). Since then, pornography has incurred a wide range of situational definitions and subsequent categorizations. Magill (1995) refers to pornography, which is most useful for the purposes of this chapter, as "written, visual, or spoken material that shows or describes sexual acts or the genitals and is intended to be arousing to the viewer" (p. 985). Pornography, therefore, involves a dynamic range of magazines, books, photographs, film, video, video games, poetry, animation, paintings, drawings, sculptures, sound recordings, postcards, posters, websites, and other media.

23.3 Categorizing Pornography

Similar to defining pornography, categorizing pornography has a tenuous social and political history in terms of regulation, deregulation, obscenity laws, and its role in anti and pro-porn debates. There is also disagreement as to the utility of categorizing pornography, as doing so has the potential to reify dichotomies and enforce positioned contexts rather than encourage multiple representations of sexuality. Nonetheless, pornography is usually categorized in a number of different ways, whether it be in terms of the method of production, type of media, distribution source, or its content.

In terms of production, heterosexual pornography can be divided into three categories: professional, pro-amateur, and amateur (Abbott 2010). Sabo (2012) refers to porn as either high gloss (big production) or amateur, which can also be considered either professional or homemade porn. Types of pornographic media can be broadly categorized as still-image (as in print/photography) or moving-image (as in film/video) (Williams 2004) and are distributed to consumers who may rent or purchase content through a wide range of paid cable, digital, and satellite services, video-on-demand, theatres, mail delivery, direct sales, adult stores, and especially the Internet. Tibbals (2014) describes two primary forms of web-based pornography: pre-produced scenes (clips) that are sold for streaming and/or downloading, and live performances (web-cams) that can be archived for later sale/distribution.

Pornography is most often categorized in terms of its content, focusing on the degree of depiction of sexual acts, genitalia, plot (or lack thereof), and level of objectification or degradation. The two most common ways of classifying pornography involve distinctions between hard core and soft core, and also juxtaposing erotica and pornography. Hard core porn usually shows nudity, genitalia, actual penetration, has little plot or narrative, and is often regarded as more aggressive, explicit, and to some, violent. Soft core porn usually shows some nudity but rarely focuses on genitalia, suggests penetration, is likely to have more plot or narrative, and is considered less explicit. Hard core pornography has traditionally received the most attention from early scholars of porn and is usually the topic of anti-porn debates and activism. It also generates the most revenue for the industry (Williams 2004).

Erotica, like soft core porn, is often regarded as more sexually suggestive rather than explicit in terms of content and imagery. Erotica has been described as respectful, nonviolent, and non-degrading (Dalecki and Price 1994), artistic and stylized (Huntley 1998), and rarely depicts penetration or detailed sexual organs (Magill 1995). Crooks and Baur (2002) denote that erotica involves representations of sexuality that are based on mutual respect, affection, and personal connectedness. Since erotica is more suggestive than explicit, tends to reflect normative sexual interactions/acts, and rarely involves degrading or violent sexual imagery, it seems to be more socially acceptable and may be regarded as a healthy alternative to other forms of pornography. Erotica is therefore not typically the focus of anti-pornography debates (Corneau and Van Der Meulen 2014) and is sometimes considered more female-friendly than other kinds of pornography because there is less sexually graphic imagery and more of a focus on dyadic intimacy, sensuality, and mutual pleasure.

Rather than reinforce polarized notions of sexually explicit material, some suggest situating porn on a continuum in order to draw distinctions while simultaneously recognizing multiplicity. Corneau and Van der Meulen (2014) refer to "the porn continuum," with one end involving suggestive material or basic nudity and the other end involving explicit imagery and/or violent pornography. Erotica is placed on one end due to its rare depiction of sexual acts and organs, representations of sexuality and customary presentation of consensual sex in nonviolent, non-degrading contexts. Pornography is placed on the other due to its explicit representation of sexual acts, genitalia, and seemingly impersonal sex. While a porn continuum may be useful in conceptualizing a range of diverse adult materials, it also reinforces the polarization of suggestive versus graphic (and therefore "good" versus "bad") content.

Even though pornographic materials vary widely in terms of media, content, and production, hard core moving image pornography (feature length films, videos, and clips) remains the most common and has received the bulk of scholarly focus, theorizing, and criticism. Perhaps this is due to its explicit, extreme, and highly controversial depictions of gender, race/ethnicity, age, sexuality, and sexual imagery. Current academic trends, however, include addressing other forms of pornography (soft core, erotica, print) empirically and theoretically.

23.4 Main Dialogues Surrounding Pornography

Pornography has been and continues to be a significant aspect of modern culture (Hardy 2004). Several note the evolution and key landmarks of pornography's history in ancient times and more modern national, international, and global contexts (e.g., see Nathan 2007; McNair 2009; Taormino et al. 2013). This history includes technological developments (print, photography, film, videotape, television, computers, the Internet, smart devices), legal battles and decisions about obscenity, free speech, censorship, nudity, and morality, and cultural shifts in race/ethnicity, gender, sexual identity, and class that have shaped pornography's past and present. While some may characterize porn's omnipresence as problematic for the future of sexualities, others are poised for its continued expansion and possible trajectories.

When photography was invented in 1827, some of the first pictures taken were of people naked or having sex, which were subsequently printed on post cards for mass consumption (Nathan 2007). The early 1900s in America brought the first hard core "stag" films for men's consumption. Publications showing explicit comics, nude photos, and pin-up photos were popular by the middle of the twentieth century, especially men's magazines like Hugh Hefner's *Playboy* (first published in 1953), Larry Flynt's *Hustler* (first published in 1974), and Bob Guccione's *Penthouse* (published in America in 1969). "Peep shows" were originally shown in private booths and adult bookstores for customers (men) to watch short, looped films and masturbate. By

the end of the 1960s, Hollywood was producing widely-distributed films with explicit sex scenes like *Midnight Cowboy* (1969). Pornographic feature films were shown in public theatres, such as *Deep Throat (1972)*, *Behind the Green Door (1972), The Devil in Miss Jones (1973),* and *Debbie Does Dallas (1978),* which drew both male and female audiences. Porn actors like Ron Jeremy, Annie Sprinkle, John C. Holmes, Linda Lovelace, and Candida Royalle gained considerable notoriety due to the popularity of mainstream cinematic films during the 1970s, which is often referred to as the "golden age of porn." When videotape was invented in the late 1970s, the porn movie industry essentially collapsed in favor of more easily produced videos that could be rented or viewed in the privacy of one's residence. The early to mid-1980s brought the HIV/AIDS crisis, the sexual counterrevolution, and porn wars, which emerged out of debates between feminists about the role of sexualized media representation in American society. Anti-pornography feminists condemned porn as exploitative, degrading, and harmful to women in terms of their physical, emotional, and sexual well-being. Pro-pornography feminists heralded porn as potentially liberating and important for women's sexuality, pleasure, and social advancement. The California Supreme Court legalized porn shoots in 1988, considering performers as actors rather than prostitutes. And, most recently, the invention of computers and the Internet have made a striking impact on porn's production, distribution, and consumption (Paasonen and Saarenmaa 2007; Nathan 2007).

Pornography is sometimes discussed in terms of its contemporary cultural significance and impact, especially over the past 30 years. Western mass media incorporates language and iconography customarily associated with porn, routinely advertises sexual services and sexual commodities, and emphasizes sex through pornographic imagery, gestures and esthetics in mainstream media. Scholars have characterized this as pornographication (McNair 1996), pornification (Paul 2005), and porno chic (Duits and van Zoonen 2006; McNair 2013). Paasonen et al. (2007) identify three levels of pornification; the first of which concerns developments in media technology and the expansion of the porn industry. The second acknowledges porn's shift from periphery to center in terms of mainstream publicity, media and public spaces, newspapers, magazines, and television, and therefore involves both regulation and deregulation of media policies consistent with this shift. The third layer connects to the sexualization of culture more generally in terms of more visibility of hardcore and soft-core pornographies, pastiche or parody of porn, homage to porn, and an overall increase in sexually explicit representations, which McNair (2013) refers to as *porno chic*. Attwood (2002) notes (perhaps with caution) that perceiving a shift toward the sexually explicit in mainstream mass media reintroduces debates on the definition and status of pornography, as well as the significance of new technologies for contemporary sexual representation.

Attwood (2002) also characterizes a paradigm shift in pornography theory and research from what she refers to as a "focus on 'texts' and 'effects' to that which attempts to contextualize the consumption of pornography and other sexual representation" (p. 104). Debates over pornography impacted initial trends in research and theorizing, which made it difficult to examine pornography and other representations of sexuality from multiple perspectives. Most early scholars focused on why pornography exists, the history of pornography and sexually explicit art, whether it is obscene and should therefore be regulated, its negative impact on viewers and society at large, and the role it plays in objectification and sexual violence. Attwood refers to Walter Kendrick's *The Secret Museum: Pornography in Modern Culture* and Linda William's *Hard Core: Power, Pleasure and the 'Frenzy of the Visible'* as key contributors to a shift that continued in the late 1990s involving a re-examination of pornography, noting works by Laura Kipnis (1996), Brian McNair (1996), Laurence O'Toole (1998), Simon Hardy (1998), and Jane Juffer (1998) that focus on pornography, culture, gender, and technology. Attwood also suggests that contemporary work on pornography incorporates a broader range of theoretical perspectives from the social sciences, as well as cultural studies,

gender studies, and queer studies. The definitions of pornography, its significance as a cultural category/discourse/genres, concerns over pornography's effects, its changing status in relation to mainstream representations and technological developments, and also assessments of diverse texts and porn consumers are all components of this paradigmatic shift.

23.4.1 Empirical Approaches to Pornography

A brief review of empirical research on pornography reveals a range of quantitative, qualitative, and mixed-methods approaches. Researchers routinely employ surveys to measure attitudes, perceptions, experiences, effects, consumption patterns, and trends concerning pornography (see Paik, Chap. 6, this volume). For example, studies have examined the public's perception of pornography (Davis and Smith 1986), attitudes toward pornography (Herman and Border 1983; Kirkpatrick and Zurcher 1983; Wood and Hughes 1984), viewers' reactions to antipornographic films (Bart et al. 1985), reasons for viewing porn (Poulsen et al. 2013), ideologies concerning pornography (Cottle et al. 1989), porn exposure and risky sexual behaviors (Sinkovic et al. 2013), internet porn addiction (Griffiths 2001), as well as men's porn consumption, predictors, and correlates (Wright 2013). Main criticisms of quantitative research on pornography concern reliability, validity, problems with accuracy and self-reporting, minimal diversity in terms of research samples and data analysis, and subjective meanings surrounding porn, sexual behaviors, and identities. The Internet has revolutionized large-scale sampling techniques and self-reporting processes for sexualities studies. Online questionnaires combine demographic, closed and open-ended questions to effectively assess perceptions and attitudes toward pornography, why consumers access porn, and porn viewers' experiences and habits (Barker 2014; Rothman et al. 2014).

Qualitative researchers have a rich history exploring sexualities and the sex industry as a whole, and typically use in-depth interviews, participant observation and other ethnographic methods (see Frank, Chap. 8, this volume) to investigate topics like feminist porn markets (Comella 2013), motivations for seeking a career in porn (Abbott 2010), black women's experiences working in porn (Miller-Young 2010), and whether images constitute art or pornography for viewers (Armstrong and Weinberg 2006). Qualitative methods are ideal for fully understanding the micro-level intricacies of pornographic production, perceptions, and consumption. They allow for probing questions, detailed observations and exchanges between context, subject, and researcher. However, conducting interviews, observations and extensive field work in sexualized settings may involve ethical issues regarding safety, power, bias, and reciprocity between researchers and subjects (see Perez-y-Perez, Chap. 7, this volume).

Content analysis is perhaps the most common method employed in pornographic research and is typically used to assess a range of texts, images, scenes, trends and content in porn films, videos, websites, magazines, and stories. William's (1989) ground-breaking examination of hard-core porn, as well as studies like Kangasvuo's (2007) on bisexuality in porn magazines, Carnes's (2007) on anal sex instructional videos for women, Barron and Kimmel's (2000) comparison of violent pornography in porn magazines, and Vannier et al.'s (2014) examination of free "teen" and "MILF" online pornography all utilize different content analysis techniques. Humanities scholars have long utilized textual and content analysis in exploring a range of pornographic media, which has undoubtedly formed bodies of literature with which social scientists continue to dialogue, engage, draw from and build upon.

Several studies employ multiple research methods in order to gather data for purposes of triangulation. For example, Georgina Voss (2012) combined ethnographic observation, interviews, and a "grey" literature review (information from mainstream media like news articles and documentaries) in order to gather "rich and nuanced material about the history, structure, and social dynamics of the pornography industry" (p. 396). Dana Collins (1989) draws on both textual analysis and in-depth interviews to assess lesbian sex publications and several women involved in their production. As with any empirical research, using mixed-methods provides an ideal opportunity to combine quantitative and qualitative evidence for comprehensive analysis and conclusions. Mixed-methods, however, continue to warrant considerable training, skill, time and financial investment for researchers.

23.4.2   Key Factors: Gender and Sexual Orientation

Researchers report substantial gender differences in relation to perceptions, consumption, and experiences with pornography. Men tend to have more permissive attitudes toward porn, are more likely to seek out visual pornographic images online and use them for masturbation, and have greater access to pornography than women (Paul 2009). This is certainly a direction for future research, however, given that women's sex industry consumption continues to expand and more pornographic content is both women-made and targeted specifically to women. There are several studies that look at both gender and sexual orientation as variables or predictors with regard to pornography, although there is need for further assessing social patterns and individual experiences. Gender has been the primary focus in a number of studies looking at pornography's portrayal of unequal distribution of power, depiction of physical violence and coerced sex, objectification, and degrading or humiliating content. Scholars have also addressed the complexity of women's responses to their partners' porn use, suggesting that while some are accepting or neutral, others report negative experiences and emotions (Shaw 1999). Benjamin and Tlusten's (2010) interviews with twenty Israeli Jewish women illustrate that some embrace pornography as a tool for developing couples' intimacy and sexual fulfillment.

Like gender, sexual orientation is a main factor in predicting, assessing, and explaining consumption patterns and experiences with pornography. While most research relies on heterosexual perceptions, attitudes, and viewing practices, some research does investigate these topics among people who identify as gay, lesbian, bisexual, or queer. Further, gender and sexual orientation/identities have expanded porn genres and subgenres to reflect a range of interests, resources, and representations. There are differences between mainstream porn involving same-gender content (like girl-on-girl, bisexual, gay-for-pay) and that which is produced by gay, lesbian, bisexual, or queer studios, directors, or involves self-identified queer individuals. While some suggest that diverse gender and sexual identities have revolutionized, politicized, and transgressed traditional pornography, others maintain that they inevitably reinforce heteronormative sexual scripts and perpetuate exploitation and objectification regardless of gender.

Interestingly, a majority of research on pornography has looked at content, workers, consumers, media, youth, and the general public rather than the industry itself. Voss (2012) describes existing data on the porn industry as "primarily historical, drawing on secondary, non-peer-reviewed sources, and do not provide a rich description of the industry itself either in terms of its social dynamics, the industry structure, or the revenue models used" (p. 393). This is certainly a direction for future research, especially in terms of sociology, business, consumer/consumption, and marketing literatures.

23.5 Pornographic Genres, Subgenres, and Niches

There are several pornographic genres, subgenres, and niches based primarily on specific acts/interactions/behaviors depicted, actor/performer/model characteristics (i.e. race, age, gender, body type, ability, height, hair), fetish (power, props, bodily functions), sexual orientation (lesbian, gay, bisexual), gender (men, women, transgender), performer combinations (solo, dyadic, multiple partners) and the overall target audience or consumer. Established pornography genres include reality (real scenes or those staged to emulate amateur sex), alt (alternative subcultures), fetish (BDSM, kink), ethnic and/or interracial, gay/bisexual male, female-friendly, lesbian/bisexual female, and porn that is women-made. There are hundreds of porn subgenres and niches that represent an array of industry and viewer interests and tastes. Porn websites, in particular, have facilitated consumer access to such niches through categorizing their web-based content in searchable formats that are continually changing.

Point of View (POV) or gonzo is sometimes referred to as a specific genre of porn wherein the person (usually male) holds the camera in order to capture the sexual scene, which allows the viewer (also usually male) the sense that he is engaging in the sexual experience rather than simply watching it. According to Tibbals (2014), gonzo porn is loosely scripted, generally inexpensive to make, and involves the person holding the camera giving verbal directions or making comments to performers. While some have referred to gonzo as a demeaning hard-core pornography genre (see Dines 2010), Tibbals cautions that gonzo is not a genre, but rather a filmmaking form that for some can be both progressive and ethical in content (2014).

There has been considerable debate over a number of porn subgenres deemed degrading, violent, objectifying, obscene, offensive, and perpetuate prejudice and stereotyping based on race/ethnicity, gender and/or sexual identity, age, body size, or nationality. Indeed, much of the criticism surrounding the sex industry as a whole, and specifically pornography, involves the inherent inequalities that exist not only in terms of production and consumer base, but specifically in terms of particular genre and subgenre content, narrative, and imagery. Studies by Mireille Miller-Young (2010) document the marginalization of black female performers and directors, and it is well known that there are different pay scales, employment opportunities, career advancement, and concerns with image branding for those engaged in interracial scenes. Scholars are paying more attention to assessing the particulars and viewer impact of certain subgenres, such as Vannier et al.'s (2014) analysis of free "teen" and "MILF" online porn.

While the sex industry produces pornography in genres that present same-gender desire and characterize content as gay, bisexual, or lesbian, there are differences between specific genres that are made by women, lesbians, bisexuals, gay men, trans and queer folk that involve a range of sexual identities, desires, content, and intention. There are genre-specific publications, trade associations, studios, directors, talent, and even awards shows that serve each genres production and consumer base. Such genres, in particular, exemplify socio-cultural shifts and the transforming landscape of contemporary sexualities, especially in regard to sexual commerce and pornographic representations of sexual diversity and change. This is especially true in the context of gay/bisexual male, women-made, female-friendly, lesbian/dyke/bisexual, and trans/genderqueer pornographies.

23.5.1 Gay and Bisexual Male Pornography

What literature exists on gay and bisexual male pornography somewhat mirrors that of mainstream heterosexual porn. Publications can be categorized in terms of biographic accounts of experiences in the industry (Cohler 2004; O'Hara 1997; Poole 2000), analysis of content in gay pornographic magazines and films (Celline and Duncan 1988), the role of porn in gay and bisexual men's lives (Burger 1995; Mowlabocus 2007), porn consumption patterns (Rosser et al. 2013; Stein et al. 2012), and questioning whether the existence of gay and bisexual male porn is inherently political and central to gay and bisexual male collective identity (Isola 2013).

Pornography continues to be an important part of gay and bisexual male culture (Corneau and Van Der Meulen 2014). In *One-Handed Histories: The Eroto-Politics of Gay Male Video Pornography*, John Burger explores the significance of specifically commercial gay male film and video porn, suggesting that it documents the state of sexual existence gay men enjoy while subsequently presenting idealized fantasy images of

such existence, and therefore serves as both a cultural document and erotic tool (1995).

A recent study by Stein et al. (2012) examines porn consumption among a sample of 2552 men who have sex with men (MSM) in New York, finding almost all viewed gay porn (99 %) especially on the Internet (96 %). Rosser et al. (2013) similarly find that 98 % of their 1,291 respondents had viewed gay sexually explicit material (SEM) within the past ninety days. While gay and bisexual men have a consistent history of using the Internet for sexual purposes, Grov et al. (2014) note research is lacking on gay and bisexual men's pornography consumption, especially in terms of the mediums through which they access porn.

Similar to heterosexual porn, pro-and anti-gay pornography discourses center on porn's content and impact. Anti-gay porn sentiments suggest that gay porn is harmful, does not depict reality, perpetuates power relations and homophobia, engenders body dissatisfaction, reinforces gender and racial/ethnic stereotypes, and endorses unprotected sexual behavior. Pro-gay porn advocates suggest gay porn increases visibility and works to liberate gay male sexuality, is more equitable and reciprocal than heterosexual porn, educates gay men on sex and pleasure, and validates a range of sexualities (see Corneau and Van Der Meulen 2014).

Mercer (2004) articulates gay porn's main function as "the production of fantasy and the solicitation of desire," (pp. 155–156) identifying six main discourses prominent in gay porn films that facilitate a mythology of homosexual desire. The *all-male environment* is most popular, invoking settings like locker rooms, dormitories, prisons, military barracks, and gyms. *Heterosexual scenarios* that involve the possibility of conversion or discovery of same-sex desire are also common, as is the *urban gay lifestyle* depicting youth, attractiveness and promiscuity that idealize geographic locations like California, San Francisco, and well-known gay communities. The *luxury fantasy* involves porn scenes in glamorous locations, beaches, and other affluent arenas like country clubs, which Mercer suggests conveys an economy of abundance to the viewer, which is juxtaposed with *the idyll,* a discourse centered on nature and scenic landscapes complimenting beautiful bodies and effective sexual performances, such as those in rural locations between farmhands. The final discourse, *sadomasochism,* involves scenes of power play, dungeons, leathermen, and group sex, and is often interwoven with other discourses. Mercer refers to these discursive categories as a "gay mythology in pornographic video" (p. 161) that helps to situate same-sex desire as plural and celebratory.

A recent study by Corneau and Van Der Meulen (2014) draws on interviews with twenty Canadian gay men who consume porn to articulate five different conceptualizations of pornography. In addition to effectively categorizing typical gay porn content, the study also allows for more agentic viewer definitions of pornography. Interviewees characterized a range of scenes as *mellow, commercial, raunch, amateur,* and *bareback,* reinforcing gay pornography as a "diverse and heterogeneous phenomenon" (2014, p. 505).

Bareback porn, in particular, has garnered recent scholarly attention. Bareback porn depicts unprotected anal sex between men, and, according to Mowlabocus et al. (2013), is perhaps the most controversial shift in terms of gay porn content. Bareback porn emerged in the late 1990s as a niche and quickly moved to a feature within a wide variety of films. Although studios had been enforcing the condom code since the 1980s, the representation and demand for bareback porn (marketed as "raw," "risky," "bareback," or "condom-free") (Escoffier 2007) has become more mainstream today as a specific porn genre (Mowlabocus et al. 2013). This shift is not without contention, however, as some consider whether representations of unprotected anal intercourse in gay porn has negative effects on the sexual health of not only the performers but especially the viewers who watch it (Rosser et al. 2013; Stein et al. 2012).

Burger (1995) uses the term *pornlore* to refer to the "rumors, stories, truths, and anecdotes surrounding the icons and images in the gay porn industry" (p. 49). While heterosexual porn certainly produces its fair share of celebrity porn stars, those within gay porn acquire large reputations. A performer's sexuality (gay, bisexual, or straight), for example, becomes central to the narrative, marketing, and consumption of particular films. Whether performers are actually gay or bisexual, as opposed to "gay for pay," is often beside the point, and can enhance the draw of particular films that showcase "straight dudes" engaging in sexual situations with other men.

While gay porn has been criticized for replicating normative imagery, racism, and ageism customary in heterosexual porn, it has also been at the forefront of representing a range of subcultures, as with sadomasochism and bondage/dominance (Burger 1995). Other genres that involve women-made porn, female-friendly content, and focus on same-gender and multiple-gender desire and imagery have also played an integral role in such expansion.

23.5.2   Female-Friendly, Women-Made, and Lesbian/Bisexual Pornographies

Candida Royalle founded Femme Productions in 1984 to create porn produced from a woman's point of view aimed at women and couples. Royalle's experience as a performer combined with her sex-positive and sex-education based approach to produce softer and more romantic films that involved plot/storylines, high production value, and an emphasis on female sexual pleasure without visual imagery like male ejaculation. That same year, Nina Hartley, another mainstream performer and registered nurse, began her own line of sex education videos for Adam and Eve. The success of Royalle and Hartley's "couples porn" genre signified a shift in the industry toward acknowledging female sexual desire, viewing, and consumption (Taormino 2013).

The genre of couple's porn has more recently been reframed as female-friendly or woman-centered, especially since the genre has expanded to appeal to a wider range of women's sexual desires and needs that exist aside from partnered contexts. While female-friendly porn generated wider appeal for women, it also reinforced normative notions of gender by "softening" women's pornographic tastes. Michelle Carnes (2007) takes issue with characterizing Candida Royalle's pornography as 'what women want to see,' arguing her explicit films for women "seem to dispel a common, gendered assertion that women's sexual lives exist primarily in our heads, that we need soft-core sex with character development and plot, or at least a narrative-based context for hardcore imagery" (p. 152).

Female-friendly porn need not be directed or produced by women in order for it to be considered woman-centered; although the genre emerged from women's efforts behind (as well as in front of) the camera. Women-*made* porn, however, is regarded as a more politicized, activist oriented genre that sometimes overlaps with female-friendly porn in terms of production, intent, and consumer base. According to Jill Bakehorn, the world of women-made pornography is somewhat fragmented because it lacks a central location for production and is less established than mainstream porn (2010). At the same time, this may be beneficial in diversifying an industry criticized for lacking in fragmentation and diversity. Women-made porn typically includes photography, magazines, film (including DVD and streaming video online), and websites with photos, streaming video, message boards, blogs, and chat rooms. Some women have "single girl websites" that are more personal and include a biography, blog, chat room, live feeds, and essays on social issues. Women-made porn is usually categorized as hard core, soft core, or educational (which can involve a range of hard and soft core content). Some films are feature length with plot and characterization while others are pov/gonzo, all-sex, or educational.

Bakehorn examined women who make pornography (particularly those who make porn for a female audience) through ethnographic field work on six different porn film production sites in San Francisco, 72 interviews with mostly women directors and producers, actors, crew members, distributors, and personnel. She identifies five main factors that work individually or overlap in beginning a career in women-made porn: a background in sex education, an activist stance,

an artistic background, previous involvement in sex work, and a connection to porn through a friend or lover. Most of her interviewees discussed their motivations to make pornography that is an alternative to the mainstream industry and would be educational for viewers. They typically described their work as "by women" and "for women," regarding women as their audience and women's enjoyment as their goal, often drawing from their own experiences and desires in creating content. They were also less likely than mainstream actors to make porn for the purposes of fame and money (Abbott 2010).

There is limited empirical work on the issue of women's pornography consumption, especially in terms of social differences among women pornographic consumers (Parvez 2006; Sonnet 1999). Even less is known about consumer practices and experiences in genres like female-friendly, women-made, and lesbian/bisexual pornography.

According to Dana Collins, the first lesbian-produced pornographic images arose in the 1980s amidst anti/pro-porn debates and discussions about women's sexual desire (1998). Collins sought to assess the complexities of lesbian sexual visibility though investigating the emergence of lesbian porn out of the feminist sexuality debates, actual sexual imagery/text from three lesbian sex publications (*On Our Backs*, *Venus Infers*, and *Brat Attack*) and interviews with women involved in the production process of each publication. She finds that while such publications were not conventionally political projects, they inevitably became politicized due to historical timing and cultural emphasis of their content, production, and consumption.

Similarly, Heather Butler's (2004) investigation of cinematic lesbian sex acts and pornographic films from 1968 to 2000 illustrates certain transformations in lesbian and dyke pornography. Her analysis focuses on the butch/femme dyad, the dildo, the concept of authenticity, and creating a specifically lesbian discursive place/space to explore the historical presence and evolution of lesbians' participation in a particular genre of pornography. Butler argues that lesbian porn (because it is lesbian made, and also represents queer sexuality) has the potential to contribute to reexamining and reworking notions and representations of sex that have traditionally been marginalized, ignored, or simplified in reference to dominant male sexuality (2004). This is also the case with transgender and genderqueer pornography.

23.5.3 Transgender and Genderqueer Pornography

The erotic identities and sex lives of trans and genderqueer people have been largely omitted or fetishized in mainstream culture, and pathologized or considered problematic (e.g. a health risk) in academic scholarship. Emergent work on trans sexualities and intimate relationships, however, is expanding and garnering a fair amount of scholarly attention. "Tranny" or "shemale" porn is a particular subgenre that tends to sensationalize trans bodies and sexualities, and trans women and men are rarely cast in mainstream pornographic productions (Hill-Meyer 2013). Specifically trans-focused and trans-affirming pornography is therefore important for representing a range of bodies and sexualities in more authentic, agentic, empowered ways (Pfeffer 2014).

Tristan Taormino's (2011) *Take Me There: Trans and Genderqueer Erotica* is an edited collection of explicit narratives "for and about transfolk, FtMs, MTFs, genderqueers, gender outlaws, as well as two-spirit, intersex and gender-variant people. It is about people who like to genderfuck and fuck gender" (p. x). Taormino (2011) and Pfeffer (2014) both note an expansion in trans pornography, citing a body of independent trans porn generated by studios like Pink & White Productions, T-Wood Pictures, Morty Diamond Productions, and Handbasket Productions. Buck Angel has become a successful FtM porn star who has made tremendous strides to increase the visibility of transmen in mainstream porn (Angel 2013; Taormino 2011).

Trans pornography involves a wide presentation and representation bodies, genders, behaviors, sex acts, power, kink practices, safer sex methods, toys, tools, positions, transgressions,

replications, and intentions. Genderqueer or queer porn, in addition to feminist porn, are spaces for authentic sexual representations and present opportunities to examine bodies and sexualities in a myriad of innovative ways (Hill-Meyer 2013). However, there is little empirical attention to what trans and genderqueer porn content looks like, its effects on viewers, experiences with producing it, and especially data on consumer viewing and consumption practices and experiences; these are certainly directions for future scholarship.

Some have characterized genres like women-made, lesbian/bisexual, female-centered/female-friendly, and trans/genderqueer porn as "feminist pornography" because they create alternative images and develop their own aesthetics and iconography to expand established sexual norms and discourses. Additional qualities of feminist porn include the acknowledgement of multiple female (and other) viewers with different perspectives, attention to labor and production practices that create safe, fair, ethical, and consensual work environments and collaboration with their participants, and considers itself a site for resistance, intervention, and change (Taormino et al. 2013). Further, Bakehorn's study on women-made porn finds that there is overlap between women who make a range of lesbian, bisexual, transgender, and heterosexual porn, which illustrates the interconnectedness of feminist porn in production and content. Many of the questions that feminist porn scholars ask in their theorizing, research, and teaching are likely directions for further inquiry for the sex industry as a whole.

23.6 Technology and Pornography

There is particular scholarly interest in the relationship between pornography and technology. Some suggest that pornography has been at the forefront of developing, adopting and diffusing new technologies (Coopersmith 1998), perhaps because it is quick to recognize the economic potential of new technologies (Kendrick 1997) and has a consumer base willing to pay top prices and purchase expensive equipment to gain access (Lane 2001).

While technological evolution has taken pornography through a range of media, the internet has had a major impact in terms of availability, production, revenue, content, and cultural implications. Indeed internet porn has largely replaced magazine pornography (Patterson 2004) and may easily render print porn obsolete. Attwood argues that the migration of porn to the internet complicates current models of cultural production and consumption and makes it harder to classify as a form of commercial sex since it is freely available online (2007).

Devices like laptops, smartphones, and tablets have revolutionized how individuals can access porn in more personal, private settings. High-speed internet services, unlimited data packages and interactive computer technologies are also contributing to the ways in which consumers interact with porn. Dennis Waskul (2015) refers to *techno-sexuality* as the "increasingly ubiquitous use of technology to gather sexual information, express sexual desires, view or expose sexual bodies, experience sexual pleasure, and explore sexual fantasies" (p. 94). Waskul's empirical studies on the erotic uses of new media and communication technologies illustrate that while the Internet is both a space for sexual exploration and mediation, it has permeated the "realities of everyday erotic life and lived experiences of sexual selves" (p. 106) (see Waskul 2002, 2004; Waskul and Radeloff 2009). By recognizing how technology functions in the processes of anticipatory sexual socialization, Waskul notes that when young people become sexually aware, they use the Internet out of curiosity, to gain sexual knowledge (that may compensate for inexperience), and also for immediate arousal and masturbatory inspiration.

Some suggest that technology has impacted the relationship between the viewer or consumer and the material itself, especially with regard to internet porn. Website interfaces, search engines, ways in which content is visually presented and organized, streaming, pop-ups, daily limits on free access to clips, and physical habits like pointing and clicking or refreshing webcams contribute to a viewer's pornographic experience (Patterson 2004). Others note that the near limit-less amount of content online creates a continual need to search for new, different, or more sensational content, which may contribute to compulsive or even addictive behavior (Paul 2009).

There has also been considerable controversy surrounding pornography and the internet, namely in terms of child pornography and young people's access to readily available sexually explicit materials online. A series of legal decisions and battles in the mid 1990s occurred over what is considered child pornography and who has access to online porn (Nathan 2007). The mainstream sex industry has long maintained, however, that they have no involvement with producing or distributing child porn, and have actually worked with lawmakers to prohibit, criminalize, and eradicate such material. They are also in favor of and have abided by efforts to limit minors' access to pornography.

Technology has clearly revolutionized contemporary sexualities, and the relationships between pornography, technological invention, social trends and cultural ideologies are central for current academics in a range of fields and disciplines.

23.7   The Business of Pornography

Pornography is a highly lucrative and expansive business. There are hundreds of production companies and studios throughout the United States and internationally that produce a range of films, videos, and print porn that reflect particular genres and subgenres and cater to specific consumers. Some specialize in heterosexual content while others produce a variety of gay, lesbian, bisexual and transgender material. The industry has its own trade journals, media networks, organizations, a wide range of corporations, small businesses, news outlets, conventions, industry awards, and trade associations.

Adult Video News (AVN) and *XBIZ World* are the two leading trade journals for the porn industry. According to AVN.com, "AVN sets the standard for the business of pleasure by delivering unparalleled content that reaches industry professionals, mainstream media, and across diverse spectrums of consumer groups and communities." AVN hosts several annual expos, such as InterNEXT (for digital media), AVN Novelty Expo (for products and accessories), and the AVN Adult Entertainment Expo (AEE), which attracts hundreds of exhibitors and over 30,000 attendees like retailers, producers, manufacturers, talent, fans, public relations experts, and media consultants. AVN also began sponsoring its own Awards Show (self-described as the "Oscars" of Porn) in 1984, conferring a wide range of awards for bests in production, performers, specific scenes, technical production, marketing, and specialty release categories (AVN.com).

Similarly, XBIZ describes itself as the "global leader in adult entertainment industry news," providing current industry coverage on their website as well as two monthly trade publications for the Internet and technology (XBIZ World) and the retail market (XBIZ Premiere) (XBIZ.com). XBiz hosts four trade events annually that include the XBIZ Awards, which honor influential companies and performers in a red carpet event like AVN's awards ceremony. XBIZ.net serves as the industry's social network, connecting adult industry professionals with community news, information and business opportunities around the world (Xbizworld.com).

Lynn Comella (2010) suggests that trade shows like those of AVN and XBIZ offer a "sociologically rich window into the marketing and mainstreaming of sex in American society" and provides "an opportunity to assess the challenges confronting the industry" like internet piracy and declining DVD sales (p. 286). Indeed, her ethnographic research on the women's market for sex toys and pornography involved attending three tradeshows to gather data from industry professionals and trade events and seminars, which she argues are the "best way to gauge what is new, what is notable, and, importantly, what direction the industry is headed" (p. 303).

The Free Speech Coalition (FSC) is the adult entertainment industry's advocacy group and manages a range of legal, ethical, legislative, financial, and health issues for its members (Penley 2013). The FSC also administers the PASS (Performer Availability Scheduling Services), which provides industry producers and performers with a reliable protocol and database for STI testing. Industry talent/performers must be regularly (often weekly and monthly) screened for certain STDs/STIs at approved testing facilities, which are then held in a secure database for producers and agents to access before shooting scenes. The FSC works with an advisory council, IT specialists, medical consultants, and PASS coordinators to provide services for industry professionals (fscpass.com). The FSC also works with organizations like the California Department of Public Health to declare production moratoria when HIV infections are discovered among talent.

Several recent confirmed HIV-positive cases among heterosexual adult film actors have warranted production moratoria to assess the origins of contraction and prevent further transmission to fellow performers. The infections transpired during what has been characterized as a major decline in porn filming in Los Angeles County thanks to the 2012 passage of a law requiring porn actors to use condoms during filmmakers. The AIDS Healthcare Foundation, the organization behind the initiative to require mandatory on-camera condom use, has been highly critical of how the industry has resisted mandatory condoms and HIV testing in the past. However, the industry routinely notes that a majority of STD/STI infections, including the HIV ones in question, were believed to have occurred in the performers' private lives rather than during film shoots (Dalton 2014).

The issue of condom use in pornographic films has been one of contention in both heterosexual and gay porn contexts. Gay porn companies began enforcing condom use during shoots to protect the actors and company reputations in the 1980s in response to the HIV/AIDS crisis, well before heterosexual porn studios adopted safer sex on-screen practices (whether by choice or jurisdiction) (Mowlabocus et al. 2013). There has been considerable push back from the FSC and major production studios on mandatory condom use, citing the industry has its own internal safer sex regulations and regular screening processes to protect performers. The industry has been concerned with whether mandatory condoms break the viewer's fantasy and therefore impact sales, as well as concerns over whether local health authorities are willing or able to monitor shoots and enforce such monitoring (Carroll 2013). On-screen safer sex practices are, for a number of especially feminist porn companies, central to politicizing pornography and intentional in sub-verting gender, sexual, and pornographic norms. It is not uncommon to see the use of dental dam, latex gloves, condoms, and other barrier-protec-tion methods in a range of scenes in feminist and transgressive pornographies.

Those who work in the porn industry are em-ployed in a range of "behind-the-camera" jobs that include directors, producers, distributers, marketers, editors, agents, writers, camera per-sonnel, make-up and clothing personnel, assis-tants, and medical staff. A majority of research has been conducted, however, on those in front of the camera, who are often referred to as porn talent, actors, performers, models, or stars (de-pending on their success and self-identified ap-peal). Some scholars and industry professionals challenge terms like performer or actor, espe-cially with amateur porn, because they suggest a lack of authenticity or reality inherent in certain on-camera scenes. A majority of female directors and producers began working in the industry in front of the camera before changing direction or focus, and several have lucrative production companies and dominate a variety of subgenre production as a result.

There is growing research on the personal lives of those who work in the industry, espe-cially in relation to their sexual and intimate off-screen lives. Some studies have examined how individuals perceive porn performers (Ev-ans-DeCicco and Cowan 2001; Polk and Cowan 1996), which is customarily negative and as-sumes that porn actresses, in particular, come from sexually and physically abusive back-grounds and are perceived negatively in terms of health and self-esteem. A recent study by Griffith et al. (2013) gathered self-reported data from 117 porn actresses compared to a sample of women matched in age, ethnicity, and marital status to assess whether they had increased psychological problems, drug use, and higher rates of childhood

sexual abuse. Findings show that porn actresses had higher levels of self-esteem, positive feel-ings, social support, and sexual satisfaction than the matched group. They also were more likely to use certain drugs, be concerned with contracting an STI/STD, and had more sexual partners. More scholarship is needed on exploring performers' agency in their career choices and trajectories, how their personal and professional sex lives in-tersect, diverge, and inform one another, and also assess industry standards to ensure the safety and well-being of its employees.

23.8 Conclusions and Directions for Future Research

The social sciences are an ideal lens for dialogu-ing, theorizing, researching, and writing about pornography. Tibbals (2014) notes the reciprocal relationship between porn and broader social cul-ture, suggesting both react to and interact with one another. That wider social narratives and trends are reflected in pornography is not surpris-ing to Tibbals, especially since porn has taken in-spiration from a variety of mainstream narratives throughout history.

Research on pornography has increased ex-ponentially within the past few decades and will undoubtedly continue, especially among social scientists. There is a real need for empirical data on pornography gathered through large-scale quantitative methods, micro-level qualitative and ethnographic approaches, and also mixed method research designs. Sociologists play an important role in contributing to theoretical and empiri-cal discourses surrounding pornography. Work-ing within, aside from, and among frameworks already established by humanities scholars may further interdisciplinary dialogues about pornog-raphy.

Sexualities studies in general have become an interesting vehicle for innovative research meth-odologies that challenge normative approaches to data collection and analysis. For example, Lynn Comella (2013) suggests employing a par-ticular research approach, which she terms "porn studies-in-action," that involves scholars actually spending time in places where pornography is made, distributed, and consumed. Porn studies-in-action, asserts Comella, is a form of engaged scholarship that can therefore expand the understanding of cultural discourses and practices in specific institutional and organizational contexts, while "empirically deepening porn studies archives" (p. 64).

It is also important to expand the contexts where research and theorizing on pornography is published and disseminated. Studying pornography is becoming less peripheral in a number of contemporary scholarly fields. Peer-reviewed journals like the *Journal of Sex Research, Sexualities,* and the *Journal of Homosexuality* have traditionally published the bulk of porn research, and the recently inaugurated journal *Porn Studies* is a peer-reviewed forum for focused, interdisciplinary scholarly attention to pornography. Sex research conferences and seminars have also been supportive arenas for disseminating a wide range of scholarly efforts on pornography. Sociology journals, publications, and conferences in specific could also expand on including topics related to pornography and the sex industry.

Linda Williams (2014) notes that the current state of pornography studies involves limited work on heterosexual pornographies (and a newer abundance of work on gay porn), an underrepresented focus on soft core in favor of hard core, a need for more single-authored books, a lack of an effective archive of pornography, and the potential for the field to align itself too closely with the porn industry and thus be considered "pro-porn," which she cautions against. McKee (2014) calls for more interdisciplinary discussion and diversification with regard to methodologies employed for porn research. More generally, particular attention should be given to researchers' positionalities, unique obstacles with conducting research in hypersexualized settings, ethical considerations, and also the institutional, professional, and personal implications for scholars studying pornography.

Given that porn studies are still emerging especially in the social sciences, there are a multitude of possibilities for further exploration. While this chapter has previously articulated several ideas

warranting inquiry, specific directions for future research involve investigating consumer practices, porn business particulars, technological developments, amateur pornography, and also the relationship between pedagogy and pornography.

In terms of consumer practices, studies could examine what consumers view, purchase, download, upload, pirate, request, demand, and reject in terms of content, material, media, and production. Researchers may investigate how and where consumers use porn, such as location access, duration, private vs. public settings, devices utilized, alone or with partner(s), and what changes may occur in porn use throughout the life course. While recent studies consider the relationship between pornography consumption and actual behavior, causality remains a concern in establishing conclusions about what viewers watch and subsequently do in their actual sex lives. There is also surprisingly limited empirical data on individuals' reasons for watching porn. Barker's (2014) sample of 5490 online questionnaires regarding peoples' choices, likes and dislikes, and history with porn identified four main reasons for looking at porn: feeling horny, boredom/insomnia/restlessness, wanting to feel horny, and recognition of one's sexual interests. The role of porn in expanding and/or complicating peoples' sexual repertoires, pleasure, sex frequency, masturbation, fantasizing, and sexual decision-making are additional areas of focus. Researchers who focus on porn consumer and viewing habits could expand and diversify study samples to include more data on underrepresented populations, especially in terms of racial/ethnic identities, ages, religions, socio-economics, gender and sexual identities, and even urban/rural contexts.

Given the incredible diversity of porn's genres, subgenres, and niches, there are a multitude of unanswered questions about their content, impact, production, consumer base, and relationship to socio-sexual trends. For example, Morrison (2004) suggests that research on gay and bisexual male pornography should explore the relationship between exposure to sexually explicit material and self-assessments of attractiveness, viewers' perceptions as they relate to pornography and messages about gay male sexuality, gender, the ageing process, and safer sex, whether porn serves an important educative function, and finally what importance it has in relation to gay male culture. Corneau and Van Der Meulen (2014) also suggest a need for refining and clarifying definitions of pornography, an expanded focus on other sexually explicit materials like books, literature, and photography, and further investigation into the impact of bareback porn on its performers and viewers.

Porn business particulars are also a likely direction for future research, such as how the industry establishes best practices, provides employee health care and minimizes safety risks, and negotiates mainstream visibility and media relations. There is also a need for accurate, reliable data on industry revenue. Indeed, Comella (2013) argues that it is time to move beyond a focus on the texts and imagery of pornography in order to examine the wider industry context that gives rise to contemporary porn cultures. While a handful of scholars have touched upon porn sets, sex toy shops, direct-sales of adult novelties, adult expos, and erotic film festivals, there is ample opportunity to further contribute to pornography literatures with empirical exploration of these and similar venues. Researchers might also consider conducting ethnographic, quantitative, and mixed- method studies that investigate the personal and professional lives of performers, producers, and others working in porn, paying particular attention to intersections of race/ethnicity, class, gender, sexuality, age, and education.

Technology is a fruitful direction for future research on pornography. Scholars may explore how technology has and continues to impact consumer practices with online porn, such as with content, accessibility, and duration of use. Studies should also consider the existence, appeal, or rejection of certain online porn subgenres and viewers' responses and relations to them. Interactive technologies like webcams, chatrooms, and internet video/voice calling software are also of interest.

Several researchers have suggested more empirical focus on porn piracy, noting that consumers' decreased willingness to pay complicates supply-and-demand models typical for porn producers and may be even more problematic than the increase in amateur porn uploads (Brown 2014; Watson et al. 2014). While digital piracy is problematic for a range of media (music, software, movies), academics have yet to assess its impact on pornography in specific (Craig et al. 2005).

Scholars must consider adapting research methods to constantly shifting technologies (Grov et al. 2014). Consumer patterns, particularly in terms of gender, sexual orientation, age, and similarities by gender, sexual orientation, age, and race/ethnicity, can also provide insights and assist in meeting the needs of those who consume porn. Qualitatively investigating the experiences of those who access porn online from a myriad of devices may yield insights into the most effective technologies for private porn consumption and sexual arousal, satisfaction, and behavior. Technology has also necessitated questions about private versus public porn use, and has revolutionized individuals' access to high-quality cameras and recording devices used to capture personal pictures, behaviors, and interactions in sexualized contexts. Researchers have yet to fully address the impact of sexy selfies and especially amateur content like pictures and videos in mainstream culture and for the sex industry as a whole.

In effect, technological advancements like hand-held video cameras facilitated the advent of amateur pornography, which gained popularity in the 1980s. Professional porn actors or models are paid or compensated for their work, whereas amateur porn is described as showing average people engaging in unpaid sex for their own pleasure (McKee et al. 2008). However, a majority of amateur porn is actually commercially produced by porn companies, and is therefore referred to as "pro-amateur," "so-called" or "fake" amateur porn. Amateur porn is often considered appealing because it involves authentic representations of "real" people having "real" sex, is rarely scripted, allows for more individual sexual agency and provides considerable insight into peoples' contemporary sexual lives. Further, heterosexual amateur porn is often assumed to be more egalitarian and less objectifying, especially to women, than commercial porn (Attwood 2009).

A recent study by Van Doorn (2010), however, suggests that amateur porn is more similar to commercial pornography in perpetuating normative gender ideologies. His qualitative analysis of 100 user-generated amateur videos on YouPorn (an adult video-sharing site) shows that content reflects heteronormative "pornoscripts" that reifies traditional notions of gender and sexuality rather than providing opportunities for more authentic, emancipated versions (p. 411). Klaassen and Peter's (2014) content analysis of 400 popular Internet porn videos examines the presence of images that represent gender inequality (specifically objectification, power, and violence), noting comparisons between amateur and commercial porn content. Data show amateur porn contained more women's gender inequality than did commercial porn, which they suggest could be due to amateurs basing their on-camera performances on what they think porn should entail, as well as failing to consider their production efforts as subversive or progressive and therefore reproducing gender stereotypes in their content.

Amateur pornography is an interesting context to further explore dynamics of gender and sexual identities, power, sexual scripts, media, performance, spectacle, agency, authenticity, pleasure, desire, fantasy, and reflexivity. Further, amateur porn's existence is a technological testament and personal recording devices have essentially transformed labor, the means of production, and consumption in sexual commerce. For example, Henry Jenkins (2006) argues that commercial and amateur porn exist in tandem as people continue to harness new media technologies to construct their own communities that represent and validate a range of sexualities. Scholars can therefore use amateur porn as a lens through which to examine cultural production and consumption, labor and sexual commodities, and may yield further insights on its individual, social, and economic impact.

Finally, recent scholarly attention explores pornography's educational benefits such as Rothman et al.'s (2014) examination of porn and young people's sex education and Grove et al.'s (2014) assessment of porn's impact on adult sexual knowledge, behavior, and identity formation. Heffernan (2013) suggests that the niche marketing of home video has facilitated sexually explicit educational materials created by women as "how-to" videos by performers like Nina Hartley and author/sex educators like Tristan Taormino. Studies could focus on what viewers are learning about sexuality and their bodies in relation to what they access and consume in their private lives. Researchers may address the role, significance, utility, and consequences of incorporating pornography into formal sexual education curricula in middle and high school settings. Sexualities courses are increasingly offered in various departments at many universities and colleges, and there are several institutions that offer courses specifically devoted to pornography. Albury (2014) notes that academics have yet to fully assess what porn teaches or what can be learned from porn, and future research could further investigate how differences in sexual tastes and cultures impact audiences' reception of pornographic texts, as well as how pornography can reshape the broader curriculum of formal sex and intimate relationships. Some suggest that teaching with sexually explicit texts has the potential to challenge hegemonic meanings and customary cultural discourses of sexuality (Smith 2009).

There is a developing body of literature on the pedagogy of pornography that should further consider instructors' experiences teaching porn (e.g. Smith's (2009) study on teachers' own experiences using porn in the classroom), generating effective student discussion and debate, what pornographic materials instructors decide to show (and how they make such choices), experiences teaching porn to small classes and large lectures, negotiating potential student and institutional blowback, mentoring student research on pornography, and generating data on the scholarship of teaching and learning in sexualized contexts. McNair (2009) notes that while teaching pornography may no longer be "a dangerous pedagogical act in itself" (p. 566), it remains important both in and aside from the academy. Exploring the impact of teaching sexually explicit material on students and professors alike may contribute to further understanding sexual pedagogies in broader, more experiential contexts.

This chapter attempts to provide a comprehensive look at pornography in brief historical, present, and future contexts, with particular attention placed on its empirical significance. While porn has been widely contested, criticized, regulated, and debated, it has and continues to be a central fixture in national and global economies, societies and cultures throughout the world, and in the lives of numerous individuals who create, produce, consume, theorize, research, and teach about pornography. Such proliferation has undoubtedly necessitated new and different ways to approach, contextualize and experience the pornographic. Some suggest that perhaps the best way to move forward is to "turn toward a more nuanced conceptualization of pornography as pornograph*ies*" (Klaassen and Peter 2014, p. 11) and think of porn futures in the plural in order to remain dedicated to contextualization and sensitive to histories, aesthetics, discourses, contexts of production, distribution and consumption when conceptualizing pornographic texts and phenomena (Paasonen 2007).

References

Abbott, S. A. (2010). Motivations for pursuing a career in pornography. In R. Weitzer (Ed.), *Sex for sale: Prostitution, pornography, and the sex industry* (pp. 47–66). New York: Routledge.

Angel, B. (2013). The power of my vagina. In T. Taormino, C. Penley, C. Shimizu, & M. Miller-Young (Eds.), *The feminist porn book: The politics of producing pleasure* (pp. 284–286). New York: The Feminist Press.

Albury, K. (2014). Porn and sex education, porn as sex education. *Porn Studies, 1*(1–2), 172–181.

Armstrong, E. A., & Weinberg, M. S. (2006). Identity and competence: The use of culture in the interpretation of sexual images. *Sociological Perspectives, 49*(3), 411–432.

Attwood, F. (2002). Reading porn: The paradigm shift in pornography research. *Sexualities, 5*(10), 91–105.

Attwood, F. (2009). *Mainstreaming sex: The sexualization of western culture*. London: I.B. Tauris.

AVN.com. (2014). http://avn.com. Accessed 28 Dec 2014.

Bakehorn, J. A. (2010). Women-made pornography. In R. Weitzer (Ed.), *Sex for sale: Prostitution, pornog-raphy, and the sex industry* (pp. 91–114), New York: Routledge.

Barker, M. (2014). The 'problem' of sexual fantasies. *Porn Studies, 1*(1–2), 143–160.

Barron, M., & Kimmel, M. (2000). Sexual violence in three pornographic media: Toward a sociological explanation. *Journal of Sex Research, 37*(2), 161–168.

Bart, P. B., Freeman, L., & Kimball, P. (1985). The different worlds of women and men: Attitudes toward pornography and responses to not a love story-a film about pornography. *Women's Studies International Forum, 8,* 307–322.

Benjamin, O., & Tlusten, D. (2010). Intimacy and/or degradation: Heterosexual images of togetherness and women's embracement of pornography. *Sexualities, 13*(5), 599–623.

Brown, S. C. (2014). Porn piracy: An overlooked phenomenon in need of academic investigation. *Porn Studies, 1*(3), 326–330.

Butler, H. (2004). What do you call a lesbian with long fingers? The development of lesbian and dyke pornography. In L. Williams (Ed.), *Porn studies* (pp. 167–197). Durham: Duke University Press.

Burger, J. R. (1995). *One-handed histories: The eroto-politics of gay male video pornography*. New York: Harrington Park Press.

Carnes, M. (2007). Bend over boyfriend: Anal sex instructional videos for women. In K. Nikunen, S. Paasonen, & L. Saarenmaa (Eds.), *Pornification: Sex and sexuality in media culture* (pp. 151–160). Oxford: Berg.

Carroll, R. (2013). New HIV outbreak in US porn industry leaves insiders divided over condoms. http://www.theguardian.com/culture/2013/sep/12/porn-industry-california-hiv-condoms. Accessed 1 Jan 2015.

Celline, H. B., & Duncan, D. F. (1988). Homosexual pornography: Trends in content and form over a twenty-five year period. *Psychology: A Journal of Human Behavior, 25*(3–4), 37–41.

Cohler, B. J. (2004). Memoir and performance. *Journal of Homosexuality, 47*(3–4), 7–43.

Collins, D. (1998). Lesbian pornographic production: Creating social/cultural space for subverting representations of sexuality. *Berkeley Journal of Sociology, 43,* 31–62.

Comella, L. (2010). Remaking the sex industry: The adult expo as a microcosm. In R. Weitzer (Ed.), *Sex for sale: Prostitution, pornography, and the sex industry* (pp. 285–306). New York: Routledge.

Comella, L. (2013). From text to context: Feminist porn and the making of a market. In T. Taormino, C. Penley, C. Shimizu, & M. Miller-Young (Eds.), *The feminist porn book: The politics of producing pleasure* (pp. 79–96). New York: The Feminist Press.

Corneau, S., & van der Meulen, E. (2014). Some like it mellow: On gay men complicating pornography discourses. *Journal of Homosexuality, 61*(4), 491–510.

Coopersmith, J. (1998). Pornography, technology and progress. *Icon, 4,* 94–125.

Crooks, R., & Baur, K. (2007). *Our sexuality*. Cengage Learning.

Cottle, C. E., Searles, P., Berger, R. J., & Pierce, B. A. (1989). Conflicting ideologies and the politics of pornography. *Gender and Society, 3*(3), 303–333.

Craig, P., Honick, R., & Burnett, M. (Eds.). (2005). *Software piracy exposed: Secrets from the dark side revealed.* New York: Syngress.

Dalecki, M. G., & Price, J. (1994). Dimensions of pornography. *Sociological Spectrum, 14*(3), 205–219.

Dalton, A. (2014). "Very strong evidence" of HIV transmission during porn shoot. Huffington Post. http://www.huffingtonpost.com/2014/12/30/hiv-transmission-porn_n_6396066.html. Accessed 1 Jan 2015.

Davis, J. A., & Smith, T. W. (1986). *General social surveys: Cumulative codebook.* Chicago: National Opinion Research Center, University of Chicago.

Dines, G. (2010). *Pornland: How porn has hijacked our sexuality.* Beacon Press.

Duits, L., & Van Zoonen, L. (2006). Headscarves and porno-chic disciplining girls' bodies in the European multicultural society. *European Journal of Women's Studies, 13*(2), 103–117.

Escoffier, J. (2007). Porn star/stripper/escort: Economic and sexual dynamics in a sex work career. *Journal of Homosexuality, 53*(1–2), 173–200.

Evans-DeCicco, J. A., & Cowan, G. (2001). Attitudes toward pornography and the characteristics attributed to pornography actors. *Sex Roles, 44*(5–6), 351–361.

FSCPass. (2014). http://fscpass.com/about_us. Accessed 28 Dec 2014.

Griffith, J. D., Mitchell, S., Hart, C. L., Adams, L. T., & Gu, L. L. (2013). Pornography actresses: An assessment of the damaged goods hypothesis. *Journal of Sex Research, 50*(7), 621–632.

Griffiths, M. (2001). Sex on the internet: Observations and implications for internet sex addiction. *Journal of Sex Research, 38*(4), 333–342.

Grov, C., Breslow, A. S., Newcomb, M. E., Rosenberger, J. G., & Bauermeister, J. A. (2014). Gay and bisexual men's use of the internet: Research from the 1990s through 2013. *Journal of Sex Research, 51*(4), 390–409.

Hardy, S. (1998). *The reader, the author, his woman, and her lover: soft-core pornography and heterosexual men.* Continuum Intl Pub Group.

Hardy, S. (2004). Reading pornography. *Sex Education: Sexuality, Society and Learning, 4*(1), 3–18.

Heffernan, K. (2013). From "It could happen to someone you love" to "Do you speak ass?": Women and discourses of sex education in erotic film and video. In T. Taormino, C. Penley, C. Shimizu, & M. Miller-Young (Eds.), *The feminist porn book: The politics of producing pleasure* (pp. 237–254). New York: The Feminist Press.

Herman, M. S., & Border, D. C. (1983). Attitudes toward pornography in a southern community. *Criminology, 21,* 349–374.

Herman, M. S., & Bordner, D. C. (2013). Attitudes toward pornography in a southern community. *Criminology, 21,* 349–374.

Hill-Meyer, T. (2013). Where the trans women aren't: The slow inclusion of trans women in feminist and queer porn. In T. Taormino, C. Penley, C. Shimizu, & M. Miller-Young (Eds.), *The feminist porn book: The politics of producing pleasure* (pp. 155–163). New York: The Feminist Press.

Hines, C., & Kerr, D. (Eds.). (2012). *Hard to swallow: hard-core pornography on screen.* London: Wallflower.

Huntley, R. (1998). Slippery when wet: The shifting boundaries of the pornographic (a class analysis). *Continuum: Journal of Media and Cultural Studies, 12*(1), 69–81.

Isola, M. J. (2013). 'The string of this one story': Erotica, HIV, and the construction of safe sex in gay male popular memory. *Journal of Homosexuality, 60*(8), 1185–1219.

Jenkins, H. (2006). *Convergence culture: Where old and new media collide.* New York: New York University Press.

Juffer, J. (1998). At home with Pornography: Women, sex, and everyday life. New York: New York University Press.

Kangasvuo, J. (2007). Insatiable sluts and almost gay guys: Bisexuality in porn magazines. In K. Nikunen, S. Paasonen, & L., Saarenmaa (Eds.), *Pornification: sex and sexuality in media culture* (pp. 139–150). Oxford: Berg.

Kendrick, W. (1997). *The secret museum: Pornography in modern culture.* New York: Viking.

Kipnis, L. (1996). *Bound and gagged: Pornography and the politics of fantasy in America.* New York: Grove Press.

Kirkpatrick, R. G., & Zurcher, L. A. (1983). Women against pornography: Feminist anti-pornography crusades in American society. *International Journal of Sociology and Social Policy, 3,* 1–30.

Klaassen, M. J., & Peter, J. (2014). Gender (in) equality in internet pornography: A content analysis of popular pornographic internet videos. *The Journal of Sex Research, 0*(0), 1–15.

Lane, F. S. (2001). *Obscene profits: Entrepreneurs of pornography in the cyber age: Entrepreneurs of pornography in the cyber age.* New York: Routledge.

Laumann, E. O., Gagnon, J. H., Michael, R. T, & Michaels, S. (1994). *The social organization of sexuality: Social practices in the United States.* Chicago: University of Chicago Press.

Magill, F. N. (1995). Pornography. *International Encyclopedia of Sociology* (pp. 985–988). Chicago: Fitzroy Dearborn.

McKee, A., Albury, K., & Lumby, C. (2008). *The porn report.* Melbourne: University of Melbourne Press.

McKee, A. (2009). Social scientists don't say "Titwank". *Sexualities, 12*(5), 629–646.

McKee, A. (2014). Humanities and social scientific research methods in porn studies. *Porn Studies, 1*(1–2), 53–63.

McNair, B. (1996). *Mediated sex: Pornography and postmodern culture.* London: Arnold.

McNair, B. (2009). Teaching porn. *Sexualities, 12*(5), 558–567.

McNair, B. (2013). *Porno? Chic! How pornography changed the world and made it a better place.* New York: Routledge.

Mercer, J. (2004). In the slammer. *Journal of Homosexuality, 47*(3–4), 151–166.

Miller-Young, M. (2010). Putting hypersexuality to work: Black women and illicit eroticism in pornography. *Sexualities, 13*(2), 219–235.

Morrison, T. G. (2004). "He was treating me like trash, and I was loving it…": Perspectives on gay male pornography. *Journal of Homosexuality, 47*(3–4), 167–183.

Mowlabocus, S. (2007). Gay men and the pornification of everyday life. In K. Nikunen, S. Paasonen, & L. Saarenmaa (Eds.), *Pornification: Sex and sexuality in media culture* (pp. 61–72). Oxford: Berg.

Mowlabocus, S., Harbottle, J., & Witzel, C. (2013). Porn laid bare: Gay men, pornography and bareback sex. *Sexualities, 16*(5/6), 523–547.

Nagle, J. (1997). Introduction. In J. Nagle (Ed.), *Whores and other feminists* (pp. 1–18). New York: Routledge.

Nathan, D. (2007). *Pornography: A groundwork guide.* Toronto: Groundwood Books.

O'Hara, S. (1997). *Autopornography: A memoir of life in the lust lane.* New York: Harrington Park Press.

O'Toole, L. (1998). *Pornocopia: Porn, sex, technology and desire.* London: Serpent's Tail.

Paasonen, S. (2007). Epilogue: Porn futures. In K. Nikunen, S. Paasonen, & L. Saarenmaa (Eds.), *Pornification: Sex and sexuality in media culture* (pp. 161–170). Oxford: Berg.

Paasonen, S., & Saarenmaa. L. (2007). The golden age of porn: Nostalgia and history in cinema. In K. Nikunen, S. Paasonen, & L. Saarenmaa (Eds.), *Pornification: Sex and sexuality in media culture* (pp. 23–32). Oxford: Berg.

Paasonen, S., Nikunen, K., & Saarenmaa, L. (2007). Pornification and the education of desire. In K. Nikunen, S. Paasonen, & L. Saarenmaa (Eds.), *Pornification: Sex and sexuality in media culture* (pp. 1–22). Oxford: Berg.

Parvez, F. Z. (2006). The labor of pleasure: How perceptions of emotional labor impact women's enjoyment of pornography. *Gender and Society, 20*(5), 605–631.

Patterson, Z. (2004). Going on-line: Consuming pornography in the digital era. In L. Williams (Ed.), *Porn studies* (pp. 104–126). Durham: Duke University Press.

Paul, P. (2005). *Pornified: How pornography is transforming our lives, our relationships, and our families.* New York: Times Books.

Paul, B. (2009). Predicting internet pornography use and arousal: The role of individual difference variables. *Journal of Sex Research, 46*(4), 344–357.

Penley, C. (2013). "A feminist teaching pornography? That's like scopes teaching evolution!" In T. Taormino, C. Penley, C. Shimizu, & M. Miller-Young (Eds.), *The*

feminist porn book: The politics of producing pleasure (pp. 179–199). New York: The Feminist Press.

Pfeffer, C. A. (2014). Making space for trans sexualities. *Journal of Homosexuality, 61*(5), 597–604.

Polk, R. K., & Cowan, G. (1996). Perceptions of female pornography stars. *Canadian Journal of Human Sexuality, 5*(3), 221–229.

Poole, W. (2000). *Dirty Poole: The autobiography of a gay porn pioneer.* Los Angeles: Alyson Publications.

Pornography [Orig.]. (n.d.). Merriam-Webster.com. http://www.merriamwebster.com/dictionary/pornography. Accessed 1 Jan 2015.

Poulsen, F. O., Busby, D. M., & Galovan, A. M. (2013). Pornography use: Who uses it and how it is associated with couple outcomes. *Journal of Sex Research, 50*(1), 72–83.

Rosser, B. R. S., Smolenski, D. J., Erickson, D., Iantaffi, A., Brady, S. S., Grey, J. A., & Hald, G. M., et al. (2013). The effects of gay sexually explicit media on the HIV risk behavior of men who have sex with men. *AIDS and Behavior, 17*(4), 1488–1498.

Rothman, E. F., Kaczmarsky, C., Burke, N., Jansen, E., & Baughman, A. (2014). "Without porn…I wouldn't know half the things I know now:" A qualitative study of pornography use among a sample of urban, low-income, black and Hispanic youth. *Journal of Sex Research, 0*(0), 1–11.

Sinkovic, M., Stulhofer, A., & Bozic, J. (2013). Revisiting the association between pornography use and risky sexual behaviors: The role of early exposure to pornography and sexual sensation seeking. *Journal of Sex Research, 50*(7), 633–641.

Sabo, A. G. (2012). *After pornified: How women are transforming pornography & why it really matters.* Winchester. UK: Zero Books.

Shaw, S. M. (1999). Men's leisure and women's lives: The impact of pornography on women. *Leisure Studies, 18,* 197–212.

Smith, C. (2009). Pleasure and distance: Exploring sexual cultures in the classroom. *Sexualities, 12*(5), 568–585.

Sonnet, E. (1999). Erotic fiction by women for women: The pleasures of post-feminist heterosexuality. *Sexualities, 2*(2), 167–187.

Stein, D., Silvera, R., Hagerty, R., & Marmor, M. (2012). Viewing pornography depicting unprotected anal intercourse: Are there implications for HIV prevention among men who have sex with men? *Archives of Sexual Behavior, 41,* 411–419.

Taormino, T. (Ed.). (2011). *Take me there: Trans and genderqueer erotica.* Berkeley: Cleis Press.

Taormino, T. (2013). Calling the shots: Feminist porn in theory and practice. In T. Taormino, C. Penley, C. Shimizu, & M. Miller-Young (Eds.), *The feminist porn book: The politics of producing pleasure* (pp. 255–264). New York: The Feminist Press.

Taormino, T., Penley, C., Shimizu, C., & Miller-Young, M. (Eds.). (2013). *The feminist porn book: The politics of producing pleasure.* New York: The Feminist Press.

Tibbals, C. A. (2014). Gonzo, trannys, and teens: Current trends in US adult content production, distribution, and consumption. *Porn Studies, 1*(1–2), 127–135.

Van Doorn, N. (2010). Keeping it real: user-generated pornography, gender reification, and visual pleasure. *Convergence, 16,* 411–430.

Vannier, S. A., Currie, A. B., & O'Sullivan, L. (2014). Schoolgirls and soccer moms: a content analysis of free "teen" and "MILF" online pornography. *Journal of Sex Research, 51*(3), 253–264.

Voss, G. (2012). 'Treating it as a normal business': Researching the pornography industry. *Sexualities, 15*(3/4), 391–410.

Waskul, D. (2002). The naked self: Being a body in tele-video cybersex. *Symbolic Interaction, 25*(2), 199–227.

Waskul, D. (Ed.). (2004). *Net.seXXX: readings on sex, pornography, and the internet.* New York: Peter Lang.

Waskul, D. (2015). Techno-sexuality: The sexual pragmatists of the technological age. In T. S. Weinberg & S. Newmahr (Eds.), *Selves, symbols, and sexualities: An interactionist anthology* (pp. 77–88). Los Angeles: Sage.

Waskul, D., & Radeloff, C. (2009). 'How do I rate?' Nude 'rate me' websites and gendered looking glasses. In F. Attwood (Ed.), *Porn.Com: Making sense of online pornography* (pp. 202–216). New York: Peter Lang.

Watson, P., Zizzo, D., & Fleming, P. (2014). *Determinants and welfare implications of unlawful file sharing: A scoping review.* Glasgow: CREATe.

Weitzer, R. (2010). Sex work: Paradigms and policies. In R. Weitzer (Ed.), *Sex for sale: Prostitution, pornography, and the sex industry* (pp. 1–45). New York: Routledge.

Williams, L. (1989). *Hard core: Power, pleasure, and the "frenzy of the invisible."* Los Angeles: University of California Press.

Williams, L. (Ed.). (2004). *Porn Studies.* Durham: Duke University Press.

Williams, L. (2014). Pornography, porno, porn: Thoughts on a weedy field. *Porn Studies, 1*(1–2), 24–40.

Wood, M., & Hughes, M. (1984). The moral bias of moral reform: Status discontent vs. culture and socialization as explanations of anti-pornography social movement adherence. *American Sociological Review, 49,* 86–99.

Wosick-Correa, K., & Joseph, L. J. (2008). Sexy ladies sexing ladies: Women as consumers in strip clubs. *Journal of Sex Research, 45*(3), 201–216.

Wright, Paul J. (2013). U.S. males and pornography, 1973–2010: Consumption, predictors, correlates. *Journal of Sex Research, 50*(1), 60–71.

Xbizworld.com. (2014). http://xbizworld.com/editorial.php. Accessed 28 Dec 2014.

XBIZ.com. (2014). http://xbiz.com. Accessed 28 Dec 2014.

The Medicalization of Sexual Deviance, Reproduction, and Functioning

24

Thea Cacchioni

24.1 Introduction

Beginning in the late nineteenth century, western science, medicine, and the emergent fields of psychiatry and sexology began to supersede custom and religion as *the* authorities on sex. Since this period, sexuality has been subjected to increased diagnosis, classification, surveillance, and intervention, including psychiatric, psychoanalytic, surgical, and pharmaceutical. Medicine's influence on sexuality has been most evident in its classification, treatment, and monopolization over (1) sexualities deemed as deviant (2) sexual reproduction and (3) sexual functioning. This chapter will examine the medicalization of sex as it has unfolded in these arenas, primarily within Anglo Europe and North America where these trends have been most prevalent. It explains the medicalization thesis, traces evolving theoretical frameworks and methodologies used in scientific research and clinical practice focused on sexuality, and identifies questions for further research. As we will see, medical understandings and approaches to deviance, reproduction, and sexual functioning are not static, but have changed over time. These shifts belie the influence of social, political, and economic factors in shaping sup-

posedly "objective," "value-free" scientific and clinical epistemologies.

Throughout the chapter, I highlight various nuances in the medicalization of sex, noting examples of sexual medicalization that existed as only fringe practices, and others that have been and continue to be normalized. Additionally, while I describe the enormous power and resilience of medicalizing influences (i.e. of medical concepts, institutions, practitioners, and therapies), I note instances of resistance to reproductive and sexual medicalization by an increasingly reflexive lay populace. Indeed, we will see several examples of reproductive and sexual *de*medicalization. Finally, my discussion will underscore the ways in which medicalization has targeted some, and neglected other populations, with various consequences, and according to social differences in gender, race, class, ethnicity, sexuality, and (dis) ability.

24.2 The Medicalization Thesis

The medicalization of sexuality is part and parcel of the wider medicalization of everyday life. *Medicalization* is "a process whereby nonmedical problems become defined and treated as medical problems, usually in terms of illnesses or disorders" (Conrad 1992, p. 210), or the process wherein "more and more areas of everyday life have come under medical dominion, influence,

T. Cacchioni (✉)
Department of Women's Studies, University of Victoria, Victoria, BC, Canada
e-mail: tcacchio@uvic.ca

J. DeLamater, R.F. Plante (eds.), *Handbook of the Sociology of Sexualities,* Handbooks of Sociology and Social Research, DOI 10.1007/978-3-319-17341-2_24, © Springer International Publishing Switzerland 2015

and supervision" (Zola 1983, p. 295). Traditionally, most definitions of medicalization have implied "a critique of medicalization" as in "overmedicalization" (Conrad 1992, p. 210), although some use the term to discuss the benefits of medicalization (Williams 2001). Critics argue that in the past two centuries, a range of behaviors and practices once judged in moral terms, are now understood within the rubric of health and illness.

Since the 1960s, Foucault's writings (1965, 1973, 1978) have deconstructed medical frameworks in similar terms, as well as unique ways, that set them apart from what some term "orthodox" writings on medicalization (Williams 2001). Like others who position medicalization as a contemporary form of "social control" (Conrad 1992), Foucault (1978) argues that "biopower," the administration of bodies and the calculated management of life, is a pervasive mode of governmentality exclusive to modern capitalist nation states. However, Foucault utilizes a stronger version of social constructionism as compared to his orthodox counterparts. He questions the assumption that there is in fact any "authentic" or underlying "natural," biophysical reality of the body, untouched by ideological, discursive, and/ or disciplinary trappings.

Since the 1970s, feminist research on medicalization has also taken a slightly different point of emphasis compared to orthodox critics. Feminist writings position medicine as a male-dominated institution employing androcentric definitions of illness and disease, thus maintaining the relative inequality of women (see for example, Ehrenreich and English 1979). Scholars writing from a feminist perspective have argued that medicine has exercised power over women's life processes more so than men's, particularly in regard to their reproductive cycles (Oakley 1984; Martin 1987; Houck 2003). Women are also argued to be more susceptible to medicalization due to their roles in supervising the health care of families (Riessman 1983). Ironically, while Foucault largely ignores gender in his writing, feminists have found his theories useful for discussing the multiplicity of ways in which medicine disciplines women's bodies (see for example, Lupton 1997).

A growing body of literature refers to *biomedicalization* (Clarke et al. 2003). According to biomedicalization theorists, advertising agencies, public relations firms, HMOs, and insurance companies now join doctors and hospitals in the push towards medicalization. Drug companies exercise the most power in shaping health research agendas and clinical practice, with pharmaceutical companies now funding the vast majority of medical research, conferences, and Continuing Medical Education (CME). Pharmaceutical companies do not simply develop and sell pharmaceuticals—they now also hire medical spokespeople, public relations, marketing and advertising firms for the direct-to-consumer advertising of drugs and the conditions they claim to treat (Loe 2004). Again, feminist critics argue that women, in particular, are targets of biomedicalization with ever-increasing pressure to use the HPV vaccination, pharmaceutical means of birth control, and Hormone Replacement Therapy (Rochon-Ford and Saibil 2009).

Indeed, critical discussions of (bio) medicalization have also focused on the medicalization of reproductive and sexual behaviours, identities, and practices (Cacchioni and Tiefer 2012). Critics note that medicine, psychology, psychiatry, and more recently, geneticists, pharmacologists, and drug companies, have been active in classification, management, and surveillance of sexual medicalization. They also highlight striking examples of sexual *demedicalization* following the rise of mid-twentieth century grassroots social movements, and *remedicalization* following the growth of late-twentieth century biotechnologies and the industries that surround them.

24.3 The Medicalization of Sexual Deviance

The medicalization of sexual deviance includes scientific, medical, psychoanalytic, and psychiatric attempts at defining and classifying "normal" sexual desire and expression across social locations of gender, race, class, and so forth. As with most forms of sexual medicalization, the medicalization of sexual deviance can be traced to the late nineteenth century. Sexology, "the study and classification of sexual behaviours, identities, and relations" (Bland and Doan 1998,

p. 1), emerged at this time with an emphasis on sexual perversions. Similarly, psychiatry, another relatively new area of medical specialization, attempted to "create an increasingly fine nosology" of sexual pathologies (Digby 1989, p. 185). When assessing the criteria used to distinguish "deviance" from "normalcy," the influence of social, political, and economic factors is evident. As with other forms of sexual medicalization, a general pattern can be traced wherein sexual deviance was chalked up to visible biological markers in the nineteenth century, whereas Freudian psychoanalytic theories dominated in the early twentieth century. In the late twentieth century, some sexualities were de-medicalized, while others have been subjected to new biological theories and drug interventions.

24.3.1 Nineteenth Century Perspectives

While an active white middle and upper class male sexuality was assumed and normalized in nineteenth century medical literature, white middle-class women were constructed as naturally "passionless" (Cott 1978), and some women of colour and sex workers were framed as physiologically predisposed to hyper-sexuality (Fausto-Sterling 1999). Theories of biological racism were used as political tools as Europeans sought to justify colonial expansion through the Darwinian notion of the "survival of the fittest." In this context, Sartjie Bartman, a Khoikhoi woman from South Africa, was captured and sold to European scientists, who publicly displayed her wearing only a cloth to cover her genitals. Advertised as the "Hottentot Venus," she was billed as having large buttocks and long labia, physical attributes taken as a sign of her innate sexualization. After her death by undetermined causes in 1815, she was dissected and her skeleton, preserved genitals, and brain were displayed at the Paris *Musee De L'Homme* until 1974. In a similar vein, W. H. Flower and James Murie (1867) published "an Account of the Dissection of a Bushwoman" which located racial difference "through the sexual and reproductive anatomy of

the African female body," mainly her hips, buttocks, and labia (Summerville 1994, p. 252).

Nineteenth century writings about the bodies of sex workers similarly connected literal excess of bodily tissue with sexual excess. As a result of the increased mobility of bourgeois men living in urban centres following the industrial revolution, this century witnessed the rising popularity and elaboration of the sex industry. As part of the moral and public health panic that surrounded this booming industry, medical and social scientific writings focused on the physiology of sex workers, in an effort to construct them as naturally deviant. For instance, Adrien Charpy's (1870) influential essay published in a French *Journal of Dermatology and Syphilology*, based on his analysis of 800 sex workers in France, concluded that "there is an elongation of the labia majora in prostitutes" that is comparable to the "disgusting" genetalia of the "Hottentot." The work of Casare Lombroso and G. Ferrero (1893), an Italian criminologist and author of *La Donna Deliquente,* was also widely read in the European medical community. He wrote, "The prostitute's labia are throwbacks of the Hottentot, if not the chimpanzee." According to Gilman (1985), there was some disagreement in the medical community as to whether sex worker bodies were *naturally* predisposed to excessive tissue, or whether they were subject to specific pathologies of their genitalia through sexually transmitted disease.

By contrast, white middle class women in the nineteenth century could be diagnosed with nymphomania for veering from the ideal of "passionlessness," thought to be the norm for their bodily constitutions. In Groneman's (1994) analysis of one hundred case studies of nymphomania in Britain and the US, she found that white women who displayed higher levels of sexual expression than their husbands, confided in their husbands or doctors about sexual passions, bore illegitimate children, were victims of sexual assault or rape, were widows, or were divorced, expressed the wish to have gynecological examinations, were promiscuous, experienced clitoral orgasm, or masturbated were at risk of this diagnosis.[1]

---

[1] While this criteria would make vast populations of women eligible for the nymphomania diagnostic criteria,

Although overall a fringe practice, treatments included the application of leeches to the vagina, "diets, drugs, bloodletting, cold baths," and confinement to the asylum. And while frowned upon by the mainstream medical community, between 1859 and 1886, Dr. Issac Baker Brown, a member of the Obstetrical Society of London, performed clitoridectomies on women diagnosed with nymphomania. He was eventually barred from his practice following outcry by fellow physicians.

Homosexuality was also defined and treated as a biological state of sexual deviance beginning in the late nineteenth century (Chauncey 1989). In Richard von Krafft-Ebing's book titled *Psychopathia Sexualis* (1886), he theorized homosexuals to be physically degenerative, although he also argued that "self-abuse" (masturbation) could lead to homosexuality. Based on a case study method, many entries included drawings of what were seen as anatomical peculiarities of homosexual bodies. This book was used a key reference point for psychiatrists, physicians, and doctors in the late nineteenth century, when judging how to interpret and approach sexualities deemed "perverse."

The next generation of sexologists, including Havelock Ellis and J. A. Symonds (1897), and Magnus Hirschfeld (1914) believed in the physical differences between homosexuals and heterosexuals, but were more compassionate in their attitudes and approach. Ellis, in particular, positioned his writings on the physiological markers of homosexuality in direct protest to new laws criminalizing homosexuality. Rather than pathologizing the object choice of homosexuals, he believed that homosexuality was a case of "sexual inversion," wherein, for instance, men were entirely effeminate in dress, tastes, and behavior, or outwardly masculine, but feminine in sexual terms. Hirschfeld believed that homosexuals were an "intermediate sex," combining qualities of male and female. It is difficult for historians to know how these subjects of sexological investigation perceived their sexual and/or gender identities.

Lesbians were also examined for forensic difference beginning in the nineteenth century, pathologized as sexual inverts for their transgression from gender norms. Ellis and Symonds (1897) and other sexologists of the time believed that every lesbian couple involved a sexual invert or "mannish woman." In keeping with the sexological methods in this period, he inspected the hymen, clitoris, labia, and vagina for anatomical differences of those who identified as or were labeled as lesbians. Ellis believed that every lesbian coupling must include a masculine invert and a feminine woman who was duped by the sexual aggression of sexual inverts. Perhaps because of the firmly entrenched view of women as naturally "passionless," the connection of lesbian sex to sexual inversion remained stronger in early twentieth century sexological works about sex between females as compared to sex between males. Decades later, Dickinson and Beam's (1931) Sex Variant Study analyzed notes from over 2000 gynecological records, once again, looking for signs of genital abnormality as well as masculine behavior among lesbian women (Terry 1999).

24.3.2 Twentieth Century Perspectives

With that said, by the early twentieth century, Freud's psychoanalytic perspective of sexual deviance was most popular. Moving away from the nineteenth century tendency towards biological determinism, Freud believed that we are all born bisexual, but that normal psychosexual development would lead us to heterosexuality. He understood homosexuality as an arrested and sometimes narcissistic impulse. The idea of homosexuality as a mental illness was given institutional validity through its inclusion in the American Psychiatric Association's (APA) *Diagnostic and Statistical Manual of Mental Disorders* (*DSM*). In the *DSM I* (1952) homosexuality was labeled as a sociopathic personality disorder.

Eventually, Kinsey's mid-century large-scale surveys of sexual behavior in America gave rise to a behaviorist model of sex, highlighting and even celebrating sexual variation. While initially met with great skepticism, Kinsey's work

---

as Groneman (1994) argues, it is difficult to know how often the diagnosis was directly applied to individual women.

represented a major shift in thinking about sexual deviancy. Based on thousands of interviews with a wide cross-section of men, *Sexual Behavior in the Human Male* (1948) argued that 10% of men in his research had some kind of sexual experience with another man. In stark contrast to biological and psychoanalytic perspectives, he separated homosexual identity and practice, proposing a six point scale continuum of sexual behavior starting with exclusively heterosexual and ending with exclusively homosexual. At the time of Kinsey's mid-twentieth century writings, conversion therapies for homosexuality were still popular, despite not being successful in their goals, often leading to severe psychological trauma.

Kinsey's work and grassroots social movements such as second wave feminism, the sexual revolution, and the gay and lesbian liberation movement are credited with the demedicalization of homosexuality in the early 1970s. These social movements ushered in what Tiefer (2006) refers to as a "humanistic" approach to understanding and exploring sex, emphasizing the importance of sexual pleasure, and validating a wide range of sexual expression for consenting adults (Tiefer 2006). In 1973, the revised *DSM II* removed homosexuality as a diagnostic category (Gordon 2008), replacing it with "Sexual Orientation Disturbance" disorder, positioning same sex attraction as diseased only when it led to personal distress. A similar category titled "Ego Dystonic Homosexuality" followed in the *DSM III* (1980), but was removed as of the *DSM III R* (1987).

The demedicalization of homosexuality as a mental illness did not prevent biological explanations of homosexuality from continuing to circulate. Rather, the HIV pandemic of the 1980s, first labelled as a "gay plague," brought new forms of medical surveillance to gay populations (Giami and Perry 2012). In 1993, Dean Hamer published an article in the journal *Science* (1993), which marked a return to biological theories of sexual orientation through the rubric of genetics. Based on Hamer's study of 40 gay brothers, he claimed to have isolated a genetic marker of homosexuality which he termed xq28. While the methods and conclusions drawn by this study have been heavily refuted, "the myth of the gay gene" lives on

in popular culture and pseudo-scientific writings (O'Riordan 2012).

Moreover, just as homosexuality was making its way out of the *DSM,* Gender Identity Disorder first appeared in the *DSM III* (1980) (Drescher 2010). As mentioned, gender non-conformity was first pathologized in the late nineteenth century in connection with sexual inversion. Beginning in the 1950s, medicine facilitated hormonal and surgical body modifications as sought out by numerous trans* and gender queer individuals. However, it also made access to these technologies dependent on outwardly adhering to a medical view of gender non-conformity as a mental illness, as spelled out in diagnoses like "Gender Identity Disorder," now termed "Gender Dysphoria" in the *DSM 5* (2013).

A broad range of *paraphilias* continue to be medicalized through the power and authority of the *DSM*. The term "paraphilia" was first used in Richard von Krafft-Ebbing's *Psychopathia Sexualis* (1886), to refer to "perverse" sexualities, which he claimed were directly synonymous with non-reproductive sexualities. As he wrote, "every expression of it [sexuality] that does not correspond with the purpose of nature- i.e., propagation,- must be regarded as perverse." Reflecting the popularity of Freud in the mid twentieth century, the *DSM I* (1952) included the category "Sexual Deviation" under the larger heading of "Personality Disorders," wherein transvestism, pedophilia, fetishism, and sexual sadism were included alongside homosexuality. The most recent *DSM 5* (2013) has reduced the categories of "paraphilic disorders" to apply only in cases where individuals feel "personal distress about their interests, not only distress resulting from society's disapproval," or in cases where "a sexual desire or behavior that involves another person's psychological distress, injury, or death, or a desire for sexual behaviors involving unwilling persons or persons unable to give legal consent."

However, even with these stipulations, there is great debate over how to conceptualize and approach so-called "paraphilias" (Gordon 2008). Some argue that sexual activities involving consenting adults should not be listed as a paraphilia in any way, even if there is personal distress.

Some also believe that sexual fantasies and desires that are based on breaching sexual consent are essentially harmless and should be left alone, while others argue that fantasies may precipitate action. Additional debates surround whether acts which breech sexual consent should be criminalized, medicalized, or both. Treatment options, which have spanned surgical castration, various hormone therapies, and cognitive behavioral measures, have also spurred disagreement on intellectual, political, and ethical grounds. Surgical castration has been replaced as a treatment for acts of sexual violence by less invasive means such as the injection of luteinizing hormone releasing hormone (LHRH) agonists to reduce the level of circulating testosterone. However, treating sexual violence by altering hormones erroneously assumes that sexual violence is a phenomenon related to sexual desire (as opposed to power and domination), and that sexual desire is a strictly hormonal phenomenon.

24.4 The Medicalization of Reproduction

The medicalization of women's reproductive cycles is the most widespread form of medicalization and can be credited with the normalization of medical intervention into women's everyday lives. The medicalization of reproduction includes medical involvement with pregnancy and birth, birth control, menstruation, and menopause. The medicalization of reproduction has also shifted over time, to modes of increasingly technological, complex, and expensive biomedicalized approaches, now understood and/or marketed as necessary by an increasing range of practitioners, social institutions, private industries, and lay individuals.

24.4.1 Pregnancy and Birth

Pregnancy and birth, traditionally the domain of women's support and expertise, were among the first of women's reproductive capacities to be medicalized. As Wertz and Wertz (1989) explain,

cross culturally and throughout history, pregnancy and birth were managed by female midwives, with laywomen in the extended family and community offering emotional and household support during a "lying in" period of recovery. The English term "widwife" literally translates as "with women." These women were selected for several reasons—knowledge, dexterity, sensitivity, interest, and in most cases, the time afforded by not having children of one's own. Midwives brought with them knowledge of the science and art of birthing, using some herbs and tinctures and low-tech devices such as the birthing stool. This knowledge was translated through oral traditions, experiential learning, and via some written texts.

Birthing was first transformed into medical practice in the eighteenth century in Europe and North America. As Digby (1989) argues, the Age of Enlightenment "validated the role of the professional" (p. 195). During this period, medicine began to "professionalize." By creating formalized training programs, university accreditation systems, and professional associations, doctors attempted to set themselves apart from female healers and other "quacks" (Cahill 2001). As part of the expansion and professionalization of medicine, physicians sought to expand their practices (and incomes) by including more areas of "women's health." By the nineteenth century, newly formed medical professional associations launched a systematic assault on women's competencies in the areas of birth, a relatively simple task given that midwives were never formally or collectively organized (Wertz and Wertz 1989). Female midwives were legally barred from using new birth technologies such as forceps, and in any event, they could not afford them, and for the most part, did not view them as necessary. Unfortunately, forceps often did more harm than good as male doctors experimented with using these new devices. However, the use of such new technologies imbued doctors with the impression of progress to a growing middle and upper class lay populace. By 1955, childbirth had almost fully migrated from home to hospital, and today, upwards of 95 % of women give birth in an institutional setting in North America (Leavitt 1986; Parry 2008).

Throughout the twentieth century, the drug industry profited from the popularity of various drug interventions into pregnancy and birth, many of which have resulted in severe health consequences. Thalidomide was a drug prescribed first in 1957 as a sedative and later as an anti-nausea and morning sickness treatment. By the end of 1961, it was taken off European markets because of thousands of birth abnormalities and deaths that occurred as the result of women having taken this drug while pregnant (Goldman 2001). Similarly, Diethylstilbestrol (DES) was prescribed widely to healthy pregnant women between the 1940s and 1970s. DES was a synthesized estrogen approved by the US FDA as a hormonal balancer to prevent miscarriages. As early as 1953, several studies demonstrated the ineffectiveness of DES to prevent miscarriages and premature births. While eight cases of an extremely rare cancer (clear cell adenocarcinoma, CCAC) were reported in DES daughters between 1966 and 1969, DES continued to be prescribed to women for decades. It is now estimated that in one in one thousand DES daughters developed CCAC (Veurink et al. 2005).

Pain management drugs now commonly used during birth have been linked to rising rates of Caesarian sections (C-sections). The World Health Organization recommends optimal C-section rates for women and babies as between 5 and 10 %, and considers rates above 15 % to be doing more unnecessary harm than good (Althabe and Belizan 2006). In 1965, U.S. national C-section rates were measured within an optimal range at four and a half percent; by 2011, they had rapidly grown to 32.8 % (National Partnership for Women 2013). Synthetic oxytocin (Pitocin), used in the majority of hospital births in North America, induces and speeds up labor. One of the side effects of Pitocin is that it makes contractions stronger and more powerful than they would be otherwise, hence, the growing popularity of epidural analgesia for pain. This cascade of interventions which speed up and then slow down birth have been directly linked to the rising rate of C-sections (National Partnership for Women 2013).

There have been long-standing and growing efforts to demedicalize birth or at least resist its most fully medicalized form. The "natural" childbirth movement, burgeoning since the '40s, and popularized as part of the 1970s feminist health movement, has made attempts to reclaim home birth. As Boscoe et al. (2004) argue, the feminist health movement:

> began with exposing how lack of information prevented women from making informed decisions; how the power dynamics between health professions (doctors [usually male] and nurses [female]) and between physicians and patients made it hard to question professional expertise or refuse treatment; how sexism, racism, paternalism, and other power oppressions within the system led to our priorities not being addressed; how the growing pervasiveness of drugs and other technologies distorted the treatment and prevention programs women really needed. (p. 8)

As resistance to the colonization of birth, indigenous women are now reclaiming traditional birth practices (Van Wagner et al. 2007). For instance, in Canada, until recently, Indigenous women in Northern territories were required by the state to be evacuated at 36 weeks. This meant giving birth in communities far away from one's community and networks of support. As a way of resisting paternalistic colonial policies and restoring birthing autonomy, an extensive network of indigenous midwives now offer services within Northern locations, including those considered to be remote.

Midwives in general have recently professionalized using the same strategies as medicine: creating university accreditation programs, formalizing certifications, and forming professional associations. The midwifery model conceptualizes birth as a healthy activity, wherein medical interventions should be the exception rather than the norm (Parry 2008). Midwives emphasize women's agency in birthing, encourage more active birthing positions, and (often with the help of a doula) offer emotional support alongside technical knowledge. They also provide greater continuity of care with more visits before and after birth than a doctor typically provides. Overall, their success rates with respect to maternal and infant health tend to be on par or greater than medical rates, while resting on far fewer expensive and risky medical interventions (Janssen et al. 2002). And yet, in North America, they continue to be used as the exception rather than the norm.

24.4.2 Birth Control

While contraceptive technologies of various kinds have been used throughout history, widespread medical involvement in birth control stems from three intertwined sources: (1) early twentieth century concerns over population control leading to the development of eugenics; (2) feminist campaigns for planned parenthood; and (3) the pharmaceutical industry's efforts to capitalize on the lucrative market of pregnancy prevention.

The medicalization of birth control was directly linked to the rise of eugenics in the early twentieth century (Moss et al. 2013). As the *fin de siècle* witnessed rapid urbanization and population growth, European nations began to turn their attention to the "population question," drawing on the work of economists such as Thomas Malthus (1798), who theorized that there would not be enough food supplies to meet the world's growing population. While Malthus himself did not advocate for eugenics, his ideas added to existing xenophobic concerns over population control and efforts to limit population growth (Ordover 2003). Eugenics refers to controlling reproductive patterns to meet demographic needs. "Negative eugenics" is the effort to limit the population growth in certain areas or among particular groups, whereas "positive eugenics" refers to efforts to encourage population growth in particular areas or among specific groups. Examples of negative eugenics include the forced or coerced sterilization of African American women (particularly in the Southern US), indigenous women in North America (especially those institutionalized in Residential Schools and hospitals), Puerto Rican women (during the US presidency of Franklin Delano Roosevelt), and people with disabilities (still a widespread practice). The Nazi German encouragement of the "Aryan" race is one example of so-called "positive" eugenics.

Feminist birth control campaigners in the early twentieth century are most well-known for advocating for what British born Marie Stopes referred to as "voluntary motherhood" and what US born Margaret Sanger eventually termed "planned parenthood" (Moss et al. 2013). While these women are known for their efforts to empower women with access to contraception, both were also associated with eugenic efforts. Stopes wrote about "racial purification" through reproductive control. Sanger, the same woman who lobbied scientists and drug companies to develop the oral contraceptive pill, believed in the sterilization of poor women and women of color.

The pharmaceuticalization of birth control is often lauded as a panacea for the reproductive autonomy of all women, however, not all women have benefited from this miracle drug. The Pill was first tested in clinical trials performed in Puerto Rico, selected for its poverty, dense population, and lack of anti-birth control laws (Gazit 2003). Gregory Pincus and John Rock dispensed the Pill to 265 Puerto Rican women without informing them that they were part of a clinical trial for an experimental drug with unknown side effects. The trials, which involved a hormone dosage that is ten times what is administered today, resulted in a 100 % success rate in terms of preventing pregnancies, but also three deaths, as well as nausea, vomiting, dizziness, headaches, and stomach pain in 17 % of women in the trial. In the rush to bring the drug to market, these side effects were dismissed as psychosomatic, and minor in relation to the drug's social benefits. In a supposedly value-free "risk/ benefit" ratio, the risks to women's health were seen as worth the social and economic benefits of population control and drug company profits.

As evidence of the ways in which profit and social control have trumped concerns over women's health and well-being since the early days of the sexual pharmaceutical industry, the FDA's approval of such a high dose hormonal contraceptive pill was made without warning of the drug's side effects. From the outset, women began experiencing blood clots, heart attacks, strokes, depression, suicide, obesity, and lowered sex drive—prompting journalist and feminist activist Barbara Seaman's book *The Doctor's Case Against the Pill* (1969). In large part due to pressures by Seaman and other feminist activists, senate hearings were called in 1970 to investigate the dangers of the Pill—a hearing which included drug manufacturer testimony, but no testimonies by laywomen who had taken the Pill. A number of health activists took the Senate to task on this matter (Sigal 1970). Women staged their own hearings for testimony about the safety of the pill. Based on these hearings, and to satiate the demand for informed consent, the Senate made it a requirement to include side-effects warnings in each package of the Pill.

There is no denying that the Pill has played a pivotal role in increasing women's reproductive autonomy (Black et al. 2009). The pill is now the leading contraceptive method for women aged 15–29 in North America, used by nearly 20 % of women between the ages of 15 and 49. However, as Tone (2012) argues, the ubiquity of "the Pill" has created an enormous market of otherwise-healthy young women's bodies for medical interaction and monitoring, and eased mainstream attitudes towards drug interventions for non-medical problems. Representing a consumer approach to marketing and choosing drugs, oral contraceptives are now marketed as "miracle drugs," that not only prevent pregnancies, but offer added value in fixing acne, regulating menstrual cycles, and more. Crucially, the efficacy of barrier methods are often downplayed by pharmaceutical drug marketers (Lippman 2004, p. 9).

24.4.3 Menstruation

The ancient Greek word for uterus, "hyster" is the etymology of "hysteria" and "hysterical," implicating the uterus as the primary source of blame for unstable emotions in women. The definition of hysteria, a popular medical diagnosis in the late nineteenth and early twentieth centuries, was based on the observation of many symptoms including hysterical fits. Feminist historians such as Ehrenreich and English (1979) theorize nineteenth century "hysteria" as caused by middle-class women's boredom with their restric-

tive social roles as well as physical illness born of little physical activity and organ restricting corseting. However, medical writings at the time connect hysteria to mood swings associated with women's menstrual cycles and nervous systems.

The widespread medicalization of menstruation coincided with increasing demands by middle-class women for access to professional education in the late nineteenth century (Groneman 1999). During this period, physicians such as Sir Henry Maudsley made claims such as, "monthly activity of the ovaries which marks the advent of puberty in women has a notable effect upon the mind and body wherefore it may become an important cause of mental and physical derangement" (as cited in Studd 2006, p. 412). In 1872, the first radical oophorectomy (the removal of a woman's ovaries) was performed to relieve "menstrual madness" in women. Oophorectomy—known as "Battey's operation"—became a gynecological trend, effectively sterilizing thousands of women well into the twentieth century (Studd 2006).

Psychiatry in the twentieth century continued to link menstruation with mental illness. (Derry 2013). The term "premenstrual tension" was introduced into psychiatric discourse in 1931 and "premenstrual syndrome" (PMS) in 1964. Two decades later, the APA's *DSM IIIR* (1987) included the label "late luteal phase dysphoric disorder." The *DSM IV* (1994) listed "premenstrual dysphoric disorder" (PMDD) as an offshoot of depressive disorder. The most recent *DSM 5* (2013) includes "premenstrual dysphoric disorder" as its own category. Signaling the growing partnership between psychiatry and the drug industry, even prior to classification in official literature, the pharmaceutical company Eli Lilly introduced a treatment for the (by their own admission) poorly understood condition of PMDD in 2002 (Moynihan and Cassels 2006). Sarafem has identical ingredients and dosage recommendations as Prozac, the Selective Serotonin Reuptake Inhibitor (SSRI) drug which is argued to be the first "lifestyle" drug to reach blockbuster success in the 1990s (Loe 2004). With Sarafem, Eli Lilly effectively broadened their market share by introducing PMDD patients to the vast market of those diagnosed with depressive and anxiety disorders.

More recently, the birth control pills Yaz, Yasmin, and Seasonale have been marketed as treatments for the negative effects associated with menstruation, positioned as a bodily nuisance, no longer necessary and wholly avoidable (Mamo and Fosket 2009). These contraceptives are widely advertised as having the "convenience effects" of lightening and shortening one's period (Yaz and Yasmin) or eliminating it altogether (Seasonale). Yaz and Yasmin have since been linked to fatal blood clotting with large class action lawsuits pending, but are still among the most prescribed oral contraceptives on the market. As a sign of the loosening regulations on direct to consumer drug advertising in the US, slick television and print advertising campaigns use feminist rhetoric to promise women more control over their bodies.

24.4.4 Menopause

Menopause remained an entirely demedicalized element of women's reproductive cycles until the 1960s, when it was pathologized as an estrogen deficiency disorder. In 1963, Robert A. Wilson, a Brooklyn based gynecologist, and his wife Thelma, wrote an article published in the *Journal of American Geriatrics Society,* in which they argued that Estrogen Replacement Therapy (ERT) is a must for women who wish to remain "fully sexed" (as cited in Houck 2003, p. 18). These ideas gained broader appeal when R. A. Wilson published the popular best-selling book *Feminine Forever* (1966). In this book he portrayed menopause as a deficiency disease, which had detrimental health effects, but also robbed women of their youth, femininity, and sexuality. The need for ERT was also championed by several feminists as useful tools in women's quest for sexual liberation. Many women who identified as feminist argued that ERT could help women "control the biology that had for so long controlled them" and thus be able to "compete [...] on something like equal terms to men" (Cooper 1975, p. 16).

However, feminist applause for ERT was short-lived as the link between ERT use and cancer became evident. By 1975, two articles in the *New England Journal of Medicine* challenged the safety of ERT, already widely prescribed to hundreds of thousands of women. Each of these articles reported on studies, conducted independently of the other, which demonstrated the link between ERT and endometrial cancer. The drug industry responded by combining estrogen and progesterone, billing widely used prescription Hormone Replacement Therapy (HRT) such as Premarin and Prempro, as a safer alternative in the 1990s. In the early 2000s, HRT medications were linked to increased risk of breast cancer, heart disease, stoke, and blood clots. It has since been revealed that many of the journal articles publishing research on the efficacy and safety of HRT were penned by public relations and communications specialists given the go ahead to use the names of respected medical doctors (Fugh-Berman 2010). It is unknown how many academics participate in this practice, or how many articles in peer-reviewed medical journals are ghostwritten, but there is concern that the practice may be extensive.

24.5 The Medicalization of Sexual Functioning

Whereas psychological and psychoanalytic perspectives on the sexual functioning of men and women prevailed in the early twentieth century, the invention of new sexual enhancement technologies and drugs ushered in the biomedicalization of sexual functioning at the dawn of the millennium.

24.5.1 The Medicalization of Men's Sexual Functioning

Prior to the twentieth century, men's erectile abilities were augmented with various tinctures and foods (Loe 2004). The early twentieth century view of men's erectile difficulties as the fault of a frigid female partner shifted by the 1970s, as the diagnosis "frigidity" fell out of popularity. Impotence was then framed as caused by men's own psychological issues, best treated by stress reduction, sex therapy techniques, sex education, or acceptance.

However, as early as the 1960s, Masters and Johnson's work focused on the physiological workings of sexual functioning. Masters and Johnson theorized what they termed the Human Sexual Response Cycle (HSRC) as a sexual norm for most humans, developed as a result of clinical observations of human sexual intercourse and masturbation. But while claiming to chart a "universal" sexual response cycle in their research, Masters and Johnson used a fairly small, homogeneous sample, and coached their research subjects on what would be considered to be "successful" outcomes (Tiefer 2001). Hence, the now scientifically validated norm of sexual response as necessarily following a linear path of excitement, plateau, orgasm, and resolution was somewhat of a foregone conclusion. Even still, despite their emphasis on the measurement of genital response using high-tech devices, Masters and Johnson and other well-known sexologists mainly recommended psychosexual education and behavioral therapy in order to improve sexual functioning and satisfaction.

By the 1980s, a hydraulic approach to men's sexual problems was brewing as seen in the development of penile vacuum pumps and augmentation surgeries (Loe 2004). At the 1983 American Urology Association meeting, Giles Brindley, a physician in his 70s, shocked the audience by dropping his pants and revealing his erect penis, achieved through an injection of a substance called alprostadil. A decade later, penile injections made their way onto markets, first under the brand name Caverject, and then MUSE. The former had to be injected, whereas the latter was inserted as an intraurethral pellet. Thus, while alprostadil was effective in producing erections, its delivery mechanism left much to be desired.

During Pfizer Inc.'s clinical trials testing of sildenafil citrate as a treatment for Angina, participants noted the onset of erections as an unexpected side effect. Pfizer immediately set about researching, developing, and branding Viagra, the name inspired by words "Vigor" and "Niagara." In marketing Viagra, Pfizer was careful to set this drug apart from previously-known, non-medically recognized sex potions, employing sophisticated marketing techniques. The use of former US presidential candidate (and senator) Bob Dole as the early face of Viagra was an example of their efforts to market the drug to a conservative, "family values" demographic. They also hired medical doctors to do more research into the physiology of erections, thus establishing Erectile Dysfunction (ED) as a medically-known diagnosis treatable by Viagra. Ad campaigns to the public included disease awareness campaigns about ED as well. Whereas men's erectile difficulties were once framed by doctors in psychogenic terms as "impotence," best accepted as "normal" or treated by stress reduction, sex positive education, or sex therapy, the ED diagnosis assumes erectile difficulties to be physiologically-based and best treated with a pill.

But seldom discussed in the popular press, Viagra use has led to several health consequences and is not effective in solving all men's sexual difficulties. As reported in an article published in the *Journal of the American Medical Association* (JAMA) (Mitka 2000), over 500 Viagra users died of heart failure in the first year of Viagra's release, prior to the inclusion of warning labels about Viagra use and heart conditions. In 2010, an FDA audit noted that Pfizer "failed to submit reports of vision loss associated with Viagra in a timely fashion or downgraded the seriousness of those reports even though they involved 'blindness' and 'visual acuity loss/ reduction'" (Edwards 2010, para. 1). Further, men's issues with "premature ejaculation" or low desire will not be solved with Viagra (or one of the copycat drugs such as Cialis or Levitra). Makers of Androgel, a testosterone gel approved only for men with the rare condition "hypogandism," are currently rebranding men's sexual problems as testosterone deficiencies. Sales of Androgel almost surpassed Viagra in 2012, as a result of off-label use by men convinced that they "Got Low T," as the Abbott funded online and print campaigns shouted in newspapers around the world (Dubowitz et al. 2012).

24.5.2 The Medicalization of Women's Sexual Functioning

As part of growing medical interest and jurisdiction over women's bodies, women's sexual functioning was pathologized under the rubric of frigidity as theorized by the inter-connected fields of sexology, gynecology, psychiatry, and psychoanalysis in the late nineteenth century (Angel 2010). Translated literally as "coldness," this diagnosis reflected the belief that (particularly, white middle class women) were naturally "cold," but could be heated up by the passions of their husbands (Cryle and Moore 2011). While it may seem strange that this term would gain such popularity during a time when this particular group of women were assumed to be "passionless" in the first place, this trend belies the very fine line of sexual restraint and compliance that women were expected to negotiate. Women who would not have sex with their husbands, experienced no sexual desire for men, did not experience orgasm from any kind of stimulation, were sickly, or infertile were at risk of being labeled frigid.

Freud's turn of the century theories on psychosexual development profoundly changed how experts and lay people understood frigidity. Whereas previous definitions were focused on women's capacity for sexual heat, as discussed in his *Three Essays on the Theory of Sexuality* (Freud 1905, 1949), Freud believed that women who did not orgasm vaginally were sexually immature. His theory was that young girls consciously or unconsciously recognize their clitoris as a site of pleasure, mimicking a "little man" with a penis. Through puberty, she was supposed to realize that her clitoris is not adequate in function or size. He believed that she would enter a sexually latent period and then complete an "erotic transfer" signaled by a fully eroticized vagina.

By the end of World War II, Freud's ideas (and various interpretations of them) were widely accepted by psychoanalysts, psychiatrists, doctors, and popular writers who published marriage and sex guides. As Neuhaus (2000) notes in her analysis of sex manuals from the 1800s onwards, marriage and sex manuals written before the mid twentieth century placed the success of heterosexual intercourse under men's responsibility. Men were called on in these texts to ensure that their wives were comfortable, well stimulated (clitorally), and ready to enjoy intercourse. But Anglo sex manuals published during the 50s and 60s constructed women who did not desire or enjoy sex as in a state of sexual immaturity or neurosis. They also blamed women for their *partners'* sexual problems. In just a few decades, the importance of clitoral stimulation as a means of realizing women's sexual pleasure was seldom discussed, replaced by the 'myth of the vaginal orgasm' (Gerhard 2000).

Several forces converged to dispel the myth of the vaginal orgasm as validated through the frigidity diagnosis. In his publication *Sexual Behaviour in the Human Female* (1953), Kinsey and his colleagues were adamant that women were as sexual as men and that most women orgasmed as a result of clitoral stimulation. They went so far as to state that the vagina was of "minimum importance in contributing to the erotic responses of the female [...] and may even contribute more to the arousal of the male than it does to the arousal of the female" (in Gerhard 2000, p. 462). Masters and Johnson (1966) came to similar conclusions when researching sexual response. Last but not least, second wave feminists took frigidity to task in their re-writings of women's medical histories and sharing of their own experiences through various grassroots forums and writings (see for example, Koedt 1973). Although sexual dysfunction in women has been included in every edition of the *DSM* under various rubrics (first in psychoanalytic terms, then in increasingly biological terms), according to Angel (2012), reference to frigidity or sexual dysfunction in women could be found in medical and scientific journals less than 10 times in the 1970s and at the same rate in the 1980s. Frigidity was for the most part successfully demedicalized.

However, as drug companies race to find a sexual enhancement drug for women in the wake of the success of Viagra, there have been new efforts to remedicalize women's sexual functioning. At the time of writing, there is no approved sexual enhancement drug for women, but efforts are afoot to "pre-organize" (Fishman 2004) a market of women diagnosed with Female Sexual Dysfunction (FSD). FSD is an umbrella term to describe dysfunction in the areas of desire/arousal/interest, orgasm, and pain. As Tiefer (2001) has documented, coinciding with Viagra's early blockbuster profits, a host of medical conferences were convened to build consensus on how exactly to define FSD. Only physicians with links to drug company funding were invited to these conferences. Since then, the vast majority of Continuing Medical Education (CME) on sexual dysfunction has been pharma funded.

Industry sponsored doctors continue to widely cite the much disputed statistic that 43 % of women suffer from FSD. This statistic was taken from a sociological survey of sexual patterns in the U.S. (Laumann et al. 1994). One part of this survey asked women if they had experienced any sexual difficulties in the past year, for example, lacking interest in sex, feeling anxious about their sexual performance, having trouble with lubrication, failing to orgasm, coming to orgasm too quickly, or experiencing pain with intercourse. Forty-three percent of women surveyed answered "yes" to at least one of these questions.

Medical theorizing over the etiology of FSD seems to change as each drug hopeful enters the pipeline for FDA approval. For instance, when at first, Pfizer hoped that Viagra itself would enhance women's arousal, research on FSD was rooted in a vascular understanding of women's sexual problems as problems related to genital blood flow and arousal (Loe 2004). Researchers began to switch tack when they realized that vascular drugs did not have the same effect on women's arousal as on men's. However, only the Eros Clitoral Therapy Device, a highly medicalized and expensive sex toy has been FDA approved to treat women's sexual arousal difficulties (Fishman and Mamo 2001). The Eros has not proven popular or led to the blockbuster profits that the sexual pharmaceutical industry and its supporters are aiming for.

Therefore, as of 2000, when clinical trial results for a testosterone patch called Intrinsa were about to be released, industry sponsored doctors began to theorize that women's sexual problems are more likely to be related to desire as shaped by hormone levels (Loe 2004). However, in 2004, Intrinsa was denied FDA approval based on a high placebo effect and safety concerns regarding HRT.

In 2010, the notion that women's sexual problems were mainly issues of desire as shaped by neurological hardwiring took hold. Not surprisingly, this was the same year that Flibanserin was up for FDA approval. Flibanserin is a drug which failed FDA approval as an SSRI anti-depressant drug, and was then repackaged as a treatment for women's low desire. However, the data gleaned from clinical trials testing the drug on 5,000 premenopausal women diagnosed with low desire did not match the media hype regarding the efficacy and life changing possibilities of Flibanserin. As compared to the placebo, women taking Flibanserin noted only an increase of 0.7 Sexually Satisfying Events (SSEs) per month, however SSEs were subjectively interpreted. There were also safety concerns with a drug that would have to be taken daily and warranted a 14 % dropout rate from clinical trials due to adverse events. Flibanserin was denied FDA approval in 2010, but new owners of the patent are planning to resubmit it.

Without an approved sexual pharmaceutical drug aimed at increasing women's arousal or desire, sexual medicine physicians tend to prescribe drugs approved for other uses off-label (Hartley 2006). Physicians specializing in sexual medicine frequently prescribe women Viagra, Levitra, Cialis, and testosterone replacements such as AndroGel, despite there being no evidence of their efficacy in women (Goldstein et al. 2006).

24.5.3 Debating The Medicalization of Sexual Functioning

The medicalization of sexual function and dysfunction has been the subject of vast excitement, controversy, debate, and critique. With regard to the use of drugs, drug companies and the medical spokespeople they hire defend them as serious drugs treating medical illnesses like any others. According to these experts, sexual functioning is an integral part of sexual health, as well as wider physical and mental health.

Some sexual medicine specialists also view their work towards finding a sexual pharmaceutical drug for women in liberal feminist terms. Dr. Jennifer Berman, a urologist, and her sister Laura Berman, a sex therapist, both heavily sponsored by drug companies, have appeared on major television talk shows, interviewed in major women's magazines, and have written best-selling books, espousing the necessity of a sexual pharmaceutical for women as a path towards sexual liberation. They argue that if men have access to such drugs, women deserve the same (Berman et al. 2001). Recently, the International Society for the Study of Women's Sexual Health (ISSWSH), a heavily pharma funded group, launched the Your Voice, Your Wish (WISH) campaign. Using feminist rhetoric of equality and choice, the WISH campaign circulates a petition pleading for FSD and a drug cure for it, to be taken seriously. Similarly, a group of "consumer advocates" and drug companies launched the "Even the Score Campaign" (http://eventhescore.org). This campaign is asking the FDA to approve a sex drug for women based on the claim that 26 drugs have been approved for men's sexual problems (a false statistic which counts drugs that have *not* been FDA approved). At the heart of these campaigns, women's choices are viewed in individual and commercial terms. Equality is seen as equal access to an equal number of drug choices, without focus on the safety or efficacy of these drugs.

However, from the initial debut of Viagra, feminist health practitioners, academics, and activists have launched a major critique of sexual pharmaceutical drugs, the industry which surrounds them, and the figures who are responsible for their success. Leonore Tiefer is perhaps the most well known, publically vocal critic. Tiefer is a former medical sexology insider turned feminist sex therapist turned activist. She is also prolific in her academic publications. Tiefer rejects the medicalized view of sexual functioning,

claiming that, "sex is more like dancing than digestion." Before Viagra was approved in 1998, she had already published a critique of the biological turn in understanding and treating men's sexual erectile difficulties (Tiefer 1986). Following the success of Viagra, and the race to find a sexuopharmaceutical drug for women, Tiefer began to expose the drug company financial support behind efforts to classify FSD as a legitimate diagnosis.

In 2000, Tiefer joined with other feminists to form "The Working Group For a New View of Women's Sexual Problems." The mandate of the New View is to "challenge the distorted and oversimplified messages about sexuality that the pharmaceutical industry relies on to sell its new drugs" and "to expose biased research and promotional methods that serve corporate profit rather than people's pleasure and satisfaction" (www.newviewcampaign.org). Tiefer and other New View supporters testified against the FDA approval of both Intrinsa and Flibanserin.

The New View critiques universal models of sexual functioning as based on flawed methodology, reflecting social constructions more so than objective, biological facts (Kaschak and Tiefer 2001). According to the New View, understanding the interpersonal, social, economic, and political factors which tend to diminish sexual enjoyment, particularly for women, is a less lucrative, but more accurate, starting point for addressing sexual displeasure. They argue that the best medicine for widespread sexual enjoyment is to challenge social inequalities, deconstruct sexual norms, recognize sexual variation, support sexual human rights, and make accurate, informative sex education accessible.

A vast body of recent academic literature supports Tiefer's arguments through empirical evidence. Numerous quantitative studies based on surveys of large numbers conclude that interpersonal and social factors are the prime determinants of women's sexual problems (for instance, DeLamater and Sill 2005; Hayes et al. 2008; Koch et al. 2005; Carvalho and Nobre 2010). Qualitative studies based on in-depth interviews with smaller numbers of women (for instance, Cacchioni 2007; Nicholls 2008; Kleinplatz et al.

2009) have led to similar conclusions. Studies like these highlight numerous social, political, economic, and interpersonal factors and expectations that hamper women's enjoyment of sex. Far less research considers how men's sexual problems are shaped by similar factors. Both the medical literature on sexual functioning and works critiquing it have very much used the language "men's sexuality" and "women's sexuality," focusing the conversation in mainly heterosexual and gender binary terms.

24.6 Conclusions and Further Research

Some key themes run through the medicalization of sexual deviance, reproduction, and functioning. The late nineteenth century marks the birth of widespread medicalization in each of these areas. Whereas nineteenth century understandings were mainly rooted in a forensic, biological determinism, Freud's ideas of psychosexual development dominated the early to mid twentieth century. The demedicalization of many sexualities and reproductive processes coincided with the rise of powerful grassroots social movements in the late twentieth century, such as various forms of feminism, the natural childbirth movement, the sexual revolution, and LGBTQ activist movements. Nevertheless, biologically reductionist approaches to sexuality continue to flourish. To a large extent, this focus reflects the growing influence of the pharmaceutical industry on medical education, research, and clinical practice. Other influences include an attempt to apply genetics frameworks to the complex world of sexuality.

And yet, even before the pharmaceutical industry wielded so much influence in the realm of sex and reproduction, career expansion, the enhancement of professional status, and profit have motivated reproductive and sexual medicalization from their inception. Clearly, these instances of medicalization must be contextualized within a broader socio-political context. Many macro factors such as colonialism, capitalism, and patriarchy have influenced the rise of scientific and medical epistemologies and the diminishing of other ways of knowing and managing sexual health.

Sexual medicalization is a way of protecting social norms such as hegemonic constructions of gender and heterosexuality. Diagnostic labels such as homosexuality, inversion, sadism, masochism, nymphomania, hysteria, frigidity, erectile dysfunction, and female sexual dysfunction all serve to bolster gender binaries, reproductive heterosex, and the institutions which surround these constructions as societal ideals and norm. But sexual and reproductive medicalization clearly affects different groups in different ways. The bodies of women have been prime targets of medical scrutiny and surveillance, but the form and intensity of scrutiny has been divided according to sexuality, race, class, nationality, and (dis) ability.

For further research, as the drug industry plays an increasing role in sexual health research agendas, the bodies, lives, and concerns of middle and upper class people with purchasing power will be increasingly (bio) medicalized. What does it mean to be targeted or neglected by (bio) medicalization? For instance, are the pressing sexual health concerns of groups without consumer power being neglected?

Much of the medicalization of sex has been targeted at the maintenance of reproductive heterosexuality. As LGBTQ sexualities are increasingly demedicalized as a form of deviance, will they be subjected to new forms of medical surveillance, perhaps the medicalization of sexual functioning? Currently sexual pharmaceuticals are marketed squarely towards heterosexual monogamous couples, but will LGBTQ subjects be targeted as a new demographic? By contrast, what are the subversive uses of sexual pharmaceuticals, if any?

At the heart of much theorizing on medicalization, is the assumption that medicine has overstepped its boundaries when it comes to intervening in deviance, reproduction, and functioning. What does this negative portrayal mean for bodies that are technologically mediated, for example, the bodies of trans* people? People with disabilities? Women who have had emergency or elective C sections? How can we interpret medicalization as a process that offers empowering possibilities without drawing on the simplistic rubric of individual "choice" as promoted by many pro-medicalization figures?

These are complex questions that play out on political, economic, interpersonal, and individual axes. While these questions are not easily resolved, it is important for academic scholars and grassroots activists involved in challenging medicalization to face these complexities and address these nuances.

Acknowledgements I would like to thank Amber Hui for her detailed and insightful RA work on this chapter.

References

Althabe, F., & Belizan, J. F. (2006). Caesarian section: The paradox. *The Lancet, 268,* 1472–1473.

American Psychiatric Association. (1952). *Diagnostic and statistical manual of mental disorders.* Washington, DC: Author.

Angel, K. (2010). The history of 'female sexual dysfunction' as a mental disorder in the 20th century. *Current opinion in psychiatry, 23*(6), 536.

Berman, J., Berman, L., & Bumiller, E. (2001). *For women only: A revolutionary guide to overcoming sexual dysfunction and reclaiming your sex life.* New York: Henry Holt.

Black, A., Yang, Q., Wen, S. W., Lalonde, A. B., Guilbert, E., & Fisher, W. (2009). Contraceptive use among Canadian women of reproductive age: Results of a national survery. *Journal of Obstetrics and Gynaecology Canada, 31*(7), 627–640.

Bland, L., & Doan, L. (1998). *Sexology in culture: Labelling bodies and desires.* Chicago: University of Chicago Press.

Boscoe, M., Basen, G., Alleyne, G., Bourrier-Lacroix, B., & White, S. (2004). The women's health movement in Canada: Looking back and moving forward. *Canadian Women's Studies, 24*(1), 7–13.

Cacchioni, T. (2007). Heterosexuality and "the labour of love:" A contribution to recent debates of female sexual dysfunction. *Sexualities, 10,* 299–320.

Cacchioni, T., & Tiefer, L. (2012). Why medicalization? Introduction to the special issue on the medicalization of sex. *Journal of Sex Research, 49,* 307–310.

Cahill, H. A. (2001). Male appropriation and medicalization of childbirth: An historical analysis. *Journal of Advanced Nursing, 33*(3), 334–342.

Carvalho, J., & Nobre, P. (2010). Sexual desire in women: An integrative approach regarding psychological, medical, and relationship dimensions. *The Journal of Sexual Medicine, 7*(5), 1807–1815.

Charpy, A. (1870). Des organes génitaux externes chez les prostituées. *Annales des Dermatologie, 3,* 271–279.

Chauncey, G. (1989). From sexual inversion to homosexuality: The changing medical conceptualization of female deviance. In K. Peiss, C. Simmons, & R. Padgug (Eds.), *Passion and power: Sexuality in history* (pp. 87–117). Philadelphia: Temple University Press.

Clarke, A. E., Shim, J. K., Mamo, L., Fosket, J. R., & Fishman, J. R. (2003). Biomedicalization: Technoscientific transformations of health, illness, in the US. *American Sociological Review, 68,* 161–194.

Conrad, P. (1992). Medicalization and social control. *Annual Review of Sociology, 18,* 209–232.

Cooper, W. (1975). *Don't change: A biological revolution for women.* New York: Stein and Day.

Cott, N. F. (1978). Passionlessness: An interpretation of Victorial sexual ideology, 1790–1850. *Signs, 4*(2), 219–236.

Cryle, P., & Moore, A. (2011). *Frigidity: An intellectual history.* Basingstoke: Palgrave Macmillan.

DeLamater, J. D., & Sill, M. (2005). Sexual desire in later life. *The Journal of Sex Research, 42*(2), 138–149.

Derry, P. S. (2013, February). *The medicalization of the menstrual cycle.* Paper presented at Selling Sickness, Washington, D.C.

Dickinson, R. L., & Beam, L. (1931). *A thousand marriages: A medical study of sex adjustment.* Baltimore: Williams & Wilkins.

Digby, A. (1989). Women's biological straightjacket. In S. Mendus & J. Rendall (Eds.), *Sexuality and subordination: Interdisciplinary studies of gender in the nineteenth century* (pp. 192–220). London: Routledge.

Drescher, J. (2010). Queer diagnoses: Parallels and contrasts in the history of homosexuality, gender variance, and the Diagnostic and Statistical Manual. *Archives of Sexual Behavior, 39,* 427–460.

Dubowitz, N., Puretz, M., Fugh-Berman, A. (2012, August 20). Low-T, high profit? [Web log post.] *Bioethics Forum.* http://www.thehastingscenter.org/Bioethicsforum/Post.aspx?id=5941&blogid=140. Accessed 1 Sep 2012.

Edwards, J. (2010, June 16). Viagra and blindness: Now the FDA is accusing Pfizer of covering up eye problems. *CBS News.* http://www.cbsnews.com/8301-505123_162-42844959/viagra-and-blindness-now-the-fda-is-accusing-pfizer-of-covering-up-eye-problems/. Accessed 1 Sep 2012.

Ellis, H., & Symonds, J. A. (1897). From sexual inversion. *The Columbia Anthology of Gay Literature: Readings from Western Antiquity to the Present Day, 328.*

Ehrenreich, B., & English, D. (1979). *For her own good: one hundred and fifty years of the experts' advice to women.* London: Pluto.

Fausto-Sterling, A. (1999). Gender, race, and nation: The comparative anatomy of 'Hottentot' women in Europe, 1815–1817. In J. Terry & J. Urla (Eds.), *Deviant bodies: Critical perspectives on difference in science and popular culture* (pp. 19–44). Indiana: Indiana University Press.

Fishman, J. & Mamo, R. (2001). What's in a disorder: A cultural analysis of medical and pharmaceutical constructions of male and female sexual dysfunction. In E. Kaschak & L. Tiefer (Eds.), *A New View of women's sexual problems*. Binhampton: Haworth Press.

Fishman, J. R. (2004). Manufacturing desire: The commodification of female sexual dysfunction. *Social Studies of Science, 34,* 187–218.

Flower, W. H., & Murie, J. (1867). Account of the dissection of a bushwoman. *Journal of Anatomy and Physiology, 1*(2), 189–208.

Foucault, M. (1965). *Madness and civilization: A history of insanity in the age of reason*. New York: Pantheon Books.

Foucault, M. (1973). *Birth of a clinic: An archeology of the human sciences*. New York: Pantheon Books.

Foucault, M. (1978). *The history of sexuality: Vol. 1.* London: Allen Lane.

Freud, S. (1949). *Three essays on the theory of sexuality*. (J. Strachey, Trans.). Albury Court: Imago Publishing. (Original work published 1905).

Freud, S. (1905). Three essays on sexuality. Standard.

Fugh-Berman, A. (2010). The haunting of medical journals: How ghostwriting sold "HRT." *PLoS Med, 7*(9). doi: 10.1371/journal.pmed.1000335

Gazit, C. (Writer & Director). (Feb 17, 2003). The *American experience: The Pill* [Television broadcast]. In C. Gazit, D. Steward, & H. Klotz (Producer). Arlington: Public Broadcasting Service.

Gerhard, J. (2000). Revisiting Anne Koedt's "The myth of the vaginal orgasm." *Feminist Studies, 26,* 449–476.

Giami, A., & Perry, C. (2012). Transformations in the medicalization of sex: HIV prevention between discipline and biopolitics. *Journal of Sex Research, 49*(4), 353–361.

Gilman, S. L. (1985). *Difference and pathology: Stereotypes of sexuality, race, and madness*. Ithaca: Cornell.

Goldman, D. (2001). Thalidomide use: Past history and current implications for practice. *Oncology Nursing Forum, 28*(3), 471–479.

Goldstein, I., Meston, C. M., Davis, S., & Traish, A. (2006). *Women's sexual function and dysfunction: Study, diagnosis and treatment*. United Kingdom: Taylor and Francis Group.

Gordon, H. (2008). The treatment of paraphilias: An historical perspective. *Criminal behavior and mental health, 18*(2), 79–87.

Groneman, C. (1994). Nymphomania: The historical construction of female sexuality. *Signs: Journal of Women in Culture and Society, 19,* 337–367.

Hamer, D. H., Hu, S., Magnuson, V. L., Hu, N., & Pattatucci, A. M. (1993). A linkage between DNA markers on the X chromosome and male sexual orientation. *Science, 261*(5119), 321–327.

Hartley, H. (2006). The pinking of Viagra culture: Drug industry efforts to create and repackage. *Sexualities, 9,* 363–378.

Hayes, R. D., Dennerstein, L., Bennett, C. M., Sidat, M., Gurrin, L., & Fairley, C. K. (2008). Risk factors for Female Sexual Dysfunction in the general population: Exploring factors associated with low sexual function and sexual distress. *Journal of Sexual Medicine, 5*(7), 1681–1693.

Hirschfield, M. (1914). *Die Homosexualität des Mannes und des Weibes*. Berlin: Louis Marcus Verlagsbuchhandlung.

Houck, J. A. (2003). "What do these women want?" Feminist responses to Feminine Forever, 1963–1980. *Bulletin of the history of medicine, 77*(1), 103–132.

Janssen, P. A., Lee, S. K., Ryan, E. M., Etches, D. J., Farquharson, D. F., Peacock, D., & Klein, M. C. (2002). Outcomes of planned home births versus planned hospital births after regulation of midwifery in British Columbia. *Canadian Medical Association Journal, 166*(3), 315–323.

Kaschak, E., & Tiefer, L. (2001). *A new view of women's sexual problems*. Binghamton: The Haworth Press.

Koch, P. B., Mansfield, P. K., Thurau, D., & Carey, M. (2005). "Feeling frumpy": The relationships between body image and sexual response changes in midlife women. *Journal of Sex Research, 42*(3), 215–223.

Koedt, A. (1973). The myth of the vaginal orgasm. In A. Koedt, E. Levine, & A. Rapone (Eds.), *Radical feminism* (pp. 198–207). New York: Quadrangle Books.

Kinsey, A. C., Pomeroy, W. B., & Martin, C. E. (1948). *Sexual behaviour in the human male*. Philadelphia: W. B. Saunders Co.

Kinsey, A. C., Pomeroy, W. B., Martin, C. E., & Gebhard, P. H. (1953). *Sexual behaviour in the human female*. Philadelphia: W. B. Saunders Co.

Kleinplatz, P. J., Menard, A. D., Paquet, M., Paradis, N., Campbell, M., Zuccarino, D., & Mehak, L. (2009). The components of optimal sexuality: A portrait of "great sex." *The Canadian Journal of Human Sexuality, 18,* 1–13.

Laumann, E. O., Gagnon, J. M., & Michaels, S. (1994). *The social organization of sexuality: Sexual practices in the United States*. Chicago: University of Chicago Press.

Leavitt, J. W. (1986). *Brought to bed: Childbearing in America 1750–1950*. Cambridge: Oxford University Press.

Lippman, A. (2004). Women's cycles up for sale: Neomedicalization and women's reproductive health. *Canadian Women's Health Network, 6,* 8–11.

Loe, M. (2004). *The rise of Viagra: How the little blue pill changed sex in America*. New York: New York University Press.

Lombroso, C., & Ferrero, G. (1893). *La donna delinquente: La prostituta e la donna normale*. Torino: Fratelli Bocca Editori.

Lupton, D. (1997). Foucault and the medicalization critique. In A. Petersen & R. Bunton (Eds.) *Foucault, health, and medicine* (pp. 94–110). London: Routledge.

Malthus, T. (1798). *An essay on the principle of population, as it affects the future improvement of society*. London: J. Johnson.

Mamo, L., & Fosket, J. R. (2009). Scripting the body: Pharmaceuticals and the (re)making of menstruation.

Signs: Journal of Women in Culture & Society, 34(4), 925–949.

Martin, E. (1987). *Woman in the body: A cultural analysis of reproduction.* Boston: Beacon Press.

Masters, W. H., & Johnson, V. E. (1966). *Human sexual response.* Boston: Little, Brown.

Mitka, M. (2000). Some men who take Viagra die—why? *Journal of the American Medical Association, 283,* 590–593.

Moss, E. L., Stam, H. J., & Kattevilder, D. (2013). From suffrage to sterilization: Eugenics and the women's movement in 20th century Alberta. *Canadian psychology/Psychologie Canadienne, 54*(2), 105–114.

Moynihan, R., & Cassels, A. (2006). *Selling sickness: How the world's biggest pharmaceutical companies are turning us all into patients.* New York: Nation Books.

National Partnership for Women. (2013). Caesarian section: Why is the national U.S. Caesarian rate so high? http://www.childbirthconnection.org/article.asp?ck=10456. Accessed 7 July 2014

Neuhaus, J. (2000). The importance of being orgasmic: Sexuality, gender, and marital sex manuals in the United States. *Journal of the History of Sexuality, 9,* 447–473.

Nicholls, L. (2008). Putting the New View classification scheme to an empirical test. *Feminism & Psychology, 18,* 515–526.

Oakley, A. (1984). *Captured womb: A History of the medical care of women.* Oxford: B. Blackwell.

Ordover, N. (2003). *American eugenics: Race, queer anatomy, and the science of nationalism.* Minneapolis: University of Minnesota Press.

O'Riordan, K. (2012). The life of the gay gene: From hypothetical genetic marker to social reality. *Journal of Sex Research, 49*(4), 362–368.

Parry, D. C. (2008). "We wanted a birth experience, not a medical experience:" Exploring Canadian women's use of midwifery. *Health care for Women International, 29,* 784–806.

Riessman, C. K. (1983). Women and medicalization: A new perspective. *Social Policy, 14,* 3–18.

Rochon-Ford, A., & Saibil, D. (Eds.). (2009). *The push to prescribe.* Toronto: Women's Press.

Sigal, R. (1970). Politics of the pill. *Off Our Backs, 1*(1), 3.

Studd, J. (2006). Ovariotomy for medical madness and premenstrual syndrome-19th century history and lessons for current practice. *Gynecological endocrinology, 22*(8), 411–415.

Summerville, S. (1994). Scientific racism and the emergence of the homosexual body. *Journal of the History of Sexuality, 5*(2), 243–266.

Terry, J. (1999). *An American obsession: Science, medicine, and homosexuality in modern society.* Chicago: University of Chicago Press.

Tiefer, L. (1986). In pursuit of the perfect penis: The medicalization of male sexuality. *American Behavioral Scientist, 29,* 579–599.

Tiefer, L. (2001). Arriving at a "New View" of women's sexual problems: Background, theory, and activism. In E. Kaschak & L. Tiefer (Eds.), *A new view of women's sexual problems* (pp. 63–98). Binghampton: Haworth Press.

Tiefer, L. (2006). Sex therapy as a humanistic enterprise. *Sexual & relationship therapy, 21*(3), 359–375.

Tone, A. (2012). Medicalizing reproduction: The pill and home pregnancy tests. *Journal of Sex Research, 49*(4), 319–327.

Van Wagner, V., Epoo, B., Nastapoka, J., & Harney, E. (2007). Reclaiming birth, health, and community: Midwifery in the Inuit villages of Nunavik, Canada. *American College of Nurse-Midwives, 52*(4), 384–391.

Veurink, M., Koster, M., & de Jong-van den Berg, T. W. (2005). The history of DES, lessons to be learned. *Pharm World, 27,* 139–143.

von Krafft-Ebing, R. (1886). *Psychopathia sexualis: eine klinisch-forensische Studie.* Enke.

Wertz, R. W., & Wertz, D. C. (1989). *Lying-in: A history of childbirth in America.* New Haven: Yale University Press.

Williams, S. J. (2001). Sociological imperialism and the profession of medicine revisited: Where are we now? *Sociology of Health & Illness, 23*(2), 135–158.

Zola, I. K. (1983). *Socio-medical inquiries.* Philadelphia: Temple University Press.

Sexualities and Social Movements: Three Decades of Sex and Social Change

Amy L. Stone and Jill D. Weinberg

In her germinal work "Thinking Sex" Gayle Rubin ([1984] 2011a) constructed a hierarchy of sexual practices and identities that reflected the status quo in the early 1980s. Rubin analyzed how sexuality was organized in a "charmed circle" in which heterosexual, procreative, monogamous, and married sexuality was privileged as charmed, good, salubrious, and natural. Other sexualities, particularly non-relational sex that happened in public, involved same-sex partners, was inter-generational, kinky, or involved toys was considered inherently perilous and on the "outer limits" of the charmed circle. Although Rubin acknowledged that there was constant social contention about where to draw the line between "good" and "bad" sex, some sex was automatically assumed to be charmed and was uncontested. Rubin theorized about the charmed circle of sexuality in the height of the HIV/AIDS epidemic at a moment in which sexual panics were woven into sexual discourse. Her theorization expanded the existing understandings of heteronormativity, or the way that heterosexuality can be marked as natural and salubrious, to argue that only certain kinds of heterosexuality were considered charmed.

Much has changed in the past 30 years. HIV/AIDS turned into a chronic, manageable illness. The acceptance of non-relational or non-marital sex has changed dramatically since the early 1980s (Giddens 1992). The decrease of legal and normative restrictions on homosexuality, the dramatic legalization of same-sex marriage, and increase in public visibility of same-sex couples has potentially moved homosexuality out of the nebulous "outer limits" of the charmed circle (Seidman 2002). The broader acceptance and visibility of polyamorous, swinger, and BDSM practices has made these practices less stigmatized (Sheff 2005; Weiss 2006). The normalization of pornography and sex toys has been abetted by internet availability of both (Hooi 2008; Quinn and Forsyth 2005). Although many of these sexualities are still not "charmed" in the same way that relational, monogamous heterosexuality is, there are more possibilities for legal support, positive identities, and cultural visibility than there were 30 years ago.

This transformation has not impacted all aspects of the "outer limits" evenly. Although relational sex has been challenged by the rise of non-marital sexuality, in the past decade, reproductive and procreative sex has been reasserted as the natural, appropriate mode of sexuality by attacks on insurance coverage of contraceptives and state targeted regulation of abortion providers (TRAP) laws. Prostitution is still illegal in almost all states, and sex work more generally remains stigmatized (Barton 2006). Public sex is still heavily regulated (Berlant and Warner 1998).

A. L. Stone (✉)
Sociology and Anthropology, One Trinity Place, Trinity University, San Antonio, TX 78212, USA
e-mail: astone@trinity.edu

J. D. Weinberg
Sociology, DePaul University, American Bar Foundation, Chicago, IL 60614, USA
e-mail: jweinberg@abfn.org

J. DeLamater, R.F. Plante (eds.), *Handbook of the Sociology of Sexualities,* Handbooks of Sociology and Social Research, DOI 10.1007/978-3-319-17341-2_25, © Springer International Publishing Switzerland 2015

One of the most dramatic transformations has been the increasing regulation of intergenerational sex, which has been fueled by sexual panics about children (Lancaster 2011). In a follow-up to "Thinking Sex", Rubin ([1993] 2011b) admits that she underestimated in her original analysis the extent to which sexual panics about youth would shape sex laws and public discourse. The escalated legal regulation of intergenerational sex and the creation of the "sex offender" as a legible, stigmatized subject have all become part of the social landscape (Leon 2011).

25.1 The Role of Social Movements in Sexual Change

This vast transformation of gender and sexuality is complex. This chapter focuses on the role of social movements—particularly the lesbian, gay, bisexual, transgender, and queer (LGBTQ) movement— in motivating these changes. The effectiveness of these social movements is embedded in other large-scale social processes in the last 30 years, specifically the detraditionalization of society and rise of the internet.

Many scholars have theorized about the detraditionalization of marriage and intimacy in the United States. This detraditionalization has included the decline of early marriages and open participation in nonmarital childbearing, rearing, and sexual activity. Neil Gross (2005) argues that detraditionalization is only partial. Gross (2005) argues that detraditionalization has mainly transformed the regulative traditions that excludes sexual deviants from moral communities, such that nonmarital childbearing is no longer a stigmatized identity and same-sex couples are more integrated into community life. However detraditionalization has not transformed the meaning-constitutive traditions of intimacy and romantic life—for example there remains a strong idealization of heteronormative romantic married life. The causes of this detraditionalization are complex, and scholars have attributed it to social forces such as globalization and late capitalism (see Gross 2005 for overview; Giddens 1992). One of causes has been the denaturalizing tropes

deployed by social movements (Castells 2000; Gross 2005) that challenge the essentialization of gender and sexuality.

Technology and the role of the internet have also transformed both sexual practices (Quinn and Forsyth 2005) and social movements (Castells 2013; Van De Donk et al. 2004). The internet has increased the connection of gender and sexual minorities with one another, regardless of geography. This connection has been most remarkable for intersex and transgender individuals (Shapiro 2003), along with individuals involved in extremely marginalized sexual practices such as barebacking (Halkitis and Parsons 2003) and pedophilia (Durkin et al. 2006). In his research on leather culture, Nathan Rambukkana (2007) asserts that the availability of a BDSM counterpublic online obliterates the need for experience in a leather bar community. The internet has transformed sexual practices or made them more accessible to the general public, including the ready availability of heretofore scarce sexual materials like sex toys and pornography. In her qualitative study of sex work, Elizabeth Bernstein (2007) argues that middle-class sex workers have been able to benefit from the organization of sex work on the internet, including making it easier "to work without third-party management, to conduct one's business with minimal interference from the criminal justice system, and to reap greater profits by honing one's sales pitch to a more elite and more specialized audience" (p. 93). The internet has also been used to help mobilize social movement organizing and protest, along with increasing social support and building national movements (Nip 2004; Shapiro 2003).

This chapter focuses on the role of social movements in transforming sexual practices, behaviors, and identities for the past 30 years. Social movements that advance or restrict gender and sexual rights are a key part of understanding these transformations. These movements—including the feminist movement, reproductive rights, reproductive justice, and LGBTQ movement—have been critical in advancing law and transforming public opinion.

The second and third wave of the feminist movement advocated for women's sexual rights, including the framing, prevention, and criminalization of sexualized violence, including incest, domestic violence, and rape (see Reger 2012, 2014; Whittier 2009, 2010) . Second wave radical feminist organizing was known for challenging monogamous relationships and developing a positive, middle-class lesbian identity (Stein 1997). More contemporary feminist efforts, such as the "slut walk" protest, have worked as an anti-rape activism to counter the sexual double standard and rape culture (Reger 2014; Ringrose and Renold 2012). Overall, the feminist movement, reproductive rights, and reproductive justice movements have been critical for destabilizing the privileging of procreative sex as well, allowing women and men to benefit from widely available birth control options (Luna and Luker 2013; Staggenborg 1994).

The creation of advocacy organizations to advocate for the rights of sex workers (Bernstein 2010; Chateauvert 2014; Jenness 1993; Weitzer 1991), BDSM practitioners (Weiss 2008), and pedophiles (DeYoung 1989) have had less impact on law and policies; most of this mobilization has been the creation of isolated social movement organizations or the enactment of personal politics in the daily lives of marginalized individuals. However, the creation of advocacy organizations may be beneficial for members of these marginalized groups.

One of the largest social movements, the LGBTQ movement, has been mobilized on a large scale since the early 1970s to address issues like the decriminalization of sodomy, the normalization of homosexuality and bisexuality, and legal and policy changes to support members of the LGBTQ community (for an overview, see Armstrong 2002; Fetner 2008; Ghaziani 2008). Subsumed within the long history of the LGBTQ movement are multiple smaller movements. The gay liberationist movement operated in the late 1960s and early 1970s as a radical departure from Cold War homophile activism; gay liberationist politics emphasize gay pride, coming out, and the intersectionality of gay issues with the New Left (see D'Emilio 2012 [1982]). Lesbian feminism peaked in the 1970s and 1980s as a schism from radical feminist organizing that focused on personal politics and the development of a posi-

tive lesbian identity (Stein 1997). Queer activism began in the late 1980s and early 1990s as a form of direct action, radical politics that challenged the homonormativity of lesbian and gay politics and advocated for the inclusion of marginalized groups within the LGBTQ community (Armstrong 2002; Gamson 1989).

All of these movements have been impacted by movements working to restrict gender and sexual rights, including the anti-gay Religious Right and pro-life movements. Both of these movements were mobilized in the mid-1970s as a response to the growing visibility of gay liberationist politics, the Equal Rights Amendment, and the Roe v. Wade (1973) Supreme Court decision (Diamond 1995). The Religious Right has a long history of affecting the agenda, tactics, and framing of LGBTQ activism (Fetner 2008; Stone 2012).

This chapter disproportionately focuses on the LGBTQ movement and feminist movement with some attention to activism to support the legalization of alternative sexualities like BDSM and polyamory. These movements have played a successful role in transforming gender and sexual practices, identities, and communities for the last 30 years. The earliest definitions of social movement success focused on the passage of beneficial laws and recognition by political elites (Gamson 1975); since then, the understanding of social movement outcomes has spread to include mobilizations outcomes, cultural outcomes, and political or policy outcomes (see Bernstein 2003; Staggenborg 1995, 2001). The multi-institutional politics approach to social movements emphasizes the way movement targets multiple social, cultural, and political institutions (Armstrong and Bernstein 2008). Not only have social movements influenced dramatic legal and policy change but they have also been part of the transformation of public opinion, increasing cultural visibility, and the transformation of individual and collective identities.

25.1.1 Legal and Political Change

Legal and political change for marginalized sexualities, particularly for LGBTQ persons, has undergone significant transformation since the mid-twentieth century. From the liberalization of abortion to the decriminalization of sodomy, there has been a general expansion of gender and sexual rights. Social movements have been at the forefront of achieving these legal and political changes. This section will primarily focus on the gains for the LGBTQ movement, giving an overview of research on the role of the movement in achieving formal legal and political rights or the process of acquiring these rights (Barclay et al. 2009; Carpenter 2012; Negro et al. 2013). The LGBTQ movement operates in multiple arenas—the ballot box, the courtroom, the city council chambers, and congress—to advocate for expanded gender and sexual rights.

In each of these arenas of contention, the LGBTQ movement clashes with the Religious Right. For the Right, the ballot measure or referendum/initiative process is its most successful arena (Werum and Winders 2001), and this arena is frequently used to curtail LGBTQ rights (Stone 2012). Anti-gay ballot measures vary in their focus. Forty percent of these ballot measures are an attempt to rescind municipal or state nondiscrimination laws that include sexual orientation or gender identity/expression. Gender identity/expression is a way of protecting transgender individuals and other individuals with non-normative gender expression. Almost one-quarter of these ballot measures are legal restrictive ballot measures, which were attempts to prevent all future LGBTQ nondiscrimination laws in a given state or municipality. An additional 30% of all ballot measures are related to same-sex marriage or domestic partnerships. The most common form of these relationship recognition ballot measures is state constitutional amendments to ban same-sex marriage. These same-sex marriage bans are put on the ballot by the legislature or a citizen petition process, depending on the requirements of each state. This form of ballot measure was the most successful strategy until recently when attorneys filed a series of challenges in the federal courts. There have also been ballot measures on other subjects that impact the LGBTQ movement, including a spate of ballot measures about HIV/AIDS in California in the 1980s (Stone 2012).

Social movements are critical for legal reform and transformation (Barclay et al. 2009). The LGBTQ movement has been most successful at the state level, although there has been limited impact on federal law and policy. Some of the most dramatic federal victories include the passage of laws including the Hate Crimes Statistics Act (1990), which required the United States Attorney General to collect crime data on offenses that "manifest prejudice based on race, religion, sexual orientation, or ethnicity," as well as the Ryan White Comprehensive AIDS Resources Emergency Act (1990), the largest federally funded program to provide services for individuals living with HIV/AIDS. Another dramatic federal policy change has been the allowance of gay and lesbian military members. From 1993 to 2011, a policy popularly called "Don't Ask, Don't Tell" (DADT) permitted closeted gay and lesbian to serve while prohibited those who were openly gay and lesbian. The Supreme Court never directly considered a challenge to DADT but two federal cases held that DADT was unconstitutional as applied to a service member who had been discharged for homosexual conduct (*Log Cabin Republicans v. United States* 2010; *Witt v. United States Department of the Air Force* 2008). These decisions prompted the Congress and President Obama to repeal the military policy in 2010.

Most LGBTQ rights laws have been workplace antidiscrimination laws passed at the local- and state-level, with protections for sexual orientation and/or gender identity and expression (Button et al. 1997; Stone 2009). Regional, state, and local social movement organizations have been critical for passing these laws and defending them when they are challenged by referendums or initiatives (Stone 2012). As of 2014, 21 states passed legislation that legally prohibits employment discrimination on the basis of sexual orientation and hundreds of municipalities have passed similar laws, which are often inclusive of gender identity and expression. Even though federal lawmakers have introduced the Employment Non-Discrimination Act (ENDA) in every session since 1994, there has yet to be a federal law that protects LGBTQ persons from workplace discrimination. Federal courts have been unwilling to interpret sex discrimination to apply to LGBTQ employees, but the Supreme Court did expand the scope of sexual harassment to include same-sex sexual harassment (*Oncale v. Sundowner* 1998).

One of the most contested areas of law and sexualities involves the legal and cultural meaning of family and relationships, including the legalization of adoptions by LGBTQ individuals and same-sex marriage. To accomplish same-sex marriage, the LGBTQ movement had to operate through multiple arenas of contention (see Bernstein and Taylor 2013; Rimmerman and Wilcox 2007). The movement focus on same-sex marriage emerged after the Hawaii State Supreme Court prohibited the denial of marriage licenses to same-sex couples on the basis of equal protection (*Baehr v. Lewin* 1993) and voters quickly approved a constitutional amendment granting the Hawaii State Legislature the power to reserve marriage to opposite-sex couples. The federal government also responded by enacting the Defense of Marriage Act (DOMA) in 1996, a law that defined marriage as between a man and woman for federal purposes. The enactment of DOMA and possibility of same-sex marriage in Hawaii unleashed a wave of state constitutional amendments across the country that resulted in 30 states passing constitutional definitions of marriage that excluded same-sex couples (Camp 2008; McVeigh and Diaz 2009; Stone 2012). Despite the strength of this Religious Right backlash against same-sex marriage, the LGBTQ movement has been successful in the legislature and courts in legalizing same-sex marriage. In 1999, the Vermont Supreme Court declared that same-sex couples were entitled to the same legal rights as heterosexual married couples under its state constitution. The Vermont legislature enacted a law creating the status of "civil unions," making it the first U.S. State to provide committed same-sex couples with marital rights. Other states and municipalities also enacted domestic partnership or civil union laws. After facing a series of setbacks including voter referendums to amend state constitutions and ban same-sex marriage and court decisions that affirmed these amendments a majority of states and Washing-

ton, D.C. allow marriage for same-sex couples. Much of this progress is a result of the 2013 Supreme Court decision *United States v. Windsor* that struck down the Defense of Marriage Act (DOMA) which defined marriage as between a man and a woman and therefore not entitled to federal benefits.

Many of these successful court decisions relied on an aggressive litigation strategy based on two constitutional theories. The first involved the right to privacy afforded by the due process clause of the Fourteenth Amendment and the "penumbra" of rights implied in the United States Constitution (*Griswold v. Connecticut* 1965). Under this framework, legal framing focused on a strategy of tolerance and freedom from government intrusion. The second approach focused on Equal Protection contained in the Fourteenth Amendment. This approach centered on equality of opportunity and viewing individuals as full members of society in the eyes of the law. The first argument about privacy was critical in the repeal of sodomy laws. Invalidating criminal sodomy laws had been a goal since the 1960s but efforts increased when organizations such as Lambda Legal Defense and Education Fund, the National Gay and Lesbian Task Force (NGLTF), and the American Civil Liberties Union (ACLU) tackled decriminalization at the state level (see Bernstein 2003). In 2003, the United States Supreme Court invalidated the remaining sodomy statutes and overruled *Bowers v. Hardwick* (1986), a decision that held homosexual conduct was not constitutionally protected. The Court established that intimate conduct is protected by a fundamental right to privacy, analogizing conduct involving contraception, abortion, and interracial marriage (*Griswold v. Connecticut* 1965; *Roe v. Wade* 1973; *Loving v. Virginia* 1963), while sidestepping the legal question of Equal Protection. *Lawrence v. Texas* was a pivotal moment because it moved the juridical discourse about homosexuality from one of stigma to protected conduct (see Carpenter 2012). Given LGBTQ persons faced ongoing discrimination in public arenas—employment, open military service, and the family—lawyers refocused efforts to Equal Protection and make a case for formal equality, which was successful in previous cases where prohibiting the extension of antidiscrimination protections based on sexual orientation was ruled unconstitutional (*Romer v. Evans* 1996). In more recent decisions, courts have adopted an Equal Protection framework to overturn any same-sex marriage bans. The California federal district court's opinion in *Perry v. Schwarzeneggar* (2010) shows this shift from privacy rights to equal protection, where Judge Vaughn Walker noted that "the movement of marriage away from a gendered institution and toward an institution free from state-mandated gender roles reflects an evolution in the understanding of gender rather than a change in marriage" (p. 993).

These legal advances and setbacks within the LGBTQ movement often invigorated the movement. For example, the repeal of the anti-gay initiative, Colorado Amendment 2, in the Supreme Court case *Romer v. Evans* (1992) empowered members of the LGBTQ movement and transformed Religious Right tactics (Stone 2012). Conversely, the negative ruling of *Bowers v. Hardwick* (1986) also impacted social movement activism. According to Deborah Gould (2001, 2009) in her study of AIDS Coalition to Unleash Power (ACT UP), this negative ruling evoked strong feelings of anger in gay and lesbian communities, which escalated activism and the beginning of ACT UP.

These legal advances are also intertwined with the increase in the number of LGBTQ politicians and judges at the local, state, and federal-levels. An LGBTQ person has been elected to a political office in all 50 states, and with 41 serving in state legislatures. Eleven openly gay individuals have served in the United States Congress, including Tammy Baldwin who served in both the House of Representatives and the U.S. Senate. Since 1994, two openly gay individuals have been appointed to the federal judiciary and two to state Supreme Court positions.

Even though this period marked an expansion for LGBTQ rights, it narrowed rights for other sexual minorities. Sexual sadomasochism remains subject to criminal assault and battery laws even in circumstances involving consenting adults in private settings (*Govan v. State*, 2009;

People v. Febrissy 2006; *State v. Van* 2004). Intergenerational sex remains controversial and law makers' concern for sexual assault against children lead to a series of state and federal laws, informally referred to as "Megan's Laws" in memory of a 7-year girl who was raped and murdered by a repeat sex offender (Leon 2011). These laws require sex offenders to register with local authorities their residence, place of employment, and vehicle information (e.g., Adam Walsh Child Protection and Safety Act 1996; Sexually Violent Offender Registration Act of 1994; Sexual Offender (Jacob Wetterling) Act 1994).

25.1.2 Public Opinion

Social movements have also been critical in impacting public opinion about marginalized sexual practices, identities and communities. Part of detraditionalization has been the alteration of traditional attitudes toward gender and sexuality, particularly strict gender roles and sexual mores. However, positive public opinion is uneven, and some marginalized sexual communities still experience extreme stigmatization.

In the last 30 years there has been a dramatic increase in public support for LGBTQ rights (Herek 2002; Loftus 2001; Yang 1997). This public opinion shift includes a surge of support for same-sex marriage in the 2000s and 2010s such that by 2013 a majority of adult Americans supported same-sex marriage (PEW 2014). However, this support is uneven. In his book *Same Sex, Different Politics*, Gary Mucciaroni (2009) documents the consistently lower support for homosexual practices and same-sex families than civil liberties like employment. Mucciaroni (2009) suggests that sexual practices and family life is more morally complex than public opinion about civil liberties.

Although there has been a general detraditionalization of attitudes towards non-relational sex, other marginalized sexual communities continue to be stigmatized. For example, there is a continued stigmatization of sex work, including prostitution, call girls, and stripping (Barton 2006; Weitzer 2009). In her book *Stripped*, Bernadette

Barton (2006) analyzes the way strippers face stigma from family members, sexual partners, and the public. Scholars have also found that individuals engaged in BDSM, polyamory, or other sexual practices frequently employ stigma management techniques to combat public ridicule (Bezreh et al. 2012). It is unclear whether behaviors that have become more common due to the internet (e.g., watching pornography, buying sex toys) are still stigmatized (see Hefley 2007). Individuals engaged in intergenerational sex have faced increasing stigmatization, penalization, and criminalization as sex offenders, often with a lifetime stigma (Jenkins 2004; Leon 2011).

Social movements play a role in forming these public opinions. In her analysis of public opinion shifts about lesbian and gay rights between the 1970s and late 1990s, Loftus (2001) suggests that half of this change can be accounted for by demographics and cultural ideological shifts about gender and sexuality associated with detraditionalization and the secularization of society. Other scholars have argued that these public opinion shifts are a consequence of social movement activism (Epstein 1999). Many types of social movement activism are focused on the de-stigmatization of identities and practices and creation of positive public images, including education campaigns. In her study of campaigns to fight anti-gay referendums and initiatives, Amy Stone (2012) documents the way these LGBTQ campaigns worked to change the "hearts and minds" of heterosexual voters about same-sex marriage through door-to-door canvassing and educational campaigns.

Public support can also impact social movement gains. Low public opinion has accounted for uneven LGBTQ legal gains, including challenges with the decriminalization of sodomy in state legislatures, the legalization of same-sex marriage (Mucciaroni 2009), and the defense of anti-gay ballot measures around issues like non-discrimination laws (Stone 2012). On the other hand, the increasing public support of same-sex marriage has played a central role in amicus briefs and court rulings about the legality of same-sex marriage.

25.1.3 Culture and Visibility

Part of the detraditionalization of society is the growing acceptability of sexual explicitness and sexual storytelling (Plummer 1995). From "the love that dare not speak its name" to the clever musings of out gay actor Neil Patrick Harris while hosting the Tony Awards, there has been an explosion of cultural visibility around LGBTQ lives in the last 30 years. Overall, there has been an overwhelming increase in the representation of gay and lesbian life in the movies, television, news, and documentaries, and coverage of celebrities, politicians, and other facets of social and political life. Coverage of alternative sexualities such as BDSM, polyamory, and swingers has contradictory visibility with an increase in fictional and reality television coverage of marginalized sexual practices (Weiss 2006; Wilkinson 2009) but significantly less public visibility of "out" members who participate in these practices.

This cultural visibility may not be positive. For BDSM, media coverage is becoming more widespread but also "pornonormative" in the types of depictions (Wilkinson 2009). Depictions of BDSM that rely on narratives of immutability to explain why people participate in these sexual activities may also lead to greater stigmatization in public opinion (Weiss 2006). Similarly, positive portrayals of LGBTQ lives in the media are often disproportionately white, middle-class, and homonormative, privileging representations of respectability, reproduction, and family life. Gender non-conformity was one of the first kinds of gay and lesbian cultural visibility in the 1950s and 1960s (Chauncey 1994; Davis and Kennedy 1993). However, gender non-conformity, effeminacy, and transgender lives are frequently used as comic relief in media portrayals of LGBTQ individuals (Walters 2014). In his book *Times Square Red, Times Square Blue*, scholar Samuel Delany (1999) argues that the less palatable forms of queer life—those that are lower class and sexual—are regulated out of public spaces, creating less visibility for queer lives.

Although this cultural visibility may not always be positive, many scholars have suggested that this visibility, including the presence of more visible public figures, media representations, and newspaper coverage, has benefited the LGBTQ community and marginalized sexual communities more broadly (Walters 2014; Weiss 2006). Visibility is constructed as a necessary precondition for equality (Walters 2014) and social movement progress. Joshua Gamson (1998) in his book *Freaks Talk Back* argues that even talk shows, a contradictory site for the representation of LGBTQ lives, is part of cultural visibility and the democratization of television, because talk shows "let people who have largely been excluded from the public conversation appear on national TV and talk about their sex lives, their family fights, sometimes their literal dirty laundry" (pp. 14–15).

Social movement activism has been a critical part of this surge of cultural visibility. Starting with the Stonewall riots of 1969, cultural visibility has become a central goal of the LGBTQ movement. Gay liberationist traditions of "coming out" and "pride" (Armstrong 2002) and lesbian feminist commitments to personal politics, language, and cultural representations (Echols 1989; Stein 1997) created the preconditions for a contemporary LGBTQ movement that frames cultural visibility as an important goal. This cultural visibility includes the normalization of "coming out" as a personal form of cultural visibility in order to dispel stereotypes about LGBTQ people and use identity as a form of education (Bernstein 1997), which asserts "the public relevance of what others deem private" (Gamson 1998, p. 200).

"Coming out" may operate as a master frame (Snow and Benford 1992) as part of social movement spillover (Meyer and Whittier 1994) in which frames developed by the LGBTQ movement are deployed by activism advocating for other marginalized sexualities. This use of "coming out" as a master frame may be more likely when the frame resonates across multiple settings or situations (Snow and Benford 1992) or there are overlapping constituencies between the social movements (Meyer and Whittier 1994). "Coming out" has been used as a frame to disclose being fat (Saguy and Ward 2011), disabled (Erevelles 2011), kinky (Nichols 2006), a stripper (Barton 2006), polyamorous (Rambukkana 2004), and a swinger (Lind 2005), among other possibilities.

The LGBTQ movement also incorporates cultural visibility into strategies and tactics of the movement. In the 1980s and 1990s, groups like ACT UP and Queer Nation used public demonstrations to increase visibility and public awareness (Gould 2009); these protests included the infamous chant "We're Here, We're Queer, Get Used to It." Marches, whether they be annual Pride marches or less frequent Marches on Washington, often are used to heighten LGBTQ visibility (Bruce, forthcoming; Ghaziani 2008). One of the many goals of Pride marches is the physical presence of the LGBTQ community in the public sphere.

25.1.4 Identity

Social movements have been critical for the development of positive, affirming social identities, particularly for members of the LGBTQ community and those with other marginalized sexualities. The last 30 years have seen the development of positive identities for many sexualities outside the "charmed circle" as a way of counteracting the stigmatization of sexual practices, identities, and communities. Yet some sexualities have not developed into positive, affirming social identities, and there are profound limits to the development of even positive LGBTQ identities. For example, longstanding sexual tropes about black heterosexuality have challenged the development of positive black gay and lesbian identities (Collins 2004).

The LGBTQ movement has been particularly adept at harnessing and transforming the emotions (Gould 2009) and identities (Stein 1997) of social movement participants. Sometimes the creation of a positive identity is the primary goal of social movement organizing (Bernstein 1997; Taylor and Whitter 1998). Gay liberation and lesbian feminism of the 1970s played a role in creating affirming identities. Gay liberationist organizers were the first to articulate "gay pride" and the reconstruction of homosexuality and bisexuality as valued, positive identities. Sentiments of pride are able to transform features of gay and lesbian life that were previously considered shameful into anger or pride (Britt and Heise 2000). Arlene Stein (1997) in her book *Sex and*

Sensibility argues that the lesbian feminist movement played a role in creating a vibrant lesbian culture and positive middle-class lesbian identity, creating lesbianism as an affirmative identity that evoked resistance against heteronormativity.

The development and deployment of identity is critical to much LGBTQ activism (Bernstein 1997). In her book *Forging Gay Identities*, sociologist Elizabeth Armstrong (2002) argues that there is prevalent "identity logic" in the LGBTQ movement as it developed after 1970. This identity logic could be seen on the organizational level as there was the growth of "organizations whose central goal was the elaboration or display of identity" and "the use of explicit sexual identity in organization names" (p. 21). Pride marches and Marches on Washington are one part of this identity deployment and celebration (see Ghaziani 2008; Bruce 2013).

Similar to "coming out", "pride" may operate as a master frame for other marginalized sexualities that creates and reinforces positive sexual identities. Margot Weiss (2008) argues that notions of sexual freedom based on privacy and equality may be partially borrowed by BDSM organizations from LGBTQ activism, including arguments made in the *Lawrence v. Texas* Supreme Court decision, along with notions of pride. Within marginalized sexual communities, the use of this "pride" frame or development of positive identities may vary significantly. Elizabeth Bernstein (2010) documents the growth of a positive identity for sex workers that includes recognition of the material benefits of sex work but also the opportunities for "personal growth" and deep social meaning. However, this positive identity mainly relies on the experience of white, middle-class, educated performers and a growing "sex-worker chic" among the urban middle-class (p. 109).

25.2 Methodology

Similar to the general study of social movements (see Taylor 1998), the sociological study of sexual social movements is dominated by qualitative or historical case studies of specific movements, with an emphasis on the LGBTQ movement.

These studies include interview studies of social movement participants (e.g., Stein 1997; Taylor and Whittier 1998), the study of one movement or organization over time (e.g., Armstrong 2002; Ghaziani 2008), and ethnographies of a social movement organization (e.g., Gould 2009; Lichterman 1999). Additionally, scholars craft historical comparative arguments using comparisons between multiple organizations or points in time within a movement (e.g., Bernstein 1997, 2003). The quantitative study of sexual social movements tends to be dominated by studies of public opinion and voters' responses to LGBTQ rights (e.g., Powell et al. 2010; McVeigh and Diaz 2009).

One of the strengths of this emphasis on qualitative methodology is the development and refinement of social theory. The study of sexual social movements has helped develop and refine theories about social movement collective identity, emotions, and tactics, among other phenomena. Work by Verta Taylor and Nancy Whittier (1998) on lesbian feminist identity was critical for the development of a working concept of collective identity. Mary Bernstein (1997) expanded on their work with a comparative study of collective identity deployment during phases of the LGBTQ movement in multiple cities to theorize about the conditions under which different kinds of identities are deployed. Conversely, Joshua Gamson (1995) has used queer politics to analyze the deconstruction of collective identities. Other scholars have refined theories about social movement success and failure (Bernstein 2003; Weitzer 1991), the role of dissent in movement decision-making (Ghaziani 2008) and the role of emotions in social movement mobilization and decline (Gould 2009), among other theoretical contributions.

The emphasis on case studies has created more nuanced social movement scholarship that embeds activism within a rich social and historical context. Most studies of the LGBTQ movement embed movement organizations, identities, and tactics in the visibility of and public opinions about the LGBTQ community, along with the impact of the Religious Right as a powerful countermovement. For example, Tina Fetner's

(2008) book *How the Religious Right Shaped Lesbian and Gay Activism* directly analyzes the way the Religious Right has affected the LGBTQ movement over time, pushing the movement to alter its strategies and diverting legal gains. The disadvantages of qualitative case studies include a geographical, demographic, and organizational bias, in which case studies are disproportionately conducted with a few white-dominated organizations in targeted cities in California and the North. There is an inordinate focus on studying LGBTQ activism in a few central cities (e.g., New York City, Chicago, Los Angeles, San Francisco) and the activist organizations founded in these cities (e.g., Mattachine Society, Gay Liberation Front, COYOTE, Queer Nation, ACT UP). An unchallenged assumption is that social movement activism begins at these central cities and spreads, unaltered, to other cities and rural areas. Thus bias leads to an overreliance on studies of exceptional (and often ephemeral organizations)—such as Queer Nation—rather than other social movement organizations operating (or attempting to operate) at the same time. For example, most studies of the homophile movement focus on the Mattachine Society, only one of many homophile organizations operating in the 1950s, which often obscures the experiences of LGBTQ people in other parts of the country (see Loftin 2012 for a remedy of this). Almost all of these targeted organizations were white and gay-male dominated, and most studies of sexual social movements have focused on white-dominated organizations (see Sheff and Hammers 2011; Ward 2008 for critique). Studies of sexual social communities and activism often "(unwittingly) reinforced and (re)constituted a homogenous image of these non-conformist subcultures" (Sheff and Hammers 2011, p. 198). This bias leads to the omissions of movements to legalize miscegenation, the reproductive justice movement (see Luna and Luker 2013), and transgender organizing (Stryker 2008). Early scholars embedded lesbian and gay activism in an international context (Adam 1987), which is less common in contemporary analysis. More recently, there is a growing body of literature on the national organization of the LGBTQ movement (Ghaziani 2008; Stone 2012) along with research on rural and Southern organizing (Bruce 2013; Gray 2009).

Finally, a case study focus has led to fewer connections being made between different types of sexual social movements. There is little analysis of the ways that sexualities are mobilized (or not) into social movements. Recent work by Hadar Aviram (2008) suggests that many polyamorous individuals are reluctant to join the movement to legalize same-sex marriage due to a general mistrust of the law and the legal regulation of relationships. The differential mobilization around non-monogamy, BDSM, miscegenation, and prostitution and the lack of a development of recuperative social identities around intergenerational sex and other sexualities is ripe for analysis. Several questions remain unanswered. Why do some sexual identities and behaviors require social movements in order to achieve effective legal, cultural, and social change? Why are some sexual identities and behaviors difficult to mobilize into social movements? Why are some sexual identities and behaviors able to achieve social and cultural acceptance without the operation of a viable social movement?

One possible direction for the study of sexual social movements is to take up some of these questions about the process by which sexual identities become mobilized into activism. Future studies may focus on the mobilization (or lack thereof) of marginalized sexual communities apart from the LGBTQ community, including polyamorous and BDSM practitioners, and the impact of increasing access to marginalized sexual practices on the changing sexual subjectivity of individuals. Trends in the study of sexuality, specifically the study of sexual fluidity (Diamond 2009) and the attention to sexual fields (Green 2008, see also Green, Chap. 3, this volume), would be interesting and provocative contributions to the study of sexual social movements. The study of sexual fluidity may impact the study of social movements by challenging the stable identities that are often assumed within the study of social movements.

References

Adam, B. D. (1987). *The rise of a gay and lesbian movement*. Boston: Twayne Publishers.

Armstrong, E. A. (2002). *Forging gay identities: Organizing sexuality in San Francisco, 1950–1994*. Chicago: University of Chicago Press.

Armstrong, E. A., & Bernstein, M. (2008). Culture, power, and institutions: A multi institutional politics approach to social movements. *Sociological Theory, 26*(1),74–99.

Aviram, H. (2008). Make love, now law: Perceptions of the marriage equality struggle among polyamorous activists. *Journal of Bisexuality, 7*(3–4), 261–286.

Barclay, S., Bernstein, M., & Marshall, A. (Eds.). (2009). *Queer mobilizations: LGBT activists confront the law*. New York: New York University Press.

Barton, B. (2006). *Stripped: Inside the lives of exotic dancers*. New York: New York University Press.

Berlant, L., & Warner, M. (1998). Sex in public. *Critical Inquiry, 24*, 547–566.

Bernstein, M. (1997). Celebration and suppression: The strategic uses of identity by the lesbian and gay movement. *American Journal of Sociology, 103*(3), 531–565.

Bernstein, M. (2003). Nothing ventured, nothing gained? Conceptualizing social movement "success" in the lesbian and gay movement. *Sociological Perspectives, 46*(3), 353–379.

Bernstein, E. (2007). *Temporarily yours: Intimacy, authenticity, and the commerce of sex*. Chicago: University of Chicago Press.

Bernstein, E. (2010). *Temporarily yours: Intimacy, authenticity, and the commerce of sex*. Chicago: University of Chicago Press.

Bernstein, M., & Taylor, V. A. (2013). *The marrying kind? Debating same-sex marriage within the lesbian and gay movement*. Minneapolis: University of Minnesota Press.

Bezreh, T., Weinberg, T. S., & Edgar, T. (2012). BDSM Disclosure and stigma management: Identifying opportunities for sex education. *American Journal of Sexuality Education, 7*(1), 37–61.

Britt, L., & Heise, D. (2000). From shame to pride in identity politics. In S. Stryker, T. J. Owens, & R. W. White (Eds.), *Self, identity, and social movements* (pp. 252–268). Minneapolis, University of Minnesota Press.

Bruce, K. M. (2013). LGBTQ pride as a cultural protest tactic in a southern city. *Journal of Contemporary Ethnography, 42*(5), 608–635.

Button, J. W., Rienzo, B. A., & Wald, K. (1997). *Private lives, public conflicts: Battles over gay rights in American communities*. Washington, D.C.: CQ Press.

Camp, B. J. (2008). Mobilizing the base and embarrassing the opposition: Defense of marriage referenda and cross-cutting electoral cleavages. *Sociological Perspectives, 51*(4), 713–733.

Carpenter, D. (2012). *Flagrant conduct: The story of Lawrence v. Texas: How a bedroom arrest decriminalized gay Americans* (1st ed.). New York: W.W. Norton.

Castells, M. (2000). *The power of identity*. Malden: Blackwell.

Castells, M. (2013). *Networks of outrage and hope: Social movements in the internet age*. Malden: Wiley.

Chateauvert, M. (2014). *Sex workers unite: A history of the movement from Stonewall to Slutwalk*. Boston: Beacon Press.

Chauncey, G. (1994). *Gay New York: Gender, urban culture, and the making of the gay male world, 1890–1940*. New York: Basic Books.

Collins, P. H. (2004). *Black sexual politics: African Americans, gender, and the new racism*. New York: Routledge.

Davis, M., & Kennedy, E. L. (1993). *Boots of leather, slippers of gold: The history of a lesbian community*. New York: Routledge.

Delany, S. R. (1999). *Times square red, Times Square Blue*. New York: New York University Press.

D'Emilio, J. (2012). *Sexual politics, sexual communities*. Chicago: University of Chicago Press.

DeYoung, M. (1989). The world according to NAMBLA: Accounting for deviance. *Journal of Sociology & Social Welfare, 16*(1), 111–126.

Diamond, S. (1995). *Roads to dominion: Right-wing movements and political power in the United States*. New York: Guilford Press.

Diamond, L. M. (2009). *Sexual fluidity*. Cambridge: Harvard University Press.

Durkin, K., Forsyth, C. J., & Quinn, J. F. Pathological internet communities: A new direction for sexual deviance research in a post modern era. *Sociological Spectrum, 26*(6), 595–606.

Echols, A. (1989). *Daring to be bad: Radical feminism in America, 1967–1975* (Vol. 3). Minneapolis: University of Minnesota Press.

Epstein, S. (1999). Gay and lesbian movements in the United States: Dilemmas of identity, diversity, and political strategy. In B. D. Adams, J. W. Duyvendak, & A. Krouwel (Eds.), *The global emergence of gay and lesbian politics: National imprints of a worldwide movement* (pp. 30–90). Philadelphia: Temple University Press.

Erevelles, N. (2011). "Coming out crip" in inclusive education. *Teachers College Record, 113*(10), 2155–2185.

Fetner, T. (2008). *How the religious right shaped lesbian and gay activism*. Minneapolis: University of Minnesota Press.

Gamson, W. A. (1975). *The strategy of social protest*. Homewood: Dorsey Press.

Gamson, J. (1989). Silence, death, and the invisible enemy: AIDS activism and social movement "newness". *Social Problems, 36*(4), 351–367.

Gamson, J. (1995). Must identity movements self-destruct? A queer dilemma. Must identity movements self-destruct? *A Queer Dilemma Social Problems, 42*(3), 390–407.

Gamson, J. (1998). *Freaks talk back: Tabloid talk shows and sexual nonconformity*. Chicago: University of Chicago Press.

Ghaziani, A. (2008). *The dividends of dissent: How conflict and culture work in lesbian and gay marches on Washington*. Chicago: University of Chicago Press.

Giddens, A. (1992). *The transformation of intimacy: Sexuality, love and intimacy in modern societies*. Palo Alto: Stanford University Press.

Gould, D. (2001). Rock the boat, don't rock the boat, baby: Ambivalence and the emergence of militant AIDS activism. In J. Goodwin, J. Jasper, & F. Polletta (Eds.), *Passionate politics: Emotions and social movements* (pp. 135–157). Chicago: University of Chicago Press.

Gould, D. B. (2009). *Moving politics: Emotion and ACT UP's fight against AIDS*. Chicago: University of Chicago Press.

Gray, M. L. (2009). *Out in the country: Youth, media, and queer visibility in rural America*. New York: New York University Press.

Green, A. I. (2008). The social organization of desire: The sexual fields approach. *Sociological Theory, 26*(1), 25–50.

Gross, N. (2005). The detraditionalization of intimacy reconsidered. *Sociological Theory, 23*(3), 286–311.

Halkitis, P. N., & Parsons, J. T. (2003). Intentional unsafe sex (barebacking) among HIV-positive gay men who seek sexual partners on the Internet. *AIDS Care, 15*(3), 367–378.

Hefley, K. (2007). Stigma management of male and female customers to a non-urban adult novelty store. *Deviant Behavior, 28*(1), 79–109.

Herek, G. M. (2002). Gender gaps in public opinion about lesbians and gay men. *Public Opinion Quarterly, 66*(1), 40–66.

Hooi, M. J. (2008). Substantive due process: Sex toys after Lawrence: Williams v. Morgan, 478 F.3d 1316 (11th Cir. 2007). Florida. *Law Review, 60*(2), 507–518.

Jenkins, P. (2004). *Moral panic: Changing concepts of the child molester in modern America*. New Haven: Yale University Press.

Jenness, V. (1993). *Making it work: The prostitute's rights movement in perspective*. New York: Aldine de Gruyter.

Lancaster, R. N. (2011). *Sex panic and the punitive state*. Berkeley: University of California Press.

Leon, C. S. (2011). *Sex fiends, perverts, and pedophiles: Understanding sex crime policy in America*. New York: New York University Press.

Lichterman, P. (1999). Talking identity in the public sphere: Broad visions and small spaces in sexual identity politics. *Theory and Society, 28*(1), 101–141.

Lind, G. (2005). Coming out swinging. *Journal of Bisexuality, 5*(2–3), 163–170.

Loftin, C. M. (2012). *Masked voices: Gay men and lesbians in cold war America*. Albany: SUNY Press.

Loftus, J. (2001). America's liberalization in attitudes toward homosexuality, 1973 to 1998. *American Sociological Review, 66*(5), 762–782.

Luna, Z., & Luker, K. (2013). Reproductive justice. *Annual Review of Sociology, 9,* 327–352.

McVeigh, R., & Diaz, M. E. (2009). Voting to ban same-sex marriage: Interests, values, and communities. *American Sociological Review, 74*(6), 891–915.

Meyer, D. S., & Whittier, N. (1994). Social movement spillover. *Social Problems, 41*(2), 277–298.

Mucciaroni, G. (2009). *Same sex, different politics: Success and failure in the struggles over gay rights*. Chicago: University of Chicago Press.

Negro, G., Perretti, F., & Carroll, G. R. (2013). Challenger groups, commercial organizations, and policy enactment: Local lesbian/gay rights ordinances in the United States from 1972 to 2008. *American Journal of Sociology, 119*(3), 790–832.

Nichols, M. (2006). Psychotherapeutic issues with "kinky" clients: Clinical problems, yours and theirs. *Journal of Homosexuality, 50*(2–3), 281–300.

Nip, J. (2004). The queer sisters and its electronic bulletin board: A study of the Internet for social movement mobilization. *Information, Communication & Society, 7*(1), 23–49.

Plummer, K. (1995). *Telling sexual stories: Power, change, and social worlds*. New York: Routledge.

Powell, B., Blozendahl, C., Geist, C., & Steelman, L. C. (2010). *Counted out: Same-sex relations and Americans' definitions of family*. New York: Russell Sage Foundation.

Quinn, J. F., & Forsyth, C. J. (2005). Describing sexual behavior in the era of the internet: A typology for empirical research. *Deviant Behavior, 26*(3), 191–207.

Rambukkana, N. P. (2004). Uncomfortable bridges: The bisexual politics of outing polyamory. *Journal of Bisexuality, 4*(3–4), 141–154.

Rambukkana, N. (2007). Taking the leather out of leathersex: The internet, identity, and the sadomasochistic public sphere. In K. O'Riordan & D. J. Phillips (Eds.), *Queer online: Media technology & sexuality* (pp. 67–80). New York: Peter Lang Publishing.

Reger, J. (2012). *Everywhere and nowhere: Contemporary feminism in the United States*. New York: Oxford University Press.

Reger, J. (2014). The story of a slut walk sexuality, race, and generational divisions in contemporary feminist activism. *Journal of Contemporary Ethnography*. doi:10.1177/0891241614526434.

Rimmerman, C. A., & Wilcox, C. (2007). *The politics of same-sex marriage*. Chicago: University of Chicago Press.

Ringrose, J. & Renold, E. (2012). Slut-shaming, girl power and "sexualisation:" Thinking through the politics of the international SlutWalks with teen girls. *Gender and Education, 24*(3), 333–343.

Rubin, G. S. (2011a). Thinking sex: Notes for a radical theory of the politics of sexuality. In G. Rubin (Ed.), *Deviations: A Gayle Rubin reader* (pp. 137–181). Durham: Duke University Press.

Rubin, G. S. (2011b). Postscript to 'Thinking Sex': Notes for a radical theory of the politics of sexuality. In G. Rubin (Ed.), *Deviations: A Gayle Rubin reader* (pp. 190–193). Durham: Duke University Press.

Saguy, A. C., & Ward, A. (2011). Coming out as fat rethinking stigma. *Social Psychology Quarterly, 74*(1), 53–75.

Seidman, S. (2002). *Beyond the closet: The transformation of gay and lesbian life.* New York: Routledge.

Shapiro, E. (2003). "Trans" cending barriers: Transgender organizing on the internet. *Journal of Gay & Lesbian Social Services, 16*(3–4), 165–179.

Sheff, E. (2005). Polyamorous women, sexual subjectivity and power. *Journal of Contemporary Ethnography, 34*(3), 251–283.

Sheff, E., & Hammers, C. (2011). The privilege of perversities: Race, class and education among polyamorists and kinksters. *Psychology & Sexuality, 2*(3), 198–223.

Snow, D. A., & Benford, R. D. (1992). Master frames and cycles of protest. In A. Morris & C. M. Mueller (Eds.), *Frontiers in social movement theory* (pp. 133–155). New Haven: Yale University Press.

Staggenborg, S. (1994). *The pro-choice movement: Organization and activism in the abortion conflict.* New York: Oxford University Press.

Staggenborg, S. (1995). Can feminist organizations be effective?. In M. M. Ferree & P. Y. Martin (Eds.), *Feminist organizations: Harvest of the new women's movement* (pp. 339–355). Philadelphia: Temple University Press.

Staggenborg, S. (2001). Beyond culture versus politics: A case study of a local women's movement. *Gender & Society, 15*(4), 507–530.

Stein, A. (1997). *Sex and sensibility: Stories of a lesbian generation.* Berkeley: University of California Press.

Stone, A. L. (2009). Like sexual orientation? Like gender? Transgender inclusion in non-discrimination ordinances. In S. Barclay, M. Bernstein, & A. Marshall (Eds.), *Queer mobilizations: LGBTQ activists confront the law.* New York: New York University Press.

Stone, A. L. (2012). *Gay rights at the ballot box.* Minneapolis: University of Minnesota Press.

Stryker, S. (2008). Transgender history, homonormativity, and disciplinarity. *Radical History Review, 100*(Winter 2008), 145–157.

Taylor, V. (1998). Feminist methodology in social movements research. *Qualitative Sociology, 21*(4): 357–379.

Taylor, V., & Whittier, N. (1998). Collective identity in social movement communities: Lesbian feminist mobilization. In P. M. Nardi & B. E. Schneider (Eds.), *Social perspectives in lesbian and gay studies* (pp. 349–365). New York: Routledge.

Van De Donk, W., Loader, B. D., Nixon, P. G., & Rucht, D. (Eds.). (2004). *Cyberprotest: New media, citizens and social movements.* New York: Routledge.

Walters, S. D. (2014). *The tolerance trap: How God, genes, and good intentions are sabotaging gay equality.* New York: New York University Press.

Ward, E. J. (2008). *Respectably queer: Diversity culture in LGBT activist organizations.* Nashville: Vanderbilt University Press.

Werum, R., & Winders, B. (2001). Who's "in" and Who's "Out": State fragmentation and the struggle over gay rights, 1974–1999. *Social Problems, 48*(3), 386–410.

Whittier, N. (2009). *The politics of child sexual abuse.* Oxford: Oxford University Press.

Whittier, N. (2010). *Feminist generations: The persistence of the radical women's movement.* Philadelphia: Temple University Press.

Weiss, M. D. (2006). Mainstreaming kink: The politics of BDSM representation in US popular media. *Journal of Homosexuality, 50*(2–3), 103–132.

Weiss, M. D. (2008). Gay shame and BDSM pride: Neoliberalism, privacy, and sexual politics. *Radical History Review, 100*(Winter 2008), 87–101.

Weitzer, R. (1991). Prostitutes' rights in the United States. *The Sociological Quarterly, 32*(1), 23–41.

Weitzer, R. (2009). Sociology of sex work. *Annual Review of Sociology, 35*(2009), 213–234.

Wilkinson, E. (2009). Perverting visual pleasure: Representing sadomasochism. *Sexualities 12*(2): 181–198.

Yang, A. S. (1997). Trends: Attitudes toward homosexuality. *Public Opinion Quarterly, 61*(3), 477–507.

Erratum to: Pornography

Kassia R. Wosick

Erratum to:
Chapter 23 in: J. DeLamater, R.F. Plante (eds.), *Handbook of the Sociology of Sexualities,*
Handbooks of Sociology and Social Research,
DOI 10.1007/978-3-319-17341-2_23

An entry was incorrect in the reference list. The incorrect reads:

Watson, P., Zizzo, D., & Fleming, P. (2014). Determinants and welfare implications of unlawful file sharing: A scoping review. Glasgow: CREATe.

The correct information is given below:

Watson, SJ., Zizzo, D., & Fleming, P. (2014). Determinants and welfare implications of unlawful file sharing: A scoping review. Glasgow: CREATe.

The online version of the original chapter can be found at
DOI 10.1007/978-3-319-17341-2_23

J. Fields (✉)
Sociology, San Francisco State University,
San Francisco, CA 94132, USA
e-mail: jfields@sfsu.edu

J. Gilbert
York University, Toronto, ON M3J 1P3, Canada

M. Miller
York University, Toronto, ON M6K 2W1, Canada

Index

A

Abolitionism, 390, 391
  and Progressive Era, 392
Activism, 283
  and law, 261
  and research, 269
  and sexual social communities
    studies on, 462
  gay political, 292
  gay rights movement and HIV/AIDS
    development of, 292
  lesbian and gay, 462
  LGBT, 314
  LGBTQ, 455, 461, 462
  political, 159
  social movement, 458, 460, 462
    consequences of, 459
Actor Network Theory (ANT), 110, 117, 118
  approach, 115, 119
  benefits of, 115
  objectives of, 115
  researchers, 115, 116
  toolkit, 114
Asexual, 273, 274, 275, 276, 280, 283
  black women, 275
  communities, 279
  definition of, 275
  historical perspective, 275
  identity, 274, 280
  Johnson's definition of, 275
  language, 281
  orientation, 276
  people, 273
  voices and perspectives, 279
Asexuality, 3, 274, 283
  and celibacy, 160
  as orientation, 275
  conceptualization of, 276
  definition of, 274, 277
  Diagnostic and Statistical Manual of Mental Disorders
    (DSM), 278
  historical versions of, 275
  in the popular press, 279, 280
  Joy Davidson's conceptions of, 279
  longitudinal studies on, 282
  models of, 282
  myths, 277
  research on, 281
  social scientific study of, 273
  studies on, 274, 276

B

BDSM, 459
  and polyamory, 455
  as an alternative sexuality, 459
  Hadar Aviram's conceptions of, 462
  media coverage of, 459
  networks, 296
  organizations, 461
  practices, 453
  practitioners, 455, 462
Birth control, 25
  and sterilization, 269
  Cancel Tirado' work on, 80
  historical transformations in, 25
  in mid-1990s, 206
  medicalization of, 442, 443
  pills, 215
    adverse effects of, 444
    options, 455
  reproduction medicalization, 440
  techniques used for, 442
Black feminist thought, 261, 262, 267, 269
Body norms, 153, 159
Brothel
  act of prostitution, 398
  and massage parlours, 112
  based prostitution, legalized, 402
  government regulations on, 398
  licensing/planning permission for, 291, 295
  local sex work context, 112
  opportunity-based varieties, 398

J. DeLamater, R.F. Plante (eds.), *Handbook of the Sociology of Sexualities,* Handbooks of Sociology and Social Research, DOI 10.1007/978-3-319-17341-2, © Springer International Publishing Switzerland 2015

Druck: KN Digital Printforce GmbH · Schockenriedstraße 37 · 70565 Stuttgart